HANDBOOK OF MIDDLE AMERICAN INDIANS • VOLUME 1

Natural Environment and Early Cultures

HANDBOOK OF MIDDLE AMERICAN INDIANS

EDITED AT MIDDLE AMERICAN RESEARCH INSTITUTE, TULANE UNIVERSITY, BY

ROBERT WAUCHOPE, *General Editor*

MARGARET A. L. HARRISON, *Associate Editor*

INIS PICKETT, *Administrative Assistant*

THOMAS S. SCHORR, DAVID S. PHELPS,

KENNETH E. OWEN, PAUL MOUTON,

MORRIS MORGAN, PAUL HEULLY, *Art Staff*

ASSEMBLED WITH THE AID OF A GRANT FROM THE NATIONAL SCIENCE FOUNDATION, AND UNDER THE SPONSORSHIP OF THE NATIONAL RESEARCH COUNCIL COMMITTEE ON LATIN AMERICAN ANTHROPOLOGY

HANDBOOK OF MIDDLE AMERICAN INDIANS

ROBERT WAUCHOPE, General Editor

VOLUME ONE

Natural Environment and Early Cultures

ROBERT C. WEST, Volume Editor

UNIVERSITY OF TEXAS PRESS · AUSTIN

International Standard Book Number 0–292–73259–7
Second Printing, 1971
Library of Congress Catalog Card No. 64–10316

The preparation and publication of
The Handbook of Middle American Indians
has been assisted by grants from
the National Science Foundation.

Typesetting by G&S Typesetters, Austin, Texas
Printing by Meriden Gravure Company, Meriden, Connecticut
Binding by Universal Bookbindery, Inc., San Antonio, Texas

CONTENTS

HANDBOOK OF MIDDLE AMERICAN INDIANS · VOLUME 1
Natural Environment and Early Cultures

1. Geohistory and Paleogeography of Middle America

MANUEL MALDONADO-KOERDELL

Rarely do the political limits of a region coincide with its natural limits (if there be such), and even more rarely do they do so in the area known as Mesoamerica, which extends from central Mexico approximately to Nicaragua. However, from the geological point of view a certain coincidence exists between Mesoamerica (the geographical-cultural concept established by anthropologists) and geological Middle America which includes all the territory from central Mexico to northwestern Colombia. Therefore, to cover adequately the geological and paleogeographical history of Mesoamerica it is necessary to consider all the territory roughly between the Tropic of Cancer and latitude 6° N. (fig. 1).

Geological Middle America resembles an irregularly shaped funnel with the widest part corresponding to Mexico and the narrow tube to Central America. The area reaches its maximum length of approximately 2000 km. from northwest to southeast, from the point where the Tropic of Cancer crosses the coast of Sinaloa, in Mexico, to the central part of the Department of Choco, in Colombia, at latitude 6°N. Its maximum widths are: (a) along the Tropic of Cancer between the Pacific Ocean and the Gulf of Mexico, (b) from the mouth of the Suchiate River, boundary between Mexico and Guatemala, to Cape Catoche on the Peninsula of Yucatan, and (c) between Cape Gracias a Dios in Honduras and the Peninsula of Cosigüina in Nicaragua. Its three notable narrowings occur at (a) the Isthmus of Tehuantepec in Mexico, (b) the Isthmus of Panama in the Republic of Panama, and (c) the Isthmus of Darien in Colombia.

These three main narrowings constitute the key to the geological history of Middle America, as they represent subareas of intense eustatism combined with very diverse tectonic factors that have acted on other subareas. In different geological epochs, particularly in the Cenozoic, strong volcanic activity occurred across the transverse axis of Mexico along latitude 19° N., and along an oblique line between Guatemala and Panama, which is still characteristic of geological Middle America with its sequel of associated phenomena (intense

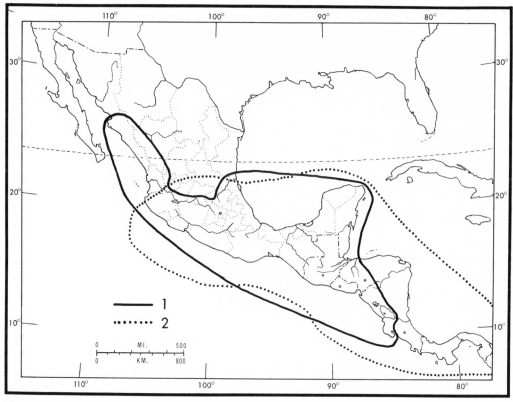

Fig. 1—AREAL CONCEPTS
Key: 1. Territory of "Cultural" Mesoamerica. 2. Geological Middle America.

seismicity). Although at times it has been broken as a continuous land mass, Middle America has functioned as a "geological bridge" between North and South America since pre-Paleozoic times.

This geological individuality of Middle America does not exclude other phenomena shared with neighboring areas; for example, one of the forked ends of the Andean chain that penetrates through the Darien to central Panama is geologically a part of South America. Moreover, certain geological events of Mexico cannot be understood without considering their relationships with North America, and many structural features of the territory between both subareas were affected by factors whose action originated in the depths of the Pacific Ocean, the Gulf of Mexico, and the Caribbean Sea.

In order to outline the course of geologic history in Middle America it is necessary

to know the distribution of its rocks, both spatially and chronologically, and its index fossils so as to learn the regional stratigraphy. Numerous studies cover both Mexico and Central America, leaving only small unimportant blanks. Geologists and paleontologists have given particular attention to the southern half of the coastal plain of the Gulf of Mexico and its southeastern part including the Peninsula of Yucatan on account of its oil-bearing importance.

The Neovolcanic Axis of Mexico is well known in its geomorphology, structural geology, and vulcanology; recently studies have been made relating this axis to the geology of the Pacific Ocean floor. We still lack regional studies on the Sierra Madre del Sur and the coastal regions of Chiapas, Oaxaca, Guerrero, Colima, Jalisco, and Nayarit. Brand (1957) has described the coast of Michoacan in a study that could well

4

serve as a model for similar research in western Mexico.

In Central America the work of the German geographer and geologist Karl Sapper is outstanding. For ten years (beginning in 1888) he explored the territory minutely, climbing the volcanoes, traveling over the plains, and compiling data which were later recorded in thousands of pages unfortunately still little known in Central America and in Mexico. Another explorer of Central America, especially of the northwestern portion near Mexico, was the German-Mexican geologist Federico K. G. Müllerried, who, under the auspices of the Pan American Institute of Geography and History, undertook geological and paleontological studies here between 1930 and 1950.

Recently with the establishment of national geological services in El Salvador, Nicaragua, and Costa Rica the exploration of these countries has been stimulated. An important contribution of over-all value for Middle America is the book by R. Weyl, of Giessen, entitled *Die Geologie Mittelamerikas* (1961). Mention should also be made of the North American geologists and paleontologists in the Panama Canal Zone, among whom W. A. Woodring, of the U. S. Geological Survey, is one of the most important.

In both southern Mexico and Central America paleogeographic reconstructions have been attempted since the latter part of the 19th century, culminating in the publication of the work of Charles Schuchert, entitled *Historical Geology of the Antillean-Caribbean Region*, still a classic since its appearance in 1935. In it Schuchert analyzed in detail the most important aspects of the regional geological history and prepared a set of paleogeographic maps that will serve as reference for the present article. After his death other maps that he had prepared were published in 1955 in a collection, *Paleogeography of North America*, but they add little to what was already known about Middle America.

In 1955 A. J. Eardley published his *Structural Geology of North America*, a basic contribution to the understanding of structural relationships of the whole of North and Central America. The most recent work is by the French workers Henri and Geneviève Termier, of the University of Paris, whose *Atlas de Paléogéographie* (1960) includes data concerning the paleogeographic conditions of Middle America in relation to the rest of the world as well as significant paleobiological information. We should also mention bibliographies concerning Mexico (Aguilar y Santillán, 1908, 1918, 1930) and Central America and northwestern South America (Maldonado-Koerdell, 1958c).

GEOLOGICAL PROVINCES

In Middle America from northwest to southeast, between the Tropic of Cancer and northwestern Colombia, the following principal geological provinces can be distinguished (Eardley, 1951, fig. 338):

1. Western Sierra Madre
2. Central High Plateau
3. Coastal Plain of the Gulf of Mexico
4. Neovolcanic Axis
5. Southern Sierra Madre
6. Isthmus of Tehuantepec
7. Peninsula of Yucatan
8. Mountains of northwestern Central America
9. Volcanoes of El Salvador and Nicaragua
10. Coastal Plains
    a. of the Pacific Ocean and
    b. of the Caribbean Sea
11. Isthmus of Costa Rica–Panama
12. Colombian Andes

These geological provinces correspond generally to the principal geomorphological features and especially to structural units. Central America has not been so widely studied in these aspects as has Mexico, and thus future investigations perhaps will modify these divisions (fig. 2). They do,

5

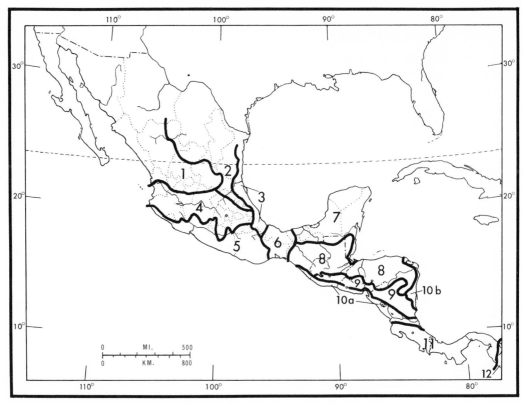

FIG. 2—PRINCIPAL GEOLOGICAL PROVINCES OF MIDDLE AMERICA
See text, p. 5, for names of numbered provinces.

however, permit a description of tectonic conditions, of the distribution of rocks, and of geological events in the paleogeographic reconstruction of this area.

In the central part of Mexico exists a great sialic block (i.e., of continental rocks) with moderate basal folds and very complex tectonic conditions that gave rise to a gigantic structure, the Western Continent, on whose western border rises the Western Sierra Madre and whose southern limits are poorly defined and covered by the immense volcanic flows of the Cenozoic. On the east, as a result of tensional forces that caused strong folding, rises the Eastern Sierra Madre following approximately the direction of the old Mexican Geosyncline of Mesozoic age, to which reference will be made later and whose eastern declivity is a coastal plain along the Gulf of Mexico. The mountainous section of southern Mexico in-

cludes a great depression, the basin of the Balsas River, separated from the Pacific Ocean by a great transverse mass—the Sierra Madre del Sur—which runs from west to east to the Isthmus of Tehuantepec.

The Peninsula of Yucatan represents the foreland of the folded mountains of northwestern Central America, closely connected in origin and development with a similar contemporary tectonic process that formed the Eastern Sierra Madre of Mexico. Also, toward the south there extends obliquely a wide volcanic belt through Guatemala, El Salvador, Nicaragua, and Costa Rica, whose southern and eastern declivities are, respectively, the coastal plains of the Pacific Ocean and of the Caribbean Sea (Bullard, 1957). An old Middle American Continent, contemporary to the Western Continent located more to the northwest, possibly underlies the vast lava flows of this volcanic

6

belt, as well as the transverse mountainous massif from Guatemala to Nicaragua; for from Costa Rica one can speak of a geological "bridgehead" directed toward Middle America from the Colombian Andes of South America, although geologically it forms a part of the same chain in structure and evolution.

There are on the floor of the Pacific Ocean, the Gulf of Mexico, and the Caribbean Sea other structural features such as the Middle American Trench, a trough that extends along the Pacific coast from Nayarit and Jalisco, in western Mexico, to Costa Rica, and farther south through a deep that includes the Gulf of Panama and the northwestern Coast of Colombia. The Gulf of Mexico can be conceived of as a depression in the form of an elongated funnel lying from west to east, in whose deepest part is the Sigsbee Trough, surrounded on the west, south, and southeast by a broad continental shelf that extends almost 200 km. off the Peninsula of Yucatan. The depths of the Caribbean Sea along the north and east coast of Central America represent a transition from the continental shelf to the great transverse depression south of the island of Cuba, the Bartlett (or Cayman) Trough. There exists, both on this side (Gulf of Mexico and Caribbean Sea) as well as on the opposite side (Pacific Ocean), an infinity of sea-mounts of various types.

PRECAMBRIAN TIMES

We can make only generalized conjectures about the distribution of rocks and paleogeographic traits of the Archeozoic in Mexico and in Central America. Formerly it was believed that certain intrusive and metamorphic rocks cropping out in various parts of Mexico along the Pacific coast, from the Peninsula of Baja California to Chiapas, were Precambrian, but later studies have demonstrated that they are of Middle or Late Mesozoic age, and even more recent. However, in Guerrero, Oaxaca, and Chiapas it appears that some of these rocks

are actually Archeozoic, as several stratigraphic units have been defined, and a crystalline and metamorphic basal complex has been recognized (Maldonado-Koerdell, 1954b, stratigraphic table).

In Guatemala, Honduras, and Nicaragua metamorphic rocks abound (Roberts and Irving, 1957) such as gneiss, schists, and quartzites, forming the "nuclei" of mountainous elevations. Their grade of metamorphism is highly varied. Sapper and Staub (1937) as well as Müllerried (1942b) considered that some could partially represent Precambrian formations and others could be of Late Paleozoic age. Schuchert (1935) mentioned that many metamorphic rocks in Guatemala and Nicaragua underlie fossiliferous deposits of obvious Paleozoic age, and therefore can be considered archaic. However, one must not lose sight of the fact that the metamorphic process could have been caused by orogenic movements and granitic intrusions during other geological periods later than the Precambrian.

PALEOZOIC ERA

Paleozoic rocks are abundant in Middle America. Through their index fossils, at least in their upper levels, their age has been determined more precisely than Precambrian rocks and stratigraphic units have been defined in many localities in Mexico (Maldonado-Koerdell, 1954b) as well as in Central America (Schuchert, 1935; Roberts and Irving, 1957). They extend practically from the northern limit of Middle America to Nicaragua; they have not yet been identified precisely farther to the southeast, although they possibly exist in Costa Rica and easternmost Panama. It is well known that a Paleozoic batholith exists in the Department of Antioquia (Colombia) of Ordovician age (Botero Arango, 1942), the principal mass of which shows predominantly metamorphic and intrusive rocks.

During Paleozoic times Middle America was subjected to strong tectonic activity (roughly contemporary to the Marathon-

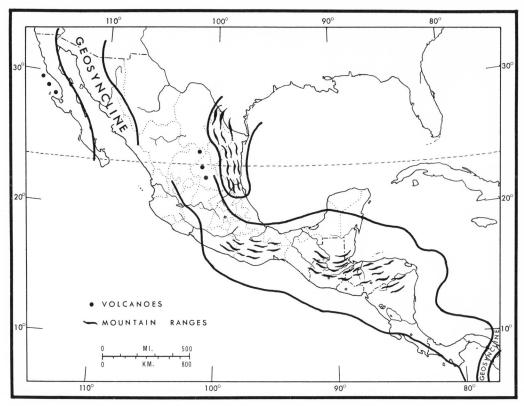

FIG. 3—LATE PALEOZOIC OROGENIC BELTS IN MIDDLE AMERICA AND ADJACENT
AREAS

Ouachita of North America), characterized by strong folding, which adopted the form of a convex arc toward the south. The west portion of the arc coincided with the territory of Guerrero and Oaxaca in Mexico; the east portion may have covered Guatemala, British Honduras, and the northwest zone of Nicaragua. In such a manner, according to Eardley (1951), one can conceive of the existence of a great orogenic belt that approximately followed the curve of the west margin of the present Gulf of Mexico, being displaced farther to the southeast in the south part to constitute what Schuchert (1935) calls "nuclear" Central America. Little is known about the nature of such forces (possibly originating in the east and dispersing to the north and south) and their relationship with the orogenic belts of the Paleozoic era in South America, although they represent the first

phases of the long geological process that formed Middle America (fig. 3).

Since the latter part of the 19th century (Dollfus and Montserrat, 1868; Manó, 1883a,b; Sapper, 1894, 1896) the existence of index fossils of the Late Paleozoic in the northwest portion of Guatemala has been known, particularly fusulinids that are important for the fixing of a precise age. On examination of these fossils many years later (Thompson and Miller, 1944; Roberts and Irving, 1957) several formations of the geologic column were defined as stratigraphic units of Late Paleozoic in Guatemala, whereas in Mexico they include part of the Mississippian-Pennsylvanian and the Permian periods, as indicated by a rich fusulinid fauna (Maldonado-Koerdell, 1952). Possibly in northern Honduras and western Nicaragua some slates, phyllites, limestones, and quartzites correspond to deposits of the

8

Permian, but their fossils are very poorly preserved and do not permit precise identification, much less the fixing of their age and correlations.

In their totality, the Precambrian and Paleozoic rocks in Middle America appear to present undoubtedly an "arched" disposition that Schuchert (1935) separated into two great structures: (1) the *pre-Paleozoic arc* whose principal segment is represented by the Sierra de las Minas in Guatemala, continued eastward by other chains in that country and in Honduras, and accompanied by minor structures in the north part of Guatemala and British Honduras, although he indicated that this refers more properly to the present orography; and (2) the *Paleozoic arc* with the highest mountains in Chiapas, in Mexico and northwest of Guatemala, formed by strong folding and faulted as a result of later intense tectonic activity. For Mexico the evidence is less clear, since the structural axis can hardly be recognized underneath the immense volcanic flows of the Cenozoic era that have covered almost all the Precambrian and Paleozoic rocks west of the Isthmus of Tehuantepec.

Extreme northwest Middle America was the southern terminus of the Cordilleran Geosyncline, a structure that extended from the ancestral Arctic Ocean N-S along the western border of the Canadian shield, and had notable permanence from Precambrian until the middle of the Mesozoic. This geosyncline received several thousands of meters of sediments from the Canadian shield as well as from the old land of Cascadia, which lay more to the west and whose southern point generally coincided with the present-day Peninsula of Lower California. Between the southern terminus of the Cordilleran Geosyncline and the extreme southern point of the Marathon-Ouachita axis there extended a low, arid land called Llanoria, much affected by intense tectonics. The history of Llanoria contains many episodes of emergence and subsidence and

vulcanism, which do not form part of the study of Middle America but which notably influenced its own evolution, especially in the latter part of the Paleozoic and the beginning of the Mesozoic.

Extreme southeast Middle America also had a complex geological history during the Precambrian and Paleozoic eras, which took place along the northwest border of the Guianan-Brazilian shield. During the Ordovician the intrusion of an enormous batholith induced strong metamorphism in the pre-existing rocks of Antioquia (Botero Arango, 1942). All northwestern Colombia and eastern Panama of the present day suffered strong isostatic movements causing geosynclinal troughs of varying direction and depth in which thousands of meters of sediments were later deposited, as in the Cordilleran Geosyncline.

Thus we can outline a Precambrian and Paleozoic Middle America of very irregular contours, the eastern part approximately following the "arched" line of the orogenic belts of those geological epochs, and the western part located between the Cordilleran Geosyncline and the geosynclines that ran along the northwest portion of the Guianan-Brazilian shield. On the north the old land of Llanoria, with its intense tectonics, would border Middle America, directly connected with it during certain stages and becoming separate as the epiric seas of the late Paleozoic advanced. The extreme southeast of Middle America is much less known, although there appear to exist Paleozoic rocks in Costa Rica and eastern Panama, now practically covered by the enormous volcanic flows of the Cenozoic.

In view of the geological history of the Antillean Islands and certain features recently discovered on the floor of the Caribbean Sea, the existence of a Caribbean Land to the east of Precambrian and Paleozoic Middle America has been suggested. The Caribbean Land would have emerged in an extensive area to the east and south-

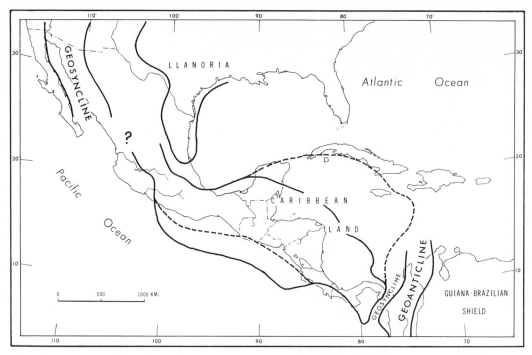

Fig. 4—LATE PALEOZOIC PALEOGEOGRAPHY OF MIDDLE AMERICA AND ADJACENT
AREAS
Broken lines represent another possible position of land mass.

east of the present Gulf of Mexico, including the Greater Antilles (up to Puerto
Rico) and Cape Catoche on the Yucatan
Peninsula and Cape Gracias a Dios in Honduras, as well as the northern half of the
present Caribbean Sea. This Caribbean
Land would really have been an eastern
continuation of the southeastern extremity
of the structural arcs already mentioned
in Guatemala and Honduras, and would
have been limited on the south by the Precambrian and Paleozoic geosynclines that
ran along the northwest border of the
Guianan-Brazilian shield (fig. 4).

MESOZOIC ERA

At the beginning of the Mesozoic (Early
Triassic), the Marathon-Ouachita axis, prolonged southward by the young Coahuila
Mountains, extended to northern Middle
America, which was united with the extreme south of the North American Continent and with the Caribbean Land toward

the east, as well as with the northwest part
of the South American Continent. That is
to say, in early Triassic Middle America
reached its maximum terrestrial area in its
geological evolution. It extended from one
continent to another, shallow epirical seas
covering it only in certain subareas, with
the exception of the Cordilleran Geosyncline, which as always was prolonged
southward and affected by intense volcanic
activity (fig. 5).

Continental deposits of the Triassic
abound in Middle America and numerous
stratigraphic units have already been recognized from Mexico to Honduras (Reeside
et al., 1957; Maldonado-Koerdell, 1958b).
These deposits are manifested in a great
variety of clastic rocks, generally red to
black, with abundant remains of plants
(ferns, cycads, etc.) and veins of coal, especially in Oaxaca, Mexico, where fossil
floras have been amply studied by Wieland
(1913, 1914), and in the vicinity of Tegu-

10

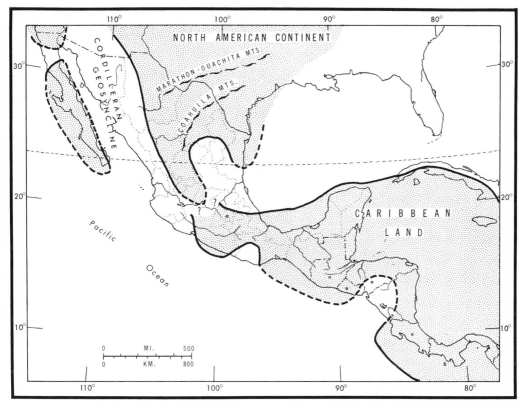

Fig. 5—EARLY TRIASSIC PALEOGEOGRAPHY OF MIDDLE AMERICA AND ADJACENT AREAS
Stippled portions indicate land.

cigalpa, Honduras (Newberry, 1888a,b; Humphreys, 1916; Maldonado-Koerdell, 1953a). It is interesting to point out the peculiar paleobiogeographic relations of such floras that possess vegetal elements of Gondwanic character, possibly originating in the southernmost portion of South America.

In the Late Triassic a number of marine transgressions occurred in northeastern Middle America from the east, and formed the Mexican Geosyncline during the latter part of Jurassic and throughout Cretaceous. On the whole, the Jurassic was a time of great marine deposition, mainly in the northern and eastern regions of present Mexico, as attested by several thousand meters of various kinds of rocks, essentially richly fossiliferous limestones. Also from

the Pacific Ocean approximately at the boundary between Michoacan and Guerrero, a small marine transgression left sediments now covered with igneous rocks of the Cenozoic, whereas on the northwest border of the Guianan-Brazilian shield minor geosynclines reappeared, thus delimiting the Caribbean Land anew.

During the Cretaceous tectonic movements began to affect both sides of northern Middle America, announcing the great changes that developed later on. The slow disappearance of the Cordilleran Geosyncline, as well as the emergence of a terrestrial belt to the west of the Mexican Geosyncline, ensured the continuity of the Caribbean Land with the northwest portion of Middle America, although at a given time (Neocomian) the Balsas Canal cut

11

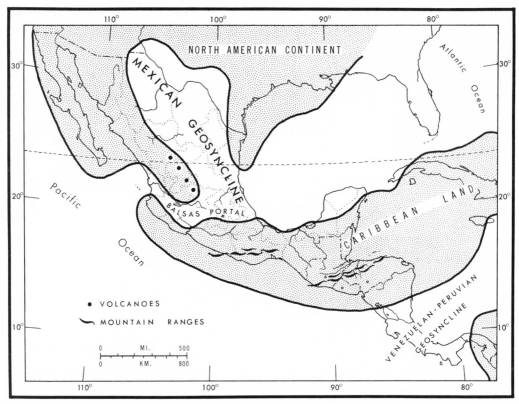

Fig. 6—MID-CRETACEOUS PALEOGEOGRAPHY OF MIDDLE AMERICA AND ADJACENT AREAS
Stippled areas indicate land.

this communication (Imlay, 1939; Erben, 1957a) establishing a marine passage between the Mexican Geosyncline and the ancestral Pacific Ocean (fig. 6).

Less known are the contemporary episodes to the southeast of the Isthmus of Tehuantepec, but as geological explorations in Central America progress, the paleogeographic phases of the Mesozoic become better defined. In Guatemala, Honduras, and Nicaragua very fossiliferous marine rocks of Jurassic and Cretaceous ages exist. These are similar in all respects to those existing in Mexico, including traits that denote the same conditions of origin and deposition (bathial deposits, reef facies, and minor orogenies). In Costa Rica and Panama, the existence of Mesozoic rocks of marine origin is known only in a few isolated localities southeast of San José; and

marking the trajectory of the old geosynclines between the Caribbean Sea and the Pacific Ocean, the same rocks with their index fossils abound in northwest Colombia.

Numerous paleontological studies have been carried out in the Mesozoic fossil floras and faunas of Middle America, particularly in Mexico, and mention has already been made of some concerning vegetal remains and veins of coal. Among the invertebrates, the group of the rudistids (mollusks connected with reef facies) have received special attention in Guatemala (MacGillavry, 1934, 1937; Müllerried, 1942a,b, 1945, 1948), as well as various groups of foraminifera and corals (see Maldonado-Koerdell, 1958c).

A certain confusion exists in nomenclature, especially in the correlation of stratigraphic units in Central America, where a

12

more detailed study of petrographic characteristics and conditions of deposition of these rocks is necessary. The best known area is in the northwest (Guatemala, El Salvador, Honduras, and Nicaragua), where the geological column has a basement of Mesozoic continental or marine-continental deposits (El Plan–Tegucigalpa, Todos Santos and Metapan formations) covered by limestones, marls, and sands (Esquias formation) in some localities, and in others only by limestones (Ixcoy and Coban formations) with folds and faults that are not satisfactorily known. In the vicinity of San Juancito, Honduras, the Cretaceous rocks have been studied in more detail, leading to the recognition of several stratigraphic units (Cantarranas, Metapan [?], Colonia, Crucero y Plancitos formations) of varying lithology and thickness, which, like the previous ones, still present problems of correlation in spite of their wealth of fossils (Carpenter, 1954; Roberts and Irving, 1957). (During the preparation of this article the Central American volume of the *International Lexicon of Stratigraphy* was published by R. Hoffstetter in Paris, 1961, in which much of this confusion has been clarified.)

This situation contrasts with the relatively good knowledge available on the Mesozoic stratigraphy in Mexico, especially in the north, the plain of the Gulf of Mexico, and Chiapas and Oaxaca, but there still remain problems in western Mexico. Possibly there are some 70 known stratigraphical units, both continental and marine, of varying lithology, many of them with numerous index fossils that also have been the object of broad studies. The principal studies published in the last quarter century are Erben, 1957a,b; Imlay, 1943, 1944a,b, 1952; Maldonado-Koerdell, 1954b, 1958b; Müller-ried, 1942b, 1944, 1947b, 1948, 1949a, some of which have paleogeographic maps of major interest.

In the extreme northwest of South America the geological history of the geosynclines

bordering the Guianan-Brazilian shield included emergence and subsidence at repeated intervals of the nearby lands, reconstructed by L. G. Weeks (1956) in a set of paleogeographic maps that extend to other subareas of that terrestrial mass. Everything seems to indicate that the Cordilleran Geosyncline located west of the present North American Continent was a counterpart of the great Chilean-Peruvian Geosyncline, which extended from the Equatorial region to the southern tip of South America, with a maximum transverse development at both extremities. Thus, the short bordering geosynclines would have really represented temporary epiric transgressions, in all aspects similar to other transisthmic marine invasions that have affected Middle America throughout geological time, a feature marking its essential structural and historical unity.

Toward the end of the Cretaceous, Middle America entered a phase of intense mountain building, initiated at various points by intrusions of diorite, granodiorite, and quartziferous monzonite that cut the sedimentary rocks previously deposited. In Mexico these intrusions were once considered of Precambrian age. However, on examination of their structure and geologic conditions in more detail and because of their being covered by Tertiary and Quaternary materials, their age was established as late Cretaceous (Peninsula of Lower California, southern portion of Mexico), although there is no doubt about the greater antiquity of other intrusions. In Guatemala, El Salvador, Honduras, and Nicaragua intrusive rocks of the same Cretaceous (or Early Tertiary) age are known (Carpenter, 1954; Roberts and Irving, 1957), identical to the intrusive rocks of Mexico.

The appearance of new mountain chains resulting from folding, particularly along the coastal plain of the Gulf of Mexico and a diagonal axis (from northwest to southeast) through Chiapas, Guatemala, and Honduras, was also characteristic of late

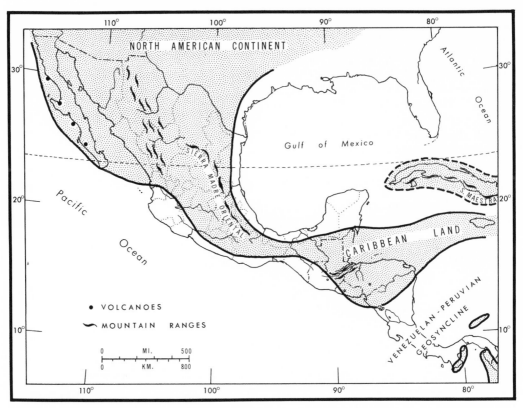

Fig. 7—EARLY TERTIARY PALEOGEOGRAPHY OF MIDDLE AMERICA AND ADJACENT AREAS
Stippled areas indicate land.

Cretaceous in Middle America. In the extreme southeast the geosynclines bordering the Guianan-Brazilian shield were closed temporarily, the seas retiring toward the northeast and southwest while mountain chains oriented obliquely toward Panama appeared. In other words, Middle America actively participated in the Laramide Revolution, with many changes in its configuration, relief, climate, floras and faunas, as did other nearby lands that also suffered the effects of that orogeny.

The Mesozoic era left a basic structural pattern for Middle America, on which successive events during Tertiary built its present physical characteristics through emergence, folding and faulting, and erosion. Nothing essential was added afterwards, except new pieces of land, a rougher relief, and a modern assortment of living forms,

caused by the extinction of many of the older ones, or the addition of many newcomers better adapted to changed environmental conditions.

CENOZOIC ERA

A most important geological event of Middle America was the continual emergence of land throughout most of Tertiary, with only occasional subsidence in the truly isthmic sections (Tehuantepec, Nicaragua, Panama). The epiric seas that still covered portions of Middle America in the latter part of Mesozoic began to recede, with small transgressive oscillations in Oligocene, giving rise approximately to the present shape of the land mass, while at the same time tectonic forces raised the high plateaus of Mexico, Guatemala-Honduras, and Costa Rica. These changes in the environment

14

caused complete extinction of many groups of plants and animals in Middle America. Other changes occurred in the nearby seas, whose physical-chemical regime was also modified by the same factors that modified the aspect of the land.

The disappearance of the Mexican Geosyncline greatly extended Middle America toward the northeast. Through folding and faulting tectonic forces raised the Sierra Madre Oriental in Mexico, and an active process of erosion caused deposition of richly fossiliferous marine formations on the present coastal plain of the Gulf of Mexico. Paleocene and Eocene were periods of marine regression, but new transgressions occurred during Oligocene, whereas the remainder of Tertiary was characterized by the complete regression of the sea and the development of the contemporary coastline. Thus, the general form of Mexico was delineated, but other events took place in Central America that delayed the development of its configuration (fig. 7).

In the extreme north-central part of Middle America, at the time of the lifting of the continental mass, red conglomerates were deposited during Early Tertiary (Edwards, 1956) as shown by fossil vertebrates. Isolated volcanic activity took place during the same epoch in southern Mexico, combined with tectonic activity that metamorphosed the ancient sediments, especially in Oaxaca, Guerrero, and Michoacan. Little is known of Central America during that time, except for the Darien region where marine deposits of Eocene age attain several hundred meters in thickness indicating emergence and intense erosion.

On the Caribbean side Middle America was subjected to a certain amount of instability, manifested by transgressions and regressions of the sea. In certain subareas along that coast bottom conditions fostered the development of reef structures rich with fossils and with a variegated lithology. It seems that little or no volcanic activity took place during the lowermost Tertiary

on this side, although it has been pointed out that on the northern part of the Caribbean Land some small volcanoes were active during Upper Eocene-Lower Oligocene but became entirely quiet by Middle Oligocene.

The existence during Eocene of a Venezuelan-Peruvian Geosyncline cutting off the Caribbean Land and the southeast tip of Middle America from the South American Continent has been established. Some islands scattered along its axis were later reunited and formed a tongue which reduced the width of that geosyncline during Oligocene times. However, an archipelago lay to the northwest, more or less in line with a large island that formed the main part of present Honduras and adjoining territories to the northwest and the southeast.

During the Paleocene and Eocene periods there was close unity between northwestern Middle America and the isthmian subarea, and no marine formations are known from a long stretch almost reaching the Venezuelan-Peruvian Geosyncline. It seems that the oscillations of that isthmus began with Oligocene and produced a wide transverse canal connecting the Gulf of Mexico with the Pacific Ocean across Tehuantepec, a forerunner of a much wider portal that lasted through Miocene. Such, at least, is the evidence gathered from the stratigraphy and paleontology of the marine formations which abound in the Isthmus of Tehuantepec, although the complete mixing of sea waters from both sides has been disputed by some workers.

Except for the marine faunas of Lower Tertiary and some plants found in the conglomerates of that age in various localities of Mexico, almost nothing is known of its paleontology in Middle America. Undoubtedly no great changes in climate or environment took place during the first epochs of the Laramide Revolution, although with the emergence of the land and the closing of the Mesozoic portals new territories be-

15

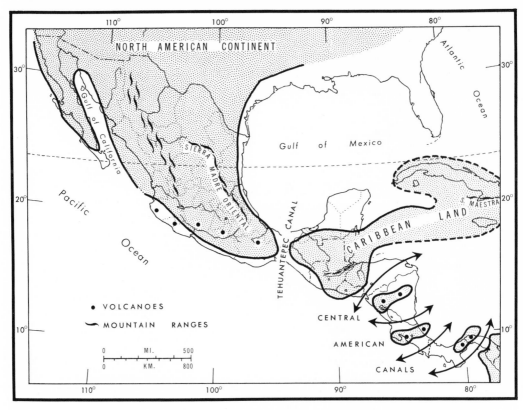

Fig. 8—MID-TERTIARY PALEOGEOGRAPHY OF MIDDLE AMERICA AND ADJACENT
AREAS
Stippled areas indicate land.

came open to the influx of living organisms. However, through both the northern entrance and the southern isthmus, plants and animals began to migrate into or cross through that territory, as indicated by the Primates, which further evolved afterwards in South America, and other forms that invaded North America from that area, long before the opening of the marine canals at the end of Oligocene.

In northwest Middle America the marine regression of Lower Tertiary caused the total disappearance of the Cordilleran Geosyncline, accompanied by a certain amount of volcanic activity to the east as shown by the stratigraphic position of lavas and pyroclastics in Sonora and Chihuahua. During Miocene very intense tectonic activity broke the coastline and separated the pres-

ent Peninsula of Lower California from the rest of Mexico, creating the San Andreas fault-line system. The invasion of the depressed surface along the fault by sea water formed the Gulf of California (or Cortez Sea), an almost unique elongated structural and sedimentary basin (fig. 8).

In the Costa Rica-Panama subarea a similar process took place probably in the same epoch, forming two small peninsulas. The larger one is the Peninsula of Nicoya, separated from the continent by a sea arm identical with the Gulf of California, whereas the smaller Osa Peninsula to the southeast is less comparable to Lower California and Nicoya. These three peninsulas have never been compared in detail, although they represent a major geologic feature of the west coast of North America

16

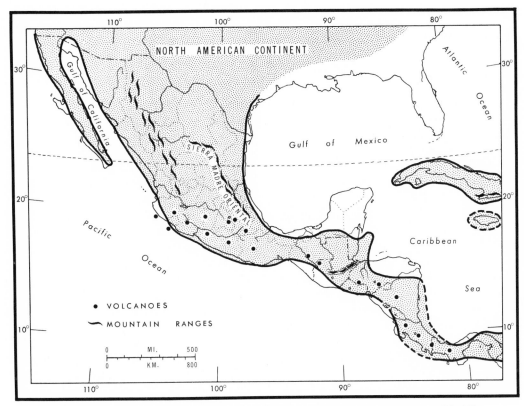

Fig. 9—MIOCENE-PLIOCENE PALEOGEOGRAPHY OF MIDDLE AMERICA AND AD-
JACENT AREAS
Stippled areas indicate land.

and were undoubtedly the result of tectonic activity that extended from one extreme to the other of the same land mass.

Miocene also marked the beginning of great igneous activity which formed the Sierra Madre Occidental in Mexico, whose southern end is situated in Jalisco, Nayarit, and Aguascalientes, south of the Tropic of Cancer. In other subareas numerous rhyolitic flows and other manifestations of vulcanism were accompanied by the progressive emergence of the Mexican Plateau (Mooser, 1957). During that period the climatic zones of the world acquired their modern characteristics, that is to say, the north and south polar areas were delimited as well as the temperate and tropical areas, thus completing the effect of geological changes on the relief, vegetation, and fauna.

The geological history of Central America during Middle Tertiary is better known. Its rocks and fossils indicate a great similarity of events with the rest of Middle America. The greatest volcanic activity was registered during Miocene-Pliocene; abundant rhyolitic flows and other volcanic manifestations appeared, while the territory was lifted more and more above sea level. Certain known intrusions in Guatemala, El Salvador, Honduras, and Nicaragua possibly also took place in that epoch (Roberts and Irving, 1957), as well as minor marine transgressions in different subareas, whose sediments are mixed with contemporary pyroclastic materials (fig. 9).

Numerous stratigraphic units of Middle Tertiary (Miocene) have been identified in Middle America, especially on the coastal

17

plain of the Gulf of Mexico and in the vicinity of the Panama Canal Zone (López Ramos, 1956; Woodring and Thompson, 1949). Most of these formations are clearly of marine origin, although some also include pyroclastic materials (Roberts and Irving, 1957). In the extreme southwest of Middle America, during Oligocene-Miocene times, communication between the Atlantic and Pacific oceans still existed south of the Caribbean Land in Panama and Colombia. A thick layer of fossiliferous sediments was deposited in these portals (Weeks, 1956; Termier and Termier, 1960), similar to the episodes in the Isthmus of Tehuantepec during Oligocene-Pliocene times (Schuchert, 1935; Termier and Termier, 1960).

Middle American flora underwent profound modification as result of the changes in relief, climate, and other environmental conditions; archaic forms incapable of adapting themselves to the new conditions disappeared and new forms appeared (by evolution or migration). In Middle Tertiary floras of the hot, temperate, and cold climates were well defined (because of altitude factors) and distributed in their respective subareas. Thus, for example, the ferns, cycads, and palms accumulated in hot, humid localities; the tree forms (sequoia, cypress) were widely distributed on the extensive plains of Middle America where there was a hot climate with alternating droughts and humidity and very marked seasons; and, finally, the conifers (fir, pine) remained in high, cold places.

Similarly the fauna suffered great changes leading to the disappearance of many groups and the appearance of new ones in that territory and its adjacent marine waters, where the hot climate of Middle Tertiary permitted the existence of forms adapted to those conditions. On the other hand, some animals migrated from north to south (equids) and others from south to north (opossums), and autoch-

thonous forms developed in this area. A number of localities (Honduras, valleys of Puebla and Toluca, Mexico) still await intensive paleontological study.

In the Caribbean Land, Upper Oligocene had continued unbroken with Miocene, but as in the rest of Middle America, strong volcanic activity developed, and its products mixed with sedimentary materials, accompanied by intrusions which contributed to the general deformation of rocks and structural features. However, during the major part of Miocene the Caribbean Land continued to be connected with the isthmian portion of Middle America, cutting off the seas to the northwest and southeast. This fact explains the similarity of certain fossil forms in both subareas, although little comparative study of paleontological remains and paleoecological conditions has been made.

The Middle Pliocene transitional epoch was characterized by a long period of volcanic quiescence and intense erosion which peneplained the landscape, as seen in the Sierra of Xochitepec in central Mexico and other localities. In Central America (highlands of Guatemala and Costa Rica mainly) a similar process took place, but these subareas are just beginning to be intensively studied. As evidence of volcanic filling old surfaces are clearly recognizable at altitudes above 3000 m., indicating the height of igneous activity attained at the end of that period and the initiation of weathering processes in Upper Tertiary.

Renewed volcanic activity began in the whole area in Upper Pliocene, depositing extensive areas of rhyolitic and dacitic lavas, which form the base of the igneous rock system of that period. Thick deposits now cover the peaks of many sierras, protecting the underlying materials of Middle Tertiary age from erosion. Originally these lavas expanded in wide valleys, but as a result of tectonic forces they were later raised and their topography was inverted. A number of Upper Pliocene lava series

18

(in regard to their nomenclature and position) have been recognized in Mexico, but they are much less known in Central America, where they should undoubtedly exist. (Some contributions of fundamental importance on the petrographic sequence of Central America, by G. Dengo, of recent years, should be consulted in this respect.)

In Mexico the volcanologic and tectonic aspects of this process have been carefully studied by Mooser (1957) in the vicinity of the national capital, where several series interfinger or adjoin. Volcanic deposits in this subarea piled up as stratified apparatuses and blocked many streams, thus beginning the development of enclosed basins. Subsequently, their own weight contributed to a complicated process of block faulting and instability, causing structural features like grabens and horsts of varied elevations, which in turn influenced climatic changes (strong rains, heavy transportation of eroded materials, extensive alluvial fans on flanks).

Thus, the rapid destruction of Lower and Middle Tertiary igneous rocks created various clastic series mixed with sands, gravels, and other materials. Pedologic phenomena formed the first "modern" soil now known as the Tarango "formation" (Bryan, 1948), easily recognizable in canyons and ravines around the Valley of Mexico and adjoining depressions. It must be noticed that lavas do not alternate with the Tarango "formation" in any place where they have been studied, indicating that volcanic activity had almost ceased at the time of development of the new soil, which was formed in a semiarid climate with scarce vegetation and fauna.

The uniform structural surface of alluvial fans was largely preserved, showing relative youth and therefore may have existed from Upper Pliocene to Lower Pleistocene. The size and thickness of such alluvial fans vary in relation to their elevation, but they have great similarity in composition with the Tarango "formation," and have been

considered as a special expression obeying differences in level. Clastic materials are lacking in them as a rule, and a pedologic process caused pedalferous soils in contrast to the pedocals found in other localities.

Pliocene also marked the appearance of the Neovolcanic Axis of Mexico, a transverse belt that extends from the Pacific coast to the Gulf of Mexico, more or less between parallels 19° and 21° N. A number of very high volcanic peaks are located along this axis: Volcan and Nevado de Colima, Pico de Tancitaro, Nevado de Toluca, Popocatepetl (with at least three Pliocene-Pleistocene episodes), Iztaccihuatl, Malinche and Pico de Orizaba, although there are many others of lesser elevation (Sánchez, 1937). These volcanoes pertain to the group of stratified volcanoes formed by successive flows; their chimneys were finally obstructed by plugs which, in many cases, caused the formation of numerous parasitic craters, some of them also very high and complex in structure.

Obviously, under such conditions, plant assemblages were directly affected in their existence and distribution, although in many subareas far from or unaffected by volcanic activity there were no modifications. South of the Tropic of Cancer the three main altitudinal climatic zones (high, medium, and low) already mentioned were preserved in many localities of Middle America. However, continuous volcanic activity inflicted heavy losses on the Middle Tertiary floras (mainly the arboreal types), which recovered or were replaced only when the Tarango soils developed over the igneous materials.

During Lower Pliocene, animals of many groups occupied Middle America, but with the beginning of volcanic activity they also suffered heavy losses, especially those that could not rapidly escape to other subareas. However, one of the strangest facts of their paleontology is the scarcity of fossil remains in the Tarango soils, which has not yet been properly explained. It might be that

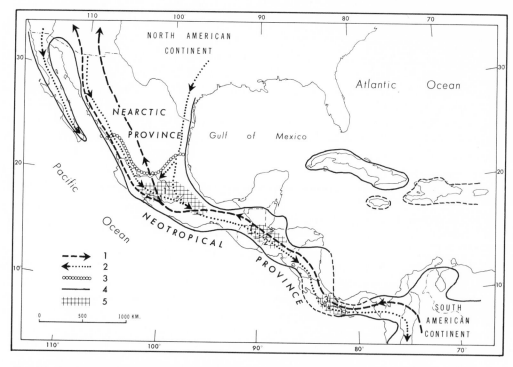

Fig. 10—MIOCENE-PLIOCENE ROUTES OF ANIMAL MIGRATIONS
Key: 1. South-north routes. 2. North-south routes. 3. Boundary between Nearctic and Neotropical Provinces. 4. Margin of Miocene-Pliocene land area. 5. Highland areas: (1) Central Mexico; (2) Guatemala-Honduras; (3) Costa Rica-Panama

the semiaridity of the climate, existing since the beginning of the period, also contributed to the limitation of their populations except in favorable localities.

The disappearance of the Venezuelan-Peruvian Geosyncline reunited the isthmian portion of Middle America with South America, allowing migration in both directions of numerous forms, plant and/or animal (fig. 10). The most convenient way for such exchanges was the eastern coastal plain, where the presence of fossil remains (Veracruz, Tabasco, and Peninsula of Yucatan in Mexico and subarea of Honduras) indicates routes of migration far from the western coast, which was directly under the influence of volcanic activity. This does not necessarily imply that plants and animals did not use other routes during intervening periods of quiescence along the central regions or the western coast itself.

Toward the end of Pliocene it seems that there was a long period of volcanic quiescence on the mainland, although both the erosive and soil-forming processes continued, causing a strong relief and facilitating the location of plants and animals. On the other hand, the complex hydrographic systems of Mexico and most probably those of Central America became established during the same epoch. On the west side of the North American Continent a revival (or continuation) of igneous activity sustained strong faulting, associated with E-W lines of weakness in the bottom of the eastern Pacific Ocean and connected with the Neovolcanic Axis of Mexico (Maldonado-Koerdell, 1958a).

In Lower Pleistocene this system of faults created transverse submarine fracture zones, which appeared on the floor of the eastern Pacific Ocean as a result of crustal bulging and breaking. One of these fracture zones (Clarion) lies in line with the

20

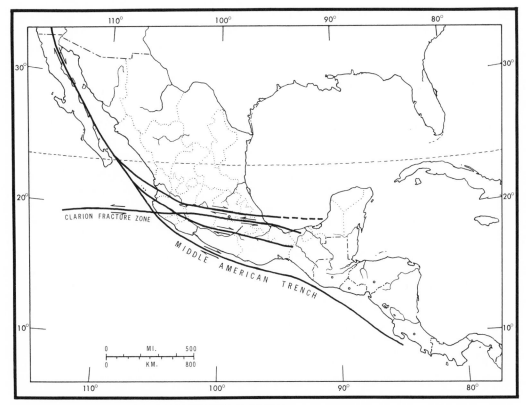

Fɪɢ. 11—FRACTURE ZONES IN MIDDLE AMERICA
Arrows indicate direction of sheer.

Neovolcanic Axis of Mexico, and was the result of a deep-seated shear-zone, "on top of which, along *en échelon* tension fractures the volcanoes appeared" (De Cserna, 1958); another fracture zone lies farther south and has a more complicated situation. Thus, much of the present relief of Mexico is due to a complex pattern of structural conditions and tectonic activity originating in the nearby Pacific Ocean and associated with the peculiar development of volcanic zones.

De Cserna (1958) has demonstrated that the combined action of submarine and continental tectonics affected southern Mexico to a great extent, displacing northwards the shore of the Gulf of Mexico and raising the Isthmus of Tehuantepec as well as the Chiapas highland. More faulting occurred (Webber and Ojeda, 1957) in those subareas, and intense uplift again started the

erosion of older structures and increased the filling of intermontane depressions with alluvium. Similar episodes took place in Central America, although it seems to have differed there, since in some cases Late Pliocene was accompanied by eruptions (Honduras) while in others there was a great break in deposition (Nicaragua, Costa Rica) (Schuchert, 1935).

At the same time, the San Andreas fault, crossing the Gulf of California from northwest to southeast, became trifurcated at the latitude of the Islas Marias off the west coast of Mexico (Mooser and Maldonado-Koerdell, 1961). The northernmost division entered the continent obliquely, and formed a transverse graben-like fault (Lake Chapala); the middle division crossed Jalisco and Michoacan and formed the Rio Balsas basin, which extends practically across Guerrero and Oaxaca. The southernmost

21

division continued along the southwest coast of Mexico as the Middle American Trench, reaching Central America and ending in front of Nicoya Peninsula in Costa Rica (fig. 11).

On the side of the Gulf of Mexico, pivoting on the Chiapas-Tabasco subarea and its strongly folded foreland, the Peninsula of Yucatan began to rise slowly from south to north by the end of Pliocene. It seems that the Caribbean Land was united with a portion of Central America during a part of that epoch, although faulting developed very soon and separated Yucatan from Cuba. The coastal plain of Mexico also sustained partial fracturing and emergence, in some cases creating horst-graben structures (Tabasco), and initiating the formation of a very extended continental shelf.

The floor of the Caribbean Sea was also affected by tectonic activity. Downfaulting formed Bartlett Trough which extends transversally from the Gulf of Honduras to the southern coast of Cuba. This island was raised during Pliocene about 1000 m. (the Sierra Maestra), while others to the east and southeast differed in vertical instability, indicating a state of tension possibly due to arching with more or less subsidence of the border portions (Schuchert, 1935). Subsidence in Panama took place only on the Caribbean side, as shown by the Chagres sandstone; in Costa Rica and Nicaragua coral reefs of Pliocene-Pleistocene age were also raised, indicating the constant elevation of beaches.

QUATERNARY PERIOD

The outline of Middle America was in general delineated when Pleistocene began about 1,000,000 years ago; or at least, it already had the form of a funnel, with the narrowest part (the tube) toward the southeast. This is a very important detail since from that time the southern portion of Mexico mixed and emptied in that direction biological "ingredients" that came down from North America, and also per-

mitted the dissemination northward of other biota coming from South America. Naturally, in the narrow isthmus of Central America both currents (and probably some autochthonous elements) must have fought hard to accommodate themselves or to continue their path.

Vulcanism and Magmatic Intrusion

If the outline was already delineated, the relief suffered constant modifications because of the combined effect of tectonics, vulcanism, and erosion that modeled and remodeled the surface of Middle America. After the long epoch of quiescence during Upper Pliocene there followed in Mexico more volcanic activity, although manifestations had never ceased completely (emission of andesites). But since Middle Pleistocene (in a considerable part of central and southern Mexico) there appeared high volcanoes of the explosive type that permitted the overflow of basaltic lavas (Mooser, 1957).

In many subareas the effects of that activity on the relief created barrage conditions and caused the development of enclosed basins. Stream erosion carried detritus to lower levels generally depositing sediments in the bottom of lakes, or on the nearby flood plains. Such was the case of the Valley of Mexico and adjacent basins, where contemporaneously with volcanic activity that produced basaltic rocks, series of lake, alluvial, and fluvial sediments were deposited during Pleistocene (Mooser, White, and Lorenzo, 1956).

Similar episodes took place in Guatemala, where basaltic rocks and alluvial-lacustrine sediments similar to those of Mexico occur. During Upper Tertiary, phases of volcanic activity and erosion had preceded basaltic eruptions and accumulation of materials in the subareas subject to such processes (Deger, 1932a,b, 1939, 1942; Williams, 1960). The same can be said of Honduras, although notably the process does not appear to have extended much after Late

22

Pleistocene, as demonstrated by the present distribution of volcanic cones.

The complex history of the Central American volcanoes (some still quite active) is not yet sufficiently known in spite of the work of Sapper, Termer, Deger, Meyer-Abich, and more recently Williams and others (Mooser, Meyer-Abich, and Mc-Birney, 1958). A good report has been published on the Masaya Volcano in Nicaragua, an impressive twin caldera south of the city of Managua, by Zoppis de Sena (1957). There are also reports on the vulcanology of Costa Rica, but Panama is less known in this respect, although there is a volcano (El Boquete or Chiriqui) on the west side which must have ceased activity in recent times.

A map of the Pleistocene and Recent volcanoes (with some of Late Tertiary) of Middle America shows their peculiar distribution (F. M. Bullard, 1957). There are two principal axes, one transverse in the north (more or less along latitude 19° N.), between the coasts of the Pacific Ocean and the Gulf of Mexico, and another diagonal extending from Chiapas, Mexico, to western Panama. In addition, in southern Mexico during Quaternary there appeared some isolated volcanoes that do not seem to fit this picture, an unexplained anomaly in the isthmus of Central America.

Evidently the location of the Mexican transverse volcanic chain was "guided" by structural factors, among which can be mentioned (1) the system of the San Andreas–Chapala line, and its continuation to the SE, and (2) the Clarion Fracture Zone (Mooser and Maldonado-Koerdell, 1961). But in Central America the alignment of volcanoes indicates the existence of another axis oriented from NW to SE, with a concentration of more than sixty igneous apparatuses extending for some 600 km. along the west coast with few interruptions. These volcanoes extruded great masses of lavas and other products during Upper Tertiary and Pleistocene (and in cases Recent) over Central America, the oldest volcanoes producing the most acid rocks while the youngest produced the most basic (Roberts and Irving, 1957).

The relative chronology of the volcanic activity in Central America during Quaternary is just becoming known through study of its petrographical characteristics and of intercalated fossiliferous layers, as in western Honduras, where Olson and McGrew (1941) found skeletons of certain fossil vertebrates (equines) of Upper Pliocene-Lower Pleistocene age in clay-sandy layers, with conglomeratic and cineritic materials. Also, in El Salvador Sayre and Taylor (1951) have established a separation of volcanic materials in various units (two of Tertiary, three of Pleistocene, and one of Recent) while studying the geohydrological problems of the Lempa River Basin; Meyer-Abich (1952–53) has supported their conclusions by the lithological composition of these volcanic flows, and Williams and Meyer-Abich (1955) by their collapse. In Costa Rica and Panama, over the granodioritic and monzonitic intrusions, it seems that high volcanic cones were raised in modern times (Sapper and Staub, 1937; Dondoli, 1940a,b; 1943a,b), principally andesitic.

In regard to volcanic activity the structural conditions of the continental mass and the nearby submarine depths have a close relationship with the intense seismicity of Central America. There were possibly the same typical relationships between the coastal geomorphology and the internal (landward) border of the Middle American Trench that have been established in Mexico, i.e., the tendency toward an "overflowing" of the continental mass toward the contiguous submarine shelf, causing one or various great oblique faults that almost represent the geometrical locus of seismic foci. Thus, a pattern of structural conditions has governed the distribution of volcanoes and explains their double alignment in Middle America.

23

The only subarea where volcanic activity seems to have almost never existed is eastern Panama, where an arm of the Andean Cordillera connects Middle America with the South American Continent. The pronounced curve that this chain of elevations inscribes is very irregular in altitude and of complex tectonic origin, and constitutes what Gerth (1955) has called a *virgation*, its origin having taken place at the beginning of Quaternary. In many aspects (geological, biological, anthropological) this mountainous virgation that extends through Panama into Costa Rica can be qualified as a South American "bridgehead" that confers odd transitional features on southeastern Middle America.

Two other subareas where extrusive rocks are not known are the northeast corner of Honduras and the Peninsula of Yucatan, whose origin and development were essentially due to action of tectonic factors during Upper Tertiary and Quaternary. In both subareas, however, continuous shoaling and/or filling of the continental shelf, and growth of coral reefs still contribute to the continuing emergence of the land. In the Peninsula of Yucatan geologists of Petróleos Mexicanos have added further evidence of geotectonic influences through the discovery of an intrusive body in the subsurface of its northern coast, under calcareous rocks of younger age.

Thus, in northwest nuclear Central America (Schuchert's sense), the "normal" process of consolidation of the earth's crust is taking place in Quaternary times. This process, as described by Stille (1955), includes the replacement of a geosyncline (the Mexican Geosyncline) by a basement (a thick geologic column of Mesozoic and possibly Paleozoic sediments is now known to exist beneath the Peninsula of Yucatan), and the development of geomagmatic phenomena (intrusives). Such interpretation of the intrusive body in the northern coast of the Peninsula of Yucatan would explain its nonorogenic nature, and its distant lo-

cation from the mountain-building belts of Middle America.

There are other intrusive bodies in Middle America, but little is known of their characteristics and age. According to De Cserna (1958), in southern Mexico there are stocks and batholiths of Paleozoic or Mesozoic (or even Tertiary) age as shown by radiometric determinations, but all belong in regions of orogenic activity, and their abundance and order of succession do not agree with the theory of Stille. In other Middle American subareas, the intrusive bodies would have an entirely different significance; that is, they would indicate the stabilization of their corresponding portions of the earth's crust during Quaternary.

These intrusive bodies have induced metamorphism in the surrounding and overlying rocks, and metasediments of various petrographic characteristics are abundant everywhere. Gneisses and micaschists, greenstone conglomerates and phyllites, in contact with the intrusive bodies, occur along the Sierra Madre del Sur in Mexico (De Cserna, 1958). Extensive belts of metamorphic rocks have been described by Williams (1960) along the volcanic chain of Guatemala, between Huehuetenango and Puerto Barrios, on the Caribbean side, representing intrusives of varying age that formed micaschists and phyllitic shales.

There is less certainty about the existence of intrusive bodies in Costa Rica and Panama, although Sapper and Staub (1937) mentioned them. More recently intrusive rocks have been found in the Cordillera de Talamanca, Costa Rica (Weyl, 1955a, 1956a), and on the San Juan del Norte River (on the borderline of Costa Rica and Nicaragua). In any case, they are relatively scarce in southeastern Middle America, which would have given it a certain structural "weakness" in comparison with nuclear Central America.

Seismic Activity

Another group of events that has taken place for centuries (perhaps millennia) in Middle America—the earthquakes—are also related to structural conditions, and to the exceedingly intense vulcanism of Quaternary. The coincidence of distribution of various types of rocks and the occurrence of earthquakes in that area was established by Sapper and Staub (1937), who also took into account the "influence" of the bottom of the Pacific Ocean as a factor associated with their origin. The modern study of earthquakes, especially of their depths, has demonstrated that the majority of Middle American earthquakes depend on the geologic conditions of the marginal zone between the landmass and the periphery of the ocean basin, along the Mexican and Central American coasts.

Now, the bottom of the eastern Pacific Ocean, at the latitude of Middle America, is much more complicated in structure than previously thought and consists of a number of regional elements. Among them, the marginal and anomalous zones have had a great part in the development of geologic events probably since the establishment of the complex system of fractures and faults, and the volcanic activity of Upper Tertiary and Quaternary. With the introduction of geophysical techniques for the exploration of the ocean floor, there was need of assembling further knowledge of the marginal zone to achieve a comprehensive explanation of seismic phenomena in Middle America.

First, the existence of a deep and elongated submarine trough, extending some 50 km. offshore between Cabo Corrientes (Mexico) and the Nicoya Peninsula (Costa Rica), was investigated. A detailed geophysical exploration by Heacock and Worzel (1955) permitted the tracing of the location, depth, and shape of the Middle American Trench, as it was finally called. With a variable width and oblique axis oriented from NNW to SSE (small irregularities do not affect this trend) the Middle American Trench reaches some 5000 m. in average depth, sharply dividing the landmass from the ocean basin (fig. 11).

Almost at the same time the exploration of the floor of the Pacific Ocean between the Hawaiian Islands and North America allowed H. W. Menard Jr. (1959) to discover the existence of four major fractures of the earth's crust. They are, from N to S, the Mendocino, Murray, Clarion, and Clipperton Fracture Zones, the latter two closely associated with the geodynamics of the Middle American Trench. Their structural complexity and great extension indicate that all were caused by circumstances connected with the composition and evolution of the earth's crust itself.

It has already been mentioned that since the latter part of Tertiary (or before), when the Gulf of California was formed, there developed another system of fractures along its major axis, the San Andreas fault system. As mentioned above, at the Islas Marias, off the west coast of Mexico, the San Andreas fault trifurcates and its southernmost arm seems to continue with the Middle American Trench. All the tectonic and volcanologic mechanisms of this complex of fractures and faults developed in Mexico have been studied by Mooser and Maldonado-Koerdell (1961), in their association with the distribution of earthquakes and volcanoes.

The marginal zone suffers all the effects of structural conditions which are the cause of its great instability (of seismic character), and induce a gradual displacement of the land mass into the Middle American Trench (Woollard and Monges Caldera, 1956). As a compensatory mechanism a fault has been produced exactly where the earthquake foci of greatest depth (between 50 and 100 km.) are located on its southern coast and vicinity. However, there is great variation in the depth of the seismic foci since some lie beneath the Moho line and

25

others are shallow on approaching the marginal zone, and for this reason the seisms are seldom catastrophic on the Mexican coast (in contrast to the heavy shocks toward the interior of the land mass).

The seismic "gap" between southern Mexico and the Central American isthmus lies across the Isthmus of Tehuantepec, whose structural characteristics indicate the existence of two land blocks from west to east. Webber and Ojeda (1957) have identified their relative position and tectonic interaction which explain the differences between Mexican and Central American earthquakes. Actually, to the west seismic movements have milder intensity and deep foci in the inland regions; whereas to the east, especially from the middle section of the Chiapas coast to Costa Rica, they acquire higher intensity and their foci are near the surface.

Once again this seismic mechanism is related to the submarine geology of the Gulf of Tehuantepec and the nearby area of the Pacific Ocean to the southwest of the Middle American Trench, through the Clipperton Fracture Zone. Menard (1959) has demonstrated that a secondary fracture, named Tehuantepec ridge, breaks off from the Clipperton Fracture Zone toward the Mexican Isthmus. Figueroa Abarca (1960) based a N-S trend of earthquake foci between Salina Cruz and Coatzacoalcos, and believes that the Tehuantepec ridge also cuts through the Mexican land mass. No geological evidence of such structure has yet been discovered, although one may correlate the narrow isthmian feature with the existence of a hidden zone of weakness in the earth's crust.

No similar research has been done in the Central American isthmus, although during the International Geophysical Year, 1957–58, the Pan American Institute of Geography and History carried out a study of gravity anomalies in that territory in collaboration with the Institute of Geophysics of the University of Mexico, the depart-

ments of Geology of the universities of Wisconsin and Cambridge, and the Cartographic Offices of Guatemala, El Salvador, Honduras, Nicaragua, Costa Rica, and Panama (Monges Caldera, 1960). The Scripps Institution of Oceanography (La Jolla, California) has continued its geological and geophysical studies in the Middle American Trench and the marginal zone of the southern coast of the Central American isthmus, and has (as of May 1961) announced its publication in the *Bulletin of the Geological Society of America*.

The volcanic activity and seismicity of Middle America were well known to pre-Hispanic inhabitants, and recorded in their traditions (the Legend of the Suns) and hieroglyphs (the sign Nahui-Ollin or 4-Movement). During the colonial and later periods of Mexico, Central America, and Panama, observations and records have been compiled (Maldonado-Koerdell, 1958c) in the study of phenomena that contributed so much to the peculiar configuration of that area in Quaternary. But, to complete that picture, consideration should now be given to the action of the climatic factors, especially glaciations, during the same lapse of time.

Glaciation and Pedogenesis

During Pleistocene a series of recurrent alterations in the general climate of the world occurred, causing the accumulation of enormous ice sheets around the polar and subpolar areas to midlatitudes in both hemispheres. Also in intermediary areas (now tropical or subtropical), on the high mountains and other places favorable to cooling, snow and ice accumulated to form large glaciers. It has been calculated that the total volume of snow and ice deposited on terrestrial areas during glacial maxima exceeded several million cubic kilometers, and that the thickness of the snow and ice sheets reached about 1600 m.

Obviously, such an immense concentration of one of the physical (or solid) forms of water on land induced many changes in the remaining forms, both atmospheric (or gaseous) and oceanic (or liquid). In the atmospheric realm, reduction of the water vapor component caused a certain amount of "dryness," alternating with more humid stages during deglaciation. As for the oceans, accumulation of snow and ice over the continents caused a lowering of sea level of some 125 m. around the world, which was again raised as the glaciers melted and receded.

Comparative studies of European and North American glaciations have shown that their rhythm and intensity were almost equivalent, so that in general terms a correlation of glacial events in both continents is possible (Ahlmann, 1953). However, there seems to have been a certain advance in Europe (or lag in America) in the timing of maximum extension of the snow and ice sheets, although a striking resemblance existed in the over-all trend of variations in the whole world. On the other hand, glaciers show tendencies to follow time patterns of their own, almost apart from the influence of climatic factors on occasions.

Such events took place during four successive epochs for the North American continent (as on the rest of the Earth) and have received special names, according to major areas of occurrence. These were the Nebraskan, Kansan, Illinoian, and Wisconsin glaciations, in this sequence, separated by interglacial periods of varying duration although it is known that the second (between the Kansan and Illinoian glaciations) was the longest. The best known of these interglacials is the third (or Sangamon) on account of several biological (appearance of "modern" man) and cultural events.

Each of the four North American glaciations (especially the last), as well as interglacials, developed irregularly, with culminations of diverse intensity. Their geochronological study is only beginning, but it is no exaggeration to estimate the duration of the Wisconsin glaciation at some

70,000 years, and somewhat less for the Illinoian. Between both, the interglacial III (Sangamon) probably lasted for some 100,000 years; that is to say, the three terminal events of Pleistocene in North America lasted for nearly a fourth of its total duration (1,000,000 years).

The geochronology of mountain glaciers in tropical and subtropical lands is little known, a fact that prevents clear correlation with continental glaciation in the northern or southern hemispheres. It is most probable that their rhythms of development were generally coincident and that the principal effect of their existence (climatic deterioration) was almost uniform throughout the world. However, various geographical conditions (altitude, relief) also influenced their development in different ways to lessen their effects on the land.

The relationships between tropical and subtropical mountain glaciers and climatic changes were probably more intimate than in the polar and subpolar areas. Rates of snow and ice accumulation and wastage at high altitudes (regardless of latitude) in those areas suffered more directly the effects of solid precipitation and temperature decrease for the first stage, and of convection (heat received from the air) and radiation for the second. These effects were still increased by topographic conditions, the stronger manifestations corresponding to the steeper gradients.

There was also the action of winds and distance from oceans or seas combined with above-mentioned factors of accumulation and wastage. Snow and ice accumulation in lower latitudes (as was probably the case of the highest Mexican mountains) may have resulted partially from steady cooling winds originating in "cold centers" in northern areas, and circulating across reliefless surfaces in the center of the North American Continent. Conversely, for wastage stages, in environments with predominantly humid and maritime climate (i.e. the Central American isthmus, with trade

27

winds from the Caribbean Sea, and monsoonal winds from the Pacific Ocean constantly affecting its narrow territory) the most important factor was convection, as indicated by Ahlmann (1953).

Accumulation and wastage of snow and ice, under the influence of climatic and topographic factors, were thus as complicated during Pleistocene as are both facets of the "life history" of glaciers at the present time. In this regard, wastage (or ablation, as it is called in glaciological terminology) with fluctuating diminution in extension and thickness of the snow and ice sheets was the crux of the matter, or at least as important as accumulation. Quaternary glaciers left many clues of their recession, such as moraines and other detritus deposited by melt water. Moreover biological events helped to characterize the postglacial (another interglacial, according to some specialists) environment of the last few thousand years.

The great recession of Late Pleistocene mountain glaciers in Middle America was due principally to the increase of transference of heat to the atmosphere because of the increased circulation of the warm winds of southern origin. In meteorological terms, what happened was that the summer precipitation was also produced at a higher temperature. Consequently, this reactivation of the general circulation of the atmosphere brought a greater humidity, increasing also the rains throughout the world, although the temperatures varied markedly in the several areas.

During Late Pleistocene relief modeling was an especially active process in the tropical and subtropical areas, with leveling off of elevations, filling of plains, and the development of erosive cycles that again remodeled the surface. In central Mexico (Mezquital Valley, near Ixmiquilpan, Hidalgo) one can still see the remains of an old alluvial plain with three Quaternary terraces, the highest marking the original level, the intermediate one an old period of reactivation of the erosive cycle with channeling and new stream cutting, and the lowest the present erosive cycle with its drainage system of recent centuries. The same relief traits, with some local variations resulting from the action of these factors, exist in the basins and valleys along the Neovolcanic Axis (Puebla, Toluca).

There were also pedogenic processes that produced peculiar soils from parent material carried down from nearby elevations during deglaciation. De Terra (1950) has described the oscillations and composition of ancient glaciers of Iztaccihuatl, in central Mexico, and indicated that ice and melt waters transported various materials to lower levels at irregular intervals. During the height of glaciation strong winds blowing downslope from the ice-covered mountains may have caused widespread aeolian erosion and deposition of loose soil particles at lower elevations.

During the Pleistocene glaciations the climatic deterioration directly affected the plants and animals over the whole world, changing their areas of distribution by forcing migration to regions of milder climatic conditions but in many cases killing them off. Some forms adapted to cold conditions, but the great majority migrated toward warmer lands. Thus, in the areas of refuge the arrival of new elements initiated a strong biological competition with the native ones, worsening the situation even more and contributing to new changes in floras and faunas.

In Mexico, Sonora was a refuge for many plants and animals, from which resulted a group of new forms that still characterize a life zone, the Sonoran. Probably in areas farther south similar processes took place, but they have not been sufficiently studied to be defined as life zones or, at least, as refuge areas during Pleistocene. Probably the deep, intermountain canyons of southern Mexico and some lake regions in the Central American isthmus maintained until very recently vegetal and animal groups of relict character throughout Quaternary.

The high mountains of central Mexico forming the Neovolcanic Axis have been carefully studied in their glaciological sequence. On these mountains, during Pleistocene, the existence of icecaps can now be proved by the terminal and lateral moraines, erratic boulders, and striated rocks. Even today glacial activity is still in process, but the lack of correlation of glacial events between these mountains and other North American areas prevent clear understanding of the phenomena.

Among the investigations of glaciation along the Neovolcanic Axis of Mexico in the last 75 years are the studies of Aguilera and Ordóñez (1895), Waitz (1910a,b), Jaeger (1925), Prister (1927), Robles Ramos (1944), de Terra (1947, 1950), de Terra, Romero, and Stewart (1949), and, on the occasion of the International Geophysical Year, 1957–58, those of Lorenzo (1959a,b). The contributions of White (1951, 1956, 1960) are also important, since he has concentrated his attention on the glacial geology of Popocatepetl and Iztaccihuatl, establishing the sequence of the snow and ice sheets, the intermediate volcanic episodes, and the relation of both types of phenomena to the sedimentology of the basin of Mexico. It is necessary to go to the Cordillera of Talamanca (Costa Rica) to find another Middle American subarea studied from the glaciological point of view in recent years (Weyl, 1955-a,b,c, 1956a,b,c), although since the latter part of the 19th century various localities in Central America have been pointed out as glaciated areas.

On the west side of Ixtaccihuatl there developed a series of multiple glaciations that alternated with volcanic activity of other nearby peaks, and possibly similar phenomena took place on the east side. To the west, the basin of Mexico, because of damming by volcanic materials, was converted into a reservoir for the waters and eroded materials, with lacustrine and eruptive phases alternating with varying duration and intensity. Even today, the remaining small glaciers advance or recede under the action of multiple factors, although an intimate correlation always existed between such phenomena and the sedimentation at the bottom of the basin.

According to White (1960), mid-Pleistocene icecaps descended to 2,450 m. (the lowest level ever reached during Quaternary time in Central Mexico) shortly before a volcanic barrage blocked drainage from the basin of Mexico toward the south, and podzolic soils began to develop at lower levels. Late Pleistocene witnessed new glaciations with moraines (now severely eroded) at a higher altitude, development of alluvial fans along the mountain front, and new podzolic soils, a process frequently interrupted by lava or ash emissions which covered glacial débris at later epochs. Final stages consisted of accumulation of multiple snow and ice sheets at 3,135–3,400 m. altitude, with development of alluvial fans, ash fall, a weak soil process, and other manifestations of this highly complex combination of glacial, volcanic, and pedogenic events.

The postglacial climatic fluctuations and associated phenomena had a direct influence on the origin of soils not only in the basin of Mexico but also in the adjoining valleys of Puebla and Toluca, and farther away along the Neovolcanic Axis. The character of these fluctuations has been much discussed in the light of recent findings and better understanding of the climatic sequence in other areas of North America. As generally viewed now, rather than extreme fluctuations (although some happened as such) material evidence reflects a progressive transition from the cold, dry environment of glacial times to the warm, humid environment of Recent, with an intermediate epoch, the *climatic optimum* (*altithermal* of Antevs-Bryan, *hypsithermal* of Deevey) of lesser precipitation and higher temperature.

Between Upper Pleistocene and Early Recent a most important factor in pedogenesis was the pluvial precipitation, the waters of which penetrated below the surface to varying depths, and caused a continuous solifluction of the essentially alkaline minerals resulting from the disintegration of basic rocks (andesites and basalts). Under certain circumstances there was a marked separation between the pluvial water infiltrated only to a shallow depth, and the phreatic water underneath, exaggerated by erosional phases which contributed to the formation of *caliche* on the surface. However, the presence of an overlying layer of water in the form of an oscillating lake came to complicate this process, and to add its influence on pedogenesis, especially during the above mentioned transitional epoch.

Soil development in the basin of Mexico in the last millennium has been examined in its geochemical aspects by Sokoloff and Lorenzo (1953), with special reference to caliche. Considering materials collected at various levels in prehistoric and archaeological localities of that subarea, they concluded that the soils of the basin of Mexico represent immature stages of a pedogenic process developing under quite uniform climatic conditions towards the end of Pleistocene. According to these authors, the formation of caliche has progressed continuously for the last ten or twelve millennia, and was only regulated by geohydrological circumstances.

Thus, in the course of time, a geologic column of diverse origin was deposited in the basin of Mexico during Upper Pleistocene and Early Recent, mainly consisting of two kinds of materials: the ancient one, or Becerra Formation of Pleistocene age, and the new one, or Totolzingo "earth" of

Recent age. Between both levels, stratigraphically speaking, a deposit of the evaporite-erosive type, Caliche III, sealing off Pleistocene beds, was formed during the climatic optimum, serving in the field as a good marker to differentiate the ancient and the new types of deposits. Below the Becerra Formation, there are clastic materials of very diverse origin, mostly volcanics, previously known under the general name of Tarango Formation and also attributed to Upper Pleistocene; at the top of the geologic column there is the modern soil.

Each one of these stratigraphic units was for some time the surface of a soil, since with few exceptions plant and animal remains have been encountered in the whole column, from the Tarango Formation to the Totolzingo "earth." The Becerra Formation, in central Mexico, is very rich in Upper Pleistocene animal fossils, and in one locality (Tepexpan) a human skeleton of prehistoric age was found in 1947; in other nearby places great masses of mammoth bones have been collected in association with stone artifacts of the same cultural level. The Totolzingo "earth" contains only numerous pottery sherds of the epochs identified by archaeologists as Formative and Preclassic (Archaic, in the nomenclature prior to 1955), thus "closing" the stratigraphic-cultural sequence for the prehistoric-protohistoric transitional period in the best known subarea of Middle America.

The esential geohydrological trait of the basin of Mexico, in Late Pleistocene and Early Recent, was the existence of a lake in its bottom, as a result of the accumulation of water (both of pluvial and glacial origin), and of its stagnation by volcanic damming. The oscillations of this lake, more or less well established through the study of terraces, sediments, and other evidence, characterized the nature of the environment and directed in many respects the distribution of biotas in the basin of Mexico (including the human communi-

30

ties). At the time of the arrival of the Spaniards, in the 16th century, the old lake had become fragmented into six smaller ones (Zumpango, Xaltocan, San Cristobal, Texcoco, Xochimilco, and Chalco), all of which have practically disappeared at the present time (Maldonado-Koerdell, 1954–55).

Before entering its final stage of evolution, however, the old lake was also severely affected by climatic and environmental factors, and at least on one occasion at the end of Pleistocene, it became almost dry. This was due to the climatic optimum (between 8000 and 5000 B.C.) which left so many clues of its influence in the whole of North America. In this epoch the pedogenic process continued, dominated by deposition of caliche, and the extinction of a great number of plant and animal species which changed the aspect of the environment (Maldonado-Koerdell, 1953b).

The richness of plant and animal life previous to this period has been demonstrated through the studies of Díaz Lozano (1917, 1920) on diatoms of the old lacustrine sediments in several localities of the basin of Mexico. Such materials indicate a long period of sedimentation under relatively quiet conditions of uniform climate, as proved also by the thick deposits of peat in nearby localities (Alcalá, 1906; Lozano García, 1945). Pollen analyses have completed the picture, showing that a varied population of higher plants (pine, oak) also existed in that environment, which was affected after the close of the glacial epoch by a long period of desiccation with a return to more humid conditions at a later date (Deevey, 1943; Sears, 1952).

Evidence for climatic variations has come from the examination of lacustrine sediments of Upper Pleistocene–Lower Recent age in the basin of Mexico. Sears and Clisby (1955) have examined two cores and found that their pollen content indicates a sequence of humid-dry-humid climates, as well as a correlative change in the vegetation. However, there are still certain problems in the interpretation of these data and especially in their correlation with further work for a clarification of paleoecological conditions at each successive level.

Knowledge of these conditions in adjoining zones to the west and east of the basin of Mexico, along the Neovolcanic Axis, i.e. from the Valley of Guadalajara to the high plains of Perote, is scanty and unsystematic. It seems that all were also lacustrine subareas, undergoing the same physical and biological evolution as the basin of Mexico and forming a transverse chain of paleoecological niches situated on the sinuous line between the Nearctic and the Neotropical provinces. Thus, a constant shifting of conditions enacted by "northern" and "southern" factors in this climactic and biotic battlefront added more complexity to the local circumstances and induced many changes in the whole process of transition from ancient to modern environments.

No similar studies concerning this process of transition have been made in the high mountains of Middle America south of the Neovolcanic Axis of Mexico. There are also intermountain valleys and depressions, as well as lower subareas in its territory, where cultural events have developed for several millennia, badly in need of scientific research. The highlands of Guatemala and Honduras, the Gulf of Fonseca and surrounding lowlands, and the tectonic lakes of Nicaragua are only a few examples for such investigations.

R. Weyl (1955, 1956) has begun to study the glacial geology of the Cordillera of Talamanca (Costa Rica), on the highest peaks at Cerro Chirripo (some 3400 m. above sea level) and Cerro Buena Vista, very near the former. On these mountains, during Pleistocene, glaciers of certain magnitude developed, traces of which are encountered as terminal and lateral moraines, and other deposits in the broad intermountain valleys. A pedogenic process of a periglacial type also took place, causing the development of a soil (now covered by other materials) clearly visible in a cut some 2 m. thick in a small valley.

The total extension of the glaciers of the Cordillera of Talamanca has still not been precisely determined, but the icecap covered the highest summits in all directions. Over the granitic and diorite rocks of the Cerro Chirripo, glacial erosion left three

successive moraines and other accumulations of rocky materials, and because of the local physiography, in later times bodies of water of glacial type have formed (Cerro de las Lagunas). According to Weyl, ". . . the vestiges of the glaciation (in the Cordillera of Talamanca) permit confirmation that they come from the last glaciation, i.e., the Wisconsin."

REFERENCES

Aguilar y Santillán, 1908, 1918, 1930
Aguilera and Ordóñez, 1895
Ahlmann, 1953
Alcalá, 1906
Botero Arango, 1942
Brand, 1957
Bryan, 1948
Bullard, F. M., 1957
Carpenter, 1954
De Cserna, 1958
De Terra, 1947, 1950
——, Romero, and Stewart, 1949
Deevey, 1943
Deger, 1932a,b, 1939, 1942
Díaz-Lozano, 1917, 1920
Dollfus and Montserrat, 1868
Dondoli, 1940a, 1940b, 1943a, 1943b
Eardley, 1951
Edwards, J. D., 1956
Erben, 1957a, 1957b
Figueroa Abarca, 1960
Gerth, 1955
Heacock and Worzel, 1955
Hoffstetter, 1960
Humphreys, 1916
Imlay, 1939, 1943, 1944a, 1944b, 1952
Jaeger, F., 1926
López Ramos, 1956
Lorenzo, 1959a, 1959b
Lozano García, 1945
MacGillavry, 1934, 1937
Maldonado-Koerdell, 1952, 1953a, 1953b, 1954a, 1954b, 1954-55, 1958a, 1958b, 1958c
Manó, 1883a, 1883b
Menard, 1959
Meyer-Abich, 1952, 1952-53, 1953

Monges Caldera, 1960
Mooser, 1957
—— and Maldonado-Koerdell, 1961
——, Meyer-Abich, and McBirney, 1958
——, White, and Lorenzo, 1956
Müllerried, 1942a, 1942b, 1944, 1945, 1947b, 1948, 1949a, 1949b
Newberry, 1888a, 1888b
Olson and McGrew, 1941
Prister, 1927
Reeside et al., 1957
Roberts and Irving, 1957
Robles Ramos, 1944
Sánchez, P. C., 1937
Sapper, 1894, 1896
—— and Staub, 1937
Sayre and Taylor, 1951
Schuchert, 1935
Sears, 1952
—— and Clisby, 1955
Sokoloff and Lorenzo, 1953
Stille, 1955
Termier, 1958, 1960
Thompson, M. L., and Miller, 1944
Waitz, 1910a, 1910b
Webber and Ojeda R., 1957
Weeks, 1956
Weyl, 1955a, 1955b, 1955c, 1956a, 1956b, 1956c, 1960
White, 1951, 1956, 1960
Wieland, 1913, 1914
Williams, 1960
—— and Meyer-Abich, 1955
Woodring and Thompson, 1949
Woollard and Monges Caldera, 1956
Zoppis de Sena, 1957

2. Surface Configuration and Associated Geology of Middle America

ROBERT C. WEST

Few parts of the earth of similar size have such a varied and complex surface configuration and geology as Mexico and Central America. Most of this area is high and mountainous. Plateaus bordered by steep, rugged escarpments range from 1200 to 2500 m. in altitude and individual volcanic peaks tower more than 5000 m. above the sea. Lowlands consist mainly of relatively narrow coastal strips and occasional inland depressions or deep valleys. The flattish Yucatan Peninsula is the only extensive lowland of all Middle America. The great diversity of surface configuration, together with the complex pattern of climate, vegetation, and animal life, has here afforded man a large number of natural environments in which to live.

The purpose of this chapter is to describe the surface configuration of Mexico and Central America and to interpret the origin of the varying landforms in terms of associated geology and erosional or depositional processes. Those surface forms and physiographic regions that have been significant in the development of Indian cultures will be emphasized.

STATUS OF GEOMORPHIC INVESTIGATION

As indicated in Article 1, geological knowledge of Mexico is well advanced, whereas that of Central America is still in its infancy. Preliminary geological investigations in Mexico began in the late 18th century with the founding of a school of mines, the Real Seminario de Minería (1792), and the subsequent studies of Europeans such as Alexander von Humboldt (1811) and Josef Burkart (1836) on aspects of mining geology. The late 19th century saw increased activity by Mexican geologists and the founding in 1886 of the Comisión Geológica de México; in 1891 this organization became the Instituto Geológico, which in turn was reorganized as the Instituto de Geología of the National University of Mexico in 1930. Two international geological congresses held in Mexico City (the 10th in 1906, the 20th in 1956), the importance of mining to the nation, and intensive petroleum exploration and exploitation since 1900 have given emphasis to geological investigation in Mexico by both Mexicans and North Americans as well as some Europeans. In 1949 Garfías and Chapín summarized the geology of Mexico, appending a list of nearly 600 bibliographical entries. Murray (1961) has included a masterly analysis of the geology of eastern Mexico in his recent work on the Atlantic and Gulf Coast geology of North America. Although Dollfus and Montserrat (1868) performed some of the first scientific geology in Central America, for that area one must still rely heavily on the voluminous late 19th- and early 20th-century writings of the renowned German vulcanologist and geographer, Karl Sapper. Since World War II numerous geological investigations have been undertaken in Central America by North American and European scientists, and the recent establishment of national geological surveys in the various Central American countries is an encouraging sign. Moreover, in 1958 Maldonado-Koerdell compiled a lengthy and thorough bibliography on the geology and paleontology of Central America, which will serve as a point of departure for future geological studies in that area. The most recent treatise on the geology of Central America is by the German, Richard Weyl (1961).

The geomorphology of Mexico and Central America is even less well known than the geology. Numerous researchers, however, have attempted to describe and interpret landforms and to define landform regions of Mexico and, to a lesser degree, of Central America. Since the 1870's both Mexican and foreign scientists have presented various outlines of the physiographic regions of Mexico. Of these probably that of Ezequial Ordóñez (1936, 1941) is the best known and most widely accepted. Raisz (1959) has presented one of the latest concepts of the physiographic divisions of Mexico to accompany his magnificent landform map of the country, based on aerial photography. Other physiographic outlines of Mexico have been suggested by Thayer (1916), Sanders (1921), C. L. Baker (1930), Tamayo (1941), Robles Ramos (1942) and López de Llergo (1953).

For Central American physiographic regions and descriptions of surface configuration one must again lean heavily on the work of Karl Sapper, whose numerous writings are still the best material on general geomorphology of the area. Since 1950, however, the Instituto Tropical de Investigaciones Científicas and the Servicio Geológico, both of El Salvador, have been undertaking excellent work under direction of German scientists on the geomorphology and geology of that small country.

In contrast to the numerous outlines of physiographic regions, detailed studies of particular landforms in either Mexico or Central America are few indeed. The most abundant and best work has dealt with vulcanism and volcanic forms. Early studies of volcanic landscapes include those of Aguilera (1907), Ordóñez (1906), and Sapper (1913, etc.). The latest and best work on this subject for both Mexico and Central America is by the American vulcanologist Howell Williams (1950 to 1960). Some investigations of karst forms have been made in the Yucatan Peninsula (Cole, 1910; Robles Ramos, 1950) and in the limestone areas of the Sierra Madre Oriental of Mexico (Wittich, 1935, 1935–38) and of Tabasco (Gerstenhauer, 1960). Coastal landforms of various parts of Central America have been described in geographic reports recently issued by the Department of Geography, University of California, Berkeley, under Office of Naval Research contract (C. Edwards, 1954, 1957; Vermeer, 1959; Tuan, 1960; Radley, 1960). For the coastal morphology of El Salvador one must mention the excellent work of Gierloff-Emden (1959, and his previous work cited therein).

TECTONIC OUTLINE OF MEXICO AND CENTRAL AMERICA

To understand better the major configuration of the land areas of Mexico and Central America a summary of the gross tectonic patterns of the area is outlined below. For a more detailed explanation of the tec-

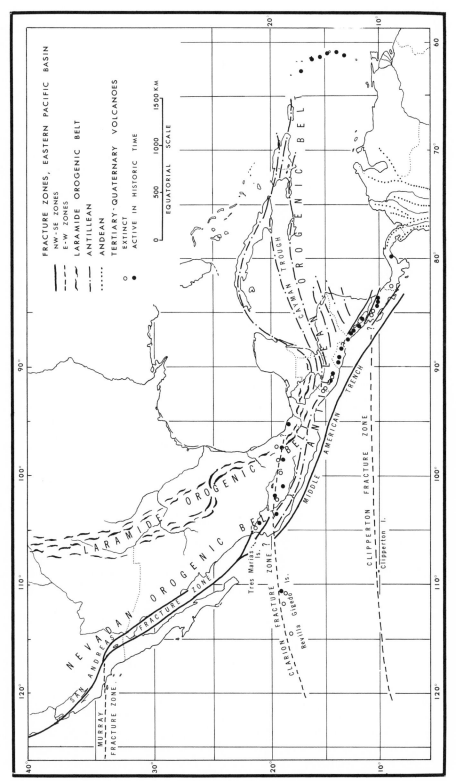

FIG. 1—MAJOR TECTONIC PATTERNS OF MIDDLE AMERICA

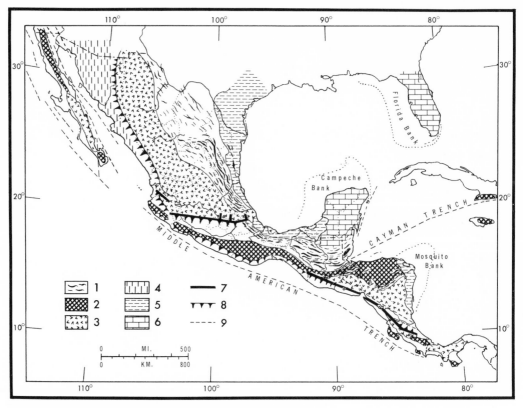

Fig. 2—MAJOR TECTONIC AREAS OF MIDDLE AMERICA

Key: 1. Folded and faulted ranges of marine clastics and limestones. 2. Crystalline, highly deformed basement complex. 3. Volcanic tablelands and ranges. 4. Sonoran basin and range structure. 5. Gulf and Mosquito coastal lowlands of young sediments. 6. Tertiary limestone platform (Yucatan and Florida). 7. Volcanic axis. 8. Major escarpment zone. 9. Major fault lines.

tonic history, the reader is referred to Article 1.

The diversity of surface forms in Middle America stems primarily from the area's complex tectonic history and its position within one of the world's regions of contemporary mountain building. At least four major tectonic patterns characterize the area's present structural and surface configuration (figs. 1, 2).

1. One tectonic pattern is formed by the great NW-SE-trending crustal fractures on the western flank of the North and Central American land mass. Along and adjacent to these fractures mountain chains have been thrust upward, large crustal blocks have moved horizontally, and in places large masses of volcanic material have been ejected to form ranges and plateaus. On the western side of Middle America the present direction of the coastline, the large depression that forms the Gulf of California, the western escarpment of the Mexican Plateau, and the long volcanic chain that borders the Pacific coast of Central America are all expressions of tectonic activity along these fractures. The largest of the NW-SE fractures is the famous San Andreas Rift, which extends from the west coast of the United States into the Gulf of California. The same fracture may continue as the deep Middle American Trench immediately off the Pacific coast of southwestern Mexico and Central America (Heacock and Worzel, 1955; Mooser and Maldonado-Koerdell, 1961). Smaller fault zones parallel the San Andreas Rift and the Middle American Trench on land and in the ocean bottom, all of which form part of the long

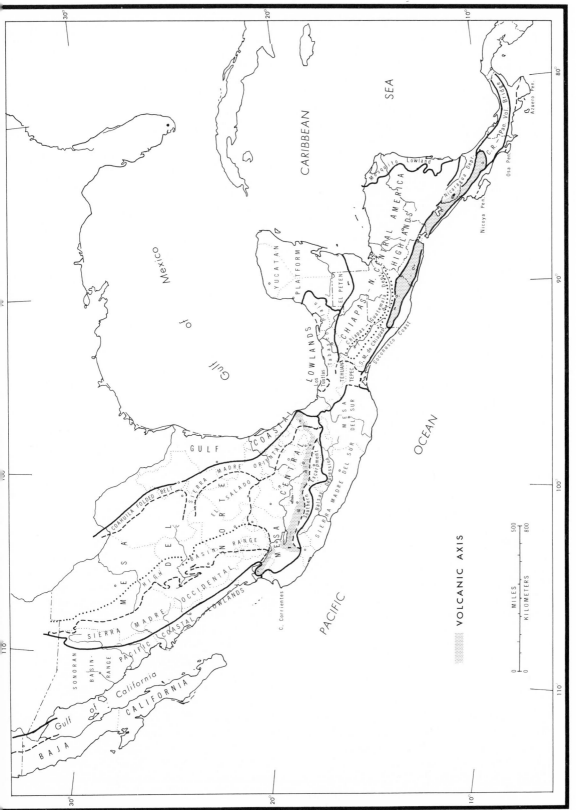

FIG. 3.—PHYSIOGRAPHIC REGIONS OF MIDDLE AMERICA

series of crustal dislocations that have occurred along the eastern side of the Pacific Basin since the Nevadan Mountain Revolution of Mesozoic times. Frequent seismic activity and occasional volcanic eruptions at various places within this zone of fracturing evince the continuance of crustal movements to the present time.

2. A second tectonic pattern consists of the predominantly N-S- and NW-SE-trending folds and overthrusts of the Sierra Madre Oriental on the eastern side of Mexico. This tectonic movement, which belongs to the Laramide Mountain Revolution, began in late Mesozoic (Cretaceous) and early Tertiary. Most geologists consider the folding of the Sierra Madre Oriental to be associated with the formation of the Rocky Mountains in the United States. Others (Eardley, 1951, 1954) believe that both the Nevadan and the Laramide and even earlier orogenies were also responsible for the E-W-trending folds and fault scarps of northern Central America and the Greater Antilles. In its northern sector the Sierra Madre Oriental structure veers suddenly westward to form the E-W-trending cross ranges of north-central Mexico.

3. Evidence for a third tectonic pattern, which has affected especially the structure of central Mexico, has only recently been confirmed. Buckling of the earth's crust in Mesozoic time resulted in a series of long E-W-trending bands of mountainous relief, called fracture zones, that occur on the ocean floor of the eastern Pacific Basin. Submarine fault-block mountains and volcanoes (which sometimes form islands) and grabens, or downfaulted blocks (which have formed deep trenches on the ocean floor), are common features of these fracture zones. One of these, called the Clarion Fracture Zone, runs for 4500 km. from the mid-Pacific along the Revilla Gigedo Islands to the west coast of Mexico south of Cabo Corrientes, where it intersects the NW-SE fault lines that border the coast. According to Menard (1955, 1960), the Clarion fracture continues across central Mexico as a sheer zone along which has developed a transverse E-W-trending volcanic axis (the Neovolcanic range) that

forms the southern edge of the Mexican Plateau. The volcanic islands of the Revilla Gigedo group are another expression of the vulcanism that has occurred along the Clarion fracture. Menard (1955) has suggested that the same structure may continue farther eastward to connect with the Cayman Trench, a deep submarine fracture which extends from northern Central America across the Caribbean Sea floor to the Greater Antilles. A thousand kilometers south of the Clarion belt is the Clipperton Fracture Zone, named from Clipperton Island, along which it passes. This fracture intersects the Middle American Trench off the northwest coast of Costa Rica. The continuance of the structure into Central America has not been confirmed, but its alignment with the E-W-trending volcanic Cordillera Central of Costa Rica is suggestive.

4. South of the Mexican Plateau a fourth tectonic pattern covers much of southern Mexico and northern Central America, and extends eastward across the Caribbean Sea to include the Greater Antilles. Often called geologically "Old Antillia," the area is characterized by predominantly E-W-trending mountain ranges paralleled by deep structural valleys. In both rock type and structure this is the oldest geologic area of Middle America. Deformation may have begun as early as Precambrian (Sapper, 1937), but greatest tectonic activity occurred in Mesozoic, when strong folding and faulting, accompanied by intrusions of large masses of granite, took place (Eardley, 1951). At that time crustal movements formed the main E-W structures of the Oaxaca Highlands, the Sierra Madre de Chiapas, and the ranges and depressions of central Guatemala, Honduras, and north-central Nicaragua. Coincident with the Laramide Revolution further deformation occurred in late Mesozoic and early Tertiary. Hess (1938) believes that the deep Cayman Trench in the Caribbean was downfaulted during middle Tertiary (Miocene). In late Tertiary and continuing to the present day, the Pacific side of Old Antillia was completely buried by great quantities of volcanic outpourings that oc-

38

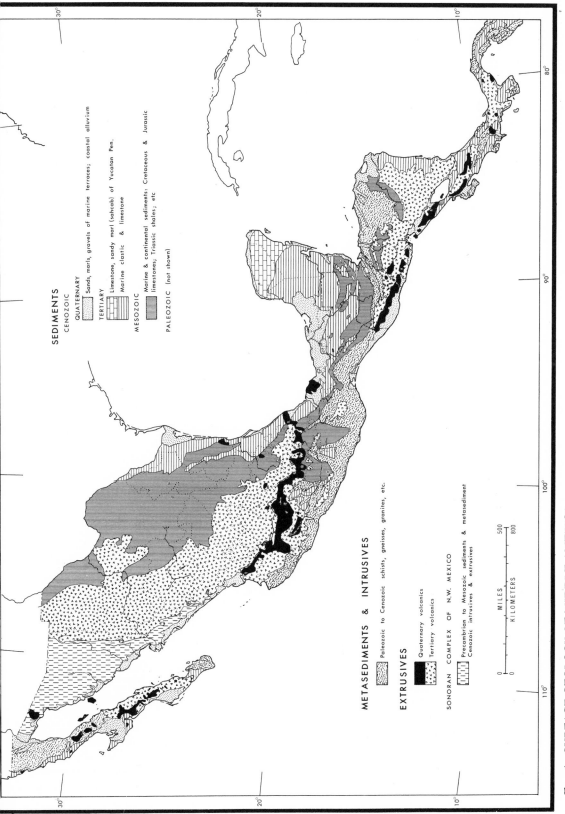

SEDIMENTS

CENOZOIC

QUATERNARY

Sands, marls, gravels of marine terraces; coastal alluvium

TERTIARY

Limestone, sandy marl (sahcab) of Yucatan Pen.

Marine clastic & limestone

MESOZOIC

Marine & continental sediments: Cretaceous & Jurassic
limestones; Triassic shales; etc

PALEOZOIC (not shown)

METASEDIMENTS & INTRUSIVES

Paleozoic to Cenozoic schists, gneisses, granites, etc.

EXTRUSIVES

Quaternary volcanics

Tertiary volcanics

SONORAN COMPLEX OF N.W. MEXICO

Precambrian to Mesozoic sediments & metasediment
Cenozoic intrusives & extrusives

MILES

0   500

0   800

KILOMETERS

FIG. 4—SURFACE GEOLOGY OF MIDDLE AMERICA
Greatly simplified from Carta Geológica de la República Mexicana, 1956; and Geologic Map of Central America, *in* Roberts and Irving, 1957.

curred along the NW-SE fracture lines described above.

PHYSIOGRAPHIC REGIONS

Because of their complexity the landform patterns of Mexico and Central America might best be described on the basis of large physiographic regions and their subdivisions, in each of which there is a general uniformity of surface characteristics. My concept of these physiographic divisions is outlined below and is depicted in figure 3. The divisions are roughly similar to but more detailed than the geological provinces (p. 5) given in Article 1. Because of its great size and cultural importance, the Mexican Plateau is treated in more detail than some of the other regions.

I. Mexican Plateau and adjacent escarpments
  A. Plateau surface
    1. Mesa Central (Altiplanicie Meridional) and the Neovolcanic range
    2. Mesa del Norte (Altiplanicie Septentrional)
      a. Western high basin and range area
      b. Central low desert area
  B. Bounding mountain ranges and escarpments
    1. Sierra Madre Oriental
    2. Sierra Madre Occidental
    3. Southern escarpment (of the Neovolcanic range)
II. Peninsula of Baja California
III. Coastal lowlands adjacent to the Mexican Plateau
  A. The Pacific coastal lowlands
  B. The Gulf coastal lowlands
IV. Old lands of southern Mexico and northern Central America
  A. Balsas-Tepalcatepec Depression
  B. Southern Mexican highlands
  C. Isthmus of Tehuantepec
  D. Highlands of Chiapas and northern Central America
V. Yucatan platform
VI. Volcanic axis of Central America
VII. Volcanic bridge of Costa Rica and Panama
VIII. Coasts of Central America
  A. Pacific lowlands
    1. Northern coastal section
    2. Southern coastal section
  B. Caribbean coastal lowlands of Central America
    1. Guatemalan-Honduran Caribbean lowlands
    2. Mosquito lowland
    3. Caribbean end of the Nicaragua depression
    4. Caribbean shore of Panama

Mexican Plateau and Adjacent Escarpments

The largest physiographic province of Middle America is the Mexican Plateau, which extends from the present United States–Mexico border southward to the latitude of Mexico City. Elevations are greatest in the southern portion of the plateau, which forms one of the world's great tropical highlands. There, many parts of the plateau surface rise over 2000 m. above the sea. Northward, elevations gradually decrease to less than 1000 m. near the present international border.

Physiographically the Mexican Plateau consists of (1) the upland surface and (2) the bounding mountain systems. The latter actually form the highly dissected upturned edges of the plateau and the steep escarpments that border on the east, west, and south. These mountain systems and adjacent escarpments are, respectively, the Sierra Madre Oriental, the Sierra Madre Occidental, and the transverse Neovolcanic range that trends E-W across the middle of Mexico.

PLATEAU SURFACE. In terms of landforms, the plateau surface consists of two major parts: (1) The arid and semiarid northern two-thirds of the Mexican Plateau, often called the Mesa del Norte, or Altiplanicie Septentrional, extends from the international border to about the latitude of Aguascalientes and San Luis Potosi, where it blends into (2) the higher and more humid south-

40

C. de Tlaloc   Ixtaccíhuatl   Popocatepetl   Puebla Basin

Amecameca

FIG. 5.—THE SNOW-CAPPED VOLCANOES OF IXTACCIHUATL AND POPOCATEPETL, LOOKING NORTHEAST
These two edifices and the Cerro de Tlaloc form the Sierra Nevada, which extends northward at right angles to the Neovolcanic Axis and separates the
Basin of Puebla from those of Amecameca and Mexico. Dissected fans composed of lahars, or volcanic mudflows, ring the base of Popocatepetl.

ern third. The latter is variously known as the Altiplanicie Meridional, the Neovolcanic Plateau, or the Mesa Central.

Mesa Central. This is a land of volcanic features par excellence. Within this small area occur almost the entire array of known volcanic forms. Although vulcanism in the western and southern parts of the Mexican Plateau began near the close of Cretaceous, the volcanic activity that has most influenced the present surface of the Mesa Central started in mid-Tertiary, reached its climax during Pleistocene, and in some localities has continued to the present time. Composed mainly of andesitic and basaltic ejecta, the more recent extrusives cover almost completely the older features of chiefly rhyolitic and andesitic rocks. The latter outcrop as worn-down hills and low mountains mainly in the northern portion of the Mesa Central (fig. 4).

Lining the southern rim of the plateau is a row of high, widely spaced volcanoes, known as the Transverse Volcanic Axis (P. C. Sánchez, 1935) or the Cordillera Neovolcanico (Robles Ramos, 1942). Among the larger volcanoes of this range are (from east to west) Orizaba, or Citlaltepetl (5750 m. elevation, the highest point in Middle America); Cofre de Perote, or Naucampatepetl (4200 m.); Malinche, or Matlalcueyetl (4400 m.); Popocatepetl (5400 m.); Ixtaccihuatl (5300 m.); Nevado de Toluca, or Xinantecatl (4600 m.); Tancitaro (3600 m.); and the Volcan de Colima (3850 m.). Most of these large volcanoes were formed in late Tertiary, but many have been active in historic time; the last large eruption of the Volcan de Colima occurred in 1913, and today steam frequently emits from the crater of Popocatepetl. These are all composite volcanoes with symmetrical, concave slopes. Each has been built up by deposition of alternate layers of lava and ash extruded from a central crater. Between or adjacent to the large volcanoes are lower mountains that have formed through the coalescing of ejecta from many small craters and vents. An example is the Sierra de Ajusco which borders the Valley of Mexico on the south; within this mass are various craters, such as that of Xitle, from which enormous quantities of ash and lava have been ejected. Mexico's newest volcano, Paricutin, which erupted in 1943 near the northwestern base of Tancitaro in Michoacan state, indicates continuing activity along the Cordillera Neovolcanica, or volcanic axis (Foshag and Gonzáles Reyna, 1956).

The peaks and upper slopes of the volcanic masses that rise above 3800 m. show evidence of Pleistocene to Recent glaciation in the form of amphitheater-like valley heads (cirques), moraines, erratic boulders, and other glacial features. Three peaks (Orizaba, Popocatepetl, and Ixtaccihuatl) still carry small patches of fern and ice at elevations above 5000 m.—remnants of Pleistocene glaciers (Lorenzo, 1959b). Until 50 years ago the *neveros*, or local ice collectors, made daily trips from Amecameca to obtain ice from the small glaciers on Ixtaccihuatl (Farrington, 1897).

As mentioned earlier, Menard (1955) believes that the main volcanic axis of Mexico is associated with the E-W-trending Clarion Fracture Zone in the Pacific Ocean floor, along which tension faults have developed, giving rise to structural weaknesses and subsequent vulcanism. Subsidiary fractures and associated volcanic activity to the north of the main axis can be traced from the Lake Chapala basin (a downfaulted, or graben, structure) westward to the deeply indented Bay of Banderas on the Pacific coast (P. C. Sánchez, 1935). Other fractures trend northwestward from the main axis to extend recent volcanic activity into Jalisco and Nayarit as far as Tepic, near which are the large volcanoes of Sanganguey and Ceboruco as well as many smaller ones. Mooser and Maldonado-Koerdell (1961) relate these northwestern fractures and associated vulcanism to offshoots from the San Andreas Fracture Zone. Although

C. Tancítaro

Fig. 6.—A PORTION OF THE TARASCAN SIERRA, MICHOACAN STATE, ALONG THE NEOVOLCANIC AXIS, WESTERN MESA CENTRAL Swarms of cinder cones and old pine- and oak-covered lava flows contrastwith the cultivated areas (light tones). The larger hills in the middle background are remnants of composite volcanoes. Cerro Tancítaro (3600 m.elevation) is the largest.

the main volcanic axis forms almost a straight line along the 19th parallel, perpendicular fractures have extended short volcanic ranges northward at right angles to the main fracture zone. Thus Cofre de Perote and intermediate volcanic forms lie directly north of the Volcan de Orizaba; Ixtaccihuatl and the Sierra Nevada that form the eastern bounds of the Valley of Mexico trend northward from Popocatepetl; and the Sierra de las Cruces lies at right angles to the Sierra de Ajusco (Felix and Lenk, 1892; Friedlaender, 1930; Williams, 1950) (fig. 5).

Besides the large composite volcanoes there are many other volcanic features that characterize the surface of the Mesa Central. On slopes and in swales between the volcanoes are numerous conical hills that vary in height from 50 to 150 m. Most of these are cinder, or explosion, cones, each with a circular flat-floored crater from which ash has been ejected. Others are scoria mounds with no craters, having been built up by the outflow of basaltic material from vents. Often cinder cones and scoria mounds occur in swarms within a given area. Around the base of Tancitaro, for example, are more than 250 such cones (Waitz, 1914–15) and nearly 800 are found in the Tarascan area between Uruapan and Morelia (Blásquez López, 1956) (fig. 6). Again, many of these conical hills occur around the base of Popocatepetl, and a line of them forms part of the picturesque Sierra de Catarina in the southern part of the Valley of Mexico. The northernmost occurrence of cone swarms within the Mesa Central is near Tepic in Nayarit and near Valle de Santiago in southern Guanajuato state. Most of the cones appear to be relatively young (Pleistocene to Recent), and are often said to represent the last stage of vulcanism within a given area. Some have been breached by either lava flows or stream erosion, but most still retain symmetrical slopes and flat-floored craters, the surfaces of which are often cultivated.

A few craters contain small, round lakes. In the eastern part of the Mesa Central within the Basin of Puebla and the Valley of Mexico cinder cones with dry craters are called *xalapazcos* (from the Nahuatl, meaning "containers of sand"); those with small lakes are known as *axalapazcos* ("containers of sand with water") (Ordóñez, 1903–06).

Much of the rolling or gently sloping surface around the bases of and between the composite volcanoes and cone swarms is composed of lava and semiconsolidated deposits of ash (tuff) and volcanic mudflows (lahars). Extensive lava flows of varying age and state of weathering cover large areas of the Mesa Central. Flows of late Tertiary and early Pleistocene are composed chiefly of andesitic rock, whereas those of late Pleistocene to Recent are mainly of olivine basalt, although the flows of newly formed Paricutin volcano in Michoacan (1943–47) and that of Ceboruco in Nayarit (1870) are andesitic (Ordóñez, 1906; Williams, 1950). The latter flows are composed of blocky, scoriaceous material, which makes their surfaces (aptly called *malpaís*) extremely rough and difficult to traverse. Even after centuries of weathering the surfaces of the lava flows retain much of their initial roughness, as evidenced by the Pedregal de San Angel flow (est. ca. 500 B.C.) on the southern edge of the Valley of Mexico (Maldonado-Koerdell, 1954a). Many of the terrace-like surfaces and low, flat-topped mesas that cover much of the Mesa Central are old, weathered lava flows. Often the surface of a highly weathered flow contains small, alluvium-filled swales; highly fertile and moisture-retentive, the soils of these small basins have been favored spots for early planting of maize since ancient times. A fine example of these features (locally called *cañadas*) occurs on the old flows south of Xochimilco in the Valley of Mexico.

Deposits of volcanic tuff, except where highly dissected by stream erosion, have

44

Fig. 7—THE NORTHERN PORTION OF TULANCINGO BASIN, NORTHEASTERN MESA CENTRAL
Natural dissection of the lacustrine floor through headward erosion by upper tributaries of the Rio Metztitlan (Rio Panuco drainage) appears in foreground. The view looks east toward the edge of the plateau escarpment.

resulted in smooth to rolling surfaces; lahars composed of highly mixed unstratified material that ranges from fine clay to large, angular boulders, have built great fans on the lower slopes of the larger volcanoes. The hummocky surface and heterogeneous composition of the lahar deposits have been mistaken for glacial debris supposedly laid down by large mountain glaciers during Pleistocene (cf. Blásquez López, 1943).

Minor volcanic features of the Mesa Central include small mud volcanoes, fumaroles (steam jets and geysers), and sulphurous hot springs, which occur either during dormancy or the final stages of volcanic activity. One of the most spectacular examples of these features on the Mesa Central is found along a line of fractures eastward from Lake Chapala across northern Michoacan, especially in the Sierra de San Andres (Waitz, 1906; Palmer, 1926; Mooser, 1958).

In terms of human habitation the most significant landforms of the Mesa Central are the flat-floored basins that today cover much of the plateau surface between surrounding volcanic features. In size these

45

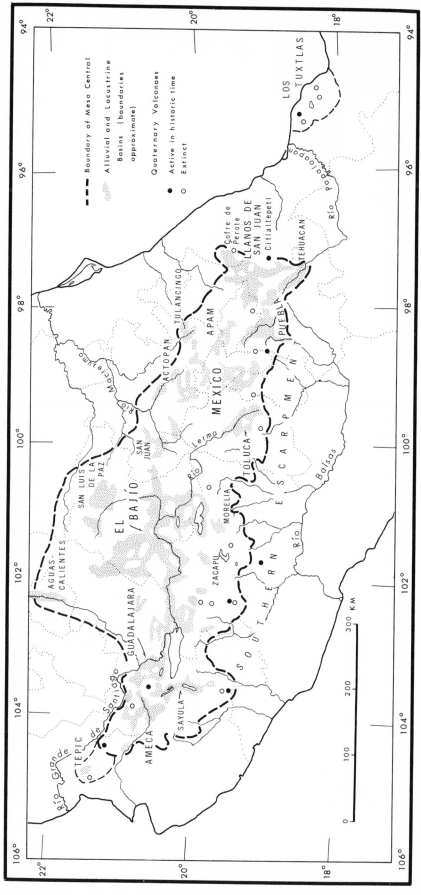

Fig. 8—THE MESA CENTRAL OF MEXICO

basins vary from small pockets of a few square kilometers to large areas such as the Valley of Mexico (45 by 75 km.) or the extensive area of interconnected basins, called the Bajio of Guanajuato near the center of the Mesa Central. In elevation the basin floors range from 1400 m. in the western part of the plateau to 2600 m. in the Valley of Toluca. All of these flattish plains are old lake basins, formed through the disruption of normal stream drainage by vulcanism. According to Waitz (1943), the formation of the basins began as early as the close of the Cretaceous through the damming of streams by lava flows, back of which formed extensive lakes. Throughout Tertiary and into Pleistocene stream-transported sediments, ash fall, and mudflows from adjacent volcanic slopes gradually filled the lakes. In the Bajio of Guanajuato ancient lake sediments are more than 300 m. in thickness (Waitz, 1943), and in the Valley of Mexico well borings have recorded basin fill to a depth of 1000 m. without encountering basement rock (Arellano, 1953b). The largest extent of the ancient lakes may have been during the last Pleistocene pluvial. At that time a continuous body of water occupied the Valley of Mexico and in the western part of the Mesa Central a huge lake joined the present Chapala, Magdalena, and Zacoalco-Sayula depressions with a water surface approximately 100 m. above that of present Lake Chapala (Waitz, 1943). Tapped by headward-eroding streams and filled by sediment, the majority of lakes have now disappeared. Their beds remain as the present level surfaces within the basins (fig. 7).

Abundant aquatic wild life in and around the remaining lakes and the fertile, easily worked soils on adjacent volcanic slopes attracted dense aboriginal settlement within the basins. Lake Patzcuaro, the center of ancient and modern Tarascan culture, and the Valley of Mexico lakes (around the shores of which are archaeological sites ranging in time from Tepexpan [8000 b.c.]

to late Aztec) give substantial evidence of the attraction of the lacustrine environment for human habitation. Today the Mexican people still obtain the bulk of their food supply from the crops cultivated in the originally fertile lacustrine soils. Figure 8 shows the extent and distribution of the more important basins, the largest of which are the Valley of Mexico, Huamantla, Puebla, Toluca, and the Bajio. Some of the basin lakes, such as the five extant in the Valley of Mexico until the end of the last century, have been drained artificially; others, such as the Laguna de Totolzingo in the Basin of Huamantla (Llanos de San Juan) in the eastern part of the plateau, are in the process of disappearing through filling and natural desiccation.

Various kinds of volcanic rock that make up many of the landforms of the Mesa Central have been useful to local inhabitants since ancient times. One of the most valuable of these materials is obsidian, a black to gray glassy volcanic rock which can be flaked by percussion or pressure to make fine, sharp prismatic blades for knives and other cutting tools or to fashion projectile points of many shapes and sizes. Rhyolitic obsidian is the most common form that occurs in the Mesa Central, where deposits are usually associated with old remnant volcanoes and lava flows of early Tertiary age. Although scattered throughout the plateau, one of the most important sources of obsidian in all Mesoamerica during ancient times was the Cerro de las Navajas, a rhyolitic hill east of Pachuca at the northernmost end of the Valley of Mexico (Aubert de la Rüe, 1958). Other especially abundant deposits are found in the Sierra de San Andres, near Ucaro, northwestern Michoacan; near Cadereyta de Montes, Queretaro; and in the Sierra de la Venta, near Magdalena, Jalisco. In preconquest times obsidian was one of the most important items traded into adjacent nonvolcanic areas. In addition, various types of andesite and basalt afforded ex-

47

cellent material for making querns or metates and for shaping building stone. Soft and easily quarried, the red tezontle (an andesitic breccia); the gray chiluca (trachytic andesite); and dark-colored, scoriaceous basalts were quarried by the ancient inhabitants of the Valley of Mexico to face religious structures in ceremonial centers within the basin.

Mesa del Norte. The northern two-thirds of the Mexican Plateau surface is a vast area of folded and faulted mountain ranges separated and half buried by deep deposits of alluvium that form extensive basin plains. Usually the northern part of this area is considered to be a southward extension of the basin and range topography of the western United States (Robles Ramos, 1942). Most of the ranges trend either N-S or NW-SE, corresponding to the general orientation of the Nevadan and Laramide tectonic patterns outlined above. In the north-central section of the plateau, however, E-W-trending ranges (e.g. the Sierra de Parras and adjacent mountains) represent a westward arcing of the Sierra Madre Oriental structure. Volcanics (chiefly rhyolite and andesite of early Tertiary age) compose most of the surface rock on the western side of the plateau. In contrast, the eastern side, being closely related to the Sierra Madre Oriental structure, is covered by clastic rocks, principally limestone (fig. 4).

At least two major landform areas can be distinguished in the northern plateau: (1) a semiarid elongated area of volcanic ranges separated by high alluvial basins adjacent to the Sierra Madre Occidental; (2) the lower central and eastern part of the plateau, an arid basin-range area with characteristic desert landforms and interior drainage.

The high basin-range area extends along the eastern side of the Sierra Madre Occidental from the vicinity of southwestern Zacatecas northwestward to the Casas Grandes district of Chihuahua near the United States border. Elevations of the detritus-filled basins vary from 1500 to 2000 m. The larger basins include those of Valparaiso and Villanueva, southwestern Zacatecas; and farther north in central Durango the plains of Guadiana, Poanas, and Guatimape. The latter contains the remnants of Lake Santiaguillo, once an extensive Pleistocene water body; lakes probably occupied other basins, but they have been drained by streams eroding headward from the Pacific or by those that flow eastward into the central desert. The adjacent NW-SE-trending ranges rise 200–700 m. above the basin floors. The bedded rhyolitic lavas and tuffs that cap many of the ranges often present steep, cliffed faces, called *bufas*, many of which served as defense sites for ancient primitives as well as for modern guerrilla bands. Along the sides of the ranges alluvial fans built by intermittent streams slope gradually into the basin flats.

The well-watered spots within the grass-covered, game-rich basins of this area afforded favorable localities for human settlement in pre-Spanish times. The Chalchihuites culture (A.D. 900–1200), represented by sites from La Quemada in southwestern Zacatecas to Zape in northern Durango, lay entirely within the high basin-range area, and is usually considered to be a northwestern extension of sedentary farming peoples from central Mexico (Lister and Howard, 1955). Similarly, the Casas Grandes culture of northwestern Chihuahua (of possible central Mexican origin) occupied the northern extremity of the high basin country. This fringe of high basins thus served as a corridor for migrations and cultural diffusion in ancient times —a function which it retained into the Spanish colonial period.

To the east of the high basin-range area lies the lower, more arid central part of the Mesa del Norte, which extends from the vicinity of San Luis Potosi northward to the U.S. border. Here aridity has been as significant as geology in molding the sur-

Cuatro Ciénegas

FIG. 9.—THE BOLSÓN OF CUATRO CIENEGAS, CENTRAL COAHUILA STATE
Fault block and folded mountains surround the desert basins, the centers of which contain barriales (white areas), often incrusted with salt deposits. A highly dissected bajada slope occurs on the extreme right.

face configuration. Because of aridity much of the area is characterized by interior drainage, and the weathering and erosive processes peculiar to arid climates have produced landforms that occur in few other parts of Middle America.

The isolated fault-block and folded mountain ranges of the Mesa del Norte appear to be partially buried by the surrounding detritus washed down from their slopes by infrequent heavy thundershowers or deposited through gravity fall and creep of weathered rock particles. Except in a few localities, such as the Samalayuca dune field in northern Chihuahua, wind has been a minor geomorphic agent within the Mesa del Norte. The larger ranges rise 500–1000 m. above the adjacent basins to elevations 2000–3000 m. above sea level. Except for the higher crests, often covered with stands of oak and pine, most of the ranges are relatively bare of vegetation, and their flanks are characterized by deep V-shaped canyons and sharp-crested spurs.

The foot of most ranges within the Mesa del Norte is defined by a sharp angle between the steep mountain face and a more gently sloping rock pediment that grades downslope into the adjacent basin. Formed by backwasting and stream and sheet erosion, the rock pediment is usually covered by a veneer of coarse sand, gravel, and small boulders deposited by flash floods that issue from the mountain canyons. The larger streams may form alluvial fans below the canyon mouths, burying the pediment under debris up to 1 m. thick. Often resistant portions of a mountain range are cut off and completely surrounded by pediment and fan material, forming residual knolls that rise above a smooth surface. After long periods of weathering and erosion under stable tectonic conditions desert ranges may be worn down to groups of isolated knolls. In such cases pediment slopes advancing headward from opposite sides may coalesce, creating "pediment passes," which afford easy access from one basin to

50

another. Several such passes are encountered along the present "super highway" that leads from Saltillo to San Luis Potosi.

In the Mesa del Norte the large desert basins, called *bolsones*, are the most extensive and conspicuous feature of the landscape (fig. 9). Rimming the basins are the rock pediments of the adjacent ranges, the gradients of which average 40 m. per km. Downslope the accumulation of water-deposited detritus increases in thickness and gradients decrease to less than 10 m. per km. This high portion of the basin is known as the *bajada*. Toward the center of the bolsón, which usually has no drainage outlet, the finest materials (clays) collect to form an almost level plain called the *barrial* (misnamed *playa* in arid portions of western U.S.). After infrequent heavy summer thundershowers, clay-laden water flowing in intermittent channels from the surrounding slopes collects in the barrial, forming a shallow ephemeral lake. The water soon evaporates, however, leaving a moist clay surface which sometimes becomes incrusted with salts. Composed of haloids of sodium, potassium, and magnesium in varying proportions, the salt crusts of the barriales were sometimes exploited by nomadic Chichimecs for trade with neighboring farmers in preconquest times (Mendizabal, 1946). The barriales of Villa de Cos and Santa Maria in eastern Zacatecas and those of Las Palomas, Los Gigantes, and Frailes in the Bolson de Mapimi (eastern Chihuahua and western Coahuila) are examples of such salt deposits. Some of the larger bolsones of north central Mexico, such as that of Parras in southern Coahuila, once contained extensive fresh-water lakes during Pleistocene. Lake Mayran in the Parras Basin, still large in the 16th century, has now practically disappeared because of artificial control of the Nazas River discharge, leaving an extensive lacustrine plain well suited for irrigated agriculture.

The southern portion of the Mesa del Norte, between the Sierra de Parras and

FIG. 10—THE FOLDED RIDGES OF THE SIERRA MADRE ORIENTAL, EASTERN NUEVO LEON STATE
Looking east toward the Gulf coastal plain. Rivers breach the tight folds to form deep transverse antecendent canyons. On the left is the Rio Potosi canyon; to the left, the Iturbide canyon, now traversed by an auto road that connects the plateau with Linares on the coastal plain.

Fig. 11—THE ARTEAGA ANTICLINORIUM FORMED BY THE SUDDEN WESTWARD FLEC-
TURE OF THE SIERRA MADRE ORIENTAL STRUCTURE IN THE VICINITY OF MONTERREY

central San Luis Potosi state, is often termed El Salado, owing to its numerous salt-incrusted barriales, especially in its western and northern portions. The eastern and southern parts of El Salado, however, dominated by a porous limestone surface, are characterized by karst topography— sink holes and disappearing intermittent streams. Low annual rainfall combined with porosity of surface has made this part of El Salado one of the most arid and desolate sections of all Mexico.

BOUNDING MOUNTAIN RANGES AND ADJA-
CENT ESCARPMENTS OF THE MEXICAN PLA-
TEAU. As indicated previously, the tectonic structures that border the Mexican Plateau on its eastern and western sides are here considered as the upturned edges and escarpments of the plateau proper.

Sierra Madre Oriental. This is a narrow belt of tightly folded, mainly N-S-trending anticlinal ridges and synclinal basins of limestone and other clastic rocks (fig. 10). Although its principal sector forms the eastern edge of the Mexican Plateau, the folded structures continue southward along the northeastern flank of the Oaxaca highlands and possibly blend into the northern side of the Chiapas highlands. In the vicinity of Teziutlan, Puebla state, and Jalapa, Veracruz, the limestone folds are completely buried by volcanic ejecta (an eastward extension of the Neovolcanic range), lava flows reaching the sea at Punta Delgada. Northward in the vicinity of Monterrey and Saltillo the main trend of the structure arcs abruptly westward to form the high anticlinorium of Arteaga and various E-W anticlinal ranges, such as the sierras of Parras and Jimulco on the plateau proper (De Cserna, 1956) (fig. 11). Low folded ranges and hills (Coahuila Marginal Folded Belt) trend northwestward from Monterrey into the Big Bend country of Texas to form the northeastern side of the plateau.

Within the Sierra Madre Oriental proper, between Teziutlan and Monterrey, anticlinal mountain ridges and intervening synclinal valleys are elongate and sinuous, some having been traced for hundreds of kilometers (Humphrey, 1956). Diastrophism has been so intense that recumbent folds and thrustfaulting are commonplace. Folding is also manifest in the low elongated foothill ranges and valleys back of the Gulf coastal plain. Westward from the foothills eight to ten major anticlinal elements, each higher and more complex than the last, form the main part of the sierra. Viewed from the coastal plain, this array of parallel ranges and gigantic overthrusts creates a formidable-looking escarpment. Although in general the crest of the Sierra Madre varies between 2000 and 3000 m., some of the overthrusts in places have elevated strata of limestone and shale to heights over 4000 m., especially between Ciudad Victoria and Saltillo.

Aside from the major forms of anticlinal ridges and synclinal valleys, various smaller erosional features are characteristic of the sierra. One of these is the short, steeply plunging anticlinal ridge or mountain that has been breached by stream erosion along its axis, forming a canoe-shaped valley, locally called a *potrero*. These features are especially common in the low folds northwest of Monterrey. In preconquest times these grassy vales were probably haunts of game animals, particularly of deer, hunted by the local nomads; since Spanish occupation the potreros have served as highland pastures for livestock and for small farming areas within the mountains.

Because limestone is the major rock type, karst forms abound in the sierra. Streams often disappear suddenly into sinkholes (*resumideros*); many anticlinal ridges are honeycombed with scores of limestone caverns, some of which contain archaeological remains (Bonet, 1953). Series of collapsed caverns and coalesced sinks have formed elongated flat-floored depressions, or *poljes*, especially on the plateau flank of the sierra (e.g. near Cardenas and Rayon, eastern San Luis Potosi state).

On the eastern or escarpment face of the sierra numerous rivers draining to the Gulf have cut across the folded structures, forming deep, narrow canyons. Examples include the Guayalejo River canyon southwest of Ciudad Victoria, the Rio Verde canyon west of Valles, and, the most spectacular one, the great canyon of the Rio Moctezuma, which has cut completely across the sierra. Upper tributaries of this river have tapped the plateau surface and are now in the process of dissecting the flat-floored highland basins.

The escarpment of the Sierra Madre Oriental is easily traversable at several points, all of which have served as important roadways connecting the plateau and Gulf lowlands since preconquest times. In the north the Paso del Aguila, between Saltillo and Monterrey, is an E-W valley that corresponds to the sudden westward arcing of the folded structures. Farther south the present highway from Antiguo Morelos to San Luis Potosi, via Ciudad Maiz, takes advantage of the low elevations of the folded ridges at that point (1500 m.). Again, along both the Zimapan-Jacala-Tamazunchale (old Pan American Highway) and Tulancingo-Huauchinango routes to the coast lowlands, the folded structures are much less complex than farther north, and the plateau edge drops off abruptly to a single escarpment slope.

Sierra Madre Occidental. The western edge and escarpment of the Mexican Plateau is generally considered to extend for 1200 km. from the U.S.–Mexican border to the Santiago River in Jalisco. Garfías and Chapín (1949), however, terminate the sierra proper at the Rio Mesquital in southern Durango, suggesting that the land configuration south thereof is more akin to the basin-range topography of the plateau. The

53

FIG. 12—LOOKING WEST TOWARD THE PACIFIC COAST DOWN THE BARRANCA DEL PRESIDIO ON THE FRAYED ESCARPMENT OF THE SIERRA MADRE OCCIDENTAL
The remnant of a flattish erosion surface in foreground indicates horizontal beds of lava flows.

early geological studies of Weed (1902) and Hovey (1905, 1907) give vivid descriptions of the fantastic configuration of the Sierra Madre.

As stated earlier, the sierra has been built up by the outpouring from vents of vast quantities of volcanic material, chiefly andesite and rhyolite of Tertiary age. These materials are between 1500 and 1800 m. thick (Albritten, 1958). From the plateau near Durango the sierra appears to be insignificant, for it rises gradually as a rolling surface to a few hundred meters above the plateau basins. Viewed from the Pacific lowlands, however, the mountain front rises as a magnificent escarpment to a maximum elevation of 2500–3000 m. above sea level. Faulting and uplift during Pleistocene created a series of NW-SE-trending ridges and valleys near the summit and eastern half of the sierra. The ridges lie only 100–200 m. above the adjacent valleys, which contain cool highland meadows. In spite of faulting, the lava beds have maintained an almost level attitude; thus the highland ridges form flat-topped mesas with steep, bufa-like cliffs. Indeed, seen from the air, the Sierra Madre appears to be a dissected plateau rather than a mountain range.

The western or escarpment side of the sierra has been frayed with scores of deep canyons, or *barrancas*, incised into the volcanic material by streams flowing to the coast (fig. 12). Some of these canyons, such as the Barranca del Cobre, carved by the Rio Urique in western Chihuahua, rival the Grand Canyon of the Colorado in depth and grandeur. The depths of many barrancas approach 1500–2000 m. The steepness of the escarpment and the presence of the deep barrancas make this section of Mexico most difficult of access. Near the bottom of the canyons ancient rocks of Precambrian (?) to Mesozoic in age have been exposed. Many of these are highly mineralized and have yielded gold possibly since preconquest times. In terms of its ruggedness, wildness, and scenic beauty, the barranca country of the Sierra Madre Occidental is one of the most spectacular areas of Middle America.

Although sparcely populated today, some 20 isolated Indian language groups, such as the Tarahumar, Tepehuan, Acaxee, Xixime, Vorohio, occupied the deep barrancas and upper basins of the Sierra in pre-Spanish times. Of these only the Tarahumar remain in any number, inhabiting the caves in the warm barrancas during winter and farming highland basin plots in summer.

Neovolcanic Range. The southern limit of the Mexican Plateau has been discussed above with the Mesa Central. Its southern flank creates a steep escarpment that overlooks the Balsas Depression. Recent lava flows, small volcanoes, and cinder cones cover much of the escarpment surface. Jorullo volcano, which formed in 1759 within a sugar hacienda in southern Michoacan, is another reminder of the recency of vulcanism on the flank of the plateau (Gadow, 1930). Paleozoic metamorphics, Cretaceous limestone, and Tertiary clastics outcrop in many parts of the escarpment. As usual, karst forms exemplified by sinks, poljes, and the large caves in Morelos state (Cacahuamilpa, Chimalacatlan, etc.) appear in the limestone outcrops (Arellano, 1948; Bretz, 1955; Fries, 1960). Streams draining

into the Balsas Depression have eroded deep gorges into many parts of the escarpment face, especially in the vicinity of Mil Cumbres, southeastern Michoacan. In places dissection is so advanced that flattish plateau remnants, such as the elevated plains of Ario and Tacambaro in southern Michoacan, stand out as peninsulas or islands, surrounded by deep canyons. In Morelos and southwestern Puebla enormous fans of volcanic ash deposited by mudflows and streams sweep down the escarpment between parallel folded ridges to form elongated sloping plains (Fries, 1960). Some of these include the famous "Valles de Morelos," such as that of Cuernavaca, Yalotepec, and Cuautla. Because of their fertile volcanic alluvium such valley fills have been significant agricultural centers for the cultivation of tropical and subtropical crops since ancient times. Furthermore, the presence of springs that issue from porous lavas near the top of the escarpment have aided materially in early agriculture and were the probable source of water for incipient aboriginal irrigation practiced on the southern escarpment at the time of the Spanish conquest. The gently sloping surface of the basin fills as well as the low passes between the large volcanoes on the highland edge made the southern approaches to the Mexican Plateau much less difficult than those on its eastern and western sides. A similar arrangement of elongated valley fills as well as steplike basins is seen in the valleys leading from the plateau to the coast via Colima; in the basins of Tepic; and the series of basins near Jalapa and Orizaba on the southeastern flank of the Mesa Central. Both ancient trails and modern communications follow these physiographic features.

Peninsula of Baja California

Consideration of this long (1300 km.) mountainous peninsula will complete the description of the major highlands of northern and central Mexico. Both Baja

55

California and the adjacent Gulf of California are products of faulting along the major NW-SE fracture zones on the eastern margin of the North Pacific Basin. The entire peninsula is a westward-tilted fault-block forming a nearly continuous mountain chain that rises in a steep escarpment along the Gulf coast and slopes gradually to the Pacific Ocean (Beal, 1948). Three distinctive physiographic sections make up the mountain chain.

The northern half is part of a huge granitic batholith, a continuation of the Peninsular Range of southern California. Elevations exceed 2000 m. in the Sierra Juarez south of the U.S. border, but increase southward in the San Pedro Martir range to 3000 m. The summit of the batholith in the Sierra Juarez represents an old erosion surface with flattish highland basins that contain lush grassy meadows among the pine forests.

Almost the entire southern half of the peninsular chain is composed of Tertiary marine sediments, in places intruded by crystallines and covered by thick layers of Quaternary volcanic flows and tuffs. Some jagged peaks along the crest of the fault scarp reach 1500 m., but elevations gradually decrease southward to the Isthmus of La Paz. Intermittent streams have cut deep, narrow valleys into the volcanic rock, leaving flat table-like interfluves. Although this mountain section is the most arid part of the peninsula (less than 100 mm. annual precipitation), springs have produced many oases in the deep valley bottoms. Such sites were the seasonal haunts of the few hunting-and-gathering bands (Ñakipa, Paipai, Kiliwa) that inhabited the central section before European contact; many of the oasis sites later became fruitful mission centers after the Spanish invasion (Aschmann, 1959).

The third physiographic section of the mountain chain is the extreme southern tip of the peninsula, usually termed the Cape Area, which rises boldly in N-S granitic

ranges to 1800 m. elevation. Physiographically the Cape highlands are somewhat similar to the northern batholith, with a few old, hilly erosion surfaces at the summit, but with deeply entrenched valleys that penetrate inward from the surrounding piedmont (Beal, 1948; Hammond, 1954).

Extensive lowlands of the peninsula are confined to the Pacific slope. The largest is the Vizcaino Desert, a basin-like depression filled with recent sediment lying between the backslope of the main fault block and the low Vizcaino Range, which juts northwestward into the Pacific near the center of the peninsula. Extremely dry and virtually devoid of vegetation, the surface of the Vizcaino Desert is covered by large dune fields, some of which are 15 km. across and 30 m. high (Beal, 1948). A somewhat less extensive lowland, the Llano de la Magdalena, occupies the Pacific side of the peninsula's southern third. Barrier beaches, spits, lagoons, tombolos, and land-tied islands complicate the shoreline of these coastal lowlands. Widespread along the coasts of Baja California are series of Pleistocene to Recent marine terraces, indicating significant uplift. Most of the terraces carry abundant shell deposits, many of which are middens.

The Gulf of California occupies a tectonic trough or rift, 1500 km. long. As stated previously, the rift continues northwestward beyond the Gulf, forming the Salton Basin of California (elevation −70 m.) and lateral depressions, such as the Laguna Salada (−10 m.) in northeastern Baja California. The delta of the Colorado River forms a flat plain at the north end of the Gulf, and until its discharge was greatly reduced artificially a few decades ago, the river was rapidly extending its delta plain gulfward (Sykes, 1937). The enormous quantities of silt and sand within the lower flood plain and delta of the Colorado have furnished material for the great dune fields that cover much of the Altar Desert east of the river in Sonora.

56

Coastal Lowlands Adjacent to the Mexican Plateau

Narrow coastal lowlands fringe the eastern and western sides of the Mexican Plateau and its escarpments. Except in the extreme northern part of the country, these lowlands and adjacent escarpments to 800 m. elevation constitute the more significant areas of "tierra caliente," many sections of which have been significant in trade with neighboring highlands for millennia.

PACIFIC COASTAL LOWLANDS. The surface is composed chiefly of ranges of old crystalline rock separated by alluvial plains and basins. Widest in Sonora near the U.S. frontier, the lowland narrows southward in Sinaloa and Nayarit, where it terminates against the mountainous coast in the vicinity of San Blas. The Sonoran portion of the lowland consists of two distinct parts: (1) to the east a series of high parallel N-S ranges and narrow alluvium-filled basins, home of the Opata and Pima Indians, forming a transitional area between the Sierra Madre; and (2) the low, dry western plains and isolated ranges half buried by stream-borne alluvium. Within the latter area is the Altar Desert, or "Gran Desierto," the driest part of Mexico, with the most extensive erg, or sand dune field of the country, bordered by a barren volcanic mass, Cerro Pinacate (Ives, 1935).

Southward in Sinaloa the low, isolated N-S hills of granite, remnants of former higher ranges, dominate the narrow coastal strip. As in Sonora, these hills are half buried by the great quantity of detritus deposited by streams flowing from the Sierra Madre. Some hills abut upon the sea, in places forming natural harbors, such as those of Guaymas, Topolobampo, and Mazatlan.

In terms of human habitation, the most important landforms of the Pacific lowlands are the river flood plains and near the coast the delta plains formed by the larger streams, such as the Yaqui, Fuerte, Mayo, and Culiacan; farther south in Nayarit the flood plains of the Acaponeta, San Pedro, and Santiago rivers are significant. In the drier north the summer overflow of the streams afforded a natural means of flood irrigation farming, which the Cahita-speaking Indians practiced on the fertile alluvium. In the more humid coastal plain of southern Sinaloa and Nayarit the natural levees along the banks of the larger rivers abound in village sites once occupied by the more highly cultured Tahue and Totorame people. Moreover, from Guaymas southward numerous lagoons fronted by sand bars and fringed with mangrove, extend along the coast, affording choice habitats for tidal shellfish and crustaceans. In southern Sinaloa and Nayarit longshore currents have formed extensive series of beach ridges, some of which contain shell middens, indicating long occupation by primitive man.

GULF COASTAL LOWLANDS. The lowland on the eastern side of Mexico is geologically a continuation of the Gulf Coastal Plain of the United States. It extends from the Rio Grande for a distance of 1350 km. to the Yucatan Peninsula. In width the lowland varies from a maximum of 300 km. in northern Tamaulipas and Nuevo Leon to almost nothing in central Veracruz, where a spur of volcanic ejecta from the Mesa Central reaches the sea. Unlike its structural counterpart in the United States, the Mexican Gulf Coastal Lowland is not a continuous plains area; rather, much of its surface is made up of low mountains and hills of varying geological origin.

The major lowlands plains correspond to large tectonic embayments, each of which contains one or several large river flood plains and corresponding deltas. The northernmost is the Rio Grande embayment with its extensive delta plain that extends southward from Matamoros and Brownsville. Farther south in the Tampico embayment are extensive plains, some alluvial, such as that of the Rio Panuco and its lower

57

tributaries; other plains in the vicinity consist of undeformed upper Cretaceous and Tertiary marine marls and shales that dip gently eastward toward the Gulf (Humphrey, 1956). South of Veracruz City the Papaloapan embayment is characterized by plains of recent alluvium bordered by low Pleistocene terraces. Eastward, the wide Tabasco lowland on its seaward side consists of a series of recent flood and delta plains built up by alluvium deposited by five major rivers: Coatzacoalcos-Uspanapa, Tonala, Grijalva, Usumacinta, and Candelaria and their ancestral streams. Low Pleistocene terraces cover the inner portion of the Tabasco lowland.

Elsewhere the Gulf lowland surface is deformed by hills and low mountains that have resulted from (1) local uplift of marine sediments, in places accompanied by granitic intrusions, and (2) past volcanic activity. From the base of the Sierra Madre Oriental eastward the surface of the inner Gulf lowland is interrupted by elongated anticlinal hills and by flat-topped mesas and cuestaform ridges of Tertiary and Pleistocene gravels eroded by present streams. Between the Rio Grande and Tampico embayments the extensive but low-relief sierras of Cruillas (600 m. max. elevation), San Carlos (1500 m.), and Tamaulipas (1000 m.) are examples of folding and doming. In northern Veracruz, between the Tampico embayment and the volcanic salient of the Mexican Plateau, the coastal lowland is a complex maze of hills with a relief of some 100 m. formed by stream dissection of slightly uplifted Tertiary shales and sandstones. These hilly lowlands are locale of the Huastec and lowland Totonac, who still practice slash-burn cultivation on steep slopes. Here also are found the ruins of Tajin, one of the great cultural centers of ancient Mesoamerica.

Volcanic forms abound along the Gulf lowland. Between Ciudad Victoria and the Tampico embayment there are basalt-covered mesas of late Tertiary age that rise

150 m. above the adjacent stream-cut valleys; and on the southeastern flank of the Sierra de Tamaulipas vast outpourings of basalt have formed a lava dome in the vicinity of Aldama (Staub and Lager, 1922). Moreover, around the margins of the Tampico embayment occur scores of old basaltic necks, remnants of former volcanoes that form needle-like peaks; for example, the spectacular Bernal de Horcasitas rises 1100 m. from the surrounding plain, 100 km. northwest of Tampico (Heim, 1934, 1940). The immense volcanic salient of the Mesa Central (called locally the Sierra de Chiconquiaco) north of Veracruz City has been mentioned; geographically this highland flank of the plateau divides the Gulf lowland into a northern and a southern sector. In southern Veracruz, between the Papaloapan and Coatzacoalcos river basins, the volcanic mass of Los Tuxtlas rises like an island out of the surrounding alluvial plains. Composed of recent basaltic lava and ash ejected from a number of craters, this feature rises to a maximum elevation of 1660 m. at the summit of extinct Volcan de Santa Marta. A slightly lower volcano, San Martin, last erupted in 1793 (Waitz, 1914–15). Within the volcanic mass beautiful Lake Catemaco occupies a large extinct crater (probably a caldera) 340 m. above sea level. Geologists have long supposed that Los Tuxtlas forms the eastern outlier of the Neovolcanic Axis of Mexico (P. C. Sánchez, 1935; Friedlaender and Sonder, 1923; Ordóñez, 1936). Later studies (summarized by Murray, 1961) indicate that the volcanic mass probably represents one of the many uplifts within the Gulf coastal area that is associated with an ancient geosyncline, and that it is completely unrelated to the Neovolcanic Axis. Since ancient times Los Tuxtlas has been densely peopled, for the soil derived from the recent basaltic materials is of high fertility. Both steep slopes of volcanoes and cinder cones and flattish swales are heavily cultivated today.

58

Archaeologically Los Tuxtlas appears to have been the center of Olmec culture; near its western and southern flanks are, respectively, the renowned Olmec sites of Tres Zapotes and San Lorenzo; not far to the east on the edge of the Tabasco lowlands lies an isolated but well-known Olmec site, La Venta.

Among the various landforms found within the Gulf lowlands probably none has been more significant for human occupation than the natural levees and stream-cut terraces that border the larger rivers in their lower courses. These features usually contain the most fertile and most easily worked soil of the lowlands; moreover, within the larger flood plains the natural levees form the highest ground in the vicinity and are thus the areas least subject to frequent floods. From the Rio Tamesi, northwest of Tampico, southward to the Yucatan platform the most numerous archaeological sites in the lowland are on the natural levees in the lower stream courses and on river terraces farther upstream. Good examples are the ancient Huastec sites along the lower Panuco levees; the Totonac sites along the lower Tecolutla and Nautla rivers in central Veracruz; and those (unidentified) seen from the Veracruz-Cordoba highway along the Rio Atoyac. Much of the Tabasco lowland is composed of recent alluvium deposited by the Grijalva and Usumacinta river systems, the most voluminous in all Middle America. The lower river courses have shifted from place to place over the Tabasco plain during the past millennia. It is particularly on the levees of abandoned river channels that archaeological material is abundant, indicating the importance of riverside sites to the Indian farmers who inhabited the lowland areas. For instance, now insignificant, the Rio Seco was a former main channel of the Grijalva River before it was abandoned sometime during the 17th century. The abundance of archaeological material along the old levees suggests that the pre-Spanish population was as numerous as that of today. Away from the levees, which vary from 1 to 3 km. in width, back swamps and marshes prevail.

In the Tabasco lowlands Pleistocene terraces of highly weathered bright red and yellow material cover the inner portions of the plains area (Krynine, 1935). These deposits dip gently seaward and pass under the more recent river-deposited alluvium along the Gulf margin of the plains. Rising a few meters above the dark-colored recent alluvium are occasional remnants of red Pleistocene material, forming islands of high ground free from flood. Although the soils are highly leached and infertile, quite possibly these terrace remnants may have served as settlement sites in pre-Spanish times, just as they do today. Villahermosa, the present capital of Tabasco, is located on such an outlier of red Pleistocene material along the Grijalva River.

In the Gulf lowlands of southeastern Veracruz and western Tabasco salt masses have intruded underlying strata and occasionally have uplifted the surface material to form small structural domes that rise a few feet above the surrounding alluvial plain. These "islands" often afford good habitation sites, some of which have been utilized since preconquest times. The ancient Olmec site of La Venta occupies high ground uplifted by a salt intrusion, and a few miles southward along the Rio Tonala the mound site of El Plan lies on a similar structure. (Murray, 1961, and personal communication). The recent exploitation of petroleum deposits that customarily accumulate around salt domes should facilitate archaeological exploration in this area.

Except where volcanic forms abut against the sea, as at Punta Delgada north of Veracruz City and in the Los Tuxtlas area, the shores of the Gulf lowlands are low, with barrier beaches, beach ridges, and lagoons forming the main coastal features. The longest barrier beaches, similar to

59

those of Texas, are found along the Tamaulipas coast in northeastern Mexico. These enclose extensive lagoons, such as the Laguna Madre south of the Rio Grande, and the Laguna de Tamiahua, south of Tampico and the Panuco River. Cabo Rojo, which forms part of the barrier beach that encloses the Tamiahua Lagoon, represents a remnant of red Pleistocene sand and clay that rests possibly on an old coral reef. The reefs that presently lie off Cabo Rojo are the northernmost examples of coral growth along the northeastern shore of the Gulf of Mexico. Southward, especially beyond Tuxpan, long stretches of beach ridges line the coast, and north of Veracruz City large areas of longitudinal dunes penetrate 10–15 km. inland. South of the city a high dune ridge continues almost without interruption along the coast to the Tuxtlas area, blocking drainage to form extensive marshes landward. A similar dune ridge is seen at Coatzacoalcos. Low beach ridges are especially well developed along parts of the Tabasco coast, where they have served as habitation and farming sites probably since ancient times. They are densely settled and intensively cultivated today, and they contain numerous archaeological sites.

Old Lands of Southern Mexico and Northern Central America

South of the Mexican Plateau and the Neovolcanic Axis begins an area of ancient crystalline rocks with a structure pattern of E-W ranges and intervening depressions. This area includes southern Mexico, northern Central America, and the Greater Antilles of the Caribbean, and is often referred to as "Old Antillia," or more recently, as "Caribbean Land." Geologically it is the oldest land area and physiographically the most complex of all Middle America.

In 1892 Felix and Lenk pointed out the structural significance of the Mexican Plateau's southern escarpment as the terminus of dominant NW-SE structural lines of western North America, in contrast to the

E-W ranges of southern Mexico. Sapper (1894) was one of the first to call attention to the same dominant E-W structural trend of northern Central America, and Hill (1898) first emphasized the relationship between the E-W structural lines of the southern Mexican highlands, the mountains of northern Central America, and those of the Greater Antilles, calling the entire area the Antillean Orogenic System. Schuchert (1929, 1935) followed Hill in proposing the Antillean Geanticline and a former land connection between northern Central America and the Greater Antillean Islands. Other investigators, however, point to the extension of some NW-SE trends into or across Old Antillia. The submarine fractures and deeps off the Pacific coast of Central America and the adjacent volcanic axis were mentioned earlier. Moreover, Guzman and De Cserna (1960) consider the folded structures of the Sierra Madre Oriental to continue southeastward as the Sierra de Oaxaca and the Sierra de San Cristobal in Chiapas.

BALSAS-TEPALCATEPEC DEPRESSION. This low, hot and dry structural depression separates the Mexican Plateau from the highlands of Oaxaca and Guerrero. A jumble of low hills composed chiefly of highly dissected Paleozoic and Mesozoic metamorphosed sediments, characterizes the surface of the Balsas lowland. Twisting and turning through the hilly land, the Balsas River and its tributaries have formed sizable patches of alluvium in only a few places along their courses (fig. 13). Near the Pacific Ocean the Balsas breaks through the southern highlands to the coast, where it has built a small arcuate delta. The structural depression, however, continues WNW through southern Michoacan, where it is occupied by the Tepalcatepec River, a tributary of the Balsas. In contrast to the dissected surface of the Balsas Basin, the semiarid Tepalcatepec Basin has a wide, flattish floor of Tertiary and Pleistocene volcanic deposits, into which the main river

Coyuca

Rio Balsas

Pungarabato

Rio Cutzamala

Río

FIG. 13—ONE OF THE MORE EXTENSIVE AREAS OF ALLUVIUM AND FLATTISH SURFACES WITHIN THE BALSAS DEPRESSION AT THE CONFLUENCE OF THE BALSAS AND CUTZAMALA RIVERS, NORTHERN GUERRERO STATE
The trading towns of Pungarabato and Coyuca dominate this agricultural area.

C. Zempoaltepec

Fɪɢ. 14—A PORTION OF THE HIGHLY DISSECTED MESA DEL SUR, EAST OF OAXACA CITY
Looking north. Cerro Zempoaltepec (3,390 m. elevation) is the highest point in the Oaxaca highlands.

is now cutting a deep gorge. The plain of Apatzingan, recently developed into a highly productive irrigated farming district, forms part of the smooth basin floor. The Tepalcatepec portion of the Balsas depression may be associated with the NW-SE pattern of crustal fractures along the west flank of Mexico, whereas the Balsas proper is related to the E-W Antillean pattern. It is within this latitudinal zone (18°–20° N.) of highly complex geology that the two structure patterns appear to intersect.

Sᴏᴜᴛʜᴇʀɴ Mᴇxɪᴄᴀɴ Hɪɢʜʟᴀɴᴅs. South of the Balsas lie the southern highlands of

Mexico. The western part of this rugged area within the state of Guerrero is often called the Sierra Madre del Sur; discontinuous ranges of the same rock type and structure, such as the Sierra de Coalcoman, continue northwestward along the Pacific coast of Michoacan and Jalisco to Cabo Corrientes. The Tres Marias Islands off Nayarit possibly form a further extension of this structure, and some investigators have suggested a structural connection with the Peninsula of Baja California (Schuchert, 1935; Eardley, 1954). The wide eastern section of the southern highlands within the state of Oaxaca is known as the Mesa del Sur. A basement of ancient metamorphic rocks (gneisses and schists of Paleozoic and Mesozoic age) intruded by large granitic batholiths, much of which has been exposed by erosion, underlies most of the southern highlands. Remnant patches of Cretaceous limestone and Tertiary continental sediments are scattered on the highland surface, and in places Tertiary lavas cap the underlying metamorphics over large areas, as along the crest of the Sierra del Sur in Guerrero and in the mountains east of Oaxaca City. Average elevations of mountain crests range from 1800 to 2000 m. above the sea, some 500–1000 m. above adjacent stream valleys and basins. A few peaks, mainly remnants of Tertiary volcanics, rise above 3000 m., such as Teotepec (3700 m.) in central Guerrero and Zempoaltepec (3390 m.) in east-central Oaxaca.

There is little level land in this rugged mountain mass. The hundreds of small torrential streams that drain the highlands have carved deep V-shaped valleys into the surface, creating a land of precipitous slopes and knife-edged ridges (fig. 14). Aside from a few flat-floored poljes (a series of coalesced sinkholes in limestone), such as that of Tixtla, east of Chilpancingo, (Müllerried, 1942c) the Guerrero highlands are practically all steep slopes. In the Mesa del Sur of Oaxaca only scattered remnants

of a former plateau surface and a few structural basins have flattish floors. The Valley of Oaxaca is the largest of the highland basins—a downfaulted trench some 95 km. long and 25 km. wide, elevated some 1500 m. above the sea (fig. 15). A series of smaller basins (Tlacolula to the east and Etla to the north) interconnect with the main one, expanding the flat-to-rolling surface over a considerable area. This entire basin complex, drained by the headwaters of the Atoyac, in pre-Spanish times was one of the most culturally important areas of Middle America. It was the center of the Zapotec and Mixtec cultures, the site of the magnificent ceremonial centers of Monte Alban and Mitla. Today the basins, the soils of which have been cultivated for more than 2000 years, form one of the most densely settled rural areas of Mexico, and are still the stronghold of Zapotec-speaking Indians.

North and west of the Valley of Oaxaca lies the Mixteca Alta, the northern dissected slope of the Mesa del Sur, drained by headwaters of the Balsas. Eastward from the Valley are the Mije highlands, a complex, rugged mountain mass of volcanics, granite batholiths, and folded limestone; this area since the Spanish conquest has served as a refuge zone for many Indian language groups. Bordering the Mesa del Sur on the northeast is the highly folded and faulted range of limestone and metamorphics called the Sierra Madre de Oaxaca (3000 m. elevation), which presents a formidable barrier between the coastal lowlands of Veracruz and the Oaxaca highlands (Tamayo, 1949). Immediately west of this range lies a narrow NW-SE graben, occupied in its northern part by the elongated plain of Tehuacan, in its southern part by the highly dissected Cañon de Tomellin. Located in the rain shadow of the Sierra Madre, the graben depression is quite dry; however, since ancient times it has served as an important roadway connecting Tehuacan and the Puebla Basin with the Valley of Oaxaca. The graben is drained by

FIG. 15—NORTHERN PART OF THE VALLEY OF OAXACA
For millennia Indians have farmed the alluvium of the Rio Atoyac (center) and tributary streams. The famous archaeological site of Monte Alban (upper left) and the unidentified hilltop sites (lower left) attest to the antiquity of Indian occupation of the area.

the headwaters of the Papaloapan River, which cuts a deep gorge (canyon of Santo Domingo) through the limestone and schistose ridges of the Sierra Madre de Oaxaca.

In spite of their ruggedness and paucity of flat land and rich soils, the southern highlands of Mexico were highly regarded in both pre- and post-Spanish times for their wealth of gold. Many sections of the metamorphic rocks and especially the pe-

riphery of batholithic intrusions are highly mineralized, carrying abundant gold in quartz veins. Indians and, later, Spaniards obtained gold from placer, or stream, deposits, where it had been washed down from the mother lodes. Particularly the upper headwaters of the Balsas and the Papaloapan rivers as well as the rivers on the Pacific slope of southern Michoacan, Guerrero, and Oaxaca, were the sources of most

64

of the gold tribute that the Aztecs exacted from the southern highland towns.

Along the Pacific coast the southern highlands descend abruptly to the sea in a steep escarpment, in places forming a high, cliffed coast. Only a few short stretches of narrow coastal plain occur from Cabo Corrientes to the Isthmus of Tehuantepec. Some of the longer narrow coastal plains lie northwest (Costa Grande) and southeast (Costa Chica) from Acapulco along the shore of Guerrero. Spits and barrier beaches often line the low stretches of coast and enclose small lagoons. The juxtaposition of rocky shores, offshore islets, sand beaches, and brackish water lagoons give this coast a varied habitat and abundant animal and plant food for primitive folk (fig. 16).

ISTHMUS OF TEHUANTEPEC. This lowland depression, lying between the southern highlands of Mexico and those of Chiapas, is often taken as the physical divide between North and Central America. However, it might be better considered as a downfaulted N-S transverse block athwart the general E-W structural trends of western "Old Antillia." Although maximum elevations at the drainage divide of the isthmus approximate only 250 m., an E-W orientation prevails in the highly dissected crystalline hills (e.g. the Sierra Atravesada), suggesting a tectonic connection between the mountains of Oaxaca and those of Chiapas. Nevertheless, at the Isthmus of Tehuantepec the land mass of Middle America narrows to a width of only 200 km. Isthmian America truly begins here.

HIGHLANDS OF CHIAPAS AND NORTHERN CENTRAL AMERICA. The parallel ranges and depressions of this part of "Old Antillia," which Schuchert (1935) calls "Nuclear Central America," form an arcuate pattern. Those in Chiapas trend generally NW-SE, those in western Guatemala, E-W, and those of eastern Guatemala, British Honduras, Honduras, and northern Nicaragua, generally WSW-ENE to SW-NE (fig. 1).

Three major mountain ranges and one great structural depression can be traced through northern Central America and across the floor of the Caribbean Sea to the Greater Antilles. One range begins as the Sierra Madre de Chiapas along the Pacific coast, southeast Mexico. Passing through central Guatemala as a series of low mountains partially covered by recent volcanic ejecta, it continues as the Sierra de Omoa in northeastern Honduras, forms the Bay Islands off Honduras, and proceeds across the Caribbean as a submarine ridge to Jamaica. Farther south in Central America a series of WSW-ENE crystalline ranges cross Honduras and northern Nicaragua and dip beneath the Caribbean to form the numerous shoals and banks off coast (Mosquito Bank), coalescing with the main structural axis at Jamaica. The third mountain structure starts in northern Chiapas as the plateau-like Sierra de San Cristobal; continuing into central Guatemala as the Altos Cuchumatanes, the highlands of Alta Verapaz, and the Sierra de Santa Cruz, it descends into the Caribbean, forming the Cayman Ridge. A large number of minor ranges and intervening depressions parallel the main structure toward the north. These include the low folded ranges of southern Peten and the Maya Mountains of southern British Honduras. The latter range apparently is part of a structure that continues northeastward as low hills along the east coast of Yucatan and across the Strait of Yucatan to western Cuba (Eardley, 1951). Between the two main mountain systems of Chiapas-Guatemala occurs a tectonic depression that can be traced from the Valley of Chiapas in southern Mexico eastward through the Motagua Valley of central Guatemala, thence into the Caribbean as the Cayman Trench, a downfaulted submarine graben which in places attains depths of more than 6600 m. below sea level. In Guatemala another depression, occupied by the Negro and Polochic rivers and by Lake Izabal, parallels the Motagua.

65

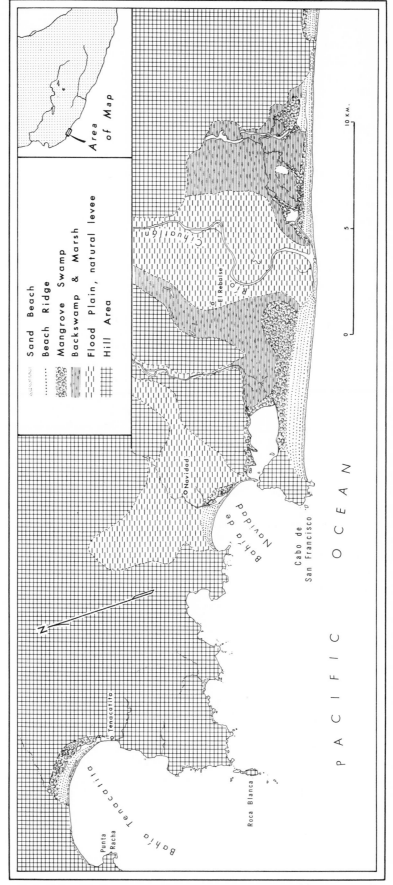

Fig. 16—PACIFIC COAST OF MEXICO, NEAR THE BORDER BETWEEN JALISCO AND COLIMA STATES, NORTHWEST OF MANZANILLO, SHOWING THE GREAT VARIETY OF SURFACE FORMS
Information from aerial photographs.

It is separated from the latter by high, narrow ridges—the Sierra de Chuacus and its continuation, the Sierra de Minas.

The Sierra Madre de Chiapas is a huge batholith of Paleozoic age, consisting chiefly of granite and diorite exposed in the northern part of the range but partially covered in its southern portion by Cretaceous sediments. Subsequent faulting has resulted in uplift and the formation of a steep escarpment overlooking the Pacific, with the backslope of the range descending gradually northeastward to the Central Valley of Chiapas. Frayed by deep, V-shaped valleys, the steep escarpment forms a difficult barrier for communication between the Pacific coast and the interior. Elevations along the sharp mountain crest increase toward the Guatemalan border, peaks ranging from 2000 to 3100 m. above sea level. Waibel (1933) has pointed out the presence of upland basins on the backslope of the range, interpreting them to be remnants of a Tertiary peneplained surface. From 600 to 700 m. elevation, these grass-covered erosion surfaces, locally called *llanos*, are today well populated, and in pre-Spanish times may have served as nuclei of Indian settlement, especially along streams. A fine example of the rolling llano surfaces can be seen in the vicinity of Cintalapa and Jiquipilas along the Pan American Highway west of Tuxtla Gutierrez in west-central Chiapas. Moreover, in contrast to the canyon-like valleys on the escarpment side of the range, rivers draining the backslope have carved rather wide alluvial valleys bordered by stream terraces.

The Guatemalan continuation of the Chiapas batholith is almost entirely hidden by a deep mantle of recent lava and ash associated with the Central American volcanic axis. Metamorphic rocks and patches of granite and serpentine outcrop in an incredibly rugged landscape on the northern side of the volcanic axis overlooking the Motagua Depression. Eastward the Sierra de Omoa (2100 m. elevation), which forms a portion of the present Guatemalan-Honduran boundary, is composed of metamorphic rocks (gneiss and schist) with steep slopes and knifelike ridges. North of the Motagua River the high and rugged sierras of Chuacus (2600 m.), Minas (3100 m.) and the lower Montaña del Mico (2000 m.) represent another arcuate chain composed of Paleozoic rocks that were further elevated and metamorphosed during Tertiary. On the northern flank of the Chuacus range the small alluvial-floored basins of Cubulco, Rabinal, Chicaj, and Salama have been significant centers of rural Indian population within the Baja Verapaz since ancient times.

The serpentine deposits within the Sierras of Chuacus, Minas, and other ancient ranges in central Guatemala and Chiapas have often been suggested as possible sources of jade, or jadeite, so important in ancient Mesoamerican cultures (Sapper, 1937). Foshag (1955a, 1955b) has described for the first time an anciently worked outcrop of jadeite near the village of Manzanal within the Motagua Valley at the base of the Sierra de las Minas.

In contrast to the steep, narrow ranges of igneous intrusives and metamorphics described above, the highlands of northern Chiapas and their continuation into Guatemala are upfaulted blocks (horsts) capped by nearly horizontal strata of Cretaceous and Tertiary limestone and other clastic rocks, forming plateau-like surfaces. The "Meseta Central," or Cretaceous plateau of San Cristobal, in northern Chiapas (2300 m. elevation) is such a feature. On its southern side this mountain mass rises abruptly as a fault scarp overlooking the Central Valley of Chiapas. On the plateau surface basins with gently rolling surfaces, such as those of San Cristobal de las Casas, Teopisca, and Comitan, alternate with faulted cuesta-like scarps. Karstic features are everywhere on the Cretaceous limestone. Sinkholes and poljes pock both steep

67

Fig. 17—LIMESTONE PLATEAU SURFACE NEAR SAN CRISTOBAL DE LAS CASAS, CHIAPAS, SHOWING KARSTIC FEATURES SUCH AS HAYSTACK HILLS AND SINK-HOLES
Few surface streams occur in this area because of underground drainage. The view looks east toward the canyon of Simojovel and the Tabasco coast on the Gulf of Mexico.

and gentle slopes; swarms of mogotes, or steep-sided haystack hills, as well as disappearing streams and limestone caverns abound in the upper Lacantum and Jatate river basins northeast of San Cristobal and Comitan (fig. 17). Similar features continue into the Altos Cuchumatanes of Guatemala, especially on the high (3000 m.), wind-swept plateau surface (Termer, 1927,

1932, 1933, 1936). Farther east in the Coban area of the Alta Verapaz severe faulting and folding has transformed the limestone surface into a series of three major E-W ranges with intervening basins; the undulating surface of the basins and lower mountain slopes are complicated by haystack hills, sinkholes, and other solution features (Termer, 1932). In the Alta Verapaz, Sapper (1901) noted the presence of volcanic ash in the larger basins, such as Coban and Tactic, and supposed it to be of aeolian origin, carried by southerly winds during past eruptions from the volcanic axis of Guatemala. In these and neighboring elongated basins the rich soil derived from the volcanic dust has attracted dense farming settlement. The entire northern limestone highland from Chiapas into Guatemala is today one of relatively dense Indian population, a probable reflection of the refuge character of the isolated highlands as well as the attraction of moderately fertile soil in basins and mountain slopes.

The northern flank of the limestone highlands of Chiapas-Guatemala is composed of a large number of elongated parallel anticlinal folds and faulted cuestas in Cretaceous to middle Tertiary sediments. The ridges and intervening basins decrease in altitude northward, until they become hills in the southern Peten of Guatemala and low mountains in northern Chiapas. Again, wherever limestone outcrops occur a karstic surface prevails (Gerstenhauer, 1960). Owing to its exposed windward position this corrugated area is drenched with rain most of the year and supports a heavy rain forest. Although today it is occupied by only scattered groups of Lacandon Indians, the folded surface of the upper and middle Usumacinta River drainage once supported large Classical Mayan ceremonial centers such as Bonampak, Piedras Negras, and Palenque.

Of the northern ranges only the NE-SW Maya Mountains of southern British Honduras exhibit extensive outcrops of underlying crystalline rocks. Sapper (1899) and Ower (1928) describe these mountains as a horst 800–1000 m. above sea level.

The great structural depression of Chiapas-Guatemala is composed of several distinctive landform areas. The westernmost is the Central Valley of Chiapas, a wide basin of chiefly Cretaceous clastic rocks,

drained by the upper Grijalva (Rio Grande de Chiapas). Waibel (1933) describes the basin surface as a partially dissected peneplain the surface of which gradually increases in elevation from 700 m. near the Mexico-Guatemala border to 900 m. in its northwestern portion. Despite the increase of elevation of the old surface northwestward, the Grijalva drainage is in the same direction; thus the main river and its tributaries become more deeply incised downstream. Most of the old basin surface is dissected into isolated flat-topped mesas, terraces, and hills. Pockets of recent alluvium occur along the Grijalva and its main tributaries, as at Chiapa de Corzo, an old aboriginal farming center, and at Tuxtla Gutierrez, the present capital of Chiapas. Downstream from the latter town the river breaks through the Sierra de San Cristobal in a deep, narrow canyon, called the "Sumidero." Farther west a tributary, the Rio de la Venta, forms a similar canyon through the range. The present physiographic picture of Chiapas indicates recent uplift and entrenchment of antecedent streams.

The eastern half of the great depression, drained by the Motagua River system, is characterized mainly by a highly faulted and folded surface and steep slopes of deeply cut valleys. Exceptions are the extreme upper and lower sections. Near the drainage divide between the Grijalva and Motagua rivers (1900–2000 m.) plain and rolling surfaces prevail, as in the vicinity of Huehuetenango and the ancient ceremonial center of Zaculeu, at the foot of the Altos Cuchumatanes. Again, at the eastern end of the depression the Motagua Valley widens to form an important finger of river flood-plain alluvium inland as far as the Mayan site of Quirigua. Farther up-basin the wide, semiarid plain of Zacapa forms part of a graben.

The cores of the parallel ranges of Honduras and northern Nicaragua are composed chiefly of old metamorphic rocks (slates, mica schists, quartzites) in places intruded by granodiorites (Powers, 1918). Such crystallines are completely exposed in the northernmost ranges of Honduras, but are mantled by thick deposits of Tertiary volcanics in most of central Honduras and in Nicaragua, where subsequent uplift followed by faulting has preserved the general E-W structural trend. Rising to elevations of 2500 m., these ranges form some of the most rugged country of Central America. In terms of human settlement the structural depressions between the ranges have been of prime significance. In northern Honduras narrow fertile alluvial lowlands, similar to the lower Motagua in Guatemala, occupy the numerous NE-SW trending depressions that open onto the Caribbean coast. The alluviation of these depressions probably was aided by rising sea level since the close of Pleistocene. Those drained by the Chamelecon and Ulua rivers, by the Lean, the Aguan, and the Sico were densely populated in pre-Spanish times, and were major sources of cacao traded into the Maya area (Chapman, 1957); today they are sites of large commercial banana plantations. The streams draining the upper portions of the depressions carry placer gold washed down from the mineralized quartz veins in the old crystalline ranges. A probable source of Aztec (and Maya?) gold in preconquest time, these placers were worked chiefly in the early colonial period, but today they are almost depleted.

In central Honduras and northern Nicaragua flat-floored, grass-covered highland basins, locally called "valles," probably never attracted Indians except for hunting, but later became important centers of Spanish settlement. Examples of such basins in Honduras are Comayagua (700 m. elevation), Otoro (600 m.), Sesenti (800 m.), and Talango (800 m.) (Sapper, 1902a). Lower "valles" (300 to 400 m.) in northeastern Honduras include Agalteca, Olancho, and Catacamas (Helbig, 1959).

In western Honduras a N-S structural depression forms a transisthmian passway from the Gulf of Fonseca, up the Goascoran river valley, through Comayagua Valley to the Ulua depression on the Caribbean coast (Sapper, 1902a).

Yucatan Platform

On the northern side of the belt of E-W crustal deformation of Central America is the recently emerged, low-lying limestone platform of the Yucatan Peninsula. Geologically this area forms part of what Schuchert (1935) calls the "Antillean Foreland," and culturally it is the locale of ancient Maya civilization and its modern derivatives. In Pleistocene the peninsula was raised out of a shallow sea and tilted westward and northward. The western and northern parts of the platform still lie under 150 m. of water, forming the extensive Campeche Banks with their numerous shoals and coral reefs.

Approximately the northern third of the peninsula has an almost level surface derived from nearly horizontal Pliocene strata of limestone, marl and gypsum with elevations up to 40 m. above sea level (fig. 18). Southward the land rises gradually with occasional weak folds and low cuestaform ridges in highly karsted Miocene and Eocene limestone, forming a low, hilly surface of some 130 m. elevation. The first significant hills are encountered in the "Sierrita de Ticul," an arcuate ridge (between Campeche City and Merida) that rises to a maximum of 50 m. above the surrounding plain. Robles Ramos (1950) believes that the Sierrita represents the littoral of Miocene time and that subsequent folding created the present ridge. In effect, the Sierrita marks the boundary between the flattish Yucatecan Plain to the north and the hilly Campeche area to the south. The highest elevations of the peninsula (up to 350 m.) occur near its center in eastern Campeche, and hilly terrain representing an advanced stage of limestone solution

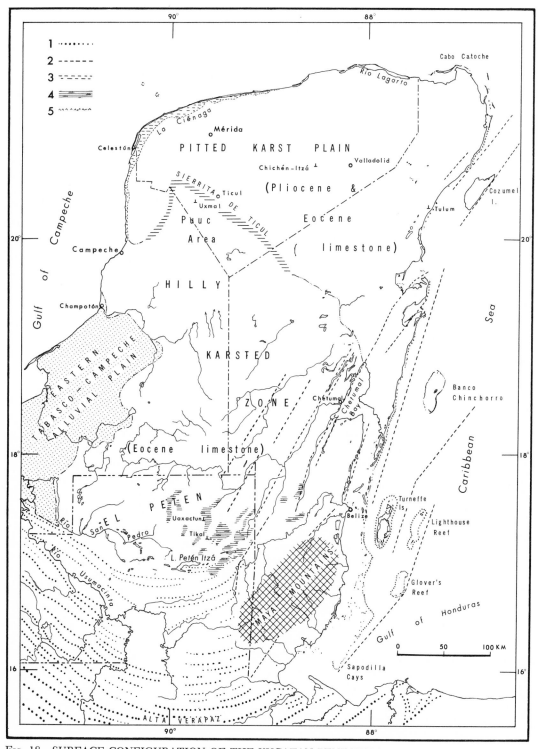

Fig. 18—SURFACE CONFIGURATION OF THE YUCATAN PENINSULA
Key: 1. Folded and faulted limestone ranges. 2. Major fault lines of eastern Yucatan. 3. Lagoonal marshes and swamps. 4. Bajos of the Peten area. 5. Coral reefs.

extends into the Peten of northern Guatemala (Sapper, 1899; Schuchert, 1935). Along the eastern side of the peninsula northward from the Maya Mountains, low limestone ridges and intervening swampy swales follow a NNE-SSW fault pattern, a part of the northernmost structural line of Old Antillia.

Most of the Yucatan Peninsula is characterized by a karstic surface. In its northern part there are no surface streams, for rainwater sinks quickly through the porous rock to form underground channels. The surface is pitted with hundreds of the famous *cenotes* (from the Maya *tz'onot*, meaning a well), or a type of sink that results from the caving of surface rock above subterranean stream channels. Robles Ramos (1950) distinguished two types of sinks in northern Yucatan: (1) the small funnel-shaped one of the normal doline type (*resumidero*) and (2) the true cenote, round or oval, 10–30 m. in diameter, vertical walls, with a visible water surface at the bottom. (The morphology and hydrography of cenotes was first clarified by Cole [1910] and further investigated by Pearse, et al. [1936].) In addition, shallow solution depressions, called *aguadas*, which usually contain small intermittent or permanent ponds, dot the peninsula's surface. As both the cenotes and aguadas are the main sources of water supply in northern Yucatan, they have been significant factors in the location of ancient and modern Mayan settlements. (See Roys [1939] for maps of southern Cupul area, eastern Yucatan state, showing distribution of cenotes and other hydrographic features in relation to ancient and modern settlement.) Other important solution features include underground caverns and caves of various sizes and stages of development. Small caverns occur in the more level northern part of the peninsula; large caves are found in abundance within the cuestaform ridges, such as the Sierrita de Ticul and south thereof in the Campeche hills (Cole, 1910; Robles

Ramos, 1950; Hatt, 1953). Replete with dripstone forms (stalactites, stalagmites, etc.), hidden chambers, and underground lakes or streams, such caves have been utilized as places of refuge during times of political stress as well as for baths and water supply in normal times.

Bare, fluted limestone is exposed over large areas of northern Yucatan; pitted and scarred by solution depressions and small ridges (lapiés or karren) that are often edged with sharp chert or flinty particles, the surface presents serious obstacles for travel, despite the apparent flatness of the landscape.

In many parts of northern Yucatan the best soils available for cultivation have accumulated through rainwash in scattered pockets, or *hoyas* on the limestone surface. Such soil pockets are larger and more abundant in the Sierrita de Ticul and in the hills of northeastern Campeche, often termed the *puuc* area (from the Maya word meaning hill). It was in this fertile hilly section of Yucatan that the flourishing Mayan Puuc ceremonial centers and towns (Uxmal, Sayil, Labna, etc.) were established probably between A.D. 800 and 900 (Termer, 1954). Farther south in central Campeche, Quintana Roo, and northern British Honduras, soils are thicker and some surface streams occur, although round and oval lakes of all sizes occupy partially alluviated sinks, aguadas, and other solution depressions.

Culturally and politically the Peten covers most of northern Guatemala, including (1) the low, E-W anticlinal ridges of Antillean affinity south of Lake Peten-Itza and (2) the rolling to hilly karsted country north of the lake. Wadell (1938), however, limits the Peten physiographically to the latter area, which is covered by Cretaceous to Miocene dolomitic limestone. Solution features are subdued because of their advanced development and the formation of a thick soil mantle. Aguadas and swampy, clay-filled swales (*bajos* or *ak'al-*

chés) occupy the depressions between isolated conical knobs (hums) (Termer, 1954). Lake- and swamp-filled NE-SW-trending depressions between faulted limestone cuestas are found in the northeastern part of the Peten in the vicinity of the Mayan sites of Uaxactun and Tikal (Sapper, 1896; W. R. Bullard, 1960). Cooke (1931) has suggested that the swampy bajos were once shallow lakes serving as important sources of water during the Classic Maya period, and that their subsequent alluviation may have been one of the causes for the abandonment of the Peten ceremonial centers during the 9th century A.D.

The limestone and associated rocks of the Yucatan Peninsula have supplied both the ancient Maya and their modern descendents with various useful materials. Chert and flint in the form of hard siliceous nodules found as accumulations in limestone were used anciently for projectile points and cutting tools; as this material breaks with a concoidal fracture, sharp cutting edges can be shaped from cores by pressure flaking. The Maya had building stone in abundance, for the soft, easily quarried limestone of the peninsula hardened on contact with air. They also burned limestone to make quicklime, which, mixed with a calcareous sand (*sascab*) and water, produced a mortar for building material and a plaster for fresco murals and stucco modeling.

Along the low northern and northwestern coasts of the Yucatan Peninsula wave action has created a series of long barrier beaches which enclose extensive lagoons and tidal swamps. The longest of the barrier beaches extends for a distance of 190 km. from near Celestun on the northwestern corner of the peninsula to beyond Dzilam on the north shore. Eastward another barrier beach, 70 km. long, encloses the wide lagoon known as Rio Lagartos. Since preconquest times various points within the shallow lagoons have been utilized for mak-

ing salt by the natural evaporation of sea water or by the washing of salt-impregnated mud. Salt from these lagoons was one of the important items of Mayan trade (Roys, 1943; Chapman, 1957; Cardos, 1959), and still today this product is manufactured by the ancient process. Diego de Landa (1938) first described the inordinately long barrier beaches, the lagoons, and salines of the north coast of Yucatan; Schott (1866) wrote the first scientific treatise on these landforms; and recently C. Edwards (1954) has redescribed them.

The east coast of the peninsula is quite different from the northern shore in forms and processes (fig. 18). In the northern portion of the east coast the limestone platform outcrops to form a low cliffed shoreline and headlands separated by beaches. The ruins of Tulum are located on such a headland (C. Edwards, 1957). The NNE-SSW pattern of faulting that is characteristic of the eastern margin of Yucatan may have influenced the trend of the northeastern shore; Cozumel Island immediately off coast is a limestone block separated from the mainland possibly by faulting. Farther south the coast is strongly embayed, again due to the fault structure. Just off the eastern shore of Yucatan lies the longest barrier reef of coral in the Atlantic tropics (C. Edwards, 1957). It extends intermittently for 650 km. from near the northeastern corner of the peninsula southward into the Gulf of Honduras. Off the coast of British Honduras the reef lies from 40 to 65 km. from the mainland, enclosing an extensive area of shallow-water lagoon and imposing a barrier to navigation by large craft. Hundreds of sand cays or islets abound in the reef; back of the reef, the shallow lagoon is dotted with mangrove cays of calcareous mud and coral in areas free from strong wave action (Vermeer, 1959). Seaward from the barrier reef are various coral banks and reef patches, some of which form atolls.

Volcanic Axis of Central America

A continuous line of Quaternary volcanoes borders the Pacific edge of Central America from the Mexico-Guatemala border into Costa Rica, a distance of nearly 1500 km. This range is the longest and most spectacular of Middle America. Its origin is closely associated with the general NW-SE structural fractures along the eastern margin of the Pacific basin. The thick deposits of volcanic ejecta spewed from the craters and fissures within the axis have buried surface evidence of the old Antillean E-W structural lines along the Pacific side of northern Central America. Within and adjacent to the volcanic axis are found some of the most fertile tropical highlands and lowlands of the Americas; chiefly for that reason this area for millennia has been densely populated (Sapper, 1902b).

According to Williams (1952a, 1952b, 1960), two phases of Cenozoic vulcanism have occurred in Central America, similar to the volcanic history of central Mexico. In the first phase—early to late Tertiary—volcanic ejecta accumulated over wide areas of Central America: southern Guatemala, El Salvador, the southern half of Honduras, and almost all of Nicaragua, save its Caribbean fringe. Most of the ejecta was andesitic and rhyolitic with some basaltic materials erupted from fissures as lava flows and pumiceous deposits laid down in glowing avalanches to form plateau-like surfaces overlying the old Cretaceous folds. The present highland surface of much of southern Honduras and north-central Nicaragua is covered by these Tertiary volcanics, now folded and faulted and highly eroded, as described previously (p. 69). Within these areas andesitic plugs and dikes in places form sharp mountain peaks, the peripheries of which are often

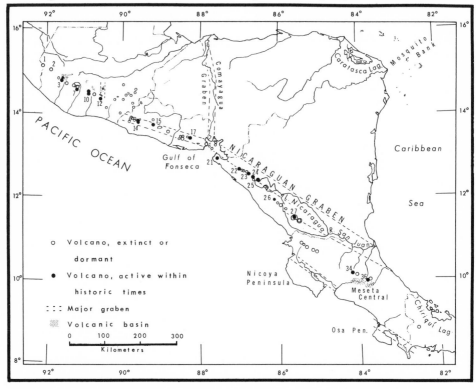

Fig. 19—VOLCANIC AXIS OF CENTRAL AMERICA AND ASSOCIATED FEATURES
Numbers refer to volcanoes listed in Table 1.

TABLE 1—MAJOR VOLCANOES OF CENTRAL AMERICA

Volcano	Elevation above sea level (m.)	Relative height, base to peak (m.)	Dates of major eruptions in historic times	Character of present activity (1950–60)
Guatemala:				
1. Tacana	4,030	2,200	None recorded	Dormant; fumarolic
2. Tajumulco	4,410	2,400	1863(?)	Dormant; slightly fumarolic
3. Santa Maria	3,768	2,200	1902, 1922–23, 1928–30, 1931–32, 1956(?)	*Active*; occasional emission of ash from adventive dome of Santiaguito; strongly fumarolic
4. Cerro Quemado (lava dome)	3,179	1,250	1785	Dormant; thermal springs
5. Zuñil	3,533	1,600	None recorded	Dormant; solfataric; thermal springs
6. San Pedro	3,024	1,500	None recorded	Extinct
7. Atitlan	3,525	2,400	1827, 1853	Dormant; fumarolic (?)
8. Toliman	3,150	1,900	None recorded	Extinct (?)
9. Acatenango	3,880	2,400	1924–27	Dormant; fumarolic
10. Fuego	3,835	2,700	1524(?), 1581–82, 1717, 1737, 1857, 1880, 1932, 1953, 1957	*Active*; occasional emission of ash and glowing avalanches; strongly fumarolic
11. Agua	3,752	2,600	None recorded	Extinct
12. Pacaya	2,544	1,600	1565, 1651, 1664, 1775, 1854 (?)	Dormant; slightly fumarolic
El Salvador:				
13. Santa Ana	2,381	1,800	1874, 1880	Dormant; slightly fumarolic
14. Izalco	1,965	800	1770 (birth), 1793, 1798, 1802–03, 1856, 1890, 1902, 1912, 1920, 1926, 1946, 1955–56	*Active*; occasional emission of ash, lava flows; strongly fumarolic
15. San Salvador–Boqueron	1,967	1,300	1659, 1671 (?), 1917	Dormant; slightly fumarolic in Boqueron crater
16. San Vicente	2,173	1,800	None recorded	Extinct
17. San Miguel	2,132	1,900	1699, 1787, 1819, 1844, 1867, 1924	Dormant; strongly fumarolic within crater; frequent emission of steam clouds
18. Usulatan	1,453	1,200	None recorded	Extinct
19. Chinameca	1,402	800	None recorded	Dormant; fumarolic; thermal springs
20. Conchagua	1,250	1,250	None recorded	Dormant; fumarolic
Nicaragua:				
21. Cosigüina	862	862	1835 (superexplosion)	Dormant
22. El Viejo	1,780	1,700	1684–85	Dormant; weakly fumarolic
23. Telica	1,038	900	1529, 1685	Dormant; strongly fumarolic
24. Las Pilas–Cerro Negro	1,071	900	1850, 1867, 1914, 1923, 1947, 1950, 1952, 1954	*Active*; occasional emission of ash; strongly fumarolic
25. Momotombo	1,258	1,200	1764, 1858–66, 1905	Dormant; fumarolic
26. Masaya (caldera)	650	...	1670, 1772, 1858–59, 1902–05, 1924, 1946	Dormant; strongly fumarolic
27. Mombacho	1,363	1,350	1560	Extinct (?)
28. Concepcion	1,557	1,557	1883–87, 1908–10, 1921, 1948 to present	*Active*; occasional emission of ash; fumarolic
29. Madera	1,329	1,329	None recorded	Dormant (?)
Costa Rica:				
30. Orosi	1,881	1,400	None recorded	Dormant; fumarolic (?)
31. Rincon de la Vieja	1,643	1,200	1863	Dormant; fumarolic
32. Miravalles	1,980	1,500	None recorded	Dormant; fumarolic; thermal springs
33. Tenorio	1,902	1,400	None recorded	Extinct (?)
34. Poas	2,644	1,600	1910, 1953	*Active*; occasional emission of ash and scoria; strong solfataric and geyser-like activity
35. Barba	2,898	1,800	1867	Dormant
36. Irazu	3,414	2,600	1723, 1917–20, 1924	Dormant; strongly fumarolic
37. Turrialba	3,342	2,500	1866	Dormant; slightly fumarolic

Sources: F. M. Bullard, 1956; McBirney, 1958; Meyer-Abich, 1956, 1958; Roy, 1957; Sapper, 1913, 1926; Williams, 1952a, 1952b, 1960.

highly mineralized, producing mother lodes of gold in northern Nicaragua and of both gold and silver in central Honduras.

The second phase of vulcanism—late Pliocene, Pleistocene, and Recent—saw the construction of the present long volcanic chain of Central America with its magnificent cones, highland basins, and beautiful lakes. Andesitic and basaltic materials make up most of the younger ejecta (in Guatemala, El Salvador, Nicaragua, and northwest Costa Rica) which has partially covered the older volcanics in a narrow band along the Pacific side of the mainland. Due to prevailing easterly winds (NE trades), most of the ash ejected from the volcanoes has been deposited on the mountain slopes and coastal lowlands south and west of the main axis; comparatively little ash has been carried by occasional southerly and westerly winds into the interior of Honduras and Nicaragua (Sapper, 1905). In Costa Rica the young volcanic chain arcs inland to form the Cordillera Central of that country.

More than 40 large symmetrical composite cones form the major portion of the volcanic chain (fig. 19). Sapper (1913) listed 101 "first order" volcanoes within the axis, including many small ones as well as lake-filled cauldrons and calderas; 25 of those listed have been active within historic times. The highest volcanoes are in Guatemala at the northwestern end of the chain, where outpouring of ejecta has been accompanied by uplift along faults. Tacana on the Mexico-Guatemala frontier towers to 4030 m. above the sea; its neighbor Tajumulco (4210 m.) is the highest point in Central America. The volcanoes decrease in elevation southeastward (Table 1). In El Salvador, Nicaragua, and northwest Costa Rica (Cordillera de Guanacaste) the main volcanoes are much lower in altitude than those of Guatemala, but their relative relief is comparable. In central Costa Rica the volcanic cones, built on the edge of an uplifted plateau, compare in elevation to those of Guatemala.

Today the Central American volcanic belt is the most active in the Americas. Within the last few years occasional eruptions of ash or small lava flows and almost continual steam clouds have emitted from Santiaguito, a large dome on the western slope of Santa Maria; from the crater of Fuego, near Guatemala City; from Izalco in El Salvador; and from Negro, Telica, and Concepcion volcanoes in Nicaragua (Meyer-Abich, 1956). Fumerolic activity is widespread along the axis. Far greater volcanic activity has occurred in the recent past and at times has inflicted catastrophic damage. In 1835 Cosigüina volcano on the Gulf of Fonseca in northwestern Nicaragua suddenly erupted in one of the world's great natural explosions; the falling ash partly buried villages and temporarily damaged farm land within a radius of 65 km. (Williams, 1952c). Much more serious destruction accompanied by the loss of possibly 6000 lives was wrought in 1902 by the eruption of Santa Maria in Guatemala (Sapper, 1903; Coleman, 1946). The volcanoes of Fuego and Izalco are two of the most active in Central America: Fuego has erupted violently ten times since the 16th century; Izalco has been almost continually active since its birth in 1770.

From the time of his first entry into this area man has had to cope with volcanic catastrophies. The discovery of artifacts dated some 3000 years ago beneath 5–30 m. of pumice near San Salvador and the presence of human footprints in consolidated mud under deep ashfall near Managua (estimated age: 2000–5000 years) attest to the ancient association of man and vulcanism in Central America (Williams and Meyer-Abich, 1955; Williams, 1952b). In the long run the benefits of rich soils derived from the weathering of basic volcanic ejecta may outweigh the damage inflicted by occasional catastrophies.

Earthquakes also plague the Pacific slope of Central America as well as of Mexico. Tremors, some of catastrophic proportions, often precede (and possibly trigger) volcanic eruptions. Seismic activity within the Pacific areas of Central America and Mexico, however, is caused by slippage of portions of the earth's crust along fault planes chiefly within the NW-SE fracture zone off coast. As mentioned previously, the down-faulted Middle American Trench off the Central American Coast is the epicenter of many strong earthquakes that affect the adjacent land areas.

The landforms that characterize the surface of the Central American volcanic belt are somewhat similar to those of central Mexico. Swarms of cinder cones and scoria mounds and extensive lava flows of various ages abound. However, calderas and small collapse pits, especially common in Nicaragua and El Salvador, are much more abundant than in Mexico, and indicate youthfulness of volcanic activity. Lakes, such as Atitlan in Guatemala and Coatepeque in El Salvador, occupy volcanic cauldrons, or depressions formed by collapse due to subterranean withdrawal of magma. Others, such as Lake Amatitlan in Guatemala and Ilopango in El Salvador, are formed in volcanic-tectonic depressions (Williams and Meyer-Abich, 1955; Williams, 1960).

Highland basins in the Central American axis are not as numerous or as extensive as in the Mesa Central of Mexico. The highest basins are those within the Los Altos region of western Guatemala, today the most densely populated Indian area of Middle America (Termer, 1936). Most of the basins lie immediately north of the main volcanic axis. Those of Quetzaltenango-Totonicapan (2400–2500 m.), Chimaltenango (1800 m.), and Tecpan (2300 m.), for example, have been partly filled with recent pumiceous ash, by glowing avalanches and mudflows, forming deposits that measure up to 300 m. thickness with flattish to rolling surfaces (Atwood, 1933; Williams, 1960). Except on their southern margins where they are bounded by large fans that extend from the Quaternary volcanoes, the basins are surrounded by eroded Tertiary volcanics (fig. 20). Streams working headward from the Pacific slope have eroded deep, steep-sided gorges (called *barrancas*) into both Recent and Tertiary volcanics in Los Altos, impeding rapid communication between settled areas. Headward erosion by barranca tributaries is rapidly cutting into soft ash of the basin floors, destroying cultivated land (Atwood, 1933; McBryde, 1947). The Valle de las Vacas, the locale of Guatemala City (1500 m. elevation), is a transverse, N-S-graben structure filled with waterlain pumice (Williams, 1960), and affords an easy pass across the volcanic range from the Pacific coastal plains to the Motagua Valley. On the outskirts of Guatemala City are the ruins of Kaminaljuyu, a large Classic ceremonial and trade center strategically located in the transverse valley.

In both El Salvador and Nicaragua basins and valleys within the volcanic belt are low in elevation, for they are located within a transisthmian depression, a large crustal fracture that rends the middle of Central America. Formed toward the end of Tertiary, this long, narrow graben trends NW-SE from the Caribbean Sea to the Pacific Ocean. It forms the lowlands of Nicaragua, the central portion of which is occupied by the largest fresh-water lakes of Middle America: lakes Managua and Nicaragua, both draining to the Caribbean via the San Juan River. The Quaternary volcanoes of Nicaragua line the southern edge of the graben and some form islands within the lakes. Surrounding the lakes and extending northwestward are plains covered with fertile soils derived from ash ejected from the volcanoes nearby. This rich lowland, the site of the ancient Chorotegan culture, has been one of the most

V. Atitlan

Pacific Coastal Plain

V Zunil

Quetzaltenango Basin

Totonicapan

FIG. 20—A PORTION OF THE VOLCANIC HIGHLANDS OF GUATEMALA, LOOKING SOUTH TOWARD THE PACIFIC OCEAN
In the background are Tertiary and Recent composite volcanoes; in the foreground dissected lava platforms and the eastern part of the volcanic basin of Totonicapan-Quetzaltenango.

densely peopled areas of Central America since pre-Columbian times. The Nicaraguan Depression continues northwestward to the Gulf of Fonseca; beyond it can be traced across El Salvador through the lowland basins of Olomega, Ilopango, Zapotitlan and, possibly, Ahuachapan, all of which lie between Quaternary volcanic cones that have risen within the depression and have partially obscured it (Williams, 1952c; Williams and Meyer-Abich, 1955).

The Meseta Central of Costa Rica is the largest of the highland basins within the Central American volcanic axis. It lies between the large Quaternary volcanoes that form the Cordillera Central to the north and a group of highly dissected hills of Tertiary intrusives and sedimentary rocks (northern portion of the Cordillera de Talamanca) to the south. It consists of two large intermontane basins separated by low volcanic hills that form a drainage divide. The smaller, higher basin of Cartago (1300–1500 m. elevation) drains to the Caribbean via the headwaters of the Reventazon River; the larger, lower western basin of San Juan (1000–1100 m.) drains to the Pacific through the Rio Grande. This river and its upper tributaries are in the process of cutting deep gorges into the soft volcanic fill on the western side of the basin. According to Williams (1952a), the floor of the San Juan Basin was built up by thick deposits of glassy pumiceous material ejected from nearby Poas and Barbas volcanoes in the form of glowing avalanches. In turn the pumice was overlain by late Pleistocene basaltic lavas, from which have formed the rich soils that cover the basin's present rolling surface. Along the northern sides of the Meseta Central are gigantic fans constructed of mudflows (lahars) and stream deposits. Occupied by the Huetar Indian culture in pre-Hispanic times, the Meseta Central is today renowned for its fertility and prosperous dense population of European descent.

Volcanic Bridge of Costa Rica and Panama

South of the Meseta Central the volcanic axis of Central America is interrupted by a huge batholith, or granitic intrusion, which forms the Cordillera de Talamanca and extends southeastward to the Panamanian border. Within this high, rugged mountain mass 10 peaks rise more than 3000 m. above the sea, that of Chirripo Grande (3920 m.) being the highest point. Since the Spanish conquest the Cordillera de Talamanca has been a refuge area for remnant Indian groups, a few representatives of which (the Boruca, Terraba, Bribris) still live in isolated valleys.

In western Panama vulcanism resumes with the large composite volcano of Chiriqui (3478 m. elevation). Highly dissected mountains of Tertiary volcanics continue in decreasing elevation to beyond the Canal Zone, forming the dividing range (Serrania de Tabasara) through the middle of the country. In some places the Tertiary material is covered by Quaternary ejecta (e.g. the volcanoes of Chiriqui, Santiago, Valle), and occasional patches of granite outcrop in the higher peaks along the continental divide (Terry, 1956). The Canal Zone, the lowest area across Panama, occupies a transisthmian fault rift. The structure of the country east of the Canal Zone is related to a northwestern prong of the Andes characterized by low folded and faulted ranges of sedimentary and igneous rock along both the Caribbean and Pacific shores. Between these coastal ranges is a structural depression occupied by the Chucunaque and Bayamo rivers.

Schuchert (1935) has called Costa Rica and Panama a "volcanic bridge" that connects Central and South America. Formed possibly in late Jurassic or early Cretaceous, the bridge was partially submerged in early Tertiary to permit the connection of Atlantic and Pacific waters. It re-emerged in middle Tertiary (late Miocene?) through the outpouring of volcanic ejecta and intrusion of granitic batholiths, which form much of its present surface.

Coasts of Central America

PACIFIC LOWLANDS. In terms of their surface configuration the Pacific coastal lowlands of Central America might be classified into (1) a northern coastal plains section, extending from the Isthmus of Tehuantepec in southern Mexico to southern Nicaragua and (2) a southern mountainous coastal section of Costa Rica and Panama. The northern part is distinguished by its generally low coast and long, straight shore back of which extend coastal plains of varying width. The southern section, on the other hand, is a high coast with an extremely irregular shoreline: peninsulas, deeply indented bays, offshore islands, and occasional stretches of low coastal plain.

Northern Coastal Section. This begins with the wide Pacific alluvial plain of Tehuantepec, the generally level surface of which is occasionally interrupted by remnant igneous hills. Along the base of the Sierra Madre de Chiapas the coastal plain gradually widens from a few kilometers to 35 km. at Tapachula near the Mexico-Guatemala border. As it continues into Guatemala along the foot of the volcanic range the plain attains a maximum width of 50 km., but narrows once more as it approaches El Salvador. The entire coastal plain from Tehuantepec to Punta Remedios in El Salvador has been formed mainly by alluvium deposited by streams flowing from the adjacent mountains. Large fans lie between the lower level plain and the mountains. In Guatemala the fans are much larger than those in Chiapas, for in the volcanic zone gigantic flows and avalanches of water-saturated ash and cinder (lahars) have aided in their construction (Termer, 1936). Known locally as the Boca Costa, the fan slopes of the upper Guatemalan coastal plain, although in places stream-dissected, have been since pre-Spanish times areas of rich agricultural production. The native provinces of Soconusco (Xoconochco) and Suchitepequez, long famed for their cacao production in both preconquest and colonial times, made up the central portion of the Chiapas-Guatemalan coastal plain and Boca Costa.

In El Salvador and Nicaragua the coastal plain is narrow and broken by volcanic and sedimentary hills that sometimes front upon the sea forming low, cliffed coasts. In its entire stretch from Tehuantepec to Costa Rica the even coastline is broken only by the large Gulf of Fonseca, a product of downfaulting at the intersection of the N-S Comayagua and NW-SE Nicaragua grabens.

Long offshore bars and barrier beaches backed by mangrove-fringed lagoons characterize the shore of the northern Pacific coast of Central America. The most extensive lagoons are those of the Tehuantepec coast (Laguna Superior, L. Inferior, Mar Muerto), along the shores of which live the Huave Indian fishermen. In colonial days, and possibly in pre-Spanish times, salt was harvested from Guatemalan lagoons by natural evaporation of tidal sea water as is still done today.

Southern Coastal Section. The irregular and mountainous character of this section (Costa Rica and Panama) is associated with active faulting, recent rise of sea level, and, in places, vulcanism. In Costa Rica the twin peninsulas of Nicoya and Osa and their adjacent gulfs and structural lowlands (Golfo de Nicoya-Guanacaste plain; Golfo Dulce-Palmar lowland) are products of a NW-SE fault system that has separated the old granitic rocks of the peninsulas from the young volcanics and sedimentaries of the interior. Drained by the Rio Tempisque, the Guanacaste plain was the center of pre-Spanish Chorotegan culture, which extended northward into the lake lowlands of Nicaragua. Except for accumulation of mudflats within the gulfs and along the adjacent lowland coasts, almost the entire Pacific shore of Costa Rica is mountainous, with short crescentic sand beaches and small river deltas occupying coves between rocky headlands (Pittier, 1912).

In western and central Panama a large lowland plain, interrupted frequently by low hills, extends from David eastward to the Gulf of Panama. Around David the plain is constructed chiefly of volcanic ejecta and lahars from adjacent Chiriqui volcano, making this area one of Panama's most fertile. Eastward much of the lowland is rolling, made up of dissected alluvium and erosion surfaces of Tertiary volcanics; the eastern portion lies as a trough between the central cordillera and the mountainous Azuero Peninsula, and in preconquest days was the center of the Cocle Indian culture, famed for its beautiful polychrome pottery and exquisite gold-work.

The Gulf of Chiriqui abounds in islets, wave-eroded remnants of the mainland invaded by rise of sea level since Pleistocene. Along the shores of both the Gulf of Chiriqui and that of Panama extensive mudflats and abrasion platforms fringe wave-cut cliffs and benches, indicating, possibly, a slight withdrawal of the sea in recent times (Tuan, 1960). West of the Canal Zone, however, a low, straight cliffed coast has developed by wave erosion of soft ejecta erupted from Volcan del Valle. Except for a narrow coastal plain on its eastern side, the shores of the Azuero Peninsula are high and rocky.

CARIBBEAN COASTAL LOWLANDS OF CENTRAL AMERICA. From Guatemala to Panama the Caribbean coast may be divided into four general sectors according to landforms: (1) the Guatemala-Honduras coast; (2) the Mosquito (or Miskito) Coast of northeastern Honduras and Nicaragua; (3) the eastern lowlands of the Nicaraguan Depression and its Costa Rican appendage; (4) the coast of southeastern Costa Rica and Panama.

Guatemalan-Honduran Caribbean Lowlands. This coastal sector, mentioned pre-

viously in connection with the Antillean ranges and depressions of northern Central America, is notable for the elongated fingers of river alluvium that extend inland from the coast within structural depressions. The cultural significance of these coastal valleys has already been discussed. In the immediate coast small arcuate river deltas and short stretches of narrow coastal plain alternate with rocky headlands formed where mountain ranges reach the sea.

Mosquito Lowland. The morphology of most of the Mosquito lowland was the subject of a recent monograph by Radley (1960). Nearly 1000 km. long and in places 150 km. wide, this area forms one of the most extensive coastal plains of Middle America. It is widest in northeastern Nicaragua between the Coco and Grande rivers; it tapers to a narrow strip south of Bluefields, where volcanic hills approach the sea. Composed chiefly of Pliocene gravels and sandy clays of marine origin, the plain slopes gradually upward from the coast to the foothills of the interior highlands. Erosion has given most of its present surface a low mesa-like appearance, with laterite-capped escarpments standing above narrow shallowly entrenched stream valleys. Strips of alluvium extend along the larger rivers, the banks of which are inhabited by remnant groups of Miskito, Sumo, and Paya Indians.

In the northern part of the Mosquito Coast the Patuca and Coco rivers have built large deltas, that of the Coco forming Cabo Gracias a Dios. Owing to the great volume of sediment carried by these rivers, and the shallowness of the offshore areas, their deltas are rapidly prograding. Between the two advancing deltas is large Caratasca Lagoon which occupies a subsiding delta-flank depression. Immediately offshore lies the Rosaline or Mosquito Bank (an expression of part of the Antillean structure), which accounts for the shallow offshore waters, rarely exceeding 100 m. in depth. Hundreds of coral reefs and cays rise from

81

the bank, presenting hazards for navigation.

South of the Coco delta the Mosquito shore is a series of long spits, bar and beach ridges, formed from the abundant silt and sand discharged from the rivers and carried southward by prevailing longshore currents. Back of the bars lie numerous lagoons.

Caribbean End of the Nicaraguan Depression. The salient landform feature of this area is the large San Juan River delta, with its numerous distributaries, lagoons, and backswamps. Most of the alluvium that the San Juan carries to build its delta comes from the right-bank tributaries that drain the northern slopes of the Costa Rican Cordillera Central, composed of loose, easily erodible volcanic ejecta.

Longshore currents have carried much of the San Juan alluvium southeastward from the delta, and together with the material deposited by local streams, has built out the wide coastal plain of northeastern Costa Rica. This plain narrows to a few kilometers' width within the vicinity of Limon and disappears entirely at Punta Cahuita, where mountains reach the sea. Coral reefs abound offshore; old reefs are found inland within the coastal plain, indicating recent uplift (Pittier, 1912).

Caribbean Shore of Panama. Southeast of Punta Cahuita in Costa Rica and along the entire Caribbean shore of Panama the coast is mountainous, broken only by the coalesced deltas of the Sixaola and Changuinola rivers, the deeply indented Chiriqui Lagoon, and the small Rio Chagres delta at the Canal Zone. East of the Zone the rocky shore is fringed with coral reefs and hundreds of small cays or islets, forming the Archipelago de las Mulatas off the San Blas coast. A large part of the remaining Cuna Indians of Panama now occupy this coast and the coral islets offshore.

REFERENCES

Aguilera, 1907
Albritten, 1958
Arellano, 1948, 1953b
Aschmann, 1959
Atwood, 1933
Aubert de la Rüe, 1958
Baker, C. L., 1930
Beal, 1948
Blásquez López, 1943, 1956
Bonet, 1953
Bretz, 1955
Bullard, F. M., 1956
Bullard, W. R., 1960
Burkart, 1836
Cardos de M., 1959
Chapman, A., 1957
Cole, 1910
Coleman, 1946
Congreso Geológico Internacional, 1956
Cooke, 1931
De Cserna, 1956
Dollfus and Montserrat, 1868
Eardley, 1951, 1954
Edwards, C., 1954, 1957
Farrington, 1897

Felix and Lenk, 1892
Foshag, 1955a, 1955b
——— and Gonzáles Reyna, 1956
Friedlaender, 1930
——— and Sonder, 1923
Fries, 1960
Gadow, 1930
Garfías and Chapín, 1949
Gerstenhauer, 1960
Gierloff-Emden, 1959
Guzman and De Cserna, 1960
Hammond, 1954
Hatt, 1953
Heacock and Worzel, 1955
Heim, 1934, 1940
Helbig, 1959
Hess, 1938
Hill, 1898
Hovey, 1905, 1907
Humboldt, 1811
Humphrey, 1956
Ives, 1935
Krynine, 1935
Landa, 1938
Lister and Howard, 1955

López de Llergo, 1953
Lorenzo, 1959b
McBirney, 1958
McBryde, 1947
Maldonado-Koerdell, 1954a, 1958c
Menard, 1955, 1960
Mendizabal, 1946
Meyer-Abich, 1956, 1958
Mooser, 1958
—— and Maldonado-Koerdell, 1961
Müllerried, 1942c
Murray, 1961
Ordóñez, 1903-06, 1906, 1936, 1941
Ower, 1928
Palmer, 1926
Pearse et al., 1936
Pittier, 1912
Polanyi et al., 1957
Powers, 1918
Radley, 1960
Raisz, 1959
Roberts and Irving, 1957
Robles Ramos, 1942, 1950
Roy, 1957

Roys, 1939, 1943
Sánchez, P. C., 1935
Sanders, E. M., 1921
Sapper, 1894, 1896, 1899, 1901, 1902a, 1902b, 1903, 1905, 1913, 1926, 1937
Schott, 1866
Schuchert, 1929, 1935
Staub and Lager, 1922
Sykes, 1937
Tamayo, 1941, 1949
Termer, 1927, 1932, 1933, 1936, 1954
Terry, 1956
Thayer, 1916
Tuan, 1960
Vermeer, 1959
Wadell, 1938
Waibel, 1933
Waitz, 1906, 1914-15, 1943
Weed, 1902
Weyl, 1961
Williams, 1950, 1952a, 1952b, 1952c, 1960
—— and Meyer-Abich, 1955
Wittich, 1935, 1935-38

3. The Hydrography of Middle America

JORGE L. TAMAYO
in collaboration with
ROBERT C. WEST

IN KEEPING WITH its diversity of geology, surface configuration, and climate, Middle America is characterized by a large variety of terrestrial water features. Surface streams range from the ephemeral channels of the northern deserts to the wide, perennial rivers of the wet eastern versant of southern Mexico and Central America. In areas of porous limestone, such as Yucatan, underground water channels, not surface streams, typify the drainage. In much of the arid northern plateau of Mexico and in districts of recent vulcanism streams flow into interior basins rather than to the sea. Lakes of many types and in various stages of development are found throughout Middle America. Springs are prevalent particularly in both young volcanic and limestone regions, where they often form sources of headwater streams. In few other parts of the world of similar size is found such an array of hydrographic features.

The terrestrial hydrography of Mexico and Central America has been of special significance to man since Pleistocene, and continues to be so today. In preconquest times the streams, lakes, and springs afforded man water for sustenance, aquatic plant and animal life for food, moisture for rudimentary irrigation, and in some places a water surface for transport. Under special conditions even salt was obtained from dry lake beds and from springs. As elsewhere in the world, availability of water has been a prime causal factor in the distribution and growth of human settlement. Today, although the manner of exploitation of water resources has greatly changed, with emphasis on the harnessing of streams for irrigation and hydroelectric power and the tapping of ground water by wells, many people here still rely on rivers, lakes, and springs and their products much as they did in ancient times. It is in emphasizing significant relationships to aboriginal life that we now examine the more important hydrographic features of Mexico and Central America.

HYDROGRAPHIC STUDIES IN MEXICO AND CENTRAL AMERICA

Many short descriptions of the lakes and rivers of Middle America have been made in the past 150 years. Most of these, however, have been based on scientific observations of short duration. Alexander von Humboldt, in his renowned *Political Essay on the Kingdom of New Spain* (1811), was an early scientific traveler who reported on the hydrography of Mexico; I subsequently (1946) published one of the first complete modern descriptions. In the mid-19th century Dollfus and Montserrat (1868) briefly considered the hydrography of Guatemala and El Salvador. The most recent comprehensive summary of the hydrologic resources of Mexico is that of the engineers Benassini and García Quintero (1955–57), given here as Table 1, p. 117.

Because of its peculiar drainage problems, the Valley of Mexico probably claims more hydrographic interest than any other single area of Mexico. The earliest scientific hydrologic study of the basin was that of Joaquín Velázquez de León y Cárdenas, who wrote in the late 18th century. Nineteenth-century treatises on drainage problems in the Valley of Mexico include those of Orozco y Berra (1864) and Peñafiel (1884). The Yucatan Peninsula has attracted attention to its unusual subsurface drainage and relationship to Maya culture (Heilprin, 1891; Sapper, 1896; Cole, 1910; Pearse et al., 1936). Recently several limnologic studies have been directed to various lakes in both Mexico and Central America (De Buen, 1943, 1944, 1945; Deevey, 1955, 1957). In Mexico ground-water supply studies of numerous small areas appear in publications of the Instituto Geológico de México and more recently in those of the Secretaría de Recursos Hidráulicos.

Unfortunately few modern scientific hydrologic studies have been made in Mexico and the Central American countries. Except for a few rivers and lakes, where relatively short records are available, systematic observation of water stages based on gauge readings are practically nonexistent. Consequently an accurate over-all study of river regimes in Middle America is not possible. For the most part only estimates of average annual stream discharges for the rivers of Mexico and for a few in Central America can be given. Moreover, in many sections of Middle America streams and lakes have not yet been adequately mapped. Lacking a reliable topographic survey, it is hardly possible to determine accurately stream gradients and to construct meaningful profiles of equilibrium needed in hydrologic studies. Fortunately, an accurate topographic mapping of most of the Middle American countries is now in progress and within a few years should be completed.

Hydrologic records of over 35 years' duration are available for only a few Mexican rivers. At the present time, however, about 75 per cent of the more important streams are being investigated by the Secretaría de Recursos Hidráulicos. In the Central American countries long-term studies have been made only for streams associated with the Nicaraguan Canal Project and for those that are at present utilized in the operation of the Panama Canal. During the last few years hydrologic studies have been initiated in Honduras, El Salvador, and Panama; it would be desirable to extend such investigations to neighboring Central American countries (Dirección General de Irrigación, 1954–55; Panama, Inst. de Fomento Económico, 1958).

CLASSIFICATION OF HYDROGRAPHIC FEATURES

In Middle America water features have been classified customarily by drainage types and by watersheds.

1. Streams and lakes of *exterior drainage* (or those that drain to the sea) are grossly divided into:
   a. Those of the Atlantic watershed (draining to Gulf of Mexico and Caribbean Sea) and
   b. Those of the Pacific watershed, including the streams of the Peninsula of Baja California that drain into the Pacific and Gulf of California.
2. Streams and lakes of *interior drainage* (or those that have no outlet to the sea) are found in:

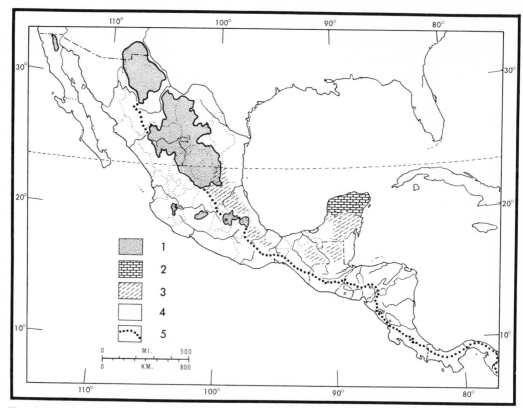

Fɪɢ. 1—DRAINAGE TYPES IN MIDDLE AMERICA
1. Interior drainage. 2. Subsurface drainage (karst). 3. Partially subsurface drainage (karst and limestone). 4. Exterior drainage. 5. Continental divide.

a. The large desert basins of arid northern Mexico and

b. Within areas of recent vulcanism, such as the Neovolcanic axis of Central Mexico and, to a lesser degree, the volcanic axis of Central America. In both regions the areas of interior drainage are at present confined to small lake basins.

3. Areas of *subsurface drainage* in Middle America are found principally in regions of porous limestone rock (karst areas), such as the Yucatan Peninsula and, to a lesser extent, sections of the limestone mountains of Mexico and Guatemala.

Streams might also be classified according to character of flow and variation of water levels.

1. *Ephemeral* streams (those that flow through indefinite channels for a short while only after heavy rains) are found

chiefly in extremely arid sections of northern Mexico, and secondarily in limestone (karst) areas.

2. *Intermittent* streams (those with defined channels, but which cease to flow during the dry period of the year) are confined mainly to small courses in those areas of Middle America that have a definite wet and dry season.

3. *Perennial* streams (those of continuous year-round flow) make up the greater part of the surface drainage area of Mexico and Central America. These streams may be further classified on the basis of regime (seasonal variation in volume of discharge).

a. *Seasonal regime.* Most of the perennial streams of Middle America are characterized by a definite seasonal regime. Most of the discharge is concentrated in the rainy period, whereas during the dry season water level is at a minimum, the slight flow

86

being received chiefly from ground-water seepage and from springs. Such a regime is typical of most tropical areas with wet and dry seasons.

b. *Uniform regime.* In areas of abundant precipitation, and slight dry period, especially the Atlantic watershed of southeastern Mexico and Central America, the river regime is more uniform than in other areas of Middle America. The larger streams are full-flowing for the entire year, especially in their lower courses, although the greatest discharge occurs during the rainier part of the year.

c. *Complex regime.* Some streams of northern Mexico show double maximum and minimum periods of discharge during the year. This is particularly true of those that drain the northern Sierra Madre Occidental, where the spring melt of winter snow, as well as occasional midlatitude frontal storms, cause rise of streams in February and April. In July and August a greater maximum discharge occurs during the height of the summer rainy season. A similar regime is characteristic of small torrential streams that drain the slopes of high, snow-covered mountain peaks, such as Popocatepetl and Orizaba in central Mexico.

Figure 1 shows in general the major watersheds and drainage types in Middle America. The position of the continental divide indicates that in northern and central Mexico the area of the Atlantic watershed is somewhat less than that of the Pacific. But in Central America from the Isthmus of Tehuantepec as far as Panama, the presence of high mountains near the western shore confines the Pacific watershed to a small strip characterized by short, torrential streams; whereas the wide Atlantic watershed of southeastern Mexico and most of Central America is drained by much longer and more voluminous rivers. The basins of interior drainage in northern

Mexico and within the volcanic axes, and the limestone platform of Yucatan with its peculiar subsurface drainage, stand apart from the normal exterior drainage areas that cover most of Middle America.

DESCRIPTION OF HYDROGRAPHIC FEATURES

The subsequent discussion of the hydrography of Middle America is organized on the basis of watersheds and areas of major drainage types in the following order: (1) exterior drainage systems of the Atlantic Watershed, (2) areas of subsurface drainage of the Atlantic Watershed, notably the Yucatan Peninsula, (3) exterior drainage systems of the Pacific Watershed, and (4) areas of interior drainage. A statement of the general hydrographic characteristics of the watershed area is followed by a description of the more important streams and lakes and their drainage basins (fig. 2).

Atlantic Watershed

The Atlantic watershed of Middle America begins in the north with the Rio Grande (Rio Bravo), an international stream the lower and middle courses of which mark the boundary between Mexico and the United States. Because of its peculiar individuality, however, the Rio Grande drainage will be considered below as a special case.

South of the Rio Grande the rivers that flow into the Gulf of Mexico and the Caribbean Sea, although of moderate length, are the most voluminous streams in Middle America. Nearly 65 per cent of the total river discharge in Mexico occurs within the Atlantic watershed,[1] and nearly one-half of the nation's total runoff is carried by four rivers of great volume: the Papaloapan, the Coatzacoalcos, the Grijalva, and the Usumacinta, which drain southern Vera-

[1] Total average annual discharge of the Atlantic watershed of Mexico, exclusive of that from the Rio Grande, is 231,169 million cu. m.; total for Mexico is 357,257 million cu. m. (Benassini and García Quintero, 1955–57).

cruz, northeastern Oaxaca, Tabasco, most of Chiapas, and a portion of Guatemala. Although data are not available, undoubtedly by far the greater percentage of stream discharge of the Central American countries occurs within the Caribbean drainage area. Obviously, this enormous discharge of water is a function of annual precipitation, size of drainage area, and amount of evapo-transpiration. As explained in the article on weather and climate, the Gulf and Caribbean versant is the wettest sector of Middle America.

Except for a few small rivers in northeastern Mexico, the streams of the Atlantic drainage of Middle America are perennial, although most show a definite seasonal regime of water flow. In the Mexican streams the high water period occurs in September and October, coincident with the heavy rainfall associated with tropical cyclonic storms (often hurricanes) that sweep in from the Gulf of Mexico and the Caribbean Sea. At this time the larger rivers often overflow their banks in their lower portions, causing disastrous floods in the surrounding coastal plains. The low water period occurs from March through May, the driest part of the year. The upper sections, to be sure, exhibit a much greater seasonal fluctuation of water stages than any other portion of the streams. The middle and lower sections of most streams from the Panuco River at Tampico southward maintain a relatively large discharge even during the drier winter months, when occasional rains occur with the invasion of cool air from the north (*norte* storms). The Central American streams of the Caribbean drainage have a fairly uniform flow throughout the year, owing to the increasing length of the rainy season equatorward.

Most of the larger rivers of the Atlantic drainage are characterized by a normal longitudinal profile of steep gradient and consequent torrential flow in their upper courses, with more gentle gradients in the middle and lower courses. In Mexico from

south of the Rio Grande to southern Veracruz the rivers originate on the steep eastern escarpment of the Sierra Madre Oriental, where the headwaters flow through deep, narrow canyons in which rapids and waterfalls abound. The middle and lower courses of these rivers are within the sierra foothills and the Gulf coastal plain, and thus have gentle gradients, relatively deep channels, and smooth flow. Among these streams the Panuco River, navigable in its lower section, is outstanding. These characteristics are accentuated within the plain of the Sotavento coast (southern Veracruz) and the extensive alluvial plain of Tabasco. The rivers of these areas are characterized by minimum gradients in their lower courses, where meandering, shifting, and bifurcation of river channels has built up a large deltaic area. The lower Papaloapan, Coatzacoalcos, Tonala, Usumacinta, and Grijalva rivers are all sufficiently deep for navigation. Unfortunately, owing to coastwise currents and wave action, bars have formed at the mouths of practically all Mexican rivers that debouch into the Gulf, presenting important obstacles for sea-river navigation. The rivers of southern Veracruz rise in the Sierra de Oaxaca, and thus their upper courses are steep and torrential. The Tabasco rivers (principally the Usumacinta and Grijalva), those that drain the Caribbean slope of Guatemala (e.g. the Polochic and Motagua), of Honduras (the Chamelecon, Ulua, Aguan, Patuca, etc.), and Nicaragua (the Coco and San Juan), drain large structural depressions within the interior highlands; thus their upper courses lack the steep gradients and torrential flow characteristic of most of the Mexican rivers. The lower courses of the Guatemalan, Honduran, and Nicaraguan rivers, like those of southeastern Mexico, are wide, fairly deep, and voluminous, and therefore navigable for small craft. The San Juan River, which forms part of the international boundary between Nicaragua and Costa Rica, is atypical in that it drains the large Nicaraguan lakes. The rivers of the steep Caribbean watershed of Costa Rica are like those of Mexico, having torrential upper courses within the mountain section and gentle gradients with deep, navigable channels in the lower coastal plain sections. Although short and of small drainage area, these rivers carry a large discharge, owing to heavy annual rainfall on the windward Caribbean slopes.

RIO GRANDE DRAINAGE. The Rio Grande is a river of special importance for both Mexico and the United States, for not only have its middle and lower sections formed the international boundary between these two countries since 1848, but it also furnishes an abundant discharge of water that is now utilized on both sides of the border for extensive irrigation projects.

The Rio Grande rises in the Rocky Mountains at 4,000 m. elevation in Colorado within the interior of the United States. The drainage basin covers an area of 472,000 sq. km., 51 per cent of which is included within Mexican territory. It is estimated that 48 per cent of the river discharge originates in Mexico; from Ciudad Juarez to the Gulf the Mexican tributaries contribute much more water to the main stream than do those on the American side, where only two tributaries, the Pecos and the Devil's rivers, are of importance.[2]

The upper Rio Grande is entirely within present United States territory (Colorado and New Mexico). This sector of the river receives much of its water from snow melt of the Rocky Mountains, the period of maximum flow being in April and May. Late spring and early summer floods were of prime importance to the Pueblo Indian farmers, who relied partly on flood irrigation for raising crops in the arid upper Rio Grande Valley.

The middle course of the river cuts across northwest-southeast-trending moun-

tain ranges to form a series of deep, steeply walled canyons. Below Piedras Negras the lower section of the river forms a narrow alluvial valley that widens considerably within the Gulf coastal plain. The large right bank (Mexican) tributaries, such as the Conchos, Salado, Alamo, and San Juan, furnish nearly half the total discharge of the Rio Grande. The period of maximum discharge of these rivers is in July, August, and September; thus they change the regime of the Rio Grande from a spring maximum discharge characteristic of its upper section to one with a complicated double maximum in its lower course, where the major flood period is in late summer and early fall.

The major tributary is the Conchos, which rises in the Sierra Madre Occidental and flows across the desert of eastern Chihuahua to the Rio Grande. This river alone supplies 18 per cent of the total flow of the Rio Grande. Most of its discharge derives from the heavy precipitation of the Sierra and springs in the eastern foothills and is carried by the main headwaters tributaries, the San Pedro, San Juan, Parral, and Florido of southern Chihuahua. Within the desert the Conchos forms a river oasis, sections of which were occupied by the Conchos Indians, who lived in part by rudimentary agriculture, planting in the moist river margins after recession of the summer floods. Within the past 30 years the middle Conchos drainage has become an important agricultural section of northern Mexico, with the construction of reservoirs and the utilization of its water for extensive irrigation projects.

With the exception of the Conchos, the middle and lower drainage of the Rio Grande was occupied in pre-European times by nomadic hunters and gatherers— the northern "Chichimec" Indians. These nomads utilized the river water only for drinking and occasional fishing. Throughout the lower Rio Grande drainage, North American food fish, especially cats, suckers,

[2] The total annual discharge of the Rio Grande is 12,135 million cu. m.; 5,810 million cu. m. is derived from Mexican tributaries.

89

and sunfish, abound. The primitives who lived in this area obtained a large portion of their food by river fishing (Mendizabal, 1946).

The lower Rio Grande has now become one of the most important agricultural areas of Mexico, with the construction of reservoirs for irrigation water on the larger tributaries (San Marcos reservoir on the Salado; El Azucar, or Marte R. Gomez, reservoir on the San Juan), as well as on the main stream (the international Falcón Dam). The latter and the proposed Devil's or Amistad dam farther upstream will serve to regulate flood waters, which previously ravaged periodically the Mexican side of the lower Rio Grande. Before the construction of the dams and reservoirs the lower portion of the Rio Grande was navigable for small craft.

DRAINAGE BASINS OF THE NORTHERN GULF AREA. South of the Rio Grande the first important drainage basin of the Atlantic watershed that is totally within Mexican territory is the Conchos–San Fernando River. Its headwaters, which rise in the Sierra Madre Oriental, are the Potosi, Linares, and Conchos, the upper portions of which are intermittent, carrying water only after rains. After a course of 300 km. the river empties into the Laguna Madre on the Gulf Coast.

Another important river of Tamaulipas is the Soto la Marina, which rises in Nuevo Leon within the Sierra Madre from the limestone spring, El Salto; the stream continues through the canyon of El Cuervo in Nuevo Leon where it tumbles over three large falls. Called La Purificacion farther downstream, it is joined by other tributaries flowing from the Sierra de Tamaulipas and finally becomes the Sota la Marina after it passes the town of that name.

Farther south the Rio Tamesi originates in the Sierra Madre Oriental as the Guayalejo River, and receives tributaries that begin from springs and subterranean streams in the porous limestone rock of the mountains. One of the most notable subterranean streams is the headwater of the Rio Mante, which gushes forth from its underground channel at a place called El Nacimiento. Such underground channels and copious springs of the vauclusian type are typical of mountainous limestone areas, such as the Sierra Madre Oriental of Mexico. Near the Gulf the Tamesi debouches into a series of tidal lagoons and its waters eventually reach the sea through the mouth of the Panuco River.

Within the middle and lower drainage areas of northern and central Tamaulipas hundreds of small intermittent stream channels scar the rolling limestone foothills and lowlands; such streams carry water for only short periods after heavy rains, and for much of the year are completely dry or carry isolated pools or *charcos* of stagnant water. Such pools were undoubtedly important sources of water for the primitive nomads who inhabited Tamaulipas in preconquest and colonial times. These people also utilized the larger permanent streams for fishing to supplement their diet gained from hunting game and gathering seeds and roots.

The Panuco drainage basin (66,300 sq. km.) is one of the largest of Mexico's Atlantic watershed, being exceeded in area only by the extensive Grijalva-Usumacinta system farther south. Most of the headwaters of the Panuco have eroded headward to reach the surface of the central plateau, where they have captured former highland lake basins. Much of the northeastern edge of the plateau thus drains into the Panuco system.

One of the largest of the Panuco tributaries is the Rio Moctezuma, which has carved an enormous canyon into the eastern escarpment of the Sierra. One of its headwater streams, the Rio Tula, penetrates the flat surface of the plateau and has captured the San Juan del Rio River, which formerly flowed westward into the Lerma River system.

90

By means of artificial drainage completed in 1900 the Valley of Mexico, by nature an enclosed basin, now drains into the headwaters of the Moctezuma and has thus been converted into the present source of the Panuco River. Beginning with the sewer system of Mexico City, which feeds into the Gran Canal del Desagüe, the new headwater receives the river called Avenidas de Pachuca, flows through the tunnel of Tequixquiac, and discharges into the Rio Salado, one of the upper tributaries of the Moctezuma. Another new headwater stream of this system is the Rio Cuautitlan, which rises in the northwestern part of the Valley of Mexico and leaves it via the artificial Tajo de Nochixtongo, which in turn discharges as the Rio del Salto into the Tepeji and thence into the Tula River.

Other large tributaries of the Moctezuma include the Estorax, which also has eroded headward into the plateau surface in San Luis Potosi; and the Tempoal, which drains the foothills of the sierra and the coastal lowlands of northern Veracruz.

Other important streams of the Panuco system are the Rio Tamuin–Santa Maria and its tributaries, the Verde and El Salto, which drain the Sierra Madre Oriental in eastern San Luis Potosi, sometimes called the Huasteca Potosiana, home of the highland Huastec Indians. All these streams receive water from springs and underground channels in the limestone of the sierra. The headwaters of the Santa Maria penetrate the plateau surface south of the city of San Luis Potosi, tapping basins of former interior drainage.

Within the coastal lowlands the Panuco and the lower parts of its main tributaries, the Tamuin, Santa Maria, Moctezuma, and Tempoal, have slight gradients; thus they have developed extensive meander belts and during frequent floods have shifted their courses occasionally. Consequently an extensive series of river flood plains have been established within the coastal area immediately between Tampico and the Sierra foothills. The natural levees of both active and abandoned channels of these rivers bear scores of archaeological sites, indicating favored spots for agriculture and settlements of the former lowland Huastec culture. The lower portions of nearly every other sizable river southward along the coastal plain of Veracruz exhibits similar features with numerous archaeological sites along the natural levees or adjacent river terraces.

The lower course of the Panuco is important for sea navigation, and at the present time, despite the presence of a river-mouth bar, ships of deep draft come up river as far as the port of Tampico, 12 km. upstream. Ships of shallow draft can reach as far as the confluence of the Moctezuma and Tamuin rivers. Recent studies indicate the possibility of extending navigation of the Panuco and its tributaries as far as 242 km. upstream with depths varying from 1 to 8 m., contingent on the completion of various projects. It is thought that by so revamping the river system water communication could be established between the Huasteca and the southeastern part of the Mexican plateau.

CENTRAL GULF DRAINAGE BASINS. Between the Panuco River system and that of the Papaloapan is a series of short but voluminous streams, each with a relatively small basin, that drain the steep rainy escarpment of the central plateau of Mexico. The Tuxpan, Cazones, Tecolutla, and Nautla of northern Veracruz state are the larger of these rivers. Each has an extremely steep gradient in its upper course, the headwaters being characterized by falls and rapids, some of which are utilized for the generation of electrical power. On the Rio Necaxa, an upper tributary of the Tecolutla, Mexico's first large hydroelectric generating plant was established in 1903, utilizing the steep gradient and the water stored within a small reservoir. The water flow in the middle portion of the river courses is relatively swift, but in the narrow coastal plain the short lower portions become slow and meandering, bordered by natural levees. During highwater stage of August and September the rivers often overflow, inundating the surrounding lowland. Although river-mouth bars impede ocean traffic, the lower portions are often navigable and small river ports are found a short distance upstream from the barred mouths.

The lowland area crossed by the rivers was inhabited by the Huastec culture in preconquest times, and is thus called the Huasteca. As in the lower Panuco drainage, archaeological sites abound along the rivers on the natural levees in the narrow coastal plain, and farther upstream in the rolling hill country stream terraces that overlook the present river channels also contain many sites.

In central Veracruz relatively small streams drain the watershed which becomes quite narrow. Among these are the Actopan; La Antigua, which empties into the Gulf near the site of the old port of Veracruz, north of the present city; the Rio Blanco, the falls in its upper and middle courses being used for generating hydroelective power and along the banks of which have been established the industrial towns of Santa Rosa, Nogales, Rio Blanco, and Orizaba.

SOUTHERN GULF DRAINAGE BASINS. As indicated previously, this area probably contains the most voluminous streams of Middle America. One of the most important is the Papaloapan, which rises in the Sierra de Juarez, eastern Oaxaca. Its headwaters (Salado and Tomellin) drain the interior structural basins of Tehuacan and Cuicatlan; as the Rio Santo Domingo, the river breaks through the Sierra Madre de Oaxaca via a deep and narrow canyon (Santo Domingo); at Valle Nacional it takes the name of Papoloapan, and after receiving many large tributaries debouches into the Laguna de Alvarado on the Gulf coast.

The lower portion of the Papaloapan and many of its tributaries (the Playa Vicente,

San Juan Evangelista, and Tonto in particular) cross the Gulf coastal plain which widens considerably south of Veracruz. A tributary of the San Juan drains Lake Catemaco, which occupies a small basin in the volcanic highlands of Los Tuxtlas, southern Veracruz. For 80 km. the lowland streams slowly meander, flooding the large areas of surrounding countryside during periods of high water (August through September), only the higher natural levees along the river banks being free from inundation. Within the coastal flood plain the fertile levees were probably favored sites for Indian settlement in preconquest times; the famous site of Tres Zapotes occurs on the eastern margin of the lower river flood plain. From Valle Nacional upstream the Papoloapan drainage basin is still occupied by many indigenous groups, among which are the Chinantec of Valle Nacional, and groups of the Mije, Zapotec, and Mazatec who inhabit the mountainous upper portion of the basin in Oaxaca.

The Papoloapan drainage basin contains one of the largest potential water resources of Mexico; fortunately this potential is now being utilized with the construction of enormous projects, among which the Temascal dam and reservoir has a storage capacity of 8,000 million cu. m. This project now helps to control floods in the lower portion of the basin and generates electric power for the industries of Veracruz.

In the Isthmus of Tehuantepec the Coatzacoalcos River rises on the northeast slope of the Sierra de Oaxaca in the headwaters of its main tributary, the Rio Jaltepec. Within the coastal plain the main river is joined by the Jaltepec, the Uxpanapa, and several smaller tributaries. Although smaller in drainage area and discharge than the Papoloapan, it is far more voluminous than the Panuco farther north. The lower section of the river is navigable, the port cities of Coatzacoalcos and Minatitlan occupying the left bank. Since colonial times, the construction of an interoceanic canal has been projected across the Isthmus of Tehuante-pec to connect the Atlantic and Pacific Oceans, utilizing the lower Coatzacoalcos as part of the project.

The wide, flat Tabasco lowlands receive the waters of the two most voluminous river systems of Middle America: the Grijalva (Mezcalapa) and the Usumacinta. Because of the special character of the lowland drainage, characterized by interconnected distributaries and swamps of both stream systems, the lower sections of the rivers will be considered later as a unit. The middle and upper sections of each system will be treated separately below.

The Mezcalapa system drains the Central Valley of Chiapas, one of the major structural depressions of Middle America. The main headwater stream, the Chejel, rises in the Guatemalan Sierra de los Cuchuma-tanes. Within the Valley of Chiapas the stream is called the Rio Grande de Chiapas, and, as it leaves the valley through a narrow defile toward the coastal plain, it takes the name Mezcalapa. At the exit of this canyon the river's yearly mean discharge is 22,740 million cu. m., or about one-fifth of the total discharge of the combined Grijalva-Usumacinta system. The Mezcalapa once drained to the Gulf through the present Río Seco. During the 17th century the river diverted its waters into the Río Grijalva to form part of its present course. In 1932 the Mezcalapa again diverted, creating the distributary Rio Samaria, which many times since has flooded large sections of the Tabasco lowland.

Within the lower coastal plain the main river channel is known as the Grijalva and is joined by the voluminous tributaries, the Teapa and the Tacotalpa, which drain the rain-drenched northern escarpment of the central plateau of Chiapas. These rivers, together with the independent system of the Macuspana and Tulija rivers, carry the runoff from the wettest spot in Mexico, which receives nearly 5,000 mm. of rainfall annually. Despite a period of less rain-fall in March and April, the flow of these rivers remains fairly uniform through the year.

The Usumacinta in terms of discharge is the most important river in Middle America. The upper and middle drainage basin of this river system, one-third of which lies in northwestern Guatemala, is the largest (102,828 sq. km.) of any in the Gulf area. Its headwaters, called the Rio Salinas, rise on the eastern slope of Los Altos · in northwestern Guatemala in the department of Huehuetenango. Farther downstream the name of the main stream changes to the Chixoy, which drains the Alta Verapaz of Guatemala. This river serves to delimit part of the international boundary between Mexico and Guatemala. At the confluence with the Rio de la Pasion it finally receives the name of Usumacinta. On its right bank the main river is joined by tributaries (the Pasion and San Pedro) that rise in the low-lying lake plains of the Peten in northern Guatemala. Although they carry much water, these streams are sluggish. On its left bank the Usumacinta system is fed by numerous tributaries that originate on the northern and eastern slopes of the Chiapas highlands. The headwaters of these streams often rise from springs and underground channels that characterize the limestone surface of the highlands. Draining small structural depressions within the highlands, some of which contain sizable lakes, these swift tributaries, such as the Jatate and Lacanji, flow southeastward to the Lacantun, which joins the Usumacinta. At Boca del Cerro, where the Usumacinta breaks out into the coastal lowlands, the average annual discharge approximates 28,118 million cu. m. The regime of the upper and middle portions of the river system is seasonal; the maximum discharge in September, when the river overflows its banks, has reached 5,600 cu. m./sec., whereas the minimum in May has measured only 280 cu. m./sec.

The middle and upper Usumacinta drain-

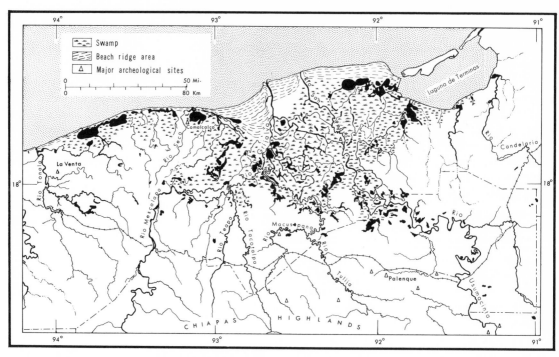

FIG. 3—DRAINAGE OF THE TABASCO LOWLANDS

age system was the locale of a large number of Classic Mayan ceremonial centers. On the banks of the main river are the ruins of the metropolises Piedras Negras and Yaxchilan; the headwaters of the Jatate contain the complex of Tonina; and near the lower drainage basin the city of Palenque was founded on one of the small tributaries of the Usumacinta. Water supply was undoubtedly one of the main attractions of such sites, especially in the upper tributary sections, while water transport may have been an added inducement to settlement on the main river.

The lower drainage area of the combined Grijalva-Usumacinta systems within the Tabasco lowlands is a maze of bifurcating channels and distributaries, abandoned meanders, overflow lakes, marshes and swamps. Figure 3 indicates the great complexity of drainage pattern within this area. The main distributary of the Usumacinta joins the Grijalva about 20 km. upstream from the mouth. The combined yearly discharge of these two rivers as measured

near the mouth is 105,200 million cu. m., or nearly 30 per cent of the entire river discharge for all of Mexico. All the main distributary channels are deep and navigable. Prior to the construction of flood protection dikes (1952), during the period of heavy rains (September-November) almost the entire lowland between the Rio Seco and the lower Grijalva was inundated by an extensive sheet of water from river overflow; only the higher natural levees and small hillocks on which the inhabitants constructed their houses, remained free from flood. The wasteful abundance of water that nature bestows upon the area during the rainy period contrasts with a marked diminution of flow in all the distributaries during the dry season, the period when navigation is made difficult, the fields desiccate, malaria is intensified, and all the appearance of wealth and euphoria is converted to desolation. The flood-ridden Tabasco lowland apparently was moderately populated in preconquest times, just as it is today. Although only a few Maya sites

94

of any note (e.g. Comalcalco and Jonuta) are found in the lower river sections, hundreds of smaller mound groups dot the natural levees of both active and abandoned river channels throughout the alluvial lowland. Moreover, the La Venta site of early Olmec culture (800 B.C.) occupies an island of high ground within the backswamp of the Rio Tonala. This and similar sites within the low coastal areas may have been chosen for ceremonial centers more because of their isolation than their favorable living conditions.

The Rio Candelaria, immediately southwest of the Yucatan Peninsula, is the last major stream in the southern Gulf drainage area. Its headwaters rise in the Peten lowlands of Guatemala, and the main stream flows through the state of Campeche. It is characterized by a marked seasonal regime, carrying a torrential flow during the rainy period, but most of the year its discharge is small. In preconquest times the Candelaria formed part of the main Aztec-Maya trade route that led from the great market center of Xicalango on the Tabasco coast across the Peten to Honduras.

CARIBBEAN DRAINAGE OF THE ATLANTIC WATERSHED.[3] This vast drainage area includes the entire Caribbean versant of Central America. Separating the Gulf drainage area from that of Caribbean is the limestone platform of the Yucatan Peninsula, which because of its peculiar hydrographic character will be considered later as a separate unit.

The first important stream of the Caribbean drainage is the Rio Hondo, which forms the international boundary between Mexico and British Honduras. The headwaters of the Hondo rise in the Peten lowlands of southern Campeche and northern Guatemala, where it is called the Rio Azul.

<hr>

[3] Much of the hydrographic data herein presented for both the Atlantic and Pacific watersheds of the Central American countries were taken from volume 18, "Mexico y Centro America," of the *Geografía Universal* and revised (Tamayo, 1959b).

After the main stream is joined by the Xmoscha River, it is called the Hondo, and debouches into the Bay of Chetumal. Other short rivers of small drainage area and moderate discharge, such as the Belize and the Sibun, rise in the Maya or Cockscomb Mountains of British Honduras. The Sarstoon River, which marks the boundary between Guatemala and British Honduras, drains a small structural depression between the Cockscomb Mountains and the Sierra de Santa Cruz. The regime of all these small rivers is seasonal, in flood during the wet period and reduced to small, clear streams in the dry season. Most of their lower sectors, however, are fairly deep and navigable for small craft.

The rivers that drain the Caribbean versant of Guatemala and Honduras each flow through a large structural basin that usually trends southeast-northwest, in accordance with the general tectonic alignment of northern Central America. Since most of these rivers drain areas of heavy rainfall, they discharge enormous quantities of water, floods being characteristic from August through November, the rainiest part of the year. Unfortunately in neither Guatemala nor Honduras have systematic hydrometric studies been undertaken or, at least, data have not been published; thus drainage area and discharge figures are not available for exact comparisons with Mexican streams.

The first of the structural-depression rivers is the Polochic, the headwaters of which are torrential streams draining the eastern part of the Verapaz limestone highlands where springs, disappearing channels, and underground drainage abound. Following its structural valley, the Polochic empties into Lake Izabal, which occupies the eastern end of the depression. In turn the lake drains to the sea through the Rio Dulce, a short, deep, entrenched outlet, which marks the final section of the Polochic system. The Rio Dulce, Lake Izabal, and the lower Polochic to the village of Panzos are navigable, and have played an important role in sea and river commerce in both preconquest and colonial times. At the mouth of the Rio Dulce was the large Maya trading center of Nito, reached mainly by river and sea canoe traffic.

The Motagua River system, the largest in Guatemala, occupies an even greater structural depression, which tectonically forms an eastern continuation of the same structure of the Valley of Chiapas. The Motagua headwaters originate in Quiche highlands near Chichicastenango and the main river flows northeastward for 300 km. to the Gulf of Honduras, where it has built an extensive delta. In its upper course it forms a torrential stream, but with small discharge owing to the comparative aridity of its drainage area. In its lower course, however, abundant rainfall gives it a heavy discharge; its width widens from 60 to 200 m. and its depth increases from 2 to 5 m. However, because of its heavy load of sediment and the formation of shifting point bars within its channel, navigation is difficult. Its lower valley appears to have been a former marine inlet, now filled by river sediment. During the period of high water (October–November) the lower Motagua overflows its banks, building up a set of wide natural levees of fertile alluvial soil, which, since preconquest times, have been important for agriculture (Contreras and Cerezo, 1958).

In Honduras the Rio Ulua, the largest and most important river system in the country, also occupies a large structural depression which tends almost directly north-south. The same depression is followed by the lower part of the Rio Chamelecon, which rises in the western highlands of Honduras and parallels the Ulua in its lower portion. Both rivers are voluminous, but the Ulua is by far the larger. Together they have built an extensive flood plain within the lower part of the depression, the fertile soils of which gave rise in preconquest times to a dense Indian population occu-

pied in growing cacao for the Maya trade. Today the natural levees and terraces of the lower Ulua and Chamelecon are the site of great banana and sugar cane plantations of the United Fruit Company.

The numerous headwaters of the Ulua rise in the western and central highlands of Honduras, former home of the Lenca Indians. The largest highland affluent is the Rio Grande de Otoro, which drains much of the western part of Honduras as well as Lake Yojoa, important archaeologically for its site of highland Maya culture. Another highland tributary of almost equal size is the Humuya, the upper part of which drains the Valley of Comayagua. Other interior highland basins, such as Talanga and Siria, are drained by tributaries of the Humuya. The largest western tributary of the Ulua system is the Rio Jicatuyo, the upper portions of which (Alash Higuito and Mejocote rivers) drain much of the southwestern highlands of Honduras. The combined Chamelecon-Ulua drainage basin is probably the largest in Central America.

The Aguan River is still another large Caribbean stream in northern Honduras that occupies a large structural basin. Its headwaters rise near the town of Yoro in the north-central highlands, the river running through the narrow structural corridor for 200 km. before debouching into the sea east of Trujillo. Like the Ulua, it has built an extensive flood plain and adjacent terraces, densely inhabited by cacao farmers in preconquest times. The middle Aguan is now the site of many banana plantations owned and operated by North American fruit companies.

Eastward from the Aguan a large number of rivers drain the eastern highlands of Honduras. Some occupy southwest-northeast–trending structural basins; others have eroded through divides to tap various highland basins. The largest of these stream systems is the Patuca, the drainage basin of which rivals that of the Ulua in size. Like the Aguan, it rises in the north central

Honduran highlands, and takes the name of Patuca below the confluence with the Rio Guayape, debouching into Brewers Lagoon on the Caribbean shore. The most celebrated tributary of the Patuca is the Rio Guayape, famed for its placer gold deposits, the probable source of much of the gold that entered preconquest Aztec-Maya trade and was intensively exploited in colonial times.

South of the Patuca another long river system of equal drainage area is variously called the Coco, Wanks or Huanqui, Bodega, Segovia, Yare, Cabo Gracias a Dios, and even other names. According to the arbitration of the King of Spain, 1906, the Coco was designated as the international limit between Honduras and Nicaragua, a decision long unrecognized by Nicaragua, which claimed the Patuca as the rightful boundary. The Coco headwaters rise in the northwestern highlands of Nicaragua, only 75 km. from the Pacific coast. From that point the main river flows 750 km. to the Caribbean, where it has built an arcuate delta, the seawardmost point of which is called Cape Gracias a Dios. Although hydrometric data are lacking, the Coco must discharge an enormous quantity of water during the flood period being from August to December. It is navigable in small craft for a distance of 500 km. from the sea.

The entire Caribbean versant of Nicaragua is drained by rivers similar to the Coco in terms of regime and longitudinal profile, but they are much shorter in length. They rise in the central Nicaraguan highlands as torrential streams and become deep and meandering as they cross the gentle gradient of the wide Mosquito coastal plain. The most important of these rivers south of the Coco are the Wawa, Cuculaya, Prinzapolca, Grande, Curinguas, Escondido, Cucra, and Punta Gorda. The last of the long Nicaragua rivers, the San Juan has a much different hydrographic character and will be considered separately below.

In their lower and middle courses the rivers of the Mosquito coast have been of special significance for human settlement. Most of the forest Indians of northeastern Honduras and eastern Nicaragua, such as the Paya, Sumo, Misquito, and Rama, were riverine people living along the main streams and their tributaries. These people cultivated the fertile alluvium of natural levees and exploited the abundant riverine tropical fish resources. They were also excellent canoemen, the rivers serving as highways for trade and migration.

The San Juan River, the lower course of which marks the international boundary between Nicaragua and Costa Rica, is different from the other Caribbean streams of Middle America in that it drains the two large lakes that occupy the Nicaraguan depression, a great structural lowland that rends the Central American isthmus. Lake Managua (or Lake Xolotlan) has an average depth of 20 m.; since the lake surface is 40 m. elevation, its bottom is still above sea level. Formerly Lake Managua drained into the Gulf of Fonseca on the Pacific coast via the Estero Real, but its outlet was blocked by lava from the volcano of Momotombo. It now drains into the larger and deeper Lake Nicaragua (or L. Cocibolca) (area 8,000 sq. km., elevation 35 m., depth 70 m.) by way of the 30-km.-long Rio Tipitapa. As the level of Lake Nicaragua varies seasonally only from one to one-half meter, its discharge into the San Juan is fairly regular. In the geologic past the lake appears to have been connected with the Pacific Ocean, for among its present aquatic fauna is a species of marine shark that has adapted itself to the fresh-water habitat. The two lakes also contain a variety of food fish, among which are the tropical grunter (*Pomadasis* sp.); many cichlids, including the red species *Cichlasoma managuense*; and the sardine-like *Melaniris sardina*, found in abundance along the shallow shores; all of these have been exploited since preconquest times by the lakeshore dwellers. The fertile shores of both lakes

97

Managua and Nicaragua were densely occupied before and after the conquest by the advanced Nicarao and Mangue Indians of Mesoamerican affinity.

The San Juan River, sometimes known as the Desaguadero, can be divided hydrographically into two sections. (1) The upper section was once a former tributary of the lake and subsequently was captured by the lower San Juan eroding headward from the Caribbean; the old drainage divide, just east of the village of El Castillo, can still be identified by a series of rapids between Toro and Machuca. (2) The second section lies within the coastal plain, where it has built a large flood plain, having filled a former bay of the sea. In most of its upper course the channel of the San Juan is wide and deep, except for the rapids near Castillo, which encumber navigation. At its mouth the river has formed a sizable delta, the main distributary of which is 130 m. wide. When in flood (September–November) the river discharges six times more water than is received from Lake Nicaragua.

This additional discharge is furnished mainly by the numerous right-bank tributaries that drain the rain-drenched windward slopes of the volcanic cordilleras Guanacaste and Central of Costa Rica. The largest of the Costa Rican streams is the Rio San Carlos, which heads in the Cordillera Central, but receives the important tributary, the Rio Arenal, the source of which is the highland Lake Arenal in the Cordillera de Guanacaste. Other large Costa Rican rivers that flow into the San Juan are the Sarapiqui, which rises on the slopes of Barba Volcano, and the Chirripo, which drains the northern slope of Volcan Irazu. These tributaries have a decidedly seasonal regime and carry large amounts of sediment eroded from the soft volcanic materials through which they flow, most of which is dumped into the San Juan. Thus from the confluence of the San Carlos to its mouth, the San Juan is a shallow stream

with a sandy, shifting bed; in low water the river is so shoal as to impede navigation (A. P. Davis, 1900; Merz, 1906).

Since colonial times an interoceanic canal through the Nicaraguan depression has been projected. Plans have envisioned the use of either one or both of the large lakes for natural means of transport; the canalization and deepening of the San Juan River; and the construction of an artificial canal at one of various suggested points across the narrow isthmus that separates the lakes from the Pacific Ocean. At the present time most of these projects have been abandoned.

South of the San Juan River the streams of the Caribbean drainage in Costa Rica and Panama are composed of short but voluminous rivers that drain the steep windward side of the central highlands. Thus gradients of these rivers are extremely steep and the flow is torrential in their upper and middle courses. The lower courses on the narrow coastal plain are quite short and have had little chance to build extensive flood plains. Owing to a long rainy period in the mountain slopes and a dense forest cover, these streams maintain a steady flow. The Reventazon River, 155 km. long, is the most important of the Caribbean streams in Costa Rica, for its valley has long been used for communication between the Meseta Central and the Caribbean coast. It heads in the Cordillera de Talamanca, and one of its tributaries has eroded headward to tap the highland basin of Cartago. At the Panamanian border the Rio Sixaola is the largest of the Caribbean streams south of Nicaragua. Rising as a torrential stream in the Sierra de Talamanca, it has built one of the larger river flood plains on the Caribbean lowlands. Its meandering lower course, 20 km. of which is navigable for small craft, serves as the northern part of the present international boundary between Costa Rica and Panama.

The Caribbean slope of Panama is drained by 153 short streams that debouch into the sea. Except for those associated with the Panama Canal, little is known of the hydrology of these streams; since 1954, however, studies have begun with the formation of the newly established Office of Hydraulic Resources. (See Terry, 1956.)

The most renowned river system of Panama is that of the Chagres. Today its waters have been dammed to form the immense reservoir of Gatun Lake, an integral part of the Panama Canal system, utilized as a portion of the canal route and furnishing water for the lock system.

Areas of Subsurface Drainage of the Atlantic Watershed

Located between the Gulf and Caribbean surface drainage areas, the Yucatan Peninsula is the most extensive area of underground drainage associated with karst topography in Middle America. Nevertheless, hydrographically it is within the Atlantic watershed, for much of the ground water eventually reaches the sea through subsurface seepage or flow. The peculiar drainage features of the peninsula (the locale of Maya civilization) have played an important role in the location of settlement and in the development of economies since ancient times.

The Yucatan Peninsula is an extensive platform of limestone with little soil, particularly in its northern half. Although the area receives a substantial amount of rainfall, the water penetrates rapidly into the porous surface and is lost in caverns and underground solution channels within the limestone. In terms of hydrography the peninsula may be divided into two large type areas: (1) the drier northern section, which lacks surface streams, and (2) the wetter southern section, including the Petén of Guatemala, where thick soils and dense vegetation permit a rudimentary surface drainage system and the formation of large lakes.

NORTHERN YUCATAN. North of a line drawn approximately northeastward from the Champoton River in Campeche to the Caribbean shore opposite Cozumel Island, the main natural sources of water are the famous *cenotes* (from the Maya, dz'onot), or round, deep sinkholes (dolines), formed by the collapse of roofs that cover underground caverns and channels dissolved from the soft limestone. The bottom portion of the cenotes contains water of varying depths supplied by the subterranean channels and ground-water seepage. The cenotes vary greatly in size and shape, but the cylindrical type with nearly vertical walls is most common. The greatest density of these forms is found in the north-central and northeastern part of the peninsula. In this area almost every important Maya ceremonial center and many present-day villages are located near the edge of a cenote where drinking water can be obtained.

It is often believed in Yucatan that the water level of the cenotes as well as the general subterranean water level coincide with sea level. However, in the interior the water levels vary considerably in cenotes, although there is a general increase in depth from the coast inland (Sapper, 1896; Heilprin, 1891; Casares, 1905). The water in most of the cenotes is fresh and appears to derive from seepage through underground channels. In some, however, the water is stagnant and layered in terms of temperature and chemical composition, indicating a lack of subsurface flow (Pearse et al., 1936). Biological investigations of several cenotes of northern Yucatan indicate the presence of several species of small perchlike fish (cichlids), a tropical catfish (*Rhamdia*), and various crustacea, which may have furnished human food in ancient times (Pearse et al., 1936).

Another water source in the northern area are the *aguadas*, shallow but usually permanent ponds of water that occupy surface depressions where a layer of stiff, impermeable clay has sealed the fissures in the underlying limestone. Moreover, old

99

cenotes, filled with sediment and organic debris, may eventually become aguadas. Within various Maya ceremonial centers are remains of artificial ponds, or aguadas, constructed to collect rain water, which during the dry season becomes stagnant with suspended organic material.

Still another important water supply for the ancient Maya were limestone caves (*actuns*), which abound in the western part of the peninsula, especially in the Serrania, a series of low ridges north of Uxmal. Most of the caves contain fresh water, some being as deep as 75 m. below the surface. The abundance of artifacts and worn footpaths within these caves is evidence that they were used as water supply for the nearby villages or ceremonial centers (Hatt, 1953).

Minor hydrographic features of the northern part of the peninsula, some of which were significant for water supply before the construction of wells in colonial and modern times, include the *sartenejas* (*haltuns*), natural hollows in outcropping limestone that temporarily fill with rain water during showers. Other features are incipient stream channels, called *arroyos*, worn into the limestone by rain water but containing running water only after heavy rains, the runoff rapidly disappearing through fissures. Moreover, along the northern coast of Yucatan occurs a remarkable phenomenon of offshore fresh-water springs called *pozas*. These are formed by water from underground channels which discharges into the sea below the surface and wells up through the salty sea water just off coast or on beaches at low tide mark. Some of the more important pozas are near Conil, Sisal, and Dzilan on the north coast, and according to the 16th-century chronicler, Oviedo y Valdés (1851-55, bk. 32, ch. 2), these were used in pre-Spanish times for water supply by the coastal people.

In the northern area the only permanent streams that feed into the sea occur as short, insignificant channels near the east-ern coast. These maintain their flow probably through the influence of heavy forest cover and relatively thick soil; some may be the result of coalesced sinkholes, forming narrow uvalas or elongated depressions, the channel floor coinciding with the high-ground water table near the sea.

SOUTHERN YUCATAN. The southern section of the peninsula, although partly characterized by subsurface drainage, is noted for its lakes and swamps, disappearing streams, and sluggish (often intermittent) headwaters of rivers that drain to either the Gulf of Mexico or the Caribbean Sea. The development of surface-water features in this area appears to be the result of heavy precipitation, dense forest cover, thick soil, and an undulating or hilly terrain. Several short streams rise in the relatively high south-central part of the peninsula (300 m. elevation) in eastern Campeche and western Quintana Roo and flow northward to empty into small lakes and swamps or to disappear into fissures within the limestone surface. Many of the lakes of this area are elongated in shape, and may be the result of collapse of several aligned sinkholes to form a water-filled uvala; or they may be due to faulting. Lake Chichancanab in north-central Quintana Roo is such an elongated feature probably formed along a fault-depression. Other elongated fault lakes are Lake Bacalar near the Caribbean coast in Quintana Roo, and in the Peten there is an east-west series of fault lakes that begins with Lake Yaxha and continues through Lake Macanche to Lake Peten Itza (Sapper, 1899; Wadell, 1938). Some of the lakes contain fresh water, but many such as Lake Chichancanab, are alkaline with a large concentration of magnesium sulphate, which gives the water a "gippy" taste and a purgative character; other lakes near the coast are saline, such as Lake Bacalar.

The most notable area of lakes within the southern part of the peninsula is in the Peten, which Guatemalan geographers have called the "Comarca Lacustre," or Lake Region. The shores of many of these lakes were sites of Maya ceremonial centers of the Classic period. The largest lake is that of Peten Itza, which with many others occurs in a large depression of interior drainage. Lake Peten Itza is more than 36 km. long and 16 km. wide, and consists of two elongated parts; depths vary from extremely shallow water in the southern part to more than 50 m. near the fault zone along the northern shore (Wadell, 1938). Flores Island in the southern section contained a sizable Maya town in preconquest times and today is the largest settlement of the Peten.

The water level of most of the Peten lakes varies seasonally. In Lake Peten Itza there is a difference of about 0.5 m. between dry and wet season levels, whereas Lake Yaxha is considerably reduced during the drier part of the year. A secular variation (50-year cycles) of water level in Lake Peten has also been noted (Sapper, 1894). The lakes have no surface outlets, but since their levels are fairly constant it is probable that they drain through underground fissures.

In most of the lakes small tropical fish, mainly cichlids, killifishes, and at least one catfish abound. These and other aquatic and amphibious animals like turtles, frogs, and iguanas, afforded a plentiful supply of protein food for the advanced Maya population that once inhabited this now sparsely peopled lake area.

Another hydrographic feature, called *akalché*, is common in the Peten and in the southeastern part of the Yucatan Peninsula. These are very low, clay-filled depressions within the present forests, and are covered with a thin sheet of water only during the rainy period. In size they vary from a few meters to 4.5 km. in diameter (Sapper, 1896, 1899). They may be old lake beds now filled by alluviation and organic growth, but more probably they are nothing more than old aguadas. These inter-

mittent swamps add to the difficulty of travel in the Peten during the wet season. It is significant that the major locale of Classic Maya civilization reached its apogee in the lake and akalché area of the Peten. The homeland of the Maya appears to have been a water environment, elements of which, such as aquatic plants and animals, held an important place in Maya art.

OTHER AREAS OF SUBSURFACE DRAINAGE IN KARST. These include the mountainous regions of limestone, such as the Alta Verapaz and the Cuchumatanes of Guatemala, the plateau of Chiapas, the Sierra de Oaxaca, and many sections of the Sierra Madre Oriental, all within the Atlantic watershed. Disappearing streams, vauclusian springs, and lakes with subterranean drainage are common hydrographic features of such areas. Lake Tepancuapan in the highland basin of Comitan in eastern Chiapas is a good example of a karst lake in a mountainous area.

Pacific Watershed

Receiving less rainfall and covering much less area than the Atlantic slope, the Pacific watershed of Middle America is characterized by surface streams of relatively small discharge. Only two large drainage basins occur within the Pacific versant: the Santiago-Lerma and the Balsas systems, both in Mexico. In Central America the largest river draining to the Pacific is the Rio Lempa of El Salvador. The Pacific watershed of Mexico discharges less than one-third of the total surface waters of the nation, and in the Central American countries probably a smaller proportion of the total surface runoff reaches the Pacific Ocean. Moreover, a marked seasonal regime characterizes most of the permanent streams of the Pacific watershed, in accordance with the long winter dry season (five to seven months) and the summer rainy period. Many of the smaller rivers are intermittent, not only in dry northwest-

101

ern Mexico, but also in southwestern Mexico and northern Central America. The Pacific watershed includes at least one river system, the Santiago-Lerma, draining much of the Altiplanicie Meridional[4] of Mexico, the lakes and streams of which have had a significant bearing on the growth of both preconquest Indian and modern population and economy in the central highlands of Mexico.

DRAINAGE OF BAJA CALIFORNIA. The arid peninsula of northwestern Mexico is comparatively insignificant, with only 0.16 per cent of the total discharge of the country. The Gulf of California watershed of the peninsula is extremely narrow and contains few definite stream courses. The Pacific watershed is much wider, the most significant streams in the northern part being those that originate on the western slope of the Sierra de Juarez, where winter rains and summer drought prevail. Most of these small streams are intermittent, but the Rio Guadalupe, north of Ensenada, and the Tijuana River, near the United States–Mexican border, are perennial with marked seasonal flow in their middle and lower courses. In the central desert intermittent arroyos may lack running water for years, but springs form occasional waterholes in the deeper valleys, from which the few desert nomads who roamed this area in preconquest times obtained drinking water. In the southern part of the peninsula permanent streams are not found except in the southern tip, where the Rio San Jose del Cabo drains the eastern and southern slopes of the high mountains.

COLORADO RIVER. This river, which empties into the head of the Gulf of California, has only 1 per cent of its drainage area in Mexico. This small area is limited to the delta. The latter is subject to the erratic floods that characterize the Colorado, but the construction of protective levees in the

river's lower course and the completion of the Boulder Dam upstream have perhaps solved the flood problem. Recently the Morelos Dam and reservoir were built to permit the utilization of the river water for irrigating 140,000 hectares in Mexico. Part of the lower course of the Colorado River serves as an international boundary between Mexico and the United States.

NORTHERN PACIFIC DRAINAGE OF MEXICO. This includes the small streams of the Altar Desert of northwestern Sonora and the larger rivers that rise in the Sierra Madre Occidental and cross the coastal lowlands from Sonora to central Nayarit. These larger rivers in southern Sonora and northern Sinaloa have a complex regime with two periods of maximum discharge. The period of highest water and floods occurs during the summer rainy season; secondary and much lower minimum occurs during January and February, when occasional winter cyclonic rains (*equipatas*) and snow melt from the higher mountain areas furnish some runoff. Farther south the rivers of southern Sinaloa and northern Nayarit have but one period of maximum discharge in summer (July–October), normal for most of the streams of Middle America.

The Rio Concepcion in northern Sonora is transitional between the ill-defined erratic stream courses of the Altar Desert and the normal streams that reach the sea. Rising in the sierra foothills near Nogales, the Concepcion flows as a permanent stream through the well-watered Magdalena Valley, but before reaching the sea it disappears in the coastal sands. Other streams of this area have the same characteristics; the larger Rio Sonora, for example, rises across the border in Arizona and flows through one of the north-south–trending foothill basins of the sierra; after passing by Hermosillo, its waters are gradually absorbed in the porous sands and gravels near the coast. Like the disappearing streams in karst topography, such rivers are often termed "cryptoric," but in the case of the Sonoran

---

[4] The term "Altiplanicie Meridional" is used hereinafter to mean the central plateau of Mexico, often formerly called the "Mesa Central."

streams disappearance is due to both evaporation and highly absorptive character of sand. As in many dry stream channels of the desert, the water table is close to the surface, and drinking water can be obtained by digging a few feet into the sand and gravel.

The Guaymas River is the first of the major streams of northwestern Mexico that has a definite lower course, permitting a discharge into the sea. From that basin southward all the rivers of the north Pacific drainage rise in the Sierra Madre Occidental, where they have carved deep canyons or *barrancas* into the steep western escarpment. The two largest river systems are the Yaqui and the Mesquital. The headwaters of both systems have eroded through the crest of the sierra to capture streams of the northern plateau that once flowed eastward to the Rio Grande or into the central desert. Interestingly, the captured headwaters of both the Yaqui and the Mesquital contain North American fish species that belong to the Rio Grande drainage, in contrast to the tropical fish typical of the middle and lower courses of the Pacific rivers (Meek, 1904; Osorio Tafall, 1946). The headwaters of the Yaqui belong to the upper Papigochic River in southwestern Chihuahua. After passing through the deep, narrow barranca of the Papigochic in present Tarahumar Indian country, the stream enters the state of Sonora as the Rio Yaqui, receiving as right-bank tributaries several streams (e.g. the Bavispe, Nacori, and Moctezuma-Nacozari) that drain north-south basins of the northeastern part of the state. The headwaters of the Mezquital rise in the plains around Durango City on the plateau surface. The captured streams include the gently flowing Poanas, Suchil, Tunal, and others, most of them fed by permanent springs that issue from recent volcanic rocks. Like the Papigochic, the Mesquital flows through a deep barranca before breaking out onto the coastal plain in Nayarit, where it takes the name San Pedro.

Between the Yaqui and the Mesquital are scores of other north Pacific rivers that head in the Sierra Madre. The more important of these include (from north to south) the Rio Mayo, Fuerte, Sinaloa, Culiacan, San Lorenzo, Piaxtla, Presidio, Baluarte, and Acaponeta, most of which flow through the state of Sinaloa. All are characterized by a seasonal regime, but the flow tends to become more voluminous and uniform southward, due to the increasing amount of annual rainfall.

In terms of preconquest Indian culture the most important aspect of the north Pacific rivers was annual summer flooding. In particular the primitive agricultural Indians in the dry north, such as the Yaqui, Mayo, and Cahita groups of the coastal lowlands, relied on the summer floods to moisten the river-bank soils where, after recession of high water, crops were planted. Farther south, within the coastal lowlands, where summer rains were sufficient for non-irrigated crops, the Indians of more advanced culture, such as the Tahue and Totorame, inhabited the flood-free river terraces, and higher parts of the natural levees. In both situations crops were cultivated, but the larger archaeological sites that indicate former dense populations along the rivers are invariably on the terraces.

Today these rivers, especially those in the more arid north, have become one of Mexico's most important economic assets. Dams and reservoirs have been constructed or are under construction on practically every major stream from the Sonora River to the Culiacan to furnish water for irrigation and control floods. On the Sonora River the dam Abelardo Rodríguez Luján, an important reservoir of 210 million cu. m., which retains the river's total discharge, has been constructed near Hermosillo. Within the Yaqui River drainage a large reservoir called La Angostura with a capacity of 270 million cu. m. is located on the Rio Bavispe 75 km. south of the United States frontier. On the lower Yaqui at the

103

beginning of the coastal plain, the dam of Alvaro Obregón was built to hold 3,000 million cu. m., one of the largest reservoirs in Mexico. From an economic point of view the Yaqui River is one of the most important streams in the entire country. Recently the Mocuzari dam and reservoir has been completed on the Mayo River to regulate its flow and furnish water for irrigating its fertile alluvial flood plain. Again, the Rio Fuerte's flow is regulated by the recent Miguel Hidalgo dam. The completion of another dam (the Jaina project) on the Sinaloa River will permit the irrigation of 250,000 hectares of new farming land. The Sinalona dam and reservoir, which holds 745 million cu. m., has been constructed on the Tamazula, the main tributary of the Culiacan River. Another dam and reservoir is planned for the Rio San Lorenzo farther south.

LERMA-SANTIAGO RIVER SYSTEM. Draining most of the Altiplanicie Meridional, the southern and most populous part of the Mexican Plateau, this is one of the largest hydrographic basins of Middle America. Although its average annual discharge is comparatively small (only 3.4 per cent of the national total), it is one of the most significant water features of Mexico in terms of economic use. It is divided into two sections by Lake Chapala: the upper, or Lerma, portion drains the plateau surface; the lower, or Santiago, section flows from Lake Chapala down the western plateau escarpment to the Pacific. This division has led some geographers and geologists to consider each section as a separate hydrographic system, an erroneous interpretation. To be sure, there is no doubt that the Lerma and Santiago rivers were independent drainage systems in the geologic past, but since the capture of the Lerma basin by the Rio Santiago, both drainages now form part of the same system.

The Lerma section in previous geological times (mid-Tertiary to Pleistocene) consti-

tuted a succession of large lakes arranged in steplike fashion with decreasing elevation from east to west. These lakes were formed by the damming of a previous normal river system by volcanic outpourings (Waitz, 1943; Osorio Tafall, 1946). Subsequently the lakes drained westward, one into the other, Lake Chapala and the Zacoalco-Sayula depression in Jalisco being the westernmost water bodies; eventually their waters found an outlet to the Pacific (possibly via the present Rio Ameca, according to Osorio Tafall). Subsequent deposition of volcanic sediment within the lakes plus the gradual draining by river capture and desiccation through increasing aridity, gave rise to the present magnificent flat-floored valleys with rich lacustrine soils that characterize the surface in the western part of the central plateau: Toluca, Tepuxtepec, Solis, Acambaro, Salvatierra, the series of small connected basins called the Bajio, and the marshes of Chapala. These fertile valleys were occupied possibly in late Pleistocene by some of the first migrants into central Mexico. Archaeological evidence indicates that between 1500 and 500 B.C. there were sedentary people practicing agriculture in the valleys of northern Michoacan (Noguera, 1948).

Within and adjacent to the present Lerma drainage are many lake basins that still lack natural surface outlets. These include the basins of Patzcuaro, Cuitzeo, and the Valley of Mexico, all of which probably once were part of the prevolcanic Tertiary Lerma drainage. Because of their great importance to early Indian culture, these lake basins of interior drainage are discussed more fully below.

The present Lerma drainage system originates in the spring-fed marshes and lakes in the southern end of Toluca Valley. Downstream the river receives many small tributaries, transversing portions of the states of Mexico, Queretaro, Guanajuato, Michoacan, and Jalisco. From Acambaro to La Piedad the Lerma flows through the

Bajio. It enters Lake Chapala at its eastern end, where it has built a large delta, formerly covered by extensive marsh.

Although the Lerma has a definite seasonal regime with a period of maximum discharge from June through October, it is a sluggish stream with slight gradient and many meanders along its course. Its water is now utilized almost completely along most of its course, although it still discharges an average annual 2,148 million cu. m. into Lake Chapala. At its headwaters its original springs are now tapped to provide water for Mexico City via the Lerma tunnel through the Sierra de las Cruces to the east; in the upper portion of its course the dam and reservoir of Tepuxtepec has been constructed; near Acambaro is the dam of Solis; and by means of a diversion channel and floodgates near Ojuelos, water is carried as far as Lake Yuriria. This lake is an artificial reservoir built by the Augustinian friar Diego de Chávez in the 16th century; surely this is the oldest man-made lake in Mexico and probably in the Americas.

Lake Chapala is a large natural storage basin 80 km. long, east to west, at 1500 m. elevation, formed in a tectonic trench (graben). It is the only remnant of the series of late Tertiary stepped basins, the capture of which has formed the present Lerma drainage system. Lake Chapala receives an appreciable discharge from the Lerma, Duero, and Zula rivers, as well as from its own local drainage area (9,040 sq. km.). Although shallow (average depth 8 m.), the average capacity of the lake is 6,000 million cu. m., but in exceptionally dry years its volume has decreased to 5,300 million cu. m., with some recession of the shoreline. The maximum volumes recently recorded were 11,678 million m. in October, 1926, and 11,491 cu. m. in October, 1935, accompanied by a marked expansion of the shoreline, inundating farm land around its edges. Were it not for the discharge of the Lerma River, the lake would gradually desiccate, for loss from surface evaporation exceeds runoff from its local drainage basin.

Since ancient times the fish resource of Lake Chapala has helped to support the farming population that has settled around its margins. Unfortunately, within the past few years water hyacinth (*Eichhornia* sp.) has invaded the northern and western shores of the lake, almost blocking canoe navigation and adversely affecting fishing.

The second portion of the Lerma-Santiago system lies below Lake Chapala. It is called the Rio Grande de Santiago (or the Rio Tololotlan) and begins from the outlet from the lake at Poncitlan, where since 1900 a diversion channel and floodgates have controlled the outflow for the purposes of irrigation and generation of hydroelectrical power. A few miles downstream are the falls of Juanacatlan, the first cataract of the Santiago as it begins to plunge over the plateau escarpment. The river crosses the southern end of the Sierra Madre Occidental in a northwesterly direction, proceeding down the escarpment through a narrow canyon which at times becomes a gorge; in Nayarit the river turns abruptly westward and crosses the narrow coastal plain to discharge an average 8,596 million cu. m. of water yearly into the Pacific Ocean a few kilometers north of the port of San Blas. The left-bank tributaries are of little importance, whereas those of the right bank carry large discharges. The most outstanding of these are the Verde, Juchipila, Bolaños, Apozolco, and Guaynamota rivers, all of which meet the main stream within the Sierra Madre or its foothills. The lower course of the Santiago within Nayarit is navigable for small craft, but access to the sea is difficult, due to the bars that impede traffic at the river mouth.

CENTRAL PACIFIC DRAINAGE AREA OF MEXICO. This area lies between the Lerma-Santiago and the Balsas basins. The streams are short and torrential, plunging down the steep slopes of the plateau escarpment. From north to south the largest streams are the Rio Ameca in Jalisco, the upper tributaries of which have eroded headward into the westernmost basins of the plateau surface; the Rio Armeria, which rises in western Jalisco and flows through Colima, furnishing water for irrigation along its lower course; and the Rio Coahuayana, the lower portion of which forms the boundary between Colima and Michoacan. Many of the smaller streams, especially those that drain the Pacific versant of Michoacan, were exploited for their rich gold placers in both preconquest and early colonial days.

The Balsas River system drains a large basin of 105,900 sq. km., an area almost as large as that of the Lerma-Santiago and one of the largest in Middle America. Despite the size of its drainage area, the Balsas system empties into the Pacific only 4.5 per cent of the total river discharge of Mexico. The main river flows through a large east-west trending geosyncline, bounded by the volcanic axis of Mexico (Cordillera Neovolcánica), the Sierra de Oaxaca, and the Sierra Madre del Sur. As it is thus cut off from moisture-bearing winds, the basin is comparatively dry. Most of the discharge is contributed by tributaries that drain the surrounding high mountains and plateau escarpments. Discharge is distinctly seasonal, with high water period during August, September, and October; during February and March the water stage of the middle and lower courses of the Balsas is greatly reduced.

The uppermost tributary (Atoyac Poblano) of the Balsas has eroded headward into the southeastern part of the Cordillera Neovolcánica to tap the basin of Puebla at 2150 m. elevation. Other important northern Balsas tributaries are the Nexapa, Amacuzac, Zitacuaro, and Tepalcatepec. The last-named occupies the northwestern extension of the Balsas geosyncline. These tributaries furnish a large part of the Balsas water, for they are fed by springs that issue from the porous volcanic lavas of the plateau, which contain enormous

106

quantities of ground water. One stream in particular, the Rio de Marques, a Tepalcatepec tributary, rises as the Cupatitzio River near Uruapan, Michoacan, and maintains a steady spring-fed flow of water much of which is utilized for irrigation. Such streams were used even in pre-Hispanic times for small-scale irrigation. Today they have a large power potential, and hydroelectric plants have already been established on some of them.

The eastern tributaries of the Balsas drain the dry western slope of the Sierra de Oaxaca; the southern ones drain the northern side of the Sierra Madre del Sur. In preconquest times the principal asset of these streams lay in their rich gold placers, exploited by local inhabitants to fill tribute requirements for the Nahua overlords in Tenochtitlan. Likely the streams of the Mixteca Alta and Baja were also the source of much of the gold fashioned into artifacts by Zapotec metallurgists of central Oaxaca.

The main stream of the Balsas system is called the Mezcala in its eastern portion; it receives the name Balsas only after passing the village of that name in its middle course. At its lower end the river breaks through the sierra to the ocean in a confined valley. Little use has been made of the Balsas water for agricultural ends; since the river flows through rugged terrain for most of its length, extensive arable flood plains are not available.

SOUTHERN PACIFIC DRAINAGE OF MEXICO. The narrow versant in Guerrero, Oaxaca, and Chiapas is characterized by short, turbulent streams that flood during the summer rainy period and are almost dry during the winter. Despite the lack of large streams, the relatively heavy rainfall of southwestern Mexico gives the rivers of that area a voluminous flow during the summer period, so that the combined discharge accounts for 12.3 per cent of the total for the country. The three largest streams of this drainage area are the Papagayo in Guerrero, the Verde and Tehuantepec in Oaxaca. In terms of human occupation the headwaters of the Verde are the most significant, for one of its tributaries, the Atoyac, drains the highland basin of Oaxaca, the seat of the preconquest Zapotec civilization. As it flows down the escarpment to the Pacific, however, the lower course of this river runs through deep valleys that have offered little in the way of agricultural possibilities, but do afford chances for the development of hydroelectric power. The Tehuantepec River, which flows from the Oaxaca highlands southeastward to the isthmian plains, is now being developed through the construction of a large dam and reservoir at El Marques, just below the confluence with the Rio Tequistlan.

PACIFIC DRAINAGE OF CENTRAL AMERICA. As indicated previously, an extremely narrow drainage area characterizes the Pacific versant of the Central American countries. Thus with few exceptions the streams are short and turbulent as they rush down the steep slopes of the high mountains that border the Pacific coast. Drainage basins are small, but heavy summer precipitation and abundance of springs induce a perennial flow in the larger rivers. This type of stream actually begins just east of the Isthmus of Tehuantepec in the narrow Pacific slope of Chiapas in Mexico and continues into Panama. Some of the longer Pacific streams, by means of headward erosion, have tapped various lakes and highland basins within the volcanic axis of Central America. For instance, many of the highland basins of the southern Guatemalan highlands formerly of interior drainage, now flow to the Pacific. Lake Amatitlan in Guatemala and those of Ilopango and Güija in El Salvador are examples of lake capture by Pacific streams. The lower courses of the rivers often have built up extensive alluvial fans and flood plains of fertile volcanic alluvium, which have afforded choice sites for former Indian as well as modern agricultural settlement.

The largest of the Pacific rivers in Central America are those that drain elongated structural basins. One of the best examples is the Rio Lempa, the largest river in El Salvador. The Lempa, 300 km. long, drains the lowland depression that separates the recent volcanic axis near the Pacific from the Sierra Madre of the Central American interior. The river rises in Guatemala near Esquipulas and enters the structural depression in northwestern El Salvador; a tributary, the Rio Desagüe, drains Lake Güija into the Lempa system. Following the depression eastward for some distance, the main river turns abruptly southward across the volcanic axis to the Pacific. Wide and turbulent, the lower part of the Lempa has been a physical barrier that separated Pipil and Lenca cultures in preconquest times and the provinces of San Salvador and San Miguel in colonial days. Recently the large dam and reservoir, "5 de Noviembre," was completed in the middle course of the river to regulate floods and generate electricity.[5]

Only short streams drain the Pacific side of Nicaragua, where the continental divide approaches within 20 km. of the coast. The largest river is the Estero Real, which drains the northern end of the Nicaraguan depression. On approaching the Gulf of Fonseca the waters of the Estero Real bifurcate into a maze of tidal channels bordered by mangrove swamp. Farther south the western side of the narrow volcanic isthmus that separates the lakes from the sea is drained by short, turbulent streams of small volume.

The Rio Tempisque and the Rio Diquis

[5] Hydrometric studies of the Rio Lempa and other rivers of El Salvador were begun in 1952 by the Centro Nacional de Agronomía and continued by a foreign engineering company. The Lempa is the only river in the country with several gauging stations along its course; during 1955–56 the minimum flow in its lower course was 43 cu. m./sec. The Instituto Tropical de Investigaciones Científicas in San Salvador has recently undertaken limnologic studies of various Salvadorean lakes.

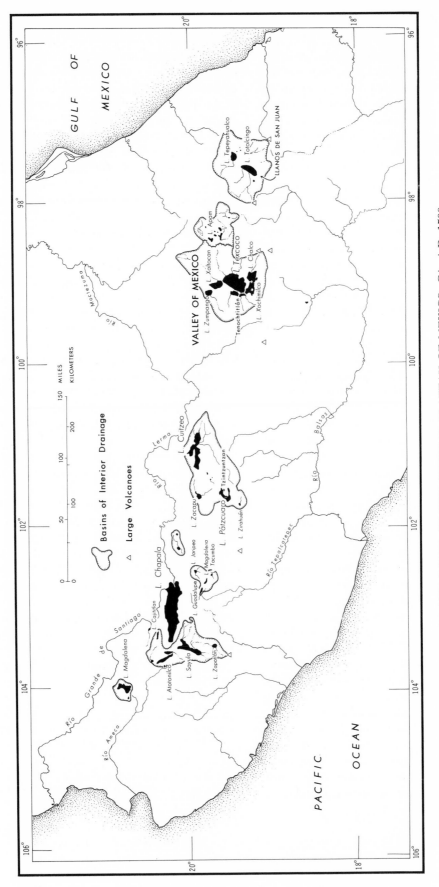

Fig. 4—AREAS OF INTERIOR DRAINAGE AND LAKES OF THE CENTRAL PLATEAU OF MEXICO, CA. A.D. 1500

are the largest streams of Costa Rica's Pacific versant; both drain structural depressions. The Tempisque, navigable in its lower course, drains the Guanacaste plain between the Peninsula of Nicoya and the volcanic axis, and flows into the Gulf of Nicoya. The headwaters of the Diquis rise in the Cordillera de Talamanca and as the Rio General flows through the depression of that name. The Diquis has a voluminous flow, as it drains areas of heavy rainfall. In its lower course it has built up an extensive flood plain, the natural levees of which have been developed for banana plantations.

Although 325 small voluminous streams drain the Pacific slope of Panama, the largest rivers are the Chepo, the Chucunaque, and the Tuira in the eastern part of the country. All three drain a continuous structural depression, which represents the northernmost extent of Andean orogeny. All are voluminous streams and are navigable in their lower courses; small craft can navigate the Tuira from its mouth on the Gulf of San Miguel upstream for a distance of 130 km. These rivers were the home of the Cuna Indians and later of the Choco, both riverine peoples and expert canoemen.

Areas of Interior Drainage

As mentioned previously, the areas of interior drainage in Middle America are of two types: (1) the arid basins of northern Mexico, where lack of sufficient precipitation has prevented the development of streams large enough to reach the sea; and (2) the small lake basins within the areas of recent volcanic activity, in particular the basins of the Neovolcanic Axis of central Mexico, where during the geologic past normal exterior drainage has been disrupted by lava dams. A third type of interior drainage, associated with karst hydrography and exemplified by the Peten basin and lakes of northern Guatemala, has been discussed above in the section on subsurface drainage.

LAKE BASINS OF VOLCANIC ORIGIN. Although small in area, these basins have since ancient times been of far greater significance to man than the larger desert basins. The greatest number of the volcanic lakes are found in central Mexico. Geologically most of these are closely associated with the late Tertiary Lerma drainage, discussed above. These include: the Zacoalco-Sayula and the Magdalena lake basins of Jalisco; a large number of lakes in Michoacan (some now drained artificially) including those of Magdalena (near Cotija), Zacapu, Zirahuen, Patzcuaro, and Cuitzeo; and, according to some authors, the Valley of Mexico (fig. 4).

The evidence for a former connection of the present lakes with the Lerma drainage is biological. Certain species of small Nearctic fish are peculiar to both the present Lerma system and the lakes, indicating a former connection (Meek, 1904). As indicated above, a series of large Tertiary and early Pleistocene lakes covered much of the Altiplanicie Meridional, being formed by the volcanic disruption of a mid-Tertiary stream system that extended from the Valley of Mexico to Jalisco. Most of these lakes were eventually drained by the present Lerma River, but those that now form interior drainage systems remained untapped. The fish that are common to both the Lerma River and the lakes consist mainly of two families: a group of small killifishes (Goodeidae) and the silversides (Atherinidae); the latter include the small *pescado blanco* (*Chirostoma* spp.), which for centuries has been one of the most important sources of protein food for the aboriginal population of central Mexico.

Most of the lakes of west-central Mexico have been gradually drying up since preconquest times through natural desiccation and alluviation; within the past 60 years some have been drained artificially, such as Lake Texcoco in the Valley of Mexico. In western Jalisco, Lake Magdalena, which in 1900 was still supplying large quantities

Fig. 5—REMNANTS OF LARGE PLEISTOCENE LAKES THAT OCCUPY DOWN-FAULTED DEPRESSIONS IN THE WESTERN PART OF THE ALTIPLANICIE MERIDIONAL (MESA CENTRAL)

Only the western tip of Lake Chapala, which occupies an E-W structural depression, appears. On the left are two shallow lake remnants that occur in the N-S Zacoalco-Savula graben.

of *pescado blanco* to the Guadalajara area, has now completely disappeared, as has Lake Zacapu in northern Michoacan. Both Lake Sayula of southwestern Jalisco and Lake Cuitzeo of northern Michoacan are greatly diminished in size during the dry season (fig. 5). The latter occupies a relatively large basin that includes the Valley of Morelia; it is fed by the Rio Grande de Morelia, which rises in the Serrania de Mil Cumbres north of Tacambaro, and by the short Rio Querendaro, which enters the lake from the east. Since the modern dam of Cointzio retains most of the water of the Rio Grande de Morelia, and most of the water of the Rio Querendaro is diverted for irrigation, Lake Cuitzeo now receives only a third of the former discharge from its tributary streams.

Of the lakes of interior drainage in west-central Mexico only Patzcuaro and Zirahuen in Michoacan appear to be maintaining their levels. Lake Zirahuen, a few kilometers southwest of Patzcuaro, is the youngest of the lakes, having been dammed by a lava flow that is quite visible today (fig. 6). It is the deepest of the volcanic lakes, having a maximum depth of 45 m. Lake Patzcuaro, one of the centers of Tarascan culture and one of the few remaining places of native lake fishing, is a much older water body, its maximum depth being only 15 m.; its periphery has shrunk appreciably since the 16th century (De Buen, 1944; Deevey, 1955).

The lake area of central Mexico coincides with the most important locale of highland Indian civilization in Mesoamerica, represented on the eve of the conquest by the cores of the Aztec and Tarascan states. The capital center of each state lay within or on the shores of lakes: Tenochtitlan of the Aztecs on Lake Texcoco and Tzintzuntzan of the Tarascans on Lake Patzcuaro. As Deevey (1955) intimates, the lake habitat was indeed significant in the development of large sedentary populations. Not only was the fish resource important for food

supply, but other aquatic animals—frogs, the salamander (*axolotl*), crayfish, shrimps, as well as water birds, such as ducks, grebes, coots, and herons that nested in the marshy lake shores—were taken for food in all the lakes. Moreover, at least in the lakes of the Valley of Mexico, the Indian inhabitants both before and after the conquest gathered and cultivated eggs and larvae of waterbugs (*Ahuautlea mexicana*), deposited on tule reeds within the lakes, to prepare the famous *ahuautli*, or Aztec "caviar," rich in protein and essential vitamins. Even algal scum (*techilatli*) was harvested from the lake surface, dried and eaten as small cakes (Deevey, 1955). Besides food, the marshy lake shores supplied a dense growth of tule reeds (*Typha* sp., *Scirpus* sp.) used throughout Mesoamerica for making mats (*petates*).

The Valley of Mexico was one of the largest of the basins of interior drainage within the neovolcanic axis until its artificial drainage was finally completed in 1900. At the time of the Spanish conquest five large lakes, fed by springs from surrounding porous volcanic materials and by short streams that drained the enclosing mountains, occupied the lower part of the basin. Saline Lake Texcoco was the largest and lowest, receiving the discharge of the neighboring lakes. In the southern part of the basin the fresh-water Xochimilco-Chalco lake system was important for the development of chinampa agriculture. In the northern section of the basin the saline lakes of Zumpango and Xaltocan were already in the process of desiccation. By the 15th century the Nahuatl inhabitants of the basin had become expert hydrologists, with the construction of aqueducts to bring potable water from the springs of Chapultepec to the island capital of Tenochtitlan, the construction of the famous dike of Nezahualcoyotl to regulate the lake level around the capital city, and the development of the chinampa agricultural system.

Bordering the Valley of Mexico on the

111

Zirahuen

Fig. 6.—LAKE ZIRAHUEN IN THE TARASCAN SIERRA, SOUTH OF LAKE PATZCUARO

A lava flow (upper right) blocked normal drainage to help form this deep lake.

northeast is a series of small interior basins known collectively as the Llanos de Apam, near which are the ruins of the immense ceremonial center of Teotihuacan. In each basin are lakes, some now partially desiccated, including Lake Apam, the lakes of Soltepec, Lake Atocha, Lake Tecocomulco, Lake Puerco, and Lake Huehuechoca.

In the eastern part of the volcanic plateau of central Mexico is a group of highland plains of interior drainage, called the Llanos de San Juan, or the "Region del Seco." Located entirely within the dry eastern part of the state of Puebla, these basins cover an area of approximately 8,000 sq. km. and drain into a former lake, Totolcingo, which has now dried to a soggy, saline marsh. At the eastern limits of the Llanos de San Juan are found many small, round crater lakes, called *axalpascos*, which also occur elsewhere in the neovolcanic range. These water bodies occupy the craters of cinder cones. When the crater lakes finally disappear through natural desiccation, the landforms with their dry lake bed are locally known as *xalapascos*.

Small lake basins of interior drainage also occur in the volcanic axis of Central America, particularly in Guatemala and El Salvador. As in Mexico, most of these lakes have formed in depressions of former exterior drainage subsequently blocked by lava dams. Some of the smaller lakes have formed in craters of cinder cones or have resulted from subsidence in sections of active vulcanism. As brought out above, many lakes of previous interior drainage within the Central American volcanic axis have now been captured by streams eroding headward from the Pacific.

Atitlan, often said to be the world's most beautiful lake, is the largest volcanic water body in Guatemala. Located at 1500 m. elevation, it was probably formed by eruptions of the volcanoes Atitlan and Toliman to the south, which blocked former drainage to the Pacific. It is the deepest highland lake in Middle America, with a maximum sounding of over 320 m. The surrounding steep mountain slopes give the lake an extraordinary setting, but the abrupt banks and deep offshore waters have prevented the accumulation of large areas of sediment and the growth of water grass, reeds, and algae that serve for feeding and spawning grounds for fish. Moreover, the low temperature and relatively high mineral content of the water probably have an adverse effect on fish life. The lake's fish resource is thus meager, with only three species represented: two small killifishes (*Poeçilia* and *Fundulus*) and one tropical cichlid (*Cichlasoma*); crabs are also present. Today of the many Indian villages on the lakeshore, only one (Santa Catarina Palopo) specializes in fishing; in preconquest times this lake appears to have attracted few inhabitants, in contrast to the importance of lacustrine environments in Mexico.

The smaller and shallower (40 m. maximum depth) Lake Amatitlan, lies south of Guatemala City. Although now tapped by a Pacific stream, it is considered here, for the surrounding archaeological sites suggest the lake's environmental importance in the pre-Spanish period. Despite a high mineral content of the water caused by adjacent hot springs, the abundance of aquatic vegetation around its shores gives it a good fish habitat and a much more abundant fish population than Lake Atitlan. The fishes are represented by seven species, including the cichlids and one tropical catfish (*Rhamdia*). Many smaller volcanic lakes are found in western Guatemala: Lake Ayarza (150 m. deep), the crater lake, Lake Azufrado (or Ixpaco), Lake Atescatempa, Lake Güija (now drained by a tributary of the Rio Lempa), and at least eight others.

In El Salvador Lake Coatepeque is the largest one without a natural surface outlet. Formed within a tectonic depression that was blocked by volcanic outpourings, it has a maximum depth of 120 m. and its water is slightly alkaline. The small lake of Cuscachapa near the archaeological site

113

of Tazumal represents a lake in its last stage of development; only 4 m. deep and 200 m. across, it will soon disappear. Former Lake Zapotitan, west of San Salvador, is now a marsh, having been tapped by a tributary of the Lempa River. Ilopango, the principal lake of El Salvador, also occupies a structural depression dammed by lava flows, but is drained by the Rio Jiboa to the Pacific. Most of the Salvadoran lakes at present are poor in food resources, which may be the result of overexploitation. The most common food fishes are the small perchlike cichlids (*Cichlasoma* spp., locally called *mojarras*) found in all the lakes (Hildebrand, 1925).

In Nicaragua the lakes of interior drainage are confined to small craters, similar to the Mexican *axalpascos*, found in the low, narrow volcanic range between the Pacific and the structural lowland. Like those of El Salvador, the lakes Asososco, Masaya, and Apoyo contain several species of cichlids, important food fish.

ARID BASINS OF INTERIOR DRAINAGE. These make up most of the Altiplanicie Septentrional, or northern plateau, surface; they represent the southernmost extent of the interior basins of western North America. In Mexico interior drainage extends from beyond the international boundary with the United States southeastward for 1350 km. to latitude 22°N., south of the city of San Luis Potosi. The Conchos River system, draining to the Rio Grande, divides this large area into (1) a northern section that covers northwestern Chihuahua and a small part of New Mexico and (2) a larger southern section that includes parts of the states of Chihuahua, Coahuila, Durango, Zacatecas, Nuevo Leon, and San Luis Potosi. Within these two sections streams flow from surrounding mountains and discharge into permanent and intermittent lakes that form in the lower parts of structural basins. In addition, during occasional rains water may flow in intermittent and ephemeral channels within the interior desert; some

discharge into intermittent lakes, others disappear in the desert gravels by absorption and evaporation.

The northern section of interior drainage of northwestern Chihuahua is dominated by three sizable rivers that head in the Sierra Madre Occidental and flow northward to discharge into permanent alkaline lakes. The Casas Grandes River begins on the eastern slopes of the sierra as the Rio San Miguel and empties into the Laguna de Guzman, a basin in an advanced stage of natural desiccation. From a distance saline deposits of whitish color can be seen ringing the diminishing shores of the lake. The second river is the Santa Maria which rises between two spurs of the sierra as the Rio San Jose, finally discharging its waters into the Laguna de Santa Maria, which like the Laguna de Guzman is gradually drying up. Since a substantial amount of the river water is used for irrigation, its flow into the lake has been markedly reduced. Finally, the Carmen River originates as the Santa Clara near the town of Tepehuanes in Durango; it empties into the Laguna de los Patos, which also shows evidence of becoming extinct. The combined average annual discharge of these three rivers is only 750 million cu. m.; nevertheless the ancient Casas Grandes people of northwestern Chihuahua utilized the flood-moistened riverbanks for cultivation, and later nomadic invaders fished the streams for food supply. Moreover, nomadic Jumanos gathered salt from the lakes for local use and for trade (Mendizábal, 1946). Today the river courses are lined with irrigated farms.

During the Pluvial period of the Pleistocene these streams probably were tributaries of the Rio Grande (or formed enormous lakes that spilled into the Rio Grande), for today they contain fish species that belong to that river system (Meek, 1904). With increasing dryness after the last ice retreat, the once voluminous rivers shrank to their present size; some authors (Meek,

114

1904; Osorio Tafall, 1946) believe that the capture of the headwaters of these streams by the vigorous Papigochic, which flows to the Pacific, helped to decrease their discharge.

In spite of its great size, the southern section of interior drainage has only three streams which carry appreciable amounts of water from the Sierra Madre Occidental into permanent lakes in the desert. Of these the Rio Nazas is the largest and one of the streams of major importance in the modern history of Mexico. Its lower course flows through an arid zone that has high quality soils. Thus in this area with the utilization of the river water for irrigation it has been possible to establish one of the most important agricultural centers of the country —the La Laguna District or Comarca Lagunera—and one which now shows signs of progressive industrialization.

The Nazas rises in the state of Durango on the eastern slopes of the Sierra Madre Occidental, where its headwaters are formed by the confluence of the Oro and Ramos rivers. It flows westward and enters the Comarca Lagunera near Ciudad Lerdo. It passes between the cities of Gomez Palacio and Torreon, and near the agricultural center of San Pedro de las Colonias it debouches into the remnant of the once extensive Laguna de Mayran. In its lower part the channel of the Nazas was a devious one, and there is still surface evidence that at one time it emptied into the Laguna de Tlahualilo to the north, and possibly once flowed into the Laguna de Viesca to the south. At the present time the lower channel has been canalized as it enters the Laguna de Mayran. This lake, however, is disappearing, due to the storage of the Nazas water behind the dam of Lazaro Cardenas, recently constructed at El Palmito on the upper course of the river. This reservoir has a capacity of 3000 million cu. m., which regulates the discharge, now utilized almost entirely for irrigating the extensive cotton and wheat fields in the Comarca Lagunera. The average annual discharge of the Nazas is about 1300 million cu. m., or somewhat more than half that of the Conchos, but more than the total discharge of all other streams that enter the arid interior basins of northern Mexico.

The other two sierra streams that flow into the central desert are the Rio Aguanaval and the Arroyo de la Parida. The former rises in the state of Zacatecas and flowing northward as an intermittent stream empties into the Laguna de Viesca, just south of the Comarca Lagunera. The upper course of this river is ephemeral, most of its flow disappearing in gravel and sand; only the higher flood waters of summer succeed in crossing the desert to the lake. The intermittent flow in its lower course is formed by the discharge from the tributary arroyos of Las Cruces and Sain Alto. The Laguna de Viesca shows strong signs of desiccation, which has been accelerated due to the increased utilization of the Aguanaval water for irrigation. In preconquest times the Irritilas Indians of the vicinity gathered salt encrusted along the shores of this lake for extensive trade (Mendizábal, 1946).

To the north the intermittent Arroyo de la Parida rises from springs in the sierra foothills of southern Chihuahua and northern Durango and flows northwestward into the Laguna de las Palomas, an intermittent desert lake, once important for its salt deposits.

Like the streams of northwestern Chihuahua, the Nazas, the Aguanaval, and their respective lakes contain Rio Grande types of fish, biological evidence for a former connection with that river system. It is known that the Laguna de Mayran extended over a vast area of Parras Basin during Pleistocene; probably at that time it had an outlet to the Rio Grande. The capture of the headwaters of the Nazas by the more aggressive Mesquital in Durango possibly aided the increasingly dry climate to de-

115

crease the flow into the lake after the close of the Pleistocene (Osorio Tafall, 1946).

Two large areas of deficient surface streams occur within the southern section of interior drainage in northern Mexico. One is the Bolson de Mapimi of southeastern Chihuahua and western Coahuila within the heart of the central desert. The area is characterized by extreme aridity (less than 250 mm. of rain annually). There are no well-defined stream channels. Stream beds are formed after infrequent heavy rainstorms, but they are obliterated by wind action after months of dryness. In the eastern part of the region there exist important ground water resources, which are now being utilized.

The second area deficient in streams is called El Salado, a vast basin and range section of the plateau that extends from the Comarca Lagunera southward to San Luis Potosi. In this area there are few indications of stream courses, for the intermittent arroyos that descend from mountain flanks disappear in the plains without forming definite channels. Morphologically, the eastern part of this region constitutes a karstic area developed in the prevailing limestone rocks that characterize the geology of much of eastern Mexico. Thus the surface discharge is quite ephemeral, for the water almost immediately penetrates into the porous limestone. Within the flattish plains areas, after heavy showers rain water covers wide areas without forming definite channels. Such flats are locally called *bajios*. In the lower sections of the bajios wherever an impermeable clay surface develops, intermittent lakes and salt flats occur. Salt flats are most common in the western part of El Salado, where some, such as those of Santa Maria and Peñol Blanco east of Zacatecas, have been used since colonial days for salt supply. The combination of karst topography and meager rainfall makes the El Salado area one of the poorest agricultural areas of Mexico. In preconquest times it was sparcely inhabited by desert nomads, and today is largely devoted to stockraising.

REFERENCES

Benassini and García Quintero, 1955-57
Casares, 1905
Cole, 1910
Contreras and Cerezo, 1958
Davis, A. P., 1900
De Buen, 1943, 1944, 1945
Deevey, 1955, 1957
Dirección General de Irrigación, 1954-55
Dollfus and Montserrat, 1868
Hatt, 1953
Heilprin, 1891
Hildebrand, 1925
Humboldt, 1811
Meek, S. E., 1904, 1907, 1908
Mejía, 1927
Mendizábal, 1946
Merz, 1906
Meza Calix, 1916
Morley, 1938
Noguera, 1948
Orozco y Berra, 1864
Osorio Tafall, 1946
Oviedo y Valdés, 1851-55
Panama, Inst. de Fomento Económico, 1958
Pearse et al., 1936
Peñafiel, 1884
Sapper, 1894, 1896, 1899
Tamayo, 1946, 1949, 1958, 1959a, 1959b
Terry, 1956
Wadell, 1938
Waitz, 1943

TABLE 1—ESTIMATE OF SURFACE WATER RESOURCES (GROSS DISCHARGE) IN
RIVERS OF THE REPUBLIC OF MEXICO ARRANGED ACCORDING
TO HYDROLOGIC AREAS*

Hydrologic Area and Associated Rivers	Station	Basin Area, km²	Mean Annual Discharge in Millions M³	Discharge/ km² Thousands of M³	Period of Observation
1	2	3	4	5	6
1. *Baja California, northern zone:*		37,260	312		
Rio Tijuana	At mouth, excluding Barret Reservoir, U.S.A.	3,780	25	6.5	1937-55 (excluding 1941)
Rio Guadalupe	Near mouth	2,530	19	7.3	1937-55 (excluding 1941)
Streams between the Guadalupe and Sto. Domingo (S. Carlos, Sto. Tomas, S. Vicente, and S. Rafael	Near mouth	7,280	100	13.8	1937-55 (excluding 1941)
Rio Santo Domingo	Near mouth	990	20	20.2	1937-55 (excluding 1941)
Streams south of the Sto. Domingo to the southern limit of southern zone, both watersheds (arroyos Rosario, Sta. Catarina, Delfino, San Andres, S. Miguel, etc.)	Near mouth	22,680	148	6.5	1937-55 (excluding 1941)
2. *Baja California, southern zone:* Streams within area limited on north by northern zone and on south by southern zone (the rainiest section). (arroyos S. Venancio, Sto. Domingo, S. Luis, Salado, Malva, Conejo, Ballenas, etc.)	Near mouth	22,120	145	6.5	1937-55 (excluding 1941)
Streams within rainiest section of southern zone.	Near mouth	5,800	117	20.2	1937-55 (excluding 1941)
3. *Colorado River:* Colorado River	Between U.S.A. boundary and mouth	3,840	1,850		
4. *Northern Pacific, northern zone:*		155,220	4,258	5.6	1929-55
Rio Sonoyta	Near mouth	3,360	19	5.6	1929-55
Streams between the Sonoyta and the Concepcion	Near mouth	2,280	13	5.6	1929-55
Rio Concepcion	Near mouth	25,440	151	5.9	1929-55
Rio San Ignacio	Near mouth	2,560	14	5.6	1929-55
Rio Bacavachic, etc.	Near mouth	8,880	49	7.6	1929-55
Rio Sonora	Hermosillo	21,560	171	7.9	1929-55
Rio Guaymas	Near mouth	5,160	41	7.9	1929-55
Streams between the Sonora and the Guaymas	Near mouth	2,640	15	5.6	1929-55
Rio Yaqui	Chiculi (A. Obregon Reservoir)	69,960	2,790	39.9	1929-55
Arroyo Cocoraqui	Near mouth	1,300	58	44.6	1929-55
Rio Mayo	Navojoa (near mouth)	12,080	937	77.6	1929-55

*After Benassini and García Quintero (1955–57), with additions and corrections.

(Continued through p. 121)

Hydrologic Area and Associated Rivers	Station	Basin Area, km²	Mean Annual Discharge in Millions M³	Discharge/ km² Thousands of M³	Period of Observation
1	2	3	4	5	6
5. *Northern Pacific, southern zone:*		*106,140*	*22,600*		
Rio Fuerte	San Blas (near mouth)	34,640	5,933	171.3	1924-55
Rio Sinaloa	Near mouth	13,240	2,176	164.3	1924-55
Rio Mocorito	Guamuchil (near mouth)	1,730	131	75.6	1924-55
Streams south of the Mocorito (Rio Tule, etc.)	Near mouth	2,280	172	75.6	1924-55
Rio Culiacan	Southern Pacific Railroad Bridge	16,400	3,357	204.7	1924-55
Rio San Lorenzo	Near mouth	10,030	1,941	193.6	1924-55
Streams between the S. Lorenzo and the Elota (Venadillo, etc.)....	Near mouth	1,400	311	222.3	1924-55
Rio Elota	Near mouth	1,970	494	251.1	1924-55
Rio Piaxtla	Near mouth	6,870	2,034	296.2	1924-55
Rio Quelite	Near mouth	1,400	498	350.1	1924-55
Rio Presidio	Near mouth	5,080	1,779	350.1	1924-55
Rio Cañas, etc. (between the Baluarte and the Acaponeta).....	Near mouth	1,160	343	295.9	1924-55
Rio Baluarte	Near mouth	4,610	1,861	404.0	
Rio Acaponeta	Near mouth	5,330	1,578	295.9	
6. *Rio Mezquital (San Pedro) system:*		*27,980*	*2,642*		
Laguna San Bartolo	Laguna San Bartolo	330	11	33.0	1943-55
Area between the San Pedro and the Acaponeta	Near mouth	1,840	175	95.0	1944-55
Rio Mezquital (San Pedro)	San Pedro (near mouth)	25,810	2,456	95.0	1944-55
7.A. *Rio Lerma system:*		*37,990*	*2,561*		
Rio Lerma	Yurecuaro	33,800	2,148	63.6	1929-55
Rio Grande de Morelia	Quirio	1,280	146	114.6	1942-54
Lake Cuitzeo	Individual basin of Lake Cuitzeo	2,030	186	91.7	1942-54
Lake Patzcuaro	Individual basin	880	81	91.7	1942-54
B. *Lake Chapala-Rio Santiago system:*		*86,780*	*9,507*		
Lake Chapala	Individual basin	9,040	713	78.9	1929-55
Laguna de Sayula	Individual basin	1,620	134	82.7	1942-55
Laguna de Atotonilco	Individual basin	380	37	97.4	1942-55
Laguna de San Marcos	Individual basin	300	27	89.1	1942-55
Rio Santiago	Corona-Yago Section (near mouth)	75,440	8,596	113.9	1929-55
8. *Central Pacific (southern Jalisco):*		*43,220*	*9,489*		
Streams between the Santiago and the Huicicila	Near mouth	920	170	185.2	1941-55
Rio Huicicila	Paso de Arocha (near mouth)	1,230	228	185.2	1941-55
Rio Ameca	Near mouth	12,520	3,599	287.5	1941-55
Streams between the Ameca and Armeria (Tomatlan, S. Nicolas, Cuetzamala, Purificacion, Cihuatlan, etc.)	Near mouth	11,080	2,690	242.8	1943-55
Rio Armeria	Near mouth	9,840	1,200	121.9	1941-55
Streams between the Armeria and Coahuayana	Near mouth	440	107	242.8	1943-55
Rio Coahuayana	Callejones (near mouth)	7,190	1,495	207.8	1941-55

118

Hydrologic Area and Associated Rivers	Station	Basin Area, km²	Mean Annual Discharge in Millions M³	Discharge/ km² Thousands of M³	Period of Observation
1	2	3	4	5	6
9. *Rio Balsas system:*		*116,460*	*16,370*		
Streams between the Coahuayana and the Balsas (Ostuta, Coalcoman, Chula, Carrizal, etc.) ....Near mouth		7,920	1,646	207.8	1941-55
Rio Balsas ....Near mouth		105,900	12,186	115.1	1928-55
Streams between the Balsas and the Jeronimito (Union, Ixtapa, etc.)		2,640	2,538	961.5	1953-55
10. *Southern Pacific, northern zone:*		*67,460*	*29,700*		
Streams between the Ixtapa and Atoyac (Jeronimito, Petatlan, Coquilla, San Luis, Tecpan, etc.)..Near mouth		4,160	4,000	961.5	1953-55
Rio Atoyac ....Las Palmas (near mouth)		730	833	1,149.0	1953-55
Streams between the Atoyac and Papagayo (Coyuca, Sabana, etc.) ....Near mouth		11,960	1,885	961.5	1953-55
Rio Papagayo ....Near mouth		7,280	5,634	773.9	1951-54
Streams between the Papagayo and Sta. Catarina (Nexpan, S. Luis, etc.) ....Near mouth		3,520	2,724	773.9	1951-54
Rio Santa Catarina (Ometepec) ....Near mouth		6,680	3,619	541.7	1951-54
Streams between the Sta. Catarina and Verde ....Near mouth		1,680	910	541.7	1951-54
Rio Verde ....Near mouth		17,680	4,130	223.6	1936-55
Streams between the Verde and the Tehuantepec (Grande, Colatepec, Copalita, etc.) ....Near mouth		8,880	2,074	223.6	1936-55
Rio Tehuantepec ....Near mouth		10,520	1,439	136.8	1936-55
Streams between the Tehuantepec and los Perros ....Near mouth		440	50	112.4	1936-55
Rio de los Perros ....Near mouth		1,010	89	88.0	1936-55
Streams between the los Perros and the Chicapa ....Near mouth		440	95	216.1	1936-55
Rio Chicapa ....Near mouth		640	220	344.2	1936-55
Rio San Jose and Niltepec ....Near mouth		640	508	793.1	1936-55
Rio Ostuta ....Near mouth		1,200	1,490	1,242.0	1936-55
11. *Southern Pacific, southern zone:*		9,905	15,998		
Streams between the Ostuta and the Pijijiapan ....Near mouth		3,120	3,875	1,242.0	1936-55
Streams between the Pijijiapan and the Cahuacan (Pijijiapan, Coapan, Novillero, Pueblo Nuevo, etc.) ....Near mouth		5,320	10,269	1,930.3	1936-55 / 1944-55
Rio Cahuacan ....Cahuacan (near mouth)		265	694	2,618.5	1944-55
Rio Suchiate† ....Suchiate (near mouth)		1,200	1,160		1944-55
12. *Rio Conchos (Rio Grande system):*		*77,090*	*2,196*		
Rio Conchos ....Ojinaga (near confluence with the Rio Grande)		77,090	2,196	28.5	1912-55
13. *Rio Salado, etc. (Rio Grande system):*		*110,060*	*1,293*		
Arroyos S. Antonio, la Costura, Caballo, Zorra, Buey, etc. ....Near mouth		27,520	268	9.7	1924-54

†Only the discharge from Mexican territory (450 km²) is considered.

119

Hydrologic Area and Associated Rivers	Station	Basin Area, km²	Mean Annual Discharge in Millions M³	Discharge/ km² Thousands of M³	Period Observa*
1	2	3	4	5	6
Arroyo de las Vacas	Villa Acuña				
	(near mouth)	930	23	24.3	1933-5
Arroyo San Diego	Jimenez (near mouth)	2,200	128	58.1	1933-5
Rio San Rodrigo	El Moral (near mouth)	1,730	62	35.7	1933-5
Rio Escondido	V. de Funte				
	(near mouth)	3,310	30	8.9	1933-5
Arroyos S. Nicolas, Texas, Resaca, Castaña, Caballero, etc.	Near mouth	9,320	125	13.4	1924-5
Rio Salado	Near mouth	65,050	657	10.1	1924-5
14. *Rios San Juan and Alamo* (*Rio Grande system*):		*38,210*	*1,291*		
Rio Alamo	Ciudad Mier				
	(near mouth)	4,380	166	37.9	1925-5
Rio San Juan	Marte R. Gomez				
	Reservoir (El Azucar)	33,830	1,125	33.3	1924-5
15. *Northern Gulf area:*		*54,450*	*5,773*		
Rio San Fernando	San Fernando				
	(near mouth)	15,640	756	48.3	1931-5
Rio Purificacion or Soto la Marina	Near mouth	20,680	2,270	109.8	1931-5
Arroyo Carrizal, etc.	Near mouth	3,440	447	103.1	1931-5
Rio Tamesi	Confluence with the Rio Panuco	17,690	2,300	130.1	1931-5
16. *Rio Panuco system:*		*66,300*	*17,300*		
Rio Panuco	Near mouth	66,300	17,300	260.9	1937-5
17. *Central Gulf area:*		*37,810*	*28,318*		
Rio Tuxpan	Near mouth	5,440	4,231	777.7	1937-5
Rio Cazones	Near mouth	2,760	2,147	777.7	1937-5
Rio Tecolutla	Near mouth	8,080	7,529	931.8	1937-5
(Other rivers)	Near mouth	3,920	3,653	931.8	1937-5
Rio Nautla	Near mouth	2,270	2,465	1,085.9	1937-5
Rios Misantla, Colipa, Juchique and others	Near mouth	1,960	1,723	879.2	1937-5
Rio Actopan	Near mouth	1,940	1,308	672.5	1947-5
Rio la Antigua	Near mouth	2,880	2,817	978.1	1947-5
Other streams	Near mouth	570	334	585.4	1947-5
Rio Jamapa	El Tejar	1,800	598	331.1	1947-5
Rio Cotaxtla	Paso del Toro	1,550	1,297	839.8	1947-5
Laguna Tepeyahualco	Individual basin	4,640	216	46.6	1937-5
18. *Southern Gulf area:*		*192,420*	*174,967*		
Rio Blanco, etc.	Near mouth	5,310	3,845	723.4	1947-5
Rio Papaloapan	Near mouth	37,380	37,290	997.7	1947-5
Rio Coatzacoalcos	Near mouth	21,120	22,394	1060.6	1947-5
Rio Tonala and others between this river and the Grijalva	Near mouth	6,680	6,238	933.9	1947-5
Rio Grijalva–Usumacinta system	Near mouth	121,930	105,200	862.8	1947-5
19. *Campeche and Quintana Roo area:*		*35,110*	*4,285*		
Rio Chumpan	Near mouth	2,000	434	217.2	1948-5
Rio Candelaria	Near mouth	7,790	1,692	217.2	1948-5
Rio Champoton	Near mouth	6,080	885	145.5	1948-5
Rio Hondo‡	Near mouth	19,240	1,275	145.5	1948-5
20 and 20A. *Altiplanicie Septentrional: basins of interior drainage, northern zone:*		*44,680*	*856*		
Rio Casas Grandes	Entire contributing basin	16,600	294	17.7	1912-5

‡Only the discharge from Mexican territory (8,754 km²) is considered.

Hydrologic Area and Associated Rivers	Station	Basin Area, km²	Mean Annual Discharge in Millions M³	Discharge/ km² Thousands of M³	Period of Observation
1	2	3	4	5	6
Rio Santa Maria	Entire contributing basin	10,680	175	16.4	1912-55
Rio del Carmen	Entire contributing basin	11,880	271	22.8	1912-55
Laguna de Bavicora	Individual basin	1,680	34	20.4	1912-55
Laguna de Bustillos	Individual basin	2,720	58	21.5	1912-55
Laguna Mexicanos	Individual basin	1,120	24	21.5	1912-55
21. *Bolson de Mapimi* (scant surface discharge)					
22. *Altiplanicie Septentrional: basins of interior drainage, southern zone:*					
Rio Nazas	Entire contributing basin	85,530	1,661	37.0	
Rio Aguanaval	La Flor	20,800	143	6.9	1912-55
Laguna de Mayran	Individual basin	6,800	23	3.4	1912-55
Laguna Viesca	Individual basin	5,760	20	3.4	1912-55
Laguna Palomas	Individual basin	18,800	104	5.6	1912-55
Laguna de Santiaguillo	Individual basin	1,790	69	38.3	1912-55
24. *El Salado* (scant surface discharge)					
25. *Valle de Mexico:*		*5,000.4*	*361.78*		
Rio de las Avenidas de Pachuca and Rio Tezontepec	Confluence of both	1,449.0	9.73	6.713	1920-56
Rio San Juan Teotihuacan	Tepexpan	505.5	6.79	13.426	1920-56
Rio Papalotla	La Grande	182.0	9.36	51.45	1920-56
Rio Xalapango	Atenco	61.2	4.02	65.74	1920-56
Rio Coxcacoaco (Magdalena)	San Andres	48.6	6.45	132.67	1920-56
Rio San Lorenzo	Texcoco	32.5	3.31	101.88	1920-56
Rio Chapingo	Chapingo	18.4	2.30	125.00	1920-56
Rio San Bernardino	Near mouth	15.0	1.59	105.98	1920-56
Rio Santa Monica	El Tejocote	38.2	3.32	86.96	1920-56
Rio Coatepec	Near mouth	109.3	7.13	65.22	1920-56
Rio de la Compañia and Arroyo San Francisco	Confluence with both	420.2	22.70	54.02	1920-56
Rio Ameca	San Luis Ameca	397.5	17.02	42.82	1920-56
Rio San Lucas y Santiago	Lake Xochimilco	150.1	13.56	90.37	1920-55
Rio S. Juan de Dios and San Buenaventura	Near the confluence with Rio Ameca	111.5	10.08	90.37	1920-55
Rio Churubusco	Xoco	179.7	22.64	126.00	1920-56
Rio Mixcoac	Mixcoac	37.0	10.63	287.16	1920-56
Rio Becerra	Viaducto	10.8	1.44	133.70	1920-52
Rio Tacubaya	Belem	10.9	1.52	139.63	1920-55
Rio Tecamachalco	Tecamachalco reservoir	11.7	1.54	132.56	1920-56
Rio San Joaquin	San Joaquin reservoir	19.3	2.62	136.27	1920-56
Rio de los Remedios	San Juan Ixhuatepec	497.3	92.48	185.96	1920-56
Rio Cuatitlan	Guadalupe reservoir	289.5	92.95	241.42	1920-56
Rio Tepozotlan	Concepcion reservoir	57.7	13.93	241.42	1920-56
25. *Laguna de Apam, etc.*		*347.5*	*4.67*	*13.426*	*1920-56*
NATIONAL TOTAL		1,472,835	353,856		

4. The American Mediterranean

ALBERT COLLIER

The oceans and the peripheral lands have stood longer than man and since his arrival they have fed him, transported him, buried him, and drowned him. Through all his time on Earth, and all through his struggles from one primitive step to another, his tools, his bones, his garbage have fallen in the dirt. The stable residues of the remains and artifacts accumulate in the soil and under the rocks, in the lakes and the rivers, and, to a degree, become scattered in the sea. In the very long run the sea will be the recipient of all of it, as the incessant and eroding rains keep washing down the exposed surfaces of the earth. But man does not need to die and be ground to bits to be received by the sea; he may live upon it and fish upon it.

It does not welcome him at all, but if he respects it and provides himself with safeguards against the loss of buoyancy and sustenance, he can survive on it for great periods. How well he learns to do this determines his success in migrating across the sea barrier from one shore to another. In an even more immediate sense it can determine the extent to which his populations can maintain themselves and multiply, for the sea, if intelligently harvested, is bountiful.

The limits within which this can be accomplished are imposed by the nature of the seaboard itself, as well as the cultural status of the peoples concerned. To determine these limits and define the complex interaction between man and the living and nonliving resources of the sea, especially in retrospect, requires some degree of knowledge concerning the nature of the sea as an environment.

In this article we are interested in the Gulf of Mexico and the Caribbean Sea as an environmental unit with a bearing on the cultures of the various groups of Middle American Indians. These two bodies of water will be mentioned collectively as the American Mediterranean. After a brief description of the combined geographical and geomorphological aspects of the system, the features deemed to be of most significance to the surrounding cultures will be discussed from the oceanographic point of view.

Basins of the American Mediterranean

The topography of the American Mediterranean falls into a series of segments which

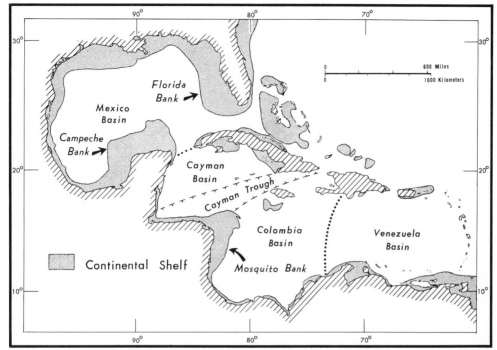

FIG. 1—OUTLINE OF THE AMERICAN MEDITERRANEAN SHOWING THE DISPOSI-
TION OF THE CONTINENTAL SHELF AND THE MAJOR BASINS

are set off from each other by ridges, some of which rise above the water surface (fig. 1).

The southern Caribbean has two such segments or basins, the easternmost being the Venezuela Basin, to the west of which lies the Colombia Basin. The Colombia Basin articulates on the Cayman Trough by means of the Jamaica Rise. North of the Cayman Trough we find the Cayman Basin, a vestibule before the entrance of the Gulf of Mexico. The Gulf of Mexico itself is a large simplified basin with no subdivisions (see p. 124).

These basins are walled in for the most part with steeply sloping sides. The eastern aspect of the Venezuela Basin, embracing the lesser Antilles, opens as a weir into the Atlantic, there being some nine or ten passages of significant depth. The deepest openings in this sector are the St. Lucia Channel, the Dominica Channel, and the Anegada Passage. Thus the Venezuela Basin is the first receiver of the water mov-

ing in from the tropical Atlantic. The north wall of this basin rises above the surface as Hispaniola and Puerto Rico. The south wall is formed by Venezuela. The separation between the Venezuela and the Colombia basins does not appear to be so well defined on the navigators' chart. However, there is a ridge which rises from the bottom and extends in a southerly direction about 320 km. from Punta Beata of Hispaniola. The appearance of this ridge as it rises from the floors of the basins would be that of a fairly respectable mountain range. At several points it slopes about 1,850 m. in less than 50 km. (3.7%), and at one point it rises nearly 1,700 m. in 16 km. (10.7%).

The Colombia Basin is encircled by the land masses of Colombia, Panama, Costa Rica, Nicaragua, and the east portion of Hispaniola. The northwest boundary is formed by the Jamaica Rise, which protrudes above the sea surface to form Jamaica Island.

The Cayman Basin is enclosed by Cuba

123

on the northeast and by Honduras, British Honduras, and the Yucatan Peninsula on the south and west. In the southern portion of the Cayman Basin the Cayman Trough extends eastward to Windward Passage.

The Caribbean, viewed as a whole, is characterized by segmentation into deep basins surrounded by steeply inclined ridges. By contrast the Gulf of Mexico has a rather uniform structure with steep slopes in only three areas: Campeche Bank, off Veracruz (Mexico), and southern Florida.

On the other hand, the Gulf of Mexico has a much greater area of continental shelf than has the Caribbean. The only place that the latter has shelves of significance are Mosquito Bank and, to a much lesser extent, the coast of Venezuela. This point may have some indirect significance to the anthropologist (see pp. 132–33).

Campeche Bank spreads out from the Yucatan Peninsula and under the waters of the Gulf of Mexico as far as 245 km. In general, it is a gradually downward-sloping plain which terminates abruptly at the 180-m. (100-fathom) contour. At this point the depth increases almost precipitously all around the bank; in one case it falls immediately from 180 to 2,560 m. (100 to 1,400 fathoms). Almost due north of Punta Yalkubu, which is near the center of the northern periphery of Yucatan Peninsula, a depth of 3,600 m. (2,000 fathoms) is found within 24 km. of the 180-m. (100-fathom) curve, a slope of 145 m. per km. (14.5%). If we draw a line southeastward from Cabo Catoche into the Cayman Basin and examine the depths along it, we will discover a slope which is of some importance in the oceanography of the Gulf of Mexico. Near the end of this line we will find a sounding of 4,320 m. (2,400 fathoms) about 8 km. from the 1,800-m. (1,000-fathom) curve—a slope of 320 m. per km. (32%); from the 1,800-m. (1,000-fathom) curve into Cabo Catoche the slope is only 12.5 m. per km. (1.25%).

Along the northern aspect of the western end of Cuba the 180-m. (100-fathom) contour is on the order of 1.5–2.5 km. from the 18-m. (10-fathom) line. Between the former and the 1,800-m. (1,000-fathom) contour the slope is about 100 m. per km. (10%), but beyond this the rate of drop decreases considerably.

To the north of Cuba lies the wide Florida Bank—an expanse of some 245 km. between the mainland and the 180-m. (100-fathom) contour. The gradient between the edge of the shelf and the principal plain of the bottom of the Gulf of Mexico is similar to that mentioned in the paragraphs above —about 114 m. per km. (11.4%).

On the opposite side of the Gulf and about 120 km. north of Tampico, there begins a constriction of the continental shelf which extends 400 km. south in the vicinity of Veracruz. The maximum constriction occurs 80 km. north of Veracruz; here the slope between dry land and the 180-m. (100-fathom) contour is 11.5 m. per km. (1.15%). Between the latter and the 1,800-m. (1,000-fathom) contour it is 68 m. per km. (6.8%) and immediately beyond this, it is about 28 m. per km. (2.8%).

The remaining underwater features of the Gulf of Mexico have already been referred to, namely the broad areas of the continental shelf. These extend entirely around the northern aspect of the Gulf and southward along the coasts of Florida and Mexico, with the exception of a somewhat restricted area between the Mississippi Delta and Cape San Blas to the east.

The dominating feature of the northern Gulf coast is, of course, the Mississippi Delta, which has encroached upon the continental shelf almost to the 180-m. (100-fathom) line, the latter being barely 15 km. from the entrance to South Pass. If an arbitrary line is drawn from Cameron, Louisiana, to Biloxi, Mississippi, with a slight inward arch, the effects of this great river on the shoreline can be appreciated.

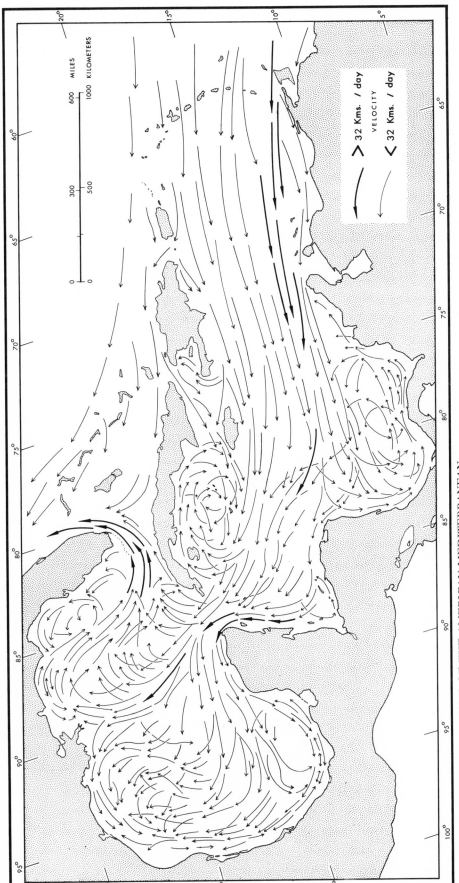

FIG. 2—SURFACE CURRENTS OF THE AMERICAN MEDITERRANEAN

This diagram is a composite of currents shown for all months of the year on pilot charts published by the U. S. Hydrographic Office. The direction and velocity of these currents are variable and the loci of the various eddy systems are subject to seasonal shifts. These variations are indicated by the direction of the arrows. The superimposition of the arrows facilitates an estimate of the dominant trends in surface currents, but at the same time does not conceal entirely the degree of deviation as would be the case with a mean indication.

SURFACE CURRENTS OF THE AMERICAN MEDITERRANEAN

The curiosity of various persons among the seafaring fraternity of Europe had been aroused by strange logs drifting onto their shores from across the sea. Among these was one who was sufficiently inquisitive and determined to trace the origin of this unknown driftwood. It is true that there were certain mercenary interests which made it worthwhile for Columbus to start on his adventures, but nevertheless he can be cited as the first oceanographer of the Caribbean. He described the currents of the Caribbean as moving parallel to the shore and charted them into the Gulf of Mexico. On the strength of these observations and the records of them, Columbus' chief pilot, Antón de Alaminos, was able to assist Cortez at a later date. Cortez had urgent need of contacting his supporters at home while he was being harassed during his operations in Mexico. Alaminos was charged with the mission and set his course from Veracruz to the north of Cuba, being able to ride the swiftly moving waters through Florida Strait, instead of taking what otherwise might have been the more obvious course back through the Caribbean (Thoulet, 1898, p. 421).

After this the development of oceanography in the American Mediterranean was largely a matter of map making and working out trade routes until the early part of the 19th century, when the old U. S. Coast Survey began operations in the Gulf of Mexico. Really modern oceanographic investigations of the American Mediterranean began with the cruises of the schooner "Mabel Taylor" in 1932. These were supported by the Bingham Oceanographic Foundation (Yale University) and included both the Caribbean and the Gulf. Since then the pace of oceanographic research in this area has increased steadily. In 1935 the research ship "Atlantis," of the Woods Hole Oceanographic Institution, made surveys in the Caribbean and Gulf areas. From 1951 through 1953 the U. S. Fish and Wildlife vessel "Alaska" completed ten research cruises in the Gulf of Mexico, seven of which were carried out with the cooperation of the Department of Oceanography, A. and M. College of Texas. In 1954 the U. S. Fish and Wildlife Service published a general treatise on the physical and biologic characteristics of the Gulf of Mexico, under the editorship of Paul S. Galtsoff.

To an oceanographer the subsurface circulation of the sea is as important as the currents which are apparent at the surface. In the American Mediterranean the movement of the deeper waters is incompletely known, and the most extensive knowledge of surface currents comes from the accumulated observations of mariners. The following description of the currents with which we are concerned comes from British Sailing Directions and U. S. Pilot Charts, and, in the main, is reliable in so far as the needs of the anthropologist are concerned (fig. 2).

The over-all picture of the surface currents in the American Mediterranean can be likened to a fountainhead. The main source of water comes into the stem of the fountain through the islands arcing from Trinidad to Antigua. Its volume and much of its power are derived from the joining of the north and south equatorial currents. With the aid of the prevailing winds the main stream is sustained with such force that at the orifice of the fountainhead (the Yucatan Channel) the waters are actually moving upslope. Leaving Yucatan Channel, the stream spreads as a fountain top into the breadth of the Gulf of Mexico. The central axis continues to the northwestward, aimed in the general direction of the delta of the Mississippi River. At this point waters from the deep Atlantic combine with those washing a large portion of continental North America to produce great quantities of seafood.

From the point of view of the oceanographer the most significant branch from

the fountainhead is the one moving directly eastward as it rounds Cape San Antonio,
the southwesterly directed finger of western
Cuba. This section, with the elevated hy-
drostatic head of the Gulf of Mexico pressing against it, picks up sufficient energy
to swing through the Florida Straits and
along the Florida Peninsula to become the
Florida Current and later the Gulf Stream.
One might conjecture that the American
Mediterranean, by means of the warm
ocean river it sends across the Atlantic, has
influenced the North Sea cultures more
than those of the circum-Caribbean areas.

The branch of the fountain swinging
eastward is matched by a weaker and less
voluminous mate turning to the west. This
branch further divides like a trident as it
rides over Campeche Bank: one division
parallels the Yucatan coast, one heads in
the direction of Veracruz, and another leads
farther north.

These branches shift around from season
to season, and, as they move into the coast-
lines, variable eddy systems are formed.
These minor currents often suddenly reverse themselves.

In the stem of the fountain the movement of water straight through the Caribbean is not dissipated as it is in the Gulf
of Mexico, and the currents are more pre-
dictable. Lateral to the main axis there are
two ancillary eddies—one south of the
down-turned palm of Cuba in the eastern
Cayman Basin, and one in the western Colombia Basin. The principal deviation
from this simplified plan is the water moving in through Windward Passage, which
lies between the eastern tip of Cuba and
Haiti.

The central axis of the current through
the Caribbean flows at an average velocity
of 31 km. per day from November to July,
and about 33 km. per day from August to
October. Within the breadth of the stream
there are local variations in velocity. In
general, the greatest velocities are found in
the southern periphery of the stream as

it moves through the Venezuela and Colombia basins. Along the northern edges
the velocities vary from 0.5 to 1.0 knots
(from 0.9 km. to 1.8 km. per hour).

The velocity at which these waters move
may be important to the anthropologist in
two ways: (1) the currents can become effective barriers to human transport between land masses if the velocities are high
enough, and (2) they may or may not
transport accidentally entrained terrestrial
animals (including aborigines) to new and
distant habitats, provided they move fast
enough for the migrant to survive the
ordeal.

*Possible Effects of Surface Currents on
Aboriginal Migration*

No strong evidence has been found for
a regular passage by preconquest craft from
the mainland of Middle America to the
Greater Antilles. In the following paragraphs this problem will be analyzed in
terms of what has been said about surface
currents.

On opposite sides of the Caribbean there
existed simultaneously an advanced people
and a less advanced people—respectively,
the Maya and the Arawak (not to mention
the even more primitive Ciboney and Carib). Why had there been no extensive interchange between these localities?

Between Yucatan and Cuba the least distance is approximately 200 km. In crossing
from Yucatan to Cuba one must take into
consideration the velocity of the current
through Yucatan Strait and the prevailing
winds. It is reasonable to assume that the
maximum sustained speed at which a primitive canoe of any size could be propelled
is 5 knots (9 km. per hour). To travel 160
km. would then require on the order of 18
hours if the water and air were motionless.
In Yucatan Strait, however, about the
first half of this journey would be in a current moving in a northerly direction at
velocities up to 3.5 knots (6.3 km. per hour)
and the latter half would encounter ve-

locities up to 1 knot (1.8 km. per hour). Assuming no correction of course and no wind, our canoe at the end of 18 hours could easily find itself in the Florida Straits and the headwaters of the Gulf Stream. This northward deflection of the course could be minimized or increased by the winds. A southerly or southeasterly wind would set the canoe deeper into the Gulf of Mexico, whereas the winds in the northeast quadrant would tend to minimize the error. However, winds of any sort are most likely to come from an unfavorable direction and would tend to slow the progress of the vessel both by opposing the propulsive force and by creating rough seas.

The possibility of a crossing in the opposite direction might be improved, but it is doubtful if the primitives resident in western Cuba had anywhere near the naval technology of their more advanced neighbors across the Yucatan Channel. The elements of geography and oceanography have combined to cause the interposition of a mere 200 km. of water surface to become a virtually impassable barrier between two neighboring cultures.

These considerations seem to support the idea that the Maya artifacts found on the western tip of Cuba were transported there by slaves captured during the conquest (Rouse, 1948, 4: 501). In any event, it does not seem likely that the Maya would have existed long as minor elements amongst the Ciboney and Arawak.

If the mainland tribes had the large craft referred to elsewhere in this article, it would seem likely that they might have made good their passage to Cuba or Florida by landing along either shore of Florida Straits. Perhaps some venturesome Maya did get caught up and carried in the eastward-moving sea and, putting ashore, rejoiced in the discovery of a new land—only to find the return home with the news impossible because of the power of the very waters that brought him there.

In summary, it appears that the habita-

tion of the West Indies by American Indians was possible only as a stepwise migration from island to island, the first step being from the shores of Trinidad to Grenada.

Coastwise Water Transport

The Ciboney perhaps used only dugout canoes, but they were the most undeveloped of all the Antillean inhabitants (Rouse, 1948, 4: 504).

The Arawak was a more advanced culture, and water transport did not deviate from the general picture. A subgroup of Arawak, the Taino, used dugout canoes (Rouse, 1948, 4: 527) but also had large vessels capable of carrying 70 or 80 persons. They did not use sails, but did travel extensively from island to island, and apparently carried on a trade in pineapples, which they grew for export. In Trinidad, Arawak as well as Carib built vessels with cabin-like structures in the center.

The Carib constructed four general classes of craft: piraguas with an average length of 25 m., large canoes, small canoes, and rafts. In historic times they are known to have provided piraguas with three masts and canoes with two masts. McKusick (1960) has shown that the Caribs' use of masts and sails was not aboriginal but was adopted from Europeans.

On the whole, these are primitive craft, but their makers were venturesome people, and their superstitions attest to the fact that they were subjected to the vicissitudes of seafaring (Rouse, 1948, 4: 553).

Unfortunately, references to water transport by mainland peoples are limited. J. Eric S. Thompson (1949) has summarized the few data on coastal navigation by the Maya; he mentions the oft-quoted account of Columbus' encounter with a large Mayan trading canoe 8 feet wide and the length of a Spanish galley, carrying 25 men, their wives and children and merchandise, near the Bay Islands 80 miles east of the Yucatan coast. Amalia Cardos de M. (1959, pp. 76–

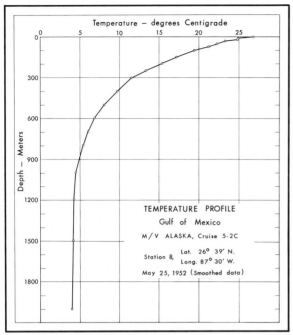

FIG. 3—TEMPERATURE PROFILE, M/V ALASKA, CRUISE 5-2C, STATION 8, MAY 25, 1952

80) indicates extensive Mayan canoe traffic on the Caribbean coast from the northern part of Yucatan to Honduras and in the Gulf of Mexico along the west side of the Yucatan Peninsula to Tabasco. The maritime activity was probably developed in connection with the active commerce the Maya carried on in the salt and cloth trade and in fishing activity.

TIDES OF THE AMERICAN MEDITERRANEAN

Without going into the theory of tide-generating forces we can say that the American Mediterranean is not of the proper length and depth to sustain significant semidiurnal oscillations, but it does provide adequate dimensions for responding to daily tide-producing forces (Marmer, 1926, p. 143). The diurnal range is from 30 to 90 cm. (lower low water to higher high water), and the mean range varies from 12 to 106 cm. (mean low water to mean high water). The lower values occur along the

mainland of Middle America and the higher values along the Florida Gulf Coast.

The tidal ranges within the bays and lagoons are dampened by narrow passages and tend to be much less than those of the open Gulf as cited above (A. Collier and Hedgpeth, 1950, pp. 170–76). As biological factors, the influence of tides will be determined to some degree by the terrain. Even small tidal fluctuations can alternately expose and cover large expanses of marsh, if the slope of the coastal areas is slight; but in a rocky and steep-sided embayment, the area involved becomes very much less and the influence of tidal fluctuations is lessened accordingly.

Meteorological conditions greatly influence the occurrence and amplitude of tides, especially along the continental shores of the Gulf of Mexico, where wind tides may be more significant than normal ones.

SOME RELATIONSHIPS BETWEEN THE OCEANOGRAPHY OF THE AMERICAN MEDITERRANEAN AND CLIMATE

The American Mediterranean embraces some 23° of latitude, beginning at 8° north of the equator. The Gulf of Mexico is the more temperate of its two components; the Caribbean is more tropical.

These waters have considerable depth, and at first glance it would seem that the cooler waters present in these deep basins would influence the climate. The temperature of the waters at the 2,000-m. level in the American Mediterranean fluctuates around 5°C., and at 300–400 m. around 13°C. (fig. 3).

These figures would be more helpful in understanding the climatic relationships if we consider the surface/volume ratio of the American Mediterranean. When we speak of the effects of the oceans on climate, we are actually thinking about contact between air and water. Amount of surface is important because the greater the area the greater the contact of the whole water mass with the air, thus allowing more efficient

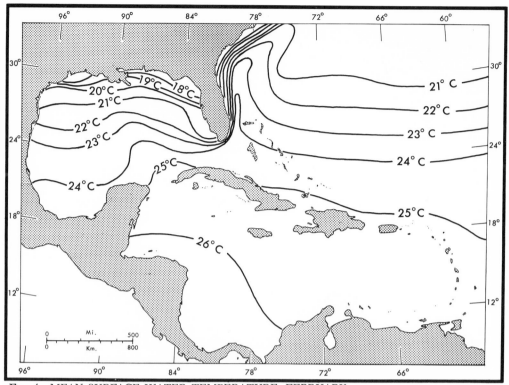

Fig. 4—MEAN SURFACE WATER TEMPERATURE, FEBRUARY
After Fuglister (1947).

heat transfer. The American Mediterranean has an area of approximately 4.3 million sq. km. and a volume of 9.6 million cu. km.—a ratio of 2.2 million cu. km. for each million square kilometers of area. The ratio for the European Mediterranean would be 1.4 million cu. km. for each million square kilometers of area.

The waters in the American Mediterranean do not show a strong tendency to mix vertically, and so there is stratification, which tends to keep the cool water isolated. This, in combination with the low surface to volume ratio, reduces the rate of heat exchange between the atmosphere and the water mass as a whole. Consequently the surface temperatures over the whole of the American Mediterannean remain relatively high throughout the year. Distributions for the extreme months of February and August are shown in figures 4 and 5. The Gulf of Mexico waters, influenced by the cold winter air from the North American conti-

nent, have the greatest temperature ranges: from 18° (along the U. S. Coast) to 25°C. in winter, but from 29°C to slightly less in summer. The Caribbean waters range from 25° and 26°C. in winter to 28° and 29°C. in summer. The high surface water temperatures especially in summer give rise to the warm, unstable tropical air mass that overlies the Gulf and Caribbean areas. The effect of this air mass on the climate of the adjacent coasts of Mexico and Central America is considered in Article 6.

Surface Salinity of the American Mediterranean

The waters of the American Mediterranean system fall into two salinity categories: those with salinity characteristics of oceanic waters, and those which are influenced by land drainage. The latter are found along the northern Gulf of Mexico, a section of the Gulf lying between Tampico and Coatzacoalcos and the south-central Caribbean.

130

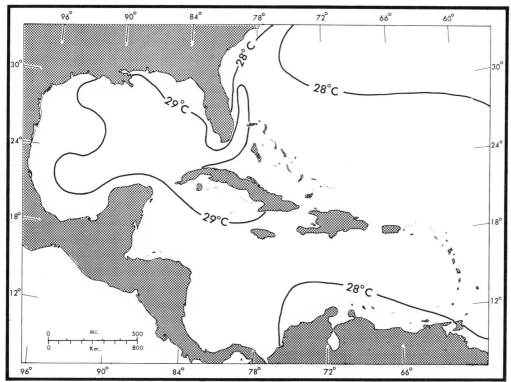

Fig. 5—MEAN SURFACE WATER TEMPERATURE, AUGUST
After Fuglister (1947).

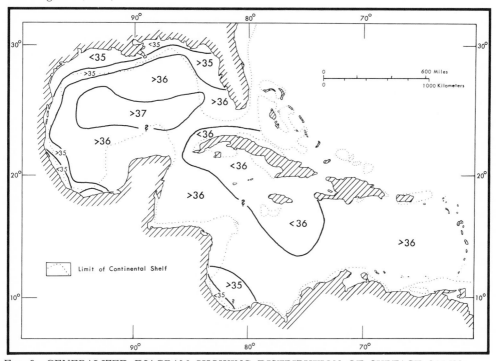

Fig. 6—GENERALIZED DIAGRAM SHOWING DISTRIBUTION OF SURFACE SALINITIES IN THE AMERICAN MEDITERRANEAN
Adapted from Parr, 1935a, b; 1937; 1938; A. Collier, 1958; Drummond and Austin, 1958.

131

These areas are indicated in figure 6 by salinities of less than 35 parts per thousand (‰).

For the most part, the Caribbean has salinities ranging between 36.00 and 36.8‰ except as indicated in figure 6. By contrast the Gulf of Mexico has a large but at present poorly defined area, which has salinities of 37.00‰ and over. Between this and the coastal waters the salinities are over 36‰, and as the shore is approached they drop to less than 35‰.

These paragraphs reflect in very general terms the regional salinity picture, but in fact these generalizations are not justified. The surveys that have been reported (Parr, 1935, 1937, 1938; A. Collier, 1958; Drummond and Austin, 1958) make it clear that there is much variation in detail according to season, and from one year to the next. At present the best generalization would be that the Caribbean has a surface salinity of around 36‰. The Gulf of Mexico is similar, except for a large central area where there is a tendency for the surface to bear waters with salinities of 37‰ and slightly over.

Salt Making

Combined climatic and geographic factors make the northwest coast of Yucatan Peninsula a favorable area for the production of sea salt, and the Maya were quite active in taking advantage of this resource (Landa, 1938, pp. 227–28).

Perhaps the most important factor is the lack of streams discharging from this part of Yucatan Peninsula. The nearest ones are Rio Champoton, on the west coast, and Rio Hondo, which empties into the Bay of Chetumal on the lower east coast of the peninsula (Carreño, 1951, map). The peninsula itself is primarily limestone, the northern part of which is especially pocked by sink holes (*cenotes*) and solution fissures, which tend to literally soak up precipitation before it can form streams and run off into the sea.

132

Compared to the inland portion of the peninsula, the northern periphery receives only moderate precipitation, being on the order of 500 mm. along the western half and from 500 to 1,000 mm. along the eastern half (Carreño, 1951, map). High insolation and the character of the trade winds create an environment in which evaporation can be expected to be rather high. The magnitude of precipitation agrees with that given by Sverdrup (1943, p. 72) for the high seas in a similar latitude, 400 mm. per year, and makes his figure for evaporation useful, although care should be exercised in synthesizing data from such diversified sources. For a latitude of 20° he shows an evaporation of 1490 mm., which is some 1,000 mm. in excess of precipitation. Available observations (Collier, 1958, p. 189) indicate salinity values of over 36.00‰ near the shore of the peninsula.

With this combination of circumstances it is not difficult to understand why the Maya are said to have enjoyed a monopoly in the salt business (Roys, 1943, p. 53). Salt was harvested in abundance in the shallow lagoons along the northern and western shores of Yucatan. Landa (1938) described this coast as an inland portion of a continuous lagoon that extended more than 70 leagues (350 km.) from the Isla de Mujeres near Cabo Catoche to the vicinity of Campeche. From these salines the Maya carried salt as far as Tabasco and Honduras (Landa, 1938, pp. 110, 227).

BIOLOGICAL PRODUCTIVITY OF MARINE WATERS

There are three general situations in which the marine environment exhibits maximal biological productivity. The most important are those areas in which chemical enrichment and maximum light intensity are coupled over the greatest areas for the greatest length of time. These are the coastal waters and estuaries. Next in productivity are the so-called "banks," those areas of ocean bottom which rise above the general level of the surrounding sea floor. These irregularities in the sea bottom do two things: they provide increased surface for the growth of small and large forage organisms, and they create a certain amount of turbulence in the flow of ocean water over them. When such areas are shallow enough to receive sufficient sunlight to drive the photosynthetic process, the productivity is greater than in the surrounding areas. The remaining general case is that in which a hydrodynamic situation causes the richer waters from the depths to rise within the range of sunlight. An example of this can be found in the equatorial current systems of the Pacific, for here the deeper, nutrient-laden waters of the midoceans are brought within reach of light. A productive, although not fully developed, tuna fishery is found in this region.

In the American Mediterranean of pre-conquest times the most important of these cases is that of fluvial enrichment, whereas the Campeche Bank and Mosquito Bank, particularly the former, offer fine examples of the case of surface irregularity. The sea turtles (p. 140) feed on algae, eel grass, and sponge, and these are the materials found most abundantly in such areas as Mosquito Bank.

Campeche Bank

Oceanographers are alert to situations in which the deeper strata of water can be transported to the surface. There are a number of physical systems which can supply the energy necessary for such an overturn. This energy may be derived from wind, heat transfer, or the force of moving water masses, either singly or in combination. It would be impossible to describe here the operation of these processes for the entire Gulf of Mexico and Caribbean even if the information were sufficiently complete to do so. As an example of the movement of deeper water towards the surface, we will describe some aspects of the oceanography of Campeche Bank.

The geomorphologic features of the pertinent sea bottom have already been described and should be kept in mind while the following paragraphs are read.

As the water flows from the Cayman Basin through the throat of Yucatan Strait it impinges with massive energy on the east shoulder of Campeche Bank. As would be expected, the deeper water is deflected upward and comes to the surface where the wind directs some of it westward. Oceanographic observations in this region show that this upwelling, as it is called, brings inorganic nitrogen and phosphorous to the surface.

By special devices an oceanographic ship can take samples of sea water from various depths and, at the same time, determine the temperature of the water at those depths. When the ship stops at a given point (called a "station") and takes a series of samples by means of devices let down into the water on a cable ("making a cast"), it obtains data which, when correlated with that at other stations, give a fair idea of the vertical distribution of certain properties.

Thus we learn that in the Gulf of Mexico just north of Campeche Bank, on a certain date, the total salt content of the water was 36‰ and over, from the surface down to about 150 m.; between 35 and 36‰ from 150 to 250 m.; and less than 35‰ at depths greater than 250 m. When points of equal salinity from other stations are joined and properly contoured, along with the other properties that are measured, the resulting patterns will tell the oceanographer much about the movements and origins of different water masses with which he is concerned. If salinity measurements and temperature determinations are applied according to certain physical principles, the relative density of the water can be determined.

On the east side of Campeche Bank the density lines and the salinity lines approach the vertical (fig. 7). This is good indication that the deep water in the Yucatan Channel

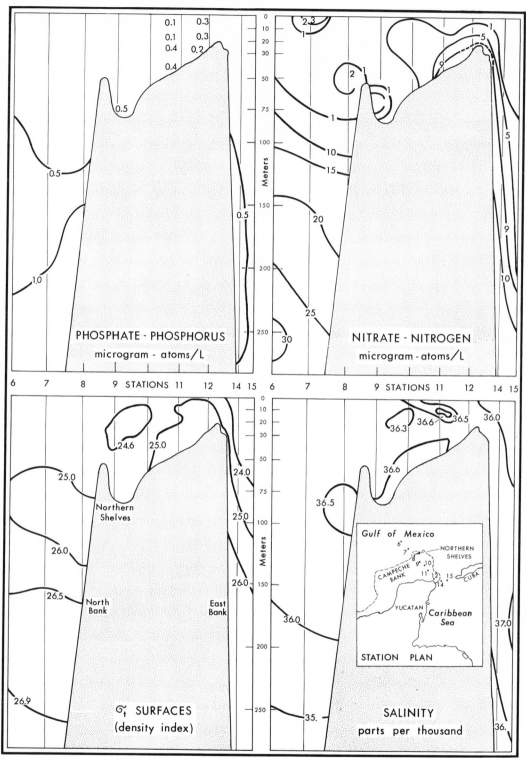

FIG. 7—PROFILES OF CAMPECHE BANK SHOWING THE VERTICAL DISTRIBUTION
OF NUTRIENTS, SALINITY, AND DENSITY

The plan of stations from which profiles were constructed is given in the insert. The steepness
of the contours on the east bank is evidence of the rise of deep water from Yucatan Channel.
Compare with fig. 2 and see text.

is being forced upward along the steep slopes of the bank (see p. 124). These waters bring up significant quantities of phosphate and nitrate. This constitutes an upwelling which derives its energy from the force of the water flowing through Yucatan Channel.

In the deep oceans the concentrations of the fertilizing elements, nitrogen and phosphorous, increase with depth below 200 m. This is as far as light will pass through even the clearest water in sufficient strength to satisfy the energy requirements of photosynthesis. This 200-m.-thick surface layer is where the food chain and all life in the deep sea, with the probable exception of some microorganisms, originate; in it there is a continual living, multiplying, and dying. Diatoms and dinoflagellates burst forth in their spring blooms and die off as quickly. The minute crustacean copepods feed on the diatoms and die according to their own cycle. As these organisms, and the others in their turn dependent on them, die and sink below the 200-m. level, they decay. In this way the chemical elements carbon, oxygen, hydrogen, nitrogen, phosphorus, and all the others required to keep even a small living creature going, are returned to the sea in one form or another.

But without light the plants cannot carry on photosynthesis, and so there is no primary producer to soak up the nitrogen and phosphorus and incorporate them anew into living matter. These elements then accumulate in the deeper waters and reach a maximum at 500–800 m., depending on the location (fig 8). A cubic kilometer of water at 500 m. contains, on some occasions, as much as 62,000 kilograms of elemental phosphorus. This is roughly equivalent to the phosphorus content of 279 metric tons of orthophosphate (mono-hydrogen). Thus, for each square kilometer of water in the American Mediterranean, which is more than 1500 m. deep, there is approximately this amount of phosphate fertilizer present.

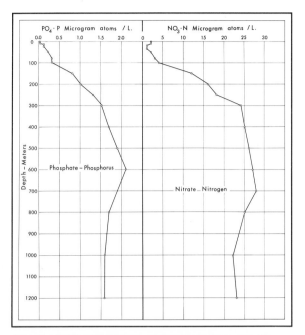

FIG. 8—THE VERTICAL DISTRIBUTION OF INORGANIC NUTRIENTS IN THE SEA
The observations from which these graphs were made came from the Gulf of Mexico (Collier, 1958) and are typical of the American Mediterranean. Individual stations will deviate from these curves to a minor extent. The tendency for the concentrations at the greater depths to decrease to a level slightly less than the maximum is characteristic.

Nitrogen in the form of nitrates is even more abundant.

Any process, such as upwelling, which can bring these stores of essential nutrients within reach of the photic zone is bound to contribute to the living resources. Thus Campeche Bank receives a perennial flow of rich water to support its corals, shrimps, snappers, and their fellow creatures in colorful array and great number.

Inshore Oceanography

From the point of view of the anthropologist the principal significance of offshore oceanography may lie in the direct effects of the oceans on climate, the indirect influence of fertility of bay waters, and more or less direct effects as barrier or transporter of peoples and cultures. Where we enter

135

into the study of the inshore oceanography the story of the interaction between man and the sea becomes at the same time more intimate and more complex. In this article we cannot describe all the significant inshore oceanography; therefore, after a consideration of certain general principles, we shall examine only certain local regions as examples.

The nature of inshore oceanography is determined mostly by local geography: the coastal geomorphology, the quantitative and qualitative natures of river discharges, and tidal fluctuation. The balance between these factors and the open sea determines the salinity levels and their seasonal variations, the hardness of the bottom, the depth and composition of the sediments, and, finally, the character of the flora and fauna.

The feature of first consideration is the degree of shoreline involution: does the shoreline run for long distances with only gentle or minor changes in line, or is it marked with channels, islands, or embayments? If it runs unbroken for miles, the water will in general have the character of that of the open sea. If there are embayments or estuaries, there will be compromises between that of the open sea and the effluents of rivers and the drainage of tidal marshes and swamps. Estuaries and lagoons or bays will, in general, be richer in flora and fauna than the open beach. They offer greater environmental variety and trap river-borne nutrients eroded from the land. In some respects a system of bays could be considered the "pantry shelf" for the animals frequenting the coastal waters.

The shallowness of bays and lagoons in comparison to their areas allows for a maximum availability of nutrients within the range of sunlight, the power that keeps all biological wheels turning through the intermediary of photosynthesis. This advantage, however, is partly negated by the increased turbidity of shoal waters. In addition, the enclosed waters act as traps for the suspended solids carried by stream

discharges, and as a dumping system for the outflow of river water into the sea. This dumping means that the ocean water entering the bay with an incoming tide is mixed with river water, the mixture leaving the bay on the falling tide. Some of the river water is held within the bay long enough for the photosynthetic organisms to absorb the inorganic nutrients. This keeps the organic richness (or the capacity of the water to produce living matter) at some maximum level which is commensurate with the particular situation under study. In short, the great fisheries of Louisiana (mainly shrimp and oysters) are there because of the tremendous discharge of the Mississippi River and the associated coastal marshlands. We may cite as an opposite extreme a lower production off the mouth of the Rio Grande, a river now discharging very little water.

After leaving the bays and estuaries the enriched waters will tend to spread along the coast to an extent, and in directions, consistent with the local ocean currents and winds. If the coast tends to be shallow and slopes gradually into the sea, these enriched waters can still provide support for a sustained and considerable organic productivity. If, on the other hand, the coast drops rapidly to great depths, the productive life of the water will be sharply attenuated in both time and space. The extremes that can be offered as examples in this connection are the north coast of the Gulf of Mexico and the coast of Panama.

The idea of an absolute value for the potential productive capacity of a body of water is a modern concept which has developed along with increasing efficiency in the exploitation of fishery resources. In so far as the significance of aquatic resources in the nourishment of primitive man is concerned this modern idea is not applicable. Marine organisms available to the modern fisherman with his large vessels and specialized gear were not in reach of the preconquest Indian shore fisher, whose tools were

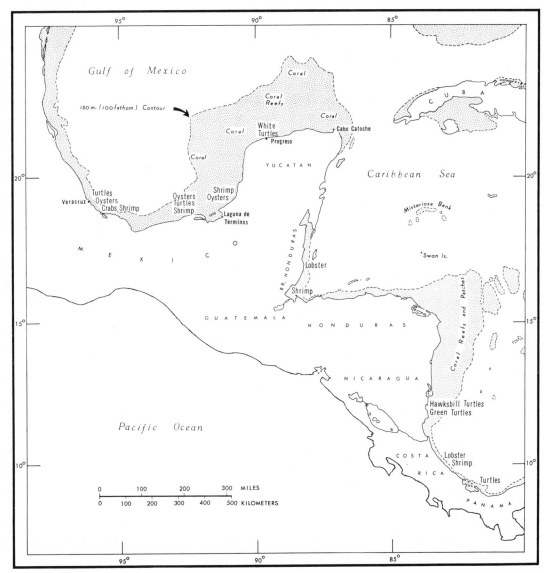

Fig. 9—THE CONTINENTAL SHELF AND AREAS OF CERTAIN FISHERIES OF CENTRAL AMERICA

limited to the harpoon, the bow and arrow, beach seines, traps, and fish poisons.

River Discharge

In the absence of data bearing on qualitative considerations, the degree of enrichment of coastal waters by terrestrial drainage may be estimated roughly from quantitative considerations. From the U. S. Geological Survey (1958) and from Benassini and García Quintero (1955–57) we have obtained some comparative figures of the mean annual discharge of various tributaries to the Gulf of Mexico. Since these values do not take seasonal fluctuations into consideration, they are, to a certain extent, misleading. During the season of high water, the nutrients are diluted more than they might be during periods of ordinary flow, and also they might be absorbed on silt and carried beyond the range of sunlight before they can be incorporated in the

137

marine food chain. If these hypothetical phenomena operate in conjunction, then the total annual discharge would have to be weighted accordingly, but even so, the latter still provide a useful index for our purpose.

The estimated total annual discharge of river water into the Gulf of Mexico is 1,045,000 million cu. m. Of this the Mississippi contributes an estimated 427,000 million cu. m., all other rivers of the United States together 313,000 million cu. m., and the Mexican rivers combined, 305,000 million cu. m. Radcliffe (1922, p. 16) gives evidence to support the idea that the area between Coatzacoalcos and Punta Frontera is particularly productive. Within these points the following rivers discharge their waters: Coatzacoalcos, Tonala, Mezcalapa-Grijalva system, the Usumacinta, and a number of lesser streams. The total annual discharge of these rivers is of the order of 151,000 million cu. m. This is 50% of the discharge of all the Mexican rivers discharging into the Gulf of Mexico and, if discharge is any clue to the productivity of a coastal area, would give reason for thinking of this area as a particularly rich one.

The few data available indicate that the discharge of Central American rivers into the Caribbean is likewise enormous and vastly exceeds the discharge of streams that flow into the Pacific.

LIVING RESOURCES OF THE AMERICAN MEDITERRANEAN

The waters of the American Mediterranean have the tropical characteristic of containing a great variety of life, but offering no great quantities of any one item. These waters may be assigned to three arbitrary divisions: the shallow coastal waters with mangrove swamps and estuaries; limited areas of continental shelf; submerged coral reefs and emergent islands surrounded with water of great depth. Each of these has its characteristic complex of life (fig. 9).

It is not within the scope of this article to give an exhaustive account of the flora and fauna of these areas, but we shall consider these life provinces in the light of recorded information about the utilization of the various species by the natives in pre-Columbian times. Table 1 lists certain data concerning fish as given by the 16th-century chroniclers, Oviedo (1851) and Landa (1938).

In addition to the fish listed in Table 1, there are others worthy of note, particularly the snappers. Besides fish, there are crustaceans, molluscs, turtles, and mammals, all of which filled certain specialized requirements.

Several important species of fish not shown in the table were probably of significance in the aboriginal economy. Most important among these are snappers (Lutianidae) and anchovies (Engraulidae). The snappers are plentiful among the coral banks, and certain species are easily obtainable among mangrove roots. The common name "snapper" or "red snapper" usually brings to mind the well-known article of commerce *Lutianus blackfordii*.

However, the availability of this fish on the general market is a result of the development of modern deep-sea fishing methods, and it was probably not within reach of the preconquest aborigine. It is reasonable to guess that the gray snapper *L. griseus*, as one of the more desirable snappers from the point of view of table use and as one more easily captured in its haunts among the mangroves, was of much greater importance to the Middle American Indian. Ginsburg (1930) mentions that the young *L. griseus* are caught with nets in shallow water, those of *L. blackfordii* are not.

It is impossible to discuss the other animals mentioned by Oviedo because of the lack of specificity of the names given. These include fish such as eels and crustaceans.

Landa (1938, p. 230) mentions an abundance of crabs in the lagoons of Yucatan and fine oyster beds in the mouth of Rio Champoton.

TABLE 1—LIST OF FISHES REPORTED AS PRECONQUEST ITEMS OF FOOD AND COMMERCE FOR THE NATIVES OF MIDDLE AMERICA

Scientific Name[1]	Local Names	Localities Mentioned	Tribes Mentioned	Author
Mugil sp. ? (mullets)	lisas	Greater Antilles Yucatan, north & west coasts	Taino Maya	Oviedo Landa
Gerres sp. ? (mojarras)	mojarra	Greater Antilles Yucatan, north & west coasts	Taino Maya	Oviedo Landa
Pomacentrus robalito ? (snook)	robalo	Greater Antilles Yucatan	Taino Maya	Oviedo Landa
Caranx sp. ? (jack fishes)	jurel caballos	Greater Antilles Yucatan	Taino Maya	Oviedo Landa
Achirus sp. ? (soles)	lenguado lenguadas	Greater Antilles Yucatan	Taino Maya	Oviedo Landa
Bairdiella sp. ? (silver perch)	corbinetas	Greater Antilles	Taino	Oviedo
Trigla sp. ? (sea robin)	bermejuela	Greater Antilles	Taino	Oviedo
Holocentrus sp. ? (squirrel fish)	dorado	Greater Antilles	Taino	Oviedo
Dasyatidae Aetobatidae Mobulidae	rayas	Greater Antilles Yucatan	Taino Maya	Oviedo Landa
Agonostomus sp. ? (fresh-water mullet)	trychas	Yucatan	Maya	Landa
Sardinella sp. ? (sardines)	sardinas	Yucatan	Maya	Landa

[1]The Spanish names for these fishes come from Oviedo and Landa, and the scientific names and English common names were derived by comparison of the former with information given by Radcliffe (1922, p. 17) and by Jordan and Evermann (1896). Some of these are difficult to identify, but it is believed that names shown are reasonable guesses.

The mullet graze on the algae which grow on the surfaces of rocks, and sift small creatures from mud and sand. They travel in large schools, which commonly enter shallow water and can be easily prepared for eating. These factors contrive to make mullet quite adaptable to a kind of domestication, which was practiced by Arawak. They are reported to have built large bamboo stockades in shallow water and to have carried on within these a considerable mullet culture (Gilmore, 1950, p. 409).

The sub-Taino must have found great amusement, if not substantial utility, in training their remoras to capture and retrieve prey for them (Oviedo, 1851, b. XIII, c. IX). The spinus dorsal fin of *Echeneis naucrates* (and other remoras) has become modified to form an organ of attachment, which operates in a fashion very similar to the common suction cup. By this structure they cling to larger fishes, turtles, and sharks, and travel with them. They can cling very tightly, as they must, to be able to stay on a large actively moving animal. The Indian allegedly put these fish on a leash and trained them to attach themselves to a victim and remain fast while they were being retrieved. This is reminiscent of the use made of cormorants in the Orient. If the

139

reports are accurate—and they seem to be well authenticated—the Arawak captured the remoras as juveniles, and trained them in a rock pool until they were large enough to be put to work.

These are rather intelligent measures made by a comparatively advanced people when viewed along with the Carib. The latter tribe, known as the "crab eaters," seem to have done most of their crabbing at night by torchlight. The crabs were eaten with a sauce called "taumalin" made from lime juice, pounded peppers and the "greenish meat next to the shell of the male crab" (Rouse, 1948, 4: 550).

The Arawak, who seem to have had the most advanced culture of the West Indies, practiced intelligent methods of agriculture. They fertilized the soil with urine and the ash from burnt trees and developed an extensive irrigation in the southwest part of Hispaniola. On Puerto Rico they cultivated pineapples for export. Such an agriculture as this, combined with their abilities as seafarers, probably provided the basis for the dominance of their race in the Indies (Hostos, 1948, 4: 540). Whether or not the more primitive Carib would have adopted these technologies with sufficient intelligence to meet their total food requirements is unknown, but their ability to harvest the sea might have made up any deficiencies.

Mollusca

In Middle America shells of many kinds of marine molluscs were widely used as ornaments, which are commonly found in Indian graves. Along the seashore shellfish afforded an important food item. However, almost no archaeological work has been done on the coastal middens, in which oysters and clams are the chief components.

It has already been mentioned that the waters of the American Mediterranean provide an abundance of species of fishes, and the same applies to the mollusca. There is no greater expression of this than is found in the ornamentation of persons and buildings

with sea shells. Outstanding among these is the so-called thorny oyster *Spondylus*. It produces colorful shell which was used for pendants, beads, and inlay work. Part of its value probably arose from difficulty in acquisition, for it is found in relatively deep water fastened to rocks (Kidder, Jennings, and Shook, 1946, pp. 146–47).

The small olive shells (*Oliva*) were gathered and traded extensively for the making of necklaces and trinkets. Other standard shells of Gulf and Caribbean origin used in trade and ornamentation included *Marginella, Murex, Cardium*, and many others. These have been found in graves in the Mexican and Guatemalan highlands, indicating an extensive preconquest trade in sea shells (Kidder, 1947; Vaillant, 1941; Smith and Kidder, 1951). One of the most spectacular of the worked shells are the famous Huastec triangular pendants, or gorgets, carved from the large gastropods *Strombus gigas* or *Fasciolaria* (Beyer, 1933; Ekholm, 1944).

Large gastropods of *Fasciolaria* were used as ceremonial trumpets. Species of this genus are found both on the east and west coasts of Middle America (Kidder, 1947, p. 61; Kidder, Jennings, and Shook, 1946, pp. 146–47).

Turtles

If any group of animals might be called the "marine staple" of the Indians, it would be the turtles. As many as five species may be available in the different environments in the American Mediterranean.

The most important as a food item is the Atlantic green turtle (*Chelonia mydas mydas*), the favorite habitat of which is shallow water with an abundance of vegetation and rocky holes scattered about. In the spring and early summer it digs large nests on the shore, in which it may lay up to 200 eggs about 2 inches in diameter. Its meat provides good food, as does its eggs, and the Indians made good use of both (Carr, 1952, p. 345).

The Atlantic Hawksbill (*Eretmochelys imbricata imbricata*) is less discriminating about its habitat and is found in shallow muddy bays with or without vegetation and rocky holes. In so far as food is concerned, its chief value is its eggs, but in addition its shell provides highly decorative materials which were already esteemed in pre-Columbian times (Carr, 1952, p. 366).

Another turtle which was undoubtedly important as a food item to the Indian was the Atlantic loggerhead (*Caretta caretta caretta*) (Carr, 1952, p. 382). This interesting turtle ranges from rivers to marshes to the high seas, and is common throughout the American Mediterranean. Both its meat and its eggs are used as food. This turtle is carnivorous and consumes crabs, oysters, sponges, and jelly fish.

The Atlantic ridley (*Lepidochelys kempii*) appears to be confined mostly to the Florida Gulf coast, particularly the mangrove swamps. It is edible, but probably contributed little to the area of interest here (Carr, 1952, p. 396).

The Atlantic leatherback (*Dermochelys coriacea coriacea*) is a comparatively rare pelagic form. Because of its rarity, it is not an important item, but its eggs are used when they can be found. In Middle America, it nests from May to August in Honduras and Nicaragua. The nesting seasons differ slightly in other localities.

More problematical because of the uncertainty of the southern limits of its range is the Diamondback terrapin (various species and varieties of the genus *Malaclemys*). Either the Florida species or the Texas species could enter the Middle American areas, and Carr (1952, p. 184) indicates his opinion that they might be found in Yucatan. Certainly the estuaries offer suitable environment.

Mammals

The sea cow or manatee (*Trichechus manatus*) was abundant in the waters of the Indies and around Yucatan. Landa

(1938, p. 230) reports that there were many manatee on the west coast of Yucatan Peninsula between Campeche and La Desconocida, where the Indians hunted them with harpoons. They were used for flesh and oil.

Another mammal, formerly abundant in the Gulf and Caribbean waters as far south as Honduras and north to the Texas coast, is the West Indian, or Caribbean, monk seal (*Monachus tropicalis*). Although probably little hunted by the aborigines, the seal was overexploited by Spaniards during the colonial period for skins and oil. This animal is now almost extinct, the Alacranes and Triangulos reefs off the northwest coast of Yucatan being one of the last remaining strongholds of a few individuals.

CATASTROPHIC FISH KILLS

Catastrophic fish kills may be regarded as one of the characteristic biologic phenomena of the Gulf of Mexico. Whether this characteristic can be applied to the Caribbean, other than on a local basis, is problematical. These fish kills may be caused by sudden lowering of water temperatures with the onset of "northers" (Gunter, 1941), or by "red tides" (Walford, 1958, pp. 175–81).

Northers

The water temperatures of the shallow coastal bays of the Gulf of Mexico tend to follow the mean daily air temperature rather closely. This is because of the very high ratio of surface area to volume and the high degree of turbulence brought about by the prevailing winds. Severe northers along the upper Gulf coast can cause water temperatures to drop very rapidly, and unless fish are located in a situation from which they can quickly migrate into deep water, they are in great peril. For instance, on January 18, 1940, a norther struck the Texas coast, and in the vicinity of Rockport the air temperature dropped from 65° to 25° F. in four hours

(Gunter, 1941, p. 204). This was part of a general cold spell that spread all over the southern United States and the upper coast of the Gulf of Mexico. There was a general fish mortality in almost all the shallow bays of the area. It is doubtful if significant mortality occurs from this cause in the southern Gulf or anywhere in the Caribbean.

Red Tide

Through general usage, the term "red tide" has come to mean discolored water, either fresh or marine, irrespective of the cause or what effect it may have on the living things in the water. An outbreak of "red tide" is not necessarily red, and the word "tide" is applied only as a figure of speech.

The best-known fish kills of this nature are those of the west coast of Florida between St. Petersburg and Cape Romano. The causative organism was identified by association as a naked dinoflagellate *Gymnodinium breve* (C. C. Davis, 1948). It was later proven to be this species by direct experiments with isolated cultures by Wilson and Collier (1955). The same organism was found to be associated with another

large fish kill in the area between Tampico and Veracruz (Ray and Wilson, 1956). Almost every living creature that comes into contact with these massive blooms or organisms is affected, either directly or indirectly. This includes shellfishes, porpoises, and birds, as well as fish. It has not been shown whether seafood gathered in the region of destruction is toxic to man.

Small-scale fish kills may occur in small bodies of water as a result of the "explosive blooms." Such a case was reported for Offats Bayou, a small arm of Galveston Bay within the city limits of Galveston, Texas. This case was reported as being caused by a species of the dinoflagellate genus *Gonyaulax* (Connell and Cross, 1950).

There appear to be no fish kills of this nature recorded for the American Mediterranean of pre-Columbian times, but undoubtedly they could have occurred much as they have since the arrival of Columbus. It is also conceivable that they could have had considerable influence on Indian life, especially where populations might have been confined to relatively small areas on some of the islands.

REFERENCES

Benassini and García Quintero, 1955–57
Beyer, 1933
Cardos de M., 1959
Carr, 1952
Carreño, 1951
Collier, A., 1958
—— and Hedgpeth, 1950
Connell and Cross, 1950
Davis, C. C., 1948
Drummond and Austin, 1958
Ekholm, 1944
Fuglister, 1947
Galtsoff, 1954
Gilmore, 1950
Ginsburg, 1930
Gunter, 1941
Hostos, 1948
Jordan and Evermann, 1896
Kidder, 1947

——, Jennings, and Shook, 1946
Landa, 1938
McKusick, 1960
Marmer, 1926
Oviedo y Valdes, 1851
Parr, 1935, 1937, 1938
Radcliffe, 1922
Ray and Wilson, 1956
Rouse, 1948
Roys, 1943
Smith, A. L., and Kidder, 1951
Sverdrup, 1943
Thompson, J. E. S., 1949
Thoulet, 1898
U. S. Geological Survey, 1958
Vaillant, 1941
Walford, 1958
Wilson and Collier, 1955

5. Oceanography and Marine Life along the Pacific Coast of Middle America[1]

CARL L. HUBBS and
GUNNAR I. RODEN

ALTHOUGH we need not accept Sir Alister Hardy's intriguing concept (1960) that man evolved more in association with water than with trees, we must bear in mind that the seas have profoundly affected his life and his customs.

The seas temper the weather; provide food, and materials for use and ornament; facilitate commerce and intercourse; and whet the imagination.

Many of the aboriginal peoples throughout Middle America were to a greater or lesser degree dependent on the Pacific Ocean and its marine life. Aschmann (1959 p. 97) elaborated on this point for Baja California and the adjacent Gulf:

All explorers and travellers have agreed that the waters on both sides of the peninsula contain a rich and varied fauna. To the extent that their technology permitted, a large number of the aboriginal inhabitants exploited this resource. Though the food that the Indians could obtain from a limited stretch of coast and coastal waters varied seasonally and annually in response to changes in currents, water temperatures, storminess, and other factors, such variations probably were small and would not be in phase with those of foods derived from the land. Thus the violence of the cyclical fluctuation from feast to famine was appreciably reduced for those rancherias which could exploit the resources of both land and sea.

[1] This paper is a Contribution from Scripps Institution of Oceanography, New Series. Many have aided us materially in its preparation. Albert Collier, Director of the Oceanographic Institute, Florida State University, has made available the drafts of his companion article, "The American Mediterranean" (Article 4). Michael D. Coe, anthropologist at Yale University, has furnished information and ideas on the probably extensive prehistorical marine trade and travel. William Neil Smith II has shared with us some results of his intimate study of the Seri. Pedro Mercado Sánchez and Julio Berdegué Aznar have provided information on primitive fishing.

In outlining the oceanography of the eastern Pacific we are indebted for suggestions and discussions to colleagues in the Scripps Institution of Oceanography: Maurice Blackburn, John D. Isaacs, Joseph L. Reid, Milner B. Schaefer, and Warren S. Wooster. The researches reported herein were supported partly by the Marine Life Research Program of Scripps Institution and partly by grants to the senior author from the National Science Foundation and from the Research Committee of the University of California.

143

Fɪɢ. 1—COASTAL MIDDEN AT PUNTA MINITAS, NORTHWESTERN BAJA CALI-
FORNIA, AT 31° 18′ 50″ NORTH LATITUDE
Radiocarbon dates, from near base to near top, are, in series: 7,020, 3,100, 2,540 or 2,500, and
1,510 years ʙ.ᴘ. (Photo by Laura C. Hubbs.)

For thousands of years food-gathering peoples relied on the sea and lived along the shores, and they traded shells and other marine products with the inhabitants of the interior. Midden shells from the Gulf side of Baja California have been dated at over 6,000 years B.P. (before present), and from the west shore of the peninsula at about 7,000 years B.P.; several dates from the southern California coast lie between 7,000 and 7,500 years. It may be assumed with considerable confidence that shellfish gatherers began to obtain their livelihood along the Baja California coast about 8,000 years ago, and have utilized seafood ever since. A single midden on the northwest coast of Baja California, at Punta Minitas (fig. 1), has been dated, from near the base to near the top, at 7,020, 3,100, 2,540 or 2,500, and 1,510 years (Hubbs, Bien, and Suess, 1960, 1962). The initial utilization of seafood by man may have been earlier, but if so, the shells have probably weathered away. The earlier and in large part still disputed traces of human activity along the coasts of southern California and of Baja California seem at present to pertain to hunters, or to food gatherers who used neither shellfishes nor food-grinding tools.

Datings along the coast south of Baja California are presently too few to warrant conclusions regarding the antiquity there of seafood eaters, but it seems plausible to assume that the sea was utilized in some way along the whole Middle American coast for at least several millennia.

A full understanding of human affairs through the ages, in any coastal region, calls for a consideration of the oceanic environment and of the abundant life that the ocean supports.

The Ocean Environment
Introduction

The ocean off the Pacific coast of Mexico and Central America is dominated by two large current systems, the California Current and the North Equatorial Current (both of which are parts of the great anticyclonic circulation of the North Pacific). The California Current, which carries water of subarctic origin southward along the coasts of California and Baja California and is augmented by upwelling, is characterized by relatively low temperatures, low salinities, and high content of dissolved oxygen. The North Equatorial Current, which transports water of tropical origin westward, is noted for its high temperatures, rather high salinities, and a low content of dissolved oxygen. Where the two current systems meet, notably in the vicinity of Cabo San Lucas and Cabo Corrientes, the temperature and salinity gradients are sharp. Superimposed on these two large current systems are local circulations, which are seasonal and which affect only the surface layers of the ocean. The most notable of these local circulations occurs along the northwest coast of Baja California and in the gulfs of California, Tehuantepec, and Panama. Since they affect inshore waters, these disturbances, though local, were no doubt of particular importance to primitive man.

The subsurface waters in the eastern tropical Pacific form three distinct layers: a very shallow upper "mixed layer," between the surface and about 20 m.; a layer of strong temperature and salinity gradients (the thermocline and the halocline), roughly between 20 and 60 m.; and the entire ocean below that depth (figs. 6, 10, 13, 14). The strong stratification induces marked vertical stability, which has some important hydrodynamic consequences in that it greatly restricts the exchange of properties between the upper and lower parts of the ocean. The waters below the layer of maximum stability are characterized by very low amounts of dissolved oxygen (much lower than on the Atlantic side) and, commonly, by a complicated distribution of salinity. At great depths the properties become rather uniformly distributed.

The driving force of the major currents

145

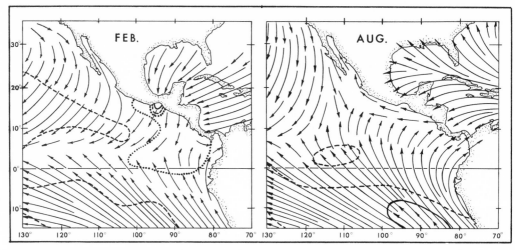

Fig. 2—PREDOMINANT WINDS IN THE EASTERN TROPICAL PACIFIC AND ADJA-
CENT AREAS
Arrows indicate wind direction only; the dotted line refers to an average wind speed of 3
m./sec., the dashed line to 7 m./sec., and the solid line to 10 m./sec.

of the region is the wind. The California Current and the North Equatorial Current are driven by the Northeast Trades and the Peru Current and the South Equatorial Current by the Southeast Trades. The trade winds (fig. 2) are a permanent feature of the atmospheric circulation, although their speed and direction at any particular place vary with the season. The Northeast Trades and the Southeast Trades are separated by a region of weak and variable winds, which region, because of its high sea-surface temperatures and humidities, constitutes an ideal breeding ground for tropical cyclones and hurricanes.

History of Oceanographic Investigations

The hydrographic exploration of the Pacific Ocean off Mexico and Central America is comparatively recent. Early in this century the inshore waters of northern Baja California were explored by McEwen (1916). Except for this local work there were, prior to 1939, few cruises, mainly into Golfo de Panama (Fleming, 1935, 1941). In 1939 a concentrated effort was directed toward a detailed study of Golfo de California (Sverdrup, 1941). This was followed by a second cruise into the Gulf in 1940 (F. P. Shepard, 1950; Revelle, 1950; and

other papers in Memoir 43 of the Geological Society of America), and by an investigation of "Panama Bight" (the region between Panama and Punta Santa Elena, Ecuador) in 1949 (Wooster, 1959). In 1949 the Scripps Institution of Oceanography of the University of California, in cooperation with the U. S. Fish and Wildlife Service, initiated a long-range program of hydrographic surveys off the coasts of California and Baja California and in Golfo de California (Reid, Roden, and Wyllie, 1958; Roden and Groves, 1959). The hydrography of the eastern tropical Pacific was explored on several cruises between 1949 and 1954 (Wooster and Jennings, 1955; Wooster and Cromwell, 1958), mainly in offshore waters. In 1955 the oceanography of the Pacific was investigated internationally between latitudes 20° and 60° N. (Reid, 1960) and along the coast off southern Mexico and Central America. The results of the Eastropic Expedition of Scripps Institution, in 1955, have been charted (E. B. Bennett, 1963). The "Island Current Survey" of 1957, by the Inter-American Tropical Tuna Commission, yielded results published by E. B. Bennett and Schaefer (1960). Since 1957 the Gulf of Tehuantepec and other localized areas have been investigated on several trips conducted by the Scripps Tuna Oceanographic Research Program of the University of California (Blackburn, 1962, 1963; Roden 1961b). A detailed investigation of Golfo de Nicoya was completed recently (Peterson, 1960). The oceanography of Baja California and Golfo de California has been reviewed by Groves and Reid (1958) and by Roden (1964). Additional treatments of the oceanography of the eastern equatorial Pacific include those of Brandhorst (1958), Cromwell and Bennett (1959), Holmes and Blackburn (1960), Blackburn and Associates (1962), and Roden (1962). General treatments of the whole area were by Schott (1935) and by Sverdrup, Johnson, and Fleming (1942). Oceanographic data from the region have been published by Scripps Institution of Oceanography (1957, 1960a,b, 1963a,b, and MS) and U. S. Bureau of Commercial Fisheries (1960).

California Current Region

The California Current, which in Middle America primarily affects Baja California, represents the eastern part of the great anticyclonic gyral of the North Pacific and lies, roughly, between the eastern edge of the subtropical high-pressure cell and the coast. The name is applied to the generally offshore, southward flow between latitudes 46° and 23° N. The boundaries of the current and its speed and direction off the west coast of Baja California vary greatly with the season (Table 1). It is strongest, with speeds averaging about 15 cm./sec., between March and May, when the direction of the current is toward the southeast or south. Between July and January the average speeds are very low and the directions are variable. Off central Baja California the currents then continue to set toward the south, but a narrow inshore countercurrent develops at the southern and northern extremes of the peninsula. The instantaneous speeds of the California Current as indicated by electromagnetic (GEK) measurements are much higher than the average speeds shown here (Reid, 1960). In winter the current extends southward to Cabo San Lucas and flows close to the coast; in summer it leaves the coast in the vicinity of Punta Eugenia and turns toward the southwest (fig. 3).

Isolated areas of very low surface temperatures constitute an outstanding feature of the California Current region. This feature was first mentioned by Thorade (1909), and has subsequently been discussed at length by McEwen (1916) and, more briefly and largely from a biotic viewpoint, by Dawson (1945, 1951, 1952, 1960), Hubbs (1948, 1960b), and others. These cold areas are generally in the wind-lee of capes, peninsulas, and other land projec-

TABLE 1—SPEED CM./SEC.) AND DIRECTION (BEARING IN DEGREES TRUE) OF THE CALIFORNIA CURRENT OFF BAJA CALIFORNIA FOR EACH MONTH OF THE YEAR
After U. S. Hydrographic Office, 1947

	Jan.	Feb.	Mar.	Apr.	May	June	July	Aug.	Sept.	Oct.	Nov.	Dec.
31°–32° N., 117°–118° W.	2.1 020	3.6 150	8.0 160	9.3 160	7.7 160	2.5 160	2.5 350	2.1 160	2.6 180	3.0 160	2.1 040	2.5 000
29°–30° N., 116°–117° W.	2.5 170	7.2 170	13.2 170	15.0 160	12.8 160	8.8 170	5.1 170	5.1 170	5.0 170	6.6 170	2.3 160	3.6 160
27°–28° N., 115°–116° W.	4.4 220	7.3 170	12.8 170	13.9 170	15.9 170	10.3 160	9.1 170	5.1 190	5.0 190	4.0 190	4.6 250	3.0 220
25°–26° N., 113°–114° W.	3.6 180	7.6 160	11.8 180	13.2 150	15.0 100	11.8 140	7.7 170	3.0 180	3.0 230	4.0 290	3.0 300	2.1 240
23°–24° N., 111°–112° W.	5.1 220	9.8 150	14.3 150	17.0 160	15.4 160	10.3 170	4.0 200	2.1 250	3.6 260	4.6 260	7.5 300	2.6 220

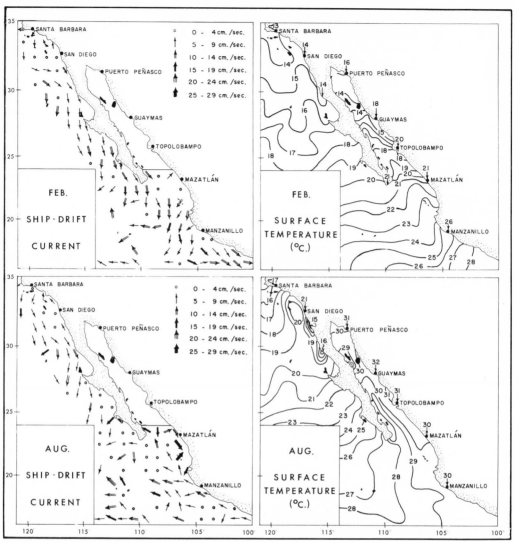

Fig. 3—SHIP-DRIFT CURRENTS (AFTER U. S. HYDROGRAPHIC OFFICE, 1947) AND
SEA-SURFACE TEMPERATURES IN THE CALIFORNIA CURRENT REGION AND IN
GOLFO DE CALIFORNIA, IN FEBRUARY AND IN AUGUST

tions. The circumstances that the low temperatures are commonly associated with high salinities and with relatively low oxygen values indicate that the source of the cool water must be below the surface. There is little definite information, however, regarding the rate of upwelling or about the depth from which the water rises to the surface. That the action close to shore may be rapid is suggested by observed changes of several degrees within a few hours, following appropriate changes in the

direction and intensity of the wind. Detailed temperature profiles and continuous temperature recordings (as by Norris and by Hubbs, unpublished data), about Punta Banda, Baja California, suggest that the cool isotherms of the shallow thermocline are deflected to the surface in the areas of upwelling.

As to the mechanism of the upwelling along shore it is generally hypothesized that the upwelling is induced by northerly, generally northwesterly, winds and by the

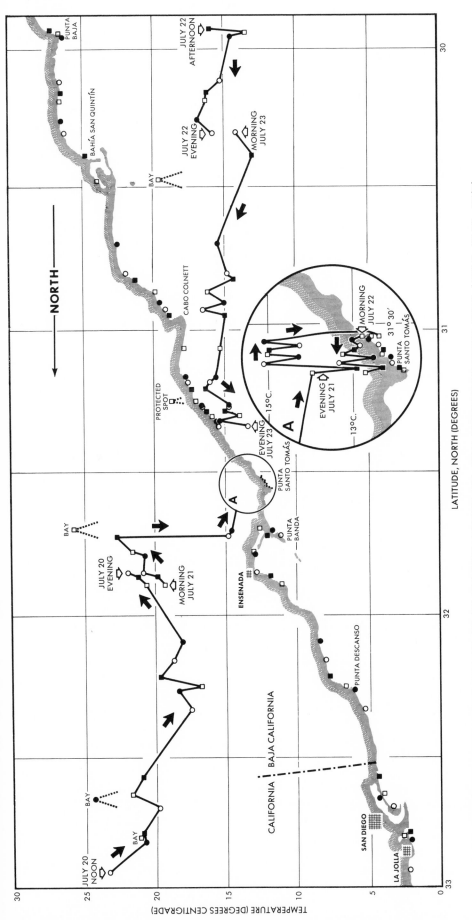

FIG. 4—PROFILE OF INSHORE SEA-SURFACE TEMPERATURES ON ONE REPRESENTATIVE RUN (JULY 20-23, 1951) BETWEEN LA JOLLA, CALIFORNIA, AND PUNTA BAJA, BAJA CALIFORNIA

Temperatures are plotted by latitude directly opposite stations, which are identified by use of corresponding symbols on the shoreline and in the temperature profile.

deflecting force of the earth's rotation. According to Ekman (1905), these winds cause the surface current to be deflected 45° and the total current 90° to the right of the wind direction. Upwelling would then be required along the coast to replace the water that has been moved away. The assumptions on which Ekman's theory is based have been seriously questioned by Sarkisyan (1960), who presented evidence that the current in a baroclinic ocean moves at all levels in approximately the same direction as the wind. Yoshida and Mao (1957) have tried to relate upwelling to the curl of the wind stress and to the planetary vorticity, but, because of inadequate observations, the validity of none of the theories can be tested.

A typical example of the monthly temperature variation in an upwelling region is furnished by the data for Arbolitos, at the southwest side of Punta Banda, not far from Ensenada, Baja California (fig. 4, Table 2). The summer temperatures at Arbolitos are usually about 4°–6°C. lower than in Ensenada, whereas winter temperatures differ relatively little at these two places. The differences in surface temperatures on the two sides of Punta Banda, a distance of only 3 km., in the summer commonly reach 5°–9°C., occasionally as much as 12°C.—a difference that one would not expect to encounter ordinarily over hundreds of miles of shoreline. This area of upwelling continues southward for many miles. Upwelling occurs also near Punta

Descanso (30 km. below the international border), to the south of Cabo Colnett, at and south of Punta Eugenia, and, to a lesser extent, on the open coast outside of Bahia Magdalena. A typical temperature survey for the summer, for the coast from La Jolla, California, to Punta Baja, Baja California is shown in figure 4. Base data for 1955–62 have been published (Anonymous, 1957; Hubbs and Hubbs, 1960–63).

Because of the low surface temperatures induced by this upwelling, the flora and fauna along the northwestern Baja California coast are largely cool-temperate. Californian types (notably rockfishes, *Sebastodes*, and embiotocids) dominate the fish fauna, which includes some central Californian species of sculpins and blennioids that avoid the warmer inshore waters of southern California (Hubbs, 1960b). During a cold period, dated at 1,600–600 years ago, the giant *Cryptochiton stelleri* also occurred along this coast, and was extensively harvested (Hubbs, 1958, 1960a; Hubbs, Bien, and Suess, 1960, 1962); in the coldest areas this northern species persisted until about 100 years ago.

In the regions of upwelling organic productivity is high. Thick beds of giant kelp (*Macrocystis*) grow, and lie close to shore because the temperatures are low. Red and brown plankton blooms are very frequent close to shore and occur every year (but apparently do not result in heavy fish kills). Of special importance to the aborigines was the abundance in this area of certain Cali-

TABLE 2—COASTAL SEA TEMPERATURES (°C.) ALONG THE WEST COAST OF BAJA
CALIFORNIA
Partly after U. S. Coast and Geodetic Survey, 1956

	Jan.	Feb.	Mar.	Apr.	May	June	July	Aug.	Sept.	Oct.	Nov.	Dec.
Ensenada	15.6	15.9	16.5	17.4	18.4	19.4	21.2	21.8	20.4	19.1	17.0	16.4
Arbolitos*	14.8	14.2	14.2	13.8	14.5	15.0	15.3	16.0	15.9	15.8	15.8	15.8
Cabo Colnett*	16.1	15.3	14.0	13.6	15.1	15.7	16.7	18.2	17.0	17.4	16.2	15.8
Isla San Benito	17.5	16.7	16.2	16.7	17.2	19.0	21.3	22.4	21.2	17.1	15.7	15.2
Isla Guadalupe	16.9	16.8	16.8	17.0	17.6	18.3	19.5	21.1	20.0	20.1	18.9	18.1
26°44′ N.,												
114°30′ W.*	18.2	17.8	15.6	14.3	14.3	14.2	17.2	20.0	21.8	22.5	20.0	18.5
Cabo San Lucas ...	21.9	21.6	22.4	21.6	23.2	23.6	26.7	28.2	29.0	28.2	26.2	22.8

*Regions of major upwelling.

fornian mollusks, notably the California mussel (*Mytilus californianus*), the pismo clam (*Tivela stultorum*), and species of abalone (*Haliotis*).

Outside the coastal areas of Baja California the seasonal temperature variation is generally less than 5°C. In the vicinity of Cabo San Lucas, however, the range is about 9°C. (in Golfo de California, toward the upper end, the seasonal range exceeds 15°C., and extreme differences are as great as 22°C.). The large seasonal range near the tip of the peninsula is attributed to the alternating effect of two water masses: the California Current water in winter and spring, and the North Equatorial Current water in summer and fall. The large range in the Gulf is discussed below.

The rather complex seasonal distribution of salinity (fig. 5) depends to a large degree on the seasonal variation in precipitation and upwelling. The rainy season and the greatly reduced upwelling cause slightly reduced salinities during winter in the north and during summer in the south. In the central region there is little seasonal variation in salinity, owing to sparse precipitation and persistent upwelling. Salinity gradients are strong in the vicinity of Cabo San Lucas, where low-salinity water from the California Current meets high-salinity water from Golfo de California.

Representative data on the distribution with depth of temperature, salinity, and oxygen along the west coast of Baja California (fig. 6), at a series of stations (fig. 7), illustrate several outstanding features of the region, particularly the shallow thermocline, between 30 and 60 m., the salinity minimum between 20 and 80 m., and the oxygen maximum in approximately the same layer. Below the thermocline, the characteristic feature is the intrusion of high-salinity and low-oxygen water from the south (Roden, 1964).

Calculations of the heat balance for the California Current region (Roden, 1959) yield estimates of the net incoming radia-

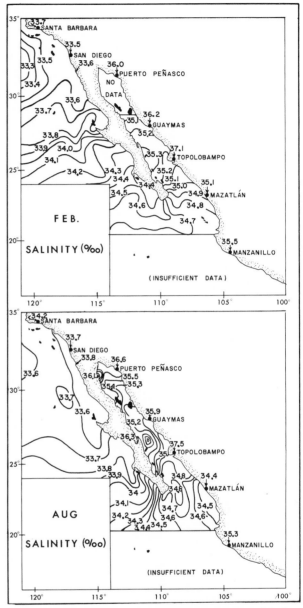

FIG. 5—SEA-SURFACE SALINITIES IN THE CALIFORNIA CURRENT REGION AND GOLFO DE CALIFORNIA, IN FEBRUARY AND IN AUGUST

tion of about 200 cal./sq. cm. day for winter and of about 400 cal./sq. cm. day for summer. Values on individual days vary considerably, owing to different amounts and types of clouds. The mean monthly variation of the incoming radiation (Q_r) indicates a net gain of heat throughout the year

151

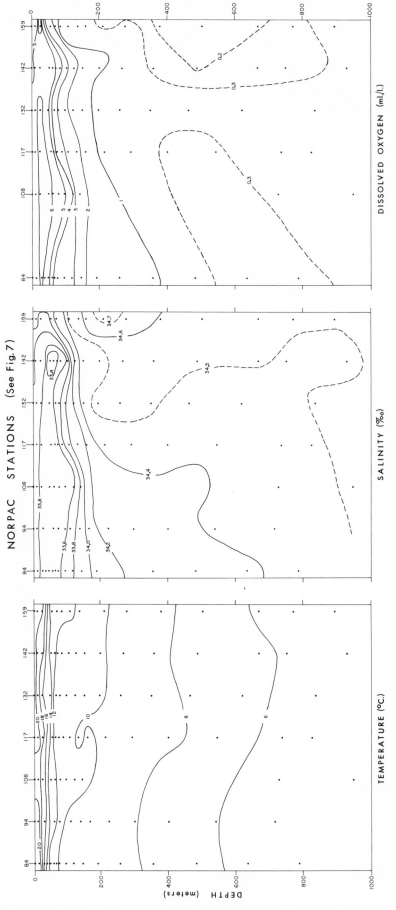

Fig. 6.—Vertical distribution of temperature, salinity, and dissolved oxygen in the California current region, at NORPAC stations shown in Fig. 7.

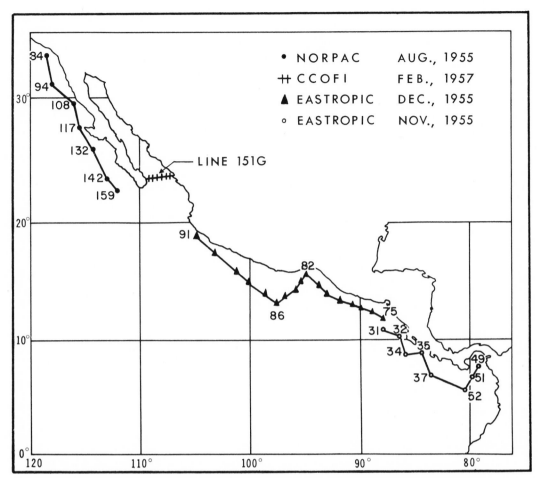

FIG. 7—LOCATION OF SECTIONS AND STATIONS, OF FOUR CRUISES, USED IN THIS INVESTIGATION
(See also figs. 6, 10, 13, 14.)

(Table 3). The loss of heat to the atmosphere (Q_a), through evaporation and conduction, varies roughly between 60 and 150 cal./sq. cm. day. Off Baja California the higher values occur in winter and spring, owing to increased wind speeds and lower humidities. At any particular place the upper layers of the ocean appear to gain heat between June and October and to lose heat between November and May. The lateness of the heating season relative to net incoming radiation can be attributed to advection of cold water by the California Current. The rate of cold advection seems to be largest between February and April and least between June and September.

Advection of warm water is observed only in the coastal area south of Punta Eugenia, where it occurs in September and amounts to about 200 cal./sq. cm. day.

Golfo de California

Golfo de California occupies an oceanographically unique position among the marginal seas of the Pacific Ocean. Because it lies between the mountainous and arid peninsula of Baja California and the similarly arid eastern shores, in Sonora and Sinaloa, the Gulf constitutes a large evaporation basin, which, at its southern end, is in open communication with the Pacific. The southern boundary of the Gulf is not

153

TABLE 3—MEAN MONTHLY NET INCOMING RADIATION (Q_r), TOTAL ENERGY EXCHANGE BETWEEN SEA SURFACE AND THE ATMOSPHERE (Q_a), LOCAL HEATING (Q_l) AND ADVECTION (Q_v)

All units in cal./sq. cm. day. After Roden, 1959

	Jan.	Feb.	Mar.	Apr.	May	June	July	Aug.	Sept.	Oct.	Nov.	Dec.
30°–35° N., 115°–120° W.												
Q_r	138	169	258	307	318	326	314	291	270	205	160	113
Q_a	−67	−74	−84	−74	−71	−63	−90	−90	−84	−88	−78	−62
Q_l	−141	−83	−32	−70	−26	173	237	166	128	51	−166	−237
Q_v	−212	−178	−206	−303	−273	−90	13	−35	−58	−66	−248	−288
25°–30° N., 110°–115° W.												
Q_r	176	208	317	356	388	389	395	408	370	288	213	154
Q_a	−128	−121	−145	−80	−105	−74	−63	−64	−85	−139	−123	−124
Q_l	−307	−205	−166	−204	−26	205	256	307	542	173	−294	−281
Q_v	−355	−292	−338	−480	−309	−110	−76	−37	257	24	−384	−311

well defined, but from oceanographic considerations it can be placed roughly on a line from Cabo San Lucas southeast to Cabo Corrientes. As thus delineated, the total surface area of the Gulf is about 250,000 sq. km. Topographically the Gulf comprises a series of basins, trenches, and ridges (Shepard, 1950). Toward the south these bottom features are sufficiently deep to permit a free exchange of water above a depth of roughly 2,000 m.; the northern depressions, which are isolated by shallower sills, have a distinctive hydrographic environment. In the vicinity of the numerous islands, particularly near the two largest (Tiburon and Angel de la Guarda), strong tidal currents, at times spectacular, induce extensive mixing with subsurface waters and keep the bottom, even where deep, largely free of soft sediments (Revelle, 1950; Francis P. Shepard, personal communication).

The surface circulation of the Gulf is predominantly wind-driven. In winter and spring the winds blow from the northwest with a speed of about 5 m./sec. and move the water southward; in summer and fall they blow from the southeast at about 3 m./sec., and induce a flow of water into the Gulf. In the northernmost part, as well as between the islands and the main coasts, tidal currents, often very strong, predominate (U. S. Hydrographic Office, 1951). Near the Gulf entrance seasonal changes in the currents are notable. According to data (Table 4) published by the Hydrographic Office (1947) and summarized cartographically in figure 8, for two areas near the entrance, the surface currents, averaged by the month, tend to be strongest (with a grand average of about 10 cm./sec. and reaching 15 cm./sec.) during winter and spring, when the general set is toward the south (to the south or south-southeast off Cabo Corrientes; to the south or southwest off Cabo San Lucas). In summer and fall the currents near the entrance are generally weaker, and the set is usually

TABLE 4—SPEED (CM./SEC.) AND DIRECTION OF CURRENTS NEAR THE ENTRANCE TO GOLFO DE CALIFORNIA, FOR EACH MONTH OF THE YEAR

After U. S. Hydrographic Office, 1947

Bearing in degrees true

	Jan.	Feb.	Mar.	Apr.	May	June	July	Aug.	Sept.	Oct.	Nov.	Dec.
22°–23° N., 110°–111° W.	4.0	10.7	12.4	15.0	11.3	5.5	4.0	4.6	4.0	6.3	7.5	6.6
	230°	170°	150°	160°	170°	180°	230°	280°	250°	240°	270°	230°
20°–21° N., 107°–108° W.	8.7	10.3	11.3	6.3	5.1	5.5	7.6	5.1	2.4	3.6	6.6	8.8
	230°	180°	180°	200°	180°	290°	290°	300°	340°	270°	290°	210°

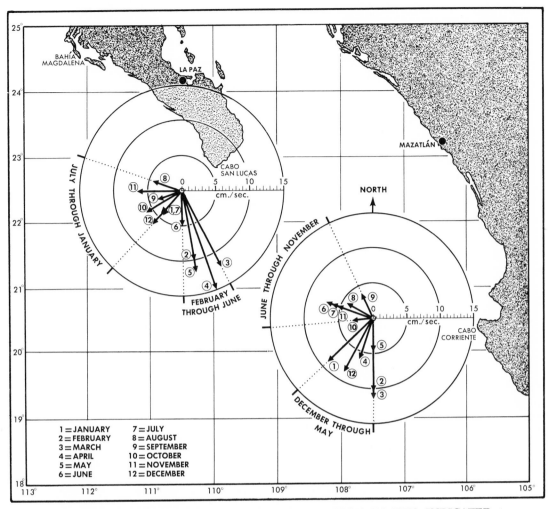

Fɪɢ. 8—SPEED AND DIRECTION OF SURFACE CURRENTS IN TWO INDICATED
AREAS NEAR THE OFFING OF GOLFO DE CALIFORNIA
Data (also recorded in upper part of Table 6) from U. S. Hydrographic Office, 1947. Lengths
of arrows indicate average strength of current for each month (1–12).

toward the west (to the west or northwest off Cabo Corrientes; to the west or southwest off Cabo San Lucas).

The surface temperatures in the Gulf (fig. 9, Table 5) are considerably influenced by the arid climate, by the surrounding land masses, and particularly by the seasonal changes in wind direction, all of which give rise to a large annual temperature range. In the open Gulf the surface temperatures vary between 14° and 20°C. in February, and between 27° and 31°C. in August. In partly enclosed waters, along the Sonoran coast, where frost occurs, surface temperatures drop greatly, occasional-

ly to as low as 12°C. In the uppermost part of the open Gulf the surface waters in winter are often as cool as the coastal waters of southern California and northwestern Baja California; and even about the mouth of the Gulf the surface temperatures are then commonly about 20°C. The upper layers usually warm rapidly in spring, and through summer and fall the temperatures throughout the Gulf approximate those of the eastern tropical Pacific (about 30°C.).

The lowest temperatures in any given month occur in the area of strong tidal mixing in Canal de las Ballenas, between the Baja California mainland and the islands

155

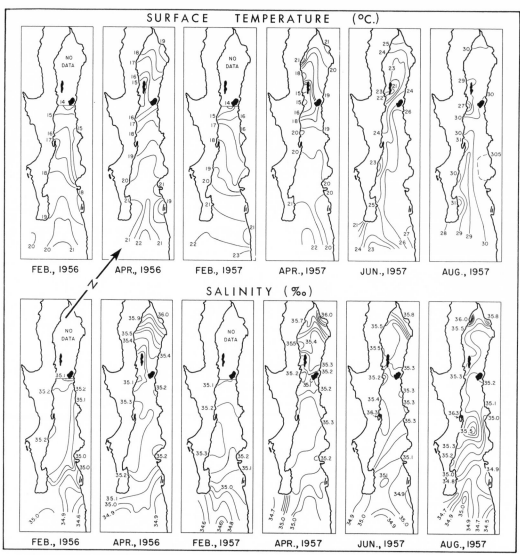

Fɪɢ. 9—SEASONAL VARIATION OF SURFACE TEMPERATURE AND SALINITY IN
GOLFO DE CALIFORNIA
(After Roden and Groves, 1959.)

of Angel de la Guarda and San Lorenzo
(Roden and Groves, 1959). Localized coastwise upwelling in the Gulf, characterized
by low temperatures and relatively low
salinities, occurs in isolated places along
the east coast in winter and along the west
coast in summer; it is not nearly as pronounced, however, as on the Pacific side
of the peninsula. The highest temperatures,
at times exceeding 34°C., occur in semi-enclosed bays and estuaries along the coast
(Osorio-Tafall, 1943). Since temperatures
as low as 12°C. have been encountered in

semi-enclosed waters along the Gulf (original data), the extreme annual range reaches
the figure, of at least 22°C., that greatly
exceeds the value for any other region
along the entire coast of western North
America.

The extraordinary range of temperatures
in Golfo de California has had a profound
effect on the character of the fauna and
flora. The biota is rather limited in number
of species, presumably largely because temperatures become too cold in winter for
many tropical types and too warm in sum-

After U. S. Coast and Geodetic Survey, 1956, 1957.
The salinities are indicative of the local environment and do not represent those of the open Gulf.

	Jan.	Feb.	Mar.	Apr.	May	June	July	Aug.	Sept.	Oct.	Nov.	Dec.
Temperatures (°C.):												
Puerto Peñasco ..	14.9	15.8	17.8	20.6	23.8	26.3	29.7	31.2	31.0	28.4	22.0	17.1
Guaymas	17.9	18.8	19.1	22.2	25.4	29.4	31.3	31.5	31.3	28.9	23.3	18.9
Topolobampo ...	19.6	20.7	20.8	23.7	26.4	29.8	31.4	31.7	31.3	30.0	22.7	20.4
Mazatlan	21.7	20.8	21.0	21.9	24.7	28.2	29.6	30.0	30.0	28.4	25.1	23.0
La Paz	20.3	20.2	21.4	22.4	24.2	25.1	27.4	29.2	29.6	28.2	25.1	21.7
Salinity (‰):												
Puerto Peñasco ..	36.0	36.0	36.3	36.6	36.4	36.6	36.6	36.6	36.7	36.6	36.6	36.0
Guaymas	36.3	36.2	36.0	36.0	36.8	37.5	37.1	35.9	36.3	36.7	36.2	36.2
Topolobampo ...	36.8	37.1	36.8	37.1	37.3	37.9	38.1	37.5	37.3	37.3	37.3	35.7
Mazatlan	35.0	35.1	35.1	35.4	35.4	35.5	34.8	34.4	32.7	34.5	35.1	35.1
La Paz	36.0	36.2	36.6	36.6	36.6	36.6	36.6	36.2	36.2	36.2	36.0	35.9

mer for most temperate types. A considerable number of tropical forms, however, have adjusted themselves to the Gulf conditions, and a number of temperate types (Pleistocene relicts or forms that still occur in moderate depths around Cabo San Lucas) maintain themselves (Hubbs, 1948, 1952, 1960b; Walker, 1960). Some fundamental physiological adaptation may have been involved, or breeding seasons may have been adjusted to allow for reproduction at appropriate times in the widely varying seasonal range in temperature. Many species can survive extremes of temperatures and other conditions, so long as they can find suitable conditions for reproduction at some time during the year. For some species, cold is limiting; for others, warmth; still others tolerate both low and high temperatures, or extremes of other environmental factors (Hutchins, 1947).

The biota of Golfo de California is characterized not only by the limited number of species, especially toward the upper half of the Gulf, where variations in temperature and other factors are extreme, but also by the peculiar mixture of temperate and tropical forms. Furthermore, as one might expect from the isolation of Pleistocene cold-water relicts and from the confinement of most forms, and from the highly varying and in some respects peculiar environmental factors, a considerable proportion of the biota is endemic.

The great seasonal range in temperature in the upper part of the Gulf is correlated with the similarly wide range in air temperatures, particularly on the northern coast of Sonora. Here is considerable frost in winter, high temperatures in summer, and, almost constantly, very low humidity. These conditions may well have served as a barrier, limiting the northwestward spread of the higher human cultures that developed in Mexico during the last two or three millennia.

The surface salinities in the Gulf are closely related to the difference between evaporation and precipitation (Roden, 1958). The average rate of evaporation is about 250 cm./year; that of precipitation, only 25 cm./year. The excess of evaporation over precipitation tends to increase the salinities, which are about 1.5 per mille higher inside than outside the Gulf. The salinity increases slightly toward the upper end of the Gulf and, offshore, reaches its highest values in the vicinity of Puerto Peñasco, where it sometimes exceeds 36 per cent (fig. 9). Salinities are consistently higher in semi-enclosed bays and lagoons than in the open Gulf (Table 5). In some northern lagoons evaporation is so rapid that salt is precipitated.

The influence of the Colorado River on salinities has been negligible in recent years, owing to the diversion of most of the water for irrigation; occasionally, for weeks at a time, no surface water reaches the

157

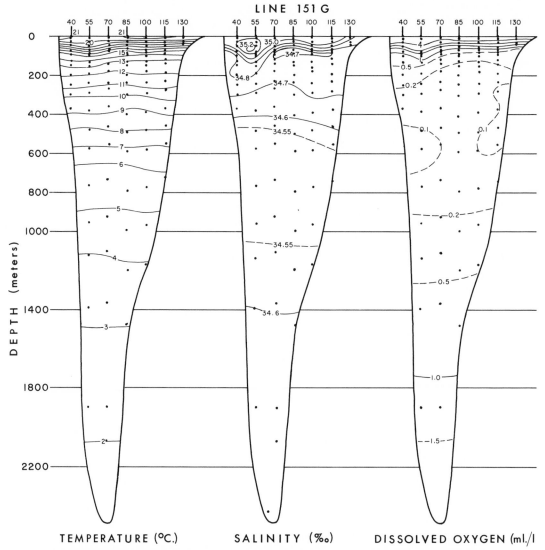

LINE 151 G

TEMPERATURE (°C.) SALINITY (‰) DISSOLVED OXYGEN (ml./l)

FIG. 10—VERTICAL DISTRIBUTION OF TEMPERATURE, SALINITY, AND DISSOLVED
OXYGEN ACROSS GOLFO DE CALIFORNIA, NEAR MOUTH, ALONG SURVEY LINE
151G OF THE CALIFORNIA COOPERATIVE OCEANIC FISHERIES INVESTIGATIONS
(SHOWN BY HATCHED LINE ON FIG. 7) AT INDICATED NAUTICAL MILES FROM
THE WEST SHORE

Gulf. Prior to the construction of various dams, the mean annual discharge at Yuma, Arizona, was about 550 cu. m./sec.; now, it is only 180 cu. m./sec. (U. S. Geological Survey, 1954). Salinities near the mouth of the Colorado River were relatively low (34.5 per cent) in 1889 (Townsend, 1901), but values that low have not been observed on recent cruises.

Temperature, salinity, and dissolved-oxygen content in the Gulf all vary significantly with depth (fig. 10). The thermocline is well developed throughout the year, generally between 10 and 50 m. Only in the northernmost, shallow part of the Gulf and in the area of strong tidal mixing does the thermocline vanish during winter months. There is salinity minimum below the thermocline, between 400 and 800 m., and an oxygen minimum between 200 and 800 m.

The content of dissolved oxygen in the minimum layer may be as low as 0.05 ml./l., and in a few analyses it was impossible to determine the amount by ordinary methods. The extremely low concentrations are attributable, at least in part, to the circumstance that the very high stability of the upper layers does not permit an exchange of oxygen with the deeper layers, into which much of the extremely rich plankton sinks, consuming oxygen as it decomposes.

Golfo de California is particularly noted for its extremely high production of aquatic life (Osorio-Tafall, 1943; Steinbeck and Ricketts, 1941). One of its names, Vermilion Sea, is based on the almost continuous plankton bloom. At times the water in the upper Gulf looks like thick soup (Hubbs once encountered extensive areas where large hydromedusae, where thickest, seemed almost to fill the water—in 17 trials with a dipnet they were found to vary from 1 to 130/cu. m., with an average of 27/cu. m.). Red blooms are especially common also in the area of maximum turbulence, about the islands of Angel de la Guarda and Tiburon; bright green blooms occasionally occur there.

Mexican Region

As defined by Schott (1935), the Mexican region lies between the Northeast Trades and the Southeast Trades, in the area from Cabo San Lucas to Golfo de Tehauntepec and seaward to the North Equatorial Current. Golfo de California, with its unique hydrographic conditions, is discussed above. Golfo de Tehuantepec, which by reason of its characteristic winter circulation belongs to the Central American region, is discussed below.

The outstanding features of the Mexican region are the weak and variable currents, the high surface temperatures, and the relatively high salinities (Table 6, figs. 11, 12). The predominant drift is toward the southeast in winter and toward the northwest in summer. The strongest southeastward-setting currents, about 15 cm./sec., occur between February and April; the strongest northwestward ones, about 20 cm./sec., between June and August. The surface temperatures are high and over most of the area vary little (about 5°C.) seasonally. The salinities appear to be rather uniform, with a seasonal range of about 3 per mille in coastal regions, but

TABLE 6—OCEANOGRAPHIC DATA FOR THE MEXICAN REGION
Speed (cm./sec.) and direction of surface currents (after U. S. Hydrographic Office, 1947) and coastal sea temperatures and salinities (after U. S. Coast and Geodetic Survey, 1956, 1957). Data on currents graphed as fig. 8.
Bearing in degrees true

	Jan.	Feb.	Mar.	Apr.	May	June	July	Aug.	Sept.	Oct.	Nov.	Dec.
Current:												
18°–19° N.,	12.8	2.6	15.4	2.1	5.6	13.3	11.3	9.8	4.7	2.1	7.7	12.4
104°–105° W.	280°	230°	250°	190°	280°	290°	290°	300°	280°	240°	280°	300°
16°–17° N.,	2.1	13.3	10.7	10.3	3.0	12.4	9.2	6.6	2.6	2.1	3.6	5.1
100°–101° W.	240°	120°	140°	130°	240°	280°	280°	290°	260°	140°	140°	150°
15°–16° N.,	12.4	16.9	13.3	12.8	6.2	20.1	12.6	2.1	2.1	2.1	13.9	4.1
97°–98° W.	130°	130°	120°	130°	270°	280°	280°	260°	190°	160°	130°	200°
Temperature (°C.):												
Manzanillo ...	26.8	26.7	25.6	25.7	26.9	28.2	28.9	30.0	29.4	28.9	27.4	27.2
Acapulco	27.3	26.8	26.1	26.3	27.7	28.8	29.5	30.0	29.7	28.8	28.3	27.8
Salinity (‰):												
Manzanillo ...	35.1	35.5	35.3	35.3	35.7	35.3	35.5	35.3	34.1	33.1	33.6	34.4
Acapulco	34.2	34.4	34.6	34.6	34.8	34.1	33.1	33.5	32.5	32.8	33.7	34.0

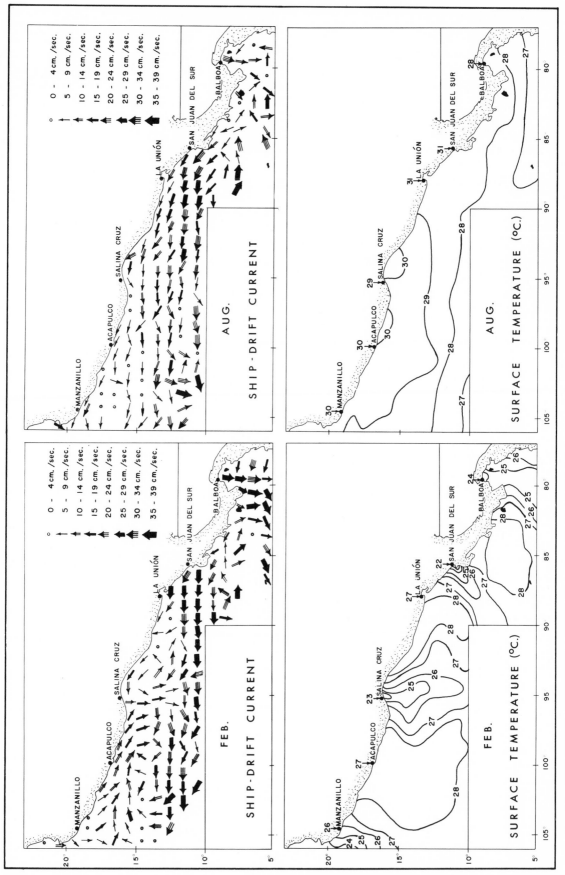

FIG. 11—SHIP-DRIFT CURRENTS (AFTER U. S. HYDROGRAPHIC OFFICE, 1947) AND SEA-SURFACE TEMPERATURES OFF SOUTHERN COAST OF MEXICO AND OFF CENTRAL AMERICA

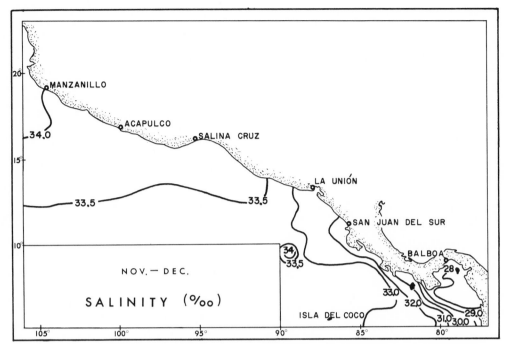

Fig. 12—SEA-SURFACE SALINITIES (NOVEMBER AND DECEMBER) OFF SOUTHERN COAST OF MEXICO AND OFF CENTRAL AMERICA

their monthly variation cannot be established from the meager data available. Salinities are lowest during the rainy season (June to October). Throughout the year the thermocline in this region is strongly developed and usually lies above 50 m. (Cromwell, 1958). Outstanding features of the variations with depth of salinity and oxygen along the coast between Cabo Corrientes and Costa Rica (exemplified by a vertical section in fig. 13) are the presence of strong halocline around 50 m., the salinity maximum between 100 and 300 m., and the low content of dissolved oxygen between the thermocline and about 800 m. The oxygen values, however, are not as low as previously reported (Sverdrup, Johnson, and Fleming, 1942).

Central American Region

The ocean off the southwest coast of Central America is influenced considerably by winds of both the Pacific and the Atlantic. Winds from the Atlantic are mostly felt during the dry season (November to April), particularly when a continental anticyclone extends far southward into the Gulf of Mexico or when the Azores high is southwest of its normal position. Under these conditions strong winds blow offshore in the gulfs of Tehuantepec, Papagayo, and Panama. The energy of the wind is derived partly from the tendency of air currents to flow around mountains and to crowd through mountain gaps, and partly from the instabilities created when cold, dense air overrides warm and less dense air beyond the gap. Such winds, which have been termed "fall winds" (Godske, Bergeron, Bjerknes, and Bundgaard, 1957), are common in the gulfs of Tehuantepec and Papagayo (Hurd, 1929a). The northerlies in Golfo de Panama, representing intensified Northeast Trades from the Atlantic (Chapel, 1927), are of a different type (essentially "gradient winds").

The effect of the strong northerly winds on the ocean surface (Roden, 1961b) is twofold: (1) they displace the surface waters to the south and thus cause entrain-

161

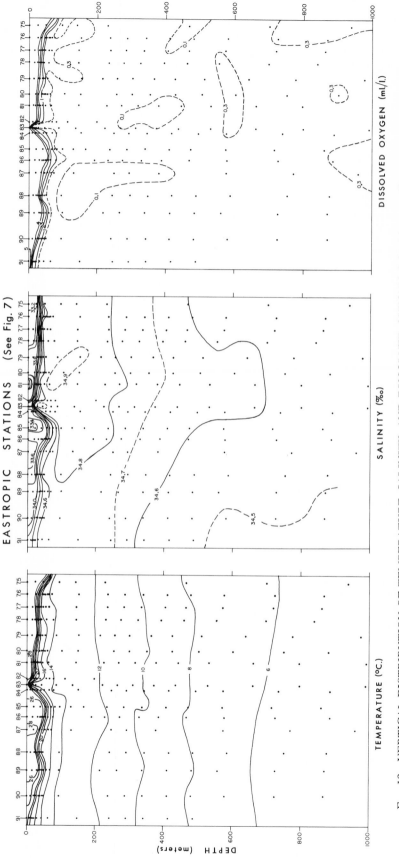

FIG. 13.—VERTICAL DISTRIBUTION OF TEMPERATURE, SALINITY, AND DISSOLVED OXYGEN OFF SOUTHWESTERN MEXICO AND OFF NORTHWESTERN CENTRAL AMERICA

ment of water from the sides and from below, and (2) they cause mixing. Both processes lead to a considerable lowering of the sea-surface temperature in the gulfs mentioned above. In the winter a southward current sets off Salina Cruz and off Balboa (fig. 11). The sea-surface temperatures in these regions are 2°–6°C. lower than elsewhere off the coast of Central America. Another, very striking center of

coastal upwelling is Golfo de Papagayo, in northern Costa Rica, and along the adjacent indentation of the coast of southern Nicaragua. The upwelling areas are characterized by low temperatures, by relatively high salinities and high phosphate concentrations, and by low oxygen content (Fleming, 1935; Schaefer, Bishop, and Howard, 1958; Blackburn, 1962, 1963). In correlation with the upwelling, the phyto-

TABLE 7—OCEANOGRAPHIC DATA FOR THE CENTRAL AMERICAN REGION
Speed (cm./sec.) and direction of surface currents (after U. S. Hydrographic Office, 1947) and coastal winds (after Servicio Meteorológico Mexicano, 1928–1941 and U. S. Hydrographic Office, 1951).
Bearing in degrees true

	Jan.	Feb.	Mar.	Apr.	May	June	July	Aug.	Sept.	Oct.	Nov.	Dec.
Current:												
14°–15° N.,	13.3	15.8	15.4	10.7	4.7	18.0	16.5	8.8	4.1	11.8	17.5	16.5
95°–96° W.	190	180	160	150	290	300	280	280	180	240	220	250
13°–14° N.,	4.7	3.0	8.1	2.1	12.8	30.8	22.0	18.4	10.7	21.6	6.2	3.0
91°–92° W.	030	350	090	320	300	290	300	290	320	330	300	330
10°–11° N.,	44.1	46.6	37.4	35.5	28.2	28.7	24.6	31.9	22.0	21.6	35.5	45.8
86°–87° W.	270	280	290	300	330	340	300	310	320	320	310	320
06°–07° N.,	56.1	56.1	47.7	42.2	14.3	24.2	19.0	18.0	14.0	3.6	26.1	34.9
80°–81° W.	230	200	200	220	200	230	200	220	180	170	160	220
08°–09° N.,	41.5	38.1	37.4	38.5	34.4	30.8	32.3	32.3	28.7	26.1	32.3	38.9
79°–80° W.	190	180	210	200	190	190	190	200	180	180	210	190
Mean wind speed (m./sec.):												
Salina Cruz	9.8	9.2	8.9	8.9	6.7	4.9	5.9	5.9	4.4	6.3	8.4	8.8
Punta Mala	9.0	9.4	8.8	7.0	4.9	4.3	3.7	3.8	4.0	4.5	5.0	6.7
Balboa	4.1	4.8	4.7	4.0	2.8	2.4	2.7	2.7	2.6	2.9	2.6	2.9
Maximum wind speed (m./sec.):												
Salina Cruz	35.4	33.7	36.2	33.9	28.1	25.6	25.5	24.6	24.0	35.0	33.3	32.2
Balboa	14.3	15.2	16.1	17.4	21.0	17.0	15.2	16.5	17.0	17.0	15.3	16.1
Mean temperature (°C.):												
Salina Cruz*	23.0	22.6	24.8	26.2	27.8	28.4	28.6	28.8	28.7	26.4	24.1	23.3
San Jose	28.1	28.1	28.6	29.3	29.8	29.8	30.0	30.0	30.0	28.8	28.9	28.6
La Union	27.2	27.3	28.4	30.0	30.3	30.1	30.2	30.6	29.9	28.8	27.8	27.2
San Juan del Sur*	24.3	21.8	22.4	25.0	27.0	28.5	27.7	28.8	30.8	29.8	27.8	25.9
Puerto Armuelles.	28.9	28.8	28.7	28.8	28.1	28.2	28.4	28.6	28.3	27.8	28.0	28.1
Naos Island* ...	26.4	24.7	23.8	25.3	28.1	28.6	28.3	28.2	28.8	28.0	27.7	27.2
Mean salinity (‰):												
Salina Cruz*	34.8	34.8	35.1	34.9	34.9	34.0	33.8	34.0	32.9	33.5	34.4	36.5
San Jose	33.6	34.1	34.5	34.5	34.4	33.5	32.4	32.7	31.9	31.1	32.7	33.3
La Union	33.8	35.0	35.8	35.9	33.7	28.4	27.6	29.1	25.2	24.4	29.7	32.3
San Juan del Sur*	34.9	34.2	34.8	35.1	34.4	33.7	34.2	34.4	34.6	34.0	34.2	34.9
Puerto Armuelles.	31.0	31.9	32.9	33.7	33.8	33.3	32.4	31.9	31.9	31.2	31.1	30.7
Naos Island* ...	31.4	33.2	34.2	34.4	32.8	30.6	29.9	30.2	28.4	27.3	27.6	28.9
Mean minimum temperature (°C.):												
Salina Cruz*	18.9	20.0	18.9	22.4	23.9	25.8	26.8	27.2	27.0	22.8	18.1	18.7
San Juan del Sur*	19.6	18.2	19.3	21.1	21.1	24.9	24.3	24.6	26.0	23.5	22.7	21.1
Naos Island* ...	24.1	21.7	21.6	22.0	26.4	27.7	27.4	27.3	27.8	26.9	26.9	26.2

* Areas of upwelling.

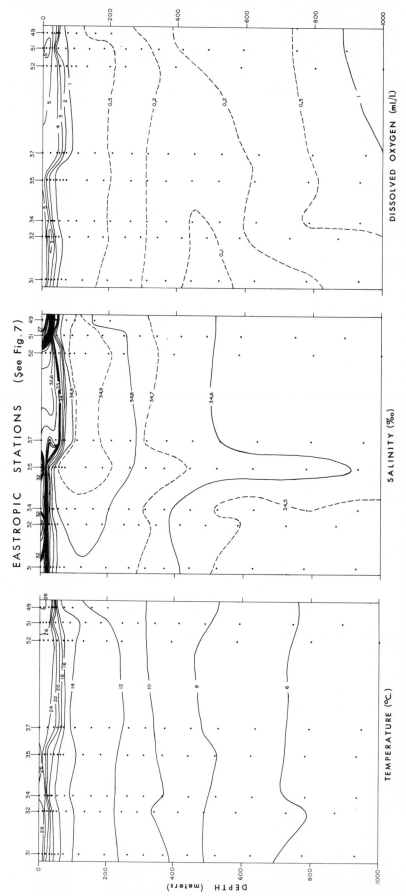

FIG. 14—VERTICAL DISTRIBUTION OF TEMPERATURE, SALINITY, AND DISSOLVED OXYGEN OFF SOUTHWESTERN COAST OF CENTRAL AMERICA

plankton is moderately rich (W. E. Allen, 1939).

Temperatures and salinities, as well as the winds and currents, vary greatly along the Central American coast (figs. 11, 12, Table 7). The highest average wind speeds, between 8 and 10 m./sec., are recorded at Salina Cruz, Mexico, and at Punta Mala, Panama, from December to March. The speed of the southward-setting current during this time varies between 15 and 20 cm./sec. in Golfo de Tehuantepec and between 40 and 60 cm./sec. in Golfo de Panama. The minimum surface temperatures vary between 18° and 21°C. in Golfo de Tehuantepec and between 20° and 23°C. in Golfo de Panama. The low-temperature area in the vicinity of Golfo de Papagayo is small and does not extend far offshore, but is noted for temperatures as surprisingly low as 16°C.

During summer the entire region off Central America is influenced by the Southeast Trades and is dominated by a west- to northwestward-setting current. The surface temperatures are high, between 27° and 29°C. In coastal areas the temperatures are sometimes even higher. Owing to abundant rainfall and considerable runoff, the salinities are low. The offshore salinities are lowest, less than 29 per mille, in Golfo de Panama, and throughout "Panama Bight." Salinities may be still lower in partly enclosed coastal recesses, such as Golfo de Nicoya (Peterson, 1960).

Outstanding subsurface features along the Central American coast are the well-developed thermocline between 30 and 60 m., the oxygen minimum between 300 and 600 m., and the salinity maximum between 100 and 300 m. (fig. 14; the very low surface salinities shown in this figure, probably lower than usual, are attributable to above-normal rainfall in 1955).

The coastal areas in the southeastern part of Golfo de Panama and throughout the "Panama Bight" are dominated by the warm northward-setting Colombia Current

(Wooster, 1959). Winter temperatures range between 25° and 26°C. and summer temperatures between 26° and 27°C. Surface salinities, depending to a large extent on rainfall, vary between 28 and 34 per mille.

In the central part of the Middle American region, between and including the gulfs of Tehuantepec and Fonseca, a long stretch of depositional shoreline appears to present a barrier against the dispersal of rocky-shore fishes (and presumably other organisms), so that faunal subregions have been distinguished on either side (Springer, 1958).

Tides and Sea Level

The tides along the Pacific coasts of Mexico and Central America are of the mixed type, with large diurnal inequalities (U. S. Coast and Geodetic Survey, 1915). The mean tidal ranges (fig. 15) are only 0.5 m. along the open coast between San Blas and Acapulco, but increase rapidly toward the interior part of Golfo de California (Roden and Groves, 1959) and, more gradually and to a much lesser degree, from near Acapulco to Golfo de Panama (Fleming, 1938). Along the west coast of Baja California the mean range lies between 1.2 and 1.8 m.

Within Golfo de California (fig. 16) the tidal ranges increase very slowly to Isla Tiburon, but thence rise very rapidly toward the mouth of Rio Colorado, where ranges exceeding 10 m. occur during spring tides. The tidal wave continues into Rio Colorado in the form of a very conspicuous bore. Twenty kilometers upstream the bore has been measured by tide gauge to heights as great as 3 m. (José G. Valenzuela, personal communication). The time of high water (fig. 16) becomes progressively later with distance up to the head of the Gulf, where it is 5.5 hours later than at its mouth. Tidal currents are very strong in the northern part of the Gulf, especially in Canal de las Ballenas, between Baja California and

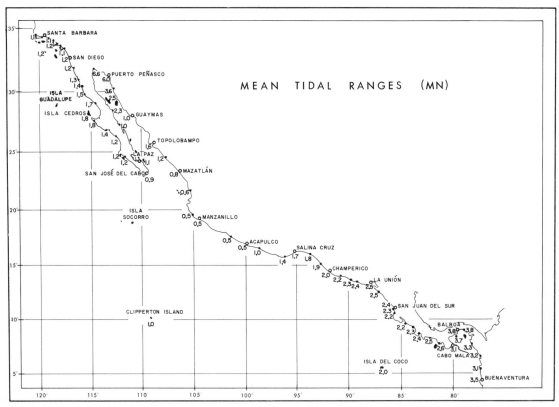

FIG. 15—MEAN TIDAL RANGES ALONG THE PACIFIC COAST FROM SOUTHERN CALIFORNIA TO COLOMBIA

Figures are in meters.

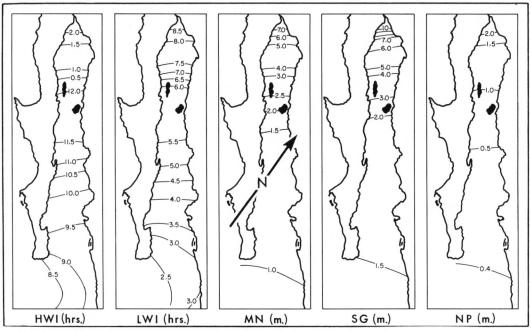

FIG. 16—TIDES IN GOLFO DE CALIFORNIA

HWI, high-water interval; LWI, low-water interval; MN, mean range; SG, spring range; NP, neap range (after Roden and Groves, 1959). Figures are in meters.

the islands of Angel de la Guarda and San Lorenzo. At times the tidal front in the southern part of this channel is said to become a high bore. These currents occasionally reach speeds of 3 m./sec. and in the narrows induce intensive mixing, which has important biological consequences.

The tides in Golfo de Panama resemble those in Golfo de California, although on a somewhat reduced scale. The mean tidal range increases from about 3 m. at Cabo Mala to 4 m. at Balboa; for the spring tides the corresponding increase is roughly from 3.5 to 5.5 m. The highest tides observed at the head of the Gulf approximate 7 m. The tides throughout the broadly open Golfo de Panama occur simultaneously.

The generally well-developed tides along the Pacific Coast of Middle America have no doubt been of long standing, and have had varied oceanographic, geomorphological, and biological effects. They cause great turbulence and much vertical mixing in the central part of Golfo de California, as already noted. They no doubt cause beach erosion and sand transport, so as to produce rocky shores. The greater extent of rocky shoreline and the greater width of the rocky habitat affected by tides appear to have conditioned the extensive speciation of certain fish groups in this habitat, for instance in the clinid blennies (Clark Hubbs, 1952, 1953; Springer, 1958); in the clingfishes (Briggs, 1951, 1955); in the emblemariid blennies (Rosenblatt, 1959); and in the brosmophycine brotulids (Boyd W. Walker,

personal communication). The tides in many ways have been a boon for man; for example, in rendering easy and effective the gathering of clams and other intertidal animals, and in making possible the capture of shrimp in the tapo net, in tidal estuaries.

The nontidal sea-level variation along the west coasts of Mexico and Central America is characterized by low levels in winter and by high levels in summer (Pattullo, Munk, Revelle, and Strong, 1955). The annual ranges vary widely from place to place (Table 8) and seem to depend on the particular environment in which the tide-gauge station is located. In shallow bays and harbors the sea-level variations follow the water temperature rather closely (Roden, 1960). Sea-level variations at Panama have recently been treated (Roden, 1963).

Sea, Swell, and Surf

Except in more or less enclosed waters, of which the largest is Golfo de California, the generally straight and openly exposed shores of Middle America are commonly lashed by moderately heavy surf, and the sea surface often is rather rough. Heavy swell comes from storms far to the north or south, and rough seas result from local storms. Such conditions affect shore features, increasing erosion and exposing rocky habitats, where erosion can reach rock, and building barrier bars or depositional shores.

Shore life abounds on the rocky reefs, owing to the abundant surface for attachment, plentiful supply of living and detrital

TABLE 8—DEVIATION OF MONTHLY SEA LEVEL FROM THE ANNUAL MEAN (CM.)

	Jan.	Feb.	Mar.	Apr.	May	June	July	Aug.	Sept.	Oct.	Nov.	Dec.
Ensenada	−1.9	−4.3	−6.5	−7.0	−5.2	−1.7	+1.6	+5.9	+6.3	+5.5	+4.7	+2.6
Guaymas	−15.2	−14.5	−13.2	−9.9	−0.1	+13.5	+19.0	+17.8	+17.7	+5.6	−9.4	−11.3
Mazatlan	−5.0	−10.3	−12.3	−11.7	−2.1	+7.7	+14.7	+12.7	+13.5	+2.9	−5.5	−4.6
La Paz	−7.3	−9.1	−11.8	−10.9	−6.3	−1.8	+6.3	+11.8	+14.1	+10.3	+6.4	−1.7
Isla Socorro ..	−0.9	−2.2	−0.2	+0.4	+2.4	+1.8	−1.5	−1.4	+2.5	+1.0	−0.5	−1.4
Manzanillo ...	−1.7	−8.9	−11.8	−12.1	−2.0	+3.0	+9.8	+7.8	+11.0	+4.1	−0.2	+1.0
Acapulco	−1.4	−7.4	−9.4	−7.5	−0.7	+4.4	+10.1	+8.0	+5.5	+1.4	−1.2	−1.8
Salina Cruz ...	−7.0	−6.5	−6.5	+0.3	+5.9	+9.5	+10.0	+9.8	+6.1	−3.8	−8.1	−9.7
San Juan del Sur	−7.0	−8.1	−10.6	−8.0	+5.6	+8.9	+4.2	+6.4	+4.6	+4.9	+1.5	−2.4
Balboa	−8.0	−16.9	−17.6	−11.4	+2.6	+7.1	+6.1	+5.0	+7.6	+10.5	+9.0	+6.0

167

food, high oxygen content, and other factors. In Baja California the surf-bound coast is very productive in the beds of giant kelp, *Macrocystis*, with a train of animal associates, and abounds in intertidal mollusks, such as the California mussel (*Mytilus californianus*), abalones (*Haliotis* spp.), limpets (*Lottia, Acmaea, Fissurella*, etc.), and rock oysters (*Pseudochama*), and in spiny lobsters (*Panulirus*). Similar growths are affected farther south, and almost everywhere intertidal rocks are rich in life. Midden remains bear mute evidence to the extensive utilization by primitive man of the animal life of the wave-washed rocky shores.

Shoreline Features

The rich rocky foreshore just mentioned is conditioned in part by heavy swell and sea, but owes its extensive development along the Pacific Coast largely to other factors. Prominent among these is the proximity of hills and mountains to the shore. Rocky structures throughout much of the coast are being directly eroded by the sea. The continental divide through most of Central America is close to the Pacific. Depositional coastal plains are much less extensive on the Pacific side than on the Atlantic.

In general much of the Pacific shoreline has a high proportion of coastal lagoons as well as of rocky shores. Both are very productive of food for man. That lagoons as well as rocky shores were extensively exploited in preconquest times is abundantly indicated by midden deposits and other remains.

Hurricanes

The hurricanes in the eastern tropical Pacific (locally known as "chubascos"), which originate mostly in the area between longitudes 95° and 105° W. and between latitude 10° N. and the coast, are related to oceanographic conditions. The hurricane season starts in late May, when the sea-

surface temperatures and the humidities are high and when the intertropical convergence has shifted northward. The peak of the season is reached in September, when as an average two storms occur. The hurricane season ends in early December, with the southward shift of the intertropical convergence and the cooling of the sea-surface temperatures.

It can be said without hesitation that hurricanes are at times the most important single factor affecting human life along the coast of southern Mexico. The severe storm in late October, 1959, left about 2,000 dead in Manzanillo and surrounding communities. The severest damage was caused not directly by wind but indirectly by an extraordinary rise in sea level and by torrential rainfall. Similar disasters have occurred previously but somehow the meteorological literature contains only a few, inadequate studies of hurricanes in this region (Hurd, 1929a,b). Occasionally, these storms were a boon: according to Aschmann (1959), a single chubasco in the desert region of Baja California may yield more rain than will fall in the next two or three years; and a chubasco may strand large numbers of shellfish on shore.

The outstanding features of the storm tracks of the hurricanes and tropical cyclones (fig. 17) are that in July and August most storms travel west to northwest and tend either to hit the southern coast of Baja California or to head seaward toward the Revillagigedo Islands, whereas in all other months most of the storms curve northeastward and affect the entire coastline from Salina Cruz in Golfo de Tehuantepec to Guaymas in Golfo de California. The speed of the storm centers varies; along straight parts of the track it is about 370–550 km./day. The speed of the winds around the center is extremely variable, 30–75 m./sec. The severest storms usually strike in October and November (Meteorological Office, London, 1956; U. S. Weather Bureau, 1955–1960).

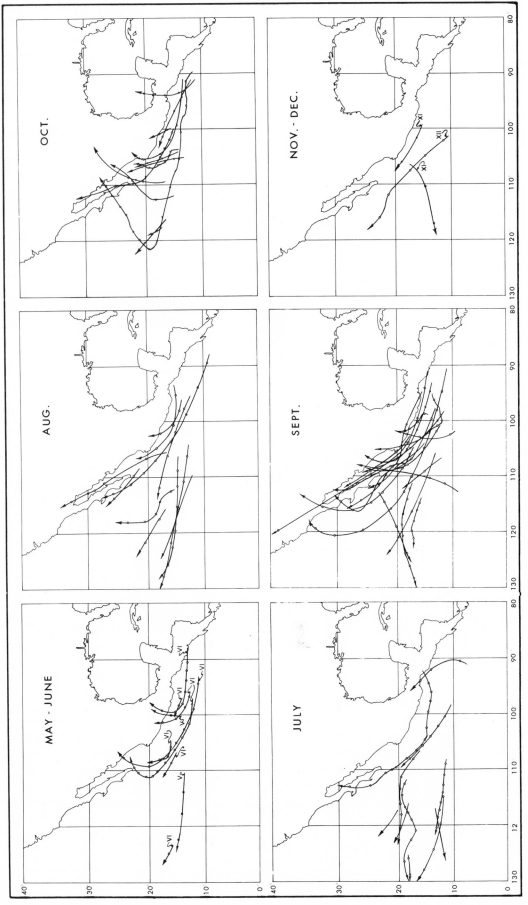

FIG. 17—HURRICANE TRACKS IN THE EASTERN TROPICAL PACIFIC
(After Meteorological Office, London, 1956, and U. S. Weather Bureau, 1955–1960). Roman numerals refer to months.

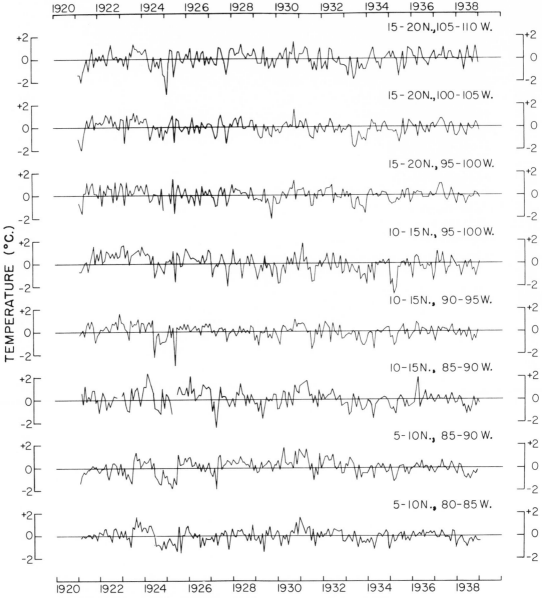

Fig. 18—MONTHLY SEA-SURFACE TEMPERATURE ANOMALIES OFF SOUTHERN
MEXICO AND CENTRAL AMERICA
(After reports of Imperial Marine Observatory, Kobe, Japan, for 1921–38).

Nonseasonal Temperature Variations

Apart from the more or less regular seasonal variations connected with solar radiation, the temperature of the sea surface undergoes nonseasonal variations due to changes in the atmospheric circulation and in the ocean currents. For the study of these variations there are only a very few, rather short-period records, some of which are shown in figure 18. The curves represent monthly anomalies from the long-term mean of respective months for several 5° squares of latitude and longitude off the southwestern coast of Mexico and Central America. Certain similarities in the anomalies along the coast are evident, particularly within the region off southern Mexico and Guatemala (the upper five graphs) and within the region farther southeast

170

(lower three graphs). The magnitude of the anomalies is in the order of 1°–2°C. The records shown here are too short to indicate any secular trends, but the observed good coherence between sea and air temperatures permits the use of air-temperature anomalies as an indication of sea-surface anomalies (Hubbs, 1948; Roden, 1961a). The yearly anomalies from the long-term yearly mean for San Diego, California, and for Mazatlan, Sinaloa (Table 9), indicate periods of temperatures above and below the normal, but long-term changes in the mean are not clearly indicated by such analysis. However, when the trends at San Diego are investigated by running means (fig. 19), it becomes evident that temperatures ran high at about the middle of the 19th century, and that the means, especially for late spring and early summer months, decreased from about 1850 to about 1910, with some possible rise since then (Hubbs, 1948). About 100 years ago the fauna at San Diego, California, included subtropical elements that are now rare or absent so far

north, and the fauna at Monterey, California, where the sea temperatures are now cold and the fauna cool-temperate, contained elements now characteristic of the warm-temperate San Diegan fauna (Hubbs, 1948).

Prehistoric Oceanographic, Climatic, and Food Conditions

Studies by the senior author of coastal middens on both sides of Baja California and in the adjacent parts of California are indicating, with increasing probability, that throughout most of Recent time, that is, since the end of the cold, wet Wisconsin Period, about 11,000 years ago (B.P.), the coastal temperatures have generally been warmer than at present. Paleotemperature (O^{18}) estimates and faunal data, from about 7,500 B.P. to the present, indicate warmer sea temperatures, which were almost surely accompanied by warmer air temperatures along the coast. The one exceptional period, when temperatures are indicated to have been colder in the sea

TABLE 9—ANNUAL AIR-TEMPERATURE ANOMALIES (°C.) FROM THE LONG-TERM ANNUAL MEAN, FOR EACH INDICATED YEAR

Values for San Diego, for months after January, 1940, are corrected to compensate for higher temperatures at the new location, but no such corrections are made for the Mazatlan data.

	0	1	2	3	4	5	6	7	8	9
San Diego (mean = 16.4°):										
1850	−0.4	....	+0.3	+1.0	+0.3	+0.5	−0.3	+0.2	−0.2	−0.2
60	−0.2	+1.0	+0.6	0	+1.0	+0.4	+0.8	+1.3	+0.8	+0.4
70	−0.2	+0.2	−0.6	−0.8	−1.1	0	−0.3	+0.4	−0.5	−0.8
80	−1.6	−0.6	−1.0	−0.2	−0.4	+0.3	−0.6	−0.5	+0.1	+0.6
90	+0.2	+0.3	−0.7	−0.5	−1.7	−0.6	+0.2	−0.3	−0.6	−0.8
1900	+0.3	−0.4	−1.0	−0.4	+0.4	−0.2	−0.2	−0.2	−1.1	−1.0
10	−0.6	−0.8	−0.7	−0.6	+0.1	−0.2	−1.2	−0.6	+0.3	−0.4
20	−0.7	−0.4	−0.6	0	−0.4	+0.1	+0.8	−0.2	−0.2	+0.5
30	+0.4	+1.4	−0.5	−1.3	+0.8	−0.2	+0.6	−0.2	+0.2	+0.6
40	+1.0	+1.0	+0.4	+0.9	−0.1	+0.4	+0.6	+0.7	−0.3	−0.1
50	+0.2	+0.3	+0.2	+0.7	+0.8	+0.3	+0.7	+1.3	+2.0	+2.1
60	+0.9	+0.8	+0.1	....	....	....	....	....	....	....
Mazatlan (mean = 24.3°):										
1880	−0.5	+0.2	−0.4	−0.3	+0.3	+0.7	−0.4	−0.7	+1.0	+1.4
90	+1.5	+1.0	+0.2	−0.1	+0.2	+0.6	+1.1	+1.3	+0.1	+0.3
1900	+1.1	+0.3	+0.4	+0.6	+0.3	+1.3	+0.9	+0.8	+0.8	−1.0
10	−0.4	+0.2	....	....	....	....	....	....	....	....
20	....	−1.1	−1.1	−0.6	−1.0	−0.5	−0.3	−0.8	−0.3	−1.1
30	−0.6	−0.3	−0.9	−1.6	−0.3	+0.2	−0.2	−0.6	−0.2	−0.4
40	+0.3	+0.6	0	0	−0.5	−0.5	+0.2	0	+0.3	−0.1
50	+0.4	+0.2	+0.3	−0.1	+0.3	−0.8	−0.1	....	....	....

171

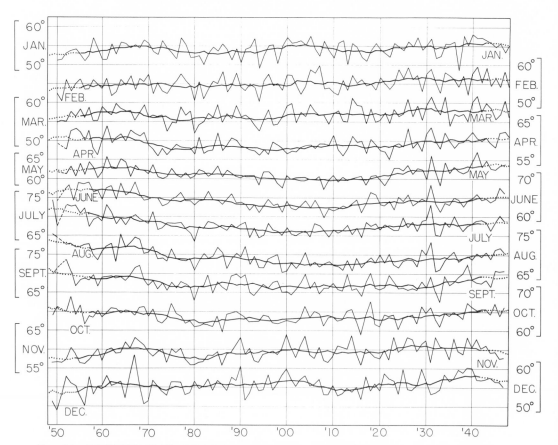

Fɪɢ. 19—FLUCTUATIONS OF MEAN MONTHLY TEMPERATURES AT SAN DIEGO,
CALIFORNIA, FROM 1849 TO 1948, WITH TRENDS COMPUTED BY RUNNING
AVERAGES OF 11 (FROM HUBBS, 1948, FIG. 1)
No compensation is made for higher temperatures at the new station occupied after January, 1940.

and presumably in the air, began after 2,500 B.P., was at a low point about 1,600 B.P., and lasted until about 600 B.P. During both this cool period and the preceding and following warm periods, there are many suggestions of less arid conditions, with enough rain to supply the drinking needs of more people than could be expected to survive under primitive conditions today. The last three or four centuries seem to have approached the present in aridity, but about a millennium ago there seems to have been substantially more rain than at present.

That rocky reefs were well developed is indicated by the circumstance that an abundance of seafood from these habitats was utilized by the local folk. A rising sea level probably maintained reefs by continuing erosion of the cliffs. On the recent approach to a steady state of sea level, beaches seem to have increased, and such reef mollusks as the California mussel (*Mytilus californianus*) were in places replaced by beach clams, particularly by *Tivela stultorum* and *Donax gouldii*. In San Diego County, just north of the border, rising sea level helped maintain coastal inlets (Shumway, Hubbs, and Moriarty, 1961), which only in recent centuries have become clogged with sediment, and it is probable that like events occurred along the adjacent coast of Baja California.

Only preliminary reports on these findings and interpretations have as yet been published (Hubbs, 1948, 1958, 1960a;

172

Hubbs, Bien, and Suess, 1960, 1962). The researches of Arnold (1957) at Laguna Seca Chapala in the interior of Baja California Norte even more dramatically indicate heavier rainfall and larger human populations in the past; other archaeological studies yield confirmatory conclusions. Aschmann (1959) analyzed the problem of the formerly large populations in the desert regions of Baja California, in reference to probably greater rainfall.

Geographic Variation in Climate Associated with Oceanographic Conditions

In general, the ocean exerts a moderating and stabilizing effect on the climate of the adjacent land. Sea and air temperatures are closely correlated (Hubbs, 1948). Throughout most of Middle America the coastal climate is favorable and free of cold. Even when coastal waters in Central America are cooled by strong offshore winds, the air remains warm; under these conditions the correlation between sea and air temperatures tends to become negative.

Tropical conditions prevail as far north as Manzanillo, and are not greatly tempered as far north as Mazatlan. Along the east coast of Golfo de California, however, there is a rapid change in air temperatures, just as there is in surface water temperatures in the Gulf. In northern Sonora frosts are common near shore during several weeks in winter, though summer temperatures are high. Here the Gulf temperatures seem to be more the cause than the result of air temperatures.

Along the Gulf and Cape shores of Baja California winter temperatures are salubrious, summer temperatures high. Proceeding northward along the outer coast of Baja California into regions of upwelling, one encounters cool and often foggy air. Where ocean temperatures are most depressed in the warmer months, the air is so foggy that the coastal shrubs are thickly clothed in green lichens, so that at a distance they appear to be in full foliage, though the leaves have then dropped off in response to the lack of ground water. Fuel is generally at a premium.

Along most of the Middle American shoreline the rainfall, like the temperature, is rather high, but toward the north falls sharply. Rain remains ample as far north as southern Sinaloa, with some apparent depression in Jalisco, south of the mountains behind Cabo Corrientes, where a rain shadow of moderate intensity is indicated by a change in vegetation, which is clearly evident from the air. North of Mazatlan the coast becomes drier, to culminate in the extreme desert around the head of the Gulf. Most of the coast of Baja California is desert or semidesert (Aschmann, 1959). The Cape region is less arid than the central part of the peninsula, and along the northwest coast the rainfall increases northward to reach about 25 cm./year at the international border.

MARINE LIFE OF THE COAST AND ITS UTILIZATION

As one would expect from oceanographic conditions, marine life generally abounds along the coasts of Middle America, providing a prime source of food and of articles for utility and ornament. The generally high phosphorus content of Pacific waters and, of probably greater significance, the upwelling of water along the eastern shore of the ocean—keeping the surface waters supplied with varied nutrients—have, along with other favorable oceanographic conditions, produced a rich and plentiful fauna and flora, including an abundance of delectable mollusks and fishes, sufficient to supply the needs of large numbers of coastal inhabitants. The living marine resources are generally abundant, particularly so in regions of greatest coastal upwelling. Aschmann (1959) elaborated on this point for Baja California and the Gulf.

Throughout Middle America, as elsewhere, primitive man obtained a considerable variety of animals and plants in vari-

173

ous shore habitats: on rocky reefs, with many kinds of mollusks and fishes; on extensive intertidal flats and on beaches of mud, sand, and cobble, with a profusion of clams; and in coastal bays, inlets, esteros, and tidal channels, with an abundance of shrimp, fish, and other organisms. As we have noted in other sections, the Indians of Baja California and the Gulf depended heavily on marine life, and many of those in southern Mexico and Central America, particularly about coastal lagoons and estuaries, no doubt depended largely on fishing and shellfish gathering for subsistence. We venture to predict that such cultures will be traced back at least 8,000 years and that they will be shown to have persisted more or less continuously ever since. A number of radiocarbon dates for midden sites as far south as northern South America support this view. M. D. Coe (1960b, p. 365) indicated a presumably early pattern of fishing, hunting, and mollusk gathering at the La Victoria site in Guatemala, and inferred a transition to settled maize agriculture by reason of finding metates and manos even in the very earliest levels (but in early times the food that was ground may not have been maize). Coe compiled some of the recent evidence on dated midden sites along the Pacific coast of South as well as Middle America.

The offshore waters, scene of great tuna fisheries today, are also prolific in fish, but the early historic evidence indicates that the coastal inhabitants did not extensively engage in high-seas fishing. They may have done so, in places, as some of the relatively recent Indians did in southern California.

The abundance of marine life, supplying food, utensils, and ornaments, may have been a mixed blessing, supplying a soft living and leading to cultural decay up and down the coast, as it almost surely did in California and Baja California. A more thorough analysis and interpretation of midden sites throughout the west coast of Middle America should clarify this point.

174

In treating the marine life we begin by summarizing its biogeographical relations, first for the area as a whole and then by regional divisions. We then take up, in series, the various groups of organisms, with some consideration of how they were utilized by aboriginal man.

Biogeographic Relations

The marine biotas on the two sides of Middle America together comprise the main segment of the distinctive New World biogeographical category. The integrity of the whole biota stems from the circumstance that until late Tertiary time Central America was not an isthmus, but a series of islands, separated by straits through which the marine life of the two bounding oceans remained in contact. Dates for the closure of the several hypothesized straits are commonly given as during various times in the Miocene and the Pliocene—long enough ago to have allowed for much differentiation, mostly on a subspecific or specific level. Paleogeographers earlier, and biogeographers (as Mayr, 1946; Darlington, 1957) more recently, have interpreted the straits as having remained open until some time in Pliocene, but invertebrate paleontologists (as Olsson, 1932; Nygren, 1950; Durham and Allison, 1960) have definitely indicated the closure as Miocene. Since the deep-sea bottom fauna is most sharply differentiated, and the shallow inshore life is least differentiated on the two sides, it seems probable that shoal-water connections, perhaps through lagoons, persisted long after the backbone of the isthmus rose in continuity nearly to the surface, perhaps as recently as early Pleistocene. But there is little reason to suspect that any such straits ever blocked the free passage of primitive man, for there is no sound evidence that man arrived in the New World prior to the Third (Sangamon) Interglacial or the Fourth (Wisconsin = Würm) Glacial period, and it is almost unthinkable to assume the existence of even a very narrow and shallow strait during the highest Sangamon sea-stand.

The faunas of the two sides, in fishes, mollusks, and other marine life utilized by man, have had enough in common to insure that human travelers across the isthmus would have been at once reasonably familiar with most forms of life that they would have encountered on the opposite shore.

The marine life of the Pacific shores of Middle America, however, contrasts rather sharply in some respects with that of the Atlantic shores, despite the fact that the biotas were interconnected until relatively recent geological time. A major contrast, resulting from oceanographic conditions, is the narrowing of the tropical faunal belt on the Pacific side, because of the equator-ward-setting major currents. As a result, there is greater latitudinal diversity of marine life zones on the Pacific side: north-western Baja California has a large element of the very rich cool-temperate biota of the northern Pacific, whereas northeastern Mexico remains subtropical.

Another contrast lies in the very weak development of coral reefs and their associated life in the eastern Pacific, where there is but a single atoll, Clipperton Island (which was apparently unknown to primitive man). It is probable that much of the tropical life was extirpated by late Pleistocene cold on both sides (Newell, 1959a,b; Hubbs, 1952), but that on the Atlantic side repopulation was possible from a more tropical refugium to the southward, whereas on the Pacific side no such refugium existed. On the other hand, the vast tropical storehouse of the Indo-Pacific has, through the Equatorial Counter Current, re-established on the islands and even on the mainland of the tropical eastern Pacific a small faunal element, which, presumably on account of the short time period involved, remains at most weakly differentiated.

Another contrast lies in the spectacular richness of certain marine groups in the eastern Pacific, attributable to several factors. The great development of lagoons and of sandy beaches has fostered a unique expansion of certain fish groups, such as anchovies (Engraulididae) and croakers (Sciaenidae) that habituate such conditions. The phenomenal richness of certain other fish groups, which inhabit rocky shores, reflects the greater extent in the Pacific of such habitats (as is indicated above, in the discussion of the greater tidal range on the Pacific side). These inshore fishes, both of soft and rocky bottoms, for various reasons were obviously better adapted than the coral-reef fishes to persist through the Wisconsin cold period. The richness of the eastern Pacific in these faunal elements largely compensates for the depauperate representatives there of coral-reef types.

In the Atlantic the island-studded waters have no doubt accelerated speciation on the micro-evolutionary level, whereas on the Pacific side the general depauperation of the biota during Wisconsin time has left an evolutionary vacuum which has allowed the residual forms to differentiate and the immigrants to become established. As apparent results, recent speciation on the two sides has been rather dissimilar, and the biotas of the two sides have diverged considerably.

Biogeographic Pattern in Middle America

The marine life of Middle America, both fauna and flora, is relatively uniform and tropical from Golfo de Panama, as also from northern Peru, Ecuador, and Colombia, through Central America to southern Mexico. This biota, the Panamanian, extends southward only about 7° south of the equator; due to the intense upwelling on the west coast of South America and to the strong northward-flowing Peru or Humboldt Current, the temperate fauna extends far northward, to northern Peru. As mentioned above (p. 167), the rocky-shore fauna of Central America is divisible into

175

F<small>IG</small>. 20—MANGROVE OYSTERS, ONE OF THE SEAFOODS READILY AVAILABLE AT
LOW TIDE ALONG THE COAST OF MIDDLE AMERICA
Photo by Lewis Wayne Walker, at Laguna Coyote, Bahía Ballenas, Baja California Sur,
February, 1948.

two subregions by reason of a long intervening area that is largely free of rocks.

With some dilution and with intrusions
from the warm-temperate (San Diegan)
biota of southern California and the outer
coast of Baja California, the tropical biota
extends into Golfo de California and occupies the Cabo San Lucas region of Baja
California. On the outer coast of the peninsula the tropical types rapidly give way to
the generally very different warm-temperate forms (Hubbs, 1960b), just as the water
temperature in summer, below the very
shallow thermocline, typically drops abruptly (for instance, in August and September,

1955, as charted by Groves and Reid, 1958,
fig. 5). In Bahia Magdalena, and more particularly in its shallow southern arm (Bahia
Almejas), tropical species still predominate,
though on the adjacent open coast, where
there is considerable upwelling, some San
Diegan forms occur. Northward a similar
situation holds: Laguna San Ignacio shelters a considerable proportion of tropical
forms, whereas along the nearby coast of
Abreojos and Punta Eugenia an essentially
San Diegan biota holds forth. In the wide
re-entrant known as Bahia Sebastian Vizcaino, and in the large connected lagoons,
many tropical forms reappear. A clockwise

176

eddy in this bay results in unusually warm surface waters in the warm season (Dawson, 1952; Groves and Reid, 1958). North of this bay the marine life has a distinctly northern aspect, in concordance with the strong upwelling that characterizes this area. Where the shallow surface layers are considerably warmed, in the inner or lagoon portion of Bahia San Quintin and in Bahia de Todos Santos, and to a lesser degree in other, smaller, somewhat protected spots, some subtropical forms persist, whereas on the open coast, where surface temperatures are extraordinarily low for such latitudes, tropical types are essentially lacking and a number of cool-temperate (Montereyan) species mingle with many warm-temperate (San Diegan) forms. These conclusions have stemmed largely from studies on the distribution of algae and of fishes, but are confirmed by researches on the distribution of other organisms, crabs for example (Garth, 1960).

The tropical element becomes reduced toward the head of Golfo de California, where the biota includes a number of warm-temperate types identical with or closely related to those of northwestern Baja California. Some of these northern types are presumably Glacial relicts, which rounded the peninsula during one or more periods of Pleistocene glaciation. The cool-water forms are particularly prominent in the "Mid-Riff," about the large islands of Tiburon and Angel de la Guarda, where strong, at times violent, horizontal and vertical turbulence markedly reduces the surface temperatures. The biota of the Gulf thus comprises a mixture of (1) tropical types, which either move in during the warm season (such migratory fishes as the sailfish, *Istiophorus greyi*, and the yellowtail, *Seriola dorsalis*), or can tolerate the cool winter temperatures, and (2) of temperate types that can withstand the tropically warm surface waters of summer or that keep cool then by descending into the lower layers. Many forms, both tropical and temperate, have failed to adjust themselves to the cool winters and warm summers, and are therefore absent. In slight compensation, endemic forms have arisen in considerable number, apparently in response to the partial isolation and the peculiarly varying environment. The biogeography of the Gulf was treated recently by Walker (1960).

Marine Plants

Certain natives along the Pacific coast made direct use of the plant resources of the sea. Canaliños of southern California made mats from dried surfgrass (*Phyllospadix*) and some of the Baja California Indians no doubt used surfgrass or eelgrass (*Zostera*). The Seri seasonally thrashed out the starch-rich seeds of *Ruppia maritima* (Dawson, 1944; William Neil Smith II, personal communication). It may be assumed that dried seaweeds were used as fuel and as bedding along the barren portions of the coast. Along the northwestern shore of Baja California great windrows of the giant kelps, including the large woody holdfasts, other algae, and surfgrass are often washed ashore, and in the coastal lagoons great masses of eelgrass are often stranded. According to McGee (1901, p. 207), the Seri ate some algae.

Shellfish

Many species of mollusks and of other shelled invertebrates, such as sea urchins and barnacles, were widely used by preconquest peoples along the coast. The chief use was for food, but the shells were also extensively employed as utensils and as ornaments.

Mollusks were a particularly important item in the food of Indians along both shores of Golfo de California and in western Baja California (Aschmann, 1959; Massey, 1947; Julio Berdegué Aznar, personal communication): the abundant and long-continued use of mollusks, in part continuously and in part periodically, is attested

177

by the frequent, in places scarcely uninterrupted, middens along the shores. Some of the shell mounds on each shore of central Baja California cover more than an acre and are up to 6 m. deep. Along the Gulf coast, to the southward, shell heaps up to about 5 m. deep cover areas several hundred meters wide. Shells, surely or apparently representing food use, often occur many miles from the shores—for example, at Laguna Seca Chapala (Arnold, 1957), and on the east side of Paso de San Matias, 72 km. in a straight line from the Gulf coast.

In many portions of the coast, particularly along both shores of Golfo de California, the Indians harvested oysters (*Ostrea*) in large quantities, in places leaving shell mounds, with oysters predominating, several meters deep. In the harvest of oysters the conservative natives in certain areas along the west coast of Mexico still persist in the primitive and very inefficient method of harvesting by diving, refusing to use diving gear or even containers on their dives. Instead, according to Julio Berdegué Aznar (personal communication), they gather a handful, which they press against their body, and then take a few more before they rise to the surface with a minor load. Other species of oysters live on the mangroves (fig. 20), and primevally were no doubt harvested by hand, as they are now, the gatherer wading at low tide.

Along the outer coast of Baja California, as in southern California, the middens show that the shellfish were derived from bays (*Pecten, Chione, Ostrea, Polinices*), from sandy beaches (*Tivela, Donax*), and from rocky shores (*Mytilus, Pseudochama, Haliotis, Lottia, Acmaea*). Some of these genera continue in middens farther south, and other genera appear there.

The pearl fisheries of the eastern tropical Pacific were prosecuted by the natives before the coming of the Spaniards, whose avaricious ways were in part incited by the pearls. The pearl fisheries were conducted at various localities from Golfo de Panama northward, but were most extensive and famous along the southern part of the Gulf coast of Baja California. In historic times pearls have been gathered chiefly about La Paz, Loreto, and other points between the vicinity of Cabo Pulmo and Mulege, but extensive pearl-oyster middens occur as far northward as Bahia San Francisquito below Bahia de los Angeles, and some occur in middens as far north as Punta San Felipe. The pearl-fishing enterprises in the Gulf were recorded by H. R. Wagner (1930), who indicated that the natives were notable divers, recovering pearls from depths as great as 15–20 fathoms. He further indicated that few pearls were collected or used by the Indians, who gathered these shellfish primarily for food, to supplement their diet of reptiles, game, and pitahaya; since the oysters were roasted, the pearls were damaged. However, several archaeologists (as Kidder, Jennings, and Shook, 1946, p. 152; Kidder, 1947, p. 66, fig. 84) have indicated that the cultured natives of Mesoamerica utilized pearls for ornament. After the Spaniards came, the skillful Indian divers were employed in harvesting pearls (Aschmann, 1959, p. 71).

Various marine shells, from the Pacific as well as from the Atlantic, were sufficiently prized, during the preconquest period, through the interior of Middle America, as far east as Yucatan, to have become products of transport and trade. Such trade has been referred to by various authorities, including Blom (1932a, pp. 531–56), Boekelman (1935a,b), Scholes and Roys (1948, pp. 23–31, 59–60), Thompson (1929, pp. 40–44), and Tozzer (1941, pp. 94–96, and notes 415–22, 488).

Marine shells, many identified as having stemmed from the Pacific, are generally reported as having been used largely as beads and other ornaments, in villages throughout Middle America; for example by Roys (1939, p. 61), Kidder, Jennings, Shook (1946, pp. 145–52, figs. 62–65), Kidder

FIG. 21—"TAPO" (SHRIMP TRAP) AT CAMERON, NEAR ESCUINAPA, MEXICO
Photo by H. Oscar Wright, 1960.

(1947, pp. 61–66, figs. 85, 86), and W. R. Coe (1959b, pp. 55–60, figs. 51–55). Structures as well as persons were ornamented with the shells. In northwestern Mexico and in the American Southwest shells for ornaments, such as olivella beads and abalone beads and pendants, represented trade material from the Pacific coast.

Clam shells, particularly large species from the tropical eastern Pacific, provided people along the coast, and those on trade routes, with a variety of tools. The Seri today, steeped in tradition, use clam shells as spoons and as knives, and in digging for water in their desert environment. Clams with edges cut sharply into serrations obviously served as combs (for instance, along the upper part of Golfo de California). Oviedo y Valdés (1851–55) wrote that "nacarones" (elongated bivalves, presumably *Pinna rugosa*), which produced pearls of low value, were used in the re-

179

gions of Golfo de Orotina (that is, Golfo de Fonseca, Costa Rica) and Cabo Blanco, Nicaragua, as hoe or spade blades in the cultivation of their fields. The same bivalve was valued for food (as it still is, under the name of "hacha").

Another molluscan product utilized in Middle America, and still occasionally employed there, is a trumpet, manufactured from shells of giant gastropods, of the genera *Fasciolaria* and *Strombus* (see, for example, Kidder, Jennings, and Shook, 1946, p. 147).

Certain rocky-shore gastropods, of the eastern tropical Pacific, particularly *Purpura patula pansa*, produce a dye, comparable to Tyrian purple, that has been used since preconquest time and is still locally utilized (Gerhard, 1964).

Still another significant use of mollusks, that was probably more important in the relatively advanced cultures, was in the manufacture of lime for mortar and plaster. Several authorities, including Landa (Tozzer, 1941), indicated that ancient Maya and other peoples burned shell to produce lime.

Crustaceans

Shrimp have been a mainstay in the diet of the Indians along the Mexican Pacific coast, and probably elsewhere in Middle America. From time immemorial they have caught shrimp, during the spawning period, in the estuaries and bayous on outgoing tides, by an ingenious type of fixed weir known as "tapo." Such a practice would seem to be destructive, but the shrimp supply has somehow maintained itself for centuries and probably millennia. This type of net and other primitive local fishing gear, still persisting, have been described by Mercado Sánchez (1959, 1961).

Along the outer coast of Baja California midden remains show that other crustaceans, especially the spiny lobster (*Panulirus interruptus*) and rock crabs (*Cancer* spp.) were often eaten. In one campsite in the Laguna Salada basin in northeastern

180

Baja California the food remains consisted almost wholly of crab. These crustaceans, like the mollusks eaten, could have been caught at low tide. The distribution of crabs in the eastern Pacific has been treated by Garth (1960, and references there cited).

Fishes

Coastal middens in general contain remains of fishes along with the shellfishes. Little has been done in the way of identifying the species of fish that were taken along the Pacific coast, or in determining in detail what gear was used in their capture. What little is known of the primeval fisheries in Baja California was reviewed by Aschmann (1959, pp. 71–76, 99–102). Much of the fishing was communal, and brush traps and poison (barbasco) were extensively employed.

In northwestern Baja California, as in southern California, species commonly used were the sheephead (*Pimelometopon pulchrum*) and rockfishes (*Sebastodes* spp.), both of which were probably taken along the rocky shores (as they still are). Various other bony fish and some sharks were also consumed. In Golfo de California corbinas (*Cynoscion* spp.) were commonly taken, as they still are.

The Seri are still accomplished fishermen, using hooks and harpoons. The few old men who retain the primeval lore of the tribe have a very detailed and accurate knowledge of the fishes and their habitats, even in areas where the Seri have not fished for many decades (William Neil Smith II, personal communication).

Fishes were probably often utilized for purposes other than food. Their vertebrae, as well as shells, served as ornaments. The Seri and probably other people utilized the caudal spines of sting rays, which have retrorse dentation. More cultural tribes made incised ornaments from these spines (Kidder, Jennings, and Shook, 1946, p. 156; Kidder, 1947, fig. 75; W. R. Coe, 1959b, pp. 64–67, fig. 56). It is probable that the pectoral spines of marine catfishes, also with retrorse dentation, were similarly utilized.

We have not encountered evidence that the coastal natives took advantage of the great offshore abundance of tuna and other large pelagic fishes. The lack of evidence of occupation of the islands far offshore, Galapagos excepted, suggests that the fisheries were all coastal.

Reptiles

The marine herpetological fauna of Middle America is limited in species and includes only one group—sea turtles—of much importance to man. *Crocodylus acutus* occurs from Sinaloa to Ecuador. A few lizards feed on beaches and occasionally enter the water, but the only truly marine species is confined to the Galapagos. The only New World representative of the poisonous marine snakes is the pelagic species *Pelamys platurus*; this snake occasionally comes to the sea margin in large numbers, as at Puerto Vallarta, Mexico, and was undoubtedly known to the aborigines.

The sea turtles (Carr, 1952) have largely compensated for the relative insignificance of their cousins. They have served man along the entire tropical Pacific coast in many ways. All lay their numerous nutritious eggs in certain tropical sand beaches, and leave a telltale trail to mark the spot. Most of the species feed in shallow water, often far north of the restricted breeding areas. They are readily found and harpooned. The eggs are extensively used in season. The flesh of the adults provides excellent meat, when variously prepared by the coastal peoples—roasted, boiled, and dried. It has long been a principal food of the Seri, who often ate the meat raw, and was used by other tribes (Aschmann, 1959, p. 98). The inedible parts have been used extensively. For instance, the Seri, in Golfo de California, who until recently hunted sea turtles from well-made balsa canoes, used the bones for implements, and the integument of the flippers for sandals. They utilized the carapace shells for roofing, umbrellas, water trays, and food storage; also as cradles for the infants and as coffins for the dead (McGee, 1901; Lindig, 1959; William Neil Smith II, personal communication).

By far the most important sea turtle is the Pacific green turtle, *Chelonia mydas agassizii*. Of lesser importance are the Pacific loggerhead, *Caretta caretta gigas*, the Pacific ridley, *Lepidochelys olivacea*, and the little Pacific hawkbill (or tortoise-shell) turtle, *Eretmochelys imbricata squamata*. The largely pelagic and rare gigantic Pacific leatherback turtle, *Dermochelys coriacea schlegelii*, has probably seldom been used by man, except occasionally, we suppose, in the egg stage.

Sea Birds

Sea birds have provided subsistence and other utilitarian products for coastal peoples on the Pacific shores of the Americas. Skeletal remains frequently occur in middens. The Seri aboriginally used pelican hides for clothing (McGee, 1901), as did other tribes (Aschmann, 1959, p. 99). They and other tribes extensively raided bird rookeries on islands, to secure either eggs or the nesting marine birds themselves. At a certain season pelicans formed a staple food of the Seri. Nesting petrels, shearwaters, auklets, murrelets, and other pelagic birds, as well as pelicans, gulls, terns, and cormorants no doubt were caught in large numbers, especially on the coastal islands, when they came ashore to breed. Detailed evidence is scanty, but some exists; for example, skeletal remains of Cassin's Auklet were found in a midden on North Coronado Island near San Diego.

Marine Mammals

Marine mammals were utilized by the Indians along the Pacific coast of Middle America, at least in Baja California, for their remains are often found in the middens.

181

The sea otter, *Enhydra lutris,* until it was nearly exterminated by white hunters early in the 19th century, abounded along the kelp beds as far south as Isla Cedros, Baja California, and was extensively hunted for food and presumably for fur in Baja California (Aschmann, 1959, pp. 72, 76, 98), as well as in southern California and northward. Skeletal remains have been found in a very recent midden on Islas Los Coronados near San Diego (Hubbs, Bien, and Suess, 1960, p. 205).

Sea lions (*Zalophus californianus*), which abound in numerous rookeries along the outer coast of Baja California and through Golfo de California, were extensively used as food, at least in northwestern Baja California (as about Santo Tomas) during the last millennium or two. Remains are numerous in certain middens. Aschmann (1959) quoted early writers on the use of sea lions, though, strangely, elephant seals (*Mirounga angustirostris*) were apparently not utilized. Harbor seals (*Phoca vitulina*) were presumably utilized in northwestern Baja California, but their remains have not been identified in the middens.

Remains of cetaceans (dolphins and whales) are rare in the middens of Baja California, and presumably represent stranded individuals. Aschmann (1959, p. 98) presented evidence that the Baja California Indians did not hunt whales but feasted on stranded ones. Strandings of sperm and pilot whales in Golfo de California seem to be relatively common (Gilmore, 1957, 1959), and presumably supplied the natives occasionally with a great feast. McGee (1901) provided the supporting evidence of a Seri legend. No definitive evidence has come to our attention on aboriginal whaling in Middle America.

Various whales occur along the coasts of Middle America, and three large species breed in separate areas on the west coast of Mexico: the gray whale, *Eschrichtius gibbosus,* in the lagoons, chiefly of western Baja California; the finback whale, *Balaenoptera physalus,* in Golfo de California; and the humpback whale, *Megaptera novaeangliae,* along the rocky shores about Cabo San Lucas and from Cabo Corrientes southward, including the offshore islands.

OTHER MARINE PRODUCTS

Aborigines along the coast no doubt utilized products of the sea other than those of plant and animal origin. The chief mineral product here, as elsewhere, was no doubt sea salt. Starr (1900, p. 65) noted that the Huave of southern Mexico make salt. Although Baja California contains great surface deposits of salt suitable for culinary purposes, the missionary accounts, according to Aschmann (1959, p. 102), agreed that the Indians of the peninsula did not utilize it. Their food apparently met their physiological needs for salt.

Traces of asphaltum have been found in middens in northwestern Baja California, indicating that this product of submarine oil seeps was utilized here to some extent, as it commonly was in southern California (Heizer, 1943; Emery, 1960, pp. 320–22). The asphaltum was used in making ornaments, waterproofing baskets, and caulking boats.

Another commonly used marine mineral product was beach cobbles, which for seven millennia were a prime source of flaked artifacts along the coast of northwestern Baja California. The type of wear and particularly the chatter-marks on the unworked cortex of chopper-scraper tools indicate beach origin. (The beach cobbles themselves are often precussively flaked by surf action during storms. Some of the products closely simulate artifacts, occasionally to a confusing degree. Such products the senior author has called "naturifacts.")

TRAVEL AND TRADE OVER THE SEA

The coastal waters of the Pacific shore of Middle America presumably served the aborigines not only as a source of food and of local transportation by canoe but also as a channel of communication, commerce, and intercourse over long distances, even between the great centers of civilization in Middle and South America. Spinden (1917) erected the hypothesis of a Nuclear America in a single sphere, thought to be in Mexico, from which maize agriculture, ceramic arts, and other cultural traditions spread in ancient time southward to Peru. Spinden's hypothesis has been extensively debated and is still under scrutiny. The problem was recently reviewed by M. D. Coe (1960b), who stressed the cultural linkages between North and South America, stating that "excavations in Peru, Middle America, and in the intervening areas have demonstrated the almost incontrovertible fact that both of the major New World civilizations rest on a single Formative base during which intimate interdiffusion of ideas and perhaps products took place." He favored the idea of a complex rather than, as Spinden proposed, a unilateral diffusion. It indeed seems plausible to assume that such intercourse took place, and that it was facilitated by boat transportation, whether along inner routes in such largely protected waters as estuaries, lagoons, bays, and gulfs, or out over the open sea, or by both routes.

The idea that at least some of the traffic was along shore in more or less enclosed waters is favored by a number of lines of evidence. In the first place, longshore lagoons are frequent and often extensive. Indications that such waters generally supported human populations and that such populations depended in part on aquatic animals lend weight to the hypothesis that inland passages were utilized by traders. Even today there are places where trading routes involve aquatic sections, wherein canoes are used, with foot-trails or pack-trails interpolated. Canoes may well have been left at either end of the water courses, for travelers to use freely, then leaving the canoes at the other end of the water course, for someone traveling in the opposite direction (as the senior author has seen dugouts left for general use on either bank of a stream mouth in the State of Washington, and at either end of a small lake on a trail route in the Peten, Guatemala).

Various lines of evidence, however, show that some of the primeval trade traffic was over the open sea. M. D. Coe (1960b, pp. 384–86) recently presented rather convincing evidence, largely on the basis of the Sailing Directions published by the U. S. Hydrographic Office, that at appropriate seasons and under favorable conditions, sea journeys in trading canoes back and forth between Central and South America would have been entirely feasible. As previously noted, storm weather along the coast is sharply seasonal. During most of the year small craft can safely ply the coast. That long journeys were at least occasionally taken is evident from the fact that primitive man somehow reached the Galapagos Archipelago (Heyerdahl and Skjölsvold, 1956).

Indeed, there is direct evidence of primeval travel over the open sea. Oviedo y Valdés (1851–55, bk. 29, ch. 32) early mentioned that large seagoing canoes, powered by sails, were used on the Pacific coast of Panama. That the Seri used seaworthy balsa rafts in Golfo de California has already been mentioned. Indians along the west coast of Baja California used ocean canoes, as did some of the tribes in southern California, where canoes seen by Spaniards in 1602 and in 1770 were so well made and so seaworthy as to have attracted special attention and note in the diaries of Sebastián Vizcaíno (Bolton, 1916, p. 87) and of Fray Crespi (Bolton, 1927, pp. 34, 159). The boatmen of Cedros Island were held by the early historians to have been very proficient (Aschmann, 1959, p. 72). Evidence for aboriginal boat-fishing and navigation along the coasts of California and of

Baja California was reviewed by Heizer and Massey (1953). No doubt many of the people who lived along the shore were rather able coastwise seamen. There is good evidence, also, of ocean navigation along the west coast of South America.

That navigation and trade were largely coastwise, however, is strongly suggested by the circumstance that the aborigines probably did not become established on the islands off the Middle American coast (Guadalupe, the Revillagigedos, Clipperton, Cocos, and Malpelo) that are far out of sight from the mainland (the exception, the Galapagos, may well have been the first reached accidentally, along the course of the Peru Current). Trading between the mainland and the islands within sight of California and Baja California was definitely involved.

Whether the ships plied inshore or offshore waters (or both), it does seem clear that coastwise trading and intercourse was accomplished on an extensive scale. A few references exemplify the evidence. West (1961) recently presented strong indications of aboriginal expeditions between the region of Guerrero in Mexico and the south. Early sources on the Chorotega and the Nicarao of the Pacific coast of Nicaragua and Costa Rica clearly indicated that the Mexican invaders, especially the Nicarao, arrived on these shores by sea (Chapman, 1960). Early colonial trade and navigation between Mexico and Peru (Borah, 1954) suggests a continuum from precolonial time.

There are intriguing but as yet not well-substantiated indications (recently briefly reviewed, with references, by Emery, 1960, pp. 1–2) of some pre-Columbian transpacific travel to the west coast of North America, involving a trace of some cultural infiltration. Many students disbelieve (or disregard) the evidence, and still more emphatically disagree with the idea of Heyerdahl that such travel and cultural infiltra-

tion took place from America to the South Sea islands.

CONTRASTS BETWEEN OCEANOGRAPHIC CONDITIONS AND MARINE LIFE ON THE WESTERN AND EASTERN SHORES

In many respects the oceanographic conditions and the biota of the western shores of Middle America contrast sharply with the conditions and the biota of what Collier has described for the eastern shores, around the "American Mediterranean." These differences undoubtedly affected aboriginal man in many ways.

Outstanding distinctions depend on the location of the shores in reference to the earth's rotation. The vast clockwise, anticyclonic circulation of the northern oceans produces the great inflow into the Caribbean, the eddies in this sea and the Gulf of Mexico, the strong flow through the Strait of Yucatan, and the vast outflow from the Gulf into the Gulf Stream: a modification, induced by the land configuration, of the northward component of the great anticyclonic circulation that would otherwise run a more regular course. The similar clockwise circulation pattern in the northeast Pacific produces, in simpler pattern, the southward-flowing California Current and the westward-flowing North Equatorial Current, which appears to derive its waters more from the Central American region than from the California Current.

A major oceanographic distinction involves the content of dissolved oxygen below the thermocline. The deep waters in the eastern Pacific are very low in oxygen, because of the long time these waters have taken to move from the surface of the Antarctic. The depletion of dissolved oxygen is much less in the Atlantic. This distinction, however, has been of no obvious significance for primitive man.

The hydrodynamic factors in the American Mediterranean, as on the western sides of oceans generally, largely prevent upwelling of nutrients, except locally as on the Campeche Bank, whereas the waters along the west coast of Middle America are among those most affected by such enrichment, indirectly by the southward flow from upwelling farther north and directly by upwelling along the Middle American shores. In compensation, the eastern waters of Middle America are enriched much more than the western shores by inflow of nutrient-rich fresh water; rainflow is generally greater to the east, and the continental divide runs far west of center.

The Pacific and Atlantic waters of Middle America differ further in that excessive fish kills seem to be confined to the Atlantic. Though it has extremely high plankton production, Golfo de California does not seem to be seriously affected by lethal "red tides." Nor have winter kills been noted—probably because the waters on the two sides of Baja California are regularly subjected to marked drops in temperature. (The fish kills in Peru, associated with the El Niño Current, are a special case.)

Another great contrast is furnished by the tides, which are generally insignificant on the east coast but, except locally in southern Mexico, have a very considerable range on the west coast. The stronger tides, as already noted, have made possible the ancient trapping of shrimp in tidal waters of the west coast by the tapo net; have permitted a very heavy take of clams and oysters; and have led over geological time to the rich development of rock-inhabiting, generally intertidal, organisms.

The Atlantic shores are largely depositional, by reason of the greater inflow of rivers, carrying much silt, whereas much rock is exposed on the Pacific shores, owing to the greater tectonic movements, the higher waves, and the stronger tidal currents, as well as to the lesser runoff. There are also long stretches of gulfs, lagoons, and estuaries on the west coast, with sandy and muddy bottoms. These differences in the shoreline are reflected in strong contrasts in the littoral fauna.

A further major difference in shore features lies in the rather extensive development of coral reefs on the Atlantic side, and the extremely poor coral growth along the Pacific shores. This is probably attributable to the more complete extirpation of coral on the west coast during the Pleistocene (Hubbs, 1948), rather than to present-day control by cold water during periods of upwelling. The difference in reef development is also strongly reflected in the fauna, as already noted.

Another basis for the marine faunal differences on the two sides of Middle America is the proximity of the Atlantic shores to the Antilles, leading to greater richness in many faunal elements. On the other hand, through the mediation of the Equatorial Counter Current, a number of distinctively Indo-Pacific animals have become established on the Pacific coast. One of the most significant of these to man is the pearl oyster (*Pintada*). To the northward, on the western coast of Baja California and to a lesser extent on the coast of Golfo de California, especially toward the north, the fauna is enriched by representatives of genera characteristic of the great North Pacific fauna.

Generally rougher seas and higher surf, paucity and wide separation of islands, less available big trees, and lesser populations of man on the adjacent shores, all probably acted to restrict travel and commerce on the Pacific, as contrasted with the Atlantic. As a consequence, the few more-offshore islands on the Pacific side (namely Guadalupe, San Benedicto, Socorro, Clarion, Clipperton, Cocos, and Malpelo), with the exception of the Galapagos, which alone could be reached by traveling down-current, remained apparently undiscovered until Caucasians sailed by.

185

REFERENCES

Allen, W. E., 1939
Anonymous, 1957
Arnold, 1957
Aschmann, 1959
Bancroft, 1876, 1886
Bennett, 1963
—— and Schaefer, 1960
Blackburn, 1962, 1963
—— and associates, 1962
Blom, 1932a
Boekelman, 1935a, 1935b
Bolton, 1916, 1927
Borah, 1954
Brandhorst, 1958
Briggs, 1951, 1955
Carr, 1952
Chapel, 1927
Chapman, Ann, 1960
Coe, M. D., 1960b
Coe, W. R., 1959b
Cromwell, 1958
—— and Bennett, 1959
Darlington, 1957
Dawson, 1944, 1945, 1951, 1952, 1960
Durham and Allison, 1960
Ekman, 1905
Emery, 1960
Fleming, 1935, 1938, 1941
Garth, 1960
Gerhard, 1964
Gilmore, 1957, 1959
Godske, Bergeron, Bjerknes, and Bundgaard, 1957
Groves and Reid, 1958
Hardy, 1960
Heizer, 1943
—— and Massey, 1953
Heyerdahl and Skjölsvold, 1956
Holmes and Blackburn, 1960
Hubbs, Carl L., 1948, 1952, 1958, 1960a, 1960b
——, Bien, and Suess, 1960, 1962
——, and L. C. Hubbs, 1960, 1961, 1962, 1963
Hubbs, Clark, 1952, 1953
Hurd, 1929a, 1929b
Hutchins, 1947
Kidder, 1947
——, Jennings, and Shook, 1946
Landa, 1864
Lindig, 1959
McEwen, 1916

McGee, 1901
Massey, 1947
Mayr, 1946
Mercado Sánchez, 1959, 1961
Meteorological Office, London, 1956
Newell, 1959a, 1959b
Nygren, 1950
Olsson, 1932
Osorio-Tafall, 1943
Oviedo y Valdés, 1851–55
Pattullo, Munk, Revelle, and Strong, 1955
Peterson, 1960
Reid, 1960
——, Roden, and Wyllie, 1958
Revelle, 1950
Roden, 1958, 1959, 1960, 1961a, 1961b, 1962, 1963, 1964
—— and Groves, 1959
Rosenblatt, 1959
Roys, 1939
Sarkisyan, 1960
Schaefer, Bishop, and Howard, 1958
Scholes and Roys, 1948
Schott, 1935
Scripps Inst. Oceanography, 1957, 1960, 1963, MS.
Shepard, F. P., 1950
Shumway, Hubbs, and Moriarty, 1961
Spinden, 1917
Springer, 1958
Starr, 1900
Steinbeck and Ricketts, 1941
Sverdrup, 1941
——, Johnson, and Fleming, 1942
Thompson, J. E. S., 1929
Thorade, 1909
Townsend, 1901
Tozzer, 1941
U. S. Bureau of Commercial Fisheries, 1960
U. S. Coast and Geodetic Survey, 1915, 1956, 1957
U. S. Geological Survey, 1954
U. S. Hydrographic Office, 1947, 1951
U. S. Weather Bureau, 1955–60
Wagner, H. R., 1930
Walker, 1960
West, 1961
Wooster, 1959
—— and Cromwell, 1958
—— and Jennings, 1955
Yoshida and Mao, 1957

6. Weather and Climate of Mexico and Central America

JORGE A. VIVÓ ESCOTO

GREAT DIVERSITY characterizes the weather and climate of Mexico and Central America. The temperature of the air and the amount of rainfall vary enormously from place to place. In short distances one can travel from hot, humid lowlands to cool, dry highlands. The windward side (*barlovento*) of a mountain may be drenched with rain; the leeward side (*sotavento*), possibly only 30 km. distant, may be semiarid. Dry northwestern Mexico, parts of which receive less than 100 mm. of rain yearly, contrasts with the Caribbean coast of Central America, where in places over 6000 mm. of rain falls annually. This diversity of temperature and precipitation is fundamental in the distribution of natural vegetation and animal life and is reflected in various facets of aboriginal culture, such as agriculture, shelter, and even in religion.[1]

The distinction between weather and climate is only one of degree, for both involve the state of the atmosphere as expressed in terms of air temperature, air pressure and winds, and precipitation and humidity of any place or area. *Weather* is the day-to-day condition of the atmosphere, whereas *climate* is a generalization of the daily weather conditions of a given area as observed over a longer period of time. The following discussion of the atmospheric conditions that characterize Mexico and Central America considers both weather and climate together.

Generally speaking, the reliability of meteorological data for most of Mexico and Central America is only fair to poor. Relatively few weather stations have continuous records for periods longer than 50 years. Usually these are confined to some of the national capitals (Mexico City, San Salvador, San Jose) or to a few of the larger cities (Puebla, Mexico; Colon, Panama, the latter with nearly a century of continuous record). Except for the records of a few of the larger towns and those kept by foreign-operated plantations and mines, the weather data for most of Central America are meager and unreliable. Most series of observations are fragmentary, length of

---

[1] With the author's approval, the volume editor has made several additions to the original article.

187

record is short (often less than 10–15 years), and stations are few and unevenly distributed. Within the last 15 years, however, the national meteorological services of the Central American countries have established many new weather stations in connection with air transport and agricultural experiment centers. Since 1921 the Servicio Meteorológico of Mexico has maintained a large network of weather stations, which now number more than 600 distributed throughout the country, but mainly within the central plateau.

Factors of Weather and Climate

The characteristics of the weather and climate of Mexico and Central America have their origin in various fundamental factors, or controls. These include latitudinal position, extent of land mass, surface configuration and altitude, and adjacent oceans and their currents.

Latitude

The land area of Mexico and Central America lies between latitude 32°43′ and 7°30′ N. and between longitude 75°30′ and 117°08′ W. One third of this entire region, including the northern half of Mexico, lies to the north of the Tropic of Cancer (29°30′ N.); in terms of weather and climate most of this area is characterized by hot summers and cold winters. In contrast, two thirds of the region, including central and southern Mexico and all of Central America, lies south of the Tropic of Cancer, where the temperature differences between the summer and winter months become less as one goes equatorward.

Extent of the Land Mass

As is evident from the map, the land mass of Mexico–Central America is wide in its northern sector and tapers to isthmian proportions toward continental South America. Humid oceanic air can easily move into the narrow portion of the land mass from Tehuantepec to Darien. Thus the isthmian

character of southernmost Mexico and all of Central America makes the climate of most of this sector quite humid, similar to the climate of the West Indian Islands.

But in central and northern Mexico, where the land mass widens to continental size, humid oceanic air does not readily extend far into the interior. Consequently, the climate of northern Mexico is relatively dry and that of central Mexico, moderately humid. Other factors, such as the position of areas of high atmospheric pressure, discussed below, also help to cause the aridity of northern Mexico.

Altitude and Surface Configuration

According to the latitudinal distribution of the land already mentioned, we might expect that north of the Tropic of Cancer the climate should be temperate, and that south thereof, it should be tropical. But this generalization does not hold, due to the configuration of the land.

As indicated in a previous article, the surface of Mexico and Central America is composed largely of mountains and intervening depressions, and to a lesser extent of plateaus and coastal lowlands. The presence of highlands extends the temperate climates far south of the Tropic of Cancer into low latitudes, for altitude strongly influences air temperature. Normally the temperature of the air decreases with altitude at the average rate of about 1° C. for every 150 m. of elevation. Thus on mountain slopes and plateau escarpments there occurs an altitudinal zonation of weather and climate. In Mexico and Central America these zones have been recognized by the people living south of the Tropic of Cancer since ancient times. Those areas below 1000 m. elevation have hot tropical temperatures and are known as *tierra caliente*; those between 1000 and 2000 m. have lower temperatures and are called *tierra templada*; while those above 2000 m. are known as *tierra fría* because of relatively cold temperatures for most of the year. In general,

188

it can be stated that north of the Tropic of Cancer latitude is the most important control of air temperature, whereas south of it altitude is the most significant determinant.

The mountainous character of the land surface of Mexico and Central America also affects the distribution of rainfall, giving rise to an extremely complicated pattern of wet and dry areas. The windward sides of mountains and escarpments tend to be humid, the leeward sides, dry. Most of the high mountain ridges are wet; adjacent depressions or valleys, shut off from moisture-bearing winds, are usually dry or moderately humid. For example, within the isthmian portion of Mexico–Central America the depression of central Chiapas and the Motagua Valley of central Guatemala are only moderately humid. Other areas, such as the Tepalcatepec-Balsas depression of southern Mexico, are in part dry.

With regard to plateaus, those of the isthmian area, such as Los Altos of Guatemala and central Chiapas, are humid; the central plateaus of Mexico are moderately humid; however, the northern plateaus of Mexico are dry, since they are located far from humid air masses that originate over the adjacent oceans.

In general, the lowlands of Mexico and Central America are coastal and are thus near the sea, the source of atmospheric moisture. Those south of the Tropic of Cancer that are below 1000 m. elevation are humid. Those north of the Tropic, regardless of elevation, are either dry, as in Sonora, Sinaloa and Baja California; or they are moderately humid, as in Tamaulipas.

Adjacent Oceans and Their Currents

These constitute a fourth control of the weather and climate of Mexico and Central America. Warm surface water characterizes both the Caribbean Sea and the Gulf of Mexico. Both receive warm water from a branch of the Atlantic North Equatorial Current. This mass of water enters the Caribbean through the Lesser Antilles and passes through the Yucatan Strait to the Gulf of Mexico. The main current flows through the Florida Strait as the Gulf Stream, which warms the southern Atlantic shores of the United States. Several smaller currents proceed from the Yucatan Strait into the Gulf of Mexico. One, called the Gulf of Mexico Current, passes clockwise along the east coast of Mexico to the United States.

These currents thus bring warm, equatorial waters to the Caribbean and most parts of the Gulf of Mexico, over which form humid tropical air masses. These air masses in turn influence the weather and climate of the eastern portions of Mexico and most of Central America. They also greatly modify cold air masses from the United States that often move southward along the east coast of Mexico and Central America in winter.

Most of the water that bathes the Pacific shores of Mexico and Central America is also warm. A branch of the Pacific Equatorial Countercurrent passes northward along the western coasts of Central America and southern Mexico. The Pacific maritime tropical air mass that forms over these warm waters brings high temperatures and often heavy rainfall to the adjacent coasts.

Farther north along the western coast of Baja California the cold California Current is in striking contrast to the warm waters that border the rest of Mexico. This cold current lowers the prevailing temperatures along the dry west coast of the peninsula, in contrast to the warm regime that characterizes the east coast on the Gulf of California. The cold current also causes the presence of a coastal fog, similar to the conditions along the Peruvian coast of South America.

DYNAMICS OF THE AIR

One of the most fundamental aspects of weather and climate of any area concerns the moisture and temperature characteris-

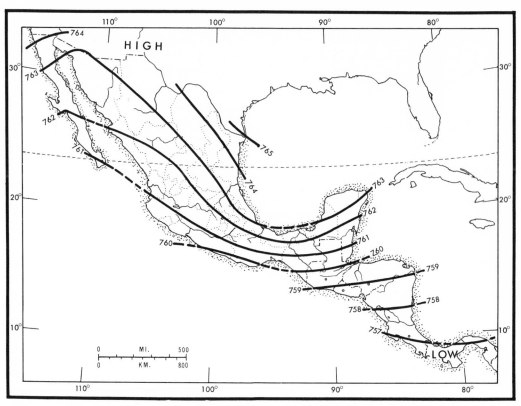

Fɪɢ. 1—AVERAGE SEA-LEVEL ATMOSPHERIC PRESSURE FOR JANUARY

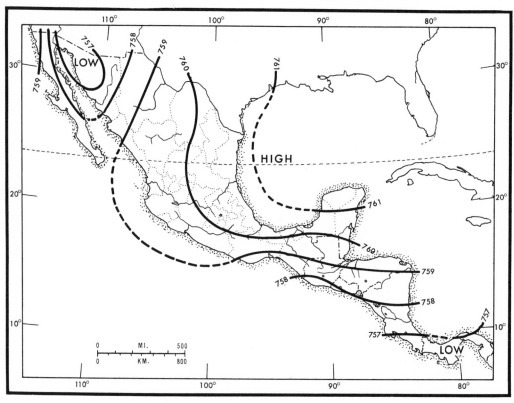

Fɪɢ. 2—AVERAGE SEA-LEVEL ATMOSPHERIC PRESSURE FOR JULY

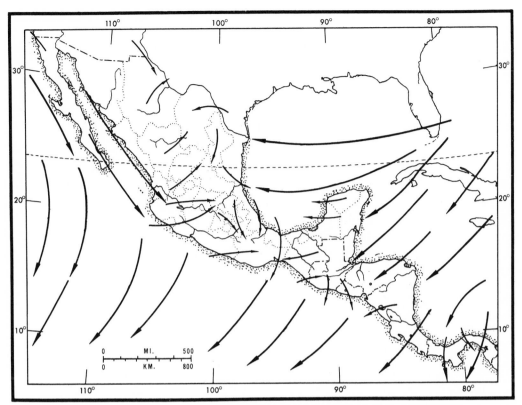

FIG. 3—AVERAGE WIND DIRECTION DURING JANUARY IN MIDDLE AMERICA

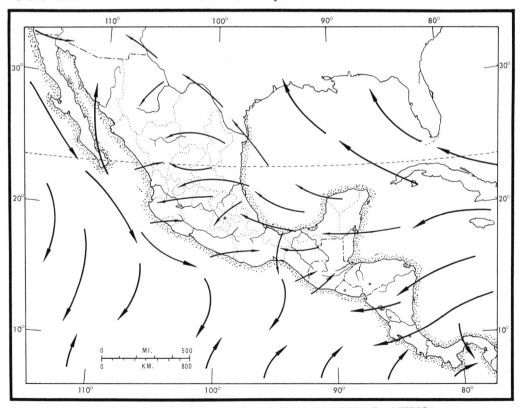

FIG. 4—AVERAGE WIND DIRECTION DURING JULY IN MIDDLE AMERICA

tics that derive from the movement of surface air. To simplify the presentation of these complex atmospheric movements, those that are related to the general or world air circulation that affect Mexico and Central America will be discussed first, followed by those of regional extent, and finally by those of local nature (figs. 1–4).

Easterlies or Trade Winds

Mexico and Central America are affected throughout the year by a gigantic flow of easterly air, commonly called the Northeast Trade Winds, a part of the general world atmospheric circulation. This air flow not only moves horizontally (advectively), but also trends upward (convectively) as it approaches the thermal equator, in which the doldrums or equatorial calms originate. This vertical movement of air within the easterlies and the increasing instability of the air mass as it approaches the doldrums cause heavy rainfall, often accompanied by thunderstorms.

As they sweep over the warm surface of the Caribbean Sea and the Gulf of Mexico, the trade winds absorb vast quantities of water vapor. Although the trades are capable of producing rainfall at all times of the year, they do so only when forced to rise and cool. Such an ascent is effected as the trades approach the rising air of the equatorial calms. When the thermal equator (along which the air is ascending) migrates northward during the months of June, July, and August, it is at this time that the trade winds reach their maximum instability, bringing on the summer rainy season over much of Middle America.

The ascending convective movement of the trades influences the weather of southern Central America most of the year. But in summer this movement also causes rainfall in central and southern Mexico and northern Central America, for at that time the thermal equator migrates northward to about latitude 12° N. During this period heavy rains fall not only on windward

mountain slopes, but also in lowlands and in valleys.

According to the foregoing analysis, then, the easterlies, or trade winds, do not produce rainfall just because they transport water vapor from the seas to the land. Rather, the rains are due mainly to convergence near the equatorial calms, resulting in ascending air which cools adiabatically with the help of local convection and produces heavy precipitation.

The trade winds are also forced to rise and cool along high, windward-facing mountain slopes. Hence, the high escarpments of Mexico from Veracruz into Chiapas along the Gulf, as well as those of Central America along the Caribbean, are enveloped in cloud and drenched with moisture for most of the year.

Subtropical Calms

During the northern hemisphere winter the heat equator migrates southward. At this time all of Mexico and the northern sector of Central America are affected by the subtropical calms, or masses of descending air, a part of the world's general circulation. Such calms originate in the belts of high atmospheric pressure that occur chiefly over the oceans around latitudes 23–35°, but also extend over some adjacent land areas. As the air subsides from the upper atmosphere it is heated adiabatically and is therefore dry and stable, incapable of either condensation or precipitation. These descending convective movements of air cause the typical dry season from December through April in both Mexico and much of Central America. During winter and spring the trade winds are also stable and incapable of producing much precipitation; for except along steep windward slopes they no longer are actually ascending winds in the latitude of Mexico and Central America, owing to the counteraction of the descending air.

The deserts and steppes of northern and northwestern Mexico are under the influence of the subtropical high pressure belt of calms during the entire year, and thus receive little rain at any period. The aridity of the north Mexican plateau results from both its interior continental position and the subsiding air of the subtropical calms. The occasional precipitation that does occur in northern and northwestern Mexico owes its origin in summer to local convectional storms and in winter to incursions of cold fronts from the United States and the Pacific Ocean.

Cold Fronts of the Westerlies

A third type of air movement associated with the world's general circulation that affects the weather of Mexico and sometimes of Central America are the incursions of cold polar air from the midlatitude frontal storms of the westerly wind belt. Such storms, which occur within extratropical cyclones, are the normal bearers of daily weather in the United States and Canada during most of the year. From October to May, however, frontal storms are deflected from their normal paths southward into Mexico, Central America, and the Caribbean. Infrequently they may reach the northern coast of Colombia and Venezuela in South America.

Most of the midlatitude frontal storms that affect Mexico and Central America originate in the Great Plains of the United States and Canada or over the North Pacific Ocean. They consist of large masses of cold polar air from the high latitudes. When the air masses penetrate into Mexico and Central America they are called northers, or *nortes*, for they are characterized by strong cold winds from the north. These cold air masses produce fronts or "storm lines" along the zone of contact with warm tropical air. Large areas of cumulous clouds and often rainfall occur in front of and along the front. After the passage of the front there is a sharp drop in temperature, especially in northern Mexico. In the mountains and higher elevations of the plateau

in northern Mexico, as in Chihuahua, the cold fronts frequently produce snowfall and in certain cases cause dust storms as far south as Zacatecas, San Luis Potosi, and other regions.

When they reach central Mexico the polar air masses are greatly modified, but they still may produce a decrease in temperatures and on contact with warmer, moister air will cause the infrequent light winter rains (called *cabañuelas* or *equipatas*) in El Bajio and other parts of the central plateau.

Furthermore the cold waves, or nortes, occur as strong, cool winds along the Mexican Gulf coast and in Central America. Extensive cloudiness and heavy rains result on contact with the warm, humid air of the Gulf, along the fronts, especially on the eastern escarpments of Mexico and northern Central America, where further uplifting takes place. The nortes often attain high velocities, 150 km. per hour having been recorded during one storm in Veracruz. These strong winds produce heavy seas off the Gulf and Caribbean shores, making coastwise navigation in small craft at best hazardous if not impossible for periods of many days during the winter months. On such occasions pre-Columbian Mayan sea trade between Yucatan, Tabasco, and Honduras must have ceased entirely. Northers also blow through the depressions across Central America, causing rough seas off the Pacific coast south of the Isthmus of Tehuantepec, the Gulf of Fonseca, and the Nicaragua lowlands. The stronger nortes pass over the highlands of Central America, causing freezes and snow storms in the plateau regions; they then descend to the Pacific coast as hot, dry winds.

Monsoon Regional Circulation

As shown in figures 1 and 2, heating of the land in summer results in the development of a semipermanent low pressure area, particularly in northern and northwestern Mexico. Conversely, cooling in winter caus-

193

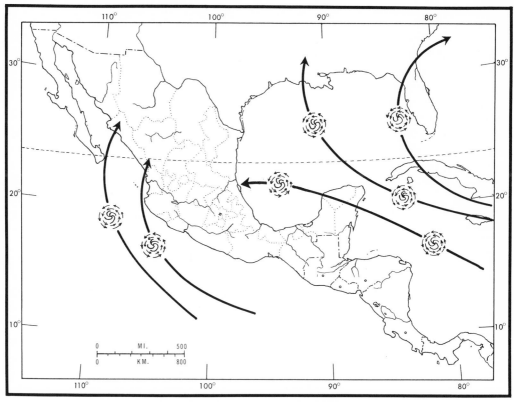

Fig. 5—NORMAL HURRICANE TRACKS, MIDDLE AMERICA

es a high pressure area to form over the land. The low pressure of summer induces regional winds to blow inland from the sea, both from the Gulf into northern Mexico and from the Pacific Ocean into the northwestern part of the country. This regional circulation causes the deflection of the trade winds during summer from northeast to southeast, bringing some humid air into the dry northern territory of northern Mexico and southwestern United States. In this case most of the precipitation occurs in the higher mountains of the Sierra Madre Oriental and the Sierra Madre Occidental. On the plateau surface heating causes local convection currents, which lift the humid marine air to form scattered thundershowers that characterize the summer rainfall in these regions. The winter high pressure area over northern Mexico induces air to flow from the land to the sea. This seasonal reversal of wind direction, inducing sum-

mer rains and winter drought, is called a monsoon because it is somewhat similar to the air of circulation of that name in southern and eastern Asia.

During winter the contrasts between the high air pressure over the cold land and the low pressure over the warmer water in the Gulf of Mexico and Caribbean Sea causes a deflection of the polar air masses and their cold fronts southward into Mexico and Central America.

Tropical Cyclones

A second type of regional air circulation has its origin in the tropical cyclones that affect mainly the Caribbean and eastern coasts of Mexico. Similar storms also occur on the Pacific coast of Mexico and northern Central America.

Tropical cyclones are whirls of air that develop around areas of abnormally low atmospheric pressure. Circulating counter-

194

clockwise in the northern hemisphere (fig. 5), winds within these storms often reach velocities well over 180 km. per hour. Although they usually measure no more than 160 km. across, they are some of the most destructive storms known. In the Caribbean area and in Mexico these storms are called *hurricanes*, a word of West Indian origin, according to some authors.

Hurricanes originate along the poleward edge of the doldrum belt principally in the Caribbean Sea and the North Atlantic Ocean; they develop as violent storms usually between 6° and 20° north of the equator. They travel slowly (15–25 km. per hour) westward with the direction of the trade winds, usually recurve poleward, and frequently follow a parabolic path. The West Indian islands bear the brunt of most of the destructive hurricanes. However, many sweep over the Yucatan Peninsula and reach the Gulf coast of Mexico from Tabasco to Tamaulipas. Recurving northward, many storms reach the Gulf and Atlantic coasts of the United States. Relatively few hurricanes have been recorded for the east coast of Central America.

In the eastern Pacific Ocean hurricanes also form off the coast of Central America and southern Mexico and travel northward into the Gulf of California. Often these storms suddenly veer northeastward causing extensive damage along the west coast of Mexico.

Hurricanes develop mainly during August through October, the maximum number occurring in September.

Hurricane destruction results not only from high wind velocity, but also from tidal waves which the winds pile up along coasts, inundating extensive areas of low elevation and making navigation impossible. Moreover, due to ascending masses of warm, humid air within the hurricane, tremendous amounts of rain fall with the passage of the storm. The most intense downpours known (more than 100 mm. per hour; 1150 mm. the 24-hour maximum) are those that oc-

cur in hurricanes. These deluges often produce destructive floods that inundate agricultural lands and urban areas.

Furthermore, the tropical cyclones cause cloudiness and precipitation over a wide area outward from their centers. Thus the coastal lowlands and the central plateaus of Mexico as well as northern Mexico and southwestern United States receive late summer and early autumn rains from such disturbances. Indeed, many regions of central and northern Mexico would be quite dry without the rains associated with hurricanes. During years of frequent tropical cyclonic disturbances reservoirs are refilled, the crops yield abundantly, and grazing flourishes. In contrast, during years of few hurricanes severe autumn drought frequently harms agriculture and stockraising in Mexico and southwestern United States. Moreover, the autumn maximum of rainfall that is characteristic of the Caribbean islands, the Gulf coast of Mexico, and northeastern Central America, as well as in some regions along the Pacific coast, is due chiefly to the moisture associated with hurricanes. Without the rains connected with the tropical cyclones many areas of central Mexico would be dry; and the arid regions of northern Mexico and southwestern United States would be more extensive. It should not be forgotten that Mexico, Central America, and the West Indies lie in the same latitudes as the Sahara and Arabian deserts.

Closely associated with tropical cyclones of the Caribbean are the recently discovered "easterly waves," perturbations in the air flow of the trades or easterlies. Of relatively low wind velocity, these disturbances often bring days of continuous rain along the Gulf and Caribbean shores of Middle America, and in northern Central America they may reach inland to the Pacific coast. As yet poorly understood, the easterly waves may be due to the same factors that cause tropical hurricanes.

The Indians of the Antilles as well as the

195

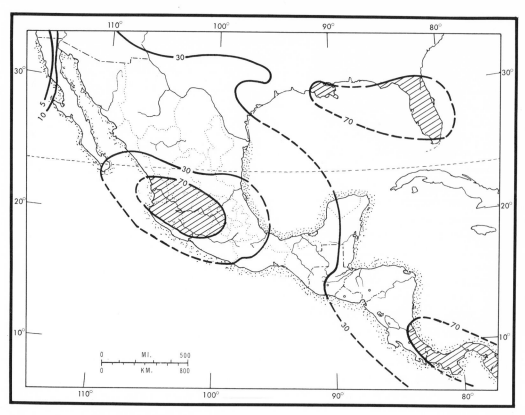

FIG. 6—THUNDERSTORM FREQUENCY
Figures indicate average annual number of days with thunderstorms.

Maya and Quiche of the Mexican and Central American mainland attached great importance to the hurricane as a natural phenomenon, and among them it was worshipped as a nature god. According to Fernando Ortiz the hurricane cult was widespread within the Caribbean. Among the Maya the god Huracan may have been derived from the cult of Tlaloc or Chac, the god of rain and thunder. In the Popol Vuh of the Quiche (edition of Adrian Recinos) the god Huracan, or hurricane, is considered to be one of three deities who made up the "Heart of Heaven."

Local Circulation

Local circulation of the air also plays an important part in the weather and climate of Mexico and Central America. The most important type of local circulation is the convective currents of rising and subsiding air that derive from local pressure differ-

ences due to heating of the land surface. Such convective currents are more frequent in low than in high latitudes; they are also more frequent in the high interior plateaus than in the coastal lowlands.

Local convection plays an important role in the development of thundershowers within the humid air masses that are carried into the interior of Mexico and Central America by the trade winds, monsoons, and the tropical cyclones. Figure 6 shows that west-central Mexico is one of the areas of greatest thunderstorm frequency in Middle America (over 70 days per year with such storms), practically all of which result from local convection. The large frequency of thunderstorms shown for southern Central America results chiefly from the unstable air associated with the equatorial calm or doldrum belt as it migrates northward during June, July, and August.

Although they are of great importance in

196

bringing rain to Mexico and Central America, thunderstorms often cause serious damage to life and property. Lightning, for example, usually connected with violent thunderstorms, kills many people yearly in Mexico.

Moreover, closely associated with intense thunderstorms is the occurrence of hail, often detrimental to crops. Within Mexico and Central America hailstones fall mainly from thunderstorms in the high plateau and mountain areas, such as the central plateau of Mexico and the highlands of Chiapas and Guatemala. Hailfall is less frequent in the lowland tropics, for the ice globules melt as they pass through warm surface air before reaching the ground. In preconquest times hail damage to crops in the tropical highlands must have been as serious as it is today.

Sudden wind squalls, also connected with local convection and thunderstorms, are frequent in northern and central Mexico. Sometimes such wind gusts may reach hurricane force (120 km. per hour), causing serious damage to crops and buildings. Wind squalls are somewhat similar to, but less destructive than, tornados, common in midwestern United States. True tornados have not been recorded for Mexico and Central America, although waterspouts occasionally occur off both the Pacific and Caribbean coasts of Middle America.

A second form of local circulation is land and sea breezes. Slight diurnal variation in atmospheric pressure between land and adjacent sea causes light winds to blow landward during the daytime and seaward during the night. These breezes are more fully developed in the tropics than in higher latitudes, and near the coast during the day sensible temperatures are lowered by the sea breeze.

A third type of local circulation is the mountain and valley winds of the interior. At high altitudes, especially on warm days, winds tend to blow upslope during the early morning and downslope in the after-

noon and sometimes at night. During the day the upslope winds may cause rainfall in the upper valleys and on the mountain sides, provided the air is sufficiently humid.

Complexity of Air Dynamics in Middle America

In contrast to the relatively simple air dynamics of the midlatitudes of North America and those of the equatorial regions of South America, the atmospheric movements of Mexico and Central America are characterized by their complex nature. This complexity is due largely to the position of Middle America between the middle and low latitudes.

Generally speaking, air movements over most of the United States and Canada are characterized by the continuous eastward succession of cyclones (low pressure areas) and anticyclones (high pressure areas); within these structures are developed frontal storms that result from the contact of cold polar air and warm tropical air. Another simple pattern of weather is seen in the equatorial areas, where convergence of the easterlies (trade winds) produces the doldrum belt with its ascending air and afternoon convective thundershowers throughout most of the year.

Located between these two areas of simplified air movements and influenced by both, Middle America has no general weather pattern that prevails throughout all seasons. During the summer months the easterly trades with their ascending winds, together with the monsoonal air movements complicated by local convection, prevail as weather bearers. In late summer and autumn tropical cyclones (hurricanes) and easterly waves add to the complexity of the weather. Taken together, all these air movements operate to bring on the rainy season in Mexico and Central America.

In late winter and spring the subsiding air of the subtropical high pressure area dominates the weather over most of Mexico and northern Central America, causing the

197

long dry season. But the dry period is often interrupted by the invasion of cold air masses from North America, resulting in weak, frontal storms which are difficult to predict. Accurate weather forecasts in most of Mexico and Central America are at best difficult even with modern meterological knowledge and equipment.

The complexity and difficult forecasting of the weather of these areas is reflected in the great importance and antiquity that weather deities had in the religion of high Indian cultures in Middle America. The gods of rain, and in some areas of the wind and the hurricane, had to be propitiated to insure favorable weather for crops. The development of cults based on the worship of weather elements, particularly rain, necessitated the formation of a priesthood to act as an intermediary between the gods and common man.

WEATHER AND CLIMATIC ELEMENTS

Temperature

As we have noted previously, not only latitude but also great differences in altitude are the main factors that control surface temperatures in Middle America (fig. 7). The highland areas located north of the Tropic of Cancer experience the warm summers and cool winters of the midlatitudes, similar to the temperature regime of south-central United States. In northern Mexico maximum temperatures occur from June through August; minimum temperatures come in December or January. Daytime summer temperatures of over 40° C. are not uncommon in Chihuahua, whereas freezing weather of less than −10° C. occurs during the winter months within the same region of the northern plateau. The temperature regime of northwestern Mexico is similar to the southern part of the arid Great Basin of western United States; in some parts of Sonora the maximum temperature in summer reaches nearly 50° C. and the minimum in winter falls to around 0° C.

South of the Tropic the differences be-

tween average temperatures of the warmest and coldest months become less as one goes equatorward. In southern Mexico and Central America monthly thermal differences are so slight that definite seasons cannot be readily distinguished on the basis of temperature. Moreover, south of the Tropic the warmest period of the year comes in March, April, or May, rather than in the normal high-sun period of June or July. This anomaly is due to the fact that the period of highest temperature occurs at the height of the dry season with clear skies and brilliant sun. With onset of the rainy period in June and July air is cooled by the presence of cloud cover and the descent of cold air from above during convective thundershowers. Such cooling is more prevalent at high altitudes on the plateaus than in the coastal lowlands.

The hot period from March to May is usually the most unpleasant of the year. Especially on the plateaus local dust storms, engendered by towering convective dust devils that range in size from the great *tolvaneras* to the smaller *remolinos*, accompany the heat and dryness. The first showers of the rainy season bring immediate relief for body comfort. The relation between lowering temperatures and precipitation is a phenomenon well recognized among the common people of Middle America.

The important relation between altitude and temperature and the resulting altitudinal temperature zones of Mexico and Central America have already been mentioned. These zones are best developed in the areas south of the Tropic of Cancer.

The tropical lowlands below 1000 m. elevation, or the tierra caliente, have average yearly temperatures between 25° and 30° C., or between 20° and 25° C. These include the coastal plains and adjacent foothills, large plains areas such as the Yucatan Peninsula, and the low interior depressions. High, but not excessive, daytime temperatures (29°–32° C.) contrast with cool nights (20°–24° C.). The common adage "night is the winter of the tropics" is quite true of the lowlands, where daily range of temperature exceeds the annual range by many degrees. The mid-latitude traveler in the lowland tropics soon comes to learn that a light blanket used by native people is welcomed comfort during the chilly nights. Frost is rare or unknown, except in lowland areas north of the Tropic of Cancer.

Many areas of the tierra caliente of Middle America were heavily populated in preconquest times, and archaeological sites abound in the low coastal areas on both the Atlantic and Pacific sides of Mexico and Central America. The well-known decrease in native population in Middle America soon after the Spanish conquest appears to have been far more drastic in the tropical lowlands than elsewhere. This phenomenon may have been due not only to the introduction of the common European contagious diseases such as smallpox, measles, and typhus, but also to the transfer of the Old World malarial parasite, *Plasmodium*, subsequently carried by the native anopheles mosquitos which thrive in hot humid conditions of the tierra caliente.

The intermediate altitudes between 1000 and 2000 m. elevation, called the tierra templada, are characterized by average yearly temperatures between 15° and 20° C. This zone constitutes the lower tropical highlands of Middle America, and includes the intermediate mountain slopes and much of the plateau surface of Mexico and Central America. During the day temperatures are mild (24°–27° C.), but in the dry period hot afternoons with temperatures over 35° often occur. Nights are cool (14°–20° C.), but near the northern margins of the tropical highlands, such as in central Mexico, periods of cold with night frosts are not uncommon in December and January. Exceptionally early frosts in October and late freezes in spring often cause severe crop damage.

The tierra fría, or the higher portions of the tropical highlands above 2000 m., usually have average temperatures of less than 15° C. A rather small part of Mexico and Central America rises above this elevation. The high plateau surfaces and mountain slopes and peaks of central Mexico, the highlands of Chiapas and Guatemala, and a few mountain peaks in other parts of Central America are the principal areas of tierra fría in Middle America. These areas have mild pleasant days (20°–27° C.) and cold nights (below 10°–15° C.). Killing frosts are common during the cooler months of November through February.

Since ancient times the humid parts of both the tierra templada and tierra fría of Mexico and Central America have been favored areas for human settlement. Especially the tierra templada was occupied in preconquest times and today is the most densely populated section of Middle America.

Pressure and Winds

Although atmospheric pressure does not exercise a direct influence on man, it is of great importance in directing the movements of air masses, as described in a previous section. Here we shall summarize briefly seasonal pressure distribution and its effect on wind direction.

Figure 1 indicates the distribution of pressure for January by means of isobars, or lines connecting points of equal pressure, and figure 3 shows wind direction in the same month. An area of high pressure lies over the cold part of northern Mexico whereas the warmer areas, the Gulf of Mexico and Central America, are characterized by low pressure. This pressure distribution of winter aids the development of the northers, or invasions of cold air from the North American continent into the tropical areas of Middle America and the Caribbean.

In contrast, the pressure distribution for July, shown on figure 2, indicates the presence of a semipermanent low pressure area

199

in northern and northwestern Mexico which develops from the high summer heating of the continental interior. This low pressure induces the winds indicated in figure 4, including the inward movement of air from the Gulf of Mexico and the Pacific Ocean, producing the summer monsoon of northern and northwestern Mexico. Another seasonal low pressure area appears during the summer period over the southern sector of Central America. This low corresponds to the northward migration of the thermal equator and the doldrum belt during the months of June, July, and August.

Relative Humidity

The amount of moisture actually contained in the air compared with the maximum possible content (at a given temperature) is called *relative humidity*, expressed as a percentage. Relative humidity is not only an important element of weather and climate. It is also one of the significant factors that determines the amount and rate of evaporation, which in turn affects the rate of moisture and temperature loss by living organisms. Hence, relative humidity is an important determinant of human comfort, particularly in areas of high temperature.

In Mexico and Central America relative humidity generally increases equatorward, is normally greater along coastal areas than in the interior, and is higher during the summer and autumn than in the spring and winter months. Figures 8 and 9 show the distribution of relative humidity for March and September, extreme months for most of the area in terms of rainfall and moisture content of the air.

Dry northern Mexico, of course, has the lowest relative humidity; despite high daytime temperatures, heat is not inordinately oppressive, except along the Gulf of California coast in summer. The presence of cold-current fog along the Pacific coast of Baja California causes high relative humidity for a desert area (over 70%), but ab-

normally low temperatures lessen oppressiveness.

The greatest seasonal contrast in relative humidity is seen in the central plateau of Mexico, where dry, desert-like air (30–50% relative humidity) prevails at the height of the drought period in March, in contrast to the more humid conditions (60–70% relative humidity) during the rainy season. A lesser degree of seasonal contrast in relative humidity is found along the Pacific side of Central America and in northern Yucatan.

It is chiefly along the Gulf and Caribbean lowlands that the air is highly moist almost all year long. There, the damp trade winds keep the relative humidity well over 80% even in the hot lowlands. In low valleys sheltered from the prevailing winds, the near-saturated condition of the air combined with high summer temperatures can make atmospheric conditions detrimental to the proper functioning of the human organism. Unable to lose moisture and temperature readily by evaporation, the body becomes rapidly overheated under such conditions. Along the immediate coast, however, atmospheric conditions can be delightful, for the sea breeze quickly evaporates surface body moisture, reducing sensible temperatures of the skin. Under such conditions as these clothing, or rather the paucity or lack thereof, becomes highly important. Apparel among the aboriginal groups living in the tropical lowlands as well as at higher elevations in Middle America has had much more of a ceremonial than a protective function.

Rainfall

The distribution of annual rainfall shown in figure 10 indicates the complicated pattern of wet and dry areas that characterizes Mexico and Central America. The most humid section lies along the eastern or windward coasts where the ascending trades are forced upward along mountain slopes or are trapped in narrow seaward-

200

facing valleys or embayments. The latter situation is exemplified by the lower San Juan Valley of Nicaragua, where the station of Greytown receives an annual rainfall of more than 6000 mm., the wettest known spot in Central America, and by Teapa, in Tabasco, with around 4000 mm., one of the wettest places in Mexico. Eastward-facing escarpments from the Huasteca in northeastern Mexico to Panama are drenched with rainfall, ranging from 2000 to 4000 mm. per year. The northern part of the protruding, flat, and low-lying Yucatan Peninsula, on the other hand, receives only moderate rainfall, with less than 1000 mm. per year, for there the trade winds are not forced to rise abruptly.

In general the Pacific coast of Mexico and Central America is drier than the windward Caribbean or Gulf coasts. Nevertheless high annual rainfall is recorded in places on the western slope of Central America, where, in summer, moist air from the Pacific Ocean is forced to rise against high escarpments (e.g. more than 4000 mm. on the steep volcanic versant of southwestern Guatemala and southeastern Chiapas; 5000 mm. in southeastern Costa Rica).

Only moderate amounts of rain (1000–2500 mm.) characterize the interior valleys and plateaus of Central America and southern and central Mexico. Some deep depressions such as the middle Motagua of Guatemala receive as little as 500 mm. yearly. Areas to the leeward of high mountains, such as the region of the central plateau of Mexico in eastern Puebla, are relatively dry, receiving less than 500 mm. annually.

Because of its aridity and its position outside the tropics, northern Mexico stands apart climatically from the rest of Middle America. Two large areas separated by the Sierra Madre Occidental comprise the dry section of the north. The high central desert of the northern plateau is bounded generally by the 250-mm. isohyet (a cartographic line connecting points of equal rainfall). The low deserts of Baja California and western Sonora in northwestern Mexico are the driest areas of Middle America. Some sections, like the Altar Desert of northwestern Sonora and the Vizcaino Desert of Baja California, annually receive less than 100 mm. of rainfall.

Seasonality of Rainfall

As we have indicated already, in most sections of Mexico and Central America rainfall is seasonal. The rainy period usually comes during the hotter months from May through October. The drier part of the year corresponds to the cooler period from December through April. March is commonly the month of least rain, whereas September is usually the rainiest month (figs. 11, 12). Over most of the plateau and Pacific coast areas of Mexico and northern Central America nearly 80 per cent of the annual rain falls between May and October. Except for small areas of irrigated farming, the entire rhythm of agricultural life among the ancient Indians of Mexico and Central America was geared to this seasonality of rainfall.

In parts of Middle America there are various modifications of the general wet and dry season regime. The humid eastern versant from the Isthmus of Tehuantepec to eastern Panama receives rain throughout the year. A period of maximum precipitation comes during September to November, when the trades blow strongly and the tropical cyclones are best developed. April to June is the period of minimum rainfall, erroneously called the "dry season" because it is a season of less rain than in autumn, rather than one of complete dryness.

Another variation in seasonal rainfall is the presence of a short dry period of one or two weeks or even more during the wet summer season in much of Central America and southern Mexico. Called the *veranillo*, or "little summer," this dry period occurs in July or August. Travelers often count on the veranillo for making trips, but sometimes it fails to materialize; other years it may en-

MARCH

100
50
25 mm

MILES

KILOMETERS

dure so long as to endanger crops by drought. The veranillo of Central America and southern Mexico is due to a southward retreat of the doldrum belt or equatorial calms.

Whereas in most of central and southern Mexico the height of the rainy season comes in late July or September, in arid northern Mexico late June and early July are often the rainiest months, due to the early summer monsoon, that is, the influx of moist air from both the Gulf of Mexico and the Pacific ocean toward the semipermanent low pressure center in the interior. The convectional thundershowers taper off during August and September, but occasional tropical cyclonic storms add to the summer precipitation. Only light drizzles of frontal origin interrupt the almost continuous drought from November to June; April or May are commonly the driest months.

The northwestern region of Baja California comes under the influence of the winter extratropical cyclonic rains and summer drought that typifies the climate of upper California. Farther south in the central desert area of the peninsula the frontal rains of winter become progressively less and light summer convective showers begin, forming still another rainfall regime characterized by scanty moisture in almost every month. In the south of the peninsula rare convectional thundershowers and occasional tropical cyclonic storms are typical.

There are few areas in Middle America that receive substantial rainfall in all months of the year with no definite dry or wet periods. One section that approaches this condition is northeastern Mexico. Although annual totals of precipitation are relatively low, winter rains occur in the form of midlatitude cyclonic storms that sweep in from Texas, whereas summer and autumn precipitation (September maximum) are brought in by the monsoon effect as well as by occasional tropical cyclonic disturbances.

As indicated earlier, other areas that re-

ceive abundant rainfall in every month are the upper eastern escarpment of southern Mexico and the Caribbean slope of Central America. In both areas the forced ascent of the moist trades up windward mountain slopes is the chief cause of this rainfall regime.

Variability of Rainfall

Of prime importance to an agricultural people is the fluctuation of yearly rainfall from the amounts normally received. In years of excessive rainfall destructive floods may occur; equally disastrous are years of drought which among nontechnical peoples may result in widespread famine.

In Mexico and Central America the areas of least rainfall variability, percentagewise, are in areas of moderate to abundant precipitation, as shown in figure 13. The areas of greatest variability correspond to the arid sections of northern Mexico, inhabited in preconquest times mainly by nonagricultural people; where farming was practiced, as in northwestern Mexico and southwestern United States, primitive forms of irrigation were employed. Significantly, the areas of well-developed agriculture in Middle America have since ancient times occupied the regions of relatively low rainfall variability, according to Wallén. Much of the central plateau of Mexico, the Guatemalan highlands, and Yucatan are outstanding in this regard.

Nonetheless, even in areas of relatively low variability of precipitation, such as central Mexico, periodic droughts do occur, as evidenced on several occasions in the last century. Moreover, in preconquest times the three-year drought of 1454–56 caused widespread famine and death among the Nahua people of central Mexico, according to S. F. Cook.

The God of Rain

The occasional droughts, floods, hailstorms and other vagaries of weather that plagued the agricultural areas of Meso-

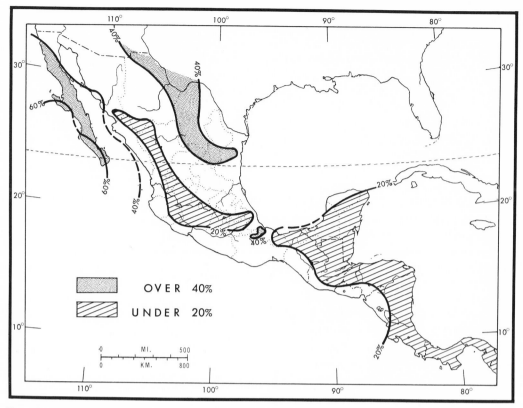

Fig. 13—RELATIVE YEAR-TO-YEAR VARIABILITY OF ANNUAL RAINFALL
(After Wallen, 1956.)

america made the god of rain the most ancient and important of the nature deities in the preconquest pantheons. Because he controlled precipitation, this god lived on high mountain tops, where rain clouds formed and where lightning and thunder were generated.

As might be expected, the rain cult appears among every agricultural people from southwestern United States to the southern limits of high culture in Central America. The development of this cult probably took place in early pre-Classic times, and was related to the cult of the jaguar in the tropical lowlands of Veracruz and Tabasco.

In central Mexico Tlaloc was the deity of rain and thunder, and was the companion of Quetzalcoatl, the god of life and fertility and inventor of agriculture, in early Teotihuacan and in the first stage of the Nahuat-Toltec cultures. During the late Teotihuacan and the late Nahuat-Toltec periods at

Tula, Tlaloc was closely associated on the altars with Xipe Totec, the god of spring planting. Still later, during the Nahuatl-Chichimec period, Tlaloc and Tezcatlipoca, the black god of the north, of evil and destruction, were grouped together on twin altars. At the height of the Nahuatl-Aztec military power during the 15th century in the temples of Tenochtitlan the rain god was associated with Huitzilopochtli, the blue Tezcatlipoca and the deity of war. Among the other associates of the rain god were Chalchihuitlicue, the wife of Tlaloc and the goddess of runoff water, of streams, lakes, and the sea; the Nahua Ehecatl, the god of wind (Tariacuri of the Tarascans), who opened the way for the rain.

Again, among the Maya the equivalent of the Nahua rain god was Chac, who was paired with Itzamna, the sky deity. Together these two gods were the principal ones in the Mayan pantheon. Chac is still a folk deity among the present Mayan farmers of northern Yucatan. Among the Totonac the same rain god was called Tajin; among the Zapotecs, Cocijo; among the Mixtec, Tzahui; and among the Tarascans, possibly Acuitze Catapeme.

The ancient priests associated with the rain god who controlled flood and drought, hail and snow, lightning and thunder, may have been the first weather "forecasters" of Middle America. With the accumulation of a large amount of weather lore through centuries of observation, the priests' task was probably not too difficult most of the time. But to deal with prolonged dry spells the propitiation of the rain deities by blood sacrifice was usually practiced, especially in late Indian times, on the eve of the Spanish conquest.

Climatic Types and Areas

As indicated previously, the climate of any particular area is determined by the combinations of the prevailing weather elements, such as temperature, precipitation, humidity, cloudiness, etc., as observed over a period of several years. Various attempts have been made to classify climates on a world-wide basis. One of the most accurate, better-known, and more easily understood classifications is that of Wladmir Koeppen. Koeppen's classification is based chiefly on annual and monthly averages of temperature and precipitation. The system also recognizes the effectiveness of precipitation for plant growth through the amount of evaporation, which varies yearly with temperature and the season of rainfall; thus, a given amount of rainfall in the hot tropical lowlands, where the rain is in summer and the rate of evaporation is high, is less effective for vegetation growth than the same amount of rainfall would be in an area of cooler temperatures, where the rain is in winter and the evaporation rate is low.

To designate climatic types Koeppen uses a system of letter symbols, each letter having a precise meaning in terms of temperature, rainfall, etc. The combination of such letters results in a formula which describes the climatic type.

According to the Koeppen system for Mexico and Central America there are three major zones of climates, each of which is composed of its respective subtypes: (1) the dry climates are represented by the letter B; (2) the letter A stands for humid tropical climates; and (3) the letter C, for the temperate climates. The boundaries of the B, or dry climates, are determined by empirical formulas of annual precipitation effectiveness that involve average annual temperature, and the season of the rainy period. Both A, macrothermal or humid tropical climate, and C, mesothermal or humid temperate climate, are determined on the basis of average monthly temperatures. For example, an A climate is one in which the average temperature of any month of the year is not less than 18° C. A C climate is one in which the average temperature of the coldest month is higher than 0° C. and that of the warmest month is more than 18° C. Other letters in the climatic formulas indicate seasonality of precipitation, average seasonal temperature extremes, and other elements. Thus, the formula Aw means a tropical humid climate, no month having an average temperature below 18° C., and a dry season during the winter. Again, Cfa signifies a temperate climate with average monthly temperatures as described above; rain in every month (f), that is, no dry season; and a hot summer period (a) in which the warmest month has an average temperature of over 22° C.

The boundaries between climatic areas as drawn on the map should not be considered as sharp lines of change, but rather as wide transition zones—a gradation of one type of climate into another. Again, these climatic boundaries are not constant, but fluctuate from year to year, according to local weather conditions. For example, the city of Monterrey, near the boundary zone between dry and humid climates, may fall into the dry climate type one year, into the humid type the next year.

In Mexico 50 per cent of the national territory, chiefly plateaus and lowlands of the north, is covered by the *B* or dry climates; approximately 25 per cent of the lowlands belong to the *A* or tropical rainy climates; and the remaining 25 per cent, mainly the higher mountains and plateaus of the central and southern part of the country, is characterized by the *C* or temperate climates.

In Central America more than 50 per cent of the land area falls into the lowlands with tropical rainy climate; the remainder is made up of plateaus and mountains having the temperate humid climates (fig. 14).

The B or Dry Climates

According to the Koeppen classification, there are two general types of dry, or *B*, climate: the true desert (*BW*) and the steppe or semiarid (*BS*). Both, of course, are distinguished by moisture deficiency. In general, however, given the same average monthly temperatures, the steppe or semiarid climate receives about double the amount of rainfall of the desert. Since the effectiveness of moisture for plant growth depends upon the rate of evaporation, which in turn is dependent upon temperature, definite amounts of rainfall cannot be used to delimit the dry climates for all areas. Rather, one must resort to the use of the empirical and somewhat unsatisfactory formulas referred to above in order to determine whether a particular area is dry or humid, or whether it is desert or steppe. The formulas devised by Koeppen for this purpose will not be elaborated on here, but they can be consulted in any standard book on climatology.

Desert Climate (BW)

In Middle America the true desert climates are confined to north-central and northwestern Mexico (figure 14). As we have seen already, northwestern Mexico, including the lowlands of western Sonora and two-thirds of Baja California, is the most arid of the two desert areas. The central desert occupies Mexico's most interior position in the middle of the northern plateau (elevation 1200 to 1500 m.) and extends southward into northeastern Zacatecas and San Luis Potosi. Both the high north-central and the low northwestern deserts and steppes are considered to be southern extensions of the arid climates of the southwestern United States. In both, the scant rainfall supports only cacti, bunch grass, and xerophytic shrubs that have developed special adaptations for aridity.

The Koeppen system divides the desert climates into two subtypes on the basis of average annual temperature. The warm desert (*BWh*) is that having an average annual temperature above 18° C.; the cool desert (*BWk*) has an average yearly temperature below 18° C.

The warm desert is best developed in the lowlands surrounding the Gulf of California, in particular the plains and coasts of western Sonora and the central region of Baja California. Some of the highest temperatures ever recorded in Mexico—up to 50° C.—occur along this lowland. In terms of high summer temperatures and position along a narrow arm of the sea, the Sonoran Desert is similar to the dry, hot lands near the Red Sea and the Persian Gulf. The little rain that falls (less than 200 mm. yearly) comes both during summer in the form of rare thundershowers and during winter with the passage of extratropical cyclonic storms from the Pacific Ocean.

Most of the interior plateau desert of northern Mexico in eastern Chihuahua and Coahuila is also classed as warm. However, due to altitude summer temperatures are not as extremely hot as in Sonora, although winters may be far colder. Rainfall is concentrated in the summer months when con-

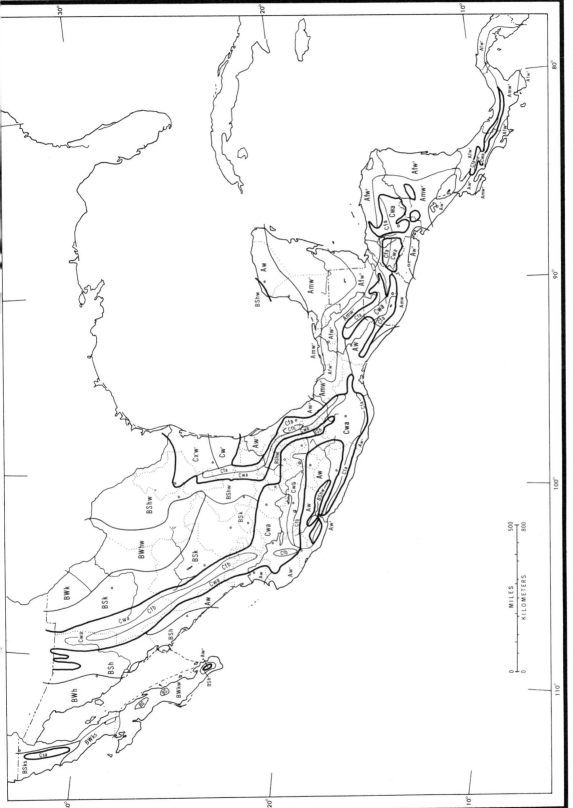

Fig. 14—DISTRIBUTION OF CLIMATIC TYPES IN MEXICO AND CENTRAL AMERICA, BASED ON THE KOEPPEN CLASSIFICATION

vective thunderstorm activity is greatest; light extratropical cyclonic rains or drizzles often occur in winter.

In both the low Sonoran and interior plateau deserts, however, the difference between day and night temperatures is extreme, owing to the clear, dry atmosphere and rapid land radiation of heat after sunset. During the winter in eastern Chihuahua, for example, midday may be uncomfortably hot, whereas at night the temperature often drops to below freezing.

The cold desert (*BWk*) is found in northern Chihuahua, extending southward from the arid lands of New Mexico.

Another cold desert (*BWk*) is formed in northwestern Baja California, where the presence of the cold California Current offshore and the occurrence of thick fog, particularly in the summer months, greatly lowers air temperature. Furthermore, because of the summer fog, there is a small seasonal and daily range of temperature, which is typical for arid regions of western coasts. The scant rainfall comes in winter from extratropical cyclonic storms, but often the summer fog is so intense that sufficient dew accumulates on the ground to induce the growth of low grasses and succulent plants. The dry but foggy weather and climate of the Pacific coast of Baja California is much like that of the Peruvian coastal desert of South America for similar reasons.

Steppe or Semiarid Climates (*BS*)

These are often considered transition zones between the true desert and the humid climates, for they occur on the margins of the more arid regions. The rainfall of the semiarid climates (twice that of adjacent deserts) is usually sufficient to induce the growth of a grass cover which can support a more varied and abundant animal life than the scrub-covered desert. Streams, although often intermittent, and springs are also more frequent than in desert lands. Moreover, given sufficient agricultural

knowledge, dry farming is possible in semiarid climate. In terms of human occupation, therefore, the steppe or semiarid areas of Middle America in general have been more significant than the deserts.

In Mexico the areas of *BS* climate are far more extensive than the deserts. Again, the largest areas are in the north, bordering the deserts. In north-central Mexico the steppe occupies two wide belts that correspond to the higher plateau surfaces.

One belt lies in central Chihuahua and Durango between the central desert and the Sierra Madre Occidental, and continues southward to include most of Zacatecas and Aguascalientes. Due to elevation (1500–2000 m.), this is a cool steppe land (*BSk*), with average annual temperatures below 18° C.

The second belt of interior steppe (*BSh*) with average yearly temperatures above 18° C. lies east of the central desert along the western flank of the Sierra Madre Oriental, in San Luis Potosi. Northward it continues into Texas and eastward into the lowlands of Nuevo Leon and northern Tamaulipas. Southward it extends as a narrow strip far into central Mexico (central Hidalgo and eastern Puebla), immediately to the leeward, or rain shadow, of the eastern Sierra. This belt is classed as a warm semiarid climate, due to the relatively high temperatures that result in part from the warm, drying winds (ending easterlies or trades) that descend westward from the eastern sierra. Both the cold western steppe of Chihuahua, Durango, and Zacatecas and the warmer eastern one receive from 300 to 500 mm. of rain yearly, mainly during the hotter summer months.

Another large area of warm steppe or semiarid climate occurs in central Sonora, between the desert on the west and the Sierra Madre Occidental on the east. This belt of steppeland continues southward along the low coastal areas of Sinaloa to the Tropic of Cancer, north of Mazatlan. Rains come in both summer and winter. Islands

208

of similar semiarid climate occur in the higher mountains of southern Baja California. Northwestern Baja California falls into a cold steppe climate, with winter rains and summer drought—an extension southward of the dry climate of southern upper California.

In southern Mexico small spots of warm steppe climate occupy either low, dry coastal areas or rain-shadow positions in deep depressions and on the leeward tip of the Yucatan Peninsula, swept by the trade winds without induced ascent. The Tepalcatepec and middle Balsas valleys are good examples of rain-shadow depressions. Were sufficient climatic data available, similar dry depressions could likely be mapped in other sections of southern Mexico and northern Central America. The central Motagua Valley of Guatemala might be an example. Although such spots might receive as much as 750 mm. of rain annually, the high temperatures and rapid evaporation in summer lowers moisture effectiveness to such an extent that the climate falls into the dry, or *B,* classification.

Dry Climates and Indian Settlement

At the time of Spanish contact most of the dry areas of northern Mexico were occupied by Indians who practiced a primitive hunting-fishing-gathering economy. The so-called "Chichimecs," nomadic hunters and gatherers speaking many Uto-Nahua (Zacateco, Guachichil, Suma) and Athabascan (Apache, Toboso) languages, lived in the north-central steppes and deserts. Indians of even lower cultural status occupied the peninsula of Baja California. Among these nomads were the Hokan-speaking Cochimi and Laymon in the north and the Guaicuran and Pericú speakers in the southern end of the peninsula. Across the Gulf the Seri fishers, also Hokan-speaking, occupied a portion of the hot, arid Sonoran mainland.

Undoubtedly both the dry northern plateau and Baja California (the rich sea fauna of the coasts bordering the Gulf of California excepted) were areas of low attraction in terms of food availability. Meager and unreliable rainfall may have been factors that helped to discourage the spread of preconquest agriculture into north-central Mexico, but conservatism or cultural resistance on the part of the desert nomads and few opportunities for trade contacts with neighboring farmers were probably far more important than environment as barriers to culture change.

On the other hand, the dry lands of Sinaloa and Sonora were settled by agriculturists—the Cahita, Yaqui, and Mayo of Uto-Nahua speech, who practiced primitive flood farming along the exotic rivers that flow from the well-watered Sierra Madre Occidental across the steppe and desert lands to the Gulf of California. The Pima and Opata of north-central Sonora and southern Arizona were expert farmers who practiced crude irrigation as well as flood and dry farming in the valleys watered by streams from the adjacent sierra. Moreover, around A.D. 600 the Hohokam people along Salt River in the desert of southern Arizona had developed an amazing system of canal irrigation, the like of which is not found elsewhere in the Americas save in the desert coast of Peru. In short, located near or within the route of northward penetration of cultural influences from central Mexico, practically the entire desert and steppe regions of Sonora and Sinaloa were occupied by Indians, depending on agriculture in the river valleys with alluvial soils, in contrast to the nomadic peoples of Baja California and the dry lands of north-central Mexico (except those living in the Conchos river valley and in La Laguna).

In the latter area archaeological evidence indicates that during the Toltec period in central Mexico a culture depending on agriculture extended northward within some of the steppes of Zacatecas, Durango, and perhaps to the Casas Grandes area of northwestern Chihuahua. With the subsequent incursion of desert nomads from the north and east, the early agricultural settlements were abandoned. At the time of Spanish contact only the Concho who lived along the river of the same name in Chihuahua, the Irritila who inhabited the borders of the interior marsh-lake of La Laguna in Coahuila, and perhaps the western Pame in San Luis Potosi were the only primitive farmers who remained in the dry area of the north. All these people practiced rudimentary planting in moist alluvial soil of river or lake banks after recession of floods. Both primitive nonagricultural nomads and semisedentary agriculture peoples thus occupied the deserts and steppes of north-central Mexico. The predominance of one economy over the other appears to have resulted from migrations of people and culture, rather than from any direct influence of climate.

Humid Temperate Climates (C)

These are confined almost entirely to the highland areas, with one or two exceptions. As explained previously, the C climates are determined on the basis of the average temperature of the coldest (above 0° C.) and warmest (above 18° C.) months. The temperate highland climates south of the Rio Grande can be divided into two large subtypes on the basis of seasonal rainfall distribution. One (Cw) is characterized by a distinct winter dry season and summer rains; the other (Cf), by rain in every month without a distinct dry period, but usually with most rain coming in the summer or autumn months. Each of these subtypes is again subclassified according to the degree of summer temperatures. The warm summer type (average temperature of warmest month over 22° C.) is indicated by adding the letter a to the climate designation; the cool summer type (average temperature of warmest month below 22° C.), is shown by the letter b. Thus the climates Cwa and Cfa refer to temperate highland

climates which occupy the lower mountain and plateau heights and usually correspond to the altitude of the tierra templada; Cwb and Cfb, the cool summer types, occupy the higher and colder elevations, and include the tierra fría zone.

The winter-dry temperate types (Cwa and Cwb) are by far the most widespread of the highland climates of Mexico and Central America. These cover the central plateau of Mexico, the highlands of Oaxaca and Chiapas, and those of northern Central America into Nicaragua. A small outlier occurs in the highlands of Costa Rica and Panama. Northward from central Mexico the same climate follows the eastern and western sierras that border either side of the great Mexican plateau.

In the highlands the rains begin usually in June (May in Central America) in the form of violent afternoon thunderstorms, often accompanied by hail, and last through the middle of October. During the rainy season mornings are usually crisp and beautifully clear. Before noon clouds begin to form over rising currents of heated air, and by midafternoon the sky may be completely overcast, the clouds pierced by lightning flashes and peals of thunder. And the downpour begins. The rain may continue intermittently until six or seven at night and drizzles may persist until nine or ten o'clock. Occasionally the summer or autumn rains continue for two or three days (temporales) without ceasing, due to the passage of a weak tropical cyclone or an easterly wave. During the height of dry season the highlands become parched and winter dust takes the place of the summer mud. Periodic cyclonic storms from the midlatitudes, however, may bring occasional light rains; rare winter snowstorms have occurred on the central plateau of Mexico as far south as the capital city, and of course, snow occurs year round on the high volcanic peaks above 4000 m. elevation. With the incursion of cold air from the north, killing frosts are common at night in the higher plateau areas as far south as Guatemala and Honduras.

The humid temperate highland climates (*Cfa* and *Cfb*) with substantial rain in all months occur mainly on high windward escarpments and mountain slopes. Such climates are best developed on the eastern escarpments of the Mexican Plateau and along the Caribbean versant of Central America, where the trade winds are forced to rise, cool, and precipitate moisture the entire year. These escarpments are almost continually in cloud, and the dampness is reflected in the eerie moss- and epiphyte-covered trees in the dense forests of these exposed altitudes. Modified *Cf* climates are found also on the Pacificward-facing escarpments and mountain tops of southern Mexico and Guatemala. Although in these areas rain falls in every month, the maximum amount is received between June and October. But even in the drier season (December–March) the higher mountain regions, such as parts of Los Altos of Guatemala, are often enveloped in cloud and mist. In Mexico the moist highland climate follows the crest of the Sierra Madre Occidental far northward, almost reaching the United States border. The summer monsoon thunderstorms and winter extratropical cyclonic rains and snows give this highland area precipitation throughout the year.

Aside from the highland temperate types, a lowland *C* climate occurs in northeastern Mexico where, better known as a humid subtropical type, it occurs in two phases. One phase (*Cx'w'*), in northern Tamaulipas and southeastern Nuevo Leon, receives a relatively small amount of rain in all months with the maximum in autumn; the other phase (*Cw'*), which occurs in southern Tamaulipas, receives a much greater yearly rainfall concentrated in late summer and autumn, but has a definite dry season in winter. These lowland temperate types might be considered to be modified southern extensions of the subtropical climates of southeastern United States. Although hot in summer, the frequent invasions of cold air masses during winter lowers November through April temperatures along the coastal lowlands of northeastern Mexico from the Rio Grande to the Panuco River (Tampico).

Temperate Climates and Indian Settlement

It is significant that most of the high Indian civilizations of Mesoamerica developed in the highland temperate climates. The locale of pre-Classic highland cultures of Mesoamerica particularly is found in the winter-dry phases (*Cwa* and *Cwb*) in the central plateau of Mexico and the uplands of Chiapas and Guatemala. From these early cultures there evolved the well-known sequence of aboriginal civilizations of highland Mesoamerica. Undoubtedly the adequacy and fair reliability of rainfall during the summer growing season, as well as the occurrence of the winter dry period—a time of rest and leisure—were important in the great achievements of these cultures. To what extent the cool, bracing air and fairly low relative humidity were instrumental in their development is hard to determine, particularly when one considers the magnificent Mayan achievements in the hot lowlands of the Peten and other tropical regions. The cool, humid plateaus of Middle America have supported a dense population since Classic times. However, other environmental factors such as soil, hydrography, and land configuration, may have been as significant as climate in attracting human settlement. Today these highlands are still centers of dense settlement and food production; they also form the social and political cores of at least two present-day nations within the old area of Mesoamerica.

The highland temperate climates, however, extend southward from the former limits of Mesoamerica into southern Central

America. Although they received stimulus from the higher cultures to the north, the Lenca and Matagalpa Indians of the Honduran and Nicaraguan highlands were less advanced. The preconquest culture of the Costa Rican and Panamanian highlands were of Chibchan affinity, although the Güetar of Costa Rica received strong Chorotegan influences from Mesoamerica. Moreover, in contrast to the high cultures of the Mesoamerican highlands, only simple agricultural peoples such as the Tarahumar and Tepehuan inhabited the temperate areas of the Sierra Madre Occidental. Much of the Sierra Madre Oriental as well as the entire lowland temperate area of northeastern Mexico was occupied by the Tamaulipec and some Coahuiltec Indians of the Hokan family, who, like their Texas relatives, were primitive nomadic hunters and gatherers.

Tropical Lowland Climates (A)

These correspond in general to the humid tierra caliente, where average monthly temperatures never fall below 18° C. and where killing frost is unknown. In fact the areas without frost begin with the A climate boundary. Usually these areas receive sufficient rainfall (normally over 1000 mm. yearly) to support a forest vegetation. Most of the areas having tropical lowland climates are found south and east of the Isthmus of Tehuantepec, where only the narrow belt of highlands that form the backbone of Chiapas and Central America interrupt its continuous extent. North and west of the Isthmus the tropical lowland climates occupy only the narrow Pacific and Gulf coastal areas and most of the hot Balsas-Tepalcatepec Depression.

Following the Koeppen system, the tropical lowland climates are divided into two large groups: (1) the tropical rainy climates with rainfall in every month (Af), but often with a period of less rain during the cooler part of the year (Am), and (2) the tropical wet-and-dry climate (Aw), with a definite and fairly long dry season in the winter

or low-sun period and in spring during the subtropical calm influence.

Tropical Wet-and-Dry Climates (Aw and Aw')

These occur mainly on the Pacific side of Mexico and Central America, extending from the western foothills of the Sierra Madre Occidental in northern Sinaloa along the entire coastal zone of western and southern Mexico and Central America to northwestern Costa Rica. Two areas of tropical wet-and-dry climate occur on the Gulf coast of Mexico: (1) the lowlands of Veracruz and easternmost San Luis Potosi to the volcanic highlands of Los Tuxtlas and (2) northern Yucatan. Most of these areas receive the maximum amount of rainfall in the months of September and October, and are thus designated by the symbol Aw'. As indicated previously the lateness of the rainy maximum is due mainly to the prevalence of tropical cyclonic disturbances in the Mexican areas and to the late retreat of the doldrum belt in the southern part of Central America. Only three areas—northern Yucatan, the lowlands of central Chiapas, and the coast of Sinaloa and Nayarit—have the normal Aw climate with the maximum rainy period during July and August.

Although clear, almost cloudless skies are the rule during the long dry season from late November into May, rain is not completely lacking. On the Pacific side occasional thundershowers may occur during the dry season, and on the Gulf lowlands of Mexico frequent rains that result from the incursion of the nortes interrupt the dry weather. The prevailing dryness, however, results in the desiccation of grass and a seasonal leaf-fall from most of the trees and shrubs, giving a drab gray-brown color to the landscape. The hottest and dustiest part of the year comes in March and April, just before the break of the rainy season. With the coming of the rains the air becomes noticeably cooler and the vegetation suddenly springs to life, changing the color of the landscape to brilliant green. As in the adjacent highlands, during the wet season afternoon rains occur almost daily, following clear, brilliant mornings.

Tropical Rainy Climates

These include the two subtypes, *Afw'* and *Amw'*. Both have rain in all months, but the latter receives the lesser amount (1500–2000 mm.) and is characterized by a short dry period of a few weeks during February or March and concentration of rain in the months of September through November. The *Afw'* climate usually receives over 2000 mm. of rain yearly, but with no dry period and a concentration of heavy rains from September through November.

These warm, rainy climates are found chiefly in the eastern lowlands of southern Mexico and Central America, where the ascending trade winds and tropical disturbances bring heavy rainfall during the late summer and fall, and where the occasional cold fronts from the north cause winter rains. They are also found on the Pacific side of Central America, particularly in Costa Rica and Panama, but also along the lower slopes of the volcanic highlands in Guatemala, El Salvador, and Nicaragua. In these climates sufficient rain falls to support a luxuriant tropical rain forest. The seasonal rhythm of vegetation growth characteristic of the tropical wet-and-dry climate (*Aw*) is lacking, in spite of a short period of less rain than usual during the cooler part of the year.

In the tropical rainy climates dampness pervades the entire landscape. Relative humidity is high for most of the year. Although most of the rain comes in the form of afternoon thunderstorms, during the wetter part of the year tropical disturbances (tropical cyclones and easterly waves) may cause overcast and prolonged downpours that continue for days with few interruptions. Contrary to popular concepts, tem-

peratures in the rainy tropics are not excessive. During the rainier part of the year daytime temperatures may be surprisingly low (25°–30° C.), due chiefly to the prevalence of overcast. On cloudless days, however, the intense heat (but rarely above 35° C.) combined with the high relative humidity (80% or more) causes considerable discomfort for the human organism. Fortunately, nighttime temperatures are cool (18°–22° C.), and during a winter *norte* early morning temperatures may fall as low as 10° C. in the Tabasco lowlands of southern Mexico.

Tropical Lowland Climates and Indian Settlement

An area having a tropical rainy climate (*Afw'* and *Amw'*) appears to have been the cradle of Indian civilization in Middle America. The Tres Zapotes–La Venta (or Olmec) cultures, the earliest-known of the Mesoamerican civilizations, evolved in the hot, damp lowlands of southern Veracruz and Tabasco within the Papaloapan, Coatzacoalcos, and Tonala river basins. As indicated by Alfonso Caso, this area was the hearth of the high cultures of Mesoamerica, and later influenced not only the Teotihuacan and Monte Alban civilizations in the adjacent highlands but also the development of Classical Maya culture in the Peten. The Maya culture of El Peten began in the upper Hondo River Basin at Tikal and Uaxactun and later expanded to other river basins, such as the Usumacinta in southeastern Mexico and Guatemala, and the Motagua in Honduras where the metropolis of Copan was built. Classical Mayan sites of less importance were also established in the Candelaria Basin in southern Campeche and in northern Yucatan, the latter in a drier tropical climate (*Aw*).

That the humid tropical climates are "unhealthful" for human habitation and for the development of higher cultures is a popular belief which probably has little foundation of truth. One of the health factors that

213

today makes much of the humid tropics of America difficult for human life is the presence of disease, particularly malaria and, earlier, yellow fever. Both of these diseases and others appear to have been introduced from the Old World after European contact.

In terms of food resources, the humid tropics are usually rich in wild edible aquatic animals and plants that thrive along the numerous watercourses, lakes, and lagoons. Moreover, once herbaceous savannas were and are opened in the forest through cutting, burning, or cultivation, game animals, such as deer, become abundant, as was the case in the ancient Peten of northern Guatemala and Yucatan. Again, owing to lack of frost and abundance of moisture, two and often three successive crops could be raised during the year.

As Morley has pointed out, however, the main problem for cultural development in the humid tropics is that of poor lateritic soils, which are leached and become exhausted quickly when cultivated. In the humid tropics young alluvial soils offer better possibilities for a thriving agriculture, and many of the Maya cities that persisted for centuries were in such soils. Morley and others believe that the decay of some Classical Mayan ceremonial sites in the Peten and other regions and the ultimate collapse of the so-called Maya Old Empire were the result of depletion of poor soils and the consequent failure of the agricultural system.

In the tropical rainy climate of eastern Central America there is no evidence of a high culture similar to that of the Classical Maya, except in those river valleys of western Honduras that received influence through trade with the contiguous Mayan areas. The Paya of northeastern Honduras, the Sumo and Miskito of eastern Nicaragua, and the tribes of eastern Costa Rica and northern Panama were primitive forest people who lived as much by rudimentary

agriculture as by hunting and fishing. The dense tropical rain forest that covers much of the eastern lowlands of Central America served as a refuge zone for these people of circum-Caribbean culture, when the expansion of high cultures took place in the isthmian regions.

Generally speaking, at the time of Spanish contact the areas of tropical wet-and-dry climates in Mexico and Central America probably contained as dense an aboriginal population as the adjacent tropical highlands. The high cultures of central Mexican affinity continued along the west coast of Mexico from Nayarit to central Sinaloa, and along the east coast to the Panuco River basin in northern Veracruz. These lowland tropical areas only became important for post-Classic theocractic cultures that developed in Mexico and Central America after the decline of Teotihuacan and of the so-called Maya Old Empire. Among these cultures were the Nahuat-Pipil and Choluteca-Mangue-Chorotega of Central America, the Nahuat of Colima in western Mexico, the Totonac centered on El Tajin in Veracruz, the Huastec culture of northern Veracruz and eastern San Luis Potosi, that of Xochicalco within the upper Balsas depression, the Chiapanec culture of the valley of the Chiapa River, and the renaissance Maya-Toltec culture in northern Yucatan.

Sauer argues that the beginning of agriculture took place in American regions within tropical wet-and-dry climates. In some respects the tropical wet-and-dry climate offers more advantages for human settlement than the tropical rainy types. In areas having the first type of climate soils are often less leached, owing to more moderate annual rains and the presence of a long dry season. Moreover, the lack of frost still permits the cultivation of at least two successive crops in the wet-and-dry tropical climate, particularly in areas of substantial rain, such as the Veracruz and

214

southern Central American lowlands. But there is no archaeological evidence for the opinion that the high cultures of Middle America have had their beginning in the tropical wet-and-dry climates.

REFERENCES

Brooks, 1925
Caso, 1953a
Clayton, 1927, 1944
—— and Clayton, 1947
Cook, S. F., 1946
Garbell, 1947
Hernández, 1923
Hurtado, 1946
Kirchhoff, 1946a, 1946b
Koeppen, 1948
—— and Geiger, 1930-39
Morley, 1956
Ortiz, 1947
Page, 1930

Petterssen, 1941
Piña Chan, 1955
Recinos, 1947
Reed, 1923, 1926
Rossby, 1954
Sapper, 1932
Sauer, 1952
Servicio Meteorológico Mexicano, 1945
Thompson, J. E. S., 1959
U. S. Weather Bureau, 1930-52, 1947, 1948, 1949, 1959
Vivó, 1958a, 1958b, 1959
—— and Gómez, 1946
Waibel, 1946
Wallén, 1955, 1956

7. Natural Vegetation of Middle America

PHILIP L. WAGNER

T HE LANDS extending from the southern border of the United States to the Panama Canal contain a rich diversity of flora and vegetation cover. Here are many great classes of vegetation, from extreme desert and tundra to tropical rain forest, reflecting a complex physical environment and varying human interference. The exact nature of distribution, environments, and man's past influence are not well known for Middle America; but within the narrow limits of our knowledge, three major questions will be considered here: (1) the spatial distribution of vegetation types, (2) the nature of the controls affecting distribution, and (3) the mutual relations of man and vegetation. The close interrelationship among the three lines of inquiry necessitates that they be taken jointly rather than in sequence.

CLASSIFICATION OF VEGETATION

Vegetation, wrote Egler (1942), is set apart for purposes of scientific study from individual organisms, the subject of floristics; from plant communities, the subject of plant sociology; from biotic communities,

the subject of bio-ecology; and from ecosystems. It can be studied by both mechanistic and probabilistic approaches. Like all life sciences, the study of vegetation considers seven questions: composition, morphology, physiology, geography, history, ecology, and taxonomy. It deals with these questions at the level of the "social organism" which is a vegetation—a self-perpetuating, self-sufficient, and more or less stable system in nature.

Modern methods of vegetation study are described by Cain and Castro (1959). Since the pioneer work of Humboldt and of Schimper, many attempts have been made to arrange known vegetations into an orderly classification. Besides the recent classification of Schmithüsen (1959), Troll has proposed (1952) a system of tropical classes based on environment; Middle America as a whole has been treated by Harshberger (1911), Holdridge (1956), and recently by Lauer (1959), except for Mexico. Of the existing floras, that of Standley on Mexico (1920-26) is most complete and is useful for all of Middle America. Those of Standley and Steyermark on Guatemala (1946–

216

62) and Woodsen, Schery, *et al.* on Panama (1943–62) are also useful, but both are still in progress. For a systematic description of the nature and distribution of timber trees Record and Hess (1943) is valuable.

Spatial distribution of species and higher taxonomic units, interesting in itself and important for the geography of vegetation, is distinct from the distribution of *aggregations* of plants, which tend to assume characteristic forms in particular local landscapes. From this point of view a category such as "tree" is far more basic than the sum of categories Quercus, Pinus, Alnus, Betula, Salix, and so on. The recording and description of vegetation rests on physical form and spatial arrangement of the plants in an aggregation, to which floristic information, the listing of characteristic and important species, is subordinate. Thus the *physiognomic* approach is distinguished from the *floristic* one.

Physiognomic Description

Because the fundamental unit of vegetation study is the aggregation, description uses terms closely paralleling the vernacular: forest, tundra, thicket, chaparral, swamp, prairie. Precise identification and definition are maintained, however, by recognition of measurable features of individual plants and of their distribution, permitting the assignment of aggregations of plants, or "stands," to defined classes, the controlled comparison of different stands, and the matching of particular vegetation classes with corresponding environmental variables.

Among the classifying features the distinction between woody plants and nonwoody ones (herbs) is primary. Woody plants can be subdivided according to their branching into shrubs and trees. The mean heights of the tallest members of a stand can be determined. The diameter of the leafy crowns of plants and the degree of separation between individual tree crowns give other diagnostic data. The number of

"stories" or layers of plants is usually consistent and well marked. The presence or absence of a leafless phase permits distinction between deciduous and evergreen types. Length of the total life cycle of the plants, position of the bud shoots of perennials with respect to the ground surface, the size, shape and texture of leaves, structure of the trunk and nature of the bark, all offer criteria for classification. The presence of peculiar forms like succulents (e.g., cacti and many euphorbs) or of epiphytes, lianes, lichens, mosses, and other specialized members in the vegetation, may also be helpful. When the vegetation of an area is already fairly well known, the occurrence of some diagnostic species or of a special habitat may give a good clue to distinctions. This and other diagnostic information is found in Beard (1944 and 1955), Cain and Castro (1959), Dansereau (1951), and Hanson (1958).

Detailed analysis of vegetation succeeds best for small areas, but may be applied on a sampling basis to large regions. Little intensive work has been undertaken in Middle America, however, and present information is general, though based on fundamental diagnostic features.

Bases of Classification

Description and classification are not necessarily the same thing. It is possible, for instance, to find faithful empirical accounts of what a particular forest looks like, with no indication of its relation to other vegetations or its environment. Likewise, systems of vegetation types have proposed affinities among the members, and relationships to habitats have guided the selection of boundaries, without showing clearly the appearance of the particular aggregations of plants. Classification need not involve the most readily recognizable characteristics, and sometimes depends not on plants themselves but on the supposed climate of their environments.

Vegetation may be classified genetically,

morphologically, or environmentally. Genetic classification is built around the notion of plant succession, employing species composition and dominance as diagnostic features. Morphological classification takes into account the numerous observable features mentioned above. Environmental classification depends on climate, soil, and drainage, among other things, for its categories. A particular stand of plants may be seen genetically as a climax forest, morphologically as a three-layered closed canopy high deciduous forest, environmentally as a mesic midlatitude forest.

An assumption which permits all three aspects of classification concerns the *structure* of the aggregation, that is, the measurable spatial properties of, and spatial relations among, the individual plants in the stand: *the structure of a stand of vegetation is an orderly and specific indicator of its development stage and of the properties of its environment.*

Beard's Classification

A structural classification applicable to the vegetation of Middle America has been proposed by J. S. Beard (1944, 1955). It is designed to cover all possible natural vegetations of tropical America except for a few "atypical" ones of small extent. It does not embrace strongly disturbed, or "secondary," vegetation.

The lowest category of the Beard classification is the *association*, a floristic grouping based on "consistent dominants of either the same or closely allied species." The plants most alike are, of course, the members of a single species; when they are the largest, most numerous, or most flourishing components of a vegetation, controlling the light relations, they are dominants. The association is a floristic unit not because the distribution of species is in itself a chief interest, but because certain species dominate distinctive aggregations. Plant associations are next grouped together according to physiognomic similarity into *formations*,

218

which reflect habitats that are in some degree similar, and are finally brought together as *formation series*. The designation of classes at each level corresponds to these emphases: "Eschweilera-Licania association," "deciduous seasonal forest [formation]," and "montane formations [series]."

These categories, though used as if discrete, are acknowledged as arbitrary ones, for Beard envisages that "there is in reality one long unbroken series, in which the formations are artificially delimited stages." Structural characters vary gradually over distance, from greatest tree height, density, number of stories, length of period in leaf, and so on, to the least. A simple description of an actual vegetation in these terms allows its assignment to the appropriate formation. The exact determination of an association requires identification of its dominants.

It should be noticed that this classification is, at the formation level, a physiognomic or morphological one, and throughout an environmental one, but especially so at the formation series level. It does not purport to be genetic, and the plant successions within each component are not treated.

The six formation series, as listed by Beard, are given in figure 1. The tropical rain forest constitutes the "optimal" formation (and a one-membered series), from which the other series depart with decreasing environmental advantage along various lines. For Middle America, a few other formations of extra-tropical affinities must be added to the classification to account for the extensions of midlatitude formation series into the northern part of the region.

The distribution of the formation series coincides with certain broad environmental zones. Each formation series embraces a continuum of physiognomic variation under the control of a few predominant features of environment that vary regularly over distance; any one formation corresponds to a particular state of the controlling en vironmental factors, for which its structural features, unlike those of any other formation, are distinctive and diagnostic indicators. This notion has been perhaps most vigorously stated by Holdridge (1947).

If the most obvious morphological resemblances between stands were the only criteria of classification, all high forests would be grouped together as against all low shrub formations. The actual gradations that occur in nature would however tend to be masked in such a classification, and no very clear significance could be assigned to the areal patterns of vegetation. But when the geographic positions of the formation series are plotted, the decisive controls for each region are indicated, and the morphological variations of vegetation can be fitted into an orderly progression, related to these controls. Trends of variation in measurable morphological features reveal themselves clearly, and provide a reliable basis for the extrapolation necessary where, as in the case of Middle America, the details of distribution are poorly known.

MAJOR CONTROLS OF VEGETATION

The larger patterns of vegetation distribution can be ascertained from what the ordinary physical map shows about latitude and longitude, land and water surfaces, and relief. In addition one must look at climate and soil. The picture of "natural vegetation" so drawn is further modified by human activity before "actual vegetation" can be seen.

Geographic Controls

The annual cycle of solar energy that varies according to latitude has a profound effect on plant life. Total annual supply of solar energy per unit surface varies inversely with latitude; the annual range of variation in the daily receipt of radiation varies directly with latitude. The amount of insolation received at a place sets the upper limit on the quantity of energy available

for photosynthesis. Despite possible cloudiness, and the small portion of the total sunlight received by the plant that is actually used in photosynthesis, there is a clear relation between amount of sunlight and rate of growth. Furthermore, the rate of chemical and biochemical activity (where moisture is adequate) varies nearly directly with temperature. Other things being equal, then, vegetation is most abundant at the equator and decreases toward the poles.

Seasonal differences in insolation and annual variation in the length of the daylight period increase with latitude. These two factors combine to cause the seasonal range of temperature to increase with distance from the equator (unless modifying factors intervene), resulting in profound effects on vegetation. The effect of photoperiodism is also well recognized, and tends to account for certain differences of physiognomy and function between plants of different latitudes which experience similar temperature and moisture regimes.

Plant life of open-water bodies is outside our present discussion, but periodic inundation of land and the waterlogging of soils near fresh or salt water exert a strong effect on land vegetation. Along sea coasts and around saline lakes plant life is subject to salinity. The degree and periodicity of inundation or the impregnation of soil with saline solutions exerts a powerful selection of species, often resulting in belted plant zones. The proximity of water bodies, especially of the sea, produces marked effects on local climate and even on soil. Salt spray in the air, moderation of temperature range, and building of sand and mud flats produce unusual conditions for plant growth.

Elevation above sea level and surface relief each work separately on vegetation. Altitude acts through climate, whereas surface configuration is reflected in soil, drainage, local climate, insolation, and so on.

Altitude affects atmospheric temperature and precipitation. In general, mountains are cooler than neighboring lowlands. The mean rate of temperature decrease with elevation is in the neighborhood of 1° C. for 100 m. in an unsaturated atmosphere. Thus, except where relative humidity is at saturation, temperature falls off regularly with elevation, a fact clearly registered in plant growth.

Total precipitation tends to increase with altitude up to a certain level, then to decrease, a condition apparent in vegetation on slopes. Furthermore, precisely because of decrease of temperature with altitude, the increase in relative humidity is often marked; there is often, especially in tropical mountains, an altitudinal zone in which moisture droplets are continually condensed in the air, so that a "cloud belt" develops, with manifest consequences for the vegetation.

Mountains thus modify climate through the effects of altitude itself. The influences of relief are more numerous and varied, creating localized conditions. In Middle America, where a large part of the terrain is mountainous, relief plays a decisive role in the determination of growing conditions, and thus in the distribution of vegetation.

Climatic Controls

The climatological characteristics of environments are related in part to the geographic conditions just discussed and in part to processes within the atmosphere itself, especially movements of air over the earth's surface.

Among the climatological variables which influence plants, temperature has already been mentioned. High temperatures are almost always associated with abundant solar energy available for photosynthesis, but moisture may intervene as a limiting factor, and so the relation between high temperature and relative density or mass of vegetation is not simple. Very low temperatures restrict plant growth. Not only does activity proceed slowly, but near freezing the cells and tissues are often rup-

tured and destroyed by expansion of the moisture they contain. The boundary between completely frost-free areas and those subject to more than a few minutes of temperatures below freezing during the year is therefore a critical one for vegetation. The frost line in most of Middle America lies at elevations well above sea level, and its effect on vegetation is correlated with relief.

The great seasonal differences of temperature characteristic of middle and higher latitudes do not occur in the Middle American tropics, though they affect northern Mexico. The cold air which reaches lower latitudes during occasional winter incursions is usually not of low enough temperature to act on vegetation. In almost all of Middle America, where deciduous vegetation occurs, it signifies seasonality in moisture rather than in temperature, with some exceptions. The mixed broad-leaf vegetation of intermediate and higher elevations in Mexico and Guatemala, for example, with moderate temperatures and adequate moisture the year round, though it resembles midlatitude vegetations and contains many northern genera, is almost entirely evergreen, like the mountain vegetations of other American tropical areas.

Seasonal periodicity is the most decisive variable in moisture supply as it relates to the distribution of vegetation, but is intimately connected with total annual precipitation. Middle American climates range from those in which there is moderate to heavy precipitation in all months, through those in which one or more pronounced dry seasons intervene, to climates with only light precipitation, confined to a few months, and sometimes rainless years. The amount and seasonal distribution of precipitation directly influence moisture supply available in the ground for plant growth, and also the relative humidity of the atmosphere near the ground. The amount of annual precipitation tends throughout Middle America to vary inversely with the number of days without rain. Total precipitation from year to year is also roughly proportional to the number of rainless days.

Permanent scarcity of water results in a sparse and meager vegetation, and a recurring annual drought is reflected in seasonal loss of leaves (deciduousness) and in reduced vegetative development.

The loss of moisture to the atmosphere through transpiration also plays a part in regulating vegetation development. In general those areas where aridity exists permanently or recurs for an extended period annually wear marks of this feature in their vegetation, in the form of structures that serve to reduce water loss through transpiration, such as reduction of leaf surface or virtual suppression of leaves, waxy coatings or hairy coverings on leaves or trunks, and similar specializations, in addition to deciduousness itself. Furthermore, where atmospheric humidity is always exceedingly high, as in cloud belts, correspondingly peculiar structures and life-forms occur in great abundance, such as the epiphytes and spreading gnarled low trees of some mountain vegetation.

The patterns of atmospheric circulation over Middle America produce a well-marked gradient of total annual precipitation approximately from southeast to northwest. Along the same line lies the gradient of total days without precipitation, from a maximum in central Baja California to almost zero in eastern Nicaragua, Costa Rica, and Panama. The regularity of the variation is of course broken by relief.

In drier areas and periods, the daily maxima and the diurnal oscillations of temperature are greater than where the atmosphere is moist. Thus high daily temperatures are attained on exposed slopes even at the northern borders of Mexico, in the deserts. Only in the extreme northwestern corner of Baja California does oceanic influence strongly moderate temperature in such a way as to permit the growth of a correspondingly specialized vegetation. However, the atmospheric circulation is such that differences between monthly mean temperatures during the course of the year are much greater in northeast Mexico than in the northwest, for the northeastern climates are much more continental than those of the northwest.

Soils are strongly influenced by climate, and apart from serpentine and limestone areas in which parent material determines soil type, the zonation of soils closely follows that of climate. The effect of soil conditions, however, is extremely pronounced in local contexts. Poorly drained soils frequently carry a different vegetation from those which are well drained; where soils become impermeable heavy seasonal rainfall often produces a seasonal swamp vegetation. Although the soils of desert areas may abound in essential minerals for plant life, lack of moisture reduces their potency; the dense tropical rain forest, in contrast, develops under a very moist climate despite intense leaching of soil minerals by heavy rains and high temperatures.

The finer variations of soil and climate that accompany minute differentiation of relief produce numerous subtle individualities in the vegetation of any locality. Because present knowledge of local conditions is extremely scanty, for an orderly accounting for such vegetations we must rely on Beard's formation series as introduced for tropical America.

Vegetation Controls and Formation Series

A summary of the major environmental influences on vegetation distribution makes possible an idealized pattern to which the actual geographic distribution of formation series closely corresponds. As a result of variations in latitude, land and water relations, and altitude, and of large atmospheric movements, a number of more or less regular types of environment appear. In uplands, the diversity of relief produces a mosaic of local situations much more intricate than in the lowlands. Areas subject to inundation, which must be segregated as a particular class of environment, tend to be most extensive in regions of greatest precipitation; these lie mostly in the south.

The distribution of the formation series, to be described in detail subsequently, is roughly as follows. (1) The *tropical rain forest*, the most luxuriant formation, occupies the optimal zone in the southeastern sector of Middle America, in which high temperatures are combined with abundant precipitation throughout the year. (2) The *montane* formation series extends up the slopes of the mountains, accommodating to decreasing temperatures and a moisture supply that remains high. To the north it merges with formations similar to those of the western mountains of the United States. (3) The *seasonal* formation series extends from the borders of the rain forest northward, and occurs chiefly on the Pacific side of Middle America. Evergreen to deciduous forests characterize this formation in Central America and southern Mexico; northward the low forests grade into thorny woodland and scrub. In the northwest, deserts represent the extreme of this formation. North-central and northeastern Mexico bear a cover of grassland and desert-like scrub, resembling the more northerly desert of the northwest, but grading into the arid formations of Texas. Grasslands reminiscent of the Great Plains are widespread below the montane formations of northeastern and central Mexico, and probably belong to the formations commonly called steppe. Thus much of the vegetation of northern Mexico, and of the middle altitudes in central Mexico, properly falls outside Beard's categories, and is related to formations north of the border which, like this vegetation, are subject to frost; the frost line describes a good boundary for the true tropical formations.

Much of the Yucatán Peninsula and the east coast of Central America carries a shrub and tree vegetation which belongs to the (4) *dry evergreen* formation series, but

222

here again there are formations reminiscent of frost-conditioned North American types. Along the coasts the (5) *swamp* series is well represented, especially in the south. Formations of the (6) *seasonal swamp* series reflect in their sporadic occurrence (from Panama to central and western Mexico) the edaphic conditions to which they are especially subject.

The map of Middle American vegetation (fig. 1) displays the approximate distribution of formation series. Although it represents a consensus of estimates from fragmentary studies and reports, this map is reasonably correct. Boundaries are necessarily based on incomplete information; their position is especially doubtful in the north of Mexico, where the classifications are admittedly arbitrary. (For a different presentation of this area, Leopold [1950] may be consulted.)

It would not be prudent, in the present state of our knowledge, to attempt to map individual formations, let alone associations. The orderly progression attributed by Beard to the vegetation within his formation series does, however, manifest itself in published descriptions of Middle American vegetation, and the more detailed pattern of vegetation of an area, within a particular formation series, can be roughly estimated along the gradients of environmental conditions. A systematic treatment of the formation series, given in later sections, will demonstrate this.

Beard's classification includes three formation series based on climatic conditions, exhibiting general geographic regularity, and three based on edaphic conditions, occurring irregularly as the effects of local influences. The actual distribution of vegetation in Middle America does not work out exactly according to theory, of course, because in addition to natural influences of soil and climate, human action has also considerably modified the plant cover. Departures from theoretical vegetation will be discussed later. At this point we emphasize

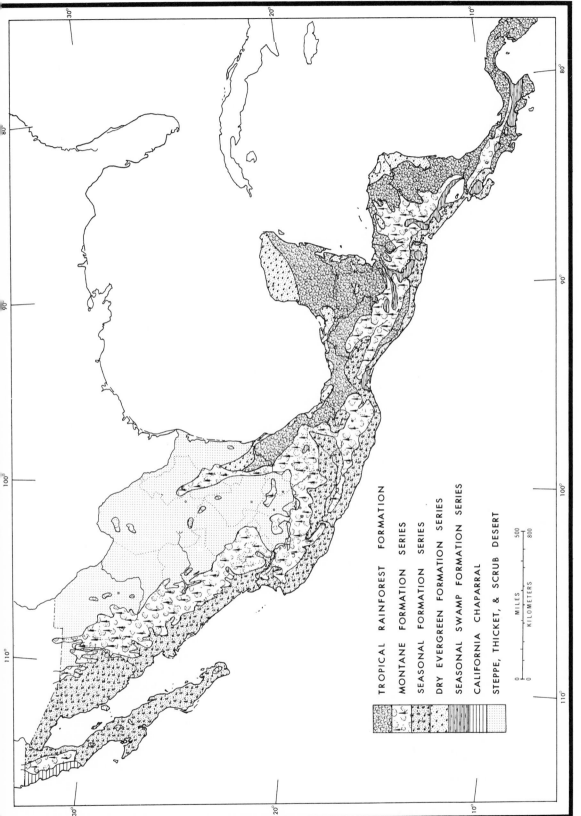

TROPICAL RAINFOREST FORMATION

MONTANE FORMATION SERIES

SEASONAL FORMATION SERIES

DRY EVERGREEN FORMATION SERIES

SEASONAL SWAMP FORMATION SERIES

CALIFORNIA CHAPARRAL

STEPPE, THICKET, & SCRUB DESERT

MILES

KILOMETERS

FIG. 1—NATURAL VEGETATION OF MIDDLE AMERICA
Formations classified after Beard and others.

what botanists have considered to be representative cases. These tend to exemplify so-called "natural" vegetation that has developed through natural processes, supposedly apart from human interference, though, as Cook (1909) long ago suggested, man has probably had much effect on most or all Middle American vegetation at some time. The spontaneous growth that takes place in nature does not for a long time produce a stabilized and more or less permanent vegetation, even in the tropics, but it may be possible to guess on occasion what it might be like. Present potential vegetation is not necessarily the same as any actual or possible vegetation of ancient times. Though they serve as satisfactory indicators for broad regions, some of the following examples show that human interference has so radically altered conditions that reconstruction of past or potential vegetations proceeds entirely by guesswork.

Our examples are taken from the few adequate descriptions, which happen to concern mostly northern Mexico, the Balsas-Papaloapan transect along parallel 18° N., Chiapas, Peten, Costa Rica, and a few smaller areas. No effort has been made to account for currently cultivated lands.

Tropical Rain Forest

Tropical rain forest: Three or four stories of evergreen trees, with dense canopy.

The tropical rain forests of Middle America constitute a vast zone at present nearly empty of population. Because much of it has hardly been visited, much less carefully explored, we can make only a general survey based on several good studies of rain forest vegetation in Middle America now available.

Rain Forests of Chiapas, Mexico

Miranda's (1952–53) extensive study of the vegetation of Chiapas covers tropical rain forests of both the Caribbean or Gulf slope and the Pacific coast. He characterizes them (including them in the "selva alta

siempre verde") as a formation of tall trees, the tallest reaching more than 20 m., evergreen, with an open story of large trees, under which is a more or less closed story at 8–20 m. (fig. 2). Some of the trees briefly lose their leaves, which are almost immediately replaced. The leaves are mostly smooth and entire, and dark green. Trees branch relatively high above the ground, and many of their trunks carry buttresses. Lianes are common, as are epiphytes—orchids, bromeliads, *Clusia*, *Ficus*, and others, including "strangler" plants. The flowers of most trees are small and inconspicuous. A large number of families, genera, and species of trees grow in scattered profusion; stands of single species are rare, and occur chiefly where man has interfered with natural growth or where special edaphic conditions obtain.

The tropical rain forest grows in a hot, moist climate, with annual mean temperatures over 20° C. and precipitation in excess of 1200 mm. annually. The true tropical rain forest does not grow where rainfall is less than 50 mm. in any one month, except where the annual total is above 2000 mm. This formation occupies deep, well-drained soils; it is less well developed where the soil is thin or subject to frequent inundation. Over one-third of the large state of Chiapas has a climate suitable for tropical rain forest, but some of the area has been cleared. There are still 10,000 sq. km. of "virgin" rain forest in the Lacandon region of eastern Chiapas alone; other similar forests are in the north and northwest and in the extreme south along the Sierra Madre.

Representative of the lush tropical rain forest of eastern Chiapas are the stands around Monte Libano. Here, on level lands in the more elevated part of the *selva lacandona*, the tallest trees, attaining 40–70 m. height, are *Terminalia*, *Guatteria*, mahogany (*Swietenia*), and *Aspidosperma*—all good timber trees. Beneath these giants, at 25–50 m. grow *Dialium*, the magnolia-like *Talauma*, *Calophyllum*, *Licania*, and Amer-

Fɪɢ. 2—HIGH EVERGREEN RAIN FOREST
This photo was taken in the Lacandon region, Chiapas, near El Cedro, some 25 km. from Bonampak, about 500 m. elevation. The large tree on the right is mahogany (*Swietenia macrophylla*), that on the left, barí (*Calophyllum brasiliense*). (Photo by F. Miranda.)

225

ican figs (*Ficus* spp.). Below is a 15–25-m. story, with *Pseudolmedia, Sideroxylon, Dipholis,* and *Brosimum,* several of which bear edible fruit. Within this story also grows *Castilla elastica,* the latex of which was the source of rubber for the aboriginal population of Mexico. In the dense shade at 5–10 m. grows a staff-tree, *Salacia.* The shrub and herb stories are composed of the young of the same trees, as well as palms (*Desmoncus* spp.), the banana-like *Heliconia,* the large aroid *Xanthosoma,* the bigleaved *Calathea,* and various members of the madder, melastoma, arum, and ginger families; the understory is thus marked by an extravagance of giant leaves and fronds. Lianes are plentiful.

On the deepest, moistest soils, a similar forest grows in which the valuable *caoba* or mahogany (*Swietenia macrophylla*) is abundant. There are many variants of this type of forest growing on particular kinds of sites. On flat rocky places the most prominent tree is *Vochysia hondurensis,* a valuable cabinet wood, with which is associated the anonaceous *Cymbopetalum penduliflorum,* the flowers of which were highly prized among the ancient Indians for flavoring and medicinal uses. In the ground story the wild yam vine (*Dioscorea*) is common. *Achras sapota,* the sapodilla tree from which chicle is derived, marks the forest in dry, rocky sites on limestone. In rugged karst the red-flowering, deciduous *Bernoullia flammea* predominates, with the shrub *Louteridium* in the understory. High ground in the karst carries a partly deciduous forest. Near Ocozocuautla, in west-central Chiapas, there is such a forest reaching 20–30 m. in height.[1] This forest probably represents a transition to the higher members of the seasonal formation series.

[1] This forest is dominated by *Celtis, Guettarda, Achras, Wimmeria, Chaetoptelea,* the smooth redbarked *Bursera, Ficus* spp., and *Linociera;* the second story, at 8–20 m., contains *Pimenta, Coccoloba, Laetia, Exothea, Fraxinus, Hippocratea, Erythroxylon,* and *Trichilia.*

226

On wet, shady slopes *Pseudolmedia oxyphyllaria* (mulberry family) may be dominant. Forests growing in dark, rocky gorges contain the milky-sapped *Brosimum alicastrum,* the bombacaceous *Quararibea funebris,* or a laurel *Licaria coriacea,* as dominant. Low places subject to flooding may have a forest 45 m. high, dominated by the pod-bearing *Vatairea Lundellii,* with numerous palms—probably a seasonal swamp forest. On the slopes of the highlands the tropical rain forest grades into a montane formation. At about 1400 m. in eastern Chiapas, a rain forest of montane type, dominated by a yellow-flowering *Sloanea* sp., grows in cool, moist conditions alongside stands of sweet gum (*Liquidambar*).

All of the associations mentioned are related ones, and all belong to eastern Chiapas. In the northern part of the state, in the vicinity of Palenque, the low moist sites are occupied by a 40-m. forest characterized by the legume *Dialium guianense,* a valuable timber tree, accompanied by *Vochysia,* and either the sapotaceous *Lucuma campechiana* or *Sterculia mexicana* of the cacao family. The underbrush contains the palmlike *Carludovica,* the giant-leaved *Calathea,* often used for wrapping material, and the palm *Chamaedorea. Dioscorea* is a prominent liane.

In the same area may be found a forest with *Tabebuia,* the legumes *Pithecolobium* and *Sweetia,* the oak *Quercus Skinnerii,* and *Carapa,* a close relative of mahogany, in the 30–40 m. story (fig. 3). There is still another story at 10–25 m. A lower forest with the acanthus *Bravaisia integerrima* at 20–25 m. grows on flat land that is periodically flooded. It is notable for the profusion of adventitious "stilt" roots of this species. Palms abound in the underbrush, and there are many lianes. This, too, apparently represents a seasonal swamp forest.

Along the streams of the eastern rain forest is a vegetation with wild figs (*Ficus*); various pod-bearing legumes such as the lacy-leaved *Lonchocarpus, Inga,* and *Pithe-*

FIG. 3—A REMNANT OF RAIN FOREST ON HIGH GROUND ALONG THE EDGE OF THE ARCHAEOLOGICAL SITE, LA VENTA, WESTERN TABASCO
Many species are represented. Most are evergreen, but the tall deciduous *Ceiba pentandra* is seen, right center. On the extreme right a large leguminous tree (probably *Pithecolobium*) forms part of the upper story. Palms and lianes abound. Swamp forest lies in the background. (Photo by R. C. West.)

colobium; the water sapote, *Pachira;* and familiar northern trees like willows (*Salix*) and sycamore (*Platanus*). Locally there are canebrakes up to 5 m. in height, composed of *Gynerium sagittatum.*

The rain forests of southern Chiapas are located near the Pacific coast on steep slopes of the Sierra Madre exposed to moisture-bearing winds. On deep, well-drained soils at altitudes 150–800 m., facing the sea, grows a high rain forest. *Terminalia amazonia,* an excellent hardwood timber tree, grows to 30 or 40 m. A story over 20 m. high is dominated by *Aspidosperma* (dogbane family); the spiny *Myroxylon;* and the legumes *Vatairea, Pithecolobium, Schizolobium,* and *Scheelea* (the latter three in specialized situations). There is an-

other tree story at 8–20 m.[2] Here, too, a transition is evident between the true rain forest and seasonal forest. On the same slopes, but at an altitude 800–1400 m., the largest trees are *Sterculia mexicana* (cacao family) and *Hasseltia guatemalensis* (flacourtia family), attaining a height of 40 m. and flanked by large buttresses. There is a luxuriant undergrowth of the arum, madder, acanthus, composite, and mallow families.

[2] The forest around Escuintla is composed of *Terminalia, Aspidosperma, Calophyllum, Ficus, Bursera, Tetrorchidium, Sterculia,* and *Cybistax,* in the story over 20 m.; the lower tree story consists of *Cupania, Guarea, Alchornea, Croton, Coccoloba, Miconia, Nectandra, Sloanea, Gilibertia, Cymbopetalum,* and *Swartzia.* A variety of this forest, growing in very moist and shady gorges, is dominated by *Virola guatemalensis.*

227

In one more situation in Chiapas a rain forest grows: the zone above 1100 m. on the inner, or northern, slopes of the Sierra Madre. Below this level the climate is too dry for the rain forest. At this altitude, however, occurs a transition to lower montane rain forest, and in the same zone grow oak-liquidambar forests of "temperate" character. The rain forest occupies only the more protected spots.[3] In the story below 20 m. are palms and tree ferns. There exist several varieties of this forest.

Rain Forests of the Peten

The forests of the Guatemalan department of El Peten, east and south of Chiapas, have been studied by Lundell (1937). Peten is a large limestone platform, with high temperatures and somewhat seasonal rainfall. The mean annual temperature is given as 26.6°C., with a variance of less than 10°C. Rainfall over a 10-year period averaged 1762 mm. annually, with few months ever entirely dry, but a highly irregular monthly distribution of precipitation from year to year. Lundell designated the vegetation of Peten as "quasi-rainforest." The degree of deciduousness of species reflects the variability of rainfall in that it differs from year to year, though most of the vegetation is essentially evergreen.

In broad and well-drained valleys or on gently undulating land, the forest grows to a height of 50 m. The larger trees stand out as emergents, but there is a more or less closed canopy in the second tree story. In the forest marked by the abundance of the ramón tree (Brosimum alicastrum), which is common on archaeological sites in Peten, the upper story emergents are chiefly mahogany, the mastic tree (Sideroxylon), and wild figs. In the middle story, Brosimum is dominant, with as many as 240 per hectare. With it are associated edible fruit-bearing

[3] Sterculia and Hasseltia appear here, as on the south slope of the mountains, along with Sloanea, Dussia, Chaetoptelea, Prunus, Sapindus, Dipholis, Tapirira, Ficus, Wimmeria, Quercus, Liquidambar, and Inga.

228

Achras, Talisia, and many other genera. The lower tree story contains, among other genera, a hackberry Celtis, the laurel Ocotea, and many palms including Opsiandra. Lianes, especially of the bignonia family, are abundant. Orchids, the aroid Anthurium, and Spanish moss (Tillandsia) are common epiphytes. This forest shows strong indications of past human interference.

Mahogany or caoba (Swietenia) and sapodilla (Achras) appear prominently in the Peten forests. The so-called caobal forest is not dominated by Swietenia, though this rather scarce tree so towers over the rest as to give the whole its name. The caobal is closely related to the forests known as zapotal, in which Achras is the dominant. This association makes up as much as 75 per cent of the upland forest of Peten.[4] In southern Peten, on the well-drained uplands in the region of Monte Santa Teresa, there grows a high forest with three tree stories, consisting of essentially the same flora as the preceding, but with different dominants. Lundell considered this as a "sub-climax."[5]

[4] The top story is composed of Calophyllum, Swietenia, Rheedia, Lucuma, Sideroxylon, and Ficus spp. In the middle story are found Achras, Vitex, Ficus, Cecropia, Bursera, Spondias, Aspidosperma, Brosimum, Pseudolmedia, and several Leguminosae and Lauraceae. In the lower story, averaging 10 m., are Trichilia, Sideroxylon, Sapium, Sebastiania, Misanteca, Parmentiera, Myriocarpa, Lucuma, Louteridium, Laetia, Deherainia, Annona, Sabal, Pimenta, Protium, Ocotea, Zanthoxylon, and species of Pithecolobium, Talisia, Cordia, and Croton. Lianes are present. The underwood is composed of such plants as Piper, Psychotria, Ruellia, Justicia, and palms. Several climbing and ground aroids occur, and the epiphytes also include orchids, bromeliads, and ferns.

[5] In the top layer, at 35–40 m., are Acacia, Dialium, Swietenia, Sideroxylon, Vitex, and Calophyllum. The middle layer consists of Sabal, Cecropia, Pera, Bombax, Oreopanax, Achras, and Linociera. In the story just above 10 m. are Chrysophyllum, Cymbopetalum, Ouratea, Rinorea, Casearia, Hasseltia, Miconia, and Symplocos. The shrubs include many Rubiaceae and Piperaceae. Lianes, epiphytes of the Orchidaceae, Piperaceae, Bromeliaceae, Cactaceae and ferns, and a ground cover of ferns, grasses, and Costus, are present.

Tropical Rain Forests in Central America

On the eastern or Caribbean side of Central America, extending continuously from the Gulf of Honduras to northern South America, lies a large and poorly explored tract of tropical rain forest. Standley (1937) characterized the upland forest of the plains of Santa Clara and San Carlos in Costa Rica, which form a part of this region, as consisting of two to four "levels of foliage" or stories, reaching a height of 30–40 m.[6] This forest occupies the zone of *tierra caliente*, reaching up to 800–1000 m. altitude, where the mean monthly temperature is well over 20°C., and precipitation is as high as 4500 mm. annually in some places, though it tends to vary considerably from year to year. The nearly level surface of the land is broken only here and there by ridges and hills.

In southern Costa Rica, near the shores of the Pacific, another area of rain forest occurs, which has been studied by Allen

(1956). The evergreen lowland forest of Golfo Dulce grows on the flood plains of the rivers in better-drained sites. Precipitation in this area is high—about 3500 mm. annually at Palmar, 5000 mm. at Esquinas; there is a more or less dry period from December to May at the former station, but none at all at Esquinas.

The tallest trees of the Golfo Dulce forest, rising to between 25 and 35 m., form a canopy, presumably at lesser height than the crowns of a few emergents. The cashew *Anacardium excelsum* makes up as much as 50 per cent of the total stand of trees in this forest.[7]

Standley (1928) provides a brief description of the Atlantic forests of the Canal Zone. On the northwest side of the Isthmus of Panama near the Canal, the annual precipitation is over 3000 mm. Where it has been preserved, as on Barro Colorado Island, the forest is composed of several stories of trees, the largest reaching 30 m. or more, and adorned with buttresses or prop-roots. Among the many large trees occur the sapotaceous *Chrysophyllum*, the legumes *Coumarouna* and *Andira*, *Ficus*, copal-bearing *Protium*, *Inophloeum*, a rubber tree (*Castilla*), and *Virola* spp., a valuable timber tree. In the lower stories are found the fast-growing softwood *Didymopanax*, the myrtle *Gustavia*, and many palms and tree ferns. Many of the herbs are endemics, but rank and common plants like *Calathea*, *Heliconia*, and *Costus* appear. Bignoniaceous lianes are common, and many epiphytes—aroids, bromeliads, orchids, mosses, hepatics, lichens, and so forth—crowd the branches of the trees.

[6] The trees of the upper layers of the Costa Rican Atlantic rain forest include *Luehea*, *Bursera*, *Swietenia*, and species of *Pentaclethra*, *Nectandra*, *Ocotea*, *Phoebe*, *Ficus*, *Coussapoa*, *Brosimum*, *Ogcodeia*, *Perebea*, *Poulsenia*, *Symphonia*, *Hippomane*, *Minquartia*, *Virola*, *Compsoneura*, *Dialyanthera*, *Prioria*, *Dialium*, *Dipteryx*, *Zanthoxylum*, *Protium*, *Vochysia*, *Terminalia*, *Manilkara*, *Jacaranda*, *Castilla*, and *Chrysophyllum*, as well as "hundreds of others." The lower stories of trees contain *Didymopanax*, *Pourouma*, *Carica*, *Inga*, *Pithecolobium*, *Dracaena*, *Ravenia*, *Olmedia*, *Guatteria*, *Theobroma*, *Guarea*, *Posoqueria*, and *Carapa*; palms of the genera *Socratea*, *Welfia*, *Astrocaryum*, *Euterpe*, *Geonoma*, *Iriartea*, *Reinhardtia*, and *Chamaedorea*; tree ferns; and the cycad *Zamia*. Among the shrubs appear various species of the genera *Piper*, *Heisteria*, *Siparium*, *Swartzia*, *Quassia*, *Neea*, *Cupania*, *Pentagonia*, *Cephaelis*, *Rudgea*, and *Psychotria*. The lianes include *Vitis*, *Marcgravia*, *Carludovica*, *Rourea*, *Entada*, *Strychnos*, *Maripa*, *Smilax*, and numbers of Bignoniaceae and Dilleniaceae. Ground herbs are frequent, including *Heliconia*, sometimes in dense thickets; *Calathea*, *Dieffenbachia*, *Renealmia*, *Costus*, *Xiphidium*, and others, a fair number of which are endemic to small areas. Such grasses as occur tend to assume a climbing habit or to produce very broad leaf blades. The epiphytes are plentiful, including *Philodendron*, *Anthurium*, *Aechmea*, *Tillandsia*, ferns, many orchids, and various Acanthaceae. *Selaginella* covers the ground in places.

[7] The genera listed, after the dominant *Anacardium excelsum*, *Brosimum alicastrum*, *B. sapiifolium*, and *B. terrabanum*, are *Bursera*, *Carapa*, *Cedrela*, *Ceiba*, *Chimarrhis*, *Chlorophora*, *Chrysophyllum*, *Cynometra*, *Dacryodes*, *Dipterodendron*, *Enterolobium*, *Ficus*, *Hernandia*, *Hieronyma*, *Homalium*, *Hura*, *Luehea*, *Pithecolobium*, *Pouteria*, *Prioria*, *Pterocarpus*, *Simarouba*, *Spondias*, *Sterculia*, *Swartzia*, *Tabebuia*, *Terminalia*, *Virola* spp., and *Vitex*. The understory genera, too numerous to list here, include many mentioned in the foregoing enumerations of rain forest elements elsewhere.

General Features of the Tropical Rain Forest

The examples of tropical rain forest described for Chiapas, Peten, Costa Rica, and Panama are all of very considerable height; in all cases except the rather eccentric Golfo Dulce forests, the maximum height of the forest is 40 m. or more. This feature, in itself, would serve to distinguish the tropical rain forest from most other vegetation in Middle America. Furthermore, the tropical rain forest consists in every case of at least three, and sometimes as many as five, stories of woody plants, one or more of which stories at or near the top of the forest forms a closed canopy. The evergreen character is also consistent.

Another striking characteristic, common to all the cases described and seldom to be found outside this formation, is the profusion of growth in addition to the large trees. In every instance the palms form a substantial part of the understory, and sometimes the palmlike *Carludovica* is present as well. Along with the palms in some stands the distinctive cycad *Zamia* and tree ferns appear. The presence of the great strangler figs of the genera *Ficus* and *Coussapoa* among the common trees in almost every description suggests another characteristic feature. The middle layer or layers of trees usually contain the highly individual foliage of the fast-growing *Cecropia* and *Didymopanax*, and the giant leaves of *Calathea, Heliconia,* and *Costus* lend an extravagant touch to the herb layer. The huge leaves of many of the aroids are likewise prominent, and often they form members of a tangle of lianes, some others of which in flower contribute almost the only spots of color to the forest. Curious epiphytes infest the branches, and send down their dangling roots.

The buttressed trunks of the large trees, the poverty of sunlight within the forest, and the spacious arrangement of the tree trunks give the rain forest at the ground an empty and almost artificial appearance. The density of the canopy prevents sunlight from reaching the lower levels, and inhibits growth there. The most luxuriant growth near the ground is found along streams and in clearings, where the flora is almost always rather unlike that of the interior of the forest.

P. W. Richards (1957) points to the heavy preponderance of woody plants as a distinctive feature of the tropical rain forest along with the great number of different species and genera represented. The numerous other special characteristics of this formation, as well as its world distribution, he treats at length.

Descriptions of rain forests cited in preceding pages are not altogether consistent. Variation in the maximum height of stands is expectable, as also in the number of stories. The tallest trees and the dominant canopy-forming species differ greatly from one place to another. A few are eminent in several areas, but the composition changes gradually with distance. Nevertheless, the Middle American tropical rain forest represents essentially one formation, though composed of different associations. A great part of the genera and even species found in one area will recur in others far away, and many extend in continuous distributions as distant as Colombia, the Guianas, and even beyond.

Some stands of rain forest mentioned show indications of a transition to other formations, or even represent not true tropical rain forest but some of its typical neighboring formations, proper to drier or cooler sites, or disturbed by man, or subject to yearly flooding. The change in structure that accompanies such habitat dissimilarities proceeds gradually, and it is difficult to draw sharp boundaries between formations.

Human Interference in the Rain Forest

The tropical rain forests of Peten, as described by Lundell (1937), reveal the past influence of man, and particularly the for-

Fɪɢ. 4—SECONDARY GROWTH (*ACAHUAL*) IN FORMER HIGH RAIN-FOREST AREA, SOUTH
OF ACAYUCAN, SOUTHERN VERACRUZ, IN THE ISTHMUS OF TEHUANTEPEC
In the foreground is guarumbo (*Cecropia obtusifolia*); the fernlike plants (right center) are
pichos (*Schizolobium parahybum*); and in the right foreground is jolotzin (*Heliocarpus donnell-
smithii*). (Photo by A. Maya, Instituto de Geografía, Universidad Nacional de México.)

mer intensive agricultural use of the land now covered by the upland forest. Some trees, particularly the useful breadnut (*Brosimum utile*), cluster on ancient Maya sites. The sapodilla (*Achras sapota*), of which some individuals are as much as 1000 years old, was apparently dispersed with the help of man. Other useful trees whose present distribution is referred by Lundell to Maya influence are the edible fruit-bearing guayo (*Talisia olivaeformis*), avocado (*Persea americana*), mamey (*Calocarpum mammosum*), and the moraceous *Pseudolmedia spuria*; perhaps the palm *Orbygnia cohune;* two incense-bearing trees, *Protium copal* and *Bursera simaruba*; and tropical cedar (*Cedrela mexicana*) and ma-

hogany (*Swietenia macrophylla*), both used for timber.

Lundell discusses the effect of slash-burn (milpa) agriculture on vegetation and soil, which was earlier raised by O. F. Cook (1909, 1921), and inclines to attribute the development of grasslands and especially of brushlands to this cause. The exploitation of *Achras* for chicle is an important influence on the vegetation at present, and *Cedrela* has been much cut for building materials. The relative scarcity of these trees in some areas may be attributed to such interference.

The secondary vegetation referred to in Peten as *acahual* has been described for Yucatan by Lundell (1934) and Bartlett

231

(1935). The succession varies considerably from one area to another, depending on manner of disturbance and on the climatic and edaphic situation. In general, in the early stages the assemblage of plants in old clearings tends to include mostly species capable of wide dispersal and of rapid growth in open sunlight. Many of these are plants that also grow normally in stream beds, where natural disturbance is frequent. A great many are spread by animals. The progression in time is from low herb cover, approximating the weeds of cultivated fields, through a dense brush to thickets, often composed of a single species, with the slow accession of the usual forest trees to dominance if the site remains thereafter undisturbed (fig. 4). Standley (1937) describes briefly a similar secondary vegetation in the Atlantic rain forests of Costa Rica.

Not much of the tropical rain forest is cleared at present in Middle America. A large part of the forest in the northern extreme of its range, Veracruz, has disappeared. Rain forests of southeastern Tabasco and northeastern Chiapas remain mostly intact, but what may once have been rain forest in the middle parts of the Yucatan Peninsula is now quite a different vegetation. On the Pacific side of southern Mexico and Guatemala, such true tropical rain forests as existed have given way to coffee plantations or have been logged. The banana plantations of southeastern Guatemala, northeastern Honduras, eastern and southern Costa Rica, and northern Panama represent the largest incursions of settlement and cultivation in the Central American tropical rain forests today, and they are foci for dispersed settlements of squatters and former laborers. The only other pressure on the rain forest in these areas is from lumbering, and in recent years considerable cuttings for balsa wood and plywood materials have been made in such places as eastern Costa Rica.

The foregoing descriptions of the tropical rain forest conform closely to those given by Richards (1957), and to the theoretical criteria of Beard. Beard's analytical key (1944, p. 156) selects tropical rain forest according to the following diagnosis: "Woody growth dominant, palms and bamboos not present in considerable numbers: Tree growth over 10 meters high: Forest entirely evergreen (or practically so): Tall forest with large trees forming a continuous canopy at 20 meters or more above ground: Tree strata 3 or 4, dominants 40 meters or more tall, leaves predominantly compound." The Middle American tropical rain forest thus corresponds to the general character of rain forests elsewhere. It is perhaps richer in palms and is certainly distinct in flora from that of tropical rain forests in other continents which are structurally similar. On the other hand, as will be seen, the tropical rain forest differs sharply from other vegetations of Middle America. In this regard, composition may be misleading, for a great many species are shared with other formations. Even in the physiognomy of individual plants, resemblances exist between the rain forest and particular other formations, notably in the presence of epiphytes, lianes, palms, and other types. It is by structural criteria alone, as Beard insists, that one can clearly define this formation, or any other.

MONTANE FORMATION SERIES

(1) *Lower montane rain forest*: Two stories of evergreen, the upper to 30 m.; leaves simple. (2) *Montane rain forest*: Two stories of evergreen trees, the upper to 20 m. (3) *Montane thicket*: Single story of evergreen trees, 10–15 m. (4) *Elfin woodland*: Dense tangle of shrubs or small trees, less than 10 m. high; evergreen. (5) *Páramo*: Partial cover of herbaceous and other low growth; evergreen.

The cardinal control affecting the vegetation of mountain areas is the variation of climate with altitude. Local relief, local atmospheric circulation, and other factors play their part in creating the climate of a place, but primarily the montane series represents the situation in which temperature, especially, decreases from the optimum of the perpetually rainy lowlands where the tropical rain forests grow.

The tropical rain forest belongs essentially to a single structural type, for it is a vegetation that develops where temperature and moisture are safely in excess of the most extreme needs of any of its component plants. Probably the limitations on height of the tallest rain forest trees, and on density of the canopy, which in turn set the conditions of growth of the rest of the aggregation, arise from inherent mechanical and biochemical properties of these preeminent and dominant trees rather than out of climatic influences. In both the montane and the seasonal series, however, climatic conditions directly restrict plant development.

The gradual decrease of temperature with increasing altitude brings successive structural impoverishments in the vegetation, though moisture is often constant, or even greater, upslope. There is a gradual decrease in the number of stories of woody plants, a thinning out of the canopy in one story and its re-establishment in a lower one, until finally there is no canopy and only one plant story.

In the tropical montane formations, bordering on the lowland rain forests, moisture is not a critical variable on the whole. The mountains of central and northern Mexico, however, lie mostly outside the regions of abundant moisture, and the climatic controls on their vegetation are more complex. Some of the formations of the montane series are therefore sometimes absent in these areas, and also farther south in Central America. With this exception, the series predicted according to theory fits satisfactorily the actual vegetational structure of almost all the mountain areas in Middle America.

Costa Rican Montane Formations

Wercklé (1909) put the division between *tierra caliente* and *tierra templada* (approx-

imately the lower limit of montane formations) at 800 m. on both the Caribbean and Pacific sides of Costa Rica. On the western side of the Meseta Central, however, around latitude 10°N., the influence of the dry region of the Pacific penetrates to 900 m. altitude. The *tierra fría*, according to Wercklé, begins at about 1500 m., with frost expectable above 2000 m. The vegetation of the tierra fría, of course, also belongs to the montane formation series.

The forests of the Meseta Central of Costa Rica, where the population has been concentrated since the conquest, have been rather thoroughly destroyed. Wercklé conjectured, on the basis of surviving remnants and by analogy with nearby areas, that this section of Costa Rica once carried a forest of mostly evergreen trees, floristically transitional to a large degree between the lowland vegetations of both coasts and those of the tierra fría. The trees included species of oaks, both evergreen and deciduous, as well as tropical cedar (*Cedrela*), laurels (*Ocotea, Nectandra*), euphorbs (*Sapium, Croton*), melastomaceous trees bearing edible fruits (*Miconia, Conostegia, Clidemia*), the legume *Inga* (now much used to shade coffee), some plants of the mulberry family, and perhaps the South American conifer *Podocarpus*, which still grows elsewhere in the highlands[8] (fig. 5).

In the mountains surrounding the Meseta Central today grow many of these same plants, together with many trees of the madder, myrtle, and myrsine families. On the southern bordering ranges are the magnolia relative *Talauma*, the South American *Drimys*, the vervain *Citharexylum*, various madders (*Calycophyllum, Palicourea, War-*

[8] Among the shrubs were Melastomaceae, Compositae, Solanaceae, Piperaceae, and Sapindaceae, with *Cassia, Mimosa*, and *Calliandra* prominent, and *Tecoma stans* occurring in the lower western portion of the Meseta Central. Lianes such as *Paullinia, Serjania, Clematis, Ipomoea, Passiflora, Cissampelos*, and *Smilax*, along with several Leguminosae and Asclepiadaceae, formed an important element.

233

Fig. 5—MONTANE RAIN FOREST BACK OF CLEARING IN THE TALAMANCA RANGE, COSTA RICA
This scene is about 50 km. south of Cartago at approximately 2500 m. elevation. Giant buttressed oaks (chiefly *Quercus costaricensis*) and laurels (*Persea* spp.) are dominants. (Photo by R. C. West.)

szewiczia), an elderberry (*Sambùcus*), an elm (*Ulmus*), and other genera among the trees; sage (*Salvia*), a madder (*Bouvardia*), and several asters (*Tithonia, Verbesina, Montanoa*) among the shrubs; a nightshade (*Solanum*), an acanthus (*Thunbergia*), and morning glory (*Ipomoea*) among the lianes. The herbs are varied and bright-flowered. In these forests epiphytes are common and include many kinds of cactus. Within the tierra templada also grow other trees such as the aster *Vernonia*, the tree-nettles *Urera* and *Myriocarpa*, the caper *Capparis*, and some palms, formerly abundant, including *Geonoma* and *Chamaedorea*. Bright-flowered *Canna* and *Maetia,* as well as aroids and bamboos, characterize the herbs, and bromeliads, aroids, orchids and ferns are the most numerous among the epiphytes.[9]

The mountain forests of southwestern Costa Rica have been described briefly by P. H. Allen (1956). Above 750 m. grows what is termed "upper montane rain forest." This formation is not sharply distinct from

[9] Standley (1937) concurred with Wercklé as to the placement of the altitudinal boundaries, but noted the impossibility of defining vegetation belts precisely. Standley, too, remarked on the thorough destruction of the forests of the Meseta Central. His list of their former trees adds *Persea, Chaetoptelea, Zanthoxylum, Engelhardtia, Alfaroa,* and *Ladenbergia* to those given by Wercklé. Additional shrubs are those in hedges, surviving as a sample of former vegetation: *Xylosma, Randia, Zanthoxylum, Iresine, Trichilia, Mauria, Acnistus, Picramnia, Cestrum, Erythrina.* To the list of epiphytes are added numerous Ericaceae and Gesneriaceae for the Atlantic-slope *tierra templada.*

234

the adjacent lower montane forest, and the same species sometimes occur in both formations. Some of the associations present have been enumerated. The deep, well-drained soils of more or less level areas carry a forest in which oaks and tropical cedar are dominant. An almost pure stand, or consociation, of *Iriartea gigantea*, a palm, appears between 800 and 1000 m. in sheltered "coves." The breadnut (*Brosimum utile*), a tree also somewhat common in the lowlands, forms consociations up to 1300 m. Around 1000 m. elevation, steep rocky walls are occupied by a consociation of rosewood (*Coccoloba roseiflora*). The madder, *Ladenbergia Brenesii*, grows in nearly pure stands on deep soils between 800 and 1000 m. An association dominated by the palm *Euterpe panamensis* and *Cespedesia macrophylla* (ochna family) occupies high slopes and crests of ridges at 1000–1300 m. elevation.[10]

At a lower elevation, adjoining these forests, grows a "lower montane rain forest" described in the same work. Here the rainfall is the same as on the lowland, and the forest grows even more densely than on the plains. The tree crowns meet in a thick canopy. More of the emergents are deciduous, however, and for a longer period. The understory contains entirely evergreen plants, with many palms. Fewer giant herbs occur at ground level in this forest than in the lowland rain forest. The upper story reaches 30–50 m. and the understory consists of three poorly differentiated tiers between 5 and 30 m., so that with the ground layer, this is a five-storied forest. Eighty-nine canopy species and 270 understory ones have been recognized.

Above 1500 m. the mountain climate is cold and moist—or, subjectively, chilling

and drippy. Fog is frequent, and in places almost eternal. Accordingly, very lush and rather eerie vegetations occur in the higher mountains. Wercklé (1909) described the forests in the rainier high regions as composed of trees of the spurge, laurel, myrtle, madder, meadow-beauty, legume, custard-apple, ginseng, nutmeg, saxifrage, soapberry, and dogbane families. In these forests, oaks are on the whole rather rare. Herbs of the begonia, gesneria, loasa, lobelia, and violet families are common, and ferns and club mosses numerous. Moss covers the branches of the trees. There are relatively few lianes, but epiphytes grow in tremendous profusion. Not only small piperaceous plants, orchids, bromeliads, and aroids grow as epiphytes, but also large shrubs of the composite, cyclanthus, cactus, heather, madder, nightshade, and acanthus families.

In the drier areas oak forests are widespread. The oak associations typically have little undergrowth and relatively few but showy epiphytes. An alder (*Alnus acuminata*) association occurs on steep bluffs of the volcanoes, and associations dominated by the lavish foliage of the ginsengs *Oreopanax* and *Dendropanax* are found elsewhere in special habitats. Oaks, the euphorb *Croton*, and some trees of the ginseng family dominate in many areas, with an undergrowth of barberry (*Berberis*), myrtle (*Myrtus*), and rubiaceous plants. Most of the epiphytes are bromeliads, which reach their maximum abundance in these forests. There are fewer ferns than in other formations, but many bright-flowered herbs, such as the red-and-yellow amaryllis (*Bomarea*), nasturtium (*Tropaeolum*), capers (*Capparis*), and various colorful representatives of the lobelia, iris, composite, and legume families.

At greater altitudes the forest is replaced by a shrub vegetation.[11] Higher still there

[10] In addition to the dominants of the various associations, other tree genera present include *Carpotroche, Coussapoa, Cymbopetalum, Guatteria, Hedyosmum, Mauria, Miconia, Nectandra, Oreopanax* spp., *Persea, Phoebe, Pourouma,* and *Stemmadenia*.

[11] With *Escallonia, Pernettya, Gaultheria, Vaccinium, Arctostaphylos, Myrtus, Senecio, Acaena, Alchemilla,* and various Compositae, Rubiaceae, and so forth.

FIG. 6—PÁRAMO VEGETATION ABOVE 3000 M., TALAMANCA RANGE, COSTA RICA
The upper limit of the montane forest, composed of stunted trees and shrubs (*Weinmannia, Myrtus, Clethra*), appears in foreground. In the páramo proper, on the upper slopes in the background, thickets of spiney bamboo (*Chusquea*) alternate with low shrubs, mosses, sedges, and lichens. (Photo by R. C. West.)

are summits covered with sphagnum moss. On the upper slopes of the volcanoes a large moisture-loving herb, *Gunnera insignis* with giant leaves up to 2 m. in width, is prominent in the vegetation.

Standley (1937) discovered numerous associations in the tierra fría. Species of oak and conifers of South American affinities (*Podocarpus oleifolius* and *P. montanus*) dominate some of these. Other associations are dominated by various low trees and shrubs (the tanbark *Weinmannia pinnata*, or the meadow-beauties *Blakea* and *Topobea*). Alder (*Alnus*) and a St. John's-wort (*Vismia*) form a thicket association, as do certain bamboos.[12]

Although Wercklé (1909) claimed that there were no true páramos in Costa Rica, this formation is in fact richly developed.

Standley (1937) lists among the components mosses, lycopods, ferns, and various herbs: lupine (*Lupinus*), *Castilleja*, the gentians *Gentiana* and *Halenia*, the rushes *Juncus* and *Luzula*, the sedge *Carex*, a grassy herb *Xyris*, a bog herb *Eriocaulon*, *Acaena* and *Alchemilla* of the rose family, the umbelliferous *Eryngium*, the South American *Puya*, and a few grasses. Floristically and physiognomically, these páramos are very similar to those of the Andes (fig. 6).

Weber (1959) has devoted a special

[12] Among the shrubs and trees, in addition to those described by Wercklé, Standley lists *Prunus, Morus, Magnolia, Eugenia, Myrica, Gaiadendron, Brunellia, Wercklea, Hydrangea, Solandra, Ilex,* and *Calatola*. The mountain flora is exceedingly rich, and very incompletely known; the associations are not well recorded.

study to the Costa Rican páramos. This formation occurs at elevations above 3000 m. in the highest mountains. The temperatures are low (monthly means from 5.4° to 7.5°C. were measured), but diurnal variation is great. Relative humidity is constantly high, and annual precipitation of more than 2800 mm. has been measured at one station of about 3000 m. elevation. Above the 2000-m. level grows a forest dominated by oaks (*Quercus costaricensis* and *Q. irazuensis*), with plentiful epiphytes. At the upper limit of this forest, around 2600 m., appear marshes, in which the fern *Lomaria* is dominant, with a cover of peat mosses (*Sphagnum*) and other plants. This vegetation is edaphic, no doubt conditioned by the high local humidity of the atmosphere.

Between 3050 and 3100 m. the páramo begins, though many of the species of the marshes continue into it, and there is even no sharp division between it and the forest. The specific composition of the páramo differs from one mountain to another, but the shrub vegetation of the Cerro de la Vuelta may be taken as representative. It consists of herbs and shrubs of the genera *Escallonia* (saxifrage family); *Weinmannia* (cunonia family); *Clethra* and *Pernettya* (heath family); the huckleberries *Vaccinium* and *Cavendishia;* a myrtle (*Myrtus*); the mistletoes *Dendrophthora* and *Gaiadendron;* and *Chusquea*, a spindly bamboo that sometimes forms dense mats. The páramo may also take the form of hummocky expanses of bunch grass or cushion plants, of saxophile "rock gardens," or of marsh.

The Costa Rican montane formations, extremely rich and better described than most others in Middle America, give a good idea of the spectrum of vegetation that makes up this formation series, but they are in many respects quite different from the mountain vegetations of other parts of Middle America. The páramo, floristically, is plainly a formation of Andean affinities, of which many components do not occur far northward of Costa Rica. It is replaced farther north by a structurally similar formation which is floristically more closely related to some found in the mountains of middle latitudes in the northern hemisphere. Even at lower altitudes, the montane formations become more similar in floristic composition to those of the United States as one proceeds northward.

Montane Formations in Chiapas

Some, though not all, of the vegetations referred to by Miranda (1952–53) as "selva alta subdecídua" belong to the lower montane rain forest formation. The forest is described as being deciduous in the upper story only, and often almost equal in height to the true tropical rain forest. One form of this forest, 12–25 m. high to which Miranda gives the name *selva de cajpoquí,* is typically lower montane. It occurs on the Mesa Central of Chiapas from 1000 to 1250 m., in the area running along the slopes behind Tuxtla Gutierrez, Berriozabal, and Ocozocuautla. The ground in this area is karstic and retains precipitation poorly.[13]

At higher altitudes appears what Miranda calls the "selva baja siempre verde." This is a dense forest with many shrubs, tree ferns, ground ferns, and mosses, reaching 15 or 20 m. The trees are evergreen, with bright coriaceous leaves. This formation

---

[13] The top story of this forest, at 12–25 m., includes *Bumelia persimilis* and species of *Ficus, Hauya, Platymiscium, Bernoullia, Guettarda, Wimmeria, Chaetoptelea, Erythrina,* and *Bursera*. The closed evergreen second story at 8–15 m. is dense, and contains *Coccoloba, Eugenia, Croton, Amyris, Schaefferia, Thouinia, Zanthoxylum, Oreopanax, Forestiera, Lonchocarpus, Inga, Ardisia, Clusia, Psidium, Ximenia, Exothea,* and *Chrysophyllum*. There occur such shrubs as *Psychotria, Mahonia,* and *Pithecolobium,* and numerous palms, aroids, cacti, orchids, and bromeliads, including many epiphytes. Various associations and consociations are present, with such dominants as *Prunus Salasii; Celtis monoica* and *Platymiscium dimorphandrum; Guettarda Combsii; Euphorbia pseudofulva;* and *Eysenhardtia adenostylis*. A related forest on the Lacandon side, to the east of the Mesa Central, grows to 40 m.; in it, *Ginoria nudifolia* accompanies many tropical rain forest species.

FIG. 7—MONTANE DECIDUOUS FOREST, SIERRA MADRE DE CHIAPAS, NORTH OF MAPASTEPEC. The dominant is sweet gum (*Liquidambar* sp.). (Photo by A. J. Sharp.)

Another and altogether different formation grows in places at the same altitudes as the *selva baja siempre verde*, with which it is frequently interdigitated. Sometimes the more usual montane formation simply becomes its understory. This is Miranda's "bosque decíduo." It is not dense, and not entirely deciduous. It grows to 25 or 30 m. and occasionally higher. The leaves of the constituent trees of the deciduous forest are soft and membranaceous, light green, and mostly serrate; they turn seasonally to bright colors. Deciduous forest occurs on northerly slopes with deep soils from 1000 or 1200 to 2000 m. The precipitation is in excess of 1200 mm., and in some places as much as 2000 mm. annually. There is little cloudiness, and frosts are frequent. Almost everywhere this vegetation is exposed to strong north winds, and in fact it does not grow where such winds are absent, as at places in the Sierra Madre where conditions are climatically otherwise appropriate (fig. 7). The tree genera include oaks (*Quercus Skinnerii* and *Q. acatenangensis*), sweet gum (*Liquidambar*, which is sometimes dominant), dogwood (*Cornus* and *Nyssa*), hornbeam (*Carpinus*), and a heath plant (*Clethra*). As mentioned before, species from the *selva baja siempre verde* may alternate with these, or constitute an understory. In some places, dogwood (*Nyssa*) is replaced by a close relative of the elm, *Chaetoptelea mexicana*. This is the tallest species in Chiapas, not excluding tropical rain forest trees. It commonly reaches 60

occurs on the slopes of the Mesa Central and the Sierra Madre at 1200–2300 m., or sometimes higher. Its habitat is cloud-bathed, wet and cool. Annual precipitation is around 2000 mm., and frost does not occur.[14]

[14] On the northern slopes of the Sierra Madre, this montane formation contains in the tree layer *Clethra, Saurauia, Turpinia, Cedrela, Toxicodendron, Zinowiewia, Phoebe, Eugenia, Prunus, Brunellia, Xylosma, Befaria, Oecopetalum, Rapanea, Persea, Dalbergia, Symplocos, Weinmannia, Inga, Oreopanax, Topobea, Cleyera, Conostegia, Gilibertia, Hedyosmum, Myrsia,* and *Rondeletia.* Some of the larger herbs and shrubs are *Besleria, Bomarea, Cavendishia, Centropogon, Cephaelis, Cobaea, Loasa, Miconia, Phyllonoma, Pilea,* and *Tropaeolum.* In clearings, *Gunnera* appears. There are many tree ferns.

The same formation grows much more widely,

however, on the slopes of the Sierra Madre, where its composition is rather different. Here the main tree genera are *Matudaea* (often dominant), *Inga, Clethra, Pithecolobium, Ilex, Podocarpus, Osmanthus, Cedrela, Olmediella, Ardisia, Conostegia, Eugenia, Hedyosmum, Nectandra, Oreopanax, Parathesis, Prunus, Rhamnus, Saurauia, Styrax,* and *Trophis.* On karst, *Oreopanax Sanderianus* is sometimes dominant in an 8–12-m. forest at 1000–2000 m. elevation, with a thick coating of mosses, lichens, and epiphytes over the trees and ground. In places on the slopes of the Mesa Central and Sierra Madre, but especially on Volcan Tacana, *Chiranthodendron pentadactylon* dominates a wet, dense forest at 2400–2500 m.

m., and individuals measuring 87 m. have been cut.

Miranda and Sharp (1950) have given a detailed description of this formation, as it occurs farther north in Mexico as well as in Chiapas, and have considered its origin and affinities. It is clear that this is a forest of very strong northern affinities: out of about 200 species sampled, 37 per cent belong essentially to north temperate genera (Miranda and Sharp, 1950, p. 330). The absence of cloud banks in the area of the deciduous forest, the prevalence of northerly winds, and the frequency of frosts, help to explain its presence in Chiapas.

The deciduous formation passes into oak and pine forests on its upper side. Oak forest vegetation in Chiapas consists of four types: tall forest, the trees with large and hard leaves; tall forest of small-leaved trees; high or low forest with large coriaceous leaves; and low forest with small-leaved trees.

The tall oak forests of *Quercus candicans*, *Q. Skinnerii*, *Q. corrugata*, and *Q. oocarpa*, all species with large and more or less hard leaves, reach 35–50 m. height. They grow where rainfall is in excess of 1200 mm. annually, and are frequently found on the borders of the lowland and the lower montane rain forest, or even within these formations. Tall, small-leaved oak forests attain their best development at elevations under 3000 m. where precipitation is less than 1200 mm. per year. The forest grows to a height of 35 m., and consists of the oak *Quercus acatenangensis*; *Daphnopsis*, a tree of the mesereum family; *Styrax*, a storax; *Oreopanax*, a ginseng shrub; madroño (*Arbutus*); manzanita (*Arctostaphylos*); blackberry brambles (*Rubus*); *Ternstroemia*, a small tree of the tea family; the groundsel shrub (*Senecio*); *Fuchsia*; and so on. Ferns and the shrubby *Baccharis* appear in clearings and the poisonous *Coriaria* herb invades scarred slopes.

Quercus brachystachys dominates a 15–25-m. forest in moister places between 2000

and 3000 m. elevation, accompanied by *Arbutus*, and with hawthorn or tejocote (*Crataegus*) and a wild cherry (*Prunus*) in the clearings. The commonest oak forest is dominated by *Q. peduncularis*, with *Q. polymorpha* and *Q. conspersa*; epiphytes are usually numerous. This forest, of medium height, grows from 700 to 2500 m. elevation. It commonly borders on savannas or on low deciduous (seasonal) formations, and like them is often strongly disturbed. Finally, a curious chaparral formation of low-growing, small-leaved oaks (*Q. sebifera*), as well as various shrubs and low trees of many other genera,[15] occurs in southern highland Chiapas around Comitan. Ordinarily this is an evergreen shrub formation 2–4 m. high, but in places it grows to only 30–60 cm., competing closely with grassland.

Pine forests are widespread in Chiapas, representing a kind of mountain vegetation that extends also into Guatemala, Honduras, and north-central Nicaragua (figs. 8 and 9). The coniferous forests, in which a single species usually forms pure stands, extend from within the tropical rainforest up to the tree line, usually occupying thinner soils than the oaks over most of this range. Certain pines, like *Pinus ayacahuite* and *P. strobus*, are restricted to humid areas (precipitation over 1200 mm. annually), where they form 35–40-m. stands, sometimes intermixed with deciduous forest. These pine forests, however, have been largely destroyed. Between 750 and 3000 m., *P. oocarpa* on drier areas, and *P. pseudostrobus* and *P. tenuifolia* on somewhat lower and moister ones, alternate with oak forest. At higher altitudes occur *P. montezumae* and *P. teocote* forests. In the very cold zone from 2800 m. to the tree line at 4000 m., *Pinus Hartwegii* and *P. rudis* grow; the wetter slopes, however, carry forests of fir (*Abies guatemalensis*). Under the pines

[15] These include *Dodonaea, Rhus, Amelanchier, Harpalyce, Ximenia, Xylosmum, Ilex, Ternstroemia,* and *Garrya.*

FIG. 8—MONTANE FOREST OF PINE AND OAK
This photo was taken in the San Cristobal highlands, Chiapas, at 1300 m. between San Geronimo and Abasolo. In this area pine grows on sandstone, oak on limestone. (Photo by A. J. Sharp.)

grows a sparse grass cover, as a rule, whereas the ground of the fir forests has a richer cover.[16]

A cypress, *Cupressus Lindleyii*, is mixed with pine or fir at 1800–3000 m. elevation, and several junipers (*Juniperus* spp.) in dry level areas between 1600 and 2200 m. occur with oak and pine. *Juniperus Standleyii*, growing 0.5–2 m. high on rocks and in cold places, forms an important element of the páramo of the peak of Tacana, at slightly over 4000 m. elevation.

The highest mountain vegetation, represented by a small area on Tacana volcano, consists of meadows one tenth to one third meter high, in which the plants are interspersed with bare soil. Besides such grasses as *Festuca* and *Calamagrostis*, these páramos contain shrubs, herbaceous plants, and the juniper already mentioned.[17]

In central Mexico around latitude 18°N. studies in the drainage of the Rio Balsas and Rio Papaloapan by Miranda (1947 and 1948, respectively) provide a transect of the montane vegetations.

Central Mexican Montane Vegetation

In general the montane formations of central Mexico are like those of Chiapas, except that the lower montane rain forest is usually lacking, and is replaced by xe-

[16] It includes *Achillea, Bidens, Centropogon, Cirsium, Eryngium, Eupatorium, Fuchsia, Gentiana, Lamourouxia, Lobelia, Pentstemon, Pernettya, Potentilla, Salvia, Senecio,* and *Vaccinium.*

[17] *Alchemilla, Arenaria, Draba, Gnaphalium, Potentilla, Senecio, Wallenia.*

Fig. 9—MONTANE FOREST OF *PINUS OOCARPA*, HIGHLANDS OF CENTRAL HON-
DURAS
This scene is east of Tegucigalpa, 1200–1800 m. elevation. In the distance above the pine is the
Montaña de Azacualpa, covered with cloud forest composed of large oaks, laurels, and the
South American conifer, *Podocarpus*. (Photo by R. C. West.)

rophytic forms. On the upper slopes around the Balsas basin, beginning at 1800 m. in the north and at 1200–1400 m. in the south, occur forests of pine (*Pinus montezumae, P. pseudostrobus*) and juniper (*Juniperus flaccida*). On limestone occur stands of the palm *Brahea dulcis*. This pine or palm forest grades upward into oak forest.

Dense forest dominated by *Quercus lanigera, Q. reticulata,* and other oaks begins at 2500–3000 m. It is rich in species, with ample underbrush and abundant epiphytes. The oaks are large-leaved deciduous trees 10–15 m. high. In the underbrush madroño (*Arbutus*), a buckhorn (*Ceanothus*) and wild cherry (*Prunus*) are common. In some places grows a tall, small-leaved evergreen oak forest 23–30 m. high, with *Q. affinis, Q. laurina,* and dogwood (*Cornus*). Forests of

Q. urbanii, with large coriaceous leaves, occur at around 2000 m., as does a chaparral of low *Q. magnoliaefolia*. On rocky outcrops is a xerophilous vegetation of *Agave, Pitcairnia, Sedum* and so forth, and in the barrancas a rich forest composed of mainly tropical genera.[18]

Fir forests of *Abies religiosa* occur at 2800–3500 m. (fig. 10). The firs are as much as 60 m. in height, and are accompanied by pine and oak. A pine forest of *P. Hartwegii,* 10–20 m. high, occurs from 3500 m. to the tree line at 4000 m.; beyond, to 4200 m.,

[18] *Meliosma, Styrax, Oreopanax, Symplocos, Zinowiewia, Bocconia, Fuchsia, Rapanea, Ardisia, Ternstroemia, Cleyera, Phoebe,* but also *Prunus, Garrya, Clethra, Ilex,* and *Morus.* Mixed with it are deciduous trees of boreal genera—hornbean (*Carpinus*), dogwood (*Cornus*), linden (*Tilia*), alder (*Alnus*), and ash (*Fraxinus*).

Fig. 10—MONTANE FOREST OF FIR (*ABIES RELIGIOSA*) AT 3200 M., NEAR MEXICO CITY (Photo by F. Miranda.)

grows a formation of juniper and other shrubs interspersed with herbs and grass—the páramo. The tundra, from 4300 m. to the permanent snow line (ca. 4800–5000 m.) contains only herbs, forming an incomplete ground cover. They include various grasses; sedge (*Carex*); and the herbs sandwort (*Arenaria*), whitlow (*Draba*), groundsel (*Senecio*), *Cirsium, Castilleja, Cerastium, Plantago, Ranunculus,* and *Sagina.* Most of these herbs are of Alpine affinities, but a few are Andean.

In the upper Papaloapan Basin the lower slopes are covered with an extremely xerophytic vegetation. Below the oak-pine forest, at elevations of 900–1400 m., the forest is a deciduous one, composed of a soft-wooded cashew, *Cyrtocarpa*; many resin-exuding species, such as *Bursera, Juliania* and the poisonous *Pseudomodingium*; the *Ceiba,* or silk-cotton tree; the yellow-flowering *Cassia,* the milky-sapped *Euphorbia, Gyrocarpus,* a legume *Leucaena,* and cacti in the open tree story, with the spiny shrubs of *Randia* (madder family), *Mimosa* and *Acacia* in the understory. In the barrancas is a 15-m.-high forest.[19] The oak forest that confines with this formation is 5–10 m. high, composed of *Quercus glaucophylla, Q. glaucoides, Q. Liebmannii, Q. obscura,* the legumes *Acacia* and *Piscidia,* and *Xylosma.* Above it is a taller (10–15 m.) oak forest with *Q. conspersa,* and sometimes mountain mahogany (*Cercocarpus*) dominant. On wetter slopes pines (*Pinus montezumae* and *P. oocarpa*) grow, with an underbrush of Ericaceae (heath family). Another pine, *P. rudis,* forms stands at high elevations.

[19] Of *Euphorbia, Cyrtocarpa, Thevetia, Ficus, Plumeria, Tabebuia, Ruprechtia, Sideroxylon, Caesalpinia,* and *Pileus.*

242

According to Miranda, these mountain vegetations are the ones found throughout the Mesa Central of Mexico, and far to the north, grading into the vegetation of the United States. Miranda (1947) suggests that even the California chaparral may be a xerophile member of the oak forest complex of Mexico.

Comparative View of Montane Formations

From these examples, the altitudinal zonation of the montane formations so widespread in Mexico and Central America can well be seen. The series begins in the lowlands with lower montane rain forest, which is lacking in much of central Mexico and altogether absent to the north thereof. The diagnostic features conform to a smoothly descending series of gradations from the lower montane rain forest uphill.

The montane rain forest formation has dominants about 20 m., as against 30 m. in the lower montane formation. Mosses and tree ferns are plentiful. This forest, too, is evergreen. The formation begins at about 750 m. in Costa Rica, about 1200 m. in Chiapas, and at elevations varying from 1400 to 2500 m. in central Mexico, where aridity, rather than temperature, sets the lower limit. The dominants throughout are mostly oaks, though a deciduous forest of northern type coexists with oak forests in eastern Mexico, and pine forests occur from far below to well above the range of the oaks. The lowland oaks of Guanacaste, in Costa Rica, are a special case which will be mentioned later.

Above the montane rain forest grows montane thicket, with a dense canopy at 10–15 m. and little understory. Above the thicket, in turn, may come elfin woodland, followed at the greatest elevations by páramos, and in high mountains by the snow line. Beard (1955, p. 44) wrote that "Mountain Pine Forest is apparently a fire-climax," derived from high mountain forests for which he possessed no structural data.

Apparently the pine and fir forests, and the deciduous forest of eastern Mexico, though they reach well into Central America, belong to a different group of formations from those treated by Beard. The extensive pine (and oak) forests of the mountains of Guatemala, Honduras, and Nicaragua have been little described. They, and some of the minor associations of the central Mexican mountains, strongly point northward to the vegetations of the United States, and they seem to occur parallel to, and be vicariants of, the formations rich in tropical genera. It is possible that the pine forest represents situations of ancient disturbance (by fire?). Denevan's (1961) study of the upland pine forest in Nicaragua supports the hypothesis of fire-climax through disturbance by man.

Human Interference in the Montane Formations

The areas of montane vegetation, except the highest zones, are often heavily populated today, and have been so no doubt in the past. The Meseta Central of Costa Rica has been so thoroughly cleared for cultivation and pasture that it was impossible to discover exactly what the former vegetation cover was. Many species must have been exterminated in this process. The floristic assemblage of the pasturelands of the Costa Rican uplands has in effect been created by man. Exploitation of the great oak forests of the Cordillera de Talamanca, between San Jose and San Isidro del General, has been opened by the building of the Inter-American Highway, and these beautiful stands are becoming converted rapidly to charcoal for sale. The skirts of the great volcanoes Barba, Irazu, Turrialba, and Poas have in recent years received a heavy influx of settlers, with the result that very large expanses of forest have been felled. Much the same has happened in the highlands of the Nicoya Peninsula. Sometimes the resulting landscape is still dominated by large trees which are used to shade coffee plantations; such is the case in the

243

middle altitudes of the Meseta Central of Costa Rica, and in parts of Nicaragua, El Salvador, Guatemala, and Chiapas. Mostly, though, settlement means removal of practically all large trees, and their replacement by cleared fields, pasture, and brush. Thus in general the oak forests are heavily disturbed by man in a large part of Middle America, and the pine forests only somewhat less so, since they are at higher elevations for the most part. Not only are the forests cleared for settlement, but beyond the settled areas they are intensively culled for certain plants, among which both palms and pines are heavy sufferers in the neighborhood of villages; and, wherever transport is feasible, the trees are burned ruthlessly to make charcoal, the whole of the forest community usually being obliterated in the process. It is possible that the assault on the montane forests is chiefly a recent phenomenon, and that the pre-Columbian inhabitants of Middle America did much less harm to vegetation in the highlands than do present folk. The ancient people of the Meseta Central of Costa Rica, some of the preconquest inhabitants of highland Guatemala and Chiapas, and above all the peoples who dwelt in the upland basins of Mexico, nevertheless, did contribute heavily to an early and thorough alteration in the vegetation of those areas, of which the work of later settlers is only an intensification.

The secondary succession in montane areas resembles that of the lowlands structurally. In general, as I have observed in Mexico and Central America, when cleared fields are abandoned a cover of grass, low shrubs, and herbs develops in the first year. If animals are regularly pastured on the land, a thin sod develops. If not, there succeeds a shrub thicket up to 2 m. high, which shades out almost completely the grass and other ground plants. A tree story arises from some members of the shrub growth as development proceeds, and stabilizes at 5–10 m., with some undergrowth. The component species of the mature forest gradu-

ally reinvade this mostly deciduous secondary woodland. Many of the oaks, however, resprout soon after cutting, and unless their roots are destroyed (which seldom occurs) a dense oak thicket, in which some thorny shrubs are often intermingled, develops in the second or third year, passing gradually to forest. In Chiapas, many of the secondary shrub and woodland stands are characterized by the prominence of genera bearing large edible fruits—hawthorns (*Crataegus*), wild plums and cherries (*Prunus*), blackberries (*Rubus*), and at relatively low elevations the guava (*Psidium*). The flora tends to be similar to the undergrowth of forests of somewhat lower elevations, with a considerable number of tropical lowland species.

Pine stands, if oak is not present, tend to give way to a persistent chaparral; if oaks were intermixed with the original pine, they repopulate the area. Solitary and much misused pine trees around villages testify to the fierce persecution of the pine by the Chiapas Indians; only on inaccessible, very steep hills and on the rocks of deep gorges are pines left to flourish, in the lower elevations.

The actual vegetation of the lower and middle slopes of the Middle American uplands consists largely of patchy secondary brush and woodland, *milpas* (slash-burn fields), and some relatively intact forests here and there, especially far removed from villages (fig. 11). The pronounced squareness of the boundaries of different stands of these various vegetations is an excellent clue to their history. Sometimes old stone walls remain, or fence posts or hedges can be recognized in the secondary vegetation. A very considerable amount of land is without woody growth, some of it serving as pasture, and a surprising amount lying almost entirely bare of plant cover. The scarred, naked lands of upland Michoacan, Oaxaca, and Chiapas, readily visible from the main highways, represent the condition of much larger areas. On the steep hillsides

FIG. 11—OAK AND PINE MONTANE FOREST NORTH OF OAXACA CITY HIGHLY DISTURBED BY SLASH-BURN CULTIVATION
(Photo by R. C. West.)

common throughout Middle America, clearing introduces a serious danger of erosion, which is all too often realized. The forests that remain are not safe from the commercial logger, especially in Chiapas and in the northern Mexican states. The total area of forest is shrinking from year to year in the Mexican mountains and in Costa Rica's uplands, as well as in areas of heavy Indian population in Guatemala, and secondary vegetations, often themselves much abused and redisturbed, are spreading.

SEASONAL FORMATION SERIES AND SAVANNAS

(1) *Evergreen seasonal forest*: Three tree stories, with canopy in the middle story. Height over 10 m. Up to one-third deciduous. (2) *Semi-evergreen seasonal forest*: Two tree stories, with the canopy in the upper story. Half to a third of the trees deciduous. (3) *Deciduous seasonal forest*: Two tree stories, no canopy, height over 10 m. Over two-thirds of the trees usually deciduous. (4) *Cactus scrub*: Low, incomplete cover of cacti and other succulents. (*Savanna*: Grassland, usually hummocky, with isolated trees of less than 10 m., bearing coriaceous leaves.)

The formations of the seasonal series in Middle America, like the savannas belonging theoretically to the seasonal swamp series, occur almost entirely in areas of Pacific drainage, which have been long and continuously settled, and since the Spanish conquest usually heavily grazed as well. A discussion of the vegetation therefore from the outset involves consideration of man's influence. Since the seasonal series and the savanna are found intermixed in the same area, and their differences are man-made as well as naturally edaphic—possibly with man-induced conditions of the soil, as well as continued pressure of burning and grazing, playing an important role in spreading the seasonal swamp vegetations —they must be treated together.

245

Seasonal Formations in Nicoya

I have observed seasonal vegetation of the Nicoya Peninsula, on the Pacific side of Costa Rica. The arrangement of formations proceeds inland from the southwestern coast in a northeasterly direction. Along the outer coast, where all but three or four months bring some rain, the forests belong to the seasonal evergreen formation, with three tree stories in which deciduous species are in a small minority. The tallest emergents are as high as 30 m., but below them is a closed canopy. Lianes and epiphytes are present but not numerous. Trees of the upper stories include mahogany (*Swietenia*), tropical cedar (*Cedrela*), *Bombacopsis*, water sapote (*Pachira*), laurels (*Cordia* and *Nectandra*), cashews (*Anacardium* and *Astronium*), *Sterculia*, sandbox (*Hura*), rubber (*Castilla*), the large leguminous *Prioria*, *Quassia*, and the sapotaceous star-apple (*Chrysophyllum*). The leguminous *Pithecolobium*, *Enterolobium*, and *Hymenaea* are rather infrequent. Plants of the bignonia, arum, morning glory, and madder families, as well as twining palms and many piperaceous vines and shrubs are common in the understory. Herbs are almost lacking, except for a few begonias.

Toward the interior of the peninsula, the tree strata become reduced to two, with a closed canopy on the low mountain ranges and a two-story open forest inland. The percentage of compound leaved trees, and of deciduous species, rises sharply. The height of the forest declines to 20 m. or less in the interior. Common upper-story trees include various legumes, such as *Pithecolobium*, *Enterolobium* (the *guanacaste*), *Albizzia*; the chinaberries, *Guarea* and *Cedrela*; the spurge, *Sapium*; and others including *Chrysophyllum*, *Terminalia*, and *Chlorophora*. Nearly all of these trees are valuable for timber. Along the streams is a somewhat higher forest dominated by the cashew *Anacardium excelsum*, with a low and open understory of star-apple (*Chrysophyllum*)

and custard-apple (*Annona*), and other trees; a mallow (*Malaviscus*) and *Piper* are common shrubs, and relatives of the begonia appear prominently among the herbs. Lianes are not infrequent, but epiphytes, ferns, and palms are almost absent. In streamside sites of drier areas grows an association dominated by *Ficus*, *Brosimum*, *Ocotea*, *Nectandra*, *Cedrela*, *Cassia*, *Enterolobium*, and so forth. Many of the trees are buttressed. The understory trees include *Andira*, *Sloanea*, *Sapranthus*, *Luehea*, *Sideroxylon*, *Inga* spp., and *Castilla*. In openings of stream beds, where natural disturbance has occurred, sandbox (*Hura*), balsa wood (*Ochroma*), and guarumo (*Cecropia*) form closed stands laced with creepers.

On the hills are associations of seasonal type, of less than 20 m. height, predominantly deciduous. The thin upper story contains the guanacaste (*Enterolobium*), and a rather scrubby assortment of *Guazuma*, *Luehea*, *Apeiba*, *Tabebuia*, *Bursera*, *Bombacopsis*, *Sterculia*, *Astronium*, *Hymenaea*, *Albizzia*, *Pithecolobium*, *Cordia*, *Cedrela*, and *Ficus*. The second tree story includes guava (*Psidium*), *Cochlospermum*, *Croton*, custard-apple (*Annona*), wild cacao (*Theobroma*), sandpaper tree (*Curatella*), *Acacia*, a madder (*Chomelia*), and hog-plum (*Spondias*). Many of the shrubs are spiny. This forest grows in areas subject to heavy disturbance by fire and grazing, and it is striking that many of the plants of the lower tree story also often occur together in thickets without tall trees. Strong disturbance, and perhaps partial recovery therefrom, is apparent in these forests. Grazing has long exerted a pressure in this area, and there is reason to suppose that it may have had an even greater impact in colonial times than at present. In the driest places, the hills carry a more or less thorny vegetation of small trees under 10 m., including *Albizzia*, *Triumfetta*, *Guazuma*, *Triplaris*, *Coccoloba*, *Cecropia*, *Byrsonima*, *Plumeria*, and a columnar cactus (*Cereus*).

In the seasonal associations of Nicoya,

which consist of genera widespread on the Pacific side of Middle America and which resemble closely the associations of most of that great region, fire and grazing have undoubtedly had much to do with vegetation development. One significant feature of these associations is the prevalence of species in them with seeds that are easily dispersed or resist fire well. In the latter category are tropical cedar, mahogany, guanacaste, *Pithecolobium*, and probably guarumo (*Cecropia*), according to local report. Light-seeded species (*Ochroma* or balsa, *Bombacopsis*) readily invade disturbed sites. Animals disperse seeds surrounded by fleshy edible fruits like those of guava (*Psidium*), guarumo (*Cecropia*), rubber (*Castilla*), the palm *Acrocomia*, *Byrsonima*, and hog-plum (*Spondias*). *Tabebuia, Hura* and some other euphorbs and many legumes have mechanical means of scattering their seeds. Animals also trample plants and destroy both foliage and some fruits. The selective effect of their action appears clearly in the development of almost pure stands of thorn bush around pens and along driving trails.

The succession on abandoned cleared fields in Nicoya probably represents well the situation in much of Middle America. The weeds present during cultivation—largely pantropical species—give way gradually in the season after abandonment to a low woody cover of sensitive-plant (*Mimosa pudica*), *Sida* spp., *Rauwolfia, Cassia, Acacia* spp., *Hyptis, Lantana, Scoparia, Physalis, Triumfetta, Chenopodium, Ageratum, Bidens, Asclepias,* and so on, most of which are suffrutescent perennial herbs. Out of the tangle of low bush less than a meter high develops, from seedlings established therein, a thicket several meters high of *Guazuma*, guava (*Psidium*), guarumo (*Cecropia*), *Chomelia, Mangifera* (near plantings of mango trees), *Coccoloba, Triplaris,* nance (*Byrsonima*), the dye-plant *Bixa,* hog-plum (*Spondias*), and other plants. After a year or more, seedlings of

forest trees begin to appear in the ground layer: *Tabebuia, Bombacopsis, Sterculia, Albizzia, Bursera,* and so on. This stage lasts for some years, until the trees break through the tangle of shrubs and creepers and form a canopy which shades out many of the shrubs, and the many creepers of the morning glory, legume, dogbane, gourd, and other families are replaced by a moderate growth of woody lianes. The same or similar secondary vegetations may readily be observed along roads and around the edges of fields.

In some of the higher forests, the presence of certain plants attests to the former presence of dwelling sites, field borders, or groves of fruit trees. There exist in some spots high concentrations of sapodilla (*Achras*) as in the Maya area, as well as of another tree with edible fruit, *Licania, Attalea* palms, and the coconut near the coasts. Abandoned banana plantations survive as well. *Castilla,* whose sap provides a kind of rubber, may represent another planted tree. In the Nicoya Peninsula, hedgerows of pineapple-like *Bromelia pinguin* frequently border the roads; there are also numerous places where more or less linear patches of this plant have maintained themselves after the forest returned. Clusters of fruit trees like *Achras sapodilla, A. sapota,* cashew (*Anacardium occidentale*), custard-apple (*Annona reticulata*) and hog-plum (*Spondias lutea*), as well as of other useful species probably not native in these forests—cannonball-tree (*Crescentia cujete*), frangipani (*Plumeria rubra*), coral tree (*Erythrina* sp.), and *Guazuma ulmifolia* (cacao family)—can often be encountered in the forest, usually in flat sites on hillsides in the vicinity of streams, that is, in places where dwellings were probably once situated.

Much of the lower floodplain of the Tempisque River, which separates the Nicoya Peninsula from the rest of Guanacaste Province, has a cover of grassland in which stand isolated small trees less than

247

10 m. high. The same formation extends beyond the river to the north, covering a large portion of the *Llanos* for which the province is noted. Almost the only trees, on the Nicoya side, are *Curatella*, *Byrsonima*, and *Acacia* spp. Across the Tempisque, however, these typical savanna species give way rather soon to oaks.[20]

The savanna develops on level surfaces of volcanic dust which cover the plains. On the terraces of the Tempisque, and in barrancas, a forest vegetation not unlike that described for Nicoya occurs, and in the immediate vicinity of the Tempisque and its main tributaries swamp forests grow, as well as mangrove from the Gulf of Nicoya up as far as the tides reach. The savanna, extending up to the Nicaraguan border and to the edge of an oak forest, undoubtedly depends at least in part on the local edaphic situation, for it is found almost exclusively on the areas of heavy accumulation of whitish, powdery volcanic dust, which when wet forms an impervious mass. Grass vegetation also covers the very steep slopes of some volcanic hills near the coast. Both the grassland of the hills and the savannas of Guanacaste have probably been maintained, if not originally developed, by the effects of grazing and burning. No other grassland except pastures frequently and laboriously cleared, and no such combination of grass and isolated small trees, can be found in Guanacaste except where cattle are run on these grasslands, which are burned over each year, and which lie on volcanic materials.

Seasonal Formations in Chiapas

A similar seasonal vegetation covers much of the western and southern slope of Central America, and has been heavily under the influence of man for a long time.

Very brief accounts of the vegetation are available by Griscom (1926) for Nicaragua, Yuncker (1945) for Honduras, and Standley (1926) and Kovar (1945) for El Salvador. Lauer (1956) has published a study of the vegetation of El Salvador, and Johannessen (1963) has treated in detail the savannas of central Honduras, both stressing the role of man in altering the distribution of vegetation types. In general, besides the encroachment of cultivation and the development of secondary vegetations, the savanna and perhaps some of the formations of the seasonal series seem to have spread at the expense of other kinds of cover where human action has been effective. Steyermark (1950) and Standley and Steyermark (1945) describe the situation in Pacific Guatemala.

In the study of the Chiapas vegetation by Miranda (1952–53), the types described as "selva alta subdecídua" include some associations of the seasonal series. The most extensive is the one in which the guanacaste tree (*Enterolobium cyclocarpum*) is characteristic. These forests, occupying deep soils in the interior basin and on the Pacific slope, have been cleared over very wide areas and are subject to much interference by men, fire, and cattle. The guanacaste itself, as well as the once-sacred *Ceiba*, are often spared in clearing, and their presence marks the former extension of the forest, after clearing has destroyed it. The forest is partly deciduous and has three stories.[21]

---

[20] The presence of oaks in this area, so near sea level, is quite startling, and even such an authority as Standley (1937) asserted that there are no oaks in Guanacaste, though Wercklé (1909) mentioned them.

[21] In the upper story, 25–40 m. high, are *Enterolobium, Licania, Astronium, Calycophyllum, Lafoensia, Albizzia, Brosimum, Cedrela, Ficus, Sideroxylon, Cybistax, Sapium, Couepia, Poeppigia*, and *Ceiba*. The second story, at 6–15 m., contains *Trichilia* spp., *Coccoloba, Annona, Swietenia, Bursera, Psidium, Inga, Exostema, Styrax, Genipa*, and *Karwinskia*. Below are *Ardisia, Eugenia*, and other small trees and shrubs.

Near streams may occur *Hymenaea, Andira, Nectandra, Ficus, Calophyllum, Brosimum*, and *Tabebuia*. Old secondary stands in this forest consist of such genera as *Luehea, Spondias, Cordia, Cecropia, Daphnopsis, Cochlospermum, Acrocomia*,

248

FIG. 12—SAVANNA GRASSLAND WITH CLUMPS OF SEMIDECIDUOUS RAIN FOREST
This photo was taken near Jaltenango, central valley of Chiapas (600 m. elevation). The tree species include totoposte (*Licania arborea*) and guapinol (*Hymenaea courbaril*). (Photo by F. Miranda.)

Two-storied deciduous forests (*selva baja decídua*) also occur widely in Chiapas. These forests, too, have been subject to much human interference. They are frequently burned, and often grazed by cattle, with the result that a very considerable selective effect is applied to their composition. On the Pacific slope of the Sierra Madre, up to 750 and 1250 m., where the precipitation totals 1200 mm. annually, the two-storied forest reaches about 12 m.[22]

There exist a number of associations marked by thorny shrubs, for which a secondary origin must again be suspected. Typical shrub vegetations of this kind are "aguanal," made up of almost pure stands of dense *Gymnopodium* (buckwheat family), a tall shrub branching from the ground and reaching 5–8 m.; "guajal," a secondary as-

and *Godmania*. A number of different associations in which many of the same genera are present characterize the drier places. *Poeppigia* and *Astronium* dominate one such association, and *Licania* and *Poeppigia* another.

[22] In the upper story are *Alvaradoa, Heliocarpus, Lysiloma, Fraxinus, Haematoxylon, Ceiba, Cochlospermum, Bursera* spp., *Pistacia, Bumelia, Gyrocarpus, Piscidia, Swietenia, Ficus,* and *Zuelania.* The 1–8-m. understory contains *Byrsonima, Com-*

ocladia, Trema, Bauhinia, Jacquinia, Ximenia, Xylosma, Stemmadenia, Psychotria, Cassia, Ardisia, Euphorbia, and *Acacia,* as well as many lianes. In the more humid barrancas, the forest reaches 15 or 20 m. Here it consists of *Bucida, Euphorbia, Pistacia, Lonchocarpus, Hauya, Colubrina, Ficus, Heliocarpus, Cochlospermum, Ceiba, Bursera,* and *Erythroxylon. Leucaena, Lysiloma, Maytenus, Bernardia, Exostema, Dalbergia, Liabum, Hyperbaena, Bourreria, Thevetia, Cordia* and so forth make up the understory, and lianes are plentiful. Several variants of this barranca vegetation occur.

249

FIG. 13—LOW DECIDUOUS SEASONAL FOREST NEAR PUERTO JUAREZ, QUINTANA ROO
Represented are the palm *Pseudo-phoenix sargentiana*, the tall lileaceous *Beaucarnea pliabilis, Bursera* (?), and many low shrubs. Disturbance by man (or hurricane?) is evident. (Photo by F. Miranda.)

sociation of the legume *Leucaena*; a dense secondary brushland of the bignonia *Tecoma* and the legumes *Cassia* and *Acacia* spp.; and cactus wastes with *Melocactus*, the cycad *Dioon*, and other strange plants. A great deal of the lowland in Chiapas is covered with these and similar deciduous thorn vegetations, or thorn woodland.

Savannas typified by grassland with isolated individuals of *Byrsonima, Curatella,* and *Acacia,* and, near the coasts, *Crescentia,* occur sporadically throughout the Chiapas lowlands, especially where human influence has been long and heavy. The savanna usually serves as pasture, though not a rich one, and is subjected to annual burning. Islands of forest commonly appear in the midst of the savanna, and these *mogotes* testify that the present vegetation is induced (fig. 12). Many species of the seasonal forest formations occur in such islands of trees on the savanna. There is, according to Miranda, no observable difference between the soils of the savanna areas and those of nearby forest land, and continued pressure of fire and grazing, as well as possible former cultivation, appear to account for the occurrence, or perhaps the tremendous spread out from small natural occurrences, of this formation.

Certain shrub formations tend to occur in much disturbed situations in the lowlands. There are large more or less pure stands of palms (*Scheelea, Sabal, Chrysophyllum,* or *Brahea*) in low lands parallel to and not far from the Pacific coast, as well as in some of the interior river valleys. These *palmares* seem also to have to do with some disturbance, and are allied to the savanna as part of the same seasonal swamp formation series.

It is not inconceivable that the extensive shrub, savanna, and palm cover in the coastal lowlands and the low-lying areas of stream valleys may be due not only to burning and pasturage since the coming of the Spaniards, but also to ancient concentrations of agricultural populations in these zones. Both in Mexico and in Central America, the early accounts mention large settlements, and rich agriculture in the lowlands, often in the same places where only cattle were raised during colonial times and there is little farming, except just along the rivers, even now.

Possibly the prevalent spiny brush, grassland, and palm forest of today mark out the gardens of ancient Indian farmers. Perhaps only a genuine eradication of forest vegetation at some time in the remote past suffices to explain the radically different lowland vegetation. Burning where it occurs in forest, or even in brushland, today does not

Fig. 14—LOW DECIDUOUS SEASONAL FOREST DOMINATED BY CUACHALALA
(JULIANIA ADSTRINGENS), BETWEEN TEHUANTEPEC AND JUCHITAN, OAXACA
The photograph was taken in May during the height of the dry season when trees and shrubs
are bare of leaves. (Photo by A. Maya, Instituto de Geografía, Universidad Nacional de México.)

produce large expanses of grass, as far as I have been able to observe (fig. 13).

Even where fields have indubitably been cleared, though, the brush and finally perhaps the forest will return if burning is not practiced. I have seen plentiful stone walls marking out old fields now submerged in the thick growth of some of the hills of central Chiapas, around Venustiano Carranza. Given a chance, the forest will progress beyond the stage where even burning will not destroy it. In the taller tree stands, a fire sweeps through and leaves the large trees alive, and the ground rapidly becomes re-vegetated. In some places in the Rio Blanco area of Chiapas, when the oak forest of the montane series has been destroyed, lowland formations of seasonal type seem to have succeeded them in some

of the same spots, probably since late colonial times. Even pine forests occurred within the memory of persons now living in places now covered with savanna or secondary seasonal woodland.

Central Mexican Seasonal Formations

Along the transect of the Balsas and Papaloapan basins (Miranda, 1947, 1948), at about 18°N., the structurally more impoverished and climatically less exigent formations of the seasonal series preponderate. In the lower parts of the Balsas region, at 800–1200 and sometimes 1800 m., the vegetation has undergone such thorough transformation at the hands of man that secondary associations are widespread. Herbaceous cover of weedy *Martynia, Encelia, Tithonia,* and other such genera on abandoned land

251

FIG. 15—LOW DECIDUOUS SEASONAL FOREST
The vegetation is composed chiefly of tall columnar cactus (*Cephalocereus mezcalensis*); izote, or yucca (*Yucca periculosa*); the flowering shrub, cacaloxochitl (*Plumeria rubra*); and many deciduous trees. Near Izucar de Matamoros, Puebla, at 1450 m. elevation. (Photo by F. Miranda.)

is eventually followed by a spiny brush of *Acacia farnesiana*. The former vegetation probably comprised two associations, in which the lugumes guamuchil (*Pithecolobium dulce*) and mesquite (*Prosopis juliflora*), respectively, were dominant. Along streams still grows a kind of gallery forest 10–30 m. high and semideciduous, with Mexican bald cypress (*Taxodium*), willow (*Salix*), and wild fig (*Ficus*). The barrancas carry a partly deciduous forest sometimes as high as 20 m., with *Brosimum*, *Trophis*, *Ficus*, *Trema*, *Cesearia*, *Licania*,

Inga, Enterolobium, Bursera, and *Celtis.* Noting the presence of a number of tropical rain forest species, Miranda (1947) suggests that this forest may represent a relic of a formerly much greater extension of the optimum formation.

All the way up into the northern Pacific lowlands of Mexico grows the low forest called by Miranda "monte mojino." The main association in the Balsas area is "cuajiotal," made up of many resin- and tannin-bearing plants, with *Ceiba, Juliania, Lysiloma,* numerous species of *Bursera, Ipomoea, Comocladia, Actinocheita,* and *Cyrtocarpa* in the top story reaching 4–10 m. and forming a more or less closed canopy, which is deciduous (fig. 14). Succulents are relatively abundant, and the second story consists of spiny leguminous shrubs and small trees interlaced with creepers. On wetter slopes grows an association in which the legume *Conzattia* is prominent. On karst, some of the same species, along with *Cochlospermum, Bombax, Swietenia,* and *Sideroxylon* form a characteristic association. On nearly level upland a poisonous cashew, *Pseudomodingium* commonly occurs, and on very rocky land are stands of ocotillo (*Fouquieria*).

The approach to lands of increasing aridity brings a growing proportion of succulents in the vegetation. In the arid slopes of the basin low spiny vegetation of *Castela, Schaefferia, Gochnatia, Forchhammeria,* and *Cercidium* grows, in the midst of which cacti are plentiful and varied in form. There are many different associations of spiny shrubs, as well as "forests" of spiny columnar cactus *Cephalocereus*.

In the upper Papaloapan drainage, west of the Continental Divide, in Oaxaca and southern Puebla, seasonal formations continue to prevail in the arid basins. *Cuicatlan,* at an elevation of 564 m., has an average annual precipitation of only 298 mm., and a mean temperature of 24.5°C.; Ixtlan de Juarez, at 1886 m., gets about 1000 mm. and has an annual mean temperature of 15.6°C., Tehuacan, 1676 m. in elevation, receives 476 mm. of precipitation, and has a mean annual temperature of 18.6°C.

In the limestone area around Tehuacan, thin-soiled rocky areas may have a vegetation in which *Yucca*, and the cacti *Cephalocereus* and *Lemaireocereus*, 4–6 m. tall, stand over a spiny shrub story 0.5–1.5 m. high. Succulents such as *Euphorbia*, *Acanthothamnus*, *Pedilanthus*, many cacti and *Agave* are well represented (fig. 15). Dense pure stands of ocotillo (*Fouquieria*), *Castela*, *Agave*, barrel cactus (*Echinocactus*), and *Ephedra* occur here and there. Barrancas in limestone country may hold a tree or shrub association.

Wind erosion markedly affects the soils of this area. The secondary vegetation of the grasses *Opizia* and *Distichlis*, with such halophile herbs as *Maytenus*, *Lycium*, *Antiphytum*, *Flaveria*, and *Viguiera*, can hardly protect the topsoil. The original cover may have been very different from that of the present, and Miranda (1948) suggests that the local climax may have been a mesquite forest of *Prosopis juliflora*.

Around Cuicatlan, where sandstones occur, hillsides below 900 m. carry a low, spiny deciduous wood less than 8 m. high. It is composed of an upper story of paloverde (*Cercidium*), mesquite (*Prosopis*), *Bursera* spp., *Chlorophora*, *Ceiba*, *Cyrtocarpa*, and *Juliania*, with an understory of spiny shrubs, few herbs, and many kinds of cacti. The barrancas in which water occasionally flows may have a vegetation of shrubby *Chlorophora*, *Podopterus*, *Zizyphus*, and *Agonandra*. The vegetation on hillsides between 900 and 1400 m. has already been described in connection with the montane formations (p. 242).

The understory plants of the forests just mentioned very often form a spiny brushland by themselves, .05–2 m. high, with many Leguminosae. Sometimes there are few spines, but a tangle of twisted, inter-

lacing branches instead. Cacti and agaves figure prominently, and there is often a sparse grass cover on the ground.[23]

Most of the basin lands of the Balsas and Papaloapan have long held dense settlements, and the present state of their vegetation reflects very profound alterations through human agency. Undoubtedly the pronounced aridity in this area makes the survival of vegetation all the more precarious and the mark of man more permanent.

Deserts of Northern Mexico

The seasonal formation runs northward along the Pacific coast of Mexico into the desert. A very similar desert occurs as well in the northern areas east of the Sierra Madre. Shreve (1934) has described the progression of vegetation types in the Pacific coastal lowlands. Associations resembling those described for the Balsas area occur up to about the Rio Mayo in southern Sonora where, between latitudes 27° and 28°N., a very rapid transition occurs. The thorn woodland to this point consists of trees up to 10 m. in height, with the dominant canopy at 7–8 m.; *Acacia macracantha* is more abundant, and the fish poison *Ichthyomethia*, paloverde (*Cercidium*), tree morning glory (*Ipomoea*), jujube (*Zizyphus*), a columnar cactus (*Pachycereus*), mesquite (*Prosopis*), *Ceiba*, *Cassia*, and a madder *Coutarea* are associated with it. Many plants, such as *Lonchocarpus*, *Bauhinia*, *Bunchosia*, *Caesalpinia*, *Croton*, dwarf palms, epiphytic *Tillandsia*, and terrestrial bromeliads occur up to the transition but no farther.

[23] Other common associations are stands of *Lemaireocereus*, groves of columnar *Cephalocereus*, and *Acacia cymbispina* wastes on exhausted lands. *Acacia unijuga*, growing to 15 m. and with an understory of *Capsicum*, *Diospyros*, *Agonandra*, *Sapium*, *Elaeodendron*, *Zizyphus*, *Thevetia*, and *Vallesia*, forms an association in dry streambeds. *Ficus* and *Taxodium* grow near the banks of streams where the water table is high. On stream banks are found thickets of *Astianthus*, *Salix*, and, where the ground is rocky, *Baccharis*.

The precipitation at Mazatlan, in Sinaloa, is recorded as 722 mm. annually. Annual rainfall decreases northward, and its variability greatly increases. Rainfall near the central coast of Sonora ranges from 250 to 375 mm. per year, and drops off to 50–125 mm. in the Colorado Delta. The concentration of precipitation in the summer months prevails in the south, but the occurrence of rain spreads over most of the year in the north. Frosts are a control of vegetation in this region; the frost line lies somewhere around latitude 26°N., near the southern boundary of Sonora. Northward of the transition zone, the vegetation consists of widely spaced xeromorphic shrubs and abundant succulents, 4–5 m. high, with *Acacia macracantha* still most abundant.[24]

Still farther north, on the lower Colorado River, creosote bush (*Larrea*) shares dominance with burro bush (*Franseria dumosa*). Little of the surface is actually shaded by the crowns of the shrubs. On sands grows sparse *Hilaria* grass, and in stream beds a thin thicket of paloverde, desert ironwood (*Olneya*), mesquite, and *Parosela*, with an understory of *Acacia, Lycium,* and *Hymenocea.*

In the extreme northwest of Baja California occurs an outlier of California chaparral.

A more extensive study of the vegetation of Sonora by Shreve (1951) distinguishes several topographic areas in the desert. It is characteristic of the desert thorn forest and cactus scrub that biotic controls are virtually absent, and each species grows exactly where climatic and soil conditions are most favorable to it, so that a mosaic of small pure stands of different plants is often encountered where relief is diverse. In the area distinguished as the "Arizona Upland," with relatively low precipitation and frosts, there is a taller and denser vegetation than on the lower Colorado. Creosote bush (*Larrea*) dominates, with many associates, including plentiful cacti and perennial grasses. In the foothills, upward from 1000 m. in the north of Sonora and from sea level in southern Sinaloa, the desert meets oaks and grassland on the east. The precipitation in these areas is mostly over 500 mm. yearly. Trees and shrubs here form dense stands, with few cacti, and some palms and grass. The Sonoran and Baja Californian coasts of the Gulf of California carry a vegetation marked by the presence of odd trees with swollen trunks, of the genera *Bursera, Jatropha,* and *Idria.* Desert ironwood, paloverde, ocotillo, and mesquite are common, and much of the shrub is deciduous. Succulents are sometimes lacking. Central Baja California contains the Vizcaino Desert, in which leaf succulents are prominent. The plants are striking and peculiar in the more favorable sites, but poor elsewhere. Representative genera are *Agave, Dudleya, Franseria, Yucca, Idria, Pachycormus, Pachycereus, Vizcainoa,* and *Glaucothea*; saltbush (*Atriplex*) and desert thorn (*Lycium*) form pure stands on poor soil. In the southern part of the peninsula, the Magdalena Desert, resembling that of mainland Sonora, gives way to a tropical thorn woodland.

The river valleys of Sonora and Sinaloa once carried forests, or at least high dense thickets of mesquite, but in many places these have been replaced by irrigated fields of cotton, barley, and alfalfa. The introduced tamarisk (*Tamarix*) tree appears widely along roads and around fields and dwellings.

In the foothills of the Sierra Madre Occidental, the desert borders to the south on

[24] In stream ways there are thickets with *Acacia, Guazuma, Ichthyomethia, Pithecolobium, Vitex, Coursetia, Haematoxylon;* the cacti *Pachycereus, Rathbunia,* and *Opuntia;* and shrubs such as *Lantana, Euphorbia, Karwinskia, Cordia, Mimosa, Cassia, Paullinia,* and *Vallesia.* Above latitude 30°N., *Larrea divaricata* is dominant in the shrub vegetation near the coast, with *Olneya, Cercidium, Prosopis, Celtis, Condalia, Encelia, Lycium, Lemaireocereus, Acacia, Jatropha, Fouquieria, Pachycereus, Opuntia,* and *Guaiacum.* Cacti are scarce, and the trees and shrubs are mostly deciduous.

254

Fɪɢ. 16—GRAMA GRASSLAND IN HIGH PLAINS (1800 M.) NORTH OF SAN LUIS POTOSI

Mesquite (*Prosopis*) and huisache (*Acacia*) shrubs and scattered cacti (*Opuntia*) are conspicuous associates. The formation, often called "steppe," is widespread in northern Mexico in areas receiving between 250 and 500 mm. of precipitation annually. (Photo by R. C. West.)

subtropical thorn woodland; on the east, at 750 m., it abuts on oak forests of *Quercus chihuahuensis;* in northeastern Sonoran river valleys, it meets a sod grassland of *Bouteloua* spp., dotted with isolated individuals of *Prosopis* and *Acacia*. Across the Sierra Madre to the east the desert vegetation reappears.

The *Bouteloua* or grama grasslands extending into northeastern Sonora belong to a widely distributed element of the vegetation of the northern part of Mexico, appearing on both sides of the mountains (fig. 16). Shreve (1939–40) has outlined the distribution and character of the Chihuahua formations. A large part of the state consists of level *bajadas*, in which a shrub cover of creosote bush alone prevails extensively.

Mesquite on the deeper soils, and elsewhere *Flourensia*, may accompany *Larrea*. On higher slopes there grows a taller and more varied vegetation with succulents, palmlike yuccas, and shrubs.[25] In the arroyos may be found trees 5–6 m. high, including mesquite, *Acacia*, hackberry (*Celtis*), and *Condalia*, with a shrub understory of *Rhus, Berberis, Porlieria, Chilopsis*, and *Acacia*. In the basins at higher altitude, around 1200–1500 m., is a low, sparse *Hilaria* grassland with islands of creosote bush, *Acacia*, and tarbush (*Flourensia*), or patches of mesquite or saltbush; cacti are few. Limestone areas in the west of Chihuahua carry a

[25] This vegetation contains the genera *Dasylirion, Fouquieria, Opuntia, Yucca, Agave, Coldenia, Euphorbia, Parthenium*, and *Jatropha*.

255

Fɪɢ. 17—DESERT FORMATION IN THE PARRAS BASIN, CENTRAL COAHUILA
In foreground is creosote bush (*Larrea divaricata*), *Agave lechuguilla,* and the tall, spindly
ocotillo (*Fouquieria splendens*). (Photo by R. C. West.)

shrub cover less than a meter high, in which *Acacia vernicosa* is dominant. It grades into a grassland on deeper loams, in which widely spaced shrubs occur. Around 1525 m. appears a zone in which shrub and grassland associations are interrupted by oak filled streamways. The *Bouteloua* grassland of this zone has been strongly affected in places by grazing, and weeds of the aster family, such as *Gutierrezia, Haplopappus,* and *Verbesina,* have invaded it.

Oak forest begins around 2150–2300 m., but the distribution of forest and grassland seems to be controlled primarily by soil conditions rather than simply by altitude, or by the climate, which is similar throughout. The oak forests are rather open and partly deciduous. They develop best on broad flat plains. These forests are rich in grasses and in shrubs that also occur in the grassland. An understory of *Rhus, Ceanothus, Mimosa, Cowania, Rhamnus, Bouvardia,* and perennial herbs is present.

Pine forests grow at elevations above 2150 m. on the eastern slope, and from 1800 m. on the western. They cover much of the mountainous part of the state of Chihuahua.[26]

According to Muller's (1947) description, the formations of Chihuahua extend eastward into Coahuila (fig. 17). Creosote bush, tarbush (*Flourensia*), *Acacia,* ocotillo, and mesquite dominate widely, and the associated species are similar to those of neighboring Chihuahua. The zonation of

[26] Many species are found: *P. apacheca, P. chihuahuana, P. cembroides, P. arizonica, P. ayacahuite,* and others. In the pine zone, *Quercus* spp., *Alnus, Populus,* and *Arbutus* occupy certain specialized habitats or grow among the pines. *Pseudotsuga, Cupressus,* and *Juniperus* likewise occur.

256

vegetation on the higher mountains resembles that described above, with grassland, chaparral and dense shrub, and forest belts. Within the grassland and desert areas of northern Mexico tall cottonwoods (*Populus*), walnut (*Juglans*), and bald cypress (*Taxodium mucronatum*) line channels of permanent streams.

The eastern portions of Coahuila exhibit another kind of vegetation, which extends down to the Gulf coast and northward into Texas. It consists of a dense shrub cover rich in species, with plentiful thorns.[27] Many of the genera occur in the tropical thorn woodland, and this vegetation may be closely related to that found so widely farther south, though it grows under a much more marked seasonal climate with which frosts are associated.

The cactus scrub and thorn woodland of the seasonal and related formations series fill a very large area in central and northern Mexico. The vegetations on the east of the Sierra Madre Occidental, though similar in places to those of the western lowlands, do not reflect the same controls as the seasonal series, and may best be considered a southernward extension of North American prairie and arid formations, subject to frost. In much of this area the variety of environmental situations over short distances is very considerable, and the pattern of vegetation distribution shows a corresponding complexity. The seasonal formations come up against both montane vegetations and the frost-conditioned grasslands and brushlands of middle latitude types. Within a single highland basin in central Mexico, an ephemeral saline lake may occupy the lowest spot, being surrounded by halophile shrubs, around which occurs a grassland with shrubs. A much disturbed stand of thorn woodland, or a secondary wasteland in which cacti, the introduced Peruvian

pepper tree (*Schinus molle*), large yucca (*Yucca australis*), and casahuate (*Ipomea murucoides*) are prominent, will surround the settlements and alternate with cornfields. Beyond grow less disturbed thorn woodland and, higher on the hillsides, oaks followed by pine. The oak and pine forests of central Mexico have been greatly depleted since the Spanish conquest. Thorny shrubs and low trees, such as mesquite and acacia, as well as cacti, have invaded extensive areas of cut-over forest and overgrazed grasslands within the central plateau. In slightly more northerly areas, the interfluves may carry a sparse grass cover, with isolated giant cacti, and thorny shrubs and small trees in the dry watercourses. Often where there has been a long history of woodcutting and cattle or goats have grazed heavily in the past, the spaces between the occasional cacti are simply bare. The former cover of such places may be indicated by the pitiful clusters of unarmed shrubs and grasses cowering in the protective radius of the long-thorned cacti, out of reach of animals.

The destruction of the desert vegetation by men, goats and cattle has proceeded remarkably far in northern Mexico. I have elsewhere described (1955) the attrition to which the desert is subject in Coahuila. Around the old mining centers, wood for fuel and mine timbers began to be cut in early colonial days, and much of the land around the old mining towns has been left barren. Currently, a great deal of the woody vegetation is being cut for charcoal. Mesquite thickets, which used to fill the more humid washes, have vanished wherever they could be cut. Some of the desert plants, like *Agave lechuguilla*, guayule (*Parthenium argentatum*), and candelilla (*Euphorbia antisyphilitica*) and *Yucca* spp. are harvested in quantity for economic uses. Goats graze the drier areas and remove much of the cover. The bean pods of mesquite, the fleshy basal leaves and stocks of agave, the fruit of the yucca, and the fruit

[27] Genera well represented are *Acacia, Leucophyllum, Porlieria, Karwinskia, Cordia, Schaefferia, Cercidium, Lippia, Parkinsonia, Castela, Colubrina,* and *Lantana.*

257

of the prickly-pear cactus (*Opuntia* spp.) have been notable foods for desert dwellers of northern Mexico, particularly in aboriginal times.

DRY EVERGREEN FORMATIONS

(1) *Dry rain forest*: Three evergreen tree stories up to 35 m. Upper story canopy. (2) *Dry evergreen woodland*: Three evergreen tree stories, with emergents to 30 m. and canopy at 12–20 m. (3) *Dry evergreen thicket*: Two tree stories with occasional emergents, and canopy at 6–12 m. (4) *Evergreen bushland*: Evergreen shrubs or small trees, under 6 m. (5) *Rock pavement vegetation*: Low scattered growth among rocks.

The dry evergreen formations occur in special edaphic situations on the eastern side of Middle America, in areas where seasonal influences are poorly developed. The character and placement of these formations in Middle America must be regarded as more doubtful than those of the other series heretofore discussed, and the assignment of the poorer east slope vegetations to this category rests on theoretical grounds rather than on actual inspection.

Aridity induced by particular soil structures, often accentuated by long-continued burning, seems to exert the strongest control on the distribution of the less tall and rich vegetation of the eastern side of the region. Though these dry evergreen formations sometimes resemble the savanna or thorn woodland formations of the seasonal swamp and seasonal series, they contain a rather different assortment of genera and live in quite dissimilar conditions, in which seasonal inundation plays no part. Secondary vegetations occur widely, and in some places, particularly in northern Yucatan, it is difficult to distinguish between natural dry evergreen formations and successional growth. Lundell (1934) has given an account of the peculiarly difficult distributional problem in Yucatan. Although disturbance has so greatly altered the vegetation of Yucatan that its original structure cannot be positively known, it seems likely that the trend of structure from the deep tropical rain forests of the southern interior runs

in accordance with Beard's dry evergreen formation series, through dry rain forest (attested also by Lundell [1937] for Peten), toward an evergreen bushland, which in this area is rich in succulents and so tends to resemble the thorn woodland and cactus scrub in appearance. In British Honduras, where a considerable element in the flora is reported by Standley (1936, p. 53) to show affinities with that of northern Yucatan, extensive pine woods exist, and it is not impossible that similar growth once occurred in the northern strip of the Yucatan Peninsula that now bears only brush.

The pine woods of British Honduras occur on more or less level lands north of the Belize River, and on hills—the "Mountain Pine Ridges"—to 1000 m., on siliceous soils. The mean annual temperature in the lowlands is around 26°C., and the precipitation ranges upward from about 1250 mm., in the south of the colony. Pine woods alternating with "savanna" occur over 15 per cent of the area of the colony, almost exclusively on sandy soils. High rain forest grows on soils with more abundant clays and on alluvium.

The identification of the pine woods and grasslands of the east coast of Central America as a vicariant of Beard's dry evergreen formations, rather than with true edaphic-climatic savannas, is proposed here because the situations conforming to the description of genuine savanna habitats carry a different sort of vegetation. Around lagoons along the coast, where the land is periodically flooded, as well as burned, grows a treeless tussock grass association. On inland sites where there is some seasonal waterlogging of the soil, sedges, and in somewhat better-drained places grasses, form the cover. The "dry" season from February to May is not completely dry, for there is usually some rain in every month, and the extreme seasonal regime common on the western side of Middle America simply does not exist here.

The *Pinus caribaea* "savanna" of British

Fig. 18—*PINUS CARIBAEA*–SAVANNA, CARIBBEAN COAST OF NICARAGUA, NEAR
THE PEARL LAGOON NORTH OF BLUEFIELDS.
(Photo by J. J. Parsons.)

Honduras resembles closely the pine woods of Florida and other southern states of the United States. It grows on very porous sandy material in company with oaks, sandpaper tree (*Curatella*), and nance (*Byrsonima*), which also occur in true savannas elsewhere. Shrubs are abundant, and there are many herbs of West Indian affinities.

The same vegetation is widespread farther south, on the Caribbean coasts of Honduras and Nicaragua (fig. 18). Here again the "savanna," as described by J. J. Parsons (1955) grows on soils derived from quartz gravels, which extend 480 km. along the coast from Cape Camaron to Bluefields and as far as 160 km. inland, though the pine belt is mostly about 48 km. wide. Where large rivers traverse the pine country, large trees of rain forest type form galleries along their banks. The precipitation in this area is very abundant, and quite sufficient to support tropical rain forest. At Bluefields it averages 3750 mm. annually, and it is everywhere above 2500 mm. There is no dry month at all at Bluefields, on the southern border of the pine belt, and though the months from February to May are relatively dry more to the north, there is seldom a month in which some rain does not fall. The boundary with the rain forests is sharp, and conforms closely to soil distribution. Even within the "savannas" occur islands of shrub and palmetto vegetation. But in these areas, as in British Honduras, lands which are seasonally inundated do not carry a pine vegetation, but rather are treeless.

According to Parsons, it is probable that fire has played a great part in the development and maintenance of the pine woods. Former large-scale agricultural use of the land is unlikely, and the simple coincidence of pine woods with soil boundaries is neither perfectly complete nor sufficient in

259

itself to explain the presence of this vegetation. It has even been suggested that certain kinds of disturbance in this area—particularly old Indian camps—might have caused pine and grass to be replaced by the restricted stands of broadleaf trees observed here and there.

The dry evergreen formations elsewhere in tropical America that have been the basis of Beard's concept of dry evergreen formation series have clearly been quite dissimilar to the pine woods of Central America. It is plain that the Middle American pine "savannas" do not conform climatically to the type of the seasonal swamp savanna formation, however, and that they are closely related to other edaphic factors than inundations, as the dry evergreen series is by definition. Rather than count these pine woods and grasslands as typical members of a dry evergreen formation, it seems more reasonable nevertheless to suppose that they, like the deciduous forests that intrude in the montane series of Chiapas, represent a vicariant formation with distant affinities. The pine woods and grasslands, in other words, replace some missing member of the dry evergreen series on the east coast of Middle America. Like the Chiapas deciduous sweet gum (*Liquidambar*) forests, they would be quite at home in the southern United States; in Middle America they are a curiosity of plant distribution.

Throughout interior Guatemala, Honduras, and Nicaragua, in all of which areas the vegetations are poorly known, exist places where the expectable tropical rain forest, or the montane or seasonal formations, are interrupted by patches of less luxuriant vegetation. The actual composition of these vegetations, which are sometimes known as "desert" (e.g., in central Guatemala), and sometimes as "savanna," is doubtful. Probably they differ greatly among themselves. In all likelihood the greater part of them represents secondary growth, for they occur in what must have been heavily populated areas since ancient

times. A long strip of such vegetation cuts through the middle of Guatemala along the bottom of the Motagua Valley. As described by Standley and Steyermark (1945), this does indeed conform to the definition of desert, i.e., thorn woodland and cactus scrub. In southeastern Guatemala occur patches of chaparral-grassland with plants of South American affinities. The valleys of the Honduran interior, according to Yuncker (1945), as around Olanchito and Comayagua, possess similar vegetations, but they are apparently locations in areas of seasonal climate, influenced by topography. The actual climates of interior Guatemala, Honduras, and Nicaragua would have to be more fully understood before the possibility of true seasonal vegetations growing on the Atlantic side of the drainage divide could be ruled out. It is probably human interference, though, that has had most to do with the origin of these seeming anomalies of distribution. The dry evergreen may simply stand for anciently disturbed cover throughout most of its range in Middle America, as in fact much of the seasonal series and the savanna do. The consequences of human interference, including burning and grazing, may well include a reduction of the differences between vegetations of different climatic and even soil regions; when man's control becomes predominant, the natural boundaries fade, and the distribution of various forms of plant cover most clearly reflects human treatment of the land.

SWAMP AND SEASONAL SWAMP FORMATIONS

A. (1) *Swamp forest*: Single tree story less than 20 m. high, with buttresses, stilt roots or pneumatophores. Inundated by fresh water. (1) *Mangrove forest*: Single tree story less than 20 m. high, with stilt roots or pneumatophores. Inundated by tidal salt water. (2) *Swamp woodland*: Single open tree stratum 3–12 m. high, bordering fresh water. (3) *Swamp thicket*: Dense woody shrub growth, submerged at high water. (4) *Herbaceous swamp*.
B. (1) *Seasonal swamp forest*: Two- or three-storied forest, with emergents at 15–25 m. and canopy at 9–15 m. Palms few, or predominant. (2) *Seasonal swamp woodland*: Two tree stories with emergent palms to 18 m., and canopy at 9–15

FIG. 19—MANGROVE SWAMP, GULF OF FONSECA, HONDURAS
The stilt roots of the solid stand of red mangrove (*Rhizophora*) form an almost impenetrable barrier to human movement. (Photo by R. C. West.)

m. (3) *Seasonal swamp thicket*: One tree story forming a thick tangle, with or without palms predominating. (4) *Savanna*: Grasses dominant. Shrubs, small trees, and sometimes palms present but scattered.

The areas occupied by swamp and seasonal swamp formations are relatively restricted, and descriptions of their vegetation are correspondingly few. P. H. Allen (1956) treats briefly the swamp forest of the Golfo Dulce area of southern Costa Rica. In this forest, floristic composition is varied and the boundaries among different swamp formations, and between the swamp formations and the lowland tropical rain forest, are unclear. Allen noted three associations. The first, dominated by *Pterocarpus officinalis* and *Carapa Slateri*, adjoins the lowland forest. Another, with *Pterocarpus officinalis* and *Mora oleifera*, occurs just behind mangrove woodlands, away

261

FIG. 20—SAVANNA OF LOW TREES (*CURATELLA AMERICANA*) AND GRASS SOUTH OF TUXTLA GUTIERREZ IN THE VALLEY OF CHIAPAS, 550 M. ELEVATION (Photo by F. Miranda.)

from the shore. A *Symphonia globulifera* consociation is found on the edges of herbaceous swamps. Palm swamp, consisting of *Raphia taedigera, Corozo oleifera,* and some of the foregoing trees, is also present. The mangrove woodland (tidal swamp), which retains remarkable uniformity all around the shores of the Pacific (as does the very similar east coast mangrove around the Atlantic), covers great areas of tidal flats and estuarine shores (fig. 19). *Rhizophora* or red mangrove is the principal component, along with *Avicennia* (black mangrove), *Conocarpus, Laguncularia, Hibiscus, Mora, Pelliciera, Pterocarpus,* and the palms *Raphia* and *Corozo.* Herbaceous swamps are composed of grasses and sedges, broad-leaved monocotyledonous herbs, and sometimes ferns, such as *Acrostichum.*

The tidal swamp formations occur on both coasts of Middle America, and for some distance up the lower reaches of the large rivers and their distributaries, as well as in coastal lagoon sites. The arrangement of formations more or less according to local microrelief is notable. On the coastal sands and rocks grows another group of formations, radically unlike those of the swamps and highly specialized for situations of edaphic aridity. These strand and rock vegetations should fall into the dry evergreen series.

The seasonal swamp formations, except for savanna, also have a very limited distribution. Presumably a truly natural savanna would be adjoined by seasonal swamp thicket, and that in turn by seasonal swamp woodland. I have observed such situations in western Costa Rica as well as in southern

Mexico. The Costa Rican instance is discussed in connection with the savanna in a preceding section. In Chiapas, a situation as follows illustrates the seasonal swamp pattern. In the bed of the perennial stream which drains a large basin, giant bald cypress (*Taxodium*) trees stand with their roots in moving water; a thin willow thicket crowds the banks near their trunks. An occasional sycamore (*Platanus*) or fig (*Ficus*), tall and solitary, rises along the bank. Small shallow bodies of still water are ringed by a thick growth of rushes, that is, herbaceous swamp. In the broad area of the basin which is inundated yearly during the high water season but not permanently submerged, a seasonal swamp thicket, consisting of a virtually pure and extremely dense stand of palms about 10 m. high, completely shades the ground. The palms grade into a lower stand with cannonball trees (*Crescentia*), until at last a pure stand of twisted and interlaced *Crescentia* trees under 7 m. high appears. The area beyond this thicket has a cover of grass with isolated small trees, including palms, which extends for a very considerable distance up the limestone hills, and merges into a seasonal forest. It appears in this case (on the Rio San Vicente near the colonial ruins of Copanaguastla, Chiapas) that the kind of clearing and burning to be seen in the

area today must have extended the savanna and associated thickets far beyond their normal edaphic limits (fig. 20).

The normal position of natural, edaphic savanna, as a member of a sequence of formations centering on water bodies or rain-catching depressions, does not characterize most of the vegetations called savannas in Middle America. Most often, though, it may be supposed that disturbance has greatly widened the area of savanna at the expense of some other formation, usually of the seasonal series. In the El General Valley of Costa Rica this is plainly the case. The savanna begins, perfectly legitimately, in the low parts of the valley near a stream that floods during the wet season. It reaches from this "normal" location far up the slopes of the hills, forming an abrupt boundary with a low montane rain forest. In this case, the other formations of the seasonal swamp series are altogether lacking, perhaps because the flooded area is small and the stream may shift from time to time. Disturbance is alone sufficient to explain the presence of a "classical" savanna, with grass, *Curatella*, and *Byrsonima*, in this area. The additional component of shrubs of the Rubiaceae, Melastomaceae, and other typical forest families, which in places even overgrows the grass, accuses human intervention even more strikingly.

REFERENCES

Allen, P. H., 1956
Bartlett, 1935
Beard, 1944, 1955
Cain and Oliveira Castro, 1959
Cook, O. F., 1909, 1921
Dansereau, 1951
Denevan, 1961
Egler, 1942
Griscom, 1926
Haden-Guest, Wright, and Teclaf, 1956
Hanson, 1958
Harshberger, 1911
Holdridge, 1947, 1956
Johannessen, 1963
Kovar, 1945
Lauer, 1956, 1959
Leopold, 1950
Lundell, 1934, 1937, 1945
Miranda, 1947, 1948, 1952-53

—— and Sharp, 1950
Muller, 1947
Parsons, J. J., 1955
Popenoe, 1926
Record and Hess, 1943
Richards, 1957
Schmithüsen, 1959
Shelford, 1926
Shreve, 1934, 1939–40, 1951
Standley, 1920–26, 1926, 1928, 1936, 1937
—— and Steyermark, 1945, 1946–62
Steyermark, 1950
Troll, 1952
Verdoorn, 1945
Wagner, P. L., 1955
Weber, 1959
Wercklé, 1909
Woodson, Schery, *et al.*, 1943–62
Yuncker, 1945

8. The Soils of Middle America and Their Relation to Indian Peoples and Cultures

RAYFRED L. STEVENS

S OIL IS ONE of the fundamental elements of the environment, for it supports the vegetation and, indirectly, the animal life from which man derives the greater part of his food supply along with much of the materials for his tools, clothing, and shelter. Yet soil is perhaps the least adequately studied of all the major features of the habitat of the Middle American Indians, partly because it is a complicated component of other environmental forces, especially intricate in this part of the world, and partly because scientific study of soil has scarcely emerged from an embryonic stage. Nevertheless, some value may derive from a synthesis of what has been learned that may serve to orient more specific and ambitious investigations.[1]

STATE OF THE INVESTIGATIONS

The beginning of soil science in Middle America owes much to Karl Sapper, who was the first to apply modern scientific concepts to study soils of a large part of the area. Primarily a geologist and geographer, Sapper was active during the formative period of soil science when geologists were forerunners in the field.[2] His work overlaps with, but never felt the full impact of, the period when the Russian school of thought, emphasizing the influence of climate in soil formation, was gaining international acceptance.

Among other scholars of international renown who were pioneers of soil science in these lands, Hugh Hammond Bennett (1925, 1926, 1945) reported briefly on various aspects of the soils of Central America and in greater detail on those of the Canal Zone and adjacent areas of Panama (1929). Later, Robert L. Pendleton (1943, 1945) studied soil and land use conditions in parts of El Salvador, Honduras, Nicaragua, and Costa Rica.

International institutions have made sig-

[1] The author gratefully acknowledges the generous support of the University of Nebraska, which provided funds for library and clerical assistance in carrying out this research, and the very helpful suggestions of numerous colleagues.

[2] Since the area covered by Sapper's major contributions to this discipline (1899, 1905), from the Isthmus of Tehuantepec through western Panama, is in large part characterized by relatively young soils, correlations between soil qualities and geologic formations are striking; a soil scientist would have to be something of a geologist in order to work in this area.

265

nificant contributions to soil science in Middle America. A comprehensive inventory of research and researchers on the soils of the area was included by the Pan American Institute of Geography and History (1953–54) in its preliminary study of the investigations on natural resources in the Americas. An agency affiliated with the Organization of American States, the Inter-American Institute of Agricultural Sciences, at Turrialba, Costa Rica, has devoted a considerable part of its program of research and technical training to soil science. A private institution with an international program, the Escuela Agrícola Panamericana at El Zamorano, Honduras, has also promoted study of the soil.

Most of the governments have initiated some sort of soil survey work. Costa Rica, El Salvador, Guatemala, and British Honduras are the most thoroughly studied countries in this regard. The small area of the first two and the large proportion of it in agricultural use make it possible for a few dedicated workers, like César Dondolí in Costa Rica and Clinton Bourne and Hans Klinge in El Salvador, to know and classify their soils. Guatemala, with a larger and less accessible area, poses a more difficult problem. Notwithstanding, a reconnaissance soil survey of the whole country was carried out by the Instituto Agropecuario Nacional, using the classification system of the U. S. Department of Agriculture and ably directed by Charles S. Simmons, of the latter agency and of the International Cooperation Administration. The report of the British Honduras Land Use Survey Team (1959) on the soils of that territory is also commendable. In terms of area surveyed, Mexico has done more than any other country, but because of its much greater extent it has the most remaining to be done. By 1955 about one-sixth of the country had been surveyed at least by reconnaissance methods.

Mapping of the more widespread great soil groups in Mexico was attempted in

1942 by Miguel Brambila, agronomist of the Comisión Nacional de Irrigación. A revision was published in 1947 and a still further elaboration was released in 1957 by the successor of that agency, the Secretaría de Recursos Hidráulicos through its Departamento de Estudios Agrológicos. The 1957 map leaves blank the areas of more than 25 per cent slope, designating them arbitrarily "complex mountain soils." Another map, postulating a further classification within the latter category, was prepared in 1959. These maps are based partly on field observations and partly on analogies suggested by the particular great soil groups identified with similar climate and vegetation zones in other parts of the world. They should not be taken for more than what the authors intended: postulations of what might be expected to occur throughout the republic, points of departure for developing more definitive maps. That they have served this function well is demonstrated by the attention which the Departamento de Estudios Agrológicos, under the direction of the same Brambila, continues to give to mapping the great soil groups in Mexico.[3]

In recent years there has been much emphasis on soil research of immediate practical importance, e.g., analysis of field samples to ascertain the productive potential for a particular crop. Leaders of these countries have pressing need to augment and reorient their agricultural production; therefore answers to academic questions, like the genesis and classification of soil, may appear to them less urgent.

The need for more effective measures toward soil conservation, felt more and more acutely with the increasing population pressure on the soil resource base in Middle America, has been pointed up recently

[3] Among other significant contributions to the study of the soils of Mexico are those of Nicolás Aguilera Herrera (1955, 1959), Mario Macías Villada (1954, 1959, 1960), Rafael Ortiz Monasterio (1950, 1957), and Ramiro Robles Ramos (1950, 1959).

266

in a Soil Erosion Survey conducted cooperatively by the Conservation Foundation and the Food and Agriculture Organization of the United Nations (1954). The Instituto Mexicano de Recursos Naturales Renovables also focuses attention on this matter as one of the fundamental features of its program. Other agencies and individuals throughout the area are likewise awakening to the problem.

So much for modern studies of the soil. What of progress in understanding the relationship between soils and Indians? Our inquiry might well begin with consideration of what the Indians themselves knew about soils before the advent of modern science. Many of their groups knew how to judge a soil's potential, guided by color, structure, occurrence of certain rocks or wild plants. They undertook irrigation projects in favored spots of the dry lands and constructed the *chinampas* or "floating gardens," in effect a sort of subsurface irrigation system, in the Valley of Mexico. The ancient Maya of Yucatan not only recognized the different kinds of soil in their peninsula but also gave them special names. Some categories in their nomenclature are in accord with modern principles of soil classification (see below, pp. 303–304). Friar Diego de Landa (1941) observed in the 16th century how the natives had adapted their agriculture to the soil resources of Yucatan. It is unfortunate that few other early chroniclers and travelers bothered to record this kind of data. Soil resource limitation has been repeatedly suggested as the answer to the perplexing question of the decline of Maya civilization. The opinions of scholars such as Ellsworth Huntington, Herbert Spinden, J. Eric S. Thompson, and Sylvanus G. Morley have been considered in preparing this topic.

In central Mexico, Sherburne F. Cook (1948, 1949a, 1949b, 1958) focused closely on questions of soil erosion in relation to population densities at various periods and places. He has relied much on field examination of buried soil profiles for clues to unravel the interwoven histories of soils and men.

The University of California at Berkeley has promoted a large number of studies that devote some attention to the soils feature of the indigenes' habitat from California to Panama. These include the abovementioned works of Cook along with studies by Woodrow Borah (1951) and Lesley B. Simpson (1948, 1952) in the Ibero-Americana series. A number of dissertations and other writings on Middle America by students, staff members and former students of the Department of Geography at that institution give appropriate, if not always adequate, treatment to the soils factor.

In Mexico, the Instituto Nacional Indigenista has sponsored studies of the soils resources of Indian communities of the Mixteca area on the coast of Guerrero (Cárdenas, 1955; Patiño, 1955). More studies of similar orientation must be completed if it is ever to be possible to answer approximately the questions on soils and Indians of major concern to readers of this *Handbook*.[4]

FACTORS OF SOIL FORMATION AT WORK IN MIDDLE AMERICA

The processes of soil formation are usually the components of several factors, principally: (A) parent material, (B) climate, (C) flora, (D) fauna, (E) relief and drainage, (F) time, and (G) man. A brief general statement of the significance of each will be followed by some observations on its work in forming the soils of Middle America.[5]

[4] Only a few forerunners of soil science in Middle America and a few representatives of particular types of research can be mentioned in this brief space. The report of the Pan American Institute of Geography and History (1954, vol. 6) includes brief biographical sketches of persons then active in the study of soils and other natural resources of the area.

[5] Use of some special terminology of soil science is unavoidable; as space does not permit defining each term, the reader is referred to the *Multilingual Vocabulary of Soil Science* (Jacks, 1954). For

TABLE 1—SOIL-FORMING POTENTIAL AND OTHER OUTSTANDING TRAITS OF
ARCHETYPES OF IGNEOUS ROCKS

ROCK	ACIDIC			BASIC
	Predominance of light-colored minerals			Predominance of dark-colored minerals
Fine-grained	RHYOLITE	TRACHYTE	ANDESITE	BASALT
	P O R P H Y R I E S			
Coarse-grained	GRANITE	SYENITE	DIORITE	GABBRO
	Poor in minerals for plant nutrition			Rich in minerals for plant nutrition

Parent Material

Parent material is the substance from which soil is made, the raw material on which the other soil-forming forces operate, removing and rearranging, decomposing and reconstituting particles. Parent rock, with rock defined in the broader geologic sense, and accumulated organic deposits together make up the parent material of soil.

The geologically diversified area of Middle America presents a wide range of rock, from old crystalline massifs and Archean sandstones in which there is a predominance of quartz (SiO_2) and other minerals of little or no value for plant nutrition; to young, basaltic lavas, rich, as the name implies, in basic minerals; and to limestones and marls newly emerged from the sea and likewise presenting a wealth of potential mineral plant food. Not all young geologic formations are rich parent materials, however; some, like the sand dunes around Veracruz, are very poor indeed. Nor is it true that older rocks are always poor in mineral plant nutrients, although this seems to be the case in much of Middle America. The old crystalline massifs in the mountains of Baja California and southern Mexico are

a readable introduction to soil study, see Charles E. Kellogg's *The Soils That Support Us* (1949a). For more technical orientation see also the U. S. Department of Agriculture Yearbook of 1938 and *Soil Science* (Kellogg, 1949b). Kellogg's work and the *Yearbook* also contain helpful glossaries.

constituted principally of quartzose and acidic, light-colored coarse-grained rocks; the dark-colored coarse-grained rocks, such as gabbro, rich in basic minerals, are not very extensive. The metamorphic rocks, widely encountered on or around these old massifs, are mostly acidic gneisses and schists, similarly poor soil-forming material.

The renowned fertility of many volcanic soils in Middle America and other lands has led to the popular misconception that all soils of volcanic origin are rich for plant growth. Actually, volcanic materials, whether extruded as showers of ash or lava flows, vary greatly in soil-forming potential (see Table 1). Rhyolite is as poor in nutrient minerals as granite, which it resembles closely in chemical composition. In Middle America the richer volcanics, basalt and andesite, are the more common. Most of the lavas and ashes extruded in Tertiary times were of the andesitic types; those erupted during the Quaternary and Recent periods (the last million years) have been mostly of the basaltic type. The abundance of the latter materials at the surface is a favorable circumstance for the development of good soils. In some places, however, as in the Mexican state of Tlaxcala, erosion has exposed at the surface older formations of volcanic materials less rich in bases.

Climate

As it affects the soil, climate perhaps may best be understood by regarding separately

268

three distinct, yet interrelated, aspects: the *temperature, moisture,* and *wind regimes.*

TEMPERATURE REGIME. Temperature contributes to soil formation in the initial breaking down of parent rock by heating and expansion, cooling and contraction. Furthermore, with increasing temperature, the velocity of physical, chemical, and biotic processes is accelerated and their effects on the soil are accentuated. Hence soils are formed and transformed more quickly under warm conditions than under cold temperatures.

Although the climate of Middle America is of immense variety, over most of the area it is quite benign, and soil formation is not subjected to the utmost effects of temperature extremes. The "baking" of soil under very high temperatures is experienced only in the drier desert areas of the north and northwest and in parts of the coastal and valley lowlands. Freezing temperatures are known at medium and high altitudes on the northern fringe, and at upper elevations farther south. "Frost heave" as an agent in the mechanical mixing of organic and mineral constituents of soil is therefore of little consequence in forming the soils of this region. As is appropriate for these latitudes, diurnal temperatures vary more widely than do the seasonal mean temperatures. With the heating of the surface by day, and cooling by night, rock and soil fragments expand and contract, sometimes fracturing and breaking apart. This mechanical weathering is more acute in dry areas where there is less moisture, and at high altitudes where there is less air to intercept the sun's rays and to retard the radiation of heat from the earth's surface at night.

MOISTURE REGIME. Extreme types of soil-moisture regimes are well represented in Middle America. A most significant distinction is whether the soil is saturated with water constantly, intermittently, or rarely. As water percolates downward through the soil it carries minerals in solution and col-

loidal clay particles in suspension. In desert and semidesert areas there is not enough water to continue this movement more than a few inches or at most a few feet. When the downward penetration ceases, some of the water may move upward by capillary action. The water evaporates, precipitating its burden of soluble minerals somewhere between the lower level of percolation and the surface. Over a period of time there may develop a soil horizon, or layer, with a concentration of mineral precipitates, usually basic, giving that part of the soil a markedly alkaline reaction. Under very dry conditions, the concentration may be so severe as to form a hardpan, scarcely penetrable to the digging stick of the Indians, the creole plow, or even to modern agricultural implements. Thus was formed, for example, the *caliche* or *tepetate* that lies at or near the surface in many parts of northern and central Mexico.

The hardpans of desert and semidesert areas were no doubt a considerable barrier to the extension of pre-Columbian agriculture. Better tools and irrigation have since brought many of these soils under cultivation, but this has been done mostly by Europeans and mestizos. Now, as then, Indian populations are more concentrated where pre-Columbian agriculture was practicable.

Under conditions of abundant moisture, soluble minerals are removed, or leached, by percolating water to depths beyond the reach of plant roots, representing, for practical purposes, a net loss of plant nutrients from the soil. Where the parent material is rich and relatively young, that is, where it has not been subjected to constant leaching for too long a time, soils of humid lands may yet retain enough basic minerals to be quite productive. Prolonged, intensive leaching, however, may leave the soil so poor in basic minerals as to render it sterile for the production of most crops. Severely leached soils cover only a small fraction of

269

Middle America, simply because in so many of the very humid areas the parent material is quite young and has not been exposed to the action of percolating water long enough to have been deprived of the soluble mineral constituents.

The intensity of precipitation as well as the total amount is significant to soil formation and conservation. When rain falls slowly, much of it percolates into the ground, and runoff is minimized. So it is with the winter rains of northern Mexico. But at other times and places, most of the rainfall of Middle America comes in torrential downpours that dislocate the soil particles exposed at the surface, puddling and carrying them away in the runoff. The erosive potential of an intense tropical rain is much greater than that of an equal amount of precipitation gently falling over a longer period of time, as is the usual meteorological pattern in temperate lands.

WIND REGIME. The role of the wind in soil formation is partly indirect, for it influences both temperature and moisture effectiveness. Winds may bring rain to the soil or hot, dry air to evaporate the soil moisture already present. In the mountains of Middle America are many cloud-forest areas; that is, where clouds strike the mountainsides from time to time, not only bringing rain but also protecting soil moisture against evaporation and even adding moisture to the soil and vegetation by direct condensation. In some areas such winds are prone to come in the dry season, and where this condition falls upon soils with a water-retentive structure, crops may be sown and well advanced in growth several weeks before the rains.

As a direct agent of soil formation, wind is especially active in the dry lands, picking up finer particles and transporting them for even hundreds of miles. Under extremely dry and windy conditions a "desert pavement" of pebbles is left behind. Often fine wind-transported silts form loess deposits, which usually have a high proportion of

mineral nutrients and consequently develop into fertile soils of good structure. The occurrence of loess in Middle America is scattered, being sometimes encountered on the leeward side of the dry lands and in volcanic areas. Winds are especially significant in distributing finer volcanic ejecta for considerable distances, sometimes to the detriment but in the case of Middle America usually to the benefit of the soils.

Flora

Without plant life and its products of decomposition there can be no soil, nor would there be need for any; conversely, without soil few land plants can exist. Mere decomposition of rock into small particles does not make soil; the incorporation of organic matter is essential. This is effected to a large extent by the activity of bacteria, fungi, and other microscopic flora, which not only contribute to the soil decaying materials from their own organisms but also change other organic residues into forms that can be taken up by plants, directly or after reacting and combining with mineral soil constituents. Microscopic flora is usually more abundant in hot, humid lands, and its activity in soil formation is more pronounced there than in the drier or cooler areas.

Over wide areas, striking correlations may be observed between the various soil characteristics and the kinds of plant cover, or vegetation. Some of the archetypes of vegetation in Middle America and their consequent interaction with the soil will be considered briefly.

DESERT VEGETATION. True deserts, defined as areas having no plant life at all or only limited and specially adapted plant life with conspicuous bare ground between individual plants, are of relatively limited extent in Middle America: portions of the Altar Desert in northwestern Sonora, the dune areas of northwestern Chihuahua, and the dry beds of saline lakes scattered throughout the arid and semiarid regions

270

of northern and central Mexico. From the sparse plant life there is no way for the soils of the desert to accumulate much organic matter. A little is supplied within the soil profile by roots of dead plants, but the scant organic debris above ground is of little benefit to the soil, for it is easily carried away by wind and rain.

SEMIDESERT. These areas evidence a closer spacing of xerophytes, shrubs, and grasses, whence more organic matter is made available than under true desert conditions. The denser cover lessens the removal of soil particles and organic debris by wind and water. Because of slightly higher rainfall, more water percolates downward, carrying some of the organic residues in suspension. Even so, soils of the semidesert are not naturally very rich in organic matter, although this can sometimes be increased by proper management.

Most of the area that anthropologists call "Arid North America" is covered by semidesert vegetation. Soils developed thereunder were little used by the aborigines for agriculture except where unusual conditions of soil texture, structure, or relief favored the conservation of soil moisture or where this might be enhanced by natural seepage or artificial irrigation.

GRASSLAND. Proceeding to somewhat more humid lands, one finds the soil better protected from erosion by a more continuous cover of grasses or of shrubs and low trees with an understory of grasses. Though many grasses are perennials, parts of the plants die back each year so that the entire root system is replaced in three or four years. The decaying roots return to the soil considerable quantities of organic matter along with assimilable mineral plant food, well distributed throughout the soil profile and easily available to feeder roots for the succeeding year's growth. The abundant decomposing organic residues react with mineral soil particles, thus making available more mineral nutrients and usually also rendering the structure of the soil more friable

so that it tills easily and new plant roots can penetrate freely.

Three general types of grassland areas may be distinguished in Middle America, each showing clearly the contribution of vegetation to soil formation. In cool or temperate highlands areas of grassy vegetation are found usually fertile soils, blackened by abundance of organic matter similar in character and productivity to the famous black soils of midlatitude areas—the Middle West of the United States, the grasslands of Russia, the pampas of Argentina. In the lowland savannas the grasses are coarser, require less soluble mineral for their development, and consequently return less to the soil. Also, under the more constantly warm conditions, breakdown of organic matter is more continuous and complete so that the role of grass in improving soil structure and fertility is less effective here than in the cooler highlands. A third type of grassland area is the aquatic, along the margins of rivers and lakes and in other, inundable areas. Here the soil is likely to have an excessive accumulation of organic matter because of the lack of oxygen to disintegrate and the absence of surface erosion to remove it.

FOREST. Soil formation under forest cover, in contrast to that under grasslands, is generally characterized by the deposition and decomposition of organic matter on the soil surface, and lesser incorporation of it within the soil profile. This decomposition releases organic acids that percolate downward with the soil water and aid in the chemical disintegration of the parent material; some of the disintegration products enter likewise into the soil solution and are removed with the downward percolation. In some cases, minerals may be redeposited at a lower horizon of the soil, and in other cases they may be leached beyond the reach of plant roots.

When subjected to long continued leaching, humid forest soils tend to be very poor in soluble mineral nutrients. At the same time, rankness of vegetation may give an absurdly optimistic idea of their fertility. Trees require relatively less mineral for their growth than do most crop plants and grasses. They can re-use the minerals released by the decay of their own leaf fall, and their larger root systems can glean from a greater volume of topsoil, or reach down to tap lower soil horizons where mineral nutrients may be more plentiful. Furthermore, trees generally have greater root activity and can extract nutrient elements that are not usually available to crop plants and grasses.

The organic debris falling from the lush tropical rain forest is considerable. Notwithstanding, the amount of organic matter incorporated into the soil is not impressive. It is broken down too quickly and thoroughly under the constantly warm and moist conditions with resulting vigorous activity of soil flora and fauna and fast chemical reactions. The mineral soil may be so altered from long-continued weathering and so thoroughly leached that it consists almost entirely of insoluble compounds, the sesquioxides of iron (Fe_2O_3) and aluminum (Al_2O_3). Most of a soil's component of mineral nutrients may actually be locked up in the biotic cycle, the living and decaying bodies of organisms, rather than in the soil itself. In these extreme situations, removal of the forest cover may leave a soil so devoid of mineral nutrients as to be virtually sterile. Tropical rain forest occurs in places along the wet windward coastal lowlands and lower mountain slopes from northern Veracruz through Tabasco, northern Guatemala, and along the Caribbean side of Central America. Smaller patches grow on the Pacific slope of Chiapas, Guatemala, southern Costa Rica, and in eastern Panama.

Another type of tall forest grows under humid conditions in the highlands made temperate because of altitude. Breakdown of organic matter under the prevailing cooler temperatures is not so rapid as in the warmer, lowland forest. While some organic matter is being incorporated into the soil, more debris is accumulating on the surface. Its decomposition releases abundant organic acids which combine with percolating water, to alter and leach away part of the mineral compounds of the upper soil horizons, gradually leaving behind a concentration of silica (SiO_2), insoluble and inert for plant growth.

Forest-Grassland Transition Zones. In lands not humid enough for tall forest, there are areas of low to medium-height trees with crooked trunks and bushy crowns variously designated as scrub, dry, or thorn forest. Trees are more or less widely spaced because of limitations of the water supply and much grassy vegetation may be growing in between. Such vegetation occurs almost continuously along the Pacific side of Middle America, from the southern tip of Baja California to the Canal Zone, with the exception of the Tapachula area; in the moderately dry interior depressions, such as the Balsas Basin; in places along the eastern side of Middle America, such as northern Veracruz and Tamaulipas; and over most of the northern half of Yucatan Peninsula. Soils developed in these lands receive benefits from both grass and tree components of the vegetation; they are usually productive for crops in so far as local relief and water supply permit their utilization.

In conclusion, it might be said that the natural vegetation of Middle America is for the most part favorable to the development of good soils, with the exception of the drier deserts where plant cover is sparse and the humid places where the dense growth may cause excessive concentration of organic matter with resulting highly acidic soil conditions.

Fauna

Although plant life is absolutely essential to the existence of soil, animal life is not. But once animals appear on the scene they must necessarily affect the soil, by interfer-

SOILS

ing with the vegetative cover and depositing waste material. The variety and abundance of fauna depends on their ultimate basic food supply—plants. As this in turn is often a direct function of water supply, we can expect to find animal life relatively sparse in the drier regions and less effective there as an agent in soil development. Even in the deserts, however, animals are of some significance in breaking down vegetative organic matter which might otherwise decay slowly owing to the lack of moisture.

Where vegetation is thick enough to support a dense population of burrowing animals, their activity is of considerable importance in modifying the soil. Earthworms, many insects, and various rodents move organic matter with them into the soil profile, opening the way for a freer entry of other organic matter, along with water, air, and fine soil particles which wind and rain may sweep into the burrows. Under close forest cover, especially, those animals are principal agents in incorporating organic matter into the soil. The beneficial contribution of burrowing animals to the soil is sometimes partly offset by their disturbance to the root systems of growing crops. The gopher (*Geomys mexicanus*) is particularly destructive in north-central Veracruz and other parts of Middle America.

In the tropical rain forest the action of abundant fauna is added to the effects of high temperature and humidity in the rapid breakdown of the organic debris, often about as fast as it accumulates above the surface soil.[6]

Relief and Drainage

Relief, or variation in surface configuration, influences soil-forming processes by controlling drainage and the effectiveness

[6] The effects of man and his domesticated animals on the soils of Middle America are more appropriately considered below under the subheading devoted to man as an agent in soil formation (p. 276) and the heading "Indian Culture Areas and their Soil Resources."

of the climatic and vegetative factors. Slopes that face the sun receive its rays more directly and tend to be warmer and drier than nearby slopes at the same elevation whereon the sun shines more obliquely. These variations imposed by microrelief on the microclimate are often reflected by the occurrence of warmer and drier types of vegetation and associated soils on the sunnier slopes.

Drainage, the movement of water on the soil surface, into or through the soil profile, is dependent not only on the degree of gradient but also on the water-absorbing capacity of the soil and vegetative cover and on the permeability of the soil and underlying strata. These factors operate together in determining whether and how much the soil will tend to erode, creep, or slide; be leached of mineral nutrients; or become burdened with accumulated organic matter.

Soil scientists regard as normal relief that which is gentle enough that erosion will not be too rapid, allowing time for the formation of substantially similar soils from parent materials of notably different chemical composition. The gradient must yet be inclined enough to permit the gradual removal of some of the accumulated organic residues and transformed mineral materials so that the soil does not become overburdened with these. Abnormal relief would thus be of the extremes, too steep and too flat. These situations will depend not only on the *degree of gradient* but also on the permeability and thickness of the soil and other loose material overlying the bedrock, on the nature of the latter, and on the vegetative cover. It will further depend on the *length of gradient*, since runoff water over long distances will attain high velocity and a great erosive capacity even on gentle slopes.

Areas of steep relief are found of course on the slopes of the great mountain ranges and on the escarpments between plains and plateaus of different elevation. Such areas

273

have an intricate distribution pattern of complex soils that defy classification in mountain areas and are usually lumped together on general soil maps as "mountain soils" or "mountain and valley" soils. Ortiz (1955–57) consigns to such a category the areas of Mexico wherein the dominant relief is of slopes in excess of 25 per cent. This includes more than one-fourth of the area of the country; the fraction must be as great for Central America. But within the mountain ranges are wide valleys and gently rolling terrain where erosion is by no means excessive, permitting some degree of soil development normal for the particular climate and vegetation. There are also enclosed valleys with restricted drainage where the local soils are developed under conditions of too flat relief. Away from the great mountain ranges and escarpments, conditions of excessive relief also occur on hilly lowlands, as on the karst landscapes of El Peten; on severely dissected plateaus, as in the Mixteca, Tlaxcala, parts of the Bajio, and the Valley of Toluca; and on the slopes of smaller volcanic ranges, as the Sierra de Tamaulipas.

On the steep slopes of Xultepec in the Sierra de Santa Catarina, in the Valley of Mexico, the loose volcanic parent materials are scarcely held in place long enough to develop soil that is normal for the climate. Yet erosion is not too severe to keep the Indians from getting good yields of corn year after year. Runoff is slight because of high porosity, and erosion merely exposes fresh parent material so that the fertility of the soil is constantly replenished. It is thus important to understand the difference between terrain that is too steep to form normal soils for that particular climate and that which is too steep for cultivation without destructive erosion. A given slope may be excessive in either sense or in both.

Whereas soils with too steep relief are characterized by rapid removal of organic matter and weathered mineral soil, under conditions of very flat relief these tend to accumulate, often to the detriment of the soil. In the swamp lands of the Tabasco, El Peten, and Caribbean lowlands, the surface soil may consist of 50 per cent or more organic matter, with resulting high acidity that precludes the growth of many crops.

Under low relief, soil permeability and water-absorptive capacity become of paramount importance. Porous soils of humid flat lands are inclined to leach, whereas the less pervious soils become highly waterlogged. Intermittent waterlogging of soils with abundant organic matter results in the formation of a yellow and gray mottled "glei" horizon by the partial oxidation and reduction of iron, a process known as gleization and especially active in the lowlands of Tabasco. In Yucatan, although many flat areas lack surface drainage, much of the soil is well drained through the porous limestone substrata. In parts of the dry lands where neither surface nor internal drainage is complete, salts dissolved in the impounded water are precipitated in the soil profile upon evaporation.

Flat areas of temperate grasslands, as in parts of the Bajio, have extremely weathered surface horizons from which much of the finer material has filtered into the subsoil forming claypans, or hardpans, so compact as to present an obstacle to the penetration of water, plant roots, and agricultural implements.

Time

Time is a factor in soil formation, not as a substance or as a force in itself, but as a measure of the expended potential of all the other forces involved. According to some observers, under given conditions of parent material, climate, flora and fauna, relief and drainage, a soil will eventually attain a state of equilibrium, or climax, after which it will undergo little or no further change in chemical or mechanical composition or in its structure unless and until one of the major factors is altered and there is a consequent change in the input of one or more of the soil-forming forces. Soils in such a state are said to be *mature* or *climax* soils for the particular environment. This concept may be valid provided its implications are regarded as theoretical. For in

actuality the forces are never more than approximately constant and the state of equilibrium of a soil is relative rather than absolute.

The length of time that the parent rock has been exposed to weathering and soil-forming processes very often decides wheth-

TABLE 2—HIGHER CATEGORIES OF SOIL CLASSIFICATION
(Thorp and Smith, 1949, p. 118)

Order	Suborder	Great Soil Groups
Zonal soils	1. Soils of the cold zone	Tundra soils
	2. Light-colored soils of arid regions	Desert soils Red desert soils Sierozem Brown soils Reddish-brown soils
	3. Dark-colored soils of semiarid, subhumid, and humid grasslands	Chestnut soils Reddish Chestnut soils Chernozem soils Prairie soils Reddish Prairie soils
	4. Soils of the forest-grassland transition	Degraded Chernozem Noncalcic Brown or Shantung Brown soils
	5. Light-colored podzolized soils of the timbered regions	Podzol soils Gray wooded, or Gray Podzolic soils* Brown Podzolic soils Gray-Brown Podzolic soils Red-Yellow Podzolic soils*
	6. Lateritic soils of forested warm-temperate and tropical regions	Reddish-Brown Lateritic soils* Yellowish-Brown Lateritic soils Laterite soils*
Intrazonal soils	1. Halomorphic (saline and alkali) soils of imperfectly drained arid regions and littoral deposits	Solonchak, or Saline soils Solonetz soils Soloth soils
	2. Hydromorphic soils of marshes, swamps, seep areas, and flats	Humic-Glei soils* (includes Wiesenboden) Alpine Meadow soils Bog soils Half-Bog soils Low-Humic Glei* soils Planosols Ground-Water Podzol soils Ground-Water Laterite soils
	3. Calcimorphic soils	Brown Forest soils (Braunerde) Rendzina soils
Azonal soils		Lithosols Regosols (includes Dry Sands) Alluvial soils

*New or recently modified great soil groups.

275

er a soil is to be classed as old or new. In some cases new soils are rich, not having had time to lose their content of basic mineral nutrients; in other cases, age may be an advantage, if undesirable concentrations of certain elements have been removed or desirable nutrients have become concentrated in more available forms.

The surface geology of Middle America is characterized by a predominance of comparatively young rocks. Yet some areas that are geologically very old have soils that are very new. For instance, parts of the rugged Sierra Madre del Sur of Mexico consist of ancient crystalline formations, from which erosion rapidly removes new soil before the parent material is completely transformed; thus the roots of plants must seek their sustenance ever deeper in the disintegrating rock, which, though geologically old, has only recently been exposed to the process of becoming soil.

Man

Of all the major soil-forming factors, man is the latest to appear on the scene. He contributes to the development of soil in the same manner as other animals do, by consuming part of the flora and fauna, by disrupting them and the soil in his quest for food, and by returning to the soil the mineral and organic wastes from his own living body and decomposing corpse. However, it is man's display of superior intelligence that requires that he be considered separately from the other animals as a soil-forming agent.

Some of man's actions are deliberate in forming, or transforming, the soils. The Tarahumara for centuries have intercepted runoff waters with small obstructions (*trincheras*) to trap material carried in suspension, and in these deposits they sow their crops. Since the Spaniards brought domestic animals, the Tarahumara have kept large herds chiefly to supply manure to enhance the fertility of their soils. The lake dwellers of the Valley of Mexico made "floating

276

gardens" (*chinampas*) enriched with dark sediments scooped from the floor of the lakes. Other effects of man on the soil, including his more destructive actions, are incidental rather than deliberate. By repeatedly setting fire to the vegetation, overgrazing with his domestic animals, turning the soil with the plow, exposing it to direct contact with sun, wind, and rain, man has accelerated erosion and destroyed a large part of the soil-resource base of his cultures.

Like other groups of men, the Middle American Indians have been both builders and destroyers of soil. Consideration of their record is given below in the section "Indian Culture Areas and their Soil Resources."

Fig. 1—DISTRIBUTION OF CALCIFICATION-PROCESS ZONAL SOILS IN MEXICO
1, "Desert and semidesert (Sierozem) soils"; 2, "Chestnut soils"; 3, "Black Soils" (Chernozem). (After Brambila, 1942, and Ortiz Monasterio, 1957.)

Areas of Category 1 include not only the Desert and Sierozem groups, properly speaking, but also other closely related and associated soils, as the Red Desert, Brown and Reddish-Brown groups, in other words, the suborder "Light-colored soils of arid regions" in the classification of Thorp and Smith (1949).

In similar fashion, the areas of Chestnut soils (Category 2) and Black soils (Category 3) include Reddish Chestnut and other closely related or associated soils. Certainly much of the "Black soil" is not Chernozem; this would give Mexico a total area of 300,000 sq. km. of these rich soils, more than one-third as much as the Chernozem area of the humid Pampa of Argentina. Such an interpretation gives a misleading, flattering impression of Mexico's wealth of soil resources. Much of the "Black soil" land of this map is severely eroded and, even though the climate and vegetation may be eminently appropriate for the formation of Chernozem, it is difficult to classify the original, normal soil in places where the only topsoil is an altered remnant of a B or C horizon.

We might think of Categories 2 and 3 of this map along with parts of the areas that have been classified as "Prairie soils" (fig. 2) as coincident with the suborder, "subhumid and humid grasslands" in the classification scheme of Thorp and Smith (1949).

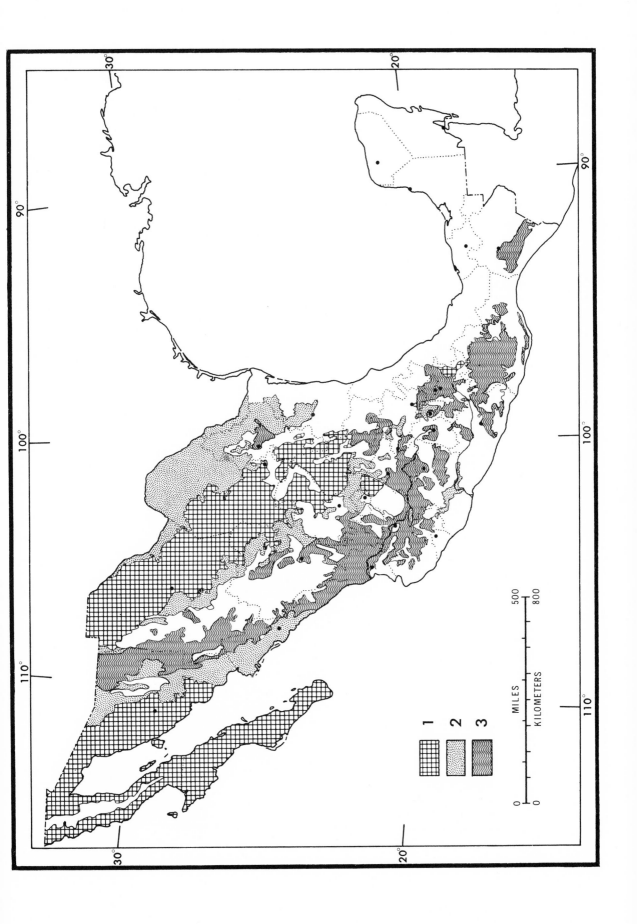

CLASSIFICATION OF THE SOILS OF MIDDLE AMERICA

We have examined summarily the factors involved in the formation of the soils of Middle America. We have seen how the different forces may complement, reinforce, or annul one another. Let us now consider some of the more typical processes, the components of these forces, and examine the nature and distribution of the soils that are their end products.

The scheme of soil classification to which the present discussion adheres is that of the U. S. Department of Agriculture (1938, pp. 979–1001) as later modified by Charles E. Kellogg (1949a, b).[7] Where possible, the nomenclature advocated by James Thorp and Guy D. Smith in the latter publication (pp. 117–26) has been used (Table 2). In some cases available data are inadequate to place particular soils of Middle America in the categories set up by the publications just mentioned. In other instances, knowledge of certain soils reveals that the system itself is inadequate to classify them.

The order of *zonal* soils embraces those developed under the influences of climate and vegetation, and their variations correspond closely to the differentiated patterns of climate and vegetation zones. Where zonal soil development is precluded by restricted drainage or persistent qualities of the parent material, soils belong to the *intrazonal* order. And where the geologic youth of parent material, as that of recent alluvial or volcanic origin, or the exposure of new parent material of whatever geolog-

[7] While this paper was in preparation a more recent system of soil classification was released by the Soil Survey Staff of the Soil Conservation Service, U. S. Department of Agriculture (1960). This will no doubt influence the nomenclature of subsequent literature, but many years will probably elapse before enough additional field work will have been done to apply the scheme intelligently to the soils of Middle America. In the meantime, the older nomenclature has been preferred for this paper, in order to orient the reader toward understanding earlier and contemporary writings on the subject.

278

ic age by rapid erosion, precludes the time necessary for climate and vegetation to make their imprints, soils are classified with the *azonal* order. Further classification distinguishes suborders in accordance with the main soil-forming conditions; great soil groups, according to major differences in the soil profile; and finally, families, series, phases, and types, according to more detailed or unique characteristics.

For a general view of the soils of an area as large as Middle America, the great soil group is a convenient category to work with. However, it is inconvenient that many of the great groups mean different things to different people and that at present they can hardly be more than tentatively classified for most of Middle America. Yet it is possible to state where the processes responsible for the various orders and suborders are most prevalent. These and some of the great soil groups that have been identified or postulated are discussed in relation to the major processes responsible for their development.

Zonal Soils

Zonal soils in Middle America are derived chiefly from three processes whose operations are circumscribed by climatic limitations: *calcification* in arid to semiarid climates, *laterization* in humid-tropical or subtropical climates, and *podzolization*, usually in cold or temperate-humid climates, although sometimes on very siliceous parent materials this process occurs in humid-tropical lands also.

CALCIFICATION-PROCESS SOILS. Calcification is the accumulation of lime carbonates ($CaCO_3$) and other basic minerals in the soil. This is possible where the soil is not continually moist so that these compounds, formed from solutes in the soil water, are precipitated by evaporation within the soil profile at a faster rate than they are removed by leaching. The great soil groups produced by the calcification process are differentiated largely according to the

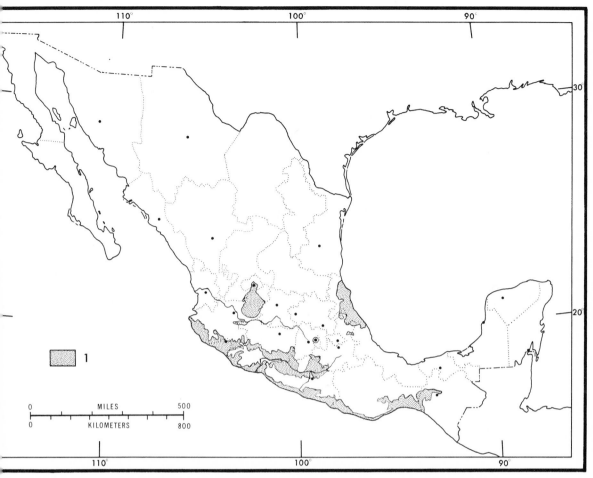

Fɪɢ. 2—PRINCIPAL AREAS OF "PRAIRIE SOILS" OF MEXICO IN THE CLASSIFICA-
TION OF BRAMBILA (1942) AND ORTIZ MONASTERIO (1957)

To these authors the term "Prairie soil" apparently means something quite different from what it does to the classification schemes followed by the present article (U. S. Department of Agriculture, 1938, especially p. 1052; Kellogg, 1949a, p. 332).

The area of the central plateau, south of Aguascalientes, is in great part shown as alkaline on a map by Ortiz Monasterio (1957, p. 44) and consequently could hardly fit the "Prairie" classification as understood by Kellogg. Lacking data for attempting a more specific classification, we prefer to consider this area simply as belonging to the suborder of "Dark-colored soils of the semiarid, subhumid and humid grasslands" (scheme of classification of Thorp and Smith, 1949).

The area of northern Veracruz shown here as having "Prairie soil" hardly belongs in the same suborder. This is actually a land of medium to tall monsoon forest. What we have observed of soil profiles along fresh road cuts suggests that Yellow Podzolic and Podzolic-Lateritic intergrades are far more widespread than profiles resembling Prairie.

It is easier to agree with the map in the case of the Balsas Depression and Pacific coastal lowlands from Cabo Corrientes through Tehuantepec, for it is reasonable that here on the numerous savannas there should be some Prairie and Reddish Prairie soil interspersed with the azonal Lithosols and Alluvial soils.

depth of the horizon of lime accumulation, its thickness and concentration. In the deserts this horizon is found at or near the surface; the concentration of calcium carbonate is considerable, sometimes forming a hardpan of near rocklike consistency

called *caliche,* and the soils are designated by the same name as the climate and vegetation, that is, *Desert* soils.[8] In the deserts of

[8] Consistent with the style of the references cited at the beginning of this section, the names of the great soil groups are capitalized.

279

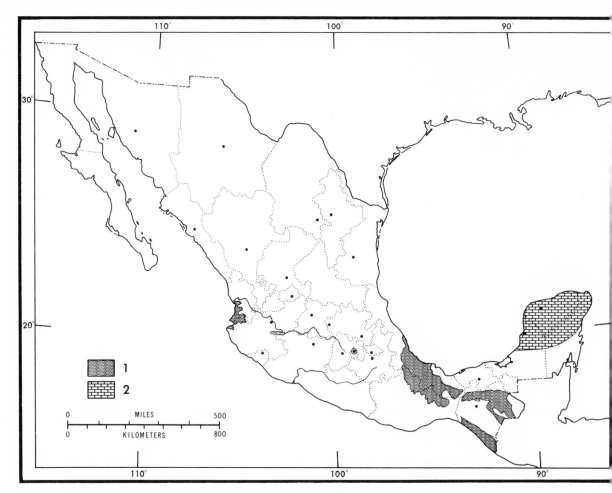

FIG. 3—MAJOR AREAS OF SOME LATERIZATION-PROCESS SOILS IN MEXICO

1, "Yellow Soils and Red Loams of the Lateritic Group"; 2, "Terra Rossa." (After Brambila, 1942, and Ortiz Monasterio, 1957.) The latter category has been regarded as part of the Red Podzolic group by Baldwin, Kellogg, and Thorp (U. S. Department of Agriculture *Yearbook*, 1938, p. 994) and as a separate great soil group by Kellogg (1949a, pp. 327, 335). Thorp and Smith's classification scheme (1949) did not take the term into account. Together the soils areas of this map comprise the greater part of the suborder "Lateritic soils of forested warm-temperate and tropical regions" (classification scheme of Thorp and Smith, 1949).

Category 1 also includes some podzolic-lateritic intergrades, but there are many other scattered areas of such transitional soils at low to medium altitudes. The Terra Rossa soils of Yucatan, as in other lands where they occur, are formed under scrub-forest vegetation in a warm, wet-dry season climate and retain a high content of available calcium as a heritage from the limestone parent material.

cooler regions, as in the high, drier parts of the Mexican plateau, soils have a characteristic gray color and may be called Gray Desert or, to use the widely accepted Russian term, *Sierozem* (fig. 1). Typical Sierozem profiles, with calcareous horizons at less than 1-foot depth, occur in the drier parts of the valleys of Mexico, Puebla, Perote, and Mezquital, and in other rain shadow areas at medium and high altitudes. In warmer desert and semidesert areas, like those of Chihuahua and Sonora, greater dehydration of the iron compounds gives the soil a decidedly reddish tinge, hence the term Red Desert soils.

Proceeding from the drier desert to the semiarid and subhumid areas, as from Matehuala to Queretaro, the effects of the cal-

280

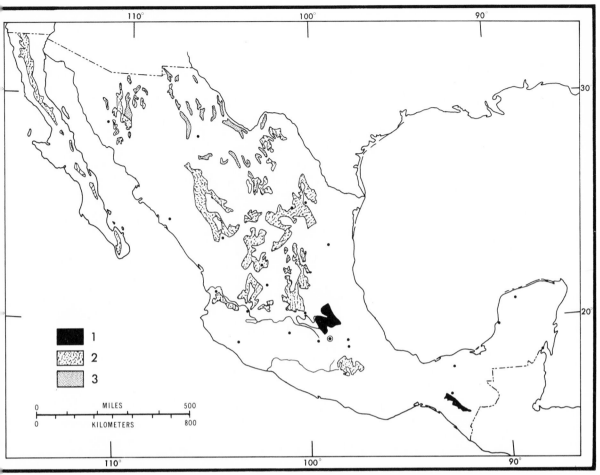

FIG. 4—MOUNTAIN ZONAL SOILS OF MEXICO IN MODERATELY HUMID TO ARID SITUATIONS

1, Prairie soils; 2, Residual soils with scrub vegetation; 3, Lithosols with desert vegetation. (After Macías Villada, 1960.) Mountain soils, because of the interference of rapid erosion on steep slopes and repeated deposition in the valleys, rarely develop into zonal soils. However, the resulting azonal soils usually show some similarities to the zonal soils that have developed under comparable conditions of climate and vegetative cover. Affini- ties with the suborders of the classification of Thorp and Smith (1949) may be stated as follows: "Prairie soils" correspond to "Dark-colored soils of semiarid, subhumid and humid grasslands." "Residual soils with scrub vegetation" approach the "Soils of the forest-grassland transition." "Lithosols with desert vegetation" are much like the suborder of "Light-colored soils of arid regions."

cification process are seen to change gradually but consistently. The horizon of lime accumulation will be found at increasingly greater depth and in less extreme concentrations. The topsoil will be thicker and darker due to the greater accumulation of organic matter made possible by the more abundant grass vegetation. Names of the great soil groups here correspond to the changing color of the topsoil, which bears a close correlation to the changing depth and degree of lime accumulation. Thus one passes from the Desert and Gray Desert (Sierozem) soils through the Brown, Chestnut, and finally to the Chernozem (from the Russian, meaning "black soil"). The transitions from the hot deserts of Chihuahua and Sonora toward the humid lands present successively the Red Desert, Reddish Brown, Reddish Chestnut, and Chernozem groups.

Altogether, the calcification process soils cover well over two-fifths of the land sur-

281

face of Middle America, which is to be expected since the wider part of the region lies within those latitudes appropriate for arid climates. Our estimates are derived from the classification reported by Rafael Ortiz M. (1957, p. 84) for the soil areas of Mexico, which has 78.5 per cent of the total land area and probably more than 95 per cent of the calcification-process soils of Middle America. The soils of about 23 per cent of the area of Mexico, or 18 per cent of Middle America, belong to Thorp and Smith's suborder "Light-colored soils of arid regions" (Desert, Red Desert, Sierozem, Brown and Reddish Brown groups). Nearly 25 per cent of the soil area of Middle America, including more than 30 per cent of that of Mexico, belongs to the suborder "Dark-colored soils of semiarid, subhumid, and humid grasslands" (Chestnut, Reddish Chestnut, and Chernozem soils, along with the Prairie and Reddish Prairie groups in which weak podzolization or even laterization may be active as well as calcification; see fig. 2).

The light-colored soils of arid regions have been of relatively little use to the Indians for agricultural purposes, either in pre-Columbian or in later times, except on the humid margins, or along rivers where rudimentary irrigation could be practiced. The same is true for much of the Chestnut, Reddish Chestnut, and Chernozem areas of northern and northwestern Mexico.

LATERIZATION-PROCESS SOILS. Laterization must be regarded as a geologic as well as a soil forming process, for it is not limited to the soil but affects underlying rock materials also, sometimes to depths of tens of meters. It results from the prolonged chemical-weathering action of water, dissolving and removing gradually much of the base mineral components, forming and leaving behind insoluble sesquioxides of iron (Fe_2O_3) and aluminum (Al_2O_3) in concentrations that in some soils may exceed 90 per cent.[9] In its extreme manifestations, the process gives a material with the rust color,

consistency and, sometimes after exposure to the sun, even the hardness of brick, to which is applied the term *laterite*, from the Latin word for brick. When capitalized the word may refer to a great soil group, which is extremely leached and sterile for plant growth. *Laterite* soils are quite sterile for most crop plants. They should be distinguished from the *lateritic* soils in which the effects of the laterization process have not been so extreme.[10]

Fortunately, Laterite soils (sometimes called true laterites) are not common in Middle America.[11] Lateritic soils, however, are extensive in both the wet-dry and continuously humid tropical lowlands (fig. 3). Some of these soils are quite productive, as in north-central Veracruz, where they supported the classic Totonac cultures of Tajin and Papantla, and in southern Veracruz, where the Olmec culture was in part established on them. Other soils of these groups lose fertility rapidly once the forest cover is removed, as in parts of the Peten and coastal areas of Central America.

PODZOLIZATION-PROCESS SOILS. Podzolization is sometimes viewed as an arrested laterization process. Unlike the latter, it is effectively limited to the true soil, or vege-

[9] In tropical lowland climates with a long dry season, an ironpan, or hard ferruginous layer, sometimes forms a meter or less below the surface.
[10] Some writers prefer the term "Latosol" in place of "Laterite" or "Lateritic" for all soils formed largely by the laterization process.
[11] Pendleton (1943, p. 404) writes of the "best laterite profile I have seen in the western hemisphere" near Puerta Cabezas, Nicaragua; Radley (1960, p. 120) reports other occurrences of Lateritic soils in the savanna-covered Mosquito coast plain on Pliocene sediments, where he observed hardpans of iron concretions just below the surface. Sáenz (1940, p. 142) reports "verdaderas lateritas" on the Pacific side of Costa Rica. Aguilera (1955, p. 6), without clarifying precisely what he means by the term, refers to the "localización probable" of "laterita pura" in the Mexican states of Aguascalientes, Nayarit, Jalisco, and Colima on the west, and in Guerrero, Oaxaca, and Chiapas on the south. Those states certainly have zones of extremely hot, wet-dry climates of the type in which, after long exposure, Laterite soils often develop.

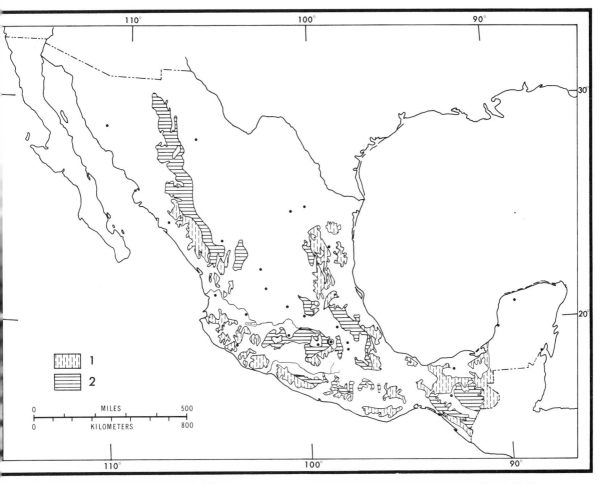

FIG. 5—MOUNTAIN ZONAL SOILS OF MEXICO IN HUMID FOREST SITUATIONS

1, Podzolic soils with coniferous vegetation; 2, Laterized humid-forest soils. (After Macías Villada, 1960.) Mountain soils, because of the interference of rapid erosion on steep slopes and repeated deposition in the valleys, rarely develop into zonal soils. However, the resulting azonal soils usually show some similarities to the zonal soils that have developed under comparable conditions of climate and vegetative cover.

By analogies with the scheme of classification of Thorp and Smith (1949), the soils of Category 1 belong to the suborder "Light-colored podzolized soils of the timbered regions," whereas Category 2 should be placed with the suborder "Lateritic soils of forested warm-temperate and tropical regions."

tation-supporting upper horizons of the mantle of loose material overlying the bedrock. Decomposition of vegetal material, which accumulates in abundance on top of the soil, releases strong organic acids that aid the percolating water in dissolving and removing metallic mineral soil constituents from the horizon just beneath the accumulated organic matter. Left behind is silica (SiO_2), insoluble under such strongly acidic conditions, giving the horizon an ashen-gray color, whence is derived the term "podzol" from a Polish word meaning ash, and the term "podzolization" to refer to the process whereby it is formed.

Podzolization exerts a maximum effect on soils of the cold, continental climates under coniferous forest vegetation, where winter freezing interrupts the breaking down of organic matter and the percolation of soil water; leaf fall continues, how-

283

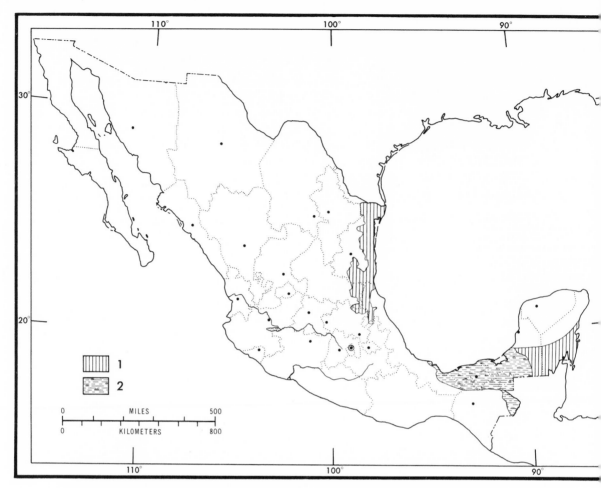

FIG. 6–PRINCIPAL AREAS OF RENDZINA (1) AND GLEI SOILS (2) IN MEXICO

(After Brambila, 1942, and Ortiz Monasterio, 1957.) These are the largest continuous blocks of intrazonal soils in Mexico (unless one regards Terra Rossa also as an intrazonal group). Scattered patches of Rendzina also occur as enclaves in the Terra Rossa area of Yucatan and on other limestone formations. Rendzinas and Lithosols resembling Rendzina occupy a large part of the Peten and constituted a major soil resource of the ancient Maya. The area mapped as "Glei soils" includes not only hydromorphic gleization-process soils, but also other hydromorphic soils not affected by gleization, as well as strips of azonal Alluvial soils on levees, terraces, and flood plains.

ever, and when decomposition resumes in summer, organic acids are released suddenly to aid in weathering and removing the minerals other than silica. Podzol soils in the classic sense can hardly be expected in the environments of Middle America except perhaps on very siliceous parent materials; but *podzolic* soils, which show some degree of podzolization, occur in many areas of gentle or moderate relief in the higher plateaus and intermontane valleys and even in parts of the tropical lowlands. Presumably the process is at work wherever the *tierra fría* and *tierra templada* areas are covered with dense, humid forest (figs. 4, 5), although on steeper slopes the removal of newly formed soil is too rapid for much effect to be observable in the soil profile.

TRANSITION SOIL GROUPS OF THE ZONAL PROCESSES. In the transition zones between the arid and humid lands calcification may take place alternately or even simultaneously with weak laterization or podzolization.

284

The case of the Prairie and Reddish Prairie groups has already been mentioned (p. 282 and fig. 2). Soils of the forest-grassland transition are spared the extreme deleterious effects of climate-induced processes of soil formation. These processes vary greatly in intensity with the weather cycles, calcification taking place in dry years, laterization or podzolization during more humid periods. Degraded Chernozems are formed where forest encroaches on a grassland, podzolization ensues, and the horizon of lime accumulation from an earlier, drier period is gradually removed. Trends of recent centuries in Middle America have been the reverse of those required for the formation of Degraded Chernozem, for the forests have mostly been retreating before, rather than advancing onto, the grasslands. Non-Calcic Brown (or Shantung Brown) soils are found in forest-grassland transition areas where calcification cannot properly take place for lack of calcium in the parent material (e.g., in eastern Sonora, along the border of Arizona).

There is no clear-cut dividing line between the zones of podzolization and laterization—nothing that would set them apart from each other as neatly as the horizon of lime accumulation distinguishes the calcification-process soils from both. Some podzolization is observable even in certain humid-tropical lowland areas. Transitional soils resulting from podzolization and laterization are widely distributed in the humid-forested *tierra templada* and parts of the *tierra caliente*. Similar soils in southeast United States and southern China have been called Red-Yellow podzolic or Red-Yellow Lateritic groups, among other proposed names. Recognizing their transitional character, we prefer to consider them "Red and Yellow Podzolic-Lateritic intergrades." The red and yellow colors correspond respectively to lesser and greater hydration. Red predominates in the drier or steeper and better-drained areas, yellow where soil conditions are more humid. Both soils have much iron sesquioxide (Fe_2O_3), but in the yellow soils a greater proportion of this will be chemically combined with water ($Fe_2O_3 \cdot 2 H_2O$).

On the map of Middle America it is difficult to separate the Reddish-Brown and Yellowish-Brown Lateritic soil groups from the Red and Yellow Podzolic-Lateritic intergrades because of the lack of adequate profile descriptions. The former groups are no doubt more widespread in the southern part of the region, especially in Costa Rica and Panama, whereas the intergrades may be more extensive in the other warm humid areas.[12]

In summary, we might emphasize that all three processes of zonal soil formation —calcification, laterization, and podzolization—in their initial stages make productive soils but in their extreme manifestations render poor soils. It is fortunate that the soils of Middle America, when compared with those of certain other large areas of the world, like northern Canada or northern Brazil, are relatively young, with extreme cases of laterization and podzolization either rare or nonexistent. On the other hand, in vast desert and semiarid lands excessive calcification has produced nearly impermeable hardpans and highly alkaline reactions that greatly restrict the land-use capacity. The Middle American Indians have cultivated all kinds of zonal soils but their most spectacular settlements may be shown to have depended on soils where neither calcification, laterization, nor podzolization have had the time or the intensity to exert their maximum effects.

---

[12] A definitive scheme based on molecular ratios of silica to aluminum sesquioxide, or silica to total sesquioxides, has been proposed for differentiating lateritic and podzolic soils. But since these substances are inert for plant nutrition, there has been little attention to them in the rather pragmatically oriented recent research in the area. Nor have other criteria of classification, based on the nature of the mineral clay components, been carefully applied.

Intrazonal Soils

Wherever surface or internal drainage is severely impeded, the action of water is altered from its characteristic role in the formation of the zonal soil corresponding to the particular climate and vegetation. Some of the resulting anomalies are so exaggerated as to warrant recognition as separate great soil groups, classified as intrazonal because of their occurrence within areas of zonal soils. The effects of restricted drainage on soil formation show marked differences accordingly as the climate is arid or humid: *halomorphic soils* (saline and alkaline) in poorly drained areas of the dry lands and tidewater areas; *hydromorphic soils* in swamps, marshes, and other areas of restricted drainage in the humid lands. Mangrove swamps and other tidewater lands (in Sinaloa and Tabasco they are quite extensive) are affected by both halomorphic and hydromorphic processes. Another suborder, the *calcimorphic soils,* are developed in areas where parent materials of highly calcareous nature preclude the development of zonal soils, even though drainage may be good and the material long subjected to weathering (fig. 6).

HALOMORPHIC SOILS. These soils are mostly to be found within the zones of calcification-process soils (fig. 1) where evaporation is in excess of precipitation, or sometimes in coastal areas. Since the water that accumulates in areas of impeded drainage in dry climates is often not abundant enough to force its way out by either surface or subsurface drainage, it stagnates in or on the soil and evaporates, leaving behind the salts carried in solution by the runoff or seepage from the watershed. Under such conditions are formed salt lakes, as Texcoco (Valley of Mexico), and Cuitzeo (Michoacan), or intermittently wet-and-dry salt lakes as Laguna del Carmen (Tlaxcala) in arid lands. The soils of adjacent slopes as well as those of the depression flats may be influenced by concentra-

tions of salt, which migrate with the water table. Use of such soils requires control of, or adjustment to, the soil-water regime; for highly saline soil solutions, particularly when they contain much sodium carbonate, are toxic to most crop plants.

The process of salt accumulation in soils is known as *salinization*, from which are derived three great soil groups differentiated according to the character of the salt and the horizons where it occurs, or has occurred, within the soil profile. These are known as *Solonchak, Solonetz,* and *Soloth,* names originally given in Hungary where they were first described. *Solonchak,* or saline soils, are those in which salinization, the salt-accumulating process, is dominant. *Solonetz* soils are developed by solonization, the leaching of part of the salts from a Solonchak, sometimes with the substitution of sodium carbonate, a substance highly toxic to most crop plants. *Soloth,* or solodized Solonetz, is formed by solodization, the further leaching of a Solonetz soil until most of the salts have been removed, giving the topsoil an acidic rather than alkaline reaction. The halomorphic soils are found throughout the arid lands in areas lacking exterior drainage and in close proximity to one another, depending on variations in microrelief and fluctuations of the water table.

A few halomorphic soils are in use by the Indians in Middle America, for example, on the shores of Lakes Cuitzeo and Texcoco and on the recently drained bed of Lake Chalco. The planners who engineered the drainage of the five fresh-water lakes in the Valley of Mexico in the latter part of the 19th century ambitiously visualized turning the lake beds into fertile farm lands. They even had hopes of leaching the salts from the bed of Lake Texcoco. Now it is realized that the fresh-water resources of the valley are inadequate for the task. In the bed of former Lake Chalco drainage has been followed by the rising of water from the lower depths by capillary action, bringing with it salts in solution which are precipitated at or near the surface during dry weather. Some parts of the old lake floor cannot be farmed at all, and in other parts yields are unreliable because of salinity. Similar disappointments attend many other efforts at reclamation of arid lands.

HYDROMORPHIC SOILS. Developed under restricted drainage in humid lands, these soils are generally characterized by high accumulation of organic matter from vegetation rank in response to the abundant moisture supply. Where only the surface drainage is blocked and vertical drainage can take place, there may be considerable leaching by either laterization, podzolization, or both, with resultant soils belonging to the Ground Water Podzol or Ground Water Laterite groups.

Another soil-forming process, involved in many of the great soil groups of this suborder, is *gleization*, usually identifiable by a bluish-gray, olive-gray, or yellow and gray mottling in the subsoil, produced by the "partial oxidation and reduction of iron caused by intermittent waterlogging" (Jacks, 1954, p. 196).

The largest area of hydromorphic soils in Middle America lies in the swamp and marshland region of Tabasco, extending in an irregular pattern into the inundable parts of the Peten (figs. 6, 7). The Bog, Half-Bog, and Ground-Water Podzol soils are no doubt the intrazonal great soil groups of widest distribution, but there is possibly some Ground-Water Laterite also. Since the Ground-Water Laterite soils by definition are developed from true laterite parent material (Kellogg, 1949a, p. 338), it is unlikely that this group would be very extensive in this or in any other part of Middle America, with the possible exception of the Mosquito Coast of Central America.

The lakeshores and other marshlands of the temperate highlands where there is no problem of salt accumulation present Bog and Half-Bog soils. Where the restricted drainage does not result in prolonged inundation the Humic Glei (formerly called "Wiesenboden" or "Meadow Soils") and Low Humic Glei soils are represented. Various forms of these groups occur in the tropical lowlands.

Alpine Meadow soils, as the name suggests, develop in the upper reaches of the mountains, in little, poorly drained valleys covered largely with bunch grasses. Such soils were of little use to the pre-Columbian peoples, except as grazing lands for the animals they hunted. Encroachments of the Europeans and mestizos and the pressures of increasing population have moved many Indians from medium altitudes to the less productive higher lands. Yet there are few indigenes in Middle America wholly dependent on Alpine Meadow soils; most mountain settlements have access to soils at various elevations and rely on the alpine meadows only for seasonal pastures.

CALCIMORPHIC SOILS. Two great soil groups—Rendzina and Brown Forest (*Braunerde*)—developed from parent materials with a superabundance of calcium which enables calcification to take place even in relatively humid climates.[13] The Rendzina group occupies much of the flat limestone platform of Yucatan Peninsula, the limestone area of Tamaulipas, and parts of adjacent states, and various scattered smaller areas of Middle America where calcareous parent material is subjected to weathering in climates ranging from cool to hot and from semiarid to humid. The Rendzinas of the Peten and Yucatan were the major soil resources for many Classic and Postclassic Maya settlements (see discussion on pp. 300–302).

Brown Forest soils, unlike most intrazonal groups, may develop under condi-

[13] There is a good case for placing Terra Rossa soils in the calcimorphic suborder, although Thorp and Smith deny them the status of a great soil group, and Kellogg (1949, pp. 327, 335) places them with the laterization-process groups. Terra Rossa soils cover much of the northwestern part of Yucatan Peninsula.

tions of good drainage; some podzolization as well as calcification may be involved. In Middle America this great soil group, or something closely resembling it, may be found at medium and high altitudes on the flanks and crests of the mountains, under broadleaf-deciduous, broadleaf-evergreen, or even coniferous vegetation. The Sierras Madres Oriental and del Sur, as well as the northern range of Guatemala, offer abundant calcareous parent materials in the appropriate situations.

Many soils of volcanic areas at various medium to high altitude locations in Mexico bear a superficial resemblance to Brown Forest soils and are sometimes called by that name, which is unacceptable in many cases if one insists, as Kellogg does (1949a, p. 339), on high availability of calcium as a qualification for the group. Some of these misnamed soils might more appropriately be placed with the Brown Podzolic group.

Azonal Soils

Azonal soils are those in which the soil-forming processes have not been sufficiently active in degree and time to change considerably the chemical composition of the mineral soil, so that parent material remains an all-important factor in determining their morphology and productivity. In Middle America there are widely scattered, but in the aggregate extensive, areas of the three great soil groups belonging to this order: *Lithosols, Regosols* (which includes the group formerly known as "Dry Sands"), and *Alluvial soils.*

LITHOSOLS. These are young soils whose chemical composition is still very similar to that of the firm rock from which they have originated. Where surface erosion is rapid, new soil in the making is removed before zonal processes have had much effect and new parent material from underneath is incorporated into the lower horizons of the vegetation-bearing soil. Lithosols are often very thin and must be managed with extreme care lest the entire

soil profile erode away, leaving only bare rock at the surface. Such care has not always been within the will or the way of the Middle American Indians, who, after having ruined the more productive lands or having been expelled from them by encroaching Europeans and mestizos, have had no recourse but to bring steep and erosible slopes under cultivation.

Marked variations in fertility correspond to the radically different parent materials of the Lithosols which cover most of the steeper mountains. The Sierra Madre Occidental consists principally of elongated volcanic edifices, fissure-type lava flows of the Tertiary period, with a predominance of andesitic-type rocks which are fairly rich in minerals for plant nutrition. On the eastern side of Mexico, the steep slopes of the Sierra Madre Oriental, an uplifted mass of folded limestone, are partly covered by thin Lithosols. Along the 19th parallel the Neovolcanic Axis is composed mainly of Quaternary basaltic materials, lavas, and fragmented ejecta, which abound in basic minerals for constituting rich soils. Similarly rich Lithosols are found on the lava flows along the volcanic axes of Central America.

Accelerated erosion, meaning that which is provoked by man's use or abuse of the land, has removed the upper horizons of zonal soils over wide areas in central Mexico (e.g., in Tlaxcala, the Mixteca, parts of Michoacan, and the Valley of Toluca) and other parts of Middle America, where it is impossible to say what was the original soil which supported the pre-Columbian cultures. Little natural vegetation is left, and erosion has been so severe on the too-frequently cultivated and overpastured lands that the entire A horizon may be missing, along with part or all of the B horizon. With the parent material thus exposed and as yet little transformed by chemical weathering, detailed soil mapping, based on what is now rather than what has been or should be, must include much of central Mexico with the Lithosols and Regosols.

288

REGOSOLS. Regosols differ from Lithosols in that the parent material consists of unconsolidated rather than massive rocks. This category includes windblown deposits (loess) and volcanic ashes and cinders on which climate and vegetation have not yet established a zonal soil because of too rapid erosion or repeated deposition of new parent material. Along the Neovolcanic Axis and in Central America, fertility of soils for miles around the active volcanoes has been frequently rejuvenated by showers of ash and cinders.

Regosols include the "Dry Sands," which earlier classifications had given the status of a distinct great soil group, found in the drier desert areas (e.g., Sonora and Chihuahua) and sometimes even in more humid areas along stream courses and windward coasts (e.g., near Veracruz city). Moving sand dunes, of course, can hardly be regarded as soil, but where vegetation has begun to fix the sand in place we may find, if internal conditions are dry enough, the "Dry Sands" soils. The extreme porosity of these soils allows rapid infiltration of the scant rainfall they receive. Porosity results in high loss of soil water by evaporation and percolation, but there is a compensation to plant life in the ease whereby its roots can penetrate long distances in search of any available soil moisture and nutrients. On bars of streams and beaches precipitation may be supplemented by seepage from the adjacent water bodies. Obviously, some soils in such situations might logically be classified either with the "Dry Sands" or the Alluvial group.

ALLUVIAL SOILS. Such soils originate from water-transported materials that have not been greatly changed by zonal or intrazonal soil-formation processes. They are often described according to the type of current or body of water depositing the material. That which simply washes down from the hillsides to lower slopes and valley bottoms is known as *colluvium*, and the resulting soils are generally considered to be a phase of the local zonal or intrazonal soil rather than categorized separately. With the Alluvial group are sometimes included soils formed of deposits left by the tides or by the receding shorelines of lakes and seas.

It is necessary to distinguish between the Alluvial great soil group and other soils of alluvial origin. The latter would include all soils developed from parent materials transported by water, whereas the former term refers only to those soils wherein these deposits have not been greatly altered by zonal and intrazonal soil-forming processes. Thus over much of the coastal lowlands and lacustrine plateaus most of the soil is of alluvial origin, but only a fraction still is classifiable with the Alluvial group.

Narrow bands of Alluvial soils lie along the shores of most lakes and rivers in Middle America. Where the sediments have been originally eroded from areas of rich soils or from rocks rich in soil-forming minerals, they are potentially productive, and they have been put to good use when occupied by agricultural Indians.

For the most part, however, Alluvial soils did not play so dramatic a role in the development of the higher cultures of Middle America as was the case in those of the Old World—along the Nile, Tigris-Euphrates, and Indus, for example—where some of the richest soils of the Alluvial group occupied extensive deltas and flood plains adjacent to wide areas of unproductive soils.

In Mesoamerica the limited and ribbon-like extent of Alluvial soils did not favor the establishment of distinct culture groups on them. Large states could not survive if dependent exclusively on such attenuated resource bases. The usual pattern was for a state to include areas of other soil groups also. In this land of relatively small rivers, Alluvial soils are often little better or worse than those of the nearby watersheds whence the sediments come. They might offer the advantage of being deeper and more water-retentive, but as a rule the same types of crops have been grown on them as on the other soils nearby.

In Arid North America, on the other hand, Alluvial soils were of considerable consequence in the development of distinctive cultures. This fact is inseparable from the coincidence of Alluvial soils with sources of water for irrigation. Actually, many of the interfluves of the Sierra Madre Occidental and the adjacent coastal plain offer soils more fertile than the Alluvials and "Dry Sands" which supported pre-Columbian agriculture (and that of the present Yaqui). It was within the limits of the Indians' technology to irrigate and cultivate the soils along the watercourses but not to bring water long distances to irrigate the zonal soils of the interfluves.

INDIAN CULTURES AND THEIR SOIL RESOURCES

The foregoing sections have been presented from the viewpoint of the soil scientist and the physical geographer. The present section will attempt to sketch the soil resource patterns of the major culture zones: (A) Arid North America, (B) Mesoamerica, and (C) the Circum-Caribbean. In so far as data and space permit, interpretations of the man-soil relationships of selected peoples and cultures will be given.

Arid North America

The zonal soils of Arid North America are predominantly calcification-process groups. Azonal enclaves of Alluvial soils lie along rivercourses and deltas, Dry Sands and other Regosols in the deserts and semideserts, and Lithosols on the steeper slopes. Humid mountain soils at upper elevations include Lithosols and podzolized profiles. Intrazonal soils of the halomorphic suborder occupy the floors of interior drainage basins, old lake beds and other depressions; a calcimorphic group, the Rendzina, occupies a great expanse between the lower Rio Grande (Rio Bravo) and the Rio Panuco, taking in most of Tamaulipas and parts of adjacent states.

The Mexico–United States boundary cuts across major cultural subdivisions of Arid North America. Our discussion focuses on the portions that lie within present-day Mexico: (1) northwest hunting-and-gathering area, (2) northwest primitive agriculture area, (3) hunting-and-gathering area of northern and northeastern Mexico.

HUNTING-AND-GATHERING AREA OF NORTHWEST MEXICO. Hunting-and-gathering cultures occupied the entire peninsula of Baja California along with the islands of the Gulf of California and exclaves on the dry coast of Sonora and northern Sinaloa. Soil formation takes place under dry conditions throughout the area except in the more humid southern tip of the peninsula, the area of winter rains around Ensenada, and some of the higher mountains. In these fairly humid areas soils are spared the harmful effects of extreme calcification, caliche formation, and severe alkalinity, which prevail over the drier lands.[14] The intermittent watercourses emerging from the mountains leave their load of detritus as alluvial fans and flood plains. Since this material is not thoroughly weathered, the Alluvial soils of the peninsula still resemble chemically the Lithosols of the igneous massifs, composed mainly of acidic rocks that are poor parent materials for soil. There are numerous outcrops of Tertiary andesites which may weather into fairly good soils. Only a small fraction of the peninsula offers truly superior parent materials like the basaltic lava flows at San Quentin. There are many areas of fertile soils that might have supported the primitive agriculture of northwest Mexico but fewer scattered spots where the scant local water resources could have been so utilized by their rudimentary technology.

The problems of the northern sierras are

14 Ortiz (1957, p. 44) shows the Cape of San Lucas area as having soils only slightly alkaline in contrast with the distinctly alkaline category in which he places the rest of the peninsula and the mainland coast of the gulf.

exemplified by the Paipai Indian Reservation southeast of Ensenada. Pebbles of granite and andesite eroded from nearby mountains cover much of the surface as "desert pavement," though many soils may still belong to the azonal Regosol and Alluvial soil groups. Even so, there are enough finer materials sufficiently weathered to make abundant nutrients available to plants. Rainfall, varying from about 250 to 500 mm. a year, would be ample for some pre-Columbian crop plants but for the fact that it is split between two unreliable seasons, June through August and November through April, neither of which is copious enough to assure a harvest. The winter rainy season has an added disadvantage of occasional freezing temperatures. These climatic conditions, rather than poverty of soil, were probably the natural factors that restricted the spread of pre-Columbian agriculture into such areas.

PRIMITIVE AGRICULTURE AREA OF NORTHWEST MEXICO. This area is cut in three by the Sierra Madre Occidental: (a) the lower slopes and foothills of the Sierra and adjacent coastal plains, (b) the upper slopes and valleys, (c) the scattered desert oases east of the Sierra.

Lower Slopes and Foothills of the Sierra Madre Occidental and Adjacent Coastal Plain. Here calcification-process soils range from Desert and Red Desert groups on the plain to the less severe manifestations of the process, Chestnut and Reddish Chestnut groups, and some Chernozem under more humid conditions at medium elevations (see the caption to fig. 1). Non-calcic Brown soils have been identified along the Arizona-Sonora border (U. S. Department of Agriculture, *Yearbook* 1938, pp. 1097–98) and probably occur widely in the forest-grassland transition areas of eastern Sonora.

The primitive agriculturists in this area confined their farming mainly but not entirely to the soils along rivers. The Yuman people practiced agriculture in desert areas outside the river valleys, growing corn, beans, melons, and pumpkins along creeks and around springs (Castetter and Bell, 1951, p. 43). Studhalter (1936, p. 116) describes Yaqui farming as "sand agriculture" practiced along the margins of the lower Yaqui River, where "even in the driest season and driest soil, a moist subsoil is reached at a depth of 6 or 8 inches."

Upper Slopes and Valleys of the Sierra Madre Occidental. In marked contrast to the relatively simpler edaphic patterns to the west and east, these areas present an immense variety of soils which will long elude definitive classification. Zonal soils probably include the Prairie and forest-grassland transition groups, along with mildly podzolized forest soils. In poorly drained valley bottoms some formation of intrazonal Humic Glei, low Humic Glei, and perhaps even Alpine Meadow soils may be found.

Much of this area, particularly the less accessible parts, is still occupied by the Tarahumara, one of the indigenous groups most successful in retaining its racial and cultural singularity. Yet they have adopted many European techniques, such as keeping domestic animals to supply manure to fertilize the otherwise unproductive sierra soil. In places so much of the volume of the surface mantle is taken up by large stones that the amount of true soil within the reach of crop plants may be limited. Nevertheless, ". . . the stoniest land yields good corn if it has been 'cured with manure'" (Zingg, 1935, p. 10).

The Tarahumara descend into the *barrancas* (canyons) on the west side of the Sierra in search of pastures and escape from the cold of the highland winters. There they raise crops of tropical and subtropical fruits as well as corn, beans, and pumpkins, in small plots perched upon the steep sides. Retaining walls, known as *trincheras*, have been constructed to conserve moisture, hold the soil in place, and even add to it by intercepting debris

291

washed down from above. The *trinchera* device has also been employed for conserving and improving the soils of the Sierra (Lumholtz, 1902, 1: 73; Kelley, 1956, p. 137).

Tens of hectares of scant sierra and barranca pastures are needed to sustain enough animals to fertilize one hectare of crop land. As the Tarahumara have much more land level enough for plowing than can possibly be fertilized, cattle rather than land come to be recognized as the primary capital resource. While giving the Tarahumara the capital and technique to enhance his soil resources, the Europeans and mestizos to some extent have forced him to do so by encroaching on his former holdings on the plateau to the east and in the lower reaches of the barrancas to the west.

Scattered Oases of the Arid Lands East of the Sierra Madre Occidental. These oases sustained agricultural enclaves and salients within an area disputed by hunting-and-gathering peoples. The agriculturists were little attracted by the calcification-process zonal soils of the interfluves and higher river terraces which could hardly be irrigated by their technology. Most of their settlements relied on Alluvial soils along stream beds, lake margins, and on alluvial fans.

Kelley (1956) has distinguished archaeologically four major settlement patterns of early farming peoples in north-central Mexico. (1) The La Quemada–Chalchihuites culture, a northwestern extension of the Mesoamerican pattern, followed the high eastern foothill basins of the Sierra Madre Occidental in Zacatecas and Durango and occupied sites with Chestnut and Mountain soils. (2) The Loma San Gabriel culture occurred generally north of the La Quemada–Chalchihuites area in northern Durango and southern Chihuahua, where, owing to lower elevations and warmer and drier conditions, soils are subject to more intensive calcification; settlements along the headwaters of the Florido and Conchos

rivers depended on alluvial soils. (3) The Conchos–Bravo Valley culture of northeastern Chihuahua was based on Alluvial soils in braided stream channels and on lower terraces of the rivers of those names. (4) The Chihuahua culture (northwestern Chihuahua) occupied one of the driest habitats of any farming people in Arid North America; the cliff dwellers in the Sierra canyons and the adobe-house dwellers along the Casas Grandes, Santa Maria, Carmen, and Piedras Verdes rivers cultivated Regosols and Alluvial soils along stream courses and on alluvial fans.

Kelley (1956, p. 139) believes that these farming cultures disappeared around A.D. 1350 and 1400, except that of the Bravo Valley at the junction of the Conchos and Grande rivers, "which survived into the historic period under exceptionally favorable environmental conditions." He also suggests that the decline may have been effected by "ecological changes triggered by comparatively minor climatic fluctuations." More thorough investigation of the soils factor might explain why certain hydrologically favored sites were abandoned while others continued to flourish. However, it must be recognized that these farmers occupied enclaves and salients within another culture zone, where their dominance was challenged by warlike hunting-and-gathering peoples whose mobile striking power was unhampered by ties to precariously balanced and spatially restricted habitats. On Spanish contact (mid-16th century) Tepehuan farmer-hunters from the Sierra Madre Occidental had reoccupied some of the high basins and stream valleys formerly cultivated by the earlier agriculturists. (Sauer, 1934).

HUNTING-AND-GATHERING AREA OF NORTHERN AND NORTHEASTERN MEXICO. The simple hunting-and-gathering peoples who wandered over northern and northeastern Mexico and other dry lands beyond the Rio Grande (Rio Bravo) had less direct concern for the soil than the agricultural peoples on whom they often waged successful forays. That the soil was a determining factor in the location of many of the fruits they gathered, and indirectly of many of the animals they hunted, was scarcely to be noted by people bent upon the chase and the unsown harvest.

Within the area of their activities the more prominent zonal groups are the Red Desert, Reddish Brown and Reddish Chestnut, with some occurrences of other soils classifiable as simply Desert, Sierozem, Brown and Chestnut in the higher and cooler areas. A few higher sierras, like that of Muzquiz, are forested and sufficiently humid to have podzolized soils. The intermontane basins which do not drain out to the sea have strong concentrations of salts left by evaporating water in the sediments washed down from the slopes, whereupon there are many halomorphic intrazonal soils. Azonal soils include the arid Lithosols of steep slopes (fig. 5), "Dry Sands," of the dune area southwest of Ciudad Juarez, and other Regosols, some of which have scarcely a trace of vegetation, as on the red hills east of Casas Grandes.

The southern and easternmost parts of the hunting-and-gathering area, except for the rain-shadow areas, have climates, soils and vegetation considerably more humid than the northern and western portions. Chestnut and Reddish Chestnut soils extend in a wide belt along the Rio Grande; Rendzinas cover the limestone formations of Tamaulipas and the Huasteca (fig. 4); scattered spots of black soils possibly include some Chernozem (near Monterrey and Ciudad Victoria). Except for early primitive part-time farming by Indians of the Tamaulipas Sierra (MacNeish, 1956), soils of northeastern Mexico remained uncultivated until the coming of the Spaniards in the 16th century.

Mesoamerica

The attainment of cultural uniformity sufficient to justify regarding the ecologically diverse area of Mesoamerica as a single culture zone is closely linked with dependence on one major staple crop—maize—which will bear fruit under widely different conditions of soil and climate. Any treatment of the soil resources of Mesoamerica must necessarily be concerned with the actualities and potentialities of maize production. Although maize yields are considerably greater from richer soils with abundant moisture, the crop was relatively dependable throughout Mesoamerica, in contrast with the vast expanses of Arid North America where its cultivation was impracticable or at best unreliable. Beyond the eastern confines of Mesoamerica, in the Circum-Caribbean culture zone, a combination of poor soils and difficulty of preserving grain under high atmospheric humidity may have influenced the preference for yuca (sweet manioc) as a more dependable staple food crop.

For purposes of this section, Mesoamerica[15] is divided into three parts: (A) western Mesoamerica (west of the Isthmus of Tehuantepec), (B) the Maya lands (from the highlands of Chiapas and Guatemala northward across the lowlands through Yucatan), and (C) southern Mesoamerica (south of the Maya Lands, along the Pacific coast and parts of the adjacent highlands from Tehuantepec through northwestern Costa Rica).

WESTERN MESOAMERICA. Western Mesoamerica is severed by mountains and valleys into small, often clearly distinct habitats. In the present state of our knowledge we dare not venture for this area such sweeping generalization as we have employed in dealing with the monotonously uniform environments, separated by broad and gradual transition zones, in Arid North

[15] Mesoamerica is here understood as that area extending across the continent south and eastward from the Sinaloa, Lerma, and Panuco rivers to northwestern Honduras and along the highlands and Pacific coast of Central America as far as the Guanacaste lowlands and the Nicoya Peninsula of Costa Rica (Kirchhoff, 1943, p. 98).

America. Though it is not possible here to appraise the soils resources of all the major culture groups of Western Mesoamerica, summary appraisals for several areas are offered, as samples of the whole and an indication of lines of inquiry for attacking the problem: (a) Otomi-Pame, (b) Teotlalpan, (c) Valley of Mexico, (d) Tarascan, (e) Ixcatecan.

Otomi-Pame Area. The Otomi and their kinsmen, the Pame, Chichimec, Mazahua, and Matlazinca, held positions geographically and technologically transitional between Mesoamerica and the simpler cultures of Arid North America. From north to south in increasingly favorable habitats, they achieved a progressively more elaborate development of culture. On the calcified soils of the far north, in the rain shadow of the Sierra Madre Oriental, where the scant precipitation was too widely scattered throughout the year for raising dependable maize crops, control was disputed with the "indios rayados," nomads reputed to have been entirely without agriculture; and some of the Pame and Chichimecs followed a seminomadic way of life, combining rudimentary agriculture with hunting and gathering. Farther south in the desertic valleys of Zimapan and Mezquital, the concentration of rainfall in one season assured some sort of harvest, while even farther south, in the *tierra fría* around Jilotepec, the Sierra de las Cruces and the Valley of Toluca, near the Neovolcanic Axis, richer soils and abundant seasonal precipitation gave a more secure resource base for cultural development. The Matlazinca branch of the family held the southernmost reaches of the Otomi-Pame area. There the soil was richer, the rainfall more abundant and reliable, and cultural development, as evidenced by the monolithic monuments of Malinalco, was the most ostentatious of the entire family and worthy to rank with the highest of Mesoamerican achievements.

Since the Spanish conquest, the Otomi-Pame peoples have been dispossessed of much of the better lands they once held, by extermination in wars and epidemics, by assimilation into the mestizo population, and by forced or voluntary withdrawal into the less-coveted lands of the mountains and deserts.

There are two principal blocks of the Modern Otomi country. The *tierra templada* areas of Zimapan and the Valley of Mezquital present dry-land types of Lithosols and Regosols on the steeper slopes and zonal Desert soils (Sierozem), along with less extremely calcified groups, in places of gentler relief. To the extent that water supply permits, these soils are fairly productive, except where the desert hardpan is extremely firm and very near the surface.[16]

The other main block of Otomi lands is at altitudes above 2500 m. in the *tierra fría* of the Sierra de las Cruces, Cerro Jilotepec, the northeastern quarter of the Valley of Toluca and intervening hills and high plains to the border of Hidalgo State. The Sierra de las Cruces is composed of predominantly andesitic lavas and ash, parent materials that naturally render quite fertile soils. On many of the higher mountain valleys are Alpine Meadow soils, somewhat boggy and usually avoided for planting but valued for pastures. Dark-colored soil groups appropriate for subhumid to humid grasslands predominate in the Otomi portion of the Valley of Toluca and the plateau of Jilotepec. Some of the densest concentrations of the Otomi, averaging in places less than two hectares per family, are found on the plain formerly occupied by Lake Lerma, where lacustrine Alluvial soils remain amazingly productive even though planted to maize for uncounted years in succession.

The Otomi around Jilotepec occupy gen-

[16] In some places pits are chopped through the hardpan to give transplanted maguey a start, by retaining runoff water and allowing the roots to penetrate quickly and deeply in search of water in looser, lower horizons. Unfortunately the streams have eroded such deep channels that the task of bringing irrigation water to the terraces is difficult.

tly rolling plains covered with a thick mantle of dark-gray to black soil, probably of the Prairie group, which is used mostly for pasture; steep, erosive slopes of scattered hills are being deforested and planted to maize. The inhabitants explain that the plains soils are unproductive without fertilizer, which they cannot afford. Though derived from basalt and other base-rich volcanic materials, the soils are evidently extremely leached. Overgrazing is responsible for considerable sheet erosion. Toward the end of the dry season after the grass has been nibbled to the ground, sheep paw the sod and eat the very roots, as no other forage is available. Loose soil accumulates 2 or 3 inches thick in places. When the rains come suddenly much topsoil is lost before it can be fixed by grass sprouting from the remaining roots.

The Modern Mazahua are scattered over the northwestern quarter of the Valley of Toluca and beyond to encompass Cerro Jocotitlan and the crests and flanks of the sierra between the states of Mexico and Michoacan. The Mazahua do not share the well-watered areas around former Lake Lerma, but occupy zones of older sedimentary formations, often very porous, dissected and well drained by the Lerma and its tributaries. Under rather treeless, grassy vegetation, the soils developed here probably range from Prairie and Chernozem through the Chestnut and Brown groups.

The pine-forested sierra soils held by the Mazahua have good structure because of the abundance of organic matter in the A horizon and they are frequently planted to maize even though pine trees may be left standing amidst the fields. Of course, with the repeated disturbance of the feeder-root systems by the creole plow many of the trees soon die (then they may be cut down without incurring the displeasure of the forest inspectors). After several years of repeated maize planting, the good soil structure is lost, the fields are abandoned, and grassland encroaches further on the forest.

The Teotlalpan. The core area of the Toltec empire of Tollan and a key area for succeeding empires encompassed about 2500 square miles lying roughly in a triangle with vertices at Tula and Actopan, Hidalgo, and Zumpango, Mexico. Sherburne F. Cook (1949a, p. 12) calculates a population of some 200,000 in the heyday of Tollan, later diminished to about 50,000 and increasing again to 477,480 on the eve of the conquest.

To have supported such a density (217 per square kilometer) by agriculture would have required a soil resource far better than present vestiges indicate to have been in the area. Today's thin, stony Lithosols, occasionally interspersed by thicker remnants of Chestnut or similar groups, afford a precarious living to an agricultural population scarcely one-fourth so numerous.

The hillsides no doubt were formerly covered by much thicker soils. Whether these were productive enough to support Cook's estimate of the preconquest population is problematical. It is not necessary to infer that such a large population must have existed in order to account for today's exhausted soil conditions. The damage need not be attributed to 500,000 people in one century when it could just as plausibly have been caused by 100,000 in five centuries.[17]

Valley of Mexico. Soils of the slopes and crests of the sierras that ring the Valley of Mexico like a giant horseshoe on the west, south, and east, are generally fertile, retaining much of the base mineral component of the parent rocks. These are predominantly basaltic in the south, where Popocatepetl, Xitle, and other volcanoes have

[17] Even so, the population of the Teotlalpan was undoubtedly more numerous in pre-Columbian times than it is today, and S. F. Cook (1949a, pp. 58–59) is probably right in maintaining that the population would have declined even without the slaughter and epidemics brought by the conquest because of "a loss in agricultural potency mediated directly by erosion and indirectly by diminution in soil water because of erosion and partial deforestation."

been active during Recent geologic times, and andesitic on the Tertiary formations elsewhere. In parts of the Las Cruces and Ajusco sierras, at elevations of 2500–2800 m., there are patches of silty soil with high moisture-retaining capacity which permits maize planting, the so-called *maíz de cajete* crop, six or eight weeks before the regular rainy season. Higher up in the sierras maize planting must be delayed not for lack of residual soil moisture but for danger of late frosts. Above 3000 m. at these latitudes cultivation of maize and maguey is not practicable because of the cold. After the conquest, the introduction of small grains, the potato, and domestic animals has enabled the Indians to utilize the Alpine Meadow and other soils of these higher elevations.

Remnants of extinct volcanoes are also scattered about the valley floor, which is filled to above 2200 m. at base level with volcanic ejecta, aeolian, alluvial, and lacustrine deposits. Some of these volcanic edifices, like the Sierra de Santa Catarina, provide base-rich parent materials. The Sierra de Guadalupe, on the plain north of Mexico City, consists largely of trachyte, one of the poorer volcanic parent materials. Aridity and a scant vegetative cover contribute further to the poor quality of the Lithosols on these and other low hills that do not rise high enough above the plain to exact much moisture from the passing clouds. From the driest part of the Valley, in the rain shadow of the Sierra de Pachuca, on the north, may be traced a gamut of soil groups ranging from Desert through Chestnut, Chernozem, and finally to podzolized profiles on the gently sloping benchlands of the rainier southern part of the basin.

A profile I examined near Tizayuca is somewhat representative of the Desert and related soil groups which abound in the northern two-thirds of the Valley. The loose mantle, only 30 cm. deep, is underlain by a desert hardpan (caliche) about 25 cm. thick resting in turn on the Tacubaya Formation, a yellowish-brown volcanic tuff and a com-

mon parent material of soils on the higher parts of the valley floor once covered by Pleistocene Lake Barcena.

During the heydays of Teotihuacan and Tollan thicker and more productive agricultural soil must have covered the northern half of the Valley. What we now think of as an A horizon may be in reality a B or C horizon in process of transformation. After the decline and fall of these empires, hegemony passed to the city states of Anahuac, the land on the edge of the water, around the margins of Lakes Chalco, Xochimilco, Zumpango, Xaltocan, San Cristobal, and Texcoco.[18] Here not only was the moisture supply more reliable, but also the lacustrine Alluvial soils were not so subject to depletion by man-made erosion. The gradients around many parts of the lakeshores were very slight so that in dry years considerably more land was available for farming than in wet years when the waters spread over a wider area. Here man became a deliberate soil-forming agent with his innovation of the *chinampas*, or "floating gardens."

Tarascan Area. Before the conquest, the Tarascans occupied most of what is now the state of Michoacan and parts of adjacent areas. The modern Tarascan area, defined by the criterion of continued use of their language, is much more restricted, lying for the most part west of Morelia and centering about Lake Patzcuaro. West (1948, pp. 9–11) gives appropriate, though brief, consideration to the soils of this habitat:

Three soil types which tend to coincide with climate and vegetation, predominate in the Tarascan area: (1) a yellowish-brown soil of the upper mountain slopes (Cwb to Cwc, pine-fir cover); (2) a dark, fine sandy loam (t'up-úri) of the lower slopes and basins in the Sierra (Cwb, oak-pine, probably grass vegetation); and (3) the reddish-brown clay soil (charán-

---

[18] Reference has already been made to the draining of these lakes in the last century and the consequent problems of salinity in soils of the old lake beds.

da) of the lower altitudes (warm phase of Cwb, Cwa, broad-leaf vegetation) around Lake Patzcuaro, in the lower elevations of the northern plateau, and in the escarpment zone. . . .

West took samples of the surface soil to a depth of 25 cm. but did not determine profiles or attempt to classify the soils according to world soil groups. Subsequently, I examined several profiles in the area, including a "charánda," 3 km. east of Quiroga, with high silica content (40–50 per cent) and a silica-sesquioxide ratio of about 1:1. In this respect, and in their color and propensity for gulley erosion, they resemble the Red Podzolic soils of southeast United States.[19]

The "yellowish-brown" soils, leached and unproductive after a few years, possibly belong to the Brown Podzolic or Gray Brown Podzolic group. The fine-sandy surface soil acts as a mulch preventing excessive evaporation. There is enough residual soil moisture toward the end of the dry season that many of these soils may be planted one or two months before the rains. Thus the corn gets a good head start on noxious weeds and grasses, but if the rains should be late, the crop may suffer for lack of moisture in a critical stage of growth.

The "t'upúri" soil found on the lower

slopes and basin plains at elevations of 2000–2400 m., differs from the "yellowish-brown" soils in having a higher content of silt and clay, a fine sandy-loam texture and greater fertility. Its structure admits water freely so that fairly steep slopes may be cultivated without serious erosion while its fine-sandy topsoil, like that of the "yellowish-brown" soils, preserves subsoil moisture from excessive evaporation so that the "t'upúri" also may be planted ahead of the rains.

The "uirás," a fibery-textured white clay soil found on Jaracuaro Island in Lake Patzcuaro, on the southwestern shore of the latter near Ihuatzio, and on the outskirts of Zacapu, is usually poor except where mingled with lacustrine deposits to form a fertile loam.

The preconquest Tarascans also held the more humid, southern part of El Bajio, on the left bank of the Lerma, and a few outposts beyond, in the "march lands" between the sedentary and nomadic culture areas. Here are some of Mexico's most classic examples of Chernozem soils, as well as other soils which resemble the Prairie and Reddish Prairie groups. There are volcanic Lithosols and Regosols on slopes, hydromorphic soil groups around Lake Yuririapundaro, and halomorphic groups around the receding shores of Lake Cuitzeo.

Much of the western half of the Balsas-Tepalcatepec depression was in the pre-Columbian Tarascan dominion. At those lower elevations, with consequently higher temperatures, evaporation is very pronounced, accentuating the aridity imposed by the rain shadows of the encompassing mountain systems, the Sierra Madre del Sur and the Sierra Volcanica Transversal. Calcification is more in evidence on the hotter, drier lowlands than on the cooler and more moist upper slopes; laterization is also discernible. Brambila and Ortiz show "Black Soils (Chernozem)," Chestnut and Prairie soils for the depression; probably a more detailed survey of the area would

[19] In the study by West (1948, p. 9n.), "All soils analyzed (including t'upúri and charánda types) were low in lime content (0.24 to 0.34 per cent), and slightly alkaline (pH values: yellow-brown mountain soils, 7.22 to 7.24; t'upúri, 7.44 to 7.71; charánda, 7.21 to 7.42; uirás, 8.05 to 8.13)." Without exception, the profiles I examined were quite the contrary: pH values of the surface horizons (A) varied from 5.55 to 6.05; and from 4.80 to 6.05 in the upper subsoil; $CaCo_3$ content was from three to five times the concentrations ascribed by West. The "yellowish-brown" profile had very high nitrogen content (0.32 in the upper 15 cm. and 0.28 at the 15–40-cm. level) in contrast to the 0.09 which West reports for the generally more fertile "t'upúri," which is to be regarded as a fair concentration for soils in Mexico. Organic matter was found to be fairly high, from 2.65 to 5.23 in the "charánda" topsoils, and 8.67 in the "yellowish-brown" profile.

show that Reddish Chestnut, Reddish Prairie, and Degraded Chernozem groups are more common (see captions for figs. 3 and 4). Lateritic profiles are also recognizable among the older soils. The influence of three major types of parent material is still apparent even on older soils; those developed from the intrusive formations around La Huacana are poor in comparison to soils developed from volcanic ashes and cinders or from Cretaceous limestone formations.

Ixcatecan Area. The Ixcatecans are a minor indigenous group in an isolated valley north of Nochistlan between the Mexico-Oaxaca railroad and the Inter-American highway. Their habitat has been intensively studied by Cook (1958), with considerable attention to soils. These are mainly derived from calcareous "tepetate" (caliche) and limestone materials. Cook's descriptions suggest that most soils still belong to the Lithosol and Alluvial groups, although they have undergone some calcification.

During the last few centuries erosion has been so severe that mature profiles are hard to find. East of Ixcatlan toward Cuicatlan and Tecomavaca, where the oak forest has not been entirely destroyed, there may be some remnants of mature profiles of the Brown Forest group. As the forest recedes, the persistent calcareous nature of the soil is evidenced by the invasion of palmetto, which has a decided preference for alkaline soils and does best on those derived from limestone. This plant furnishes the raw material for making straw hats; thus the only local industry of any consequence is intimately bound to the soil resource.

On river terraces west of Ixcatlan, Cook (1958, pp. 15–16) examined an old soil profile, with A and B horizons still intact and grading normally into *tepetate*, buried beneath a layer of sand and gravel 1 m. thick. Speculating on the history of the terrace, the author sees in it a record of aboriginal man's erosion-accelerating activities on the upper watershed.

For Ixcatlan and its subject territory, Cook (1949b, pp. 22–24; 1958, pp. 18–24) estimates the population on the eve of the conquest to have been 10,000. Of these, at least 6000 lived in the valley, which today can scarcely support 1100 people by a combination of subsistence agriculture and straw-hat manufacture. The decline was due partly to migrations and partly to epidemics. Cook holds soil exhaustion and erosion as largely responsible for these migrations and for the inability of the population to regain its former density. Though reduced in numbers, the postconquest population, aided by the plow and domestic animals, remained nonetheless active in soil destruction.

MAYA LANDS. The most elaborate developments of Maya civilization took place in three types of environment with clearly distinct soil resource bases: (a) The Classic Maya concentrated in and around El Peten, in a tropical rain forest supported by leached zonal soils interspersed with calcimorphic and hydromorphic groups as well as Lithosols; nearly all the soils of the area are derived from calcareous parent materials. (b) The Postclassic Maya were situated in northern Yucatan Peninsula, where dry seasons, flat relief, and limestone parent material of great porosity give origin to Rendzina and Terra Rossa soils. [20] (c) The highland Maya settled in the sierras of Guatemala and Chiapas where the limestone and volcanic parent materials have weathered into Lithosols and immature zonal soils of great variety in accordance with the complex patterns of climate and relief.

[20] There has been considerable disagreement as to what soils should be called "Terra Rossa" (from the Italian, meaning literally "red earth") and whether or not they should be regarded as a distinct great soil group. In this paper, the term is used for red soils developed on limestone in a warm, wet-dry season climate, which definition is broad enough to include the soils of Yucatan to which it has customarily been applied. See note 13 regarding the relationship of Terra Rossa to the other higher categories of soil classification.

298

Classic Maya Area. Spread over 45,000 sq. km., the soils of the Classic Maya Area at its peak supported about 300,000 inhabitants or about 6.6 per sq. km. (Termer, 1950, p. 237), in comparison with a density of less than one over most of these lands today. The present inhabitants, mostly Maya Indians, practice shifting agriculture in a manner little changed since the conquest. Nowhere else in Middle America is so vast an area and such a large proportion of the population still dependent on pre-Columbian technology.

About three-fourths of the Classic Maya Area was in what is now the Department of El Peten, Guatemala, and was therefore included in the recent reconnaissance soil survey of that country. The published report (Simmons, Tárano and Pinto, 1959) has furnished much of the data on which the following summary and the accompanying sketch map (fig. 7) are based, but I assume full responsibility for postulating classifications at the levels of order, suborder, and great soil groups.

Zonal soils of the laterization process are prescribed by the humid tropical climate and vegetation. However, the paucity of iron in the parent materials, chiefly residues of the disintegrating limestone platform along with colluvial and alluvial deposits of the same origin, makes it difficult for classic lateritic profiles to develop. Extreme stickiness afflicts 14 of the 26 soil series classified in El Peten. Output per worker is slowed by the adherence of heavy soil to his implements, whether these be modern plows, hoes, or simple digging sticks. This adverse trait is not usual for well-laterized soils, but in El Peten it occurs on some of the more intensely weathered series which clearly resemble the lateritic groups in other important respects.

Deeply weathered Reddish Brown Lateritic soils occupy well-drained forest and savanna lands of west-central and south-central El Peten, and northerly portions of El Quiche and Alta Verapaz. Yellowish

Brown Lateritic soils occur under similar plant cover in southwest El Peten and other lowland areas of Alta Verapaz and Izabal departments. Soils of these two groups have been well leached of mineral nutrients. In some parts of the forested areas they may be initially productive but lose fertility rapidly once the forest cover is removed. Lateritic soils of well-drained savannas in central and south-central Peten (Chachaclun and Poptun series), definitely inadequate for maize, at present are used for poor pasturage or left idle. The question arises whether or not these are remnants of forested lateritic soils, somewhat further leached and transformed under grassy vegetation following deforestation. If that is so, and if the Maya were responsible for the deforestation, there should be archaeological evidence of agricultural occupancy in well-watered sites amidst the savanna soils. Of course, since many series occur in fragmented associations, it is not easy to determine precisely which were used by an abandoned settlement.

In the south of El Peten and the north of Alta Verapaz and Izabal departments soils of the Sebol series, derived from alluvial limestone sediments, are classified with the Reddish Brown Lateritic Group; the Guapaca series, formed on clay schists, is placed with the Yellowish Brown Lateritic group. Maintaining fertility of these soils is difficult. A yield of 580 kilograms of maize per hectare is regarded as satisfactory from Guapaca soils, which support an economy based on maize and hogs. Both the Sebol and the Guapaca series offer advantages over richer nearby soils in being neither stony nor steep nor sticky. "In effect, inhabited areas in the south of El Peten may indicate the presence of Guapaca soils" (Simmons et al., 1959, p. 770).

Hydromorphic soils, which may include Ground-Water Podzols and Ground-Water Laterites as well as Bog and Half-Bog groups, are found in permanently and intermittently flooded areas, which are many

299

and vast in the forests and savannas of El
Peten, especially in the northwestern quarter. Some such soils occur even without
flooding, where perched water tables saturate the lower soil horizons. The area poses
innumerable problems of transition types
between the hydromorphic gleization-process intrazonal soils and the laterization-process zonal soils.

Where flooding does not entirely preclude agricultural land use, the productive
capacity of the hydromorphic soils is limited by the intensely leached, highly acidic,
and frustratingly sticky soil. Although simple drainage works could extend the usable
area, a great part could not have been
farmed by practices known to have been
available to the ancient Maya and therefore
must be subtracted in estimating the agricultural potential of their lands. This is
an area of karst topography, where the surface is lowered in spots as percolating water
dissolves and removes part of the underlying limestone. This process could have
extended the flooded areas, thereby reducing the soil resources available to the Maya;
in that case, there should be some evidence
of former occupancy in the areas affected.

Calcimorphic Rendzina soils, which cover
large areas in Yucatan, are not so extensive
in El Peten. The Uaxactun and Macanche
series of the northeast corner appear to be
fairly deep Rendzinas. Today the Macanche
are usually preferred for farming and the
Uaxactun are almost entirely forested. Both
series are among the potentially most productive soils of El Peten, and their usable
areas could be greatly extended by simple
drainage works.

More extensive are the areas of "black
calcareous Lithosols resembling Rendzina"
(Cuxu, Jolja, and Yaxa series) derived from
soft limestones on terrain that varies from
rolling to steep and is essentially karstic,
in eastern and central El Peten (see fig. 7).
The parent rocks are at depths usually less
than 50 cm., and rocky outcrops cover more

than 15 per cent of the surface in many
Cuxu areas. Especially on Yaxa soils, strong
winds frequently blow down many trees
that have been unable to get a firm foothold
in the thin soil (Simmons et al., 1959, p.
985). Closest to Rendzina is the Jolja
series, developed under conditions of moderate relief and good drainage in northwest,
west-central, and south-central El Peten,
fertile and tillable enough to support a
prosperous agriculture despite their stickiness and, in places, thinness of profile.

On locating the major Classic Maya ceremonial centers on the map of soils of northern Guatemala (fig. 7), we are struck by
the number situated in or between the soil
areas here classified as Rendzina and "black
calcareous Lithosols resembling Rendzina."

"Brown calcareous Lithosols" have developed from hard limestones (Chacalte
and Sacluc series) and calcareous schists
(Ixbobo series) on rolling to steep, mostly
karstic, terrain in north-central, central, and
southern El Peten; and on the foothills of
the highlands farther south. Steepness,
stoniness, and high erosiveness limit the
utility of these soils.

Noncalcareous Lithosols, though virtually
absent in El Peten, are found on the eastern and southern confines of the Classic
Maya Area. Shallow Lithosols derived from
the silicic rocks, as in the Maya-Cockscomb
Mountains, and especially those of Alta
Verapaz and Izabal formed on serpentine,
one of the poorest parent materials, have
been of little value to the indigenes from
prehistoric times to the present.

Alluvial soils in the Classic Maya Area
occur most widely along the Pasion, Usumacinta, and other large rivers of El Peten,
Campeche, and Tabasco. Having originated
mainly in limestone country, much is rich in
mineral nutrients. The older soils, where
well drained, show evidence of laterization,
whereas in poorly drained places they are
hard to distinguish from hydromorphic soils.
To the south the Alluvial group together

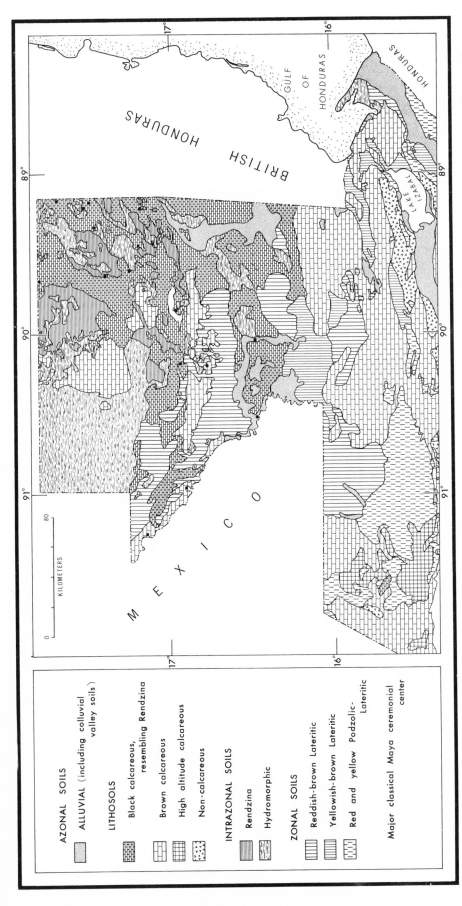

Fig. 7.—SOILS OF NORTHERN GUATEMALA

AZONAL SOILS

ALLUVIAL (including colluvial valley soils)

LITHOSOLS

Black calcareous, resembling Rendzina

Brown calcareous

High altitude calcareous

Non-calcareous

INTRAZONAL SOILS

Rendzina

Hydromorphic

ZONAL SOILS

Reddish-brown Lateritic

Yellowish-brown Lateritic

Red and yellow Podzolic-Lateritic

Major classical Maya ceremonial center

The basic data for this sketch were secured mainly from the report of the Reconnaissance Soil Survey of Guatemala (Simmons, Tárano, and Pinto, 1959). However, the attempt at relating the series descriptions to the higher categories of soil classification is my responsibility. In many instances the descriptive data on particular soils and the consensus as to what should be included or not in the various categories were both inadequate to permit definitive classifica-

tions. Though the boundaries and nomenclature are subject to change, the map shows some of the differentiated major features of the soil resource base of much of the ancient Maya lowlands and part of the adjacent highland area. Soil maps commonly show areas of prevailing kinds of soil; within these areas—especially is this true of the variegated pattern of El Petén—are scattered patches of other kinds of soil. It is sometimes difficult to ascertain whether the soils actually farmed by a given Maya settlement were of the locally prevailing types or the exceptional enclaves.

The occurrence of a great number of major Classic Maya ceremonial centers on the soil areas here classified as Rendzina (Macanche and Uaxactun series), or between those areas and the "black calcareous Lithosols resembling Rendzina" (Cuxu, Jolja, and Yaxa series), suggests that both kinds of soil were principal resources of the ancient Maya. These particular Rendzinas are not inclined to severe erosion, but it is feasible that the calcareous Lithosols may now be undergoing rejuvenation after a former period of intensive cultivation and accelerated erosion.

with colluvial valley soils line the Senin-latiu-Sarstun, Polochic-Izabal, and the lower Motagua valleys.

Termer (1950, p. 231) emphasized the concentration of Classic Maya settlements along the upper and middle course of the rivers in Tabasco and El Peten, where the banks are high enough to provide safety from floods, whereas the lower courses subject to frequent flooding were avoided. It would be interesting to know to what extent the riverine Maya of the Classic period confined their farming to the Alluvial soils of natural levees and young terraces or whether they also extended onto areas of older alluvium with more thorough zonal soil development.

Lack of surface supplies of fresh water over vast areas of karst topography in El Peten has handicapped the agricultural use of many fertile soils. Copious rains may keep the soil moist enough for crops whereas the freely percolating water quickly penetrates the porous substrata beyond the reach of men equipped with primitive technology. Study of the soils and settlement sites on the periphery of the Classic Maya Area in British Honduras by the Land Use Survey Team (1959, p. 110) suggests that ". . . unlike present day Indians, the ancient Maya placed rather less emphasis upon abundant supplies of fresh water and the 'mamulated' kind of topography that can provide an abundance of good house sites, and somewhat more emphasis on living close up against, or in the midst of, fertile soils."

The hypothesis that soil depletion caused the wholesale decline of Classic Maya is rejected by the British Honduras Land Use Survey Team (1959, p. 114), but has been supported by some leading scholars. Sylvanus G. Morley (1956, p. 71) suggests as a "possible explanation" that Classic Maya culture declined as the increase in population caused the system of shifting cultivation to be repeated too often to allow time for the impoverished lands to recuperate.

In some of the soil areas here discussed, such developments are feasible. Soils of the lateritic groups, and usable portions of the hydromorphic soils, are depleted rapidly and need a long period of recovery. But the soil areas which appear to have supported the highest Classic Maya achievements, as shown on the map (fig. 7), are the Rendzina and the "black calcareous Lithosols resembling Rendzina," soils not easily exhaustible even by continued cropping. However, these Lithosols in general are highly erosible and could be undergoing rejuvenation after a former period when intensive cultivation and accelerated erosion removed a thicker and more productive soil. As Morley (1956, p. 71) also suggests, it is feasible that "the repeated clearing and burning of areas to serve as corn lands may have gradually converted the original forests into man-made grasslands. Since the ancient Maya had no implements for breaking the sod, such areas would have become useless for agriculture." A great civilization could dwindle away before the forest could reconquer the grassland.

Far more thorough examination of the soil is needed before we can begin to interpret the ecological factors in Maya culture history. We must not overdraw conclusions based on simple comparison of settlement maps and soil maps that have not been made by coordinated investigation. The relation of settlement sites and tillable soils should be studied in the field by observers who combine an understanding of Maya agriculture with inquiry on the origin and properties of the soils actually available to each particular settlement.[21]

[21] Field studies like that of William R. Bullard (1960), relating the distribution of settlements in northeast Peten to relief, dependable water sources, and potential farm land, are to be recommended but should give more attention to the local pattern of soil variations. In another valuable pilot project, Hugh Popenoe (1960) analyzed the effects of shifting cultivation on soils in the Polochic Valley, an area ecologically transitional and culturally more akin to the highlands.

302

Postclassic Maya Area. Systematic study of the soils of the Yucatan Peninsula, wherein the Postclassic Maya Area was situated, was begun by the Maya themselves. For the various kinds of soil they developed a specific nomenclature which survives in the present-day vernacular of Yucatecan agriculturists. Ortiz (1950) has found some of the Maya terms sufficiently compatible with modern procedures of soil classification that he adapted them as names of families and series within the Terra Rossa,[22] Rendzina, and other intrazonal groups.[23]

The term *tzekel*, meaning "land very stony or full of stones and land bad for sowing" in Maya, is used by Ortiz to group in one family all the thin residual soils of Yucatan where limestone outcrops at the surface. By prefixing the modifier *kankab* (meaning "reddish earth") before the term *tzekel*, Ortiz designates a family of undifferentiated soil series transitional between the shallow Tzekel family and the deeper soils of the Kankab series. Next to the Tzekel, the Kankab-Tzekel soils are the most extensive in Yucatan State, and like the Tzekel, they are transitional between Lithosols, Rendzina, and Terra Rossa. The Kankab soil series is more distinctly Terra Rossa, as evidenced by the reddish color, clay texture, granular structure, and high content of available calcium throughout the profile, even after laterization has brought about concentration of sesquioxides of aluminum (35 per cent) and iron (10 per cent). With limestone at a depth of more than 1 m., this is the deepest of the zonal soils in Yucatan State.

The Kankab-Kat ("potter's red earth") series is a red clay soil overlying a yellow clay subsoil, observed by Ortiz (1950, p. 271), on the edge of the Sabana de X-Cumya, 40 km. south of Tekax municipio. The terrain has gentle slopes up to 5 per cent, and some colluvium is mixed with the residual soil development. The Kankab-Kat appears sufficiently laterized to be grouped with the Terra Rossa.

The Eck-Lum ("black earth") series, with a clay topsoil varying from gray through black in color overlying a yellow clay with numerous cracks partly filled with material washed down from above, occurs on argillaceous formations in very flat areas, sometimes inundated during the rainy season, with savanna grassland and bush vegetation. Not enough calcium remains in the profile to qualify this soil as the Rendzina. The series probably belongs to the Yellow Podzolic group, with intrazonal Planosol or Half-Bog soils in association.

The Chichan-Kanab series, conventionally named after the place where first described, on the receding shores of Chichan Kanab Lagoon (Ortiz, 1950, pp. 274–75), has a black topsoil overlying a pale-yellow loam. Intermittent waterlogging and organic matter accumulation suggest the formation of a Half-Bog soil.

Ortiz (1950, p. 285–86) found these soil families and series generally so rich as to require little or no fertilizers, noting only deficiencies of phosphorous in one sample of the family Kankab-Tzekel, of manganese in the Chichan-Kanab series, and of manganese and potassium in the family Tzekel.

Hester (1954; cited by Morley, 1956, p. 453) emphasized that potassium is the nutrient element in most critically short supply in the soils of Yucatan. He remarks that this element is most available on a fresh clearing after a good burn, which presumably makes available some of the potassium and phosphorous locked in otherwise insoluble compounds.[24]

[22] For clarification of the term "Terra Rossa" see notes 13 and 20.

[23] The following brief summary is based on the works of Ortiz (1950, 1957), Steggerda (1941), Aguilera (1959), and Robles (1959), and on the Diccionario de Motul (1929). Unfortunately, available data are not adequate for mapping purposes.

[24] Throughout the Maya lands, as in other zones where "fire agriculture" is practiced, farmers are very anxious to get a "good burn," that is, to heat

Kakab, the Maya name for a small settlement, is also applied to the ruins of abandoned settlements and to the soil formed thereon. The vegetal soil rests on the limestone country rock and is further fertilized by decomposition of the limestone building material of the ruins. It is regarded as a very good soil for corn and other usual crops but has a very loose structure and fine texture which causes it to dry out when rains are delayed so that sometimes the harvest is lost (Cervera, cited by Macías Villada, 1954; cited by Robles Ramos, 1959, p. 57).

Sahkab, another Maya term frequently used in describing the soils of Yucatan, refers to a highly calcareous, yellowish-gray, occasionally reddish, substratum underlying many soils. It is very porous and yet highly water-retentive so that where it is near the surface, vegetation can tap the water supply and remain green through prolonged dry periods (Aguilera Herrera, 1959, pp. 184-85).

The rapid subsurface drainage in much of Yucatan is a serious obstacle to land use. High rainfall quickly percolates beyond the reach of plants. Irrigation is rendered less effective and was impractical with pre-Columbian technology because of the lack of surface streams to be diverted for the purpose. Robles Ramos (1950, pp. 99-100) maintained that a great part of the original topsoil of the Postclassic Maya Area was eroded and filtered into innumerable cavities in the limestone. If true, there should be some archaeological relics in the soil trapped along the underground watercourses. Here is an interesting field problem challenging the combined talents of archaeologists, geologists, and speleologists

as well as soil scientists. Without further investigation, we cannot discount Robles' idea entirely, as Aguilera seems to have done (1959, p. 181).

To what extent do the foregoing descriptions apply to the soils farmed by the ancient Maya? Just after the conquest, Fray Diego de Landa (1941, p. 186) recorded a situation quite similar to that of today:

> Yucatan is the country with least earth that I have seen, since all of it is one living rock and has wonderfully little earth, so that there are few places where one can dig down an *estado* without striking great layers of very large rocks . . . the fertility of this land is so great on top of and between the stones, so that everything that grows in it grows better and more abundantly amongst the rocks than in the earth, because on the earth which happens to be in some parts, neither do trees grow nor are there any, nor do the Indians sow their seeds in it, nor is there anything except grass.

The alarmists may cite this as evidence that already before the coming of the Spaniards the soil resource of Yucatan had been robbed. The less excitable say that if the soil was so thin in Landa's time as now, 400 years have had little effect on it; therefore they find no reason to believe that the soils were much different or more abundant in the 400 years of the Postclassic period which preceded the conquest.

An experiment conducted by the Carnegie Institution of Washington for a 10-year period on a milpa at Chichen Itza showed no change in the chemical composition severe enough to account for the loss in productivity. Citing this experiment, Morley (1956, pp. 135-36) concludes that "increasing weed competition and not decreasing soil fertility is responsible for the diminishing yield from Maya milpas today."

At its peak the Postclassic area had about 500,000 inhabitants in an area of about 135,000 sq. km. (Termer, 1950, p. 229), covering most of the area now in the states of Campeche and Yucatan and the terri-

___

evenly and intensely all the ground that is to be sown. Minerals for plant nutrition are made available not only from the ash of the burning fuel but also some of those already in the soil in a "fixed" state are changed into assimilable forms by the intense heat. For more data on the effects of burning on Central American soils, see Budowski (1956), Popenoe (1960), Skutch (1950).

tory of Quintana Roo. Almost the same number of people live in this area today. On the basis of extent of land and human energy devoted to the chief export crop, henequen, it is feasible that, given different orientation, the populace could still be practicing a self-sustaining agriculture with time left over for building temples.

Other Lowland Maya Areas. Outside the Classic and Postclassic areas, Maya peoples occupied other lands in what is now British Honduras, western Campeche, Tabasco, and northern Chiapas. Were the soils of these areas less adequate for supporting high cultures? When the Classic Maya culture waned, did soil differences have anything to do with a renaissance taking place in northern Yucatan but not in the other lowlands? In some areas there is substantial evidence to the affirmative.

The British Honduras Land Use Survey Team (1959, pp. 110–223), on studying soils in relation to ancient settlement sites in that territory, suggests that the coastal settlements (possibly non-Maya) must have sustained themselves from sea foods, cocoa, yuca, and plantains, for the soils of these areas are generally inadequate for the traditional maize-beans-squash agriculture of the Maya. In the south-central part of the territory the infertile soils derived from siliceous parent materials of the Maya and Cockscomb mountains and related landforms appear to have been as devoid of agricultural settlement in former times as at present. A group of Yucatecan Maya sought to establish on the Mountain Pine Ridge in the 19th century, but by the mid-20th century only one clan-family remained.[25]

[25] The location of settlement sites in British Honduras conforms to the distribution pattern of four kinds of soil: (1) Free-draining black soils on limestone, with numerous settlements, in the western part of the territory on the periphery of the Classic Maya Area. (2) Terrace alluvium formerly subjected to seasonal flooding, mostly along rivers draining the limestone area. The preference of the Maya for middle-terrace sites, though the upper terraces were almost as near to water

Three kinds of soil predominate in the lowlands held by the Maya west of the Classic Area: Alluvial soils along the rivers and coastline; hydromorphic, gleization-process soils on the poorly drained interfluves generally inhospitable to settlement; and Red-Yellow Podzolic-Lateritic intergrades on the better-drained, rolling plains and hills of northern Chiapas, where there is archaeological evidence of former settlement far denser than that of the few Lacandon Maya remaining today. These uplands "might geographically be reckoned a sort of transitional zone but which culturally and linguistically belong with the Central [i.e. Classic] area" (Thompson, 1954, pp. 22–23).

Highland Maya Area. The principal soil regions held by the highland Maya, or in places shared with Zoque, Manque, and Nahua peoples, are distinguished by very close coincidence with conditions of relief and parent material. The soils of the limestone, northern rampart of the highlands of Chiapas and Guatemala are subject to intense leaching under the heavy rainfall—more than 3 m. annually around Coban, Alta Verapaz—brought by the trade winds to these windward slopes. Volcanic ash, transported by wind from the nearby eruptive areas, covers the surface of many of the limestone hills, alternating here, mixing there, with the calcareous parent materials.[26] Red and Yellow Podzolic-Lateritic

and much safer from floods, suggests that the people may have appreciated the renewal of soil fertility by the silt deposits of occasional floods. (3) Soils developed on the siliceous limestone with flint, which lies in a block inland from the coast north of Belice. Chipped-flint mounds indicate the settlements might have been made to secure this resource for some distant center rather than to exploit the none-too-fertile soil. (4) Soil of the cays and coastal areas of dune sands, coral limestone, and mangrove peat.

[26] The Carcha series, at elevations between 600 and 1800 m., has developed from volcanic ash overlying the limestone bedrock; the Amay series, found generally below 1200 m., has developed from limestone; while the Calante series, occurring mostly between 1800 and 2600 m. but sometimes

intergrades, with patches of Lithosols and Alluvial soils, predominate at middle elevations (1000–2000 m.). On lower margins these merge with more weathered soils, which we would assign to the Reddish- and Yellowish-Brown Lateritic groups. Soils tend to be podzolized rather than laterized on the upper reaches. The brownish profiles of the higher lands could understandably include both the zonal Brown Podzolic and the calcimorphic intrazonal Brown Forest soil groups.

Much of the northern escarpment is thinly populated today and appears to have been so at the time of the conquest. Alta Verapaz, relatively well populated then and now, presents a wide range of tropical soils. Repeated clearings through the centuries have greatly reduced the productivity of soils originally good, like the Carcha series, so that much of the land is now used only for grazing or is idle and covered with second growth fern vegetation. The extreme erosibility of most of the soils of Alta Verapaz and the poverty of its population, after a long history and prehistory of land use, make it one of the most acute and challenging problem areas for studying the relationships of soils and Indians. A commendable approach is that of Popenoe (1960), who examined the effects of shifting cultivation on natural soil constituents in the central Polochic Valley where the population is predominantly Kekchi and Poconchi Indians. "These lands produce a limited amount of crops with no apparent perma-

nent injury to the soils," he concluded. "However, shifting cultivation lands in the Polochic Valley are now saturated and further increasing population pressures will probably result in impoverishment of soil fertility and increased damage by erosion" (Popenoe, 1960, p. 139).

The principal population clusters of the highland Maya were in the intermontane valleys, filled with ejecta of volcanoes and the erosion products from the volcanic, granitoid, metamorphic, and limestone formations of the enclosing hills. The mountains are high enough to intercept the moisture-laden winds from either ocean, casting a rain shadow over the valleys. However, the climates are hardly dry enough to have produced extremely calcified great soil groups from the pumiceous ash and other parent materials that are poor in calcium to begin with. Chestnut, Chernozem, and Prairie soils of grassy spots give way on wooded lands to Degraded Chernozems and Non-Calcic Brown soils.

In Guatemala, where eruptions have been more frequent in recent times, coincidence of volcanic phenomena with soil patterns is more conspicuous than in Chiapas. Showers of volcanic ash have kept many soils productive throughout hundreds, perhaps even thousands, of years of cultivation. Where the ash is composed of minerals of the ferro-magnesian group, the continued fertility is readily understood. Studies of particular profiles in relation to their actual geologic and climatic setting are necessary in order to explain how certain soils of remarkable productivity have developed from light-colored pumiceous ash, an acidic and relatively poor parent material.[27] Thin

as low as 1100, is an example of soil of mixed alluvial and colluvial parent material of both pumiceous ash and limestone origin. Despite the differences in parent materials, the profiles of these soils are quite similar, the Amay appears transitional between Reddish Brown Lateritic and Red Podzolic, whereas the Carcha and Calante are intergrades between Yellowish-Brown Lateritic and the Yellow Podzolic soils. All are leached of calcium, which element in available form is more abundant in the upper horizon where it is released from time to time by decaying organic matter. In the Amay the concentration of calcium increases again in the lower horizons near the limestone parent material.

[27] In some places ash deposits are more than 100 m. deep. Stream beds and ground water are often far below the level of nearby crop land. Irrigation, which could give the Central Depression a 12-month instead of a 6-month growing season, thus doubling the productive potential of the soil, could be practiced only by engineering feats beyond the competence of ancient Maya technology. Unfortunately, this challenge has not been seriously accepted by the later inhabitants.

soils of the steeper, in places eroded, slopes of the Depression must still be classified as volcanic Lithosols and Regosols. Thicker and more mature profiles may also include volcanic ash soils of the kind widely distributed in Japan and described under the name "Ando."[28]

Land use has been attended by serious erosion on the steeper slopes, and even on some gentle slopes where compact horizons are near the surface. Maintenance of organic matter is another leading problem of soil management in parts of the Central Depression. Crop rotation and fallowing, obvious solutions, are difficult to effect because of increasing population pressure on the limited crop land available locally. Though many domestic animals are kept, in few areas is the manure efficiently used for maintaining soil fertility. Other soils are handicapped by a superabundance of organic matter. "Raw humus is deep and well developed in the high, undulant alpine meadows, especially above about 2,500 m." (McBryde, 1947, p. 132).

At the latitudes of Guatemala and Chiapas, the effective upper limit of maize cultivation is approximately 2800 m. above sea level. Soils above that line were an insignificant resource before the introduction of domestic animals and crop plants, especially small grains and the potato, hardy enough to withstand the high altitude climate.

[28] There has been some disagreement as to whether the "Ando" (from the Japanese, meaning "dark soils") should be recognized as a new great soil group or simply placed with the Brown Forest soils or some other group. Thorp and Smith (1949, p. 117) list Central America as one of the areas where Ando soils "have developed very widely on deposits of volcanic ash." I have found no documentation as to just where these soils are developed "very widely." Depending on precise criteria of classification, some of the series described in the report of the reconnaissance soil survey of Guatemala (Simmons, Tárano, and Pinto, 1959) might be regarded as Ando soils. The authors of that report have been reluctant to publish their opinions of the great group classifications of the soils they surveyed.

SOUTHERN MESOAMERICA. South and east of the Maya lands, from Tehuantepec to northwestern Costa Rica, the narrow plains and adjacent highlands along the Pacific coast were held by small states which at the time of the conquest were predominantly of Mangue and Nahua peoples. Little of this area is dry enough for the suborder of "light-colored soils of arid regions" but tropical types of the suborder of "dark-colored soils of semiarid, subhumid and humid grasslands" are well represented. In areas still more favored by moisture-laden winds Red-Yellow Podzolic soils grade into Reddish- and Yellowish-Brown Lateritic groups. Throughout southern Mesoamerica are Lithosols and Regosols on steep slopes and Alluvial soils in valleys, on flood plains and deltas (fig. 8).

Mature profiles are absent in much of the region where parent materials have been frequently renewed by showers of volcanic ash, by the erosion of mountain slopes, or by colluvial and alluvial deposition. Correlations between relief, parent material, soils, and land use are sharp. Volcanic ash has benefitted the soils of the Pacific side of the isthmus more than the Atlantic, for the former is in the lee, the latter to the windward, of the prevailing trade winds. Unfortunately the winds have blown much fertile ash beyond the shoreline and out to sea.

The granitic massifs of Chiapas provide poor parent rocks, but in places they are overlain by or mixed with richer volcanic and sedimentary rocks. Where weathering has not reached extreme proportions, even soils derived from gneisses and granites may be reasonably productive for maize, the main crop of indigenous shifting cultivation, or for coffee, the chief perennial crop today at medium altitudes (Waibel, 1946, p. 180).

In Guatemala the intrusive parent materials are less extensive, and recent volcanic ash is more common, so that soils are generally more productive than in Chiapas.

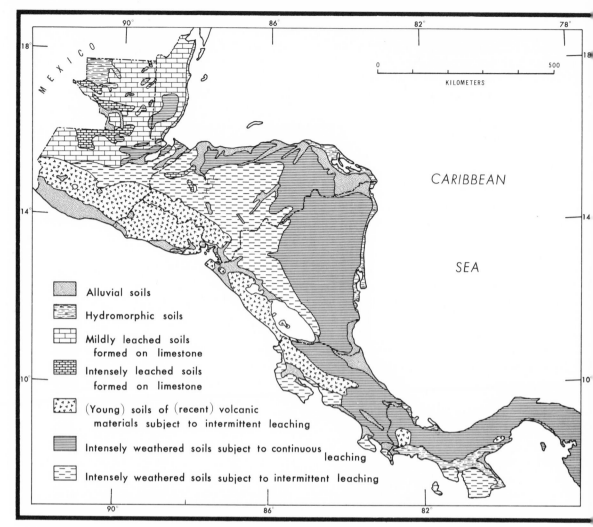

Legend:

- Alluvial soils
- Hydromorphic soils
- Mildly leached soils formed on limestone
- Intensely leached soils formed on limestone
- (Young) soils of (recent) volcanic materials subject to intermittent leaching
- Intensely weathered soils subject to continuous leaching
- Intensely weathered soils subject to intermittent leaching

FIG. 8—CONDITIONS OF SOIL FORMATION IN CENTRAL AMERICA

Almost the entire isthmus lies in the trade winds belt. The windward Caribbean side is drenched in heavy rainfall, and consequently the soil has more water available for chemical reactions and leaching. On the Pacific coast, and in much of the highlands from Costa Rica through Guatemala, weathering is interrupted by a pronounced dry season. Most of the recently active volcanoes are near the Pacific shore, in which direction much of the ejecta, potentially fertile parent material, is blown by the trade winds, some of it beyond the shoreline and out to sea. The showers of ash and cinders have rejuvenated many soils of the highlands and Pacific lowlands. The limestone hills of west-central Guatemala are partly covered by volcanic ash, presumably deposited there when the eruptions of nearby volcanoes coincided with the seasonal (monsoon) reversal of the prevailing winds. The soils of northern Guatemala are mapped in greater detail in fig. 7.

The unconsolidated mantle has been deeply dissected by the runoff from steep slopes under abundant rainfall. During the dry season, exposed soils dry out considerably so that mulching is necessary to conserve sufficient moisture for coffee. For pre-Columbian indigenous agriculture based on maize, seasonal precipitation was adequate and the problem of soil desiccation less acute.

Soils of El Salvador are generally fertile, many of them having been frequently replenished by volcanic ejecta. Radiant volcanic heat, eruptions of acid fumes, hot water and steam, with or without showers of ash, occasionally alter the land use capability of small areas near the active volcanoes. Porosity of the soil and of the underlying volcanic strata permits cultivation of many steep slopes with little erosion. Coffee is planted on 87 per cent slopes, and even maize is seen on 60 per cent slopes (Jauregui, 1948, p. 227). Notwithstanding, in parts of El Salvador erosion is a serious problem, accelerated by the clearing of the dense natural vegetation. At the same time, leaching is intensified and crop yields decline sharply within a few years, although in this land-hungry country the relatively impoverished soils might still be considered quite productive.[29]

Farther east in Honduras the predominantly volcanic parent materials are somewhat older and soil profiles tend to be more thoroughly weathered. In few places are the limestone related formations of the interior found west of the continental divide. The black color of the topsoil may mislead an observer to overestimate the fertility of many volcanic soils that are in fact severely leached and acidic.[30]

In Nicaragua volcanism has continued active until the present day, renewing the fertility of many coastal and highland soils on the Pacific side of the isthmus. Ash deposits are often very deep and porous; soils, though fertile, are subject to rapid desiccation.[31] The porous volcanic soils of the Masaya District, northwest of Lake Nicaragua, also dry out quickly.[32] Lacustrine clays around lakes Nicaragua and Managua are more water-retentive and have served as a mainstay of agriculture from pre-Columbian times to the present.

The Nicoya Peninsula of Costa Rica was held by the Chorotegas before the coming of the Spaniards. Prolonged weathering of the igneous extrusive and metamorphic rocks has produced rather mature soils of the lateritic groups. Under shifting cultivation today, clearings are productive for six, eight, or ten years at most, by methods which have changed little since the 16th century, when they were observed by Oviedo (Wagner, 1958, pp. 214–15). Yields of rice from the hill soils are low, scarcely a third as much as on the flat lands.

Connecting the Nicoya Peninsula to the mainland is the ash-filled Guanacaste lowland, overlain in the north and east by lava flows. Rain shadows of the mountains of the peninsula and of the Cordillera del Guanacaste impose the most arid climates of Costa Rica. From the driest part of the Guanacaste to the more humid, southwestern part of the province of San Jose, M. A. Sáenz (1940, p. 142) reports a full array of soils ranging from Red Desert and Reddish Brown through Chestnut, Chernozem, Reddish Prairie and finally to various Podzolic and Lateritic groups. He also notes intrazonal Solonetz soils in some dry areas.

Circum-Caribbean Culture Area

The aborigines of the Caribbean coast and adjacent parts of the interior highlands,

---

[29] The dense population of El Salvador, racially but no longer linguistically indigenous, provides abundant labor for carrying out land use practices that would be unthinkable in regions of less population pressure. Dozier (1958, pp. 115–16) writes of starting coffee trees in partly decomposed lava by planting in pits filled with sifted soil.

[30] Some of these black soils resemble the "Ando" volcanic soils of Japan. Simmons, who has done considerable field work in Honduras, in a letter to me, reports having observed only one area of distinctly Ando soils, near Rosario mine, at an elevation of 2000 m. above sea level.

[31] Wells must penetrate as much as 200 m. to tap the water table in the "sierra" southwest of Managua (Pendleton, 1943, p. 407). Where the water table is near the surface, irrigation by simple

means from shallow wells may be practiced, e.g., near Tisma, Nicaragua (Dozier, 1958, p. 80).

[32] To cultivate these soils, some form of mulching is required; banana stems, bean straw, and upland rice straw serve the purpose on coffee plantations. Bananas, plantains, and manioc, local staples of the working class, somewhat provide their own mulch, unlike the clean-tilled maize crop; they also supply a continuous, year-round harvest. Their roots tap moisture and nutrients from a greater volume of soil than can be reached by the short-lived, shallow-rooted maize plant.

east of Copan, Honduras, through Nicaragua and Costa Rica, together with the entire isthmus from southern Costa Rica through Panama, evinced many traits in common with peoples of northern South America and the Antilles, including their relation to the soil. They relied on yuca (sweet manioc) rather than maize as their leading staple crop. Although there are some areas where both crops have been produced side by side, many soils of the interior plateaus and coastlands are too infertile for maize production. Yuca makes less exacting demands so long as the soil is loose enough to permit expansion of the starchy roots. It would be interesting to trace the possible coincidence of areas of maize and yuca cultivation with soil and climatic zones in Middle America.

Much of the quartz-sandy soil on the old alluvial plains covered by pine savannas in Mosquitia, eastern Honduras and northern Nicaragua, is definitely inadequate for maize (Pendleton, 1943, p. 404). Bordering on, or interspersed with, these savannas are forested patches of broadleaf species which require a richer soil. These areas are planted to maize, using slash-and-burn methods. Clumps or small islands of broadleaf jungle that appear scattered over the open savanna are explained as former settlement sites where the accumulation of household and animal wastes gradually enriched the soil until it could support a dense vegetation, including species that could not survive on the unfertilized savanna (Pendleton, cited by Parsons, 1955). The dense growth eventually became so infested with insects that the people established new settlements on the open savanna where the trade winds could alleviate the temperatures and sweep away the swarms of insects. Once having established on these soils, the vegetation can maintain itself a long time, re-using the plant nutrients of the leaf fall. Thus, former settlements here are recognized not by abandoned clearing but by the opposite—abandoned thickets.

310

Parent materials in central and eastern Honduras and Nicaragua mainly consist of: (a) granitoid rocks, where elongated, east-west oriented batholiths pushed their way to the surface in Cretaceous times; (b) acidic volcanic materials, with tuffs, ashes, and cinders more conspicuous than lavas; (c) sedimentary rocks, particularly limestone and clay schists, in a few scattered areas; and (d) alluvial deposits, including erosion products of the above-mentioned rocks. Deposits along the emerging coastline also include very different materials eroded from distant watersheds and swept by the ocean currents from the mouths of rivers farther south and east.

Weathering is generally more advanced on the Caribbean side of the isthmus, which is drenched by the trade-wind rains and consequently has more water available for chemical reactions and leaching than do the leeward slopes and coastal plains of the Pacific side, where humid weathering is interrupted by long dry seasons. There has been little renewal of soil fertility on the Caribbean side by recent vulcanism, for the active volcanoes are very close to the Pacific shore, toward which the showers of ash and cinders are swept by the trade winds. From southern Costa Rica through Panama the differences of soil and climate on the two sides of the isthmus are not so great.

Although the climate of the eastern parts of Honduras and Nicaragua is eminently appropriate for laterization, the high silica content of many soils of the Miskito Pine Savanna and the pine uplands suggests that they be classified as podzolic. On the less extensive outcrops of basic igneous and sedimentary rocks, more thoroughly weathered soils of the Reddish-Brown and Yellowish-Brown Lateritic groups appear.[33]

[33] In parts of the savanna, Pendleton (1943, p. 404) notes weathering "in the senile, lateritic stage." Radley (1960, p. 120) regards as true laterites some of the savanna soils with well-developed ironpans.

Calcification-process soils are of very limited development in these highlands, being confined to the more pronounced rain shadow areas. The black color of many volcanic soils, as in the Danli Valley, Honduras, may give a misleading idea of their potential, for they are leached and acidic. A central point of a recent study (Denevan, 1958, pp. 37–40) holds that upland pine forests tend to coincide with areas of soils developed from acidic rocks. The "thin, rocky, eroded and acidic soils" on which appears *Pinus oocarpa,* the most common species, are regarded by farmers as poor for agriculture. Pines will grow, of course, on richer soils, but on some of these they cannot compete with more aggressive species.

Mud cracking is pronounced on the black soils of the savanna and scrub forest lands of central Honduras and Nicaragua. This is indicative of a high content of clays that are very expansile and retractile under alternately wet-dry conditions, giving the soil a massive-to-blocky structure that is difficult to till. Yet the mud cracks perform a useful function, intercepting organic debris that falls or is washed into them at the beginning of the rains, thus incorporating valuable organic matter into the soil profile. These characteristics fit well with the criteria set up by Oakes and Thorp (1950) for the "Grumusol," a term proposed for a great soil group combining various dark-clay soils of warm regions.

In Costa Rica and Panama the isthmus narrows and older formations of acidic igneous rocks no longer dominate the scene, for here the land bridge is built up largely of Tertiary and Recent volcanic materials of andesitic and basaltic composition. Only in the Talamanca Mountains and a few other places do granitoid batholiths outcrop at the surface, and sedimentary strata of limestone and clay schist are of limited extent. Costa Rica, especially, has classical examples of mature but by no means senile lateritic profiles. Relative youth and retention of basic mineral nutrients from rich parent materials make some soils productive even though intensely weathered.[34]

Soil Erosion and Conservation under Indian Land Use: Conclusion

A basic distinction must be recognized between the nature of erosion in the dry lands, especially extensive in northern and western Mexico, and that which occurs under the more humid conditions prevailing throughout most of the rest of Middle America. Where the dense vegetative cover of humid areas has not been disrupted, geologic erosion takes place gradually, so that the soil remains intact with a minimum of interference in its function as a medium for plant growth, and bare soil is seldom exposed to view. Against this background it is easy to observe where actions of man have accelerated erosion. By removing or modifying the natural vegetative cover, man exposes the soil to the direct impact of falling raindrops, which loosen soil particles that are then carried away in suspension, the runoff of water being greater in volume and rapidity where there is less vegetation to retard it. In the dry lands the natural vegetative cover, even where undisturbed by man, is not rank enough to afford the soil continuous protection from the erosive agencies of wind, rain, and runoff water. The effects of this naturally rapid geologic erosion are everywhere conspicuous and the extent of erosion attributable to man often is not clearly discernible.

The problems of differentiating normal, or geologic, erosion from accelerated, man-

---

[34] Soils so weathered that not a single grain of sand could be detected by ordinary field methods and only 0.7 or 1 per cent of the soil was found to consist of particles larger than silt, have been examined by H. H. Bennett (1925, p. 69) near Columbiana, Costa Rica. Despite this heavy texture, such soils have an easy tilth because of their friable structure and the tendency of the colloidal clay particles to form aggregates, thus allowing water to penetrate rapidly and without puddling. Plowing can be done a few hours after a heavy rain without risk of mud sticking to implements or of damage to soil structure.

311

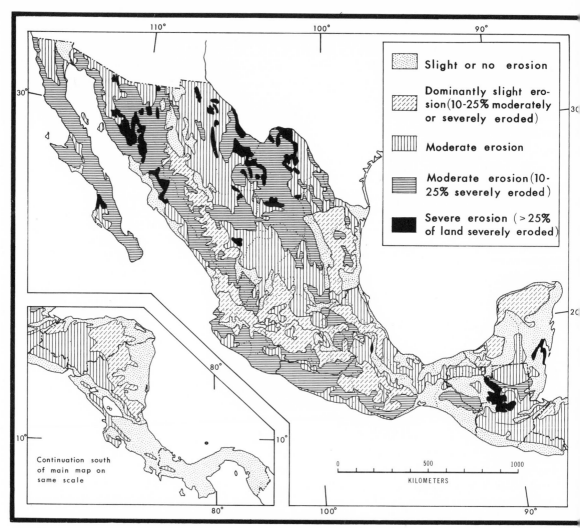

The legend on the map reads:

Slight or no erosion

Dominantly slight erosion (10-25% moderately or severely eroded)

Moderate erosion

Moderate erosion (10-25% severely eroded)

Severe erosion (>25% of land severely eroded)

Continuation south of main map on same scale

KILOMETERS

Fɪɢ. 9—SOIL EROSION IN MIDDLE AMERICA, 1950

The map is adapted from the *Soil Erosion Survey of Latin America* (The Conservation Foundation, 1954). The drier, northerly regions, which lack a continuous plant cover to protect the soil from the impact of falling raindrops, are generally more eroded than the southern and eastern regions, which have denser vegetation. There is also marked coincidence of moderate and severe erosion with areas of steep relief. Within some of the more eroded areas of Arid North America, the Indians have relied largely on Alluvial soils of relatively low erosibility. In other places, as at Jilotepec (see p. 295), the Indians have shunned plains soils of slight erosibility in favor of highly erosive but more fertile soils of steep slopes.

made erosion have been emphasized in the *Soil Erosion Survey of Latin America* (The Conservation Foundation, 1954, pp. 27–28). Unfortunately, the text of that report does not clarify to what extent it purports to have overcome those difficulties in drafting the accompanying maps (reproduced in part, with modification, in fig. 9).[35]

Most of Arid North America is mapped as moderately or severely eroded, with notable exceptions in the more densely forested upper reaches of the mountains and on the flatter parts of coastal plains. The more humid climate and vegetation types found farther south and east in Mesoamerica are less conducive to erosion, though there it is facilitated by steep slopes that dominate

[35] As an illuminating comparison, it is worth noting that no part of Middle America is mapped as "Land with soils undisturbed by man," to which category the Survey (part II) relegates large expanses of the South American continent.

312

wide areas; and furthermore, the interference of man has been more pronounced. The coastal plains in western Mesoamerica are of narrow extent and only small parts have escaped with slight or no erosion. Portions of the subalpine forest and alpine meadow lands of the Neovolcanic Axis and parts of the cloud-forest areas of the windward, eastern escarpment, may still be considered as only slightly affected by manmade erosion. We are left to wonder what criteria have led the authors to show so much of the highlands of central Mexico as "Dominantly slight erosion with 10 to 25% of land moderately to severely eroded." Nor can we concur in regarding the soils of Tlaxcala as only moderately eroded; severe erosion there seems to us more conspicuous than the map indicates.

The Maya lands, clothed as they are, in great part, by dense forest, show but slight erosion, with from 10 to 25 per cent of the land moderately or severely eroded in areas of denser settlement supported by shifting cultivation. The investigators recognize as a "complicating feature" of humid forest soil areas, that "much of the land now under natural cover may have been cultivated at one time and the soil eroded to some degree, while today that erosion may not be visible at a distance or from the air" (p. 2). Certainly this is true of large parts of the Maya area, in both lowlands and highlands. Soil rehabilitation may be facilitated by lush vegetation, but just how is one to gauge whether the soil of an abandoned clearing should be regarded as a restored rather than an eroded soil area? We doubt the propriety of classifying so much of El Peten and central Yucatan Peninsula, including marsh areas, as "moderately eroded." Since the decline of the Classic Maya culture almost a millennium ago, settlement there has been very sparse. However, we lack data for a specific revision of this part of the map. Severe accelerated erosion in the Maya lands is most prominent in semi-arid depressions of Chiapas and Guatemala,

and on the thin Lithosols and easily puddled podzolic-lateritic soils of the lower and middle elevations of the highland escarpment from eastern Chiapas through El Quiche and Alta Verapaz.

Soil erosion conditions of southern Mesoamerica and the Circum-Caribbean culture zone appear to have been properly represented by the Survey, with slight or no erosion along both coastal plains and throughout most of the interior of Costa Rica and Panama. Moderate erosion prevails over the interior highlands and escarpments of Guatemala, El Salvador, Honduras, and Nicaragua, where long dry seasons interrupt the effectiveness of the protective plant cover; of more local occurrence, steep slopes and water-repelling soil structures are also aggravating factors.

Bennett (1945, p. 166) estimated the following percentages of the arable land of the independent countries of Middle America as "ruined for cultivation, nearly ruined and severely affected": Mexico, 50; Guatemala, 30; El Salvador, 40; Honduras, 50; Nicaragua, 30; Costa Rica, 30; Panama, 20.

The material eroded from the soils of Middle America is not a total loss; much is subsequently deposited on lower slopes or along the margins of streams, lakes, and seas. Alluvial soils are thus frequently enriched by deposits of fertile topsoil transported from areas of destructive land use farther up the watershed. But alas! lands may also be rendered unproductive by the deposition of less fertile materials eroded from the substrata of the devastated areas.

Starting from the premise that many of the severely eroded areas are known to have supported much larger populations in pre-Columbian times, Cook (1948, 1949a, 1949b, 1958) assumes that other severely eroded areas must likewise have had dense populations before the conquest.[36] If so, one

---

[36] Reference has been made above to the efforts of S. F. Cook (1958, pp. 15–16) to discover in the strata of a terrace of the river Ixcatlan a record of man's use and abuse of the soils of the upper

might expect the reduction of population in the 16th century to have been accompanied by a slackening in the severity of erosion. But the survivors, equipped with new erosion accelerators from Europe, the plow and domestic animals, were enabled to lay waste in four centuries a much larger area, and to a greater degree, than could an equal number of their forebears in a like period of time. It is not justified to postulate in every case a large pre-Columbian population to account for the present devastated soil conditions. One might just as logically conclude the contrary, that the severely eroded areas would likely have been devastated too soon to have ever supported dense populations.

Recalling the thesis of Mendizábal that the Spaniards saw easier profits in livestock raising than agriculture in Teotlalpan and to that end crowded out the Indian farmers, Cook (1949b, p. 56) suggests that this redeployment of land may have been an effect rather than a cause of soil destruction. Cattle, sheep, and especially goats could glean something from whatever grass and brush grew on land abandoned as no longer fit for crop production. He insists that "it is necessary to regard livestock as a secondary and relatively minor factor contributing to the erosion process" (p. 56). Whatever the solution to this question, it should, of course, apply to an area much wider than the Teotlalpan.

We have already mentioned how the Tarahumara quickly became herders of domestic animals which enhanced rather than destroyed their soil resources by providing manure to fertilize otherwise unproductive sierra soils, a technique, curiously enough, little used by the Spanish and

watershed. Similar field investigations have been carried out by Cook (1949a, 1949b) in the Teotlalpan and other highland areas of central Mexico: in the basins of Zimapan and El Bajio; at Quiroga and Tzintzuntzan; on the Perote Plain; and in the Mixteca Alta.

mestizo settlers from whom they got the domestic animals.

Over large areas of central Mexico, livestock make amends in another way for their part in the destruction of forests and soils. Where firewood is no longer available, cattle convert grass and corn fodder into manure which is pattied into small cakes and dried in the sun for use as household fuel. Utilization of the manure in this manner, of course, precludes its being used to return to the soil nutrients taken by the pasture grasses and the corn crop.

CONCLUSION

A paramount problem confronting the Middle American Indian today is to use more productively what is left of his soil resources, to halt their destruction, rebuild and enhance them. In some areas the Indian is already extracting from the soil all that is economically feasible with his present technology. Modern agricultural science can offer better methods for cultivating some soils but not all. The humid tropical lowlands present many problems in soil management that are yet to be solved even in general terms. There, as Simmons, Tárano, and Pinto (1959) repeatedly emphasized in the reconnaissance survey of the soils of Guatemala, we must experiment and proceed with extreme caution before implementing new land use programs.

"*Soil conservation begins with the taming of raindrops.*" So formulates the Soil Erosion Survey of Latin America (The Conservation Foundation, 1954, p. 27). But it is difficult to start at the beginning in this land where a rapidly increasing population is so dependent for its sustenance on corn, a crop whose cultivation in most areas exposes the soil during many months to the beating action of rain.

Population pressure has too often resulted in expansion and intensification of soil-exhausting methods of farming rather than in the expenditure of surplus labor to conserve and improve the soil. Indigenous agriculture, as we have already pointed out, has evolved many laudable soil-conserving methods—terracing in Chihuahua and British Honduras, the *chinampas* of the Valley of Mexico, rudiments of contour farming in some highland areas of Mexico and Guatemala. It is regrettable that these techniques have not had wider acceptance and further perfections. Even the much maligned practice of "fire agriculture" is not to be discarded until one can substitute equal or better methods of fertilizing and weed control.

Those who would improve the lot of the Middle American Indian must induce him to improve and extend his old conservation practices and to accept innovations.

This is neither an easy nor an impossible task. The soil conservation movement in other lands has had to cope with ignorance, suspicion, and reluctance. In Middle America the problem is further complicated by the difficulty of communicating to peoples largely illiterate, in some areas linguistically diverse, and traditionally resistant to outside influences. Furthermore, it must be recognized that even with full implementation of the best-known agricultural techniques to the limits of economic feasibility, agriculture cannot well provide for the occupants of many soil areas with acute population pressure. Economic opportunities, alternatives to farming, are urgently needed to relieve these pressures and allow the soil resources to be restored.

REFERENCES

Aguilera Herrera, 1955, 1959
Bell, *see* Castetter and Bell, 1951
Bennett, H. H., 1925, 1926, 1929, 1945
Borah, 1951
Brambila, 1942
British Honduras Land Use Survey Team, 1959
Budowski, 1956
Bullard, W. R., 1960
Cárdenas, 1955
Castetter and Bell, 1951
Conservation Foundation, 1954
Cook, S. F., 1949a, 1949b, 1958
—— and Simpson, 1948
Denevan, 1958
Diccionario de Motul, 1929
Dozier, 1958
Hester, 1954
Jacks, 1954
Jauregui, 1948
Kelley, 1956
Kellogg, 1949a, 1949b
Kirchhoff, 1943
Landa, 1941
Lumholtz, 1902
McBryde, 1947
Macías Villada, 1954, 1960
MacNeish, 1956
Morley, 1956
Oakes and Thorp, 1950

Ortiz Monasterio, 1950, 1955–57
Pan American Inst. Geography and History, 1953-54
Parsons, J. J., 1955
Patiño, 1955
Pendleton, 1943, 1945
Pinto, *see* Simmons, Tárano, and Pinto, 1959
Popenoe, 1960
Radley, 1960
Robles Ramos, 1950, 1959
Sáenz, 1940
Sapper, 1899, 1905
Sauer, 1934
Simmons, Tárano, and Pinto, 1959
Simpson, L. B., 1952; *see* Cook and Simpson, 1948
Skutch, 1950
Smith, *see* Thorp and Smith, 1949
Soil Survey Staff, 1960
Steggerda, 1941
Studhalter, 1936
Tárano, *see* Simmons, Tárano, and Pinto, 1959
Termer, 1950
Thompson, J. E. S., 1954
Thorp and Smith, 1949; *see* Oakes and Thorp, 1950
U. S. Department of Agriculture, 1938
Wagner, 1958
Waibel, 1946
West, 1948
Zingg, *see* Bennett and Zingg, 1935

9. Fauna of Middle America

L. C. STUART

IN HIS ACCOUNT of the fauna of South America prepared for the *Handbook of South American Indians,* Gilmore (1950) was concerned primarily with the ethnozoological phases of the animal life. I do not presume to be so ambitious here. Because animals frequently serve as valuable indicators of broader environmental types that, in primitive man at least, have directed and/or limited cultural activities, the zoological data presented here are intended to serve as reference for the anthropologist seeking possible explanation of anthropological data. Only recently has intensive study of the Middle American fauna been undertaken, and summaries such as Leopold's *Wildlife of Mexico* (1959) are just beginning to appear. Some animal groups in a few areas, for example, the birds of Guatemala and Mexico, have been examined in some detail. But the existing data permit only very broad generalizations for the region as a whole, and even these generalizations must be derived frequently from extrapolation in treating of certain groups or certain areas.

Because the invertebrate groups of Middle America are as yet poorly known, this account will be largely an exposition of the vertebrates with emphasis placed primarily on their geographic behavior. It will deal first with the content and distribution of the fauna taxon by taxon to the family level and then offer a zoogeographic summary of these data. References include for the most part only major summaries, though reference is made to a few shorter, yet zoogeographically important, papers.

NATURE OF THE MIDDLE AMERICAN FAUNA

If the anthropologist, in searching into zoological literature, becomes confused by the lack of agreement on the status of various taxa, he may find comfort in the knowledge that systematic specialists are similarly perplexed. For this reason, counts of families, genera, and species are only approximate. In general I have allied myself with the conservatives and have followed the nomenclature most frequently used in the literature, e.g. *Odocoileus* rather than *Dama* for the deer. Because Darlington (1957) will probably be the zoogeographic source most readily available, his classification has been adhered to closely. Inasmuch as there is no uniformity in common names of most animal species, the ornithologists having achieved greatest standardization, an effort has been made here to modify scientific designations and to draw examples from familiar organisms wherever possible.

Vertebrates

MAMMALIA. Considered at the family level, the nonmarine mammalian fauna of Middle America is more diversified than that of either of the continental areas to the north and south (Hershkovitz, 1958). Of roughly 50 families of mammals inhabiting the New World, Middle America lacks but about 15. The reason for this diversity lies in the fact that four families of northern mammals that occur in the region do not enter South America. Conversely, about 13 families of southern mammals found in Middle America do not reach the United States, and another three are represented north of the Mexican border by but a single species each.

In their recent work on the mammals of North America, Hall and Kelson (1959) record some 520 species (exclusive of offshore island species and marine groups) from the region. These comprise from 165 to 170 genera. It may be noted, however, that this multiplicity is owing to the 60 genera of bats which, in Middle America, average only two species per genus.

The opossums (Marsupialia) are largely South American and, with the exception of the common opossum (*Didelphis*) that is widespread over much of the United States, do not extend north of the tropical lowlands of Mexico. Mouse opossums (*Marmosa*), the philander (*Philander*), and the woolly opossum (*Caluromys*) reach southern Mexico. The water opossum (*Chironectes*) extends to Honduras and El Salvador. The brown opossum (*Metachirus*), however, drops out in southern Nicaragua and the short-tailed opossum (*Monodelphis*) barely enters eastern Panama.

In contrast to the opossums, the insectivores (Insectivora) are a northern group

that is poorly represented in Middle America. The moles (Talpidae) occur no farther south than extreme northern Mexico. Of the shrews (Soricidae), the long-tails (*Sorex*) extend into the highlands of northern Central America, whereas the small-eared shrews (*Cryptotis*) have invaded South America along highland routes.

The majority of the bats (Chiroptera), like the opossums, are essentially southerners, either Neotropical or pantropical. Eight families occur within the limits of Middle America. In number of species the bats, with about 120 in the region, are exceeded only by the rodents.

Of the southerners, the American leaf-nosed bats (Phyllostomidae) and the funnel-eared bats (Natalidae) are found throughout Central America and occur on the Mexican lowlands. In general, these groups avoid the Mexican Plateau, and several small genera of leaf-nosed bats are endemic to Central America. The vespertilionid bats (Vespertilionidae) and the free-tailed bats (Molossidae) are more northern. They are widely distributed throughout the region, and a number continue southward into South America. The vampire bats (Desmodontidae) are represented in Middle America by only two species which are generally distributed in tropical areas. As vectors of rabies they are of special concern to man.

The primates (Primates), in addition to man, are represented in the region by two families, the monkeys (Cebidae) and a marmoset (Callithricidae). Of the former, the howler (*Alouatta*) and a spider monkey (*Ateles*) extend northward to the Mexican lowlands; the capuchin (*Cebus*) occurs only from Honduras south, while the douroucouli monkeys (*Aotus*) are found only south of Costa Rica. The squirrel marmoset (Cebidae, *Saimiri*) and the true marmoset (Callithricidae, *Saguinus*) are also southern and extend northward only to Costa Rica. Monkeys were practically exterminated in northern Central America by the great

317

epidemic of jungle yellow fever that swept the region in 1956–57.

The edentates (Edentata) comprise another southern group. They are represented in Middle America by seven species belonging to seven different genera. The armadillos (Dasypodidae) are found as far north as the south central United States, though there represented by but a single species. The anteaters (Myrmecophagidae) occur on the lowlands north to southeastern Mexico, but the sloths (Bradypodidae) extend only to eastern Honduras. Unlike the noisy and conspicuous monkeys, the edentates, other than armadillos, are secretive animals and only infrequently encountered. Certain species of armadillos, despite heavy predation by man, are relatively common. The flesh of the common armadillo (*Dasypus*) is highly esteemed as food, and I prefer it to that of all other game animals in the region.

Only a few lagomorphs (Lagomorpha), which include the rabbits, hares, and pikas, occur in Middle America. The last do not enter the region, and the hares (*Lepus*), represented by the jackrabbits, extend only as far south as the Isthmus of Tehuantepec. Of the rabbits, one genus, the volcano rabbit (*Romerolagus*) with but a single species, is confined to the environs of Popocatepetl. The cottontails (*Sylvilagus*), in contrast, are found throughout the region and extend into South America. Needless to say, these rabbits are prized as food.

The rodents (Rodentia), which comprise almost half of the world's mammalian species, are abundant and varied throughout Middle America. They are represented in the region by 10 families, which include 53 genera and about 280 species. They thus make up well over half the species of the Middle American mammalian fauna. The New World rodents are generally broken into three major groups or suborders. These are the Sciuromorpha (squirrels, ground squirrels, pocket gophers, pocket mice and

allies), the Myomorpha (diverse rats and mice) and the Hystricomorpha (porcupines, guinea pigs, agoutis, etc.). The former two are northern groups; the last is southern. The sciuromorphs and the myomorphs each comprise almost 50 per cent of the rodent species of the region and the hystricomorphs only about 4 per cent.

Among the Sciuromorpha, the squirrels and their allies which include the chipmunks, prairie dogs, and ground squirrels are grouped in one family, the Sciuridae. The tree squirrels (*Sciurus*) occur throughout the region and extend into South America, but the little flying squirrel (*Glaucomys volans*) is not found south of Honduras. Several small genera are endemic to Central America south of Nicaragua or continue into South America. The chipmunks (*Eutamias*) and prairie dogs (*Cynomys*) do not occur south of northern Mexico, and the ground squirrels (*Citellus*) drop out at the Isthmus of Tehuantepec.

The pocket gophers (Geomyidae) are essentially northern. Two large genera, *Thomomys* and *Geomys*, occur only in northern Mexico. Several small genera, however, are strictly Middle American. The hispid pocket gophers (*Heterogeomys*) are confined to southeastern Mexico and Guatemala; the Central American pocket gophers (*Macrogeomys*) are found only south of the Tehuantepec isthmus.

The pocket mice and their allies (Heteromyidae) repeat the above patterns. The pocket mice (*Perognathus*) and kangaroo rats (*Dipodomys*) occur from central Mexico north. One genus of spiny pocket mice (*Liomys*) extends to the Isthmus of Tehuantepec, where it is replaced by a second genus (*Heteromys*) which continues southward into South America.

The beaver (Castoridae, *Castor*) does not occur south of some of the southern tributaries of the Rio Grande.

With the exception of the exotic house mouse (*Mus*) and the true rats (*Rattus*), which have become cosmopolitan, the myomorphs are represented in Middle America by but a single family, Cricetidae. More than 130 species of these rats and mice are found in the region. In general its geographic pattern is similar to that of the sciuromorphs. The cotton rats (*Sigmodon*) and the rice rats (*Oryzomys*) are generally distributed throughout the region, though the latter tend to avoid the drier parts of the Mexican Plateau. The harvest mice (*Reithrodontomys*) and the white-footed mice (*Peromyscus*) are also widespread through Middle America, but south of Mexico they tend to be restricted to the highlands. The wood rats (*Neotoma*) are similarly upland south of the Isthmus of Tehuantepec and reach only to Nicaragua; the voles (*Microtus*) do not extend beyond Guatemala. Within the region there are also several small genera that are endemic to Central America and lowland Mexico. These include the vesper rats (*Nyctomys*), the climbing rats (*Tylomys*), the brown mice (*Scotinomys*), and the water mice (*Rheomys*).

Of the hystricomorphs, only one genus, the porcupine (*Erethizon*), occurs north of the Rio Grande. Other porcupines (Erethizontidae) are found from Mexico southward. The agoutis and the paca (Dasyproctidae) are generally distributed over the lowlands from southeastern Mexico southward. The spiny rats (Echimyidae), however, are not found north of Nicaragua, and the capybara (Hydrochaeridae) barely enters the region in eastern Panama.

Many of the rodents are utilized extensively as food. Among them are the squirrels, the pacas, and the agoutis. From a medical standpoint, of course, the exotic *Rattus* and *Mus* serve as intermediate hosts for *Trichinella*, which is communicated to man usually via the domesticated hog. These same two rodents also harbor fleas which occasionally transmit murine typhus to man.

Like the rodents, the carnivores (Carnivora) are represented in Middle America by both northern and southern elements. Among the dogs (Canidae), the kit fox (*Vulpes*) extends southward only into northern Mexico, but the gray fox (*Urocyon*) reaches South America. The coyote (*Canis*) is found southward to Costa Rica. The bush dog (*Speothos*) is a southerner and does not occur north of Panama. The bears (Ursidae) display an interesting geographic pattern. Found in the mountains south to northern Mexico, they avoid all of Central America to reappear in South America. The raccoons and their allies (Procyonidae) also show a northern-southern arrangement. The ringtails (*Bassariscus*) and the raccoons (*Procyon*) are northern, the former extending only to Panama, the latter invading South America. In contrast the olingo (*Bassaricyon*) is found northward only to Nicaragua, the kinkajou (*Potos*) reaches central Mexico, and the coati (*Nasua*) invades southwestern United States.

The weasel family (Mustelidae) parallels the Procyonidae. The badger (*Taxidea*), weasels (*Mustela*), and skunks (several genera) are northern. The badger drops out on the Mexican Plateau; skunks (*Mephitis* and *Spilogale*) continue southward to Nicaragua and Costa Rica. A hognose skunk (*Conepatus*) reaches Panama, and a weasel extends to South America. A single species of river otter (*Lutra*) is generally distributed over the lowlands of Central America and southern Mexico to South America. Two small southern genera, the tayra (*Eira*) and the grison (*Galictis*), extend northward to the Mexican lowlands.

The cats (Felidae) are both northern and southern. The bobcat (*Lynx*) is found no farther south than the Mexican Plateau, but the true cats (*Felis*) occur throughout the region. The mountain lion is the most widely distributed species of the genus, extending from Canada south to Patagonia. In

319

contrast, the ocelot, jaguar, jaguarundi and margay are southern. All occur northward from South America only to the Mexico-United States border. They are all essentially lowlanders.[1]

The tapir (*Tapirus*), the only perissodactyl (Perissodactyla) in the region other than the exotic horse, is a southerner that is spottily distributed over the lowlands from southern Mexico into South America.

The indigenous cloven-hoofed mammals (Artiodactyla) are represented in Middle America essentially by only the deer and the peccaries. Though the mountain sheep (Bovidae) and the pronghorn (Antilocapridae) enter the region, they are both restricted to northern Mexico. Of the peccaries (Tayassuidae, *Tayassu*), the collared peccary is generally distributed from southwestern United States through Mexico and Central America with the exception of the higher parts of the uplands. In Middle America the white-lipped peccary, however, is found only in extreme southeastern Mexico and in Central America. Of the deer (Cervidae, *Odocoileus*), the mule deer occurs no farther south than northern Mexico; the white-tailed deer is generally distributed through the region and enters South America. The little brockets (*Mazama*) are southerners and occur northward only to tropical lowlands of eastern Mexico. The peccaries, the deer, and the brockets are all important food items.

Only a single siren (Sirenia) occurs in the region. It is the manatee (*Trichechus*), which today is found along the east coast in shallow waters from Veracruz southward. It also occurs in Florida, and has been recorded occasionally on the Louisiana coast. Its range formerly may have been

continuous around the Gulf of Mexico. Currently it is very spotty in its distribution. It is, of course, utilized for food.

A number of species of pelagic mammals inhabit the waters off both the Atlantic and Pacific shores of Middle America. Among the seals (Pinnipedia) may be mentioned the fur seal (*Arctophoca*) and the harbour seal (*Phoca*), which are found on islands off the west coasts of Baja California and the Mexican mainland. In the Gulf of Mexico and in the Caribbean, the West Indian seal (*Monachus*) is known to occur at least as far south as Honduran waters. The whales and their allies (Cetacea) are also encountered in the coastal waters of the region. The sperm whale (Physeteridae, *Physeter*) frequents the Pacific littoral; finbacked whales (Balaenopteridae) occur in both Pacific and Caribbean waters. Porpoises and dolphins (Delphinidae) are also common off both coasts of Middle America.

AVES. Any short treatment of the extremely diverse avifauna of Middle America must be inadequate at best. In his check-list of the birds of Mexico and Central America, Eisenmann (1955) lists some 1,424 species divided among 94 families. (This work contains an excellent bibliography of Middle American ornithology.) Although some families are represented in the region by few species, these families must be considered, inasmuch as they frequently appear as conspicuous elements of the fauna. Among them may be mentioned the tinamous (Tinamidae) with five species, curassows and chachalacas (Cracidae) with eight species, and the familiar jaçana (Jacanidae) with only one species. In contrast, other families are large; five families alone, hummingbirds (Trochilidae), tyrant flycatchers (Tyrannidae), wood warblers (Parulidae), tanagers (Thraupidae), and finches and sparrows (Fringillidae), comprise almost exactly a third of the Middle American avifauna.

It is particularly difficult to treat these large families adequately. For example, it

[1] Ed. note: Skins of the lowland cats made up an important part of ancient trade and tribute in central Mexico and northern Central America, where they were used to ornament costumes of priests, warriors, and nobles. Representations of especially the jaguar (*Felis onca*) held a significant place in religious symbolism and art in almost all of the Middle American cultures.

can be said that the hummingbirds, represented in the region by 100 species divided among 46 genera, are generally distributed throughout the region. This is a true but misleading statement. Almost 20 genera occur no farther north than Nicaragua, and eight other genera breed no farther south than the same country; three genera among these eight occur in Mexico chiefly as migrants from farther north. The wood warblers are also generally distributed through Mexico and Central America, where they are represented by 80 species comprising 22 genera. In contrast to the hummingbirds, 21 genera range into Mexico, including seven genera which are merely migrants from the United States. In fact, nearly 50 per cent of the species of wood warblers recorded from Middle America only winter in the region. This seasonal movement of birds further complicates the treatment of the Middle American avifauna. What percentage of the birds recorded from the region are "accidentals," transients, and winter migrants I hesitate to compute. However, of 736 forms (species and subspecies) recorded from Guatemala by Griscom (1932), about 25 per cent are included in the above three categories. Obviously the seasonal aspect of the avifauna of the region is subject to considerable change.

Because birds, perhaps more than some other vertebrate groups, lend themselves to ecological treatment, one is tempted to follow such a plan. However, for the sake of uniformity, the classical systematic procedure will be adhered to.

The primitive tinamous (Tinamiformes) constitute a Neotropical order possibly related to the flightless rheas (Rheiformes) of South America. With one exception, the highland *Nothocercus bonapartei* of southern Central America, they are distributed over the lowlands and occur well northward in tropical woodlands on the Mexican coastal plains. Though capable of flight, these birds, so quail-like in appearance, are generally encountered on the ground.

Loons (Gaviiformes) are northerners and occur no farther south than the northern Pacific coast of Mexico where three species are known to winter in coastal waters. Grebes (Podicipediformes) are represented by several resident forms as well as winter immigrants. One interesting, almost flightless species (*Podilymbus gigas*) is confined to Lake Atitlan in Guatemala.

The order Procellariiformes is composed of oceanic birds of wide distribution. Shearwaters (Procellariidae, *in part*) and storm petrels (Hydrobatidae) occur off both the Pacific and Caribbean coasts of Middle America, but albatrosses (Diomedeidae) and petrels (Procellariidae, *in part*) are confined to the Pacific.

In the families of the order Pelecaniformes, the tropicbirds (Phaëthontidae) are truly pelagic, boobies (Sulidae) are semipelagic, frigatebirds usually fly within sight of land, and pelicans are chiefly littoral. Cormorants (Phalacrocoracidae) fish in both coastal waters and inland lakes, but anhingas (Anhingidae) are primarily freshwater birds. All families of Pelecaniformes are represented along both the Caribbean and Pacific sides of Middle America.

Herons and their allies (Ciconiiformes) are mostly shallow-water waders and are well represented throughout Middle America. Herons, egrets, and bitterns (Ardeidae), storks (Ciconiidae), and ibises and the spoonbill (Threskiornithidae) are widespread, but the flamingo (Phoenicopteridae, *Phoenicopterus ruber*) occurs within the region only on the Yucatan Peninsula.

Ducks, geese, and swans (Anseriformes) are represented for the most part by migrants from the north. Geese and swans winter no farther south than Mexico, and this is also true of a large proportion of ducks. Other ducks, however, winter throughout; several, including the masked and ruddy ducks (*Oxyura*) and tree ducks (*Dendrocygna*), are resident species. The muscovy duck (*Cairina moschata*) has, of course, been domesticated. It was originally endemic to the lowlands of Middle and South America.[2]

Vultures and birds of prey (Falconiformes) form a conspicuous element in the avifauna. Some of the genera, e.g. *Buteo* (the soaring hawks), are widely distributed in both the New and Old Worlds. Vultures (Cathartidae), as scavengers, are the sanitary police of the New World tropics and are especially abundant in and near settlements. Such hawks (Accipitridae) as occur in the region are frequently widespread in their distributions, but the harpy eagle (*Harpia harpyja*) is rare and local. This massive monkey-eating eagle is one of the largest of Central American birds; it lives in humid lowland tropical forests from South America north to near the Isthmus of Tehuantepec in southern Mexico.[3] Some falcons (Falconidae) are widespread over Middle America; the fish-eating osprey (Pandionidae, *Pandion haliaetus*) ranges coasts throughout.

Upland game birds (Galliformes) are widely distributed. Curassows, guans, and chachalacas (Cracidae) are mostly southern, but several occur well northward into Mexico, and the eastern chachalaca (*Ortalis vetula*) extends to the extreme southern tip of Texas. In the partridge family (Phasianidae), upland quails of the genus *Lophortyx* are restricted in Middle America to Mexico, where they inhabit the northwestern deserts and the Pacific slope of the Sierra Madre Occidental. The scaled quail (*Callipepla squamata*) is the most widespread native gallinaceous bird in the arid part of the Mexican Plateau, and the genus *Cyrtonyx*

ranges from the southwestern United States south through the Sierra Madres of Mexico to the highlands of northern Central America. In contrast, the wood quails (*Odontophorus*) are southern. Bobwhites (*Colinus*) are of widespread distribution. Two turkeys (Meleagrididae) are found in Middle America. The wild turkey (*Meleagris gallopavo*) is still encountered locally in northern Mexico. The ocellated turkey (*Agriocharis ocellata*) is confined to the lowlands of the Yucatan Peninsula and adjacent southeastern Mexico, British Honduras, and Guatemala. Despite the fact that it is heavily hunted as a prized food item, it remains numerous, especially in lightly populated areas, e.g. the Peten.

Among the Gruiformes, the sandhill crane (*Grus canadensis*) is a winter visitant to plains in northern Mexico. Rails (Rallidae) are represented by both migrant and resident species. Though generally distributed, they are most characteristic of marshy and swampy lowlands. Sungrebes (Heliornithidae) and sunbitterns (Eurypygidae), each with one species in Central America, extend northward locally to the humid lowlands of southeastern Mexico.

The diversified Charadriiformes comprise one of the larger groups of Middle American birds with no fewer than 11 families in the region. The majority are associated with aquatic conditions. The brightly colored jaçana (Jacanidae, *Jacana spinosa*) is generally abundant along sluggish streams and lowland marshes. Of the groups that are essentially shorebirds, plovers (Charadriidae), sandpipers and their allies (Scolopacidae), and phalaropes (Phalaropodidae) are primarily northern and the majority merely winter in the region or migrate through it. Others, as oystercatchers (Haematopodidae), the skimmer (Rhynchopidae, *Rhynchops nigra*), and the thickknee (Burhinidae, *Burhinus bistriatus*), are resident. Gulls and terns (Laridae) are predominantly littoral. The majority do not nest farther south than southern Mexico.

[2] Ed. note: Water birds, especially native and migrant ducks, geese, teals, and coots, once formed a significant source of food for Indians living near the numerous lakes that dot the plateau surface of central Mexico. The Tarascan fishermen on Lake Patzcuaro still use the ancient spearthrower (*atlatl*) to take waterfowl.

[3] Ed. note: In preconquest times the Middle American Indians associated the eagle with the warrior class, and representations of the bird enter predominantly in ancient Mexican and Mayan art.

Pigeons and doves (Columbiformes) constitute a nearly cosmopolitan land bird order; they occur throughout Middle America. The ground doves (*Columbigallina* and *Claravis*) and the quail-doves (*Geotrygon*), however, are essentially southern, and the last extend northward only to tropical Mexico.

Parrots (Psittaciformes) are pantropical woodland birds; they are abundant in the Mexican lowlands and Central America. Of 19 species recorded from Mexico, only five occur more or less regularly as high as pine-oak forest on the mountains that rim the Plateau. Twelve species do not extend farther north than Nicaragua. Of the remaining 20 species found in the Middle American region, six are generally distributed from lowland Mexico into South America.

Cuckoos and roadrunners (Cuculiformes), though occurring in midlatitudes, are, like the parrots, largely tropical lowlanders. Though several are confined to the southern part of Middle America and one is only a migrant from the United States, many of the species are widely distributed through the region.

Owls (Strigiformes) are found throughout Middle America at all elevations. However, almost half of the 30 species occurring there are confined to Mexico and northern Central America. Goatsuckers (Caprimulgiformes, Caprimulgidae) are similarly generally distributed, but the large potoos (Nyctibiidae) of the same order are confined to lower elevations from Mexico south.

Swifts and hummingbirds (Apodiformes) are, next to the passerines, the largest order of birds (in terms of species) in Middle America. Swifts (Apodidae) show geographic similarities to the cuckoos. Though almost cosmopolitan, they are best represented in the tropics. In fact, in the New World only four species are regularly found north of Mexico. In Middle America they fly over both mountains and coastal plains. Hummingbirds (Trochilidae) are endemic

to the Americas, and they, too, are largely confined to the tropics. Of the 319 currently recognized species in the world, only 15 normally range north of Mexico, and only one (*Selasphorus rufus*) regularly reaches Alaska. Even in Mexico over half of the 51 recorded species are restricted to lowlands. Despite the fact that the majority of species are lowlanders, hummingbirds are found in Middle America at all elevations. One genus (*Selasphorus*) is almost confined to high altitudes in the region. It has been recorded at 3000-3700 m. in Mexico, Guatemala, and Costa Rica.

Trogons (Trogoniformes) are pantropical forest birds, but they are best represented in the American tropics. They occur on the lowlands and highlands alike from southeastern Arizona southward. All are brightly colored, and the quetzal (*Pharomachrus mocinno*) is considered by many the most beautiful bird of the Americas. Though living in humid mountain cloud forests from Oaxaca to Panama, it is popularly associated with Guatemala, which claims it for her national emblem.[4] During the 1800's the species was heavily exploited. Its long upper tail coverts were in great demand in Europe and elsewhere to satisfy milady's vanity. As a result of slaughter of the bird to supply the feather market and of the greatly accelerated destruction by man of its habitat in the Twentieth Century, the quetzal has become rare and local.

The Coraciiformes include the kingfishers and motmots. Kingfishers (Alcedinidae), though almost cosmopolitan, are poorly represented in the New World. Only six species are found in Middle America; four of these are normally confined within the region to tropical Mexico and Central America. Motmots (Momotidae) comprise a small, tropical American family that is best represented in the Middle American

[4] Ed. note: The ancient Maya, Aztec, and their neighbors greatly prized the green feathers of the quetzal for ceremonial headdress.

region. They are found almost throughout the area but are largely lowlanders.

The Piciformes, an order comprising such diverse groups as barbets, jacamars, puffbirds, toucans, and woodpeckers, are tropical except for some woodpeckers and the wrynecks. Barbets (Capitonidae) occur no farther north than Costa Rica. Jacamars (Galbulidae) and puffbirds (Bucconidae) are both represented as far as southern Mexico; toucans range northward at low and moderate elevations in humid areas to central Mexico. Woodpeckers (Picidae) are well represented in the region. As in other near-cosmopolitan groups, however, not all the genera of the region are uniformly distributed throughout. Several occur no farther south than Mexico or northern Central America, or merely winter in the region; others barely enter Middle America from South America.

Perching birds (Passeriformes) are represented in the region by 36 families and 752 species. They thus comprise slightly more than 50 per cent of the avifauna. However, a dozen families (two of them introduced by man) contribute only one species each to the fauna, and another seven families are represented by fewer than 10 species each. In fact, three families, tyrant flycatchers (Tyrannidae), wood warblers (Parulidae), and finches and their allies (Fringillidae) comprise almost 50 per cent of the passerine birds of Middle America.

American passerines are generally divided into two suborders, the Tyranni and the Oscines (Passeres). The former suborder, though with a scattering of small genera in the Old World, appears, on the basis of its present center of distribution, to be of South American origin. Of the approximately 1,040 species of Tyranni found in the New World, only 30, all of them tyrant flycatchers, occur commonly north of the Mexican border. The Oscines, in contrast, are of diverse origins, but several families also probably evolved in South America.

Of the New World Tyranni, two small

families, tapaculos (Rhinocryptidae) and the unique sharpbill (Oxyruncidae, *Oxyruncus cristatus*) barely enter Middle America and do not occur north of Costa Rica. Though woodcreepers (Dendrocolaptidae) are mainly southern, some extend well up into Mexico, chiefly along the lowlands, and three species are even found at moderate elevations in oak woods in the Sierra Madre Oriental of northeastern Mexico. The South American ovenbirds and their allies (Furnariidae) are in Mexico, with two exceptions, strictly lowlanders. The antbirds (Formicariidae) are another very southern family; only nine of the 39 species which occur in Middle America regularly reach Mexico. Both manakins (Pipridae) and cotingas (Cotingidae) are also essentially tropical forest birds. The former range into Mexico only in the south in lowland areas. Only a single cotinga (*Platypsaris aglaiae*) penetrates northern Mexico, and this species extends sparingly to the extreme southern portions of Arizona and Texas. The remaining suboscine family, the tyrant flycatchers (Tyrannidae), will be discussed later.

It would unduly lengthen this account to comment on each of the almost 30 other families of passerines. We may depart therefore from the foregoing "check-list" approach and group certain families on the basis of their geographic characteristics.

Eight indigenous families of primarily Old World distribution are represented in Middle America by fewer than 10 species each. Of these, shrikes (Laniidae) and the wrentit (Chamaeidae, often merged into the Old World Timaliidae), each with a single species in the region, and nuthatches (Sittidae) with three species, do not occur south of Oaxaca. Titmice (Paridae) reach southern Mexico and Guatemala along highland routes; a creeper (Certhiidae) extends to Nicaragua, also only in the mountains. The dippers (Cinclidae), frequenters of clear rushing streams, are likewise montane and, though they are represented in Middle America by only one species, another species continues well southward within South America. Two other Old World groups, pipits (Motacillidae) and larks (Alaudidae), also reach South America. The former is represented by a single resident species in southern Central America (though two others winter in Middle America). The horned lark (*Eremophila alpestris*), the only member of its large family native to the New World, occurs in Mexico, skips all of Central America, and reappears in the mountains of Colombia.

Three other primarily Old World families are better represented in Middle America. These are thrushes (Turdidae), jays (Corvidae), and gnatcatchers (Sylviidae) which not only occur throughout the region but continue on into South America.

A number of families of birds found in Middle America appear to be New World elements. Of these, wrens (Troglodytidae), mockingbirds (Mimidae), and vireos (Vireonidae) are all well represented in Middle America. Wood warblers (Parulidae), although perhaps of northern origin, are similarly wide-ranging through the American tropics. In addition to many resident species of wood warblers in Middle America, a large number of familiar United States species winter in the region, and these must have a profound effect on the ecology of the resident forms. Likewise the cedar waxwing (Bombycillidae, *Bombycilla cedrorum*) winters in Middle America and its close relatives, the silky flycatchers (Ptilogonatidae), are almost confined to the region.

Three large Pan-American families are probably of South American origin. They are tanagers (Thraupidae), orioles and blackbirds (Icteridae), and tyrant flycatchers (Tyrannidae). These three comprise almost 30 per cent of the passerine fauna of Middle America. All, though generally distributed through the New World, possess certain genera that in Middle America are restricted to the extreme south or are represented only in tropical lowlands north to southern Mexico. The number of species of tanagers and tyrant flycatchers, particularly, decreases rapidly from south to north. Of the former there are 51 species in Panama, 26 in Mexico and only four in the United States. The Tyrannidae show a similar south to north decline. A fourth family, honeycreepers (Coerebidae), is considered by some to be an artificial assemblage. Honeycreepers also appear to be of South American origin and have a geographic pattern in Middle America similar to that of the previously noted woodcreepers and South American ovenbirds.

Swallows (Hirundinidae) and the diversified finch family (Fringillidae) are almost cosmopolitan. The former are poorly represented in Middle America (14 species) and almost half of these occur south of the Mexican Plateau only as migrants. The latter, with its 121 Middle American species, is the largest family of birds in the region; it is composed of subgroups of diverse origins. Cardinals and allies (Richmondeninae) appear to be a South American element that is generally distributed throughout the region but which, like the tanagers and tyrant flycatchers, decreases in number of species from south to north (only 12 north of Mexico). Sparrows of the subfamily Emberizinae make up the bulk of Middle American fringillids. Though many merely winter in Middle America, there are a number of resident species of considerable interest. Brush finches (*Atlapetes*), for example, are strictly Middle American and South American. Towhees (*Pipilo*), in contrast, do not extend south of Guatemala. Northern finches (Carduelinae), also of northern origin (probably Old World), are largely boreal in the New World. One genus (*Spinus*), however, contributes many species to the avifauna of Middle and South America.

The starling (*Sturnus vulgaris*) and the house sparrow (*Passer domesticus*), two well established imports from Europe to the United States, have spread to Mexico. They add representatives of the families Sturnidae and Ploceidae to the Middle American fauna.[5]

REPTILIA. The reptiles are well represented in Middle America. Of about 50 extant families currently recognized by herpetologists, 33 occur within the region. Three of these are restricted to Middle America and another almost so. At the present time it would be almost impossible to estimate the number of reptilian species in the area. Somewhat over 900 species have been recorded from Mexico by Smith and Taylor (1945, 1950); based on the latter's work (1951, 1956) in Costa Rica, an estimate of about 200 species for that country might be reasonable. At the specific level there would be little overlap between the two countries. It is reasonable to suspect that at least 1,200 species may occur within the region.

Exclusive of marine groups, turtles (Testudinata) are represented in Middle America by six families comprising 12 genera. Two of these families, however, barely enter the region in the north. The remaining four families, nevertheless, lend considerable diversity to the turtle fauna. But closer examination of this fauna reveals that south of Guatemala a depauperate condition obtains. Mexico, for example, counts 12 genera and 33 species, whereas southern Central America can boast no more than four genera and eight species. It is interesting to note that not a single representative of the

pantropical side-necked turtles (Pleurodira), so abundant in South America, has managed to invade even eastern Panama.

Two families of turtles, soft-shells (Trionychidae) and gopher turtles (Testudinidae), so familiar to North Americans, barely enter Middle America from the north. Neither extends south of northern Mexico, though the latter reappears in western South America and on the Galapagos islands as the giant land turtles (*Testudo*). Snapping turtles (Chelydridae), in contrast, extend the length of Middle America on the east only and continue on into northwestern South America. However, not more than two dozen specimens of this strictly New World group have been collected south of the United States.

The family Kinosternidae is confined to the Americas. Though not necessarily large in size, members of this family, which includes the mud turtles, musk turtles, and two small genera confined to northern Central America, are voracious. Mud turtles (*Kinosternon*) are the most widely distributed and most numerous of the testudines occurring in the region. South of the Mexican Plateau, however, they are confined to lowlands. Two small, related genera (*Staurotypus* and *Claudius*) occur only locally. The former is found only from southern Mexico south to Honduras and El Salvador and the latter only in southeastern Mexico and in northern Guatemala. A third small family (Dermatemydae) has a range roughly coincidental with that of *Claudius*.

The Emydidae constitute the largest family of turtles; it comprises a number of genera of diverse forms and habits. The little painted turtle (*Chrysemys*) and the genus *Clemmys* barely enter northern Mexico. The box turtles (*Terrapene*) reach southern Mexico and the Yucatan Peninsula. The genus *Geoemyda* (a small land turtle), in contrast, though occurring in southern Asia, is found in the Americas only from the lowlands of Mexico southward into northern South America. An

[5] Ed. note: Occasional reference has been made above to the economic and cultural significance of birds to the aborigines of Middle America. Aside from food derived from the taking of game fowl, the showy feathers of various tropical birds were important trade items in ancient Indian commerce. The use of the quetzal tail feathers for priestly headdresses has been mentioned. The *amateca*, or makers of the famous feather mosaics of central Mexico, used the blue, green, red, and yellow feathers of macaws and other parrots, the turquoise and purple of a cotinga, the pink of the roseate spoonbill, the iridescent colors of hummingbirds and many others.

aquatic genus *Pseudemys*, related to the painted turtles and frequently known as the "slider," is generally distributed through the region and is abundantly represented in southern United States.

The two families of sea turtles, which are worldwide, both visit the Middle American coasts locally for breeding. They are the leatherback (Dermochelyidae) and the Cheloniidae, which include the ridley (*Lepidochelys*), the loggerhead (*Caretta*), the hawksbill (*Eretmochelys*), and the green turtle (*Chelonia*).

Certain of these turtles are of considerable economic importance. The shell of the hawksbill (tortoiseshell) is widely utilized for a variety of artistic purposes. All the sea turtles are utilized as food, both meat and eggs, though there is considerable disagreement from locale to locale as to the esteem in which the various species are held. The green turtle is, of course, generally considered superior to all others as food. Carr and Giovannoli (1957) have given an excellent account of sea turtle habits and of the turtle-fishing industry of the Caribbean coast of southern Central America. Among the fresh-water turtles, the meat of many species of *Pseudemys* is held in high regard and, where it occurs, the dermatemid is also highly esteemed as a base for soup. Though they are not generally utilized for food, I have seen individuals of both *Kinosternon* and *Geoemyda* offered for sale in native markets.

Thirteen families of lizards (Lacertilia) are known to occur in Middle America. It is difficult to estimate the number of species within the region. Smith and Taylor (1950) record about 275 species from Mexico, and E. H. Taylor (1956) has listed about 70 from Costa Rica. Duplication at the specific level between the two regions is slight. These figures bring out one fact, namely that lizards are apparently better adapted to xeric than to mesic conditions. This is even better demonstrated by comparisons at the generic level. Mexico supports no fewer than 48 genera, as compared with 25 in Costa Rica. Thirteen of the Costa Rican genera, moreover, are represented by but a single species in that country. Furthermore, about half the genera recorded from Mexico do not occur south of the Isthmus of Tehuantepec.

The "geckos" are an essentially pantropical group. Three families are recognized, and all are represented in Middle America. The Sphaerodactylidae are confined to the New World. Only three genera enter the region; one occurs no farther north than Costa Rica, and the other two extend northward only to the Isthmus of Tehuantepec. These are the smallest lizards encountered in Middle America. All are found more frequently around habitations than in non-edificarian areas. One (*Sphaerodactylus*), at least, is often greatly feared because of its bright red tail. The Enblepharidae are represented in the New World by but a single genus (*Coleonyx*). This genus is best developed in northern Mexico and southwestern United States, and only one species occurs as far south as Costa Rica. The Gekkonidae are represented in Middle America by five genera. Two of these genera (*Gehyra* and *Hemidactylus*) are exotics which apparently entered the New World during the course of overseas trade. Both are restricted to coastal regions, generally in the vicinity of ports. A third genus (*Aristelliger*) is essentially West Indian and on the mainland occurs only along the Caribbean coast of the Yucatan Peninsula and Belize. A fourth genus (*Thecadactylus*) is found only south of southern Mexico. Only *Phyllodactylus* among the gekkonids is generally distributed throughout the region.

The spiny lizards and their allies (Iguanidae) comprise the bulk of the saurians of Middle America. In Mexico 60 per cent of the lizards belong to this family; in Costa Rica, 50 per cent. Tremendous diversity of size and form is encountered in this large group. Some of the little woodland anoles

(*Anolis*) are no longer than two inches, whereas the big iguana (*Iguana*) may measure over six feet. While the majority of species are rather ordinary in appearance, others are quite spectacular. The basilisk (*Basiliscus*) has a high mid-dorsal crest, the horned lizards (*Phrynosoma*) possess a number of spines that protrude from the back of the head, and the iguanas have long, flexible spines down the middle of the back.

The genera of this family are arranged more or less into two geographic groups, one northern, the other more southern. Of the northerners, such genera as the chuckwallas (*Sauromalus*), the utas (*Uta*), and the earless lizards (*Holbrookia*) occur no farther south than northern Mexico on the mainland. The horned lizards reach the Isthmus of Tehuantepec. The largest of all mainland iguanid genera, the spiny lizards (*Sceloporus*), continue as far south as Costa Rica but are represented by only two species below Guatemala. In contrast, among the southerners an anole-like genus (*Polychrus*) reaches only to Costa Rica and the crested *Corythophanes* is found only south of the Veracruz lowlands. The anoles (*Anolis*), though found in southern United States, are, north of the Tehuantepec isthmus, largely restricted to the lowlands and the plateau slopes. The large iguana and its relatives the ctenosaurs (*Ctenosaura* and related genera) are generally distributed over the lowlands from central Mexico southward to Panama and South America. Both the iguana and the ctenosaurs are prized as food, and may be purchased alive in many of the native markets throughout their ranges.

Two small families of legless lizards, the Anniellidae and the Anelytropsidae, occur only locally in Mexico. The former, with two species, is found only in southern California and northern Baja California; the latter, with but a single species, is restricted to east central Mexico. A third family of burrowers, Amphisbaenidae, also occurs

within the region. In Mexico it is represented by the genus *Bipes*, which possesses only forelegs. It is found only locally in southern Baja California. The family skips most of Central America and reappears in Panama and South America as legless forms.

The Xenosauridae are represented in the New World by only three species. Like several of the small genera noted above, these secretive little lizards are local in their distributions and are mainly restricted to the plateau slopes in the east from central Mexico south to Guatemala. Two other small families, alligator lizards (Anguidae) and so-called night lizards (Xantusidae), are northern groups. South of about Guatemala they are represented by only two species each, the former only in the highlands and the latter only on the lowlands.

Beaded lizards or Gila monsters (*Heloderma*) belong to another small family (Helodermatidae) with but two species, both of which are represented in the region. The genus occurs only from southwestern United States southward along the Pacific slope of Mexico to the Isthmus of Tehuantepec and on to Guatemala via the valley of the Rio Grijalva. Because it can inflict a fatal bite, the *escorpion*, as it is frequently known, commands considerable respect wherever it occurs. The poison of this lizard is essentially neurotoxic, especially to the respiratory centers. Various surveys of literature reveal that, though the bite can be fatal, so many factors enter into the analysis of reported fatalities that the toxicity of the venom to man cannot be properly evaluated. One author, however, has reported 23 fatalities resulting from 158 cases of bite over a period of about 65 years. Certain harmless lizards are also considered dangerous by the uninformed natives. Among these are included certain of the Xantusidae and the Xenosauridae. Brightly colored species of *Sceloporus* and even the tiny little red-tailed *Sphaerodactylus* may also be so considered in certain locales.

Whiptails and their allies (Teiidae) are essentially South American. Only eight genera enter Middle America and but three of these possibly extend north of southern Nicaragua. Two others occur only north to the Mexican lowlands. The sixth (*Cnemidophorus*) is one of the most abundant lizards of the Mexican section, but south of the Isthmus of Tehuantepec it is poorly represented.

Cosmopolitan skinks (Scincidae) are mostly a more northern group in the New World. Three genera occur in the region and two occur no farther south than Costa Rica or Panama. Best representation of the family is found in *Eumeces* but even this genus is largely confined to the Mexican section of Middle America.

Middle America has more than its share of snakes (Ophidia). The systematics of the higher categories (family and above) are in a state of flux, but a conservative herpetologist might recognize eight families of this group. All but one occur within the bounds of Middle America. It is difficult to say how many species may be found in the region. Smith and Taylor (1945) list about 330 species as occurring in Mexico, and Taylor (1951) has recorded about 125 from Costa Rica with very little duplication between the two countries. Both these lists can be said to be generous estimates.

Two families of burrowing worm snakes occur within the region. These secretive little reptiles are essentially tropical. One family (Typhlopidae) displays a geographic pattern similar to that of the amphisbaenid lizards noted above. Present in southern Mexico and Guatemalan lowlands, it skips the remainder of Middle America to reappear in South America. The second family (Leptotyphlopidae) is generally distributed throughout the region, though several small genera do not occur north of Costa Rica.

Boas (Boidae) are at best but poorly represented in Middle America. One small genus (*Lichanura*) occurs only in the north in southwestern United States, northwestern Mexico, and Baja California. Several other small genera are restricted to the Pacific sides of Mexico and Central America. None of the giant anacondas (*Eunectes*) enter the region, and the only large boa is *Boa constrictor*. It occurs on the lowlands from Mexico southward. It generally does not exceed 10 feet in length and is, surprisingly enough, a not uncommon snake over most of the region at lower elevations.

A single python (Pythonidae) occurs in the New World. This small python (*Loxocemus*) occurs only along the Pacific coast from Mexico to Costa Rica.

The Colubridae make up possibly 80 per cent of the snake fauna of Middle America. The family is extremely varied: it includes the water snakes, the racers, a number of semipoisonous forms and a multitude of small secretive genera and species. These are, for the most part, without common names, and such common names as are applied are frequently misleading. To the average Middle American, for example, any brightly colored, banded, or spotted snake is the deadly coral, whereas only a fraction of such species are true coral snakes.

In general, two geographic groups of colubrids may be recognized, one essentially southern and the other more northern. Water snakes, garter snakes, and their allies (Natricinae) are northerners. They extend as far as Costa Rica but are poorly represented south of the Mexican Plateau. In contrast a second group (Xenodontinae) are essentially southern. This subfamily includes a large number of small snakes, many secretive and abundant in leaf-mold, and frequently they are lumped together under the vernacular Spanish name *basureros*. Though several genera occur in the United States and on the Mexican Plateau, the group as a whole is more characteristic of Central and South America. Several genera may be considered semipoisonous, inasmuch as they produce a weak venom that flows down grooved teeth located in the rear of the mouth. As a result of both the impotence of the venom and the inefficient mechanism for injecting it, these snakes cannot be considered dangerous to man.

A third group of colubrids, the racers and their allies (Colubrinae), though more typically northern, are well represented in both the north and south. Included here are several of the largest of the snakes of the region. *Drymarchon* and *Spilotes* are both related to the North American whip snakes and racers, which not infrequently attain lengths of 7 feet. Like the Xenodontines, several genera are semipoisonous.

A fourth small group (Scaphiodontophinae) is represented by but a single genus. It occurs only on the lowlands of southern Mexico and Central America. It is related to a southeastern Asian group.

A single sea snake (Hydrophidae) occurs locally in bays along the Pacific from the Gulf of California southward to Chile. It, too, is apparently semipoisonous.

Coral snakes (Micruridae) are relatively common throughout Middle America. Though several occur on the Mexican Plateau north to about Mexico City as well as in the United States, the group is essentially restricted to the lowlands and lower mountain slopes. Though generally docile by nature and renitent to bite, all must be considered extremely venomous.

Pit vipers (Crotalidae) include the moccasins, rattlesnakes, the fer-de-lance and its allies, and the bushmaster. Only a single moccasin (*Agkistrodon*) occurs in the region, and it extends no farther south than Nicaragua along the Pacific lowlands. The rattlesnakes (*Crotalus* and *Sistrurus*) are strictly New World and are largely confined to North America north of the Isthmus of Tehuantepec. In fact, aside from the tropical rattlesnake of South America, only one representative of the group occurs south of Tehuantepec, and it continues only to Costa Rica in contrast to 14 species in Mexico

north of the isthmus.[6] The fer-de-lance group (*Bothrops*) is mostly southern. Though several species occur on the plateau of southern Mexico, the great majority are lowlanders or mountain slope forms. Their northern limit is Tamaulipas. The bushmaster (*Lachesis*) is the largest of the poisonous snakes of the New World. It is strictly southern and reaches its northern limit in Costa Rica or possibly southeastern Nicaragua.

With the exception of several small species of *Bothrops* and the pygmy rattlesnakes (*Sistrurus*), all the crotalids are capable of producing death from their bite. Death rate from snake bite, however, is not high in the region. In the years 1922–26 the United Fruit Company Hospital at Almirante, Panama, treated only 25 cases. This, of course, did not account for all instances of snake bite in the region, as many bitten did not seek medical treatment. However, the death rate among those 25 treated amounted to about 20 per cent. This figure seems high, since the Fruit Company reported a death rate of but 5 per cent in all Central America during the years 1938–51.

Only three crocodilians (Crocodilia) occur within the bounds of Middle America. The most widespread is *Crocodylus acutus* which is distributed over the lowlands (though more generally on the coasts) from Tamaulipas and Sinaloa, Mexico, to South America. A near relative *Crocodylus moreletti* is more of an inland species and is found only between southern Mexico and Honduras. The caiman (*Caiman*) is also largely coastal. Though found along the Pacific from South America to Oaxaca, it extends north only to Nicaragua on the Caribbean side.

AMPHIBIA. Considering the fact that the

[6] Ed. note: The ancient Middle Americans associated especially the rattlesnake with the rain cult, and representations of the animal abound as a preconquest art form in central Mexico and Yucatan.

subhumid lands of Mexico present not the best of amphibian environments yet comprise at least two-thirds of the total area of Middle America, the amphibian fauna of the region herein dealt with is surprisingly rich and varied. Of possibly 20 families occurring in the New World, only six are not represented in the area. It should be noted, however, that three northern families are not found south of the Mexican Plateau and another, the mud "eel," (Sirenidae), occurs in the region only through the courtesy of the present course of the lower Rio Grande. Two southern families, furthermore, extend no farther north than Nicaragua.

An estimate of the number of species is difficult. Smith and Taylor (1948) record about 225 from Mexico, and Taylor (1952a and 1952b) has listed about 150 from Costa Rica. Considering that duplication in the two areas amounts to little, it is not unreasonable to expect an amphibian fauna of well over 400 species in Middle America.

Caecilians (Gymnophiona, Caeciliidae), legless, burrowing amphibians, wormlike in appearance and frequently known as *tapaculo* with reference to certain unprintable habits attributed to them, are almost pantropical. Abundant in South America, only a few species enter Middle America where they extend northward only to southern Mexico.

Three families of salamanders (Caudata), in addition to the mud "eel" noted above, are present in the area. Two of these, newts (Salamandridae) and the mole salamander (Ambystomidae), however, do not occur south of the central Mexican Plateau. The aquatic larvae of certain ambystomids are of considerable scientific interest in showing neoteny in their natural environments. These are known by their Nahuatl name, *axolotl*. In parts of Mexico at least one (*Bathysiredon*) is utilized as food. The third family (Plethodontidae), so conspicuous an element in the amphibian fauna of southeastern United States, is well rep-

resented throughout Middle America and enters northern South America. In fact, southern Mexico and Central America appear to have been the center of origin of several genera, *Thorius* and *Pseudoeurycea* in Mexico and very probably *Bolitoglossa* and *Magnadigita* in Central America. Tropical members of the family are nonaquatic and are distributed from sea level to timber line. In Guatemala they are known collectively as *niño dormido,* but this may be a localism.

Frogs and toads (Anura) comprise the bulk of the Middle American amphibian fauna. Nine families occur in the region, but three of these are poorly represented and are strictly peripheral. One, spadefoots (Pelobatidae), extend southward only to Oaxaca. The other two, the Dendrobatidae and the Atelopodidae (sometimes combined as the Brachycephalidae), though well represented in South America, invade Central America northward only to Nicaragua. All are boldly colored and are certainly the gaudiest of the New World amphibians. The dermal secretion of some of these frogs is said to be more toxic than that of any other known amphibian.

A fourth family, the Rhinophrynidae, is monotypic and is found only on the Mexican lowlands, the Yucatan Peninsula, and northern Guatemala. It is a primitive frog and said to be a termite eater. These bloated creatures are well known to Maya experts whose nights during the rainy season have been rendered miserable by the brute's call which resembles nothing quite so much as the retchings of hundreds of very ill humans.

Toads (Bufonidae) are abundant throughout the region from sea level to timber line. However, all species in Middle America belong to a single, almost cosmopolitan genus, *Bufo*. One species, the marine toad (*Bufo marinus*), is certainly one of the commonest animals of the lowlands of Mexico and Central America.

The Leptodactylidae—there is no generally acceptable common name for the group or even for particular genera—is, in terms of species, the second largest family of amphibians in Middle America. Though essentially a southern element, the family is widely distributed throughout the region over lowlands and highlands alike. The largest genus, *Eleutherodactylus*, is Pan-American, but two small genera (*Syrrhophus* and *Tomodactylus*) are confined to the north and do not extend south of Guatemala. Frogs of this family show a wide diversity of form and habits. Several genera, including *Eleutherodactylus*, are the most terrestrial of the Middle American frogs, for, in so far as is known, they do not go to water for egg-laying and have thus eliminated the tadpole stage.

By far the largest family of amphibians in the region is that of tree frogs (Hylidae). Like the leptodactylids, they occur throughout Middle America, and may be found at all elevations from sea level to timber line. Despite the family's over-all wide distribution, various genera and subgenera have had different centers of origin which are mirrored in their extant distributions. Some are strictly southern, such as *Cerathyla* which does not occur north of Panama. Others are northern and do not extend much farther south than southern Mexico, for example the *eximia* group of *Hyla* (to Guatemala) and the two small genera *Diaglena* and *Pternohyla* which are confined to local areas of Mexico north of the Isthmus of Tehuantepec. A third group of genera is Central American: examples are the casque-headed *Triprion*, which is found only on the Yucatan Peninsula; and *Ptychohyla* and *Plectrohyla*, which are confined to the mountain streams of southern Mexico and northern Central America. Because of the confused systematics of the family, however, little can be said concerning its distribution other than generalizations such as the foregoing.

Several species of the genus *Phrynohyas*

are known to secrete a volatile poison from their dermal glands. This mucus has the property of producing quite violent, catarrh-like symptoms in humans.

The Centrolenellidae are a family of small, delicate, hylid-like frogs that, in Middle America, rarely attain the length of an inch. The family is restricted to the New World and is best developed in South America. Only two species occur as far north as southern Mexico as compared with eight in Costa Rica.

Narrow-mouth frogs (Microhylidae) are also essentially a southern group. Though they occur northward to the southern United States, only three genera are found in Middle America as compared with 14 in South America. However, one of the Middle American genera does not occur north of Panama. Furthermore, except along its edges, the Mexican Plateau north of about the level of Mexico City is devoid of microhylids.

Leopard frogs and their allies (Ranidae), so common in the United States, find poor representation in Middle America. All species belong to the almost cosmopolitan genus *Rana*. Though nine species are found in Mexico, only three or four occur in southern Central America and but a single species is found south of Panama.

PISCES. At this time it would be well nigh impossible to deal with all the fishlike vertebrates that inhabit the inland, littoral, and pelagic waters of Middle America. Fortunately modern ichthyologists in their zoogeographic considerations have given close attention to the ecology of their group. As a result the fishes have been divided into six ecological divisions, only two of which will be treated here—primary and secondary division fishes. Primary division fishes are those which are completely intolerant to marine waters. Secondary division fishes are those that show a slight tolerance to salt water which enables them to transcend narrow marine barriers, such as narrow straits, or permits limited alongshore movements from one drainage system to another. Thus the following remarks will be confined to essentially fresh-water groups. The remaining four divisions are chiefly comprised of fishes that show varying degrees of euryhalinity and are thus of little value in analyzing the geographic patterns displayed by inland water groups.

Roughly 20 families comprise the primary and secondary fish fauna of Middle America. It is difficult to estimate the number of species. R. R. Miller (1958) estimates over 100 species of primary fishes in Mexico, and he suggests (*in litt.*) that there are possibly 300 species of primary and secondary fishes in that country and about 100 in Guatemala. Hildebrand (1938) lists slightly over 100 in Panama. Of the intervening area little is known. The only general account of the Middle American fish fauna is that of Regan (1906–08), and he knew of only about 250 species of fresh-water fishes between the Rio Grande and Colombia.

One statement concerning the size of the fish fauna of the inland waters of Middle America, however, can be made with certainty: it is depauperate. Of 41 families comprising the fresh-water fish fauna of Mexico, only 14 may be considered primary or secondary groups. Only 10 of 35 families of the Guatemalan fauna may be similarly classified. In Panama the proportion is considerably greater because several South American families of catfishes reach their northern limits in that region. But in general, were it not for the wide-ranging top minnows (Poeciliidae) and several closely allied families (Cyprinodontidae, Goodeidae) and the *mojarras* and their allies (Cichlidae), the fish fauna of Middle America would be poor indeed. These groups comprise about 60 per cent of the species of Mexican primary and secondary division fishes, 75 per cent of the same in Guatemala, and 35 per cent of Panamanian species.

In the following account of the primary and secondary division fishes of Middle America, it will be noted that, despite the fact that we are dealing with aquatics, the broader geographic pattern displayed by this class has much in common with the patterns of terrestrial vertebrates.

The relatively primitive gars (Lepisosteidae) constitute a small family which is, nevertheless, a geographically significant element in eastern North America. This group extends only as far south as the San Juan drainage system of Nicaragua. North of the Isthmus of Tehuantepec, however, gars are found only on the Gulf of Mexico side. They have crossed over in the isthmian region and south of there are found on both the Caribbean and Pacific lowlands.

In contrast to gars, characids (Characidae), to which the voracious *piranha* of South America belongs, are a tropical group. These are mostly small, herringlike fishes which the natives lump under such vernacular names as *sardina* (*Astyanax*) or *sabalo* (*Brycon*) for some of the larger species. Only one species reaches the Rio Grande, and the group is unrepresented both on the Mexican Plateau and on the Pacific lowlands north of the Rio Armeria. Furthermore, north of Panama where 18 genera occur, the family is poorly represented. Nevertheless, where they are present, the various species occur as large populations.

The carp and minnow family (Cyprinidae), the largest of the families of fresh-water fishes, is cosmopolitan except for Central and South America. Though represented in northern Mexico by no fewer than 17 genera, the family reaches its southern limit on the Pacific slope in the Rio Balsas drainage, and only a single species extends as far south on the Atlantic slope as the upper Rio Papaloapan. Several small genera are confined to the Rio Lerma or to it and the headwaters of the Rio San Juan, a plateau tributary of the Panuco. The carp (*Cyprinus*) and the goldfish (*Carassius*) are, of course, introduced species which have become widely distributed.

Like cyprinids, suckers (Catostomidae) are a northern group. They too are well represented in northern Mexico, but have penetrated only slightly farther southward. The most southern member of the family is a species that occurs in the Rio Usumacinta.

Catfishes (Siluroidei), vernacularly known as *bagres*, are essentially southerners. In Middle America they comprise eight families. However, five of these families do not occur north of Panama; another, North American channel cats and bullheads (Ictaluridae), does not extend south of Guatemala. In fact, no single family ranges from the Rio Grande to Colombia. Though catfishes comprise about one-third of the fresh-water species of Panama, only about 10 per cent of the Guatemalan species belong to this group and, were it not for the ictalurids, only a single genus with five species would contribute to the Mexican fauna. The most extensively distributed family is naked catfishes (Pimelodidae) which range northward to the Gulf of Mexico lowlands of central Mexico, though north of Panama it is represented by only a single genus (*Rhamdia*). Mailed catfishes (Loricariidae), largest of the New World siluroid families, reach only to Costa Rica. The remaining five southern families, none of which occurs north of Panama, contribute a total of but six species to the fresh-water fish fauna of Middle America.

Killifishes (Cyprinodontidae) are on all continents except Australia. They are much more abundant, however, in the continental areas to the north and south than in Middle America. In Mexico they are, with the exception of *Profundulus*, restricted to the Gulf of Mexico side, but south of the Tehuantepec isthmus they are common to both the Pacific and Caribbean drainages. The genus *Profundulus* is endemic to the streams of upland southern Mexico, Guatemala, El Salvador, and Honduras.

Closely related to the oviparous cyprinodontids are three families. The first of these

is top minnows (Poeciliidae), almost all viviparous, to which belong the familiar "mollies" and "guppies." This family is strictly American (including the West Indies) and has a continental distribution not unlike that of the New World cyprinodontids. It is more generally distributed through Mexico, however, and contributes far more genera and species to the fish fauna of Middle America than do the oviparous forms. It is in Central America, in fact, that the family attains its maximum diversity. A number of small but distinctive genera are endemic to various sections of Middle America. Among these may be mentioned *Xenodexia*, known only from the upper Usumacinta system, and *Priapella* of southern Veracruz and Tabasco. *Xiphophorus* occurs only in eastern and southeastern Mexico eastward to northern Honduras, whereas *Carlhubbsia* is known only from southern Mexico to southern Gautemala. *Phallichthys* extends along the Caribbean lowlands from southern Guatemala to Panama and *Belonesox* from southeastern Mexico to Costa Rica.

A second family, related to the Cyprinodontidae, are goodeids (Goodeidae). This group comprises about 15 genera and some 30 species and is restricted essentially to the central portion of the Mexican Plateau. It has undergone extensive local differentiation, especially in the Rio Lerma system. A third cyprinodontid relative is the Anablepidae, which is represented in Middle America by a single species, the *cuatrojos* of Pacific Chiapas, Guatemala and El Salvador. Though it is absent from the remainder of Middle America, the family reappears on the Atlantic slope in northern South America.

Two northern families, black basses and fresh-water sunfish (Centrarchidae) and perches (Percidae), barely enter Middle America. The former does not extend southward beyond the Rio Grande system and a few of the other streams of northeastern Mexico; the latter is similarly distributed, but in addition has invaded a Pacific stream in northwestern Mexico.

Cichlids (Cichlidae) are tropical fishes which have undergone extensive radiation in both South America and Africa. In Middle America, however, the bulk of the cichlids belong to the single genus *Cichlasoma*, vernacularly known as the *mojarras*. Though the family is represented by five genera and 15 species in Panama, 11 of the species are *mojarras*. In Nicaragua, Guatemala, and Mexico the picture is even more extreme with 14 of 16, 41 of 44, and 41 of 42 species of cichlids embraced in the genus *Cichlasoma* respectively. This family reaches its northern limit in the Rio Grande system. Oddly enough, it is absent from the Lerma drainage and most of the Mexican Plateau. The *mojarras* are by far the most important food fishes of the inland waters of Middle America. They are to Middle America what the centrarchids (bass, sunfish, bluegills) are to North America.

Though the primary and secondary division fishes are of far greater importance than are peripheral fishes to zoogeographic analysis, the latter cannot be disregarded. They frequently form an important element in fresh-water faunas. For example, about one-third of the species and 27 of the 41 families of fishes of Mexican inland waters belong to peripheral division groups. In Panama, furthermore, 13 per cent of the fresh-water fish fauna are the peripheral gobies (Gobiidae). Nor can it always be said that such groups are without zoogeographic significance even when dealing with continental waters. The peripheral family Atherinidae presents such a case. Included herein is the genus *Chirostoma*, the *pescados blancos* of the Rio Lerma system. This genus, together with the goodeids, is the characterizing feature of the Lerma drainage.[7]

A number of marine groups frequently enter larger rivers and lakes where marine connections are available and many of these undoubtedly played an important role in the life of the pre-Columbian. From Lake Izabal in eastern Guatemala, for example, my colleague Dr. Robert Miller has collected the cub shark (*Carcharhinus*), the sawfish (*Pristis*), the tarpon (*Tarpon*), various anchovies (Engraulidae), snappers (Lutjanidae), several *robalos* (Centropomidae), and salt-water catfishes (Ariidae). Similarly the Nicaraguan lakes support the landlocked shark (*Carcharhinus nicaraguensis*), the sawfish, the tarpon, and grunts (Haemulidae). (For a review of the more important marine fauna along the Middle American coasts see Articles 4 and 5.)

Invertebrates

In a brief faunal account such as this it is impossible even to attempt to treat the invertebrate groups. Although 45 of the 52 volumes devoted to zoology in the *Biologia Centrali-Americana* dealt with invertebrates (38 of these being on insects), no groups below the level of the mollusks were treated. Even among such important taxa as the crustaceans, flies, and the bees and wasps, certain systematic sections were not included either owing to a lack of material or to a lack of biologists competent to handle particular groups.

Nevertheless, with the seemingly great mass of material presented in 45 volumes it would appear that a number of invertebrate groups occurring in Middle America should be fairly well known. Such, however, is not the case. Van Martens' *Biologia* volume on Mollusca (1890–1901), for example, recorded only 525 terrestrial species. From Panama he listed 26 species. In 1926 Pilsbry knew of 77 species from Panama, and in 1930 he added 12 more species to the fauna of that country. Similarly a 1930 account of the scorpions of Mexico listed almost as

---

[7] Ed. note: For millennia these small fish have furnished an important source of protein in the diet of central Mexicans. In the plateau lakes and rivers, particularly in Michoacan, native fishermen still net and dry *pescado blanco* for local use and for export to many parts of central Mexico.

many species as Pocock had recorded from all of Middle America in the *Biologia* 30 years earlier. With additions of this magnitude to our knowledge of the invertebrates over a span of but a quarter-century, it is obvious that the surface of the field of invertebrate zoology of the region even today has been only scratched.

Nevertheless, our knowledge is being extended. Local lists of various invertebrate groups and systematic revisions are appearing with increasing frequency. However, except for a few papers dealing with lower taxa, synthesis at the higher systematic levels seems, for the moment, rather futile. There are exceptions. As early as 1908 Calvert essayed a geographic treatment of dragonflies (Odonata), and recently Hovanitz (1958) reviewed the zoogeography of New World butterflies (Lepidoptera, Papilionoidea).

The last work may be summarized briefly inasmuch as it provides an example of the geographic behavior of an invertebrate group in Middle America. The Papilionoidea comprise nine families, all of which occur within the region. In his analysis Hovanitz classifies four families as tropical and five as more general in their distributions. Of the tropical families, two, morphos (Morphidae) and owl butterflies (*Caligo*) and their allies (Brassolidae), do not occur north of central Mexico; two other families, milkweed butterflies (Danaidae) and metalmarks (Erycinidae), contribute a total of only five genera to the fauna of United States. In contrast, those families of more general distribution extend well north of Mexico. The so-called "whites" (Pieridae), for example, are represented by 30 genera in the New World. Of these, 12 genera enter the United States and four are mainly confined to terrain north of the Tropic of Cancer. But, like all butterfly families, they are abundant in South America. Two families may serve to illustrate the geographic behavior of the two groups in Middle Amer-

ica, the "tropical" metal-marks (Erycinidae) and the four-footed butterflies (Nymphalidae) of more "general" distribution.

The Erycinidae are represented in the New World by 48 genera. Of these, seven are confined to South America, whereas not a single genus is confined to North America. Five genera are generally distributed throughout Middle America. Of the remaining genera they, like the major tropical vertebrate groups, invade the region from the south to varying levels northward. Twenty genera reach central Mexico, though eight occur only at elevations below 1000 m. in Mexico. Seven genera are found only south of southern Mexico and all are lowlanders. The other nine genera are also confined to the lowlands and invade the region no farther northward than southern Nicaragua. It is interesting to note that no genus is endemic to Central America.

Sixty-three of the 70 genera of New World Nymphalidae occur in Middle America. Four of these are confined to North America north of the Tropic of Cancer and another three do not reach South America. Fourteen genera are generally distributed from the United States southward into South America and all of these go well up into the mountains throughout the entire isthmian region. One genus (*Vanessa*), in fact, is found only at elevations above 2000 m. between the Tropic of Cancer and the Tropic of Capricorn. Another genus (*Argynnis*) shows a distribution similar to that of the bears and the lark. It occurs in the United States and northern Mexico but skips all of Central America only to reappear in the Andes. Nineteen genera extend from central Mexico southward, and most have a vertical range to at least 2000 m. Another three genera are not found north of southern Mexico; eight, mostly lowlanders, invade only the southern parts of Central America. Several genera appear to be endemic to Middle America or to Middle America and extreme northern South America. *Lucinia*, for example, is restricted to northern Mexico. *Morpheis* and *Balboneura* are confined to northern Central America; *Gnathotriche* and *Peria* occur only in the south and in northern South America.

The interesting feature of the distribution of the two families summarized above lies in the fact that, despite their powers of flight and the great differences in their and the vertebrates' way of life, their broad geographic behavior is remarkably similar to that of the terrestrial vertebrate groups.

It is unfortunate that it is impossible to examine the invertebrates in more detail. Certainly as part of the environment of primitive as well as of modern man the invertebrate groups had and continue to have a broader impact on man than have several vertebrate groups. This is particularly true of the present non-European and the precolonial cultural groups. As a source of food, as vectors of disease, and as contributors to certain artistic accomplishments, the invertebrates unquestionably were and continue to be of major importance in the Middle Americans' way of life.

Crustaceans and mollusks certainly must have figured heavily in the diet of precolonial man in Middle America. This was probably true of the fresh-water as well as of the marine forms. Even today the fresh-water *langosta* is a prized food item, and the inland *congrejo* is commonly sold in native markets and serves as a base for a succulent broth. The little river snail, the *jute*, is diligently sought in certain regions, and I can personally testify to its palatability. The big black carpenter ant, when swarming, contributes its abdomen to man's diet, and the traveler in Mexico soon becomes familiar with the toasted maguey worm, the larva of a moth. The wild bees and a few honey-making wasps, of course, very likely provided the major source of sweets.

Of medical importance, the arthropods must have played an important role in the life of the Middle Americans. As vectors of diseases the insects especially are of prime concern. Among endemic diseases the mosquito-borne malaria, the fly-borne leishmaniasis and trypanosomiasis (Chagas' disease) transmitted by a number of species of assassin bugs (Reduviidae) may be mentioned. Both insect-borne yellow fever and onchocerciasis were introduced into the New World by the European slave trade. The beef worm, ticks, and a variety of body insects undoubtedly made their impact felt on the life of the Indian. The black scorpion of Durango, *Centruroides suffusus*, and several other species of the same genus are even today far greater killers than all the poisonous snakes. The city of Durango between 1891 and 1931 recorded over 1700 fatalities from its sting and over 100 during the course of a single year.

Contributions of the invertebrates to the artistic accomplishments of the precolonial Middle American must also have been many. We need mention only molluscan shells, the red dye extracted from the cochineal insect, and the laque produced by the laque beetle.

I do not doubt that the anthropologist may frequently encounter puzzling distribution patterns of cultural traits that might be elucidated could the zoologist supply him with more accurate information on the zoogeography of many invertebrate groups.

GEOGRAPHY OF MIDDLE AMERICAN FAUNA

In essaying a description of the zoogeographic patterns obtaining in Middle America, two problems present themselves. The first concerns scale. Some parts of the region have been examined in considerable detail whereas other areas remain largely *terra incognita*. As a generalization, all vertebrate groups and several invertebrate groups of Mexico are fairly well known and a number of local areas have been considered in great detail. The faunas of Guatemala, El Salvador, Costa Rica, and

337

Panama are less completely known and very few local studies have been forthcoming. Aside from a few general papers and some local lists of species, however, the faunas of Honduras and Nicaragua have yet to be explored. With so much diversity in the completeness of the data, it is difficult to analyze the fauna geographically to a uniform degree of detail for the entire region.

In general the fauna of Middle America is sufficiently well known to permit geographic analysis at the chorographic level. As will be shown, there is no difficulty involved in demonstrating that the Mexican Plateau (the term "Mexican" may be utilized to avoid repetition) and Central America and the lowlands of Mexico ("Central America") represent distinct zoogeographic entities within the bounds of Middle America. It can similarly be shown that the fauna of northern Central America is very different from that of southern Central America. However, in essaying zoogeographic analysis on a larger scale, i.e. at the topographic or supratopographic level, the inequalities in our knowledge of local faunas become apparent immediately. The geographic patterns of the fishes, reptiles, birds, and mammals of the Mexican section have been studied fairly completely and both life zones and biotic provinces have been delimited. Attempts have also been made to define life zones and biotic provinces in Guatemala. Costa Rica, El Salvador, and Panama have been examined only from the life zone point of view.[8] Aside from a single account of the major

environment types of Honduras, neither that country nor Nicaragua has been examined zoogeographically. We are faced, therefore, not only with inequalities in basic data but also with diversity of treatment on larger scales.

The zoogeographer encounters a second problem in dealing with regional concepts. Geographers, or rather anthropogeographers, are wont to consider zoological regions as single-feature entities. At the geographic level, where major physical barriers have determined the nature of continental faunas, this point of view has validity. At lower levels, however, zoological regions are definitely multiple-feature in their make-up. This situation is owing to the diversity of times of origin, life forms, and life requisites of the various animal groups. The distributions of aquatics and terrestrials have been and are now controlled by very different physical factors. Even among the terrestrials, the greater vagility of birds as compared with that of reptiles and mammals has been of tremendous geographic significance. It is not difficult to understand why different groups often display different geographic patterns; the amazing fact is that we frequently encounter so great an accordance of patterns. In the following geographic analyses these problems will not be reiterated, but the reader will do well to bear these difficulties in mind.

From the faunal summations presented in the previous section, it is obvious that Middle America is not a coherent faunal region. Rather it is apparent that it is divided between two larger regions, Nearctica to the north and Neotropica to the south. Examination of the above data shows clearly that in all vertebrate groups and even in the butterflies (as exemplifying invertebrates) some orders and families and many genera find their southernmost limits on the Mexican Plateau and/or the annectent lowlands of the extreme northwest and northeast of Mexico. Conversely, other groups encounter their northernmost limits on the

---

[8] The provocative account of the biotic provinces of Central America based on the mammalian fauna (Ryan, 1963) is the initial step in remedying this situation. Though it is not entirely in accord with conclusions of my analysis which utilizes somewhat more comprehensive data, I do not doubt that it will remain a classic in the field of the regional zoogeography of Central America. For the most part, Ryan's provinces differ from mine mostly in that he fragments several of mine. I would view some of these, as does he of mine for Guatemala (and correctly so, *v.i.*), as "districts" in the sense of Dice (1943).

lowlands of Mexico south of about the levels of Tamaulipas and Sinaloa. This pattern was already known well before Sclater (1858) coined the terms Nearctica and Neotropica.

Most of the Mexican Plateau is strictly Nearctic in its faunal make-up. The same may be said of Baja California which, for the moment, will not be considered. Southward from the United States border the Nearctic element becomes increasingly more dilute (though not necessarily depauperate). A number of families and genera barely enter Mexico in the north. Among the fishes, the Percidae and Centrarchidae do not extend beyond the Rio Grande system. Of the reptiles, the Testudinidae, Trionychidae, several iguanid genera (*Holbrookia, Uma, Uta*) and such snake genera as *Heterodon, Chionactis, Arizona* and *Rhinocheilus* are all strictly northern in Mexico. The same may be said of the Castoridae, Bovidae, and Antilocapridae among the mammals and the bird family Chamaeidae. Other northern groups, however, are more widely distributed over the Mexican highlands. Some of these, the Cyprinidae, Ambystomidae, Pelobatidae, Sittidae, and the mammalian genera *Citellus* (ground squirrels), *Thomomys* (pocket gophers) and *Perognathus* (pocket mice) reach their southern limits in the transverse volcanic belt (Colima to Veracruz). Others, such as *Dipodomys* (Kangaroo rats) and *Lepus* (jackrabbits) continue southward through the Sierra Madre del Sur. In addition to these, there are a number of northern groups that occur throughout the Mexican highlands and continue southward into Central America especially in the mountains. These will be discussed later.

Even more convincing evidence of the Nearctic character of the fauna of most of the Mexican Plateau is to be found in its negative qualities. Many tropical groups, though present in the lowlands of southern and central Mexico, are either entirely wanting or but poorly represented on the

Plateau. Among the fishes, the Characidae and the Cichlidae are typical of this pattern. Other cold-bloods similarly distributed include the amphibian family Caeciliidae and the snake subfamily Scaphiodontophinae. A number of families and genera of both birds and mammals display this same geographic pattern. Among the former may be mentioned the Tinamidae, Jacanidae, and Furnariidae; the mammalian groups include *Ateles* (spider monkeys), the Dasyproctidae, *Nyctomys* (vesper rats), and *Potos* (the kinkajou). So obvious are the Nearctic relationships of the Mexican Plateau fauna that it would be diffuse to pursue the subject further.

It should be noted, however, that though the fauna of the major portion of the Mexican highlands is very similar to that of northern North America, the region supports a number of endemic groups that give it some individuality. The fish family Goodeidae is confined to the waters of central Mexico. It comprises 10 genera. In addition to these the Rio Lerma basin supports four other endemic genera. Among the amphibians, the ambystomid salamander genera *Bathysiredon, Siredon,* and *Ryachosiredon* are restricted to the southern portion of the Mexican Plateau as is the plethodontid genus *Thorius*. The frog genus *Tomodactylus* has a similar distribution. Reptiles endemic to the Plateau include the snake genera *Conopsis, Procinura,* and *Toluca* and the lizard genus *Gaigeia*. As pointed out by Griscom (1950), it is impossible to analyze the avifauna of Mexico without giving consideration to southwestern United States and the highlands of Chiapas and Guatemala. Many bird groups are endemic to that general region, but genera restricted to the Mexican Plateau area alone are few. Among these may be mentioned the banded quail (*Philortyx*), the eared trogon (*Euptilotis*), the slaty vireo (*Neochloe*), and the striped sparrow (*Oriturus*). Similarly restricted to the Mexican Plateau, or at least a portion thereof, are the volcano rabbit (*Romero-*

339

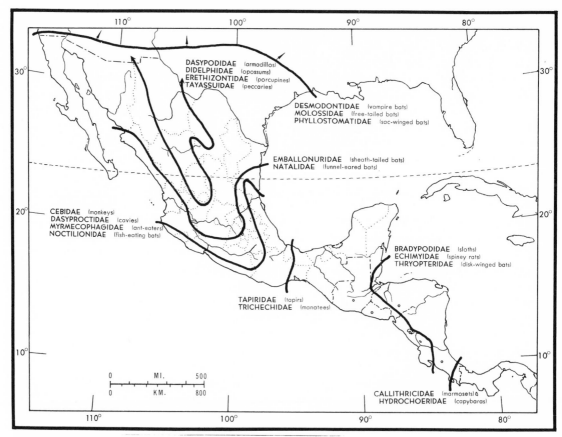

FIG. 1—THE GENERAL PATTERN OF NORTHERN LIMITS OF VARIOUS NEOTROP-
ICAL MAMMALIAN FAMILIES
(From Hall and Kelson, 1959.)

lagus), the volcano mouse (*Neotomodon*), and the wood rat genus *Nelsonia*.

The zoogeographic relationships of the Central American section of Middle America are far less clear. Since the time of Sclater the region has generally been assigned to Neotropica but with the definite understanding that it is transitional in its over-all faunal make-up. However, Schmidt (1954) in a reconsideration of the region has assigned it to Nearctica. His basis for this conclusion lay in the undeniable fact that the geological relationships of the entire isthmian link are to the north and that during the Tertiary most of Central America was a cul-de-sac into which poured a number of northern types. He has pointed out, further, that the Neotropical flavor of the Central American fauna stems from Pliocene and post-Pliocene invasions from the south. Furthermore to include the region in Neotropica would, in his opinion, weaken the distinctiveness of the last.

With his reasoning I am in complete disagreement. It is an elementary principle of regional geography that a region shall be defined by specific criteria. It is obvious that extant major zoogeographic regions must be delimited in terms of existing faunal distributions and not on past geological configurations or ancient faunal assemblages. Wallace (1876) was well aware of this concept, and Darlington (1957) has recently reiterated this point. It is true that the present character of a region has been derived from past conditions and processes, and these factors surely figure prominently in regional interpretation. But the fact re-

340

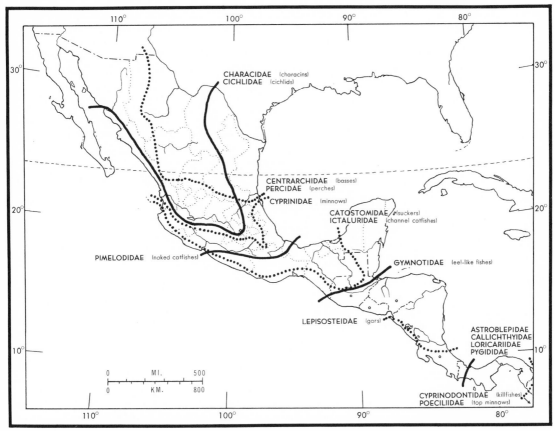

FIG. 2—THE GENERAL PATTERN OF THE NORTHERN AND SOUTHERN LIMITS OF
VARIOUS NEOTROPICAL AND NEARCTIC FISH FAMILIES RESPECTIVELY
(Based on Regan, 1906–08.) Solid boundary lines indicate northern limits; dotted boundary
lines, southern limits.

mains that extant faunal regions can be
defined and delimited only in terms of
extant faunas.

An analysis of the fauna of Central
America shows very definitely that it is
essentially Neotropical in character. The
nature of the faunal assemblage may be
brought out best through a listing of various
groups displaying accordant geographic
limits.

I. *Taxa that extend throughout Central
America and are common to both Nearctica
and Neotropica, though not necessarily to
the same degree.* Typical of this pattern are
the fish families Cyprinodontidae and Poeciliidae; the Plethodontidae and Hylidae
among the amphibians; the reptilian families Iguanidae and Colubridae; the Tyrannidae, Icteridae, and Fringillidae of the

birds; and such mammalian groups as the
Sciuridae, Felidae, and Cervidae. It may be
noted that the majority of these groups are
northerners that have invaded South America. The Hylidae and possibly the Tyrannidae and Icteridae appear to present the
reverse pattern. Actually, were all families
common to both North and South America
taken into consideration, it would be found
that the majority would be northerners. The
reasons for this are evolutionary and dispersal matters that are beyond the scope of
this account.

II. *Taxa that extend more or less throughout Central America but do not invade
Nearctica or at best barely enter Nearctica*
(figs. 1, 2). Some of these have already
been noted in the discussion of the Mexican
section. Included herein are the Characidae,

341

Cichlidae, and Pimelodidae among the fishes; the amphibian family Caeciliidae; a number of bird families which, though small, are very characteristic of the tropics, the Tinamidae, Heliornithidae, Eurypygidae, Jacanidae, Momotidae, and Furnariidae; and the mammalian groups Cebidae, Myrmecophagidae, Erethizontidae (only one species north of Mexico), Dasyproctidae, and Tapiridae.

III. *Taxa that are essentially northern but which invade Central America to varying levels* (fig. 2). Two generalized subgroups may be recognized here. The first comprises taxa that do not extend beyond northern Central America, i.e. El Salvador and Honduras as a convenient boundary. These include the Ictaluridae and Catostomidae among the fishes; the salamander genus *Pseudoeurycea*; the reptilian families Xenosauridae and Helodermatidae; the Paridae and Meleagrididae of the birds; and such mammalian genera as *Microtus* (voles) and *Glaucomys* (flying squirrels). A second group of taxa have managed to arrive in southern Central America. This group is exemplified in the fish family Lepisosteidae; the lizard families Anguidae and Xantusidae; the Certhiidae, Cinclidae, and Ptilogonatidae among the birds; and the mammalian genera *Neotoma* (woodrats) and *Mephitis* (skunks).

IV. *Taxa that are essentially southern but which invade Central America to varying levels* (figs. 1, 2). In contrast to the previous category, some groups are strictly southern, whereas others have extended their ranges well northward. Among those that are confined to the south may be mentioned the catfish families Loricariidae and Astroblepidae; the frog families Dendrobatidae and Atelopodidae; *Leposoma* (teiid lizard) and *Lachesis* (bushmaster) among the reptiles; the Oxyruncidae and Rhinocryptidae of the birds; and the mammalian families Callithricidae and Echimyidae. Taxa that extend somewhat farther north would include a number of genera. At the family level may

be noted the eels of the family Gymnotidae and the sloth family Bradypodidae. It appears, however, that once a southern group managed to attain the level of the Rio Motagua in Guatemala it was able to continue northward to at least the Mexican lowlands.

V. *Taxa that are autochthonous and certainly in many instances also endemic to Central America.* The majority of these are genera which appear to have evolved and remained more or less localized in the region. Actually many of the groups are not strictly endemic. The lowland environments of lower Central America are continuous with those of northwestern South America. As noted by Dunn (1940) and Griscom (1935), the humid forest of Caribbean Panama continues on into the very wet Choco of Pacific Colombia and Ecuador, whereas the drier Pacific forests and savannas may join those of Caribbean Colombia and Venezuela. It appears that, in accord with this environmental pattern, a number of faunal elements characteristic of Central America continue into northwestern South America. Lower Central American Pacific groups cross to northern Colombia and Venezuela, and Caribbean groups cross to northwestern Colombia and western Ecuador. Thus it must be understood that many groups that center in lower Central America may find representation to a limited extent in northern South America as well.

Both southern and northern groups have contributed to Central American endemism. However, as indicated previously, an historical analysis of the Middle American fauna is beyond the scope of this account. It may be noted, nevertheless, that two minor centers of evolution are apparent in Central America. One lies to the south and appears to have centered in the positive montane block of western Panama and Costa Rica. The second lies to the north and encompasses the similarly positive region frequently referred to as "nuclear Central America," i.e. Chiapas, Guatemala, Honduras, and northern Nicaragua. This latter, during most of the Cenozoic, formed a cul-de-sac into which many northern elements poured. It has been discussed in some detail by Schmidt (1943). Needless to say, subsequent dispersal to the north or south from these two centers has resulted in a more or less uniform distribution of many groups throughout Central America. Some, however, have remained fairly restricted. In other than exceptional cases, data are too few to allocate with any certainty all the following taxa to one center or the other.

Among the fishes, the poeciliids display the greatest amount of generic endemism in the region.[9] These include *Xenodexia, Priapella, Xiphophorus, Carlhubbsia* (all northern) and *Phallichthys* and *Belonesox* (northern and southern). The cichlid genus *Petenia* is endemic to the north, and *Neotrophus* of the same family occurs only in the Nicaraguan lakes. Another Nicaraguan lakes endemic is the characin genus *Bramocharax*. Of the Amphibia, the salamander genus *Bolitoglossa* is fairly widely distributed through the region at lower elevations, as is the hylid *Anotheca*. Other hylid genera, *Plectrohyla* and *Ptychohyla,* are particularly characteristic of upland streams in the north. The primitive toad family Rhinophrynidae and the casque-headed hylid *Triprion* are also northerners. Among the turtles, the family Dermatemydae and the kinosternid genera *Staurotypus* and *Claudius* do not extend south of Guatemala or El Salvador. The lizard genus *Laemanctus* is also northern; *Basiliscus* is found from Mexico south to Colombia. A great number of snake genera may be counted among the Central American endemics. Confined to the north are *Adelphicos* and *Tantillita,* but the great majority are more generally distributed, e.g. *Scaphiodontophis, Pliocercus, Conophis,* and *Tropidodipsas.*

Of the warm-bloods, the birds again present difficulties. However, the ocellated tur-

key (*Agriocharis ocellata*), the black chachalaca (*Penelopina nigra*), and the hummingbird genera *Abeillia, Panterpe, Microchera,* and *Lamprolaima* are each endemic to parts of the southern Mexico-Central America region. Brown jays (*Psilorhinus*) range in lowlands from northeastern Mexico (Nuevo Leon) to northwestern Panama. Among the mammalian genera, the vesper rats (*Nyctomys*), the climbing rats (*Tylomys*), and the water mice (*Rheomys*) are strictly Central American endemics.

We return, now, to the problem of the faunal allocation of Central America. Viewed as a unit, the region unquestionably supports a transitional fauna with considerable overlapping of Nearctic and Neotropical groups. However, considered at the family and genus level, Neotropical elements overshadow Nearctic elements. Of the analyzable families of the avifauna of the Americas, some 45 occur in Central America (Mayr, 1946). Twenty-five of these families are treated as either Pantropical or Neotropical, only nine are North American, whereas 10 appear to have stemmed from various Old World centers. Among the Pan-Central American amphibians and reptiles the score is roughly two thirds to one third in favor of southern groups and somewhat greater among the fishes. The mammals also display a similar pattern.

Actually, overlap of northern and southern elements is anything but uniform throughout Central America. It is most pronounced in the south Mexican-Guatemalan section. South of there the fauna is overwhelmingly Neotropical. An examination of the previously presented breakdown of the Central American fauna (Groups II, III, IV) gives ample evidence for this position. Regardless of this point, for the moment, these data strongly indicate that Schmidt's suggestion that Central America be assigned to Nearctica cannot be sustained.

On the other hand, it must be recognized that Central America by no means supports a full complement of South American

[9] For a recent extended account of this group see Rosen and Bailey, 1963.

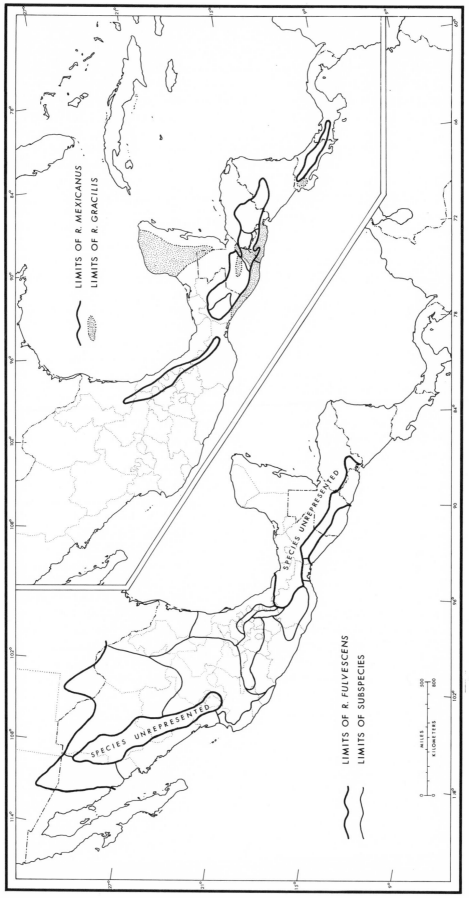

Fig. 3—GEOGRAPHIC DISTRIBUTION OF THE SUBSPECIES OF THREE SPECIES OF HARVEST MICE (*REITHRODONTOMYS*)
This pattern may be considered more or less typical of the geographic behavior of many northern groups in Middle America (After
Hooper, 1952.) *Reithrodontomys mexicanus* is essentially an upland species; *Reithrodontomys gracilis*, essentially lowland.

groups. Such fish families as the Pantropical Osteoglossidae, the characid relatives Hemiodontidae and Anostomidae, and the catfishes of the Bunocephalidae and Cetopidae do not reach to Panama. Neither do the pipid frogs (Pipidae) nor the Pantropical side-necked turtles (Pleurodira). Among birds, the trumpeters (Psophiidae), the screamers (Anhimidae), and the antpipits (Conopophagidae) are strictly South American; the guinea pigs (Caviidae) and the opossum rats (Caenolestidae) of the mammals fail to enter Central America.

In this sense Central America is faunally to South America as the Mexican Plateau is to North America. Just as Mexico supports a dilute Nearctic fauna, so does Central America support a dilute Neotropical fauna. Furthermore each region is characterized by considerable endemism, especially at the generic level. It must be noted, however, that Central America has a greater proportion of Nearctic elements than does the Mexican Plateau of Neotropical elements. Despite this last fact, Central America, particularly south of the Tehuantepec isthmian region, is something more than a region of faunal transition. In dealing with the regional concept two rough divisions of any region may be recognized, the core and the periphery (James and Jones, 1954, p. 41). There can be no denying that the Mexican Plateau is a peripheral unit of Nearctica or, more broadly, Arctogaea. In the same manner Central America seems to warrant a similar status, i.e. that of a peripheral unit of Neogaea (Neotropica).

Where, then, is faunal transition encountered? Dr. Robert R. Miller (*in litt.*), as will be brought out later, is inclined to view the general region between the Rio Panuco and the Rio Papaloapan as supporting a transitional fish fauna. In his review of Neotropical mammals, Hershkovitz (1958) would confine the zone of transition to a rough segment of southwestern Mexico west of longitude 98° and south of the Tropic of Cancer. Furthermore, data presented by Griscom (1934) suggest that the same general region may support a transitional avifauna. It would seem, therefore, that the major region of faunal transition between Nearctica and Neotropica might be sought in the mountainous region and in the annectent lowlands of southern Mexico. Certainly the Sierra Madre del Sur of Guerrero and Oaxaca, where environments run the gamut from both arid and humid tropical conditions to temperate conditions high in the mountains, presents a locale worthy of further consideration. It is unfortunate that this region is, perhaps, biologically the least known part of Mexico and northern Central America.

In the foregoing, the zoogeographic pattern of Middle America has been dealt with at the chorographic level with the distribution of families and, to a lesser extent, genera supplying the basic data. A breakdown of the several larger regions into minor faunal units necessitates analysis of the distributions of genera or, more frequently, species. It has been indicated previously that major faunal regions are single-feature regions defined in terms of faunal distributions alone. Obviously the delimitation of minor regions based on genera and species distributions would involve a task of Herculean proportions. Figure 3 illustrates the geographic pattern of three species of harvest mice. Furthermore, considering the present state of our knowledge (or, rather, lack of knowledge) concerning the systematics and distribution of the majority of Middle American animal species, the result would leave much to be desired.

It becomes necessary to depart from the purely faunal approach, therefore, and to utilize cognate criteria to aid in the establishment of minor faunal regions. Such cognate criteria may include climate, topography, soils, vegetation, and other features of the animal environment. The aim is thus to establish multiple-feature regions delimiting environment types which may be expanded to include within each a distinctive faunal assemblage. This procedure is thrust upon the zoogeographer—and with reasonable expectancy of success—when lower geographic levels and systematic taxa are considered. Dice (1952, pp. 444–45), in discussing biotic provinces, has pointed out that in any region exhibiting "peculiar ecologic conditions, the plants and animals develop certain adaptations and differentiate into local species and subspecies."

Two schemes of multiple-feature regions have proved of value to the faunal zoogeographer in varying degrees. These are the life zone scheme of Merriam (1891, 1898) and the biotic province scheme of Dice (summarized 1943). The life zone in its pristine state was conceived to be a latitudinal transcontinental belt (or vertical belt in montane regions) originally delimited on the basis of floral and faunal assemblages and later defined empirically in terms of several temperature parameters and humidity. Since the original definition, however, the life zone concept has been subjected to criminal assault by two generations of biogeographers so that the now well-violated life zone has little semblance to its early postnatal self.

Daubenmire (1938) presented a summary of the evidence against the life zone scheme as an expression of plant and animal distributions. Nevertheless as recently as 1951 Goldman essayed a life zone treatment of Mexico. In fact, the majority of the zoogeographic investigations dealing with Middle America have utilized life zone terminology, though not necessarily in the sense of Merriam. As a result, any effort to make use of such geographic data contained in many of the otherwise excellent faunal treatments of various parts of Middle America produces the ultimate in zoogeographic chaos.

The reasons for this confused situation are several. First, as indicated previously, latter-day biogeographers have not adhered to Merriam's concept of the life zone. Goldman (1951), for example, states that life

zones are "natural biogeographical areas within which consideration is given to all environmental conditions." To me this seems to be a fairly reasonable statement of the biotic province concept. Again, Griscom (1932), in dealing with the distribution of the Guatemalan avifauna, defines the Subtropical Zone (Humid Upper Tropical Zone of some authors) as a narrow band of montane rain forest (cloud forest) and the Temperate Zone (?Boreal Zone of Merriam) as an avifauna and not a temperature belt.

This concept of the Temperate Zone brings out a second reason for the life zone chaos that obtains in Middle America. Biogeographers have apparently been unable to distinguish between region and fauna. The Middle American fauna is an assemblage of organisms of diverse historical backgrounds. As shown by Dunn (1931) in dealing with the reptiles and amphibians and by Mayr (1946) in his analysis of bird life, certain taxa of the Middle American fauna have been derived from the north, others from the south. In their efforts to explain the distributions of these diverse units, certain biogeographers have essayed definition of life zones on the basis of the historical backgrounds of the several faunal elements rather than on the extant zonal arrangement of the same. In other words, they have failed to recognize that the fauna of any region, such as a life zone, may contain elements derived from several sources at different times. Having come together within the limits of a specific environment, many have differentiated taxonomically in adapting to that environment. Carriker (1910) in his geographic treatment of the Costa Rican avifauna and Griscom (1932) present typical examples of this failure to distinguish between region and fauna.

A third factor that has led to life zone confusion in Middle America is to be found in efforts that have been made to overextend any single zone. This may be owing in part to the tremendous influence of Chapman's magnificent geographic accounts of the avifaunas of Colombia and Ecuador (1917 and 1926, respectively). Though utilizing the life zone scheme, Chapman made no serious effort to extend his zones extralimitally, especially to the north. Nor did he essay a correlation of his and Merriam's life zones. But it appears that later investigators became confused as they endeavored to extend Merriam's zones southward and Chapman's northward. Turning again to Griscom's account of the Guatemalan avifauna, we note that he limited the Subtropical Zone to two small areas of cloud forest in an effort to retain Chapman's original definition of that zone. Similarly he followed Chapman in not recognizing an arid division of the Subtropical Zone. In northern South America there is, apparently, in subhumid areas a downward extension of the Temperate Zone and an upward extension of the Tropical Zone. Simply because such a situation obtains some 1500 miles to the south provides little justification for failure to recognize an arid division of the Subtropical Zone in northern Central America. Dickey and van Rossem (1938) have described such a zone in El Salvador, and I can vouch for its presence in Guatemala. Conversely Griscom abandons Chapman in dealing with the Temperate Zone. He notes that this zone in Guatemala is not commensurate with that of the northern Andes. The avifauna of the Temperate Zone of Guatemala is composed, for the most part, of Mexican and Central American endemics, whereas that of the northern Andes has been derived from the Subtropical Zone (in turn derived from the adjacent Tropical Zone) and from south Temperate (Patagonian, Chilean) groups.

Regardless of the extant confusion in the nature of basic concepts involved in life zone schemes, there can be no denying that vertical geographic patterns of animal distributions are very real. They have been utilized with good success in a number of excellent local analyses. But any scheme

of multiple-feature regionality that may be selected to aid in the expression and interpretation of faunal distributions must be capable of more than local application. It should express faunal similarities and differences throughout extensive geographic areas. It is the failure to attain this end that brings the life zone scheme to grief.

We need to examine only the Caribbean and Gulf of Mexico lowlands of Central America and Mexico to demonstrate that the life zone frequently presents a distorted expression of faunal distributions. This entire region must be and has been defined as the humid Lower Tropical Zone. That it is a distinct *ecological* region (the *biome* of modern ecologists) is not to be denied. There is, furthermore, an assemblage of animals that is fairly uniformly distributed throughout the entire region. Nevertheless, there are many differences in the faunas of, for example, the humid Lower Tropical Zone of northern Guatemala and that of eastern Panama. These faunal differences have been indicated previously. Thus even the loose faunal similarity implied in life zone terminology would be misleading.

In consideration of these facts the life zone scheme as an expression of zoogeographic patterns in Middle America must be discarded. Nevertheless, for whatever it may be worth, there is presented in figure 4 a comparative diagram of life zones of several authors who have dealt with the zoogeography of various animal groups within rather local areas in Middle America.

As we turn now to consideration of the biotic provinces as a system of zoological regionality, it becomes clear that many of the difficulties inherent in the life zone scheme may be avoided. The reason for this is obvious: biotic provinces are defined in much more comprehensive terms than are life zones. Dice (1943) states that, "each biotic province . . . covers a considerable and continuous geographic area and is characterized by the occurrence of one or

347

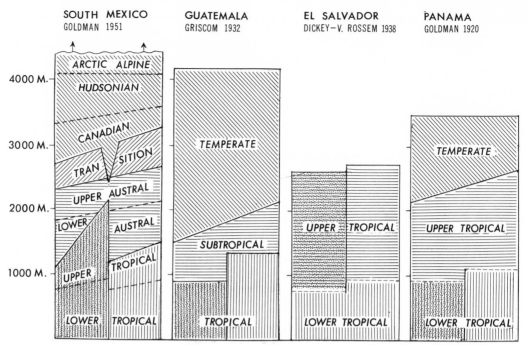

SOUTH MEXICO
GOLDMAN 1951

GUATEMALA
GRISCOM 1932

EL SALVADOR
DICKEY–V. ROSSEM 1938

PANAMA
GOLDMAN 1920

FIG. 4—COMPARATIVE REPRESENTATION OF LIFE ZONES AS DESCRIBED BY VARIOUS INVESTIGATORS CONCERNED WITH SPECIFIC AREAS IN MIDDLE AMERICA. The stippled areas represent humid subdivisions where such distinction from arid subdivisions is made.

more important ecological associations that differ, at least in proportional area covered, from associations of adjacent provinces. In general they are characterized also by peculiarities of vegetation type, ecological climax, flora, fauna, climate, physiography and soil."

In utilizing this type of multiple-feature region, problems such as the expression of zoogeographic patterns along the Caribbean lowlands, previously noted, are largely overcome. Furthermore, the biotic province system does not exclude the development of vertical life belts. It does, however, preclude the extension of any life belt beyond the limits of a single province. As a result, the difficulty that Griscom (1940) experienced in dealing with the Temperate Zone of Central America is eliminated. Certainly the biotic province scheme gives a much more realistic picture of zoogeographic patterns than do life zones.

Unfortunately, a biotic province treat-

ment of Middle America south of Guatemala has never been undertaken, and even in the north the results of excursions into this field have not proved too satisfactory.[10] In the first place, different authorities are swayed by different animal groups in zoogeographic analyses.[11] As a result, there is considerable divergence of opinion concerning not only the reality of various faunal areas but also the limits of those upon which there is agreement. Thus H. M. Smith (1949) recognized 26 biotic provinces on mainland Mexico as compared with but 16 outlined by Goldman and Moore (1946). Furthermore, Smith placed the northern boundary of the Transverse Volcanic Province 150 miles south of that of Goldman and Moore. Secondly, many of the defined "provinces" are not strictly comparable, and some of the regions previously defined as such must now be relegated to

[10] See note 8.
[11] Cf. the following and Ryan, 1963.

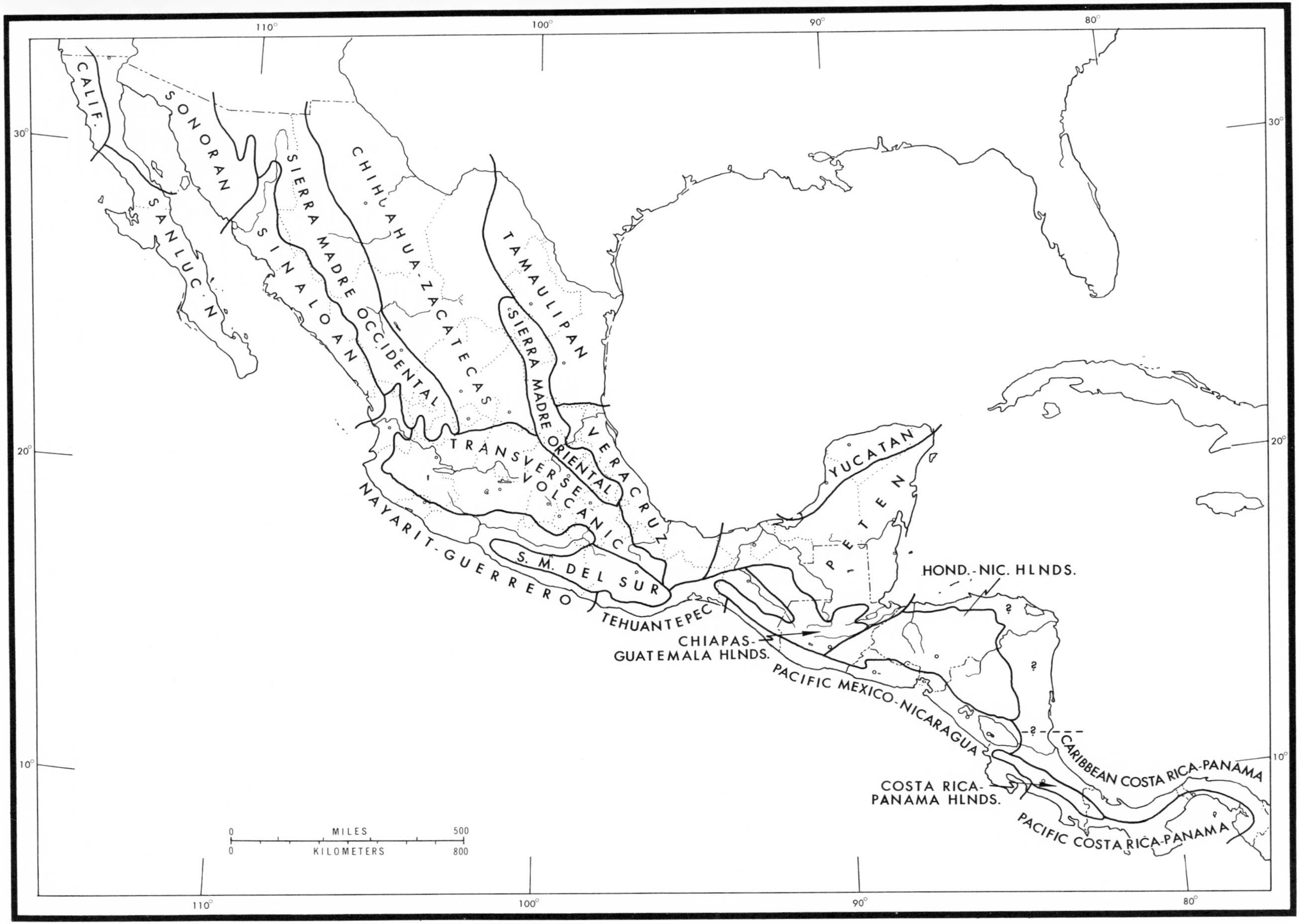

CALIF.

SONORAN

SAN LUCAN

SINALOAN

SIERRA MADRE OCCIDENTAL

CHIHUAHUA-ZACATECAS

NAYARIT-GUERRERO

TAMAULIPAN

SIERRA MADRE ORIENTAL

VERACRUZ

TRANSVERSE VOLCANIC

S. M. DEL SUR

TEHUANTEPEC

CHIAPAS-GUATEMALA HLNDS.

PACIFIC MEXICO-NICARAGUA

YUCATAN

PETEN

HOND.-NIC. HLNDS.

COSTA RICA-PANAMA HLNDS.

CARIBBEAN COSTA RICA-PANAMA

PACIFIC COSTA RICA-PANAMA

MILES

KILOMETERS

0   500
0   800

30°   80°   90°   100°   110°

110°   100°   90°   80°

30°

20°

10°

20°

10°

FIG. 5—THE BIOTIC PROVINCES OF MIDDLE AMERICA

"district" (a minor division of a province) status. This is particularly true of my Guatemalan "provinces" (1943), and it was undoubtedly that study which misled Smith into regional overdivision of southern Mexico and Guatemala.[12]

In presenting the following brief account of the biotic provinces of Middle America I have perhaps been overly conservative. This is owing to the fact that for much of the region data on landforms, soils, climate, and other features of the physical environment are at best sparse. Furthermore, the systematics of many animal groups in the region are still chaotic, and details of distributions are as yet poorly known.[13] The provinces as herein outlined should be viewed merely as a basic plan which may possibly serve to guide future workers to a more exact definition and delimitation of faunal assemblages. No uniformly concise descriptive names have been attached to the several provinces, since such could only confuse further the already confused provincial synonymy. Such boundaries as appear on the map (fig. 5) are, of course, not to be taken seriously, as they represent nothing more than the probable positions of broad areas of transition.

In his analysis of the biotic provinces of Mexico, H. M. Smith (1949) essays a grouping on the basis of major faunal relationships, i.e. Nearctic as opposed to Neotropical. This major breakdown is not too satisfactory, inasmuch as several of the provinces are faunally about equally related to the two great zoogeographic regions. Nor, in view of the foregoing discussion, does such division seem necessary at this time.

Turning first to the Mexican Plateau, we find it has been apportioned among seven provinces by H. M. Smith (1949) and among five by Goldman and Moore (1946). In my opinion the later analysis seems the

more realistic of the two. According to Goldman (1951), all life zones recognized in Mexico with the exception of the Lower Tropical occur within this major unit.

Rimming the plateau on the west from the United States border south to about Guadalajara is the Sierra Madre Occidental. Though treated as several provinces by earlier workers, both Goldman and Moore (1946) and Smith (1949) who have examined it most recently agree that it represents an entity. It is essentially the Mexican extension of Dice's (1943) Apachian Province which he assigned, for the most part, to the Durangan Province. Except locally it is encompassed within the Austral and Transition Zones of Goldman (1951).[14]

Over most of its extent it is a rolling upland, but along the western scarp it is deeply incised by rivers flowing to the Gulf of California and the Pacific. Here terrain of high relief obtains. The region is fairly dry, and snow falls on the upper slopes. At lower elevations the cover is largely oak and shrubs, while at higher elevations there are oak and pine with Douglasfir and aspen at the highest levels.

Though the province supports a number of endemic genera, the fauna is essentially related to that of southeastern Arizona and southwestern New Mexico. Some of the finest virgin highland forests in Mexico are located within the bounds of this province.

Rimming the Mexican Plateau on the east is the Sierra Madre Oriental. Physiographically, it extends from about the level of the southernmost tip of Texas south to the latitude of Veracruz city. There is some question, however, as to the extent of the encompassed biotic province. H. M. Smith (1939) drew the physiographic and biotic boundaries concordant but in 1949 set off the southern half as a separate biotic area. Dice (1943) followed Smith's earlier analysis. Goldman and Moore (1946) delimited

---

[12] As noted by Ryan, 1963. See also note 8.
[13] Well illustrated in Ryan, 1963.

[14] Baker and Greer (1962) discuss this region in some detail.

the southern extent of the biotic province at about the latitude of Tampico. I am of the opinion that Smith's original concept of the province is the more realistic of the two schemes. Within the region a complex interdigitation of life zones obtains, and these have been discussed by Goldman (1951).

Like the Sierra Madre Occidental, the eastern mountain rim appears insignificant on its inland (western) versant, but the eastern face plunges sharply to the coastal plain, producing terrain of high relief. The western section adjoining the Mexican tableland is arid. The eastern section, in contrast, is fairly humid and locally supports cloud forest even in the north. Both north-south and east-west gradients exist in environmental features, and these suggest a complex association of biotic features. It is not improbable that, when studied in detail, an interdigitation of Nearctic and Neotropical elements will be revealed, and already considerable endemism has been noted. A superb treatment of the amphibians and reptiles of the central part of the Sierra has recently been presented by Martin (1958).

The southern end of the Mexican Plateau is rimmed by the Sierra Madre del Sur (frequently called merely the Sierra del Sur), which is confined to the states of Guerrero and western Oaxaca. All authorities are in general agreement that the Sierra delimits a distinct biotic province, though Smith (1949) would extend it somewhat farther to the east to include part of the eastern portion of the Transverse Volcanic Province of R. T. Moore (1945). Because of the broken nature of the mountain mass a complex life zone pattern obtains throughout.

The region is one of extremely high relief, and elevations of 3000 m. are attained in its highest parts. Both humid and dry environments may be found within its bounds, and even cloud forest–like conditions prevail in some areas. As noted previously, this province appears to represent a major transition region between Neotropica and Nearctica. Though the region embraces one of the biologically least known parts of Mexico, R. T. Moore (1945) has noted that it is related faunally to the Transverse Volcanic Province to the north, and Griscom (1934) has further pointed out the presence of birds of southern affinities in this mountain area.

Within the rimming mountain ranges lies the Plateau of Mexico proper. It is generally agreed that it comprises two distinct biotic provinces, the Chihuahuan Province of Dice (1943) or the Chihuahua-Zacatecas Province of Goldman and Moore (1946), and the Transverse Volcanic Province of Moore (1945).

The former is a southward extension of the basin-and-range physiographic province of the western United States. Its southern limit appears to lie somewhat south of the level of San Luis Potosi city, though H. M. Smith (1949) who divided it between two provinces—the Mapimi and the Austrocentral—would place its boundary considerably farther south. It is encompassed almost in its entirety within the Lower and Upper Austral life zones of Goldman (1951). This plateau land is slightly uptilted towards the south and is broken by short mountain ranges. Subhumid conditions prevail throughout, and the vegetation cover is largely grasslands and desert shrub. The fauna is strictly Nearctic and, as is to be expected, though characterized by considerable endemism at lower systematic levels, is essentially similar to that of adjacent eastern Arizona, southern New Mexico, and western Texas.

The Transverse Volcanic Province or Austro-occidental Province of Smith (1949) is one of the most distinct of the Mexican biotic areas. Though there is no denying its reality, there is considerable question regarding its limits. As noted previously, Smith (1949) compresses its north-south extent considerably and assigns the so-called Sierra Madre de Oaxaca to the Sierra

Madre del Sur province rather than to the Transverse Volcanic Province as defined by Moore (1945). Inasmuch as the latter appears to have analyzed the region in considerable detail, his concepts are followed herein.

This province is one of high mountains and ancient lake basins and geologically is characterized by active mountain building and associated volcanic activity. No fewer than 13 peaks rise above 3500 m., and three attain about 5000 m. elevation. Climatic diversity is tremendous and, according to Goldman (1951), all the life zones of North America are represented within the region —excepting, I may add, the Lower Tropical. As a result, a variety of vegetation types obtains, though for the most part pine and oak forest predominates.

The fauna is essentially Nearctic in its composition, and endemism in this province is greater than in any other Mexican biotic area. This endemism is not confined to the specific and subspecific levels but also involves genera of amphibians, birds, and mammals as well. As will be noted later, the fish fauna of the Rio Lerma system, which in its entirety is encompassed within this province, is perhaps one of the most distinct fish assemblages of all Middle America.

If the provinces of the Mexican highlands have appeared difficult of definition, those of the annectent lowlands are even more so. The north-south clinal changes in climate and vegetation preclude the development of sharp faunal boundaries and, as a result, there has been a tendency on the part of regional zoogeographers either to overdivide or to underdivide the lowlands into faunal areas. Considering the nature of the data at my disposal, I am inclined to follow the latter course.

There is general agreement among all authors that northwestern Mexico west of the Sierra Madre Occidental and including extreme northeastern Baja California is a distinct biotic unit. This is the Sonoran

Biotic Province of Burt (1938), Dice (1943), Goldman and Moore (1946), and van Rossem (1945). Smith (1949) refers to it as the Arizonan Province. It lies entirely within the Lower Austral Zone of Goldman (1951). Its southern limit on the mainland is debatable. It has been placed as far north as Guaymas (Burt, 1938) and as far south as Mazatlan (Goldman and Moore, 1946). Bogert and Oliver (1945) have discussed the problem in some detail. Burt's conclusions are accepted herein. To the north the province extends into southeastern California and southwestern Arizona.

Relief within the region is, for the most part, low. The climate is hot and dry and the vegetation cover is largely desert shrub. Faunally the province is, perhaps, better known than any other part of Mexico. Though in its over-all aspect the fauna is essentially that characteristic of the southwestern United States, a high degree of endemism obtains. Among the mammals alone, 66 per cent of the species and/or subspecies are confined to the province (Burt, 1938) and other vertebrate groups display a similar condition.

The peninsula of Baja California is divided among several biotic provinces, but there is no general accord among investigators as to its partitioning. Nelson (1921), who has treated the region in greatest detail, recognized five faunal districts, both Dice (1943) and Goldman and Moore (1946) three, and Smith (1949) four.[15]

All recent authorities agree that the northwestern corner of the peninsula, including the Sierra San Pedro Martir, is a southern extension of Dice's (1943) Californian Province. Relief in the region varies from low along the Pacific coastal plain to high in montane regions. The climate, like that of southern California, is hot and dry and the Austral and Transition Life Zones

[15] An account of the biogeography of Baja California (in Hyman, 1960) modifies my conclusions.

352

FAUNA

are represented (Goldman and Moore, 1946). At lower elevations chaparral predominates; pine forest occurs in the higher parts of the mountains. The fauna is essentially that of the Great Valley of California and of the associated Southern Coastal Range.

There is also general agreement that the southern half of the peninsula represents a distinct biotic province. This is the Sanlucan Province of Dice (1943), Southern Baja California Province of Goldman and Moore (1946), and the Cape Province of Smith (1949). The main point of contention relating to this province arises in the allocation of the very arid Vizcaino Desert in the central part of the peninsula. Both Goldman and Moore (1946) and Smith (1949) recognize it as distinct, but Dice (1943) assigns it to his Sanlucan Province. In an effort to maintain some semblance of qualitative balance among the provinces described herein, I accept the conclusions of Dice. Relief, as in the north, is low on the coastal plains and high in the mountains. The region is xeric throughout and vegetation varies from widely spaced desert shrub at lower elevations to piñon and oak in the mountains. Faunally the province has been a cul-de-sac which has been invaded by various groups stemming from both Californian and Sonoran centers. Endemism is high on the mainland and even greater on the offshore islands.[16]

The northeastern corner of the peninsula, as previously noted, is generally assigned to the Sonoran Province.

South of the Sonoran Province on the mainland along the Pacific to about the Oaxaca-Guerrero border, the biotic province picture is extremely confused. Only very recently has much of this terrain been explored biologically, and a number of my colleagues who are currently engaged in

[16] Since the above was written a magnificent treatment of the biogeography of Baja California has appeared under the editorship of L. H. Hyman (1960).

such exploration have not yet summarized their views. Goldman and Moore (1946) recognize but two biotic provinces within the entire area, in contrast to five suggested by Smith (1949). Some concept of the difficulties involved may be gained from Peters' (1955) discussion of the distribution of the herpetofauna between southern Sinaloa and western Oaxaca. Until further data are forthcoming, it seems best to follow the scheme of Goldman and Moore. Smith's analysis is so extremely complex that no effort will be made to present a correlation of the two plans.

From about the level of San Blas extending northward on the narrow coastal plain and along the foothills of the Sierra Madre Occidental to about the Rio Yaqui and then swinging inland to include only the foothill region to about the level of Hermosillo is the Sinaloan Province of most authors (Burt, 1938; Dice, 1943; Goldman and Moore, 1946). This province also invades the canyons that cut back into the precipitous western face of the Sierra Madre. Relief is varied; climatically the chief difference between this province and the Sonoran lies in the fact that the former is frost-free. The vegetation cover consists of thorn forest along the coastal strip and tropical deciduous forest farther inland. It is almost entirely encompassed within the Arid Tropical Life Zone. Faunally, though essentially Nearctic, the province supports a number of Neotropical elements which here attain their northern limits as an assemblage of any consequence. Indications are that endemism is considerable but probably does not approach quantitatively that of the Sonoran Province to the north.

South of the Sinaloan Province to about Puerto Angel is the Nayarit-Guerrero Province of Goldman and Moore (1946). Included here are the coastal plain, probably isolate mountain ranges, (e.g. the Sierra de Coalcoman) and the Balsas "embayment" which Smith (1949) recognizes as distinct. Biologically this is one of the least known of the Mexican biotic regions. Relief is extremely varied and the climate, though essentially arid and hot, not improbably is fairly humid on some of the isolated ranges. As a result, vegetation cover also must be highly variable and patchy in its distribution. If the amphibians and reptiles may be taken as typical of other vertebrate groups, this region is one of great faunal diversity and, with the Sierra Madre del Sur previously discussed and the Veracruz region to be noted below, represents the major transition zone between faunal Nearctica and Neotropica. Peters (1955) has noted that out of a total of 79 genera of amphibians and reptiles occurring in the area, 34 southerners find their northern limits therein and nine northerners reach their southern limits. Of the roughly 150 species and subspecies of the same groups, about 25 per cent are endemic to the region.

All authors are in agreement that a very distinct biotic province centers on the southern side of the Isthmus of Tehuantepec. The limits of this province, however, have been debated. Although the western boundary is generally conceded to lie in the neighborhood of the Guerrero-Oaxaca border, the eastern boundary has been placed in the vicinity of Tonala, Chiapas, by Smith (1949), whereas Goldman and Moore (1946) extend the province along the Pacific coast into Guatemala. Furthermore, the latter authors include the Grijalva Valley of Chiapas in the province, but Smith assigns the same to his Gulf of Mexico biotic province complex. I am fully familiar with these regions (Stuart, 1954a) and am in agreement with Smith as to the eastern boundary of the province and with Goldman and Moore in their allocation of the Grijalva Valley. The northern boundary is not clear-cut but it definitely lies closer to the Pacific than to the Gulf of Mexico. The province lies entirely within the Arid Tropical Zone.

Except locally, e.g. small isolated ranges and piedmont regions, relief is low. The climate is hot and arid, and vegetation cover includes a variety of dry-land types such as desert shrub, savanna, thorn forest, and tropical scrub with oak at higher elevations. Though the fauna is relatively well known, it has never been thoroughly analyzed. It is fundamentally Neotropical, however, with a high degree of endemism.[17]

The lowlands of eastern Mexico and of extreme northern Central America are considerably more extensive than those bordering the Pacific. Furthermore, whereas xeric conditions prevail throughout the Pacific region, a clinal increase in moisture from north to south prevails in the east. Like the west, on the other hand, there is a gradual increase in Neotropical faunal elements and a decrease in Nearctic elements towards the south.

The northeastern lowlands of Mexico are to the east as the Sonoran region is to the west: both regions are essentially Nearctic. All authorities are in agreement that the region east of a line drawn from about the Big Bend of the Rio Grande southward and continuing east of the Sierra Madre Oriental to about the Rio Panuco is a distinct biotic province. The name Tamaulipan is applied almost universally to this province.

Most of the region is confined to the rolling coastal plain above which rise small, relatively low mountains and isolated mesas. North of the Sierra Madre Oriental it merges gradually with the Chihuahuan Province to the west. The climate is arid and, though killing frosts occur, hot. The vegetation cover is predominately short grass and mesquite. According to Goldman and Moore (1946), it lies entirely within the Lower Austral Life Zone. Though a number of Neotropical forms interdigitate with Nearctic elements through this region, the fauna as a whole appears to have much more in common with the north than with

[17] Duellman (1960) has presented a geographic analysis of the amphibian fauna of the isthmian region.

the south. In fact, many of the lowland southerners reported from the region are confined to the extreme south of the province. Martin (1958) has discussed this faunal interdigitation in some detail. Many of the animal species occurring in the province are found also through southern Texas and in the northern part of the Mexican Plateau, i.e. the Chihuahuan Province.

South of about the Rio Panuco on the lowlands and annectent mountain slopes, the humid tropics come into their own. The greater portion of the region from the Panuco south to northern Honduras comprises a biotic region of major proportions which contrasts sharply with a second major region in lower Central America. The northern unit has been apportioned among five biotic provinces by Smith (1949) and between only two by Goldman and Moore (1946). In my opinion—based on rather complete personal acquaintance with most of the region—three provinces are indicated.

Except in the mountain piedmonts and dissected foothills, relief is low throughout. There is a clinal increase in both temperature and rainfall towards the south and a corresponding increase in height and luxuriousness of the tropical forest. Though high wet forest of several types covered most of the region before man cleared much of it, there are extensive natural savannas scattered through the area and even a low dry forest prevails over the outer end of the Yucatan Peninsula. The entire region is encompassed within the Tropical Life Zone of Goldman (1951).

Within this major unit the Mexican state of Veracruz fairly well delimits a distinct biotic province; outer Yucatan from possibly Laguna de Terminos to the vicinity of Cape Catoche comprises another; Tabasco, eastern Chiapas, the Peten of Guatemala, British Honduras and the southern part of the Yucatan Peninsula make up a third. Of these, the last, essentially the

Peten Province recognized by me (1943) and by Smith (1949), is the most distinct and, as previously noted, appears to have been a center of considerable evolution. The most weakly defined is outer Yucatan. Here relatively dry conditions prevail, and though considerable endemism is apparent at the specific and subspecific levels, its fauna is basically very similar to that of the Peten Province. From Tamaulipas southward through Veracruz there is a gradual increase in the Neotropical element and a corresponding decrease in Nearctic elements. I am inclined to view it in very much the same light as the Nayarit-Guerrero Province along the Pacific, that is, as a region of major transition between Nearctica and Neotropica proper. There are no very sharp faunal breaks between any of these provinces. Brodkorb (1943) has discussed the transition in the avifaunas of Veracruz and the Peten, and I (1958) have dealt with the same problem as regards the herpetofaunas of the Peten and Yucatan. Aside from Paynter's (1955) study of the avifauna of Yucatan, there are no general summarizing accounts of any of these three provinces.

The Caribbean lowlands and adjacent plateau slopes of southern Central America, i.e. Costa Rica and Panama, appear to represent another major biotic unit. This unit, as noted previously, crosses over to the Pacific side in eastern Panama and continues southward into the Choco. This region is essentially the Humid Tropical Zone of both Goldman (1920) and Griscom (1935) and the Tropic Zone of Carriker (1910). Like the lowlands of the north, the region is hot and humid and supports rain forest cover. As has been indicated, however, its faunal assemblage is quite different from and notably richer than that of the north.

There are data to suggest that several biotic provinces are involved in this region. Both Goldman (1920) and Griscom (1935) indicated that there are a number of differences between both the mammal and bird faunas of eastern and western Panama. It is unfortunate that eastern Panama remains one of the biologically least known parts of the western hemisphere. Goldman (1920) suggests the Panama Canal Zone as a suitable boundary between the east and west. The northern limit of the western province is extremely obscure. From the narrow coastal strip of northern Honduras and the lowlands of the Segovia region and Mosquito Coast very little biological material has been forthcoming. If other animal groups parallel the reptiles, then there is a gradual dilution of the Neotropical element northward through Nicaragua and Honduras. In contrast, many northerners stop abruptly in the region between Laguna Izabal in eastern Guatemala and the Rio Ulua in northern Honduras. It is possible that the Caribbean lowlands of Honduras and Nicaragua may represent a distinct district of the Caribbean Costa Rica–Panama Province.[18]

On the west side of Central America south of the Tehuantepec Province, the Pacific coastal plain and adjacent piedmont and lower mountain slopes of Central America extend as a narrow strip to just beyond the Nicoya Peninsula in Costa Rica. Though divided in the north among several provinces by Stuart (1943) and Smith (1949), it was assigned to the Tehuantepec Province by Goldman and Moore, (1946). It is the Arid Tropical Zone of Griscom (1932) and of Dickey and van Rossem (1938). The Costa Rican section is the Plains Region and the North Coastal Zone

of Carriker (1910). Though drier than the Caribbean lowlands, it is no less hot and it supports a variety of cover types. In the extreme north semideciduous forest prevails; farther south are savannas and gallery forest. Only the birds of this region have been studied in any detail, though both the reptiles and amphibians of the northern section are fairly well known. Griscom (1932, 1940) believes that, owing to the high degree of endemism, the avifauna of this province is older than that of the Caribbean lowlands. Other groups have been too poorly studied to test this hypothesis.

There is some indication that the region between the levels of possibly Pijijiapan, Chiapas, and Escuintla, Guatemala, may warrant special regional recognition. This general area, especially in the piedmont and on the lower plateau slopes, is far more humid than the regions to either the north or the south.

As the Pacific versant just noted contrasts with the humid lowlands of northern Central America, so does the region south of the Nicoya Peninsula to eastern Panama along the Pacific contrast with the humid Caribbean lowlands of the south. This region is the Arid Tropical Zone of both Goldman (1920) and Griscom (1932) and the South Coastal Zone of Carriker (1910). The region is subjected to high temperatures at lower elevations, and, although rainfall is moderately heavy, there is a prolonged dry season. Vegetation cover includes both deciduous forest and extensive savannas. Aside from the birds, the fauna of this province has been poorly analyzed. Griscom (1932), however, has noted that the avifauna of this area is most closely related to that of the arid valleys and Caribbean coastal regions of northern South America. Whether or not there is faunal continuity between these latter and the Pacific versant of Panama and southern Costa Rica must await further study in eastern Panama. Endemism in the avifauna of the Pacific

---

[18] The Central American lowlands and the adjacent Costa Rica–Panama mountain system on the Caribbean versant between the Motagua Embayment (Guatemala) and South America has been divided by Ryan (1963) into three provinces. These are the Mosquito (Motagua to about Bluefields, Nicaragua), the Guatusco-Talamancan (Bluefields to beyond Bocas del Toro, Panama), and the Colon-Darien (essentially Panama and both the Caribbean and Pacific versants east of the Azuero Peninsula).

Costa Rica–Panama Province suggests that such is not the case.[19]

Two major montane regions comprise the geological framework of Central America. In the north, from east of the Isthmus of Tehuantepec to southern Nicaragua, is an ancient positive mass frequently known as "nuclear Central America." It is not a single structural unit since it includes such diverse entities as the Sierra Madre of Chiapas, the high mountain masses of northwestern Guatemala, the complex lower ranges of Honduras, and the recent volcanoes that border the uplands along the Pacific versant. In the south is a second complex of mountains that extends through Costa Rica from its northwestern border southeastward into western Panama. The two major units are separated by the lowlands of extreme southern Nicaragua.

The northern highlands appear to comprise two biotic provinces. The first and most distinct is confined to the highlands of Chiapas and of western and central Guatemala. This is the Subtropical and Temperate Zones of Griscom (1932), a complexity of life zones of Goldman (1951), the Chiapas Highlands of Goldman and Moore (1946), and a number of "biotic provinces" (more probably districts as previously indicated) of both Smith (1949) and Stuart (1943, 1956). Relief varies from low on the high plateau surfaces (generally above about 2700 m.) to high along the edges of the plateaus and on the volcanoes. The province supports a variety of cover types. Montane rain forest (cloud forest) obtains along windward slopes but the bulk of the

region is in oak and pine with pine, cypress, and fir forests on the higher ridges.

Because of the geologic and climatic complexity of the region, the Chiapas-Guatemalan Highland Province will have to be subdivided into at least five biotic districts, with considerable endemism at the subspecific and specific levels characterizing each faunally. However, viewed as a unit in so far as the birds, reptiles, and amphibians have been analyzed, the over-all character of the fauna appears to be relatively uniform throughout. As might be expected, this fauna is largely Nearctic in character and appears to have been derived postglacially from the north. There is in addition a smaller and more ancient element, highly endemic and of Neotropical relationships.

A second biotic province lies east of about the level of Guatemala City and continues through Honduras into Nicaragua. This region is the Upper Tropical Zone of Dickey and van Rossem (1938) and includes the southeastern highlands of Guatemala (Stuart, 1954b). The Honduranian portion has been described in considerable detail by Carr (1950). Like the more northern highlands, the Honduran-Nicaraguan Highland Province is geologically and climatically complex, and its chief physical difference from the Chiapas-Guatemalan Highland Province is to be found in its lower elevation. Both the general plateau level and the highest peaks lie about 1000 m. below those of the north and west. Relief throughout the area, and especially in Honduras, is high. The vegetation cover is extremely varied. Desert thorn scrub obtains in protected low valleys, but whether these should be assigned to this province or to the Caribbean lowlands remains a moot question. On the higher peaks mountain rain forest prevails, while at intermediate elevations tree savanna and oak and pine predominate.

At this time the entire region is so poorly known that even its general limits are obscure. I have taken (1954b) the 1000-m.

[19] Along the Pacific versant of Central America, with the exception of eastern Panama, Ryan (1963) recognizes three provinces. The Pacific-Nicaragua Province, as defined by me, is comprised of the Escuintla-Usulatan Province of Regan to the north and his Chinandegan Province to the south. His boundary between the two is placed at the level of the Gulf of Fonseca. Farther south from just north of the Nicoya Peninsula to east of the Azuero Peninsula extends his Punta Arenas–Chiriqui Province.

contour as a serviceable boundary between the Guatemalan section and the lowland provinces. What little is known of the fauna suggests that at lower elevations it is allied to that of the north, but there are also a number of lowlanders that enter the province. At high elevations the fauna is not unlike that of the higher elevations of the Chiapas-Guatemalan Highland Province.[20]

The second major mountain unit, that of Costa Rica and western Panama, comprises but a single biotic province, which, like the Chiapas-Guatemalan Highland Province, very probably contains a number of districts. It is the Subtropical and Temperate zones of Griscom (1932), the Upper Tropical and Temperate zones of Goldman (1920), and parts of the Tropical, Sonoran, and Boreal areas of Carriker (1910). It is almost impossible to correlate the regions of this last with any zoogeographic system. It is characterized by the complexity of its mountain systems in which volcanism has been an extremely active force, and a variety of montane climates and vegetation cover dominated by very wet montane forests at intermediate elevations and shading into páramo at the very highest elevations.

Though the fauna of the highlands of Costa Rica and western Panama is reasonably well known, there exist very few zoogeographic summaries. In fact the now-outdated account of Carriker (1910) remains the best zoogeographic treatment of the bulk of the region. It appears that the fauna includes a very few northerners, so conspicuous an element in the Chiapas-Guatemalan Highland Province, a consider-

able number of southerners related to forms in the northern Andes and a well-developed endemic element of considerable age.[21]

The foregoing regional analysis of Middle America has been undertaken with terrestrial groups primarily in mind. The freshwater fishes, though showing considerable coincidence of geographic pattern with that of terrestrial vertebrates at the chorographic level, can hardly be expected to display accordance at lower geographic levels. Their inability to transcend land barriers, except passively through stream capture, has produced geographic patterns that are generally in accord with hydrographic (i.e. drainage basin) patterns. S. E. Meek (1904) has discussed the zoogeography of Mexican fishes, and Regan (1908) reviewed the distribution of the fishes of Middle America as a whole. Dr. Miller has further supplied me with unpublished data on the Mexican section. The map of fish assemblages (fig. 6), like that of the biotic provinces, is purely tentative and has been compiled from the sources just noted.

The bulk of the Nearctic (Mexican) fish fauna appears to find its southern limits just north of the Balsas Basin on the west and somewhere between the Panuco and Papaloapan systems in the east. Dr. Miller (*in litt.*) regards the region between these last two as a broad zone of transition between the Nearctic and Neotropical (Central American) faunas.

The Rio Grande Province is by far the largest of the Nearctic subdivisions. It includes not only the extant basin of the Rio Grande but also the isolated streams and basins of Chihuahua, Coahuila, and Durango which during glacial stages probably had direct connections with the Rio Grande, e.g. via the Rio Nazas. Its limits extend from the divide of the Sierra Madre Occi-

[20] The Chiapas-Guatemalan Los Altos Province of Ryan (1963) is roughly comparable to the Chiapas–Guatemala Highlands Province as defined by me. Ryan, however, fragments my Honduran-Nicaraguan Highlands into the Lempira-Tegucigalpan Province (largely Honduras) and the Nicaraguan Montane Province (largely Nicaragua). Furthermore, a considerable portion of Ryan's Mosquito Province includes the mountain terrain of northern Honduras.

[21] Ryan (1963) does not recognize these uplands as an entity. He apportions them, rather, between his Caribbean and Pacific provinces of lower Central America, utilizing the Continental Divide as a boundary.

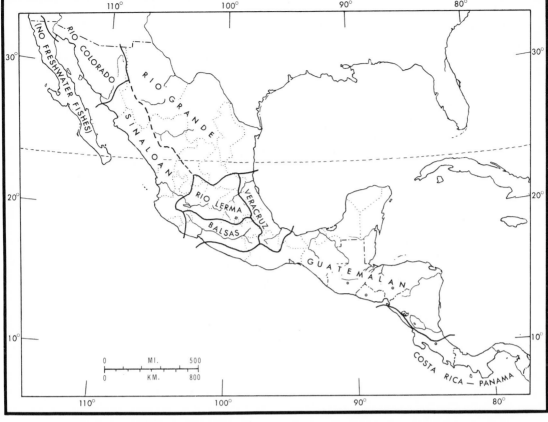

Fig. 6—THE MAJOR FISH ASSEMBLAGES OF FISH PROVINCES OF MIDDLE AMERICA
(Based on Regan, 1906–08, and Meek, 1904.)

dental on the west to the Gulf of Mexico on the east and southward to the Lerma and Panuco systems. Within these boundaries the centrarchids and percids find their southernmost limits and the characids and cichlids their northernmost limits. The minnows, killifishes, and poeciliids are all well represented, and endemism is high in the isolated streams of the system, e.g. in the shiners (*Notropis*).

To the west of the Rio Grande Province is the Rio Colorado Province. It comprises streams that arise in the northern part of the Sierra Madre Occidental and flow into the Gulf of California. The Rio Yaqui may be taken as the southern limit of the province. Suckers and minnows are abundant, and a number of the latter are either the same as or closely related to those of the Rio

Grande system. According to S. E. Meek (1904), these have entered the region as a result of stream capture.

The streams of the coastal plain from the Rio Yaqui south to the Rio Balsas appear to comprise a distinct province mostly owing to negative characteristics. Meek (1904) refers to it as a region of "shore fishes." For it Dr. Miller (*in litt.*) suggests the term Sinaloan Province. Within this region the suckers reach their southern limits in the west. The streams are almost devoid of primary and secondary division fishes, with the exception of the slightly salt-tolerant Poeciliidae, but many peripheral division groups occur in the lower courses of the streams.

Perhaps the most distinct of the Nearctic fish provinces of Mexico is that of the Lerma system. This province includes the pla-

359

teau portion of the Rio Lerma and its associated lakes and tributaries as well as some of the headwaters of the Rio Panuco. These waters support a large endemic fauna including several genera of cyprinids and great development of the genus *Chirostoma* (Atherinidae). Though the family Goodeidae is not endemic to the system, it attains its greatest taxonomic diversity therein. Furthermore, this is the only province that does not include at least one cichlid or the ubiquitous characid *Astyanax*.

A transition province, referred to previously, between about the Rio Panuco and the Rio Papaloapan supports a mixture of Nearctic and Neotropical groups. At present it is too poorly known to warrant comment.

Regan (1908) recognizes four Neotropical fish provinces within the limits of Middle America. The most northern of these is the Balsas Province. Along the Pacific, this river system or streams immediately to the north mark the southernmost limits of the suckers and the minnows and the northernmost limit of the characids in the west. This province is characterized especially by its negative qualities. The fish fauna shows extreme impoverishment. Though seven families of strictly fresh-water fishes occur in the system, the majority are represented by but a single genus and species. Most of the species, however, are endemic.

South of the Balsas Province on the west and the Nearctic-Neotropical transitional region in the east the Guatemalan Province of Regan (1908) extends southward to the Nicaraguan lakes. These last with the Rio San Juan comprise the San Juan Province of Regan; Costa Rica and Panama are included in his Isthmian Province. Actually, data more recent than those available to Regan suggest that the zoogeographic picture for the fishes is more complex than the simple statement above would make it appear.

There seems to be little question that Panama and Costa Rica do, indeed, constitute a fish province. It has been indicated that five families of South American catfishes do not extend beyond Panama and a sixth reaches only to Costa Rica. Furthermore, north of that region the characids are relatively poorly represented. In contrast the northern gars reach their southern limit in the Lake Nicaragua basin, just to the north.

The northern part of Regan's Guatemalan Province also appears to warrant regional separation. Within this area the suckers and the northern catfishes (Ictaluridae) reach their southern limits. Conversely, the naked catfishes (Pimelodidae) find their northern limit within the region, and the eel-like gymnotids just enter Guatemala. In the east the viviparous top minnows are represented by several endemic genera, and in the west anablepids are restricted to this northern section in Middle America. Furthermore *Profundulus* (Cyprinodontidae) is an endemic and characteristic genus of the highlands of southern Mexico, Guatemala, and western Honduras and El Salvador.

The intervening area between western Honduras and El Salvador and Costa Rica presents something of a regional problem. That the fish fauna finds its relationships to that of the more northern section cannot be denied. At the same time, however, there is evidence to indicate that it is not as rich as the fauna immediately to the north. Certainly endemism at the generic level is not comparable to that which obtains in southern Mexico and Guatemala. Still farther south the San Juan Province of Regan poses yet another problem. Two endemic cichlid genera, both monotypic, and an endemic characid genus with two species, together with the landlocked marine groups noted previously, seem to provide evidence that it warrants recognition as a distinct region. But it is questionable that it is to be ranked as the equivalent of northern Central America. Anthropogeographers, who as a group have given far more thought to the concept of regionality than have biogeographers, would very probably treat the

Guatemalan and San Juan provinces of Regan as a single region. They would, however, recognize the south Mexican-Guatemalan section as the core and the southern section as peripheral. Considering the sparsity of data on Honduras and Nicaragua, this method of treatment appears to be the most logical for the time being.

Before we quit this discussion of fish zoogeography, it may be well to comment briefly on vertical distribution. Throughout southern Mexico and Central America the 1500-m. contour virtually represents the upper limit of fishes. Only a single genus (*Profundulus*) occurs much above that level and it reaches 2500 m. locally. This situation is probably owing to the nature of the streams above 1500 m. In this mountainous region where the youthful stage of the erosion cycle obtains, highland streams are mostly small mountain freshets broken by falls and presenting conditions that require a high degree of specialization of their faunas. In contrast the broad plateau lands of Mexico are coursed by many streams in which environmental conditions are less demanding. The Lerma system, which supports 43 species divided among 20 genera and 7 families, is such. Yet only downstream from Lake Chapala does it drop below the 1500-m. contour, and its upper reaches in the Toluca region lie at 2800 m.

Any modern zoogeographic analysis to be complete should give consideration to such matters as dispersal centers and dispersal pathways, the historical backgrounds of various faunal elements, faunal movements and similar matters, but such treatment is beyond the scope of this account. For those interested in the historical phases of the Middle American fauna the works of Dunn (1931), Simpson (1943), Schmidt (1943), Mayr (1946), and Griscom (1940, 1950) will provide an excellent starting point.[22]

[22] The manuscript of this article was submitted for publication in 1959. During the past five years our knowledge of the fauna of Middle America has increased considerably. A number of systematic studies have appeared (Rosen and Bailey, 1963), the ranges of many taxa have been extended, scientific names have been changed, faunal summaries have been presented (Stuart, 1963), faunal analyses of several important areas have been published (Baker and Greer, 1962; Duellman, 1960; Hyman, 1960), and several very fine faunal treatments of Central and/or Middle America as a whole are now available (Baker, 1963; Ryan, 1963). Although the general conclusions presented here would not have been altered radically, I take this opportunity to explain why many pertinent studies seemingly have been overlooked. I have addended as footnotes only a few such references.

I take this opportunity to express my gratitude for the time and aid afforded me by Messrs. Reeve M. Bailey, William H. Burt, Norman L. Ford, Norman E. Hartweg, Emmet T. Hooper, Theodore H. Hubbell, Robert R. Miller, Robert W. Storer, Harrison B. Tordoff, Henry van der Schalie and Charles F. Walker, all of the Museum of Zoology, University of Michigan.

REFERENCES

Baker, 1963
—— and Greer, 1962
Bogert and Oliver, 1945
Brodkorb, 1943
Burt, 1938
Calvert, 1908
Carr, 1950
Carr and Giovannoli, 1957
Carriker, 1910
Chapman, F. M., 1917, 1926
Darlington, 1957
Daubenmire, 1938

Dice, 1943, 1952
Dickey and van Rossem, 1938
Duellman, 1960
Dunn, 1931, 1940
Eisenmann, 1955
Gilmore, 1950
Goldman, 1920, 1951
—— and Moore, 1946
Griscom, 1932, 1934, 1935, 1940, 1950
Hall and Kelson, 1959
Hershkovitz, 1958
Hildebrand, 1938

Hooper, 1952
Hovanitz, 1958
Hyman, 1960
James and Jones, 1954
Leopold, 1959
Martin, 1958
Mayr, 1946
Meek, 1904, 1907
Merriam, 1891, 1898
Miller, R. R., 1958
Moore, R. T., 1945
Nelson, 1921
Paynter, 1955
Peters, 1955
Pilsbry, 1926, 1930

Pocock, 1902
Regan, 1906–08
Rosen and Bailey, 1963
Ryan, 1963
Schmidt, 1943, 1954
Sclater, 1858
Simpson, G. G., 1943
Smith, H. M., 1939, 1949
—— and Taylor, 1945, 1948, 1950
Stuart, 1943, 1954a, 1954b, 1956, 1958, 1963
Taylor, E. H., 1951, 1952a, 1952b, 1956
van Martens, 1890–1901
van Rossem, 1945
Wallace, 1876

10. The Natural Regions of Middle America

ROBERT C. WEST

THE PRECEDING articles in this volume describe the several elements of the natural environment within Mexico and Central America and in part relate those elements to various aspects of aboriginal culture. The present article aims to coordinate the foregoing material by summarizing the total natural environment of the area and its significance to man.

The relation of the natural environment to man and his works is a fundamental, but complex, phenomenon that most social scientists recognize. The published reports of the recent symposium on ecology and anthropology arranged by Paul T. Baker (1962) is an example of increasing interest among anthropologists in human environmental relationships. In dealing with such relationships, however, we should remember that within a given context of cultural achievement physical conditions may have both restrictive and permissive relations to human activities. The more primitive the material equipment of a human group, the more direct these relations may be. Among modern anthropologists C. Daryll Forde (1934) has perhaps stated best the concepts pertaining to land-man relationships

in nontechnical societies without falling into the dangerous trap of environmental determinism. Man, the active element, adjusts to his passive physical surroundings, adopting or rejecting, for example, natural materials as resources or sites for habitation according to his cultural attributes. Although, as Forde states (1934, p. 464), physical conditions enter into every cultural development and pattern, they enter not as determinants, "but as one category of the raw material of cultural elaboration." Thus man and his works cannot be looked upon as a simple function of the natural environment.

One of the major themes emphasized in this volume has been the great geographical diversity of the elements of natural environment in Middle America. In few other areas of similar size are there such variations within short distances of landforms, climate, vegetation, soils, and animal life as are found in Mexico and Central America. The diversity of surface configuration stems chiefly from the complex geological history of the area and its position within one of the world's regions of contemporaneous mountain building. The mountainous character of the land is one of the important reasons for the complex pattern of precipitation, temperatures, and climatic types; these are reflected in the complicated distribution of vegetation and soil types. Moreover, Middle America straddles the northern limit of the tropics; thus in Mexico climates vary from midlatitude types through most of the subtropical and tropical ones, while within the tropics of Central America temperature patterns are governed mainly by differences in altitude.

One of the results of such environmental diversity has been the highly complicated interaction of man and land in Middle America. Willey (1962) has suggested that the variety of environments within small areas and the subsequent interregional exchange of goods and ideas may have been an important key to the rise of high cultures in southern Mexico and northern Central America. Earlier, Vivó (1943) pointed out that the position of Mexico within the transition zone between Nearctic and Neotropical flora and fauna afforded the aboriginal inhabitants a rich variety of plant and animal life for subsistence.

In order to simplify a summary presentation of the environmental elements in Middle America a regional approach is used in the pages that follow. Geographers and others have long debated the concept and validity of the "natural region." Ideally such an entity should represent an area characterized by a composite pattern of interrelated natural phenomena—that is, a "natural landscape"—that exhibits recognizable physical differences from adjacent areas. Such composites, however, are usually difficult to delimit. Thus in the determination of "natural regions" one or only a few interrelated physical phenomena have commonly been employed. In the United States "natural regions" have often been equated with physiographic areas (e.g., Fenneman, 1928); most writers who have presented the natural regions of Mexico and Central America have used this approach (E. M.

364

Sanders, 1921; C. L. Baker, 1930; Tamayo, 1941; Stuart, 1956). In Europe, German and English geographers have emphasized the climate and related vegetation as the most significant aspect of natural regions (Koeppen, 1900; Passarge, 1919; Herbertson, 1905). The American geographer Carl Sauer (1925), although recognizing the importance of landforms and related geology, emphasized the climatic and vegetational bases of the natural region: "We may say confidently that the resemblance or contrast between natural landscapes in the large is primarily a matter of climate" (p. 39). The relation of climate to landscape is expressed mainly through vegetation and, in part, soils and animal life. Since man is ultimately dependent on the biota for his subsistence, the distribution of vegetation types may serve as a significant key to natural regions (Aschmann, 1961). It should be apparent, however, that cultural areas in the anthropological sense and natural regions in the geographical sense rarely correspond exactly, and that two peoples with different cultures or cultural values may utilize and transform a given physical setting in quite different ways. Indeed, in Mexico and Central America the human imprint is so deep that one can reconstruct the natural landscape only with difficulty.

NATURAL REALMS OF MIDDLE AMERICA

Using climate and vegetation as the main bases for classification, one might divide Middle America into three major natural realms, as shown in figure 1 and outlined below. Each of these is further divided into natural regions and subregions on the basis of various physical phenomena.

1. The *extratropical dry lands* and adjacent subhumid areas of northern Mexico. These areas are characterized by definite winter and summer temperature seasons, by xerophytic plant assemblages of North American affinity, and by predominance of arid-type landforms.

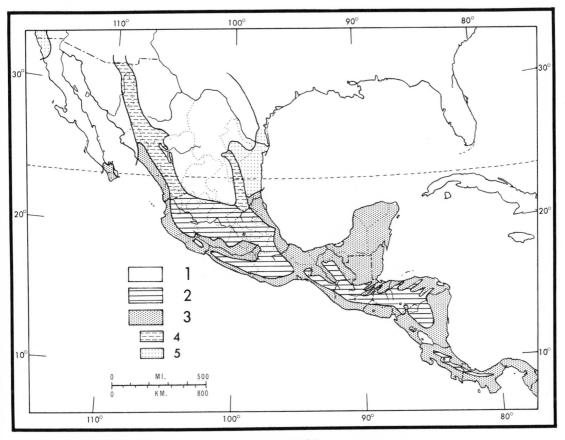

Fig. 1—NATURAL REALMS OF MIDDLE AMERICA
Key: 1, Extratropical dry lands; 2, Tropical highlands; 3, Tropical lowlands. Transitional sub-realms are indicated by 4, Extratropical highlands and 5, Subhumid extratropical lowlands.

2. The *cool tropical highlands*, including the Sierra Madre Occidental and Oriental of Mexico. From Mexico to Nicaragua oak-conifer forests of North American affinity give character to the landscape, whereas in Costa Rica and Panama a highland oak-laurel-myrtle rain forest related to South American plant assemblages prevails.

3. The *warm tropical lowlands* of Mexico and Central America. This is a complex area of many small individual units with complicated arrangements of tropical plant assemblages that range from true lowland rain forest through tropical deciduous woodland and savanna to tropical scrub, according to local relief, climatic and edaphic factors. Here the climate, characterized by relatively high temperatures throughout the year, affording frost-free conditions, is the unifying factor

Generally each of the three realms exhibits distinctive natural landscapes expressed primarily in climate and vegetation and secondarily in soils and land configuration. Less regional distinction holds for animal life. The entire region may be outlined as in key to figure 3.

By comparing figures 1 and 2 one may see but a few close correlations between the major natural realms and various aspects of preconquest Indian cultures. The closest relationship is that of the arid lands of northern Mexico to the primitive hunting-and-gathering cultures. However, an extension of agriculture into the deserts of northwestern Mexico and southwestern United States, as well as the presence of primitive cultures in subhumid northeastern Mexico and southeastern Texas, destroys a complete correlation. Obviously,

365

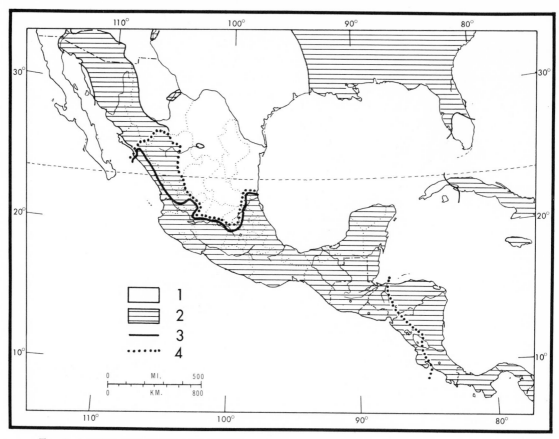

Fig. 2—MAJOR CULTURE AREAS OF MIDDLE AMERICA, CA. A.D. 1500
Key: 1, Nonagricultural areas (mainly primitive hunting-gathering-fishing); 2, Agricultural areas; 3, Northern limit of high cultures (Sauer, 1941); 4, Limits of Mesoamerican culture (Kirchhoff, 1943).

other factors in addition to environment, such as routes of cultural diffusion, human migrations, and geographical position, operated to produce these cultural distributions. The northernmost extent of high culture, on the other hand, corresponds well with the northern limits of highland and lowland tropics, but in central Mexico at the time of Spanish contact the desert nomads seem to have been pressing southward into tropical highlands on the northern edge of the Mesa Central. The southern extent of high Mesoamerican culture in Central America appears to have been largely a result of diffusion into the semideciduous tropical woodlands and savannas of the Pacific coast, whereas primitive forest cultures of South American affinity spread northward into the rain forests on the Caribbean side of Central America.

Dry Lands of Northern Mexico

Arid northern and northwestern Mexico stands apart from the rest of Middle America in terms of its distinctive physical characteristics and as the home of primitive gathering, hunting, and fishing cultures. Both physically and culturally this area might be considered a modified southern extension of the North American deserts and steppes. The Mexican portion of the dry areas is characterized by three subunits: (1) the high desert and steppe of the Mesa del Norte; (2) the low deserts of Sonora and northern Sinaloa; and (3) most of the Peninsula of Baja California.

MESA DEL NORTE. In this largest of the arid subregions (fig. 3) extensive areas of interior drainage and classic desert basin-and-range topography characterize the arid plateau surface. The relatively high elevations (1000–2000 m.) and frequent incursions of winter polar air from the north cause low winter temperatures which often descend to below freezing at night, although summer daytime temperatures may be excessive. In the eastern two-thirds of the plateau porous limestone rock combines with low precipitation (200–300 mm. annually) to form one of the harshest environments in Middle America. Over most of the eastern "limestone" desert the vegetation is composed of low, widely spaced plants, such as creosote bush (*Larrea divaricata*), various agaves (of which *Agave lechuguilla* is the most common), many species of yucca, and various cacti as dominants. On sandy soils within intermittent stream channels and along the lower portions of alluvial fans grow clumps of mesquite (*Prosopis juliflora*), the nutritious pods of which formed one of the most common foods gathered by the desert nomads. In certain areas occur veritable forests of palmillas (*Yucca*, spp.) and prickly-pear cactus (*Opuntia*, spp.), the fruit of both plants having been significant in the gathering economy. The largest of the opuntia forests, called El Gran Tunal, west of San Luis Potosi near the southern margin of the Mesa del Norte, was a favorite retreat of the Chichimec nomads (Chevalier, 1952, p. 43). The formation of large stands of single desert species, such as the opuntia cactus, may have been due as much to human action as to edaphic conditions.

Corresponding to the "High Basin-Range" subdivision of the Mesa del Norte as described by West (this volume, Article 2), the western volcanic third of the dry plateau surface adjacent to the Sierra Madre Occidental affords a less harsh environment than the lower limestone desert to the east.

The prevailing short grasslands of the western part of the plateau result from the 400–500-mm. annual precipitation and moisture retentive soils weathered from the underlying volcanic rock. Associated with the prevailing grama grasses (*Bouteloua*, spp.) are scattered clumps of acacia, mesquite bush, and opuntia cactus. Many streams, both intermittent and perennial, often lined with gallery forests of bald cypress (*Taxodium*, sp.), cottonwood, willow, and mesquite, flow from the Sierra Madre Occidental across the high steppes into the central desert. Moreover, fertile alluvium accumulates on the lower slopes of fans that form at the base of the NW-SE trending hills and ranges. As West (Article 2) and Stevens (Article 9) have indicated, the environmental basis for the northward extension of advanced La Quemada and Chalchihuites farming cultures along the steppe zone during the 10th and 12th centuries is not far to seek.

WESTERN SONORA AND NORTHWESTERN SINALOA. Separated from the plateau desert and steppe by the pine- and oak-covered Sierra Madre Occidental, western Sonora and northwestern Sinaloa form a distinct part of northern Mexico's dry lands. Although Baja California is often coupled with the Sonoran deserts in terms of climate and vegetation, contrast in surface configuration and drainage is sufficiently marked to consider the two areas as separate geographical subregions.

Vivó (Article 6) classifies the low arid lands of northwestern Mexico climatically as hot desert and steppe (Koeppen's BWh and BSh). Here occur the highest summer temperatures (over 50°C.) recorded in Middle America, whereas winter frosts sometimes occur. Annual average precipitation varies from less than 200 mm. in the Altar Desert of extreme northwestern Sonora to 400 mm. in the steppes of northern Sinaloa.

Despite scant precipitation the vegeta-

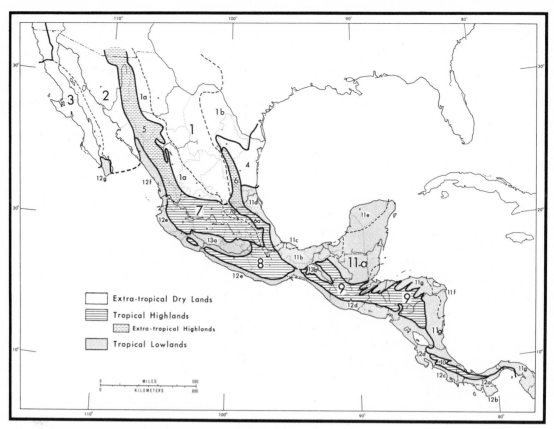

FIG. 3—THE NATURAL REGIONS OF MIDDLE AMERICA

Key to numbered subdivisions in fig. 3:

A. *Extratropical dry lands*
    1. Mesa del Norte (desert)
        1a. Steppe lands of western margin
        1b. Steppe lands of eastern Coahuila and northern Nuevo Leon
    2. Sonora and northern Sinaloa
    3. Baja California
    4. Tamaulipas subhumid lowlands

B. *Tropical highlands and extratropical appendages*
    5. Sierra Madre Occidental
    6. Sierra Madre Oriental
        6a. Tropical extension of the Sierra and eastern plateau escarpment
    7. Mesa Central
        7a. Arid rain-shadow strip
    8. Sierra and Mesa del Sur
    9. Highlands of northern Central America
    10. Highlands of Costa Rica and western Panama

C. *Tropical lowlands*
    11. Caribbean-Gulf lowlands
        11a. Peten-Yucatan rain-forest area

        11b. Southern Veracruz-Tabasco rain-forest area
        11c. Los Tuxtlas
        11d. Deciduous forest area of northern Veracruz
        11e. Northern Yucatan
        11f. Mosquito coast
        11g. Caribbean rain-forest area of Central America
    12. Pacific lowlands
        12a. Savanna of Central Panama
        12b. Azuero rain-forest area
        12c. Rain forest of southwestern Costa Rica
        12d. Volcanic lowlands of Central America
        12e. Coastal lowlands of southwestern Mexico
        12f. Coastal lowlands of Nayarit-Sinaloa
        12g. Cape region of Baja California
    13. Dry interior tropical basins
        13a. Balsas-Tepalcatepec basin
        13b. Valley of Chiapas

tion cover of most of the Sonora-Sinaloa dry lands is arboreal, or composed of treelike xerophytes (E. C. Jaeger, 1957). Thus Wagner (Article 7, fig. 1) describes the plant cover of this area as a northward continuation of the "Seasonal Formation Series" of the Pacific coast of Middle America. Low trees such as palo verde (*Cercidium*), in the more arid sections; mesquite (*Prosopis*) and huamuchil (*Pithecolobium*), in deep alluvium along streams and delta plains; treelike organ cacti such as pitahaya (various genera of the Cereus group); and large numbers of evergreen and deciduous shrubs scattered over plains and hill slopes dominate the vegetation cover. Inhabiting this lush desert growth an abundance of deer, peccary, rabbits, various rodents, quail, and occasional iguanas afforded adequate game for Indian hunters. The Neotropical jaguar and armadillo are also represented.

One of the most distinctive environmental features of the dry lands of Sonora and northern Sinaloa, however, is the drainage system and associated alluvial forms. As described in Articles 2 and 3, numerous perennial streams flow from the Sierra Madre Occidental westward athwart the general N-S structural hills in the coastal lowlands, forming narrow alluvial valleys that widen into extensive delta plains near the Gulf of California coast. For centuries before the Spanish conquest primitive farmers (Cahita, Yaqui, Mayo, Pima, and Papago) cultivated the flood plains of the Sinaloa, Fuerte, Mayo, Yaqui, and Sonora rivers. Overflowing twice yearly (in late winter due to runoff from melting snows and frontal storms in the Sierra Madre; in summer due to mountain thundershowers), the rivers on receding left rich, moist soils in which the Indians planted two crops annually. As Vivó (Article 6) avers, these primitive flood farmers lived within the Pacific coastal route of northward cultural spread (including agriculture) from central Mexico and took advantage of favor-able physical conditions to develop a farming economy in an arid environment.

BAJA CALIFORNIA. Severe aridity characterizes almost the entire length of the peninsula; only the high mountains and Pacific coastal plain in the north, which receive winter frontal rainfall, and the Cape region, moistened by late summer tropical storms, fall outside the area of desert climate. Receiving annually less than 200 mm. of rain, the central part of the peninsula is probably the most arid section of Middle America. In Baja California there are no rivers like those of Sonora to serve as a physical basis for primitive agriculture; streams are short and highly intermittent, exhibiting bare rocky or sandy beds most of the year. In the volcanic zone of the central part of the peninsula, however, many springs issue from old lava flows. In the past these sources supplied water for nomadic hunters and gatherers, and today they mark the few centers of permanent habitation, such as Mulege and Comondu.

The natural vegetation cover of the peninsula is much like that of the Sonora Desert, with an arboreal thorn forest as the dominant association. Palms (*Washingtonia* and *Erythea*) often line intermittent stream beds in the northern and southern parts of the peninsula. In the Central Desert two endemic plants, the curious cirio (*Idria columnaris*) and the corpulent elephant tree (*Pachycormus discolor*), give a weird aspect to the landscape; in the Vizcaino Desert to the west, large areas of sand dunes as well as bare rock give still another aspect to the varied surface of arid Baja California. Although fewer in actual populations, the faunal assemblage of the peninsula is again much like that of Sonora and the Colorado deserts, with mule deer, pronghorn antelope, desert big horn sheep, and rabbits as the most important game animals; the Neotropical jaguar and peccary, however, are missing. Coastal marine fauna on both the Pacific and Gulf sides is abundant; the numerous shell middens,

369

especially of the Gulf coast, attest to the importance of sea life to the primitive aboriginal inhabitants of the peninsula.

LOWLANDS OF NORTHEASTERN MEXICO. Climatically the subhumid lowlands of Tamaulipas and eastern Nuevo Leon form a transition zone between the moist subtropics of southeastern United States and the humid tropics of the Gulf and Caribbean coasts of Middle America. The passage of northern frontal storms in winter, local summer thunderstorms, and occasional hurricanes in autumn bring year-round rainfall to the lowlands, but with a fall maximum. In winter occasional light frosts, but rarely hard freezes, reach some distance below the United States border.

Bushland, often called the Tamaulipan thorn shrub, covers the lowlands and hills. Composed of shrubs and small trees such as mesquite, huisache (*Acacia*), anacahuite (*Cordia*), interspersed with opuntia and organ cactus, yucca, and various grasses, the Tamaulipas scrub is quite distinct from the desert flora of the adjacent Mesa del Norte. Thus Wagner's vegetation map (Article 7, fig. 1), which shows both the plant cover in northeastern north central Mexico as "Steppe, thicket, and scrub desert," may be misleading. Leopold (1950) indicates a zone of bluestem prairie along the Tamaulipas coast (now invaded by mesquite and cactus due to overgrazing), and Muller (1939, 1947) describes a belt of high scrub and low montane forest of oak, walnut, and pecan along the moist lower escarpment of the plateau west of the lowlands. Moreover, gallery forests of pecan, bald cypress, willow, and hackberry line most of the larger lowland stream courses. Although many plants of the central desert are present, the Tamaulipas scrub appears to be more closely related to the "brush country" of south-central Texas (Muller, 1947). Scrub oak and pine woodland occur sporadically in the higher parts of low isolated mountains, such as the San Carlos and Tamaulipas ranges. Around

and south of the latter range the scrub grades into a deciduous thorny tropical forest which continues into northern Veracruz.

In preconquest times primitive hunters, gatherers, and fishers (the Tamaulipecos, Comecrudos, etc., members of the Sioux-Hokan language groups of southeastern Texas) roamed northeastern Mexico. These people might be considered an extension of the nomadic desert cultures of northern Middle America. It was not until well after Spanish contact that the fertile rendzina soils and favorable agricultural climate of the area was utilized extensively for cultivation. The caves within the Tamaulipas Hills, however, have yielded evidence of one of the earliest farming cultures of Middle America on the northern border of the tropics (MacNeish, 1958). It may be significant that the advanced Huastec agriculturists of a later time did not advance much beyond the Rio Tamesi, the northernmost of the Mexican Gulf coast rivers with wide, easily farmed natural levees.

Tropical Highlands

Distinguished by relatively cool to cold temperatures throughout the year; by moderate amounts of precipitation that fall mainly during the warmer months; and by temperate oak-conifer forests, tropical cloud forests on high, exposed slopes, and open woods and grasses in valleys and swales, the tropical highlands formed the most significant of the natural realms of Middle America. Here developed some of the highest population densities and some of the most elaborate centers of Indian civilization in the Americas. Since in general they possess common climatic and floral characteristics, the individual highland areas are here classified physiographically. They include (1) the extratropical western and eastern sierras of Mexico as transition areas, (2) the Mesa Central, (3) the Sierra and Mesa del Sur of Oaxaca and Guerrero states, (4) the highlands of northern Central America, from Chiapas to Nicaragua, and (5) the highlands of Costa Rica and western Panama.

NORTHERN HIGHLAND APPENDAGES. Because of similarities in flora and fauna, the two extratropical extensions of the highlands—the western and eastern sierras, or the upturned edges of the Mexican plateau —are here included as subareas. Above elevations of 2200 m. pine and oak forests follow the volcanic mesas and basins of the Sierra Madre Occidental northward to the present United States border. A definite winter season with occasional snowfall occurs in the northern third of the Sierra, whereas the southern two-thirds enjoys a much lower seasonal temperature range, similar to the tropical highlands to the south. High Mesoamerican culture (e.g. the Cazcan people) extended into the southern part of the mountains (northern Jalisco). Most of the sierra, however, harbored a primitive farming population broken into numerous small linguistic groups, the Tepehuan and Tarahumar occupying the largest territories. These sierra farmers cultivated both the small, high basins and the steep hot barranca slopes that fray the western flank of the plateau escarpment. The Opata, inhabiting the high ridge and valley country of eastern Sonora (on the western flank of the sierra) represented an enclave of advanced farmers, who cultivated permanent fields by irrigation. The Sierra Madre Occidental, like the adjacent Pacific coastal lowland, lay within the western corridor of northward cultural diffusion from the tropical highlands of central and southern Mexico.

The high folded limestone ridges and intervening basins of the Sierra Madre Oriental are likewise covered by oak and pine forests, and some of the highest elevations (above 3600 m.) rise above the tree line to form spots of alpine vegetation. Unlike the Sierra Madre Occidental, however, most of the eastern range was occupied by nomadic hunters and gatherers. Farming

peoples of Mesoamerican culture extended northward only to the Moctezuma River gorge, which cuts through the sierra in northern Hidalgo state. It was not until late in the colonial period that the fertile highland basins in the central part of the sierra were finally occupied by farmers of European descent.

MESA CENTRAL. The Mesa Central of Mexico is the largest and culturally the most significant of the Middle American tropical highlands. From the archaeological record it appears that since Preclassic, or Formative, times (1500–200 B.C.) the high plateau surface has supported a large population. Here are found some of the largest of the ancient ceremonial and urban centers of Mesoamerica, particularly in the Valley of Mexico and environs on the eastern side of the plateau. Still today the Mesa Central forms the core of Mexico's population and economy.

In the first three articles of this volume two significant and closely related environmental factors of the Mesa Central were emphasized: the volcanic nature of the land and the peculiar hydrography. Within and around the margins of the Transverse Neovolcanic axis that marks the southern edge of the plateau are found the most recent forms of vulcanism. These include the large composite volcanoes, small cinder cones, and extensive lava flows. Fertile soils weathered from the basic ash and lava on the originally oak-pine clad slopes in many areas have been cultivated for centuries without showing appreciable depletion. The dry northern margin of the Mesa Central is characterized by older (Tertiary) volcanic forms of mainly acidic rocks. One of the most conspicuous landforms throughout the plateau is the flat-floored basins between volcanic hills and ranges. During much of Pleistocene time these basins contained large lakes, products of a former normal drainage disrupted by vulcanism. Many of the lakes subsequently have been drained by normal headward stream erosion

371

and gradual desiccation and filling, resulting in flattish basin floors. The remnants of the Pleistocene lakes afforded abundant aquatic animal and plant products which the Indians have utilized for millennia. The lacustrine environment of the Mesa Central was undoubtedly a significant factor in the subsistence base of the ancient plateau cultures, and is best exemplified by the Valley of Mexico.

Although altitude and resulting highland climate and temperate-type vegetation differentiates the Mesa Central from the adjacent tropical lowlands, it would hardly be correct to attribute culture growth on the plateau to cool, bracing temperatures. It should be emphasized, however, that the summer rainfall of the highlands is normally adequate for the growth of one annual crop, whereas the winter drought usually precludes cultivation of a second harvest without irrigation except in especially favored areas. Moreover, the proximity of the adjacent warm escarpments and lowland basins and coastal plains, with their varied tropical products, led to active commercial and cultural interchange that may have been the fundamental basis for the rise of civilization in central and southern Mexico.

Due to its rain-shadow position in the lee of the Sierra Madre Oriental a strip of arid climate and vegetation extends along the eastern margin of the Mesa Central, as indicated on Vivó's map (Article 6, fig. 1). The semiarid to arid Mesquital area in Hidalgo state represents a southern extension of the northern interior dry lands; the semidesert of eastern Puebla covers the sparsely inhabited Llanos de San Juan, the easternmost basin of the Mesa Central, and continues southward into the Tehuacan-Tomellin graben to Oaxaca. Columnar cacti of the Cereus group (which often form veritable forests on dry slopes), yucca, and thorny scrub plants compose the dominant vegetation of these areas.

Although now largely destroyed by human action, pine-oak forests and open woods originally covered the more humid central and western portion of the Mesa Central. A large variety of both evergreen and deciduous oaks formed open woodland in grass-floored highland basins and dense forests on slopes up to 2300 m.; mixed oak-pine and solid pine forests (composed chiefly of *Pinus montezumae*) prevailed to 3000 m., where stands of fir (*Abies religiosa*), white pine (*Pinus ayacahuite*), Douglas fir (*Pseudotsuga mucronata*), alder (*Alnus*, sp.), and stunted juniper (*Juniperus*, sp.) made up a boreal-type forest on the higher mountain peaks (Leopold, 1959). In the latitude of the Valley of Mexico the tree line approximates 4000 m., whereas above 4800 m. only low alpine grasses, lichens, and mosses can exist. In the lower altitudes of the Mesa Central where man has been destroying or altering the original vegetation for centuries, scrub oak, acacia, cactus, and grasses now dominate the wild vegetation cover. The willow-like pirul, or pepper tree (*Schinus molle*), that now forms open stands in the eastern and southern parts of the plateau, is an escaped exotic, introduced into Mexico from Peru about 1550 (Kramer, 1957).

Among the highland faunal assemblages Nearctic mammals in the open woodlands; fish, various reptiles, and amphibians; and aquatic birds and insects furnished the bulk of wild life exploited by native peoples. The white-tailed deer and rabbits were probably the mammals most hunted in ancient times; the numerous lakes furnished the small pescado blanco, frogs, salamanders, migratory ducks, geese, coots, and teals, as they do today.

TROPICAL HIGHLANDS OF SOUTHERN MEXICO. Commonly called the Sierra Madre del Sur in Guerrero, the Mesa del Sur in central Oaxaca, these highlands form a highly dissected mountain mass of old crystalline rock in places overlain by younger limestone, sandstone, and shale. As indicated in Article 2, the combined structural valleys of

Oaxaca and Tlacolula form the only extensive highland basin with flattish to rolling surfaces within this rugged region. The presence of the large Zapotec and Mixtec sites of Monte Alban, Mitla, Yagul, and others within the basin attest to its cultural importance in ancient times. Its alluvial and colluvial soils have been cultivated perhaps for more than 2000 years; and today, despite serious soil erosion induced by plow tillage since the colonial era, the basin remains the population center of highland Zapotec Indians. Even the steep mountain slopes of Oaxaca may have supported a relatively dense population in preconquest times; for, as Stevens points out in Article 9, the continual sheet erosion of the top soil exposes unleached parent material for weathering, maintaining soil fertility during the long fallow periods associated with migratory slash-burn cultivation.

Like the Mesa Central, the southern highlands of Mexico once supported a fine oak-pine forest, with solid stands of *Pinus herrerai* on the higher slopes. On moist high mountain tops above 3000 m., however, exists a cloud-forest association composed of epiphyte-draped temperate hardwoods, such as oak, sweet gum (*Liquidambar*), basswood (*Tilia*), beech (*Fagus*), mixed with an understory of large tree ferns and the South American conifer, *Podocarpus* (Sharp, 1946; Miranda and Sharp, 1950). Throughout the highlands deep valleys present an arid aspect with xerophytes (low thorny acacias and cacti of many varieties) as dominant plants; the upper Tehuantepec River drainage on the eastern side of the Mesa del Sur is representative of this situation. Centuries of human occupation have resulted in the modification of the southern highland forests. Especially in limestone areas, such as between Chilpancingo and Tixtla in Guerrero state, a low fan palm (*Brahea*, sp. ?) has taken over from the destroyed oak forests as the secondary plant cover, especially where excessive soil erosion has exposed bare, fluted bedrock.

HIGHLANDS OF NORTHERN CENTRAL AMERICA. This is a complex of many mountainous subregions. Geologically most of the area belongs to the folded and faulted Antillean structure with E-W ranges, as described in Article 2. The highlands of southern Guatemala, however, form the northern, higher end of the recent Central American volcanic axis.

Comprising the northern portion of the Antillean structure, the high (2200–3000 m.) limestone plateau of San Cristobal in Chiapas and its continuation into central Guatemala (the Altos Cuchumatanes and the folded ranges of Alta Verapaz) were important centers of Indian population probably as early as the Formative period. Karstic features ranging from extensive poljes, or coalesced solution basins, to small sink holes, complicate the hilly to mountainous surface. The few large flat-floored basins include the valley of San Cristobal, the highland plains of Comitan (both in Chiapas), and the elongated valleys of the Alta Verapaz in Guatemala.

The southern portion of the Antillean structure includes the granitic Sierra Madre de Chiapas and its abrupt southern escarpment; the volcanic highlands, or Los Altos, of southwestern Guatemala; and the ranges of eastern Guatemala, Honduras, and northern Nicaragua, all partially covered by thick deposits of volcanic material. The landforms of Los Altos of Guatemala are much like those of the Mesa Central of Mexico: lacustrine basins separated by large composite volcanoes, cinder cones, and weathered lava flows. The lower volcanic slopes and basin floors contain some of the greatest densities of Indian population in Middle America. In Honduras the highland basins (500–1200 m. elevation), called "valles," form the only flat land in this rugged area, the home of the Lenca Indians and their neighbors on the eastern margin of ancient Mesoamerican culture.

A rainy season (*invierno*) from May through November and a period of drought (*verano*) from December through April is the ordinary seasonal weather regime in most parts of the northern Central American highlands. However, south of the Isthmus of Tehuantepec a short dry period of around two to five weeks' duration, called the *veranillo,* normally occurs during July or August. Windward slopes of the higher mountains and escarpments may receive sufficient rain through the year to support a dense cloud forest discussed below.

The normal oak-pine forest that is typical of the Middle American tropical highlands extends as far as northern Nicaragua, where the Nearctic genus *Pinus* reaches its equatorward limit (Denevan, 1961). In the uplands of Chiapas, Guatemala, and Honduras *Pinus oocarpa* and *P. pseudostrobus* are the main pines that form solid stands between 1000 and 2000 m. elevation, although open forests of *P. oocarpa* often extend into the hot tropical lowlands. Elevations between 2500 and 3500 m. in western Honduras mark the equatorward limit of a boreal forest association of giant fir (*Abies guatemalensis*) and cypress (*Cupressus,* sp.), often with a Middle American pine (*Pinus ayacahuite*) intermixed.

From Chiapas southward evergreen hardwood cloud forests that occupy moist mountaintops above 2000 m. become increasingly frequent. In Honduras practically every exposed mountain height above that elevation carries a heavy forest of giant moss-draped oaks and laurels (aguacate, *Persea,* sp.), mixed with tree fern and slender *Chamaedorea* palms (Carr, 1949, 1950). Intermediate between the cloud association and the pine-oak forests (and often mixed with the latter) are found stands of deciduous sweet gum (*Liquidambar*), whose leaves turn brilliant orange and red with the first light frosts of December. The high cloud forests were probably far more extensive in pre-European times than at present, for slash-burn farmers are continually destroying the oaks and laurels for charcoal

and to open maize clearings in the deep forest soils. After cutting and burning, the hardwoods rarely regenerate; the top soil is quickly eroded, leaving a mineralized horizon that only pines and scrub will populate. It might be guessed that much of the higher lands of central Honduras and northern Nicaragua now in open pine-oak woodland were once covered by a hardwood forest. The pine cover may have been culturally induced (Denevan, 1961).

Located in the rain shadow of surrounding mountains, the interior basins (valles) of the eastern Guatemalan and central Honduran highlands reflect aridity in the prevailing thorn-scrub of mimosas, acacias, and cacti. Johannessen (1959) has shown that the extensive grassy savannas that cover many of the basin floors are probably the result of burning by man, rather than response to natural conditions.

HIGHLANDS OF COSTA RICA AND WESTERN PANAMA. The narrow, elongated upland of Costa Rica and western Panama is the smallest of the tropical highlands in Middle America and marks the southern end of the Central American volcanic axis. Fifteen hundred meters above the sea, the Meseta Central of Costa Rica was the home of the advanced Huetar Indian culture and is today the most densely settled Europeanized section of the isthmus. The highlands continue eastward as the high, forested Talamanca Range, a gigantic batholith, or granitic intrusion, today a refuge zone for isolated remnants of forest Indians of South American affinity; it is also a frontier of Costa Rican settlement that is gradually penetrating into the valleys and slopes of this rugged area. The volcanic mass of Chiriqui and the Cordillera Central of Panama form the eastern end of the highlands.

Abundant annual rainfall (2000–3500 mm.), a relatively short dry period from mid-December through April, and heavy cloud-forest vegetation differentiate the Costa Rica–Panama tropical highlands from those of northern Central America. Giant oaks and laurels with an understory of myrtle, bamboo, and tree fern are the main components of the cloud forest, a northern extension of the highland vegetation of the northern Andes. Another South American plant association is found at elevations above 3000 m., where alpine plants, such as the low bamboo-like *Chusquea*, low sedges, grasses and lichens form landscapes similar to the páramos of the Colombian Andes.

Although in general within the area of Neotropical fauna, the tropical highlands of Central America have been invaded by some Nearctic animals. Of these the white-tailed deer and a few species of rabbits and squirrels are the most important in terms of game. Associated with these as a predator is the North American cougar or puma (*Felis concolor*), who ranges into South America. True South American mammals of the lowland rain forests, such as tapirs, the spider monkey, the various tropical American cats (jaguar, margay, ocelot, etc.), anteaters, armadillo, and others, penetrate into the highland forests as far north as Guatemala and Chiapas. Among the birds, several trogons, including the beautiful quetzal, so important in ancient Mesoamerican trade and ceremony, are endemic to the Central American highlands. The limits of North and South American fishes within the isthmus are shown in Article 8, figure 2.

Tropical Lowlands

Comprising approximately one-third of the continental portion of Middle America, the tropical lowlands are geographically the most complex of the natural realms. They include the tropical areas generally below 1000–1200 m. elevation—the *tierra caliente* of the lowland plains, hill lands, and lower mountain slopes. High temperatures throughout the year and a natural vegetation composed of plants intolerant

of frost are the chief diagnostic features. In terms of climate and vegetation the tropical lowlands are here divided into three major regions, each with many subareas:

1. The wide Caribbean and Gulf coastal lands and adjacent mountain escarpments, most of which are characterized by abundant rainfall, a comparatively short dry season (Koeppen's Am to Af), and a dense rain forest cover. Exceptions are (a) the dry northern section of the Yucatan Peninsula, originally covered by scrub forest, and (b) the patches of savanna grasslands that occur sporadically from the Mosquito Coast of Nicaragua and Honduras to northern Veracruz in Mexico.

2. The narrow Pacific coastal lowlands, characterized by definite wet and dry seasons, each approximately of six months' duration (Koeppen's Aw to Am), and a semideciduous to deciduous forest with scattered patches of savanna. Only in southwestern Costa Rica and the Azuero Peninsula of Panama are there extensive areas of rain forest.

3. The dry interior lowland basins, such as the Balsas-Tepalcatepec in southwestern Mexico, the Valley of Chiapas, and the middle Motagua River valley in eastern Guatemala. Semiaridity (Koeppen's BS to Aw) is reflected in the dominant thorny scrub-cactus vegetation of these rain-shadow areas.

CARIBBEAN AND GULF LOWLANDS. These form the largest part of the Middle American *tierra caliente*. Interrupted occasionally by savanna grassland, a dense evergreen rain forest covers most of this hot, humid area from southern Veracruz to South America. Large trees of a bewildering number of species grow in scattered profusion and often form a storied structure. Thick undergrowth on the forest floor is rare, but occurs within recent windfalls and along stream banks where sunlight can penetrate. In Article 7 Wagner describes in some detail the rain forest of various well-studied areas of Middle America. Among the larger and better-known trees are the giant ceiba (*Ceiba pentandra*), a sacred tree among the Maya; mahogany (*Swietenia*); the American fig (*Ficus*); "guayabo" (*Terminalia amazonia*); and maca blanca (*Vochysia*). Smaller trees in the lower stories include the valuable rubber tree (*Castilla*); a great variety of palms; and, particularly in secondary forests, the Spanish cedar (*Cedrela*).

Throughout most of the Gulf-Caribbean rain-forest average annual precipitation is over 2000 mm. (Article 6, fig. 10). Windward slopes, such as the north-facing Chiapas escarpment in southern Mexico, receives over 4000 mm., whereas the lower San Juan basin of Nicaragua is drenched by more than 5000 mm. annually, making it the wettest spot of Middle America. Even the more humid areas, however, enjoy one or two short dry periods, or at least periods of less rain, usually from February to March (verano) and again in July or August (veranillo).

The rain forest of Caribbean Central America may be considered a distinctive subregion on the basis of botany, hydrography, and alluvial landforms. Miranda (1959) has indicated that the plant assemblage of this area contains a large number of South American species, most of which find their northern limit on the eastern and southern slopes of the Sierra Maya in British Honduras. Moreover, the numerous short but voluminous rivers that descend from the highlands to the sea have built wide natural levees along their courses within the flattish coastal plain and lowland basins. Usually free from flood and composed of fertile alluvium, the natural levees have been favored sites for human settlement since ancient times. Moreover, the river fish and amphibious mammal resource has been an added attraction. Inland from the rivers exist uninhabitable backswamps and on the forest hill slopes of the interfluves leached red-yellow clay

376

soils afford second-rate farm land. The primitive farming-hunting-fishing peoples of South American affinity who penetrated the Caribbean lowland forests of Central America to eastern Honduras built villages and cultivated slash-burn fields along the natural levees. In Honduras the Aguan, Ulua, and Chamelecon river levees and in Guatemala the banks of the lower Motagua contained the renowned cacao plantings that attracted Mayan and Aztec traders. Today these same levees are occupied by large commercial banana, sugar, and abacá plantations.

A similar alluvial coastal area within the rain forest is found in the Tabasco lowlands of Mexico. The natural levees that border the Tonala, the lower Mezcalapa, and the distributaries of the Grijalva-Usumacinta delta systems were practically the only suitable sites for human settlement within the area. Northeastward the Papaloapan River in southern Veracruz is the last of the large drainage systems within the rain forest. Along its banks are found many archaeological sites that again point up the significance of the natural levee for human habitation.

A second rain-forest area that may be differentiated in terms of landforms is the Peten of northern Guatemala and the southern two-thirds of the Yucatan Peninsula. This area is characterized by its hilly limestone configuration, numerous lakes and swamps (*akalchés*) that occupy enlarged solution depressions (*bajos*), and dark rendzina or rendzina-like soils derived from the weathering of limestone. The locale of classical Maya culture, this area supports a rain forest that seems to reflect a long period of human occupation in the predominance of chicosapote (*Achras sapota*) and breadnut (*Brosimum alicastrum*) in solid stands near archaeological sites (Lundell, 1934, 1937). Moreover, Budowski (1959a) attributes the abundance of mahogany in the rain forest of Peten and Yucatan to plant succession that has occurred since the Mayan abandonment of the area in the 10th century A.D. According to Miranda (1959), the relative geologic youth and the peculiar edaphic conditions of the Yucatan Peninsula give rise to a number of endemic plant species, which further sets the area apart as a subregion within the tropical rain-forest belt.

Another distinctive subregion within the rain-forest area is the Tuxtlas volcanic massif that rises abruptly from the coastal lowland in southern Veracruz. Although the larger volcanic peaks rise to more than 1500 m., most of Los Tuxtlas is less than 1000 m. above the sea and is thus within the *tierra caliente*. Virgin rain forest still covers much of the rain-drenched windward slopes, whereas the vegetation of the drier leeward sides has been greatly modified through centuries of slash-burn cultivation. At Spanish contact the pleasant vales of the mountainous interior and the alluvial fans on the flanks of the massif appear to have been densely occupied by people of Nahuatl and Popoloca speech. The gently sloping alluvial plains that border Los Tuxtlas on the west and south are covered with scores of mound groups, one of which is the Olmec center of Tres Zapotes.

The continuous distribution of the Caribbean-Gulf rain forest is interrupted by numerous areas of tropical savanna or tropical scrub vegetation. The largest of these areas is northern Yucatan, a distinctive natural region. With decreasing rainfall (1200–500 mm.) and the porosity of increasingly younger beds of limestone northward from southern Yucatan, the forest cover becomes progressively lower and more deciduous until a xerophytic scrub is found along the northern coast. A definite seasonal distribution of rainfall prevails, April being the driest month, September the wettest. As Wagner points out in Article 7, according to Lundell the present natural vegetation of northern Yucatan has been so modified through centuries of slash-burn cultivation by the Maya Indians that the entire area

is practically one great *acahual*, or cut-over slash-burn field in fallow. At present the tropical scrub consists of a tangle of low trees and shrubs, with torchwood or copal (*Bursera*), the mimosa-like *Albizzia*, hog plum (*Spondias*), and the spiny acacia *Pithecolobium* among the dominants on thin, rocky limestone soils (*terra rossa*). On the deeper soils of the *joyas*, or shallow solution basins (dolines), large leguminous trees, such as *Enterolobium* and the American fig (*Ficus*) are common. As indicated in Article 2, northern Yucatan comprises two karstic physiographic areas: (a) near the coast the nearly level Pleistocene-Pliocene limestone plain which has no surface streams, but is pocked by steep-sided *cenotes* and funnel-shaped sink holes (*aguadas*) that often reach the shallow water table to form natural wells; and (b) south of the Sierrita de Ticul, the older (Miocene-Eocene) limestone hill area (the Puuc), where both natural wells and surface streams are lacking, as the water table lies as much as 60 m. below the surface.

One of the most curious of the savanna enclaves within the rain-forest belt of Central America is the Mosquito Coast. Parsons (1955) and Radley (1960) have recently described this grass-pine landscape, which extends from the Caratasca Lagoon in northeastern Honduras southward in a 100-km.-wide belt to the Pearl Lagoon north of Bluefields in eastern Nicaragua. As this area receives an annual rainfall of 2000–3000 mm., with a short dry season, the occurrence of the open pine (*Pinus caribaea*) savanna is attributed to edaphic (iron pan and porous gravels) conditions and possible influence through fires set by man.

Other savanna enclaves occur in the eastern Tabasco lowlands south of the Laguna de Terminos, in northern Guatemala south of Lake Peten, and at various points along the coastal plain south of Veracruz City. The tropical scrub inland from Veracruz results largely from aridity, for the area lies in the lee of the Sierra de Chicon-

377

quiaco, an eastern extension of the Mesa Central that reaches the sea north of Veracruz City.

Although in Article 7 Wagner extends the tropical rain forest into northern Veracruz state, the vegetation of this area has been so greatly modified by man that it is practically impossible to estimate the nature of the original cover. The present wild vegetation of northern Veracruz varies from savanna grassland to tropical deciduous forest. Vivó (Article 6) classifies its climate under Koeppen's Aw, with a long dry season. As such the coastal lowlands of northern Veracruz may be considered a separate subregion. As in the Caribbean lowland of Central America, the most important landforms of the Veracruz lowlands, in terms of ancient human settlement, are the river flood plains. The present natural levees and adjacent river terraces abound in sites of preconquest Totonac and Huastec cultures, and today are still favored spots for settlement and farming.

PACIFIC COASTAL LOWLANDS. On the Pacific side of Middle America the tropical lowlands constitute a large natural region that extends from Panama to northern Sinaloa, Mexico. In general, moderate annual precipitation (1000–2000 mm.), a long dry season (five to six months), and a semi- to fully deciduous forest cover distinguishes this tropical coastal region from the Gulf and Caribbean rain-forest area.

The vegetation of the Pacific lowlands reflects both the long dry season and edaphic conditions. The *monte alto*, or high semideciduous forest once covered much of the Central American Pacific lowlands, especially those areas that receive annually more than 1500 mm. of rain and have deep, moist soils. The *monte bajo*, or low deciduous forest, corresponds to areas of less rainfall, such as the coast of southwestern Mexico, and to hill slopes that have thin, rocky soils.

In the *monte bajo* the brilliant green foliage present during the rainy season contrasts with the dull grays and browns of bare trees during the height of the dry period. Only scattered clumps of palms and an occasional evergreen broadleaf tree show spots of green amidst the drabness of the deciduous growth. Possibly in response to the length of the dry period there is a concentration of gum- and tannin-yielding plants and of dyewoods. Among these are guachumil (*Pithecolobium dulce*), cuachalala (*Juliania adstringens*), copal (*Bursera*), tepehuaje (*Lysiloma acapulcensis*), and many acacias. Milky-sapped evergreens, such as the strangler fig (*Ficus*, sp.), are also abundant. On the drier southward-facing slopes exposed to the direct sun rays cacti and thorny shrubs predominate.

In contrast to the deciduous *monte bajo* on hill slopes, the moist, deep soils of the alluvial fans and river flood plains support a luxuriant growth of trees, or *monte alto*, that is much like the rain forest. On the Pacific coastal plains of Central America the *monte alto* is composed of tall trees that include the deciduous guanacaste (*Enterolobium cyclocarpum*), the giant ceiba (*Ceiba pentandra*), mahogany (*Swietenia*), Spanish cedar (*Cedrela*), the laurels *Cordia* and *Nectandra*, many kinds of palms and other components of the tropical rain forest. The Golfo Dulce area of southwestern Costa Rica and the southern part of the Azuero Peninsula of Panama receive sufficient rainfall (up to 4000 mm.) to support true tropical rain forests similar to those of the Caribbean lowlands.

On the Pacific side of Mexico and Central America man has altered the tropical deciduous and semideciduous forests to a greater degree than he has the rain forest on the Caribbean side. The tropical wet-and-dry lands of the Pacific lowlands appear to have been a favored part of the *tierra caliente* for human occupation. It was on the Pacific side of Middle America that high Mesoamerican culture reached both its poleward and equatorward limits. From the abundance of archaeological remains along the

378

coastal plains from Sinaloa to Costa Rica and from the early Spanish accounts of the native population, this area appears to have been heavily occupied on European contact; today it supports a much denser population than the rain-forest areas. Consequently, in many sections, particularly in alluvial flood plains and the more fertile hill and fan areas, the forest has been almost completely replaced by cultivated fields or pastures. Today man-made grasslands with scattered palms and broadleaf trees cover large areas of the Pacific coastal plains of Chiapas, Guatemala, El Salvador, and the lake plains of Nicaragua, giving a false impression of natural savannas.

If natural savannas, or tropical grasslands, do occur on the Pacific side of Middle America, they are comparatively small and scattered. Following Beard's thesis, Wagner in Article 7 attributes the origin of some of the Central American savanna areas to edaphic and drainage conditions (Wagner's "seasonal swamp formation series"). Examples are the savannas of southwestern Panama, the Guanacaste of northwestern Costa Rica, and the Nicaraguan lake plains. Budowski (1959b), however, suggests that such tropical grasslands may have their origin in man-made fires; he indicates the prevalence in the savanna association of pyrophytes, such as the sandpaper tree (*Curatella*), nance (*Byrsonima*), and the gourd tree (*Cresentia*), which often occur in solid or mixed stands, forming a low, open woodland.

Another significant aspect of the Pacific lowlands vegetation of Middle America is the frequent occurrence of solid stands of palms in the coastal plains and interior valleys, usually near ancient or present habitation sites. Probably the most important of these palms in terms of food and shelter value for man is the corozo (*Orbygnia*, spp.). Johannessen (1957) attributes the distribution of wild corozo groves in the Pacific lowlands from the Gulf of Fonseca in Central America to San Blas in southern Nayarit to their protection and encouragement by man.

The brackish- and fresh-water coastal swamps along the Pacific tidal zone present another distinct tropical lowland landscape that is similar in appearance but more extensive than on the Caribbean-Gulf side of Middle America. The complex of mangrove associated with lagoons and tidal channels back of barrier beaches and between old beach ridges constitutes almost another major natural region within the lowland tropical realm. From Panama northward to the Isthmus of Tehuantepec there is a discontinuous zone of tidal swamps along the Central American coast, interrupted occasionally by marine terraces and headlands. Forests composed of the red (*Rhizophora*), black (*Avicennia*), white (*Laguncularia*), and buttonwood (*Conocarpus*) mangrove trees prevail within the brackish-water portions of the swamps. The most extensive of these are found bordering the Gulf of Chiriqui in western Panama, around the Gulf of Fonseca, within the Jilquilisco Lagoon of eastern El Salvador, and almost the entire lagoonal coast from the Guatemala–El Salvador border to the Isthmus of Tehuantepec in southern Mexico. Another large area of mangrove is found in the lagoons that extend from southern Nayarit into Sinaloa along the west coast of Mexico, where the red and black species become low, scrubby growths.

Various subregions of the Pacific lowlands can be differentiated on the basis of vegetation, landforms, and soils. In Panama the rolling to flattish savannas that extend westward from the Canal Zone contrast with the rain-forested Cordillera Central to the north and the Azuero Peninsula to the south. The eastern section of the savanna area was the locale of the preconquest Cocle culture and today forms a distinct culture area known to Panamanians as "El Interior." Northwestward lies the densely forested and mountainous Golfo Dulce coast in southwestern Costa Rica; inland, bordering on the Costa Rican highlands are less humid savanna-covered structural valleys, such as El General, heavily populated in preconquest times as evidenced by the abundance of *huacas*, or graves.

From northwestern Costa Rica to the Mexican-Guatemalan border is an almost continuous natural subregion characterized by plains, low mountains, and hills of chiefly volcanic origin. This area comprises the low central section of the Central American volcanic axis and adjacent coastal plains. It includes (1) the Guanacaste region of northwestern Costa Rica, an area of former Chorotegan Indian culture that marked the southernmost extent of Mesoamerica; (2) the Nicaraguan lake lowlands and adjacent low volcanic ranges; (3) the coastal plains, interior basins, and volcanic slopes that comprise most of present El Salvador; and (4) the coastal plains and adjacent Pacific piedmont (the Boca Costa) of Guatemala, composed of alluvium eroded from the volcanic highlands to the north. The highly fertile soils derived from volcanic materials are fundamental for the dense populations that have characterized these lowlands since ancient times.

Beyond Guatemala the narrow Pacific plains continue through Chiapas to the Isthmus of Tehuantepec to form the Soconusco Coast, renowned in preconquest and early colonial times for its productive cacao groves. In southwestern Mexico from the Isthmus of Tehuantepec to Cabo Corrientes a rugged mountainous coast prevails with narrow alluvial plains between rocky headlands. The alluvial piedmont plains of Colima (500 m. elevation) and Texcacuesco (700 m.) at the southern and western foot of the Colima volcanic massif, are the only sizable interior flattish areas associated with the mountainous Pacific lowlands of southwestern Mexico. Smaller interior basins of low elevation within the region include those of Autlan (1000 m.), Tecomate (450 m.), and Purificacion (500 m.) in southwestern Jalisco.

From southern Nayarit northward into Sinaloa the coastal lowlands of western Mexico, although 30–50 km. wide, are broken by numerous N-S trending hills and low mountains, between which are elongated alluvium-filled basins. The most important landforms of this lowland are the wide natural levees and flood plains of rivers that cut transversely across the structural grain from the Sierra Madre escarpment to the sea. In pre-Spanish times, as today, the most fertile soils and densest settlement are found along these alluvial forms. Among the more important flood plains are those of the rivers of Santiago, Acaponeta, Rosario, Presidio, and Piaxtla, along the natural levees of which are found archaeological sites in abundance. Immediately eastward from the coastal lowlands the middle and upper courses of the larger rivers have cut deep canyons (*barrancas*) into the Sierra Madre escarpment; following the river bottoms and lower canyon slopes, tropical deciduous forest and scrub form narrow, winding tongues of tierra caliente landscape far into the mountain front. As indicated above, another important feature of the Pacific coast of Mexico is the extraordinary development of barrier beaches, beach ridges, and lagoons along the sea margin. Although plagued by extensive thickets of low mangrove and myriads of pestiferous insects, the lagoonal swamps afforded an abundant and dependable food supply of fish, crustaceans, mollusca, and aquatic birds that must have attracted an early population.

The northern limit of tropical lowland landscape along the Pacific mainland of Mexico approximates the Culiacan River in northern Sinaloa. This boundary corresponds roughly to the northernmost extent of high Mesoamerican culture represented ethnographically on Spanish contact by the Uto-Aztecan Tahue Indians and archaeologically by the Culiacan polychrome pottery horizons.

In terms of climate and vegetation the

mountainous Cape Region of Baja California is placed as a subregion within the Pacific tropical lowlands. Late summer and autumnal rains of tropical origin and the occasional passage of a Pacific hurricane (*chubasco*) link the Cape climatically with the mainland. More significantly, the occurrence of tropical deciduous plants of mainland affinity, such as the wild fig (*Ficus*), various tree legumes (*Albizzia, Cassia, Mimosa, Erythrina*, etc.), many vervain shrubs, spurges, and at least one palm (*Erythea*), presents a vegetational landscape similar to the scrub cover of Sinaloa (Nelson, 1921).

DRY INTERIOR BASINS. These comprise the third major tropical lowland region of Middle America. Of these the Balsas-Tepalcatepec Basin of southwestern Mexico is the largest and most typical. Portions of the Valley of Chiapas may be considered as belonging to this dry tropical landscape, and small dry valleys of northern Central America are also typical.

Scant precipitation (500–1000 mm. average annual), a long dry season, and high evaporation rates during the hot summer rainy period combine to limit the vegetation cover to a tropical thorn scrub on the prevailingly thin, rocky soils. The resin- and tannin-bearing shrubs and low trees characteristic of the Pacific lowlands are found also in the interior basins, but in the Balsas depression species of the Leguminoseae dominate. Among these are the low cascalote tree (*Caesalpinia*), guamuchil (*Pithecolobium*), huisache (*Acacia*), and mesquite (*Prosopis*); a large variety of cacti, especially those of the columnar Cereus group, grow among the thorny shrubs on rocky hill slopes. As Wagner mentions in Article 7, Miranda (1947) suggested that the present tropical scrub of the Balsas-Tepalcatepec Basin may represent a highly disturbed or degenerate condition from a former tropical deciduous forest climax. Remnants of such a forest grow today along valley bottoms, and gallery forests of Mexi-

can bald cypress (*Taxodium*), willow (*Salix*), and wild fig (*Ficus*) are found along stream courses. Undoubtedly the rugged hill slopes of the Balsas Basin have been cultivated by slash-burn methods for centuries, as evidenced by the numerous archaeological sites in areas that now appear desolate.

The Valley of Chiapas, although slightly more humid and cooler than the hot Balsas depression, also exhibits a tropical scrub vegetation that seems to have been highly disturbed by man. Much of the dissected surface of the lowland is covered with deciduous thorny shrubs and low trees, cacti, and agaves, while uncultivated plains often support savanna with pyrophytic trees (*Byrsonima* and *Curatella*) and grasses forming open woodland pasture. Annual burning since the introduction of Old World range animals in the 16th century has surely enlarged the area of savanna in the Chiapas Valley, especially along the Grijalva River and in the slightly higher *llanos* in the eastern flank of the Sierra Madre de Chiapas.

Besides the two large interior basins described above, there are many small, deep valleys and basins in northern central America which due to rain-shadow position receive relatively scant precipitation and exhibit dry tropical scrub vegetation. One of these is the middle Motagua depression in east-central Guatemala, especially around Zacapa (less than 500 mm. annual rainfall). Stuart (1954) mentions the existence of other dry rain-shadow pockets in Guatemala, such as the canyons of the upper Grijalva and the Rio Negro, and suggests that their climates might fall within Koeppen's BS or even BW categories. As their elevations fall below 1000 m., many of the subhumid interior *valles* of eastern Guatemala and central Honduras may also be considered as dry *tierra caliente* interior subregions.

TROPICAL LOWLAND FAUNA. Since many of the same animals inhabit both the Carib-

381

bean-Gulf rain forest and the Pacific deciduous forest and savannas, the fauna of the entire tropical lowland realm is considered here. The Middle American tropical lowland fauna is mainly of Neotropical origin. The assemblages exhibit certain characteristics that may be related to tropical forest ecology. Except in open woodlands and savannas, mammals are relatively few; many are arboreal, such as the monkeys, sloths, opossums, squirrels, and the raccoon-like coati, cacomistle, and kinkajou. Among the ground mammals there are few ungulates, the largest of which is the tapir, whose Middle American range is limited to the rain forest from Panama to southern Veracruz; others are the collared and white-lipped peccaries and the small brocket deer (*Mazama*). The white-tailed deer of North America has spread southward into almost every environment of Middle America, but is more abundant in the open forests and low tropical scrub of northern Yucatan and the Pacific lowlands than in the dense Caribbean rain forests. Along the stream banks large edible rodents like the agouti and spotted cavy (paca) abound; on the Gulf coast they reach their northern limit near Tampico, and on the Pacific coast, at the Isthmus of Tehuantepec; their huge South American relative, the capybara, however, has barely crossed the Colombian border into eastern Panama. Several species of cottontail rabbits (*Sylvilagus*) are common in the tropical lowlands of Mexico and the Pacific side of Central America, and many kinds of squirrels, mice, and rats abound in the deciduous forests and savannas where the ability of sunlight to reach the forest floor produces a varied ground cover of shrubs and grasses that supply food for small rodents and lagomorphs.

All such ground mammals and some of the arboreal ones are hunted by the Neotropical cats (jaguar, ocelot, margay, and jaguarundi), all four of which have spread throughout the lowlands of Middle America (except Baja California and northwestern

Sonora) and even into some parts of the southern United States. Other predators include the ubiquitous puma of North American origin, the gray fox, and the common coyote, whose southern limit is northern Central America.

Man has been the greatest predator of Middle American mammalian fauna. Particularly the deer, peccary, tapir, agouti, rabbit, and monkey have afforded food for the lowland tropical dweller for millennia. Today overhunting has made the tapir a rarity and has driven the monkeys into isolated parts of the rain forest.[1] Although overhunted, the peccary and deer population of the tropical lowlands is still abundant (Leopold, 1959). Today in Yucatan venison is often more plentiful than beef.

As food for man the game birds of the Middle American tropical lowlands are nearly as important as the mammals. The Neotropical tinamou and curassow are rain-forest birds that keep to the Caribbean and Gulf lowlands, whereas the crested guan and chachalaca inhabit both sides of Middle America. The ocellated turkey, hunted for centuries by the Maya, is still abundant in the Yucatan Peninsula. The most important of the game birds in the lowland tropics, however, are the migratory waterfowl. On the Pacific coast the main wintering grounds for millions of ducks and geese that migrate from North America along the Pacific flyway are the lagoons and Nayarit and Sinaloa (the Marismas Nacionales) in Mexico and the tidal marshes and swamps that extend from the Isthmus of

---

[1] Of the four kinds of monkeys that inhabit the eastern lowlands of Middle America the spider monkey (*Ateles*) has the northernmost range, reaching into the dense escarpment forest of southern Tamaulipas, northeastern Mexico. The howler (*Alouata*) extends northward to the Tuxtlas volcanic massif in southern Veracruz; the northern limit of the capuchin (*Cebus*) is northeastern Honduras, and that of the douroucoulis (*Aotus*) is eastern Panama. Marmosets (*Marikina*) reach northward to the San Juan River between Costa Rica and Nicaragua (G. S. Miller and Kellogg, 1955; Leopold, 1959).

Tehuantepec to the Gulf of Fonseca in Central America. These wintering grounds must have afforded a large food supply in waterfowl for preconquest Indian population along the coast. Less significant in terms of numbers of birds are the lagoons along the Gulf Coast of Mexico (Tamaulipas and northern Veracruz) and along the west coast of the Yucatan Peninsula (Leopold, 1959).

Birds of showy plumage, of which nearly 500 species are known for the lowland tropics of Middle America, have been important to Indians for ornamentation. Among these are the colorful macaws, parrots, and parakeets; the big-billed toucan; the numerous kinds of hummingbirds; and the brilliantly colored trogons. Since the parrots and their close relatives like to feed on cultivated grains, these birds are the scourge of the tropical farmer and for that reason have been greatly depleted in numbers.

Among the numerous reptilian fauna of the tropical lowlands are some dangerous forms, such as the venomous snakes. Several other forms have furnished food for man. Examples include the large iguana which ranges from the mangrove swamps to the dry interior scrub lands; another is the green marine turtle that once nested in prodigious numbers along the Caribbean beaches of southern Mexico and Central America and on the Sonoran coast bordering the Gulf of California. In the latter area the green turtle meat and eggs formed a substantial part of the ancient Seri diet.

REFERENCES

Aschmann, 1961
Baker, C. L., 1930
Baker, P. T., 1962
Beltran, 1959
Budowski, 1959a, b
Carr, 1949, 1950
Chevalier, 1952
Denevan, 1961
Fenneman, 1928
Forde, 1934
Herbertson, 1905
Jaeger, E. C., 1957
Johannessen, 1957, 1959
Kirchhoff, 1943
Koeppen, 1900
Kramer, 1957
Leopold, 1950, 1959

Lundell, 1934, 1937
MacNeish, 1958
Miller, G. S., and Kellogg, 1955
Miranda, 1959
—— and Sharp, 1950
Muller, 1939, 1947
Nelson, 1921
Parsons, J. J., 1955
Passarge, 1919
Radley, 1960
Sanders, E. M., 1921
Sauer, 1925, 1941
Sharp, 1946
Stuart, 1954a, 1956
Tamayo, 1941
Vivó, 1943
Willey, 1962

11. The Primitive Hunters

LUIS AVELEYRA ARROYO DE ANDA[1]

THE SYSTEMATIZED and coordinated approach to Early Man studies in Middle America (and specifically in Mexico) did not begin until 1945. In this year Kirk Bryan and Alberto R. V. Arellano began their investigations of the stratigraphy of the Valley of Mexico, obtaining results that led Helmut de Terra to the discovery, in 1947, of the fossil remains of Tepexpan Man in Upper Pleistocene lacustrine deposits. A number of significant discoveries since 1947 have made it possible now to recognize a well-established level of Paleo-Indian hunters of extinct fauna in the terminal Pleistocene of this region, succeeded by a phase of early gatherers and incipient cultivators who can be placed chronologically in a large part of the post-glacial period, of Lower Recent age, before the development of the Mesoamerican Preclassic cultures.

The gathering and proto-agricultural transitional cultures (about which a number of very important discoveries have been made in recent years), the geo-paleontological background of Middle American prehistory, and aspects of the corresponding physical anthropology, are described elsewhere in this *Handbook*.

PREVIOUS STUDIES

About 1860, prehistoric studies in Mexico were initiated under the auspices of the French school of prehistoric research. The enthusiasm awakened in France by the first discoveries of fossil man in western Europe was reflected in Mexico through the works of several national and foreign scientists. During the French intervention starting in 1862, the Commission Scientifique du Mexique developed important research in several fields of science. Among its personnel were some of France's most capable and experienced geologists and paleontologists,

[1] Ed. note: Dr. Pablo Martínez del Río was to have collaborated in writing this article but was prevented by prolonged ill health. He specifically wishes to state, however, that he has gone carefully over the chapter and is in complete agreement with all observations and conclusions.

The author appreciates the cooperation of the Department of Prehistory of the Instituto Nacional de Antropología, Mexico, and of the following individuals: Alberto R. V. Arellano, Juan Armenta Camacho, Mónika Bopp, Gordon F. Ekholm, Jeremiah F. Epstein, Francisco González Rul, Alex D. Krieger, José Luis Lorenzo, Richard S. MacNeish, Manuel Maldonado-Koerdell, Federico Mooser, Florencia Müller, Frederick A. Peterson, and H. Marie Wormington. Mr. Hipólito Sánchez Vera drew the illustrations and maps.

384

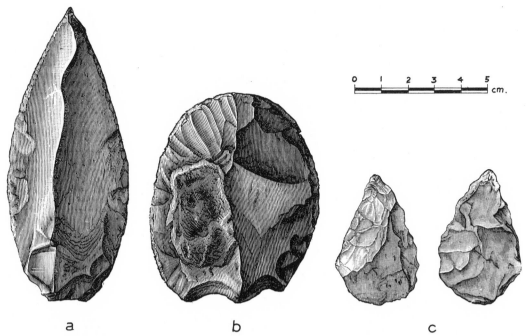

a   b   c

Fig. 1—THE FIRST PLEISTOCENE ARTIFACTS OF MEXICO, DESCRIBED IN THE PAST CENTURY

a, Cañada de Marfil, Guanajuato. *b*, Cerro de las Palmas, Tacubaya, Mexico City. *c*, Rio Juchipila, Zacatecas.

who produced some of the first evidence of the coexistence of man with extinct animals in the Upper Pleistocene of North America. The careful documentation and scientific method with which those finds were made and interpreted, nearly ten years before the celebrated investigations of Abbott in the Delaware Valley, should not be underestimated. One of the members of the Commission (Guillemin-Tarayre, 1867, pp. 406–07) expressed the following concepts:

Also in noting that at the time of the conquest, at the beginning of the 16th century, the weapons and tools of the Mexicans were made of stone, one must hasten to remark that in spite of an appearance of similarity, these objects have no identity of form or use with those used by ancient man. To judge the period of an object of this sort, one must bear in mind many considerations. The first and most important is that of the deposit, because this has absolute value. Actually, objects found in ancient alluvial deposits carry the authenticity of their origin with them, and if they are accom-

panied by the remains of extinct animals their date becomes certain.

Among other finds described by these early investigators, three are outstanding. The first was a remarkable flint blade of symmetrical lanceolate outline with fine pressure-retouching along its edges (fig. 1,*a*). The piece was found in a richly fossiliferous Quaternary deposit near the Cañada de Marfil, state of Guanajuato. The second find was a flint scraper, carefully retouched to give it a semicircular working edge (fig. 1,*b*). It was found by Eugene Boban around 1863, 8 m. deep in undisturbed Pleistocene deposits of Cerro de las Palmas, near Tacubaya in the Valley of Mexico, in sediments described as very similar to the alluvial fills of Huehuetoca and Texcoco, famous for their exceptional paleontological richness. The connection of scientists such as Boban and Doutrelaine with this discovery is of great interest. Finally, the

385

third piece of evidence offered by members of the Commission Scientifique was a small triangular flint artifact, which resembled in general form and bifacial flaking a miniature hand-axe of the Lower Middle Paleolithic of the Old World (fig. 1,c). The artifact was recovered in ancient alluvial deposits of the Juchipila River, near the village of Teul, Zacatecas (Hamy, 1878; 1884, pp. 6–9). As will be seen later, two more implements with almost identical form and in unquestionable association with fauna of Upper Pleistocene age have since been discovered in Mexico.

Soon after these pioneers, Mexican men of science became interested in the antiquity of man in their country. Among them were the geologists Antonio del Castillo and Mariano Bárcena who described, in 1884, human remains imbedded in rock from El Peñon de los Baños on the outskirts of Mexico City (Bárcena and Del Castillo, 1887; Newberry, 1887; Bárcena, 1887). Bárcena and Del Castillo maintained that the deposits in which the bones of "Peñon Man" were found were of an ancient subaquatic lacustrine formation. On the other hand, Newberry declared that the deposits were a travertine of hydrothermal origin and of recent formation. Studies carried out later in this locality have not settled this controversy (Hrdlička, 1907, pp. 32–35; Arellano, 1946a). The circumstances of this interesting find have been detailed in two publications (Maldonado-Koerdell, 1947; Aveleyra, 1950, pp. 27–32).

It should be mentioned here that the Peñon locality has yielded, very recently, additional information concerning the antiquity of man in central Mexico. In 1958 the Museo Nacional de Antropología received some strongly mineralized human bones, in fragmentary condition, which had been found by laborers building a road at El Peñon. The deposit yielding these bones was unfortunately destroyed before it could be scientifically examined. During the following summer, however, another accident-

al discovery of human remains was made while a water well was being dug in the same vicinity. On this occasion it was possible to examine the bones *in situ* and record geological conditions. The remains, those of a single individual, were not in clear anatomical relation and showed very dark coloration and considerable mineralization. Their state of preservation is excellent. The skull has extraordinarily thick walls, is pronouncedly dolichocephalic, and shows marked "primitive" features. The remains lay buried, without the possibility of later intrusion, in the lower part of a deposit, about 1.5 m. below a compact seal of overlying travertine rock, approximately 2 m. thick, and possibly the same deposit of hydrothermal origin that yielded the remains of the first Peñon Man the century before. The subtravertine deposit had two well-differentiated facies: in the upper part was a blackish-gray soil, containing little organic material and with all the characteristics of having been deposited in dry land; the lower part, which contained the bones, was a highly humitic volcanic tuff of subaquatic deposition. Evidence recovered during the exploration suggests that the bones represent a burial made at a time when the upper soil layer had been already deposited, but previous to the formation of the travertine.

The chronology of these remains presents a problem. Pottery was not found in association with the skeleton, nor were any other materials except a fragment of bird bone, taxonomically indeterminable, and the almost irrecoverable vestiges of cordage and textiles. The careful palynological sampling undertaken by paleobotanist Mónika Bopp produced profiles that clearly revealed progressive development of agricultural activity, from the bottom of the deposits upwards. In the lower part there was a high incidence of *Alnus* and *Quercus*, denoting a humid although not necessarily cold climate, and in upper strata, high values of *Pinus*, indicating a warm and drier

386

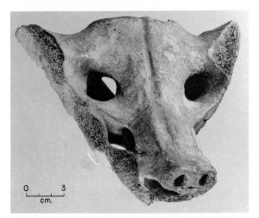

FIG. 2—FOSSIL CAMEL SACRUM WITH HU-
MAN-MADE ALTERATIONS
Found in 1870 in Upper Pleistocene deposits, Te-
quixquiac, Mexico.

phase (Bopp, 1961). Therefore, this second Peñon Man perhaps belongs to an epoch of incipient cultivators, very probably pre-ceramic, but its precise age is indetermin-able at this time.

Of the discoveries made in Mexico in the past century the "Tequixquiac bone" is probably the most famous and important. This sacrum of a fossil camelid was found in 1870, 12 m. deep in the richly fossilifer-ous Upper Pleistocene deposits of Tequix-quiac, in the northern reaches of the Valley of Mexico. Even in its natural state, the shape of this particular bone resembles the head of a carnivorous mammal like a dog or a coyote, a similarity accentuated by skillful application of certain cuts and per-forations (fig. 2). This artifact was studied in detail by Bárcena (1882) who ascribed to it Pleistocene antiquity, a judgment re-pudiated many years later by several au-thors (Plancarte y Navarrete, 1923, pp. 106–10; Cuevas, 1940, p. 2). Lost toward the end of the last century, it was redis-covered by me in 1956 in a private collec-tion. Recent examinations tend to confirm the opinion of Bárcena, in which case the Tequixquiac bone would be American pre-history's first unquestionable example of a Paleo-Indian true *art mobilier* (Aveleyra, 1964). To this we may now possibly add

the strange stone heads from Malakoff, Texas (Sellards, 1941) and the crude in-cised bone discs from Lindenmeier (Sel-lards, 1952, p. 51, fig. 23B).

Two other possible proofs of ancient man were discovered in Mexico in the last cen-tury, but in both cases the specimens have been lost for many years. The first consists of human footprints on rock in the moun-tainous region of Rincon de Guadalupe, near Amanalco de Becerra, state of Mexico. Examinations of the geological character-istics of these footprints, impressed when the rock was still plastic, suggest certain geological antiquity (J. Sánchez, 1897; León, 1921; Ordóñez, 1945; Aveleyra, 1950, pp. 33–35). Around 1890, a human infant jaw was unearthed near Xico, on the south-ern margins of Lake Texcoco. It lay in a deposit of fossiliferous sand, near a mineral-ized horse skull, *Equus excelsus* Leydi (Herrera, 1893). The discovery has addi-tional historic interest for having been the object of one of the first American applica-tions of the method of fluorine quantifica-tion for dating supposedly prehistoric bone remains. Modern fluorine tests carried out on other presumed fossil human bones from the Valley of Mexico, like Tepexpan, Chi-coloapan and others, tend to grant the jaw of Xico an antiquity comparable to them (Heizer and Cook, 1959).

INFILTRATION OF THE PALEO-INDIAN CUL-
TURES FROM NORTH AMERICA

In northern Mexico and adjoining Meso-america evidence of the penetration of Paleo-Indian hunting cultures from North America is provided by scattered findings of diagnostic Early Man projectile points. All these discoveries are from the surface and therefore lack association with a de-fined geo-paleontological context, but the typology is clear. Almost all these localities are geographically outside Mesoamerica, in northern Mexico which is linked ecological-ly and culturally with the North American Great Plains and Arid Zones.

387

Fluted Points in Mexico and Central America

In spite of their scarcity, the typological affiliation of these isolated materials south of the Rio Grande is clear, and the basic varieties into which the family of North American fluted points has been classified are well represented.

The Clovis variety, invariably associated with mammoth in the North American Llano culture postulated by Sellards (1952), occurs at two sites in northern Mexico: one (fig. 3,h) in the vicinity of the village of San Joaquin, in the central part of the peninsula of Baja California (Aschmann, 1952); the other, at Punta Blanca, near Guaymas, Sonora (Di Peso, 1955), where two good examples were found chipped from obsidian (fig. 3,b-e).

A basal fragment (fig. 3,f) of one of the celebrated Folsom points, almost always associated with fossil bison in the Great Plains, was discovered in La Mota, Samalayuca in Chihuahua, a short distance south of El Paso (Aveleyra, 1961). It represents, up to the present, the southernmost extension of the Folsom type with the exception of the specimens found at the Kincaid rock shelter, west of San Antonio, Texas (Sellards, 1952, p. 94). Also in northern Chihuahua, in the Tildio Basin not far from the Samalayuca area, finds have been reported of surface lithic material similar to that which characterizes the early gathering Cochise culture of Arizona (Brand, 1943), thus suggesting a long Paleo-Indian occupation of this region.

Three more points related to the Clovis variety are known in Mexico and Central America. The first, found in the Weicker site, near the city of Durango (Lorenzo, 1953), has a somewhat strange shape determined by a probable ancient fracture and resharpening of its distal end (fig. 3,g); the second (fig. 3,d) is supposed to have been found in Costa Rica, Central America (Swauger and Mayer-Oakes,

1952); the third was recently found on the outskirts of Guatemala City (fig. 3,a) (M. D. Coe, 1960a). A. D. Krieger, who read this article in manuscript, disagrees completely, on the basis of sound typological grounds, with the possible identification of these three points as Cumberlands as suggested by Coe (ibid.).

In addition, there are two more fragments of fluted points of the Paleo-Indian complex in Mexico, but they are difficult to classify because both lack their basal portion. In the zone which the Amistad international dam will flood, on the Rio Grande in northern Coahuila, González Rul (1959) recovered a specimen which lacks the base, part of a side, and a very small part of the tip (fig. 3,i); the general shape of this fragment and its flaking technique suggest that it is related to the Clovis type. The other fragment is a distal portion, with fluting evident on one face and doubtful on the other, found by Epstein (1961) in the Puntita Negra site, near Cadereyta, state of Nuevo Leon (fig. 3,c).

De Terra has described two projectile points to which he attributes "folsomoid affinity." One of them, found by Henry Field on the surface in Tepexpan (Field, 1948; De Terra, 1949, p. 70–71, pl. 10,E-1; 1957, p. 100), is considered part of the so-called "Tepexpan Industry" to which De Terra attributes possible preceramic antiquity, albeit on the basis of very weak stratigraphical and typological evidence. The other point, also a surface find, came from the floor at the entrance of a rock shelter in San Pedro, state of San Luis Potosi (De Terra, 1949, pp. 71, 77; 1957, p. 100). The "folsomoid affinities" of these two artifacts are wide open to argument. The Tepexpan "point" is, in fact, a small flint flake with a conchoidal scar which perhaps was mistakenly interpreted as a Folsom flute; the piece from San Pedro cave is short and thick, with a straight base and no vestiges of grooving on either of its two faces.

388

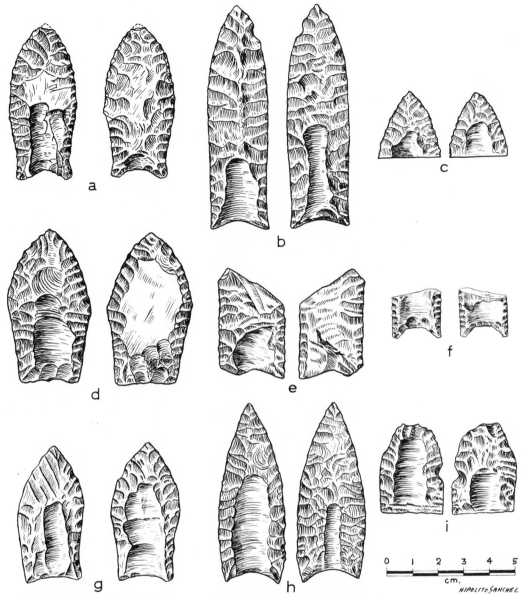

Fig. 3—FLUTED POINTS FROM MEXICO AND CENTRAL AMERICA
a, San Rafael, Guatemala. *b,e*, Cerro Guamas, near Guaymas, Sonora. *c*, Puntita Negra, near Cadereyta, Nuevo Leon. *d*, Costa Rica. *f*, La Mota, near Samalayuca, Chihuahua. *g*, Weicker site, Durango. *h*, San Joaquin, Lower California. *i*, La Chuparrosa, near Villa Acuña, Coahuila.

Other Points of Ancient Man in Mexico

In the region of the Falcon international dam, in northern Tamaulipas along the Rio Grande, an Angostura point (A. D. Krieger, personal information) and a good basal portion of a Plainview (Arguedas and Ave-leyra, 1953) (fig. 4,*e*) were found on the surface. A still more southerly range of the Plainview bison hunters is indicated by the recent discovery of four points of this type (fig. 4,*a-d*) at San Isidro site, Cadereyta, Nuevo Leon (Epstein, 1961). Another Plainview point was excavated in the level

389

corresponding to the Nogales phase of the Sierra de Tamaulipas sequence, in the cave of the same name, site Tm c 82 (MacNeish, 1958, p. 71).

The work of MacNeish in Tamaulipas revealed new types of projectile points in stratigraphic positions suggesting considerable antiquity. Most of the phases he established lie outside the chronological-cultural limits assigned to this article, for they concern cultures developed on a basis of gathering and incipient agriculture, in semi-sedentary settlements. Nevertheless, the most ancient levels in the Sierra de Tamaulipas, represented culturally by the Diablo and Lerma phases and, to a lesser extent, by the Nogales phase, reflect a mixed economy in which hunting and nomadism still played a predominant role. The Diablo phase, the earliest of all according to Mac-Neish, is still very vaguely defined on the basis of extremely scarce evidence. He gives this "phase" considerable antiquity, more than 10,000 years B.C., well within the end of the Pleistocene (MacNeish, 1958, p. 192, Table 30). The Diablo materials include crude bifacial tools such as ovoid blades and choppers worked by simple percussion, primitive pebble end scrapers, and other unifacial flake scrapers with retouching by both percussion and pressure. Mac-Neish asserts (1958, p. 152) that these materials were associated with fragments of fossil bone. A. D. Krieger (personal information) seriously questions both the stratigraphical validity and the cultural entity of this Diablo "phase." He points out that the archaeological evidence on which this stage has been postulated is scarce and insecure, and it is highly probable that the Diablo materials were nothing more than additional components of the subsequent Lerma culture of the Sierra de Tamaulipas. Krieger and geologist Glenn Evans have reported, also, that the supposed fossil bones found in that deposit and shown to them at the site were mere limestone concretions.

The subsequent Lerma phase of the Sie-

rra de Tamaulipas is much better defined archaeologically. Going back to terminal Pleistocene times, this culture is characterized by an economy based chiefly on hunting. The characteristic artifacts are laurel-leaf and lanceolate bipointed projectile points, flaked bifacially and known as Lerma points. Gathering was also practiced on this level, but subsistence depended primarily on hunting, with a nomadic settlement pattern (MacNeish, 1956, p. 143; 1958, p. 152). Association of extinct fauna with cultural materials of this phase has not been verified, in spite of the fact that there is a C14 date of 7312 ± 500 years B.C. for a hearth excavated at the Lerma level of cave Tm c 81 (MacNeish, 1958, pp. 194, 199).

In spite of the fact that the data available are still scarce, one can feel reasonably sure that Lerma points played an important role among the Paleo-Indian hunters of Mesoamerica. As we shall see later, in treating of the prehistoric discoveries in the Valley of Mexico, a point identical with these Lermas of Tamaulipas was found in association with fossil mammoth at Santa Isabel Iztapan II site, near Tepexpan (Aveleyra, 1955, 1956). Beyond the southern limit of Middle America, Lerma likenesses have been suggested in northern Venezuela (MacNeish, 1958, p. 62) in the Paleo-Indian-like culture of El Jobo (Cruxent and Rouse, 1956). These typological similarities, reinforced apparently by fairly uniform chronology, suggest correlation of these scattered finds in spite of the great distance which separates them. Nevertheless, in this particular case we must proceed with special care: from the typological as well as the technological point of view, the "Lerma" bipointed lanceolate points represent an extremely simple and primordial form, less specialized and of less diagnostic value, which easily could have been created independently in many parts of the world and at very different times.

The firm establishment of an ancient Pa-

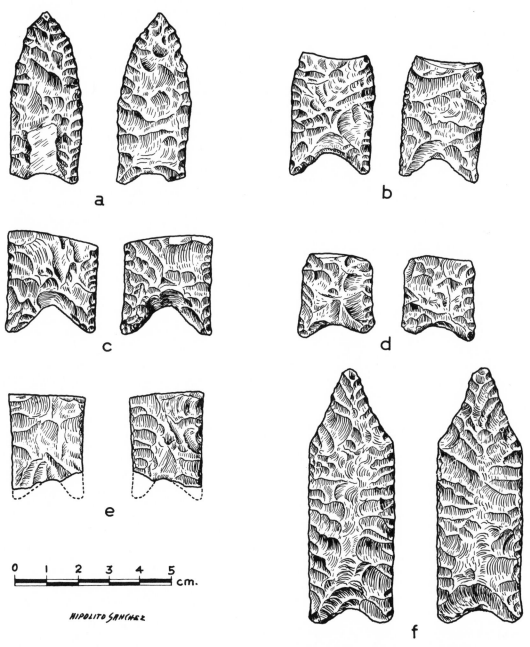

Fɪɢ. 4—OTHER PROJECTILE POINTS OF THE PALEO-INDIAN HUNTERS, MEXICO
a-d, San Isidro, near Cadereyta, Nuevo Leon. *e*, Presa Falcon, Tamaulipas. *f*, Huapalcalco, Hidalgo.

leo-Indian Lerma level, with a wide geographical range in Mesoamerica, finds additional support in the very recent results of MacNeish's excavations of the Coxcatlan and El Riego caves, near Tehuacan, Puebla. A preliminary report covering the first season's explorations (MacNeish, 1961) has

been published. It was during the second season (still unreported at the time of writing this article) that the most significant discoveries were made. The Coxcatlan cave excavations revealed a long preceramic occupation, with gathering and incipient agricultural cultures of major interest for the

391

study of the origin of cultivated plants in North America, and heretofore poorly known in Mesoamerica. The two oldest levels of occupation are of special relevance to the scope of this article. Thanks to Frederick A. Peterson, assistant director of the excavations sponsored by the Robert S. Peabody Foundation under the direction of Richard S. MacNeish, we can include here the following preliminary and still highly tentative information:

The earliest set of materials, called Ajuereado Complex, occurred only in three zones of Coxcatlan cave. Occupations were brief and two of the three were by very small groups. There was a larger proportion of bone in these levels than in others, although there was evidence that the inhabitants were also plant collectors. Lerma points are diagnostic although a Midland point occurred. Scrapers are mainly end-of-the-blade, or small snub-nosed types. . . .

The second complex, called El Riego, occurs in four zones in Coxcatlan cave as well as in the lowest zones of El Riego cave. There are a number of projectile points, including Plainview, Agate Basin, perhaps Kinney, and definitely Kent, Gary, Almagre, Abasolo, and Tortugas. Much more significant than the projectile points are scraping planes of about five types, masses of bifacial choppers, battered pebbles, skin smoothers, a flint drill, knotted nets, coiled basketry, blades and side scrapers. This horizon also produced the first mullers, bell-shaped pestles, and heavy, thick stone bowls or mortars. Vegetable materials indicate that the people were mainly plant collectors, although they knew domestic squashes [Peterson to Aveleyra, July 22, 1961].

Above these two primitive levels in Coxcatlan cave appeared the materials which combine to form the complex of the same name, with the first evidences of corn agriculture and abundant objects of a perishable nature. This Coxcatlan Complex has a C14 date of 3600 B.C. ± 250 (MacNeish, 1961, p. 24).

The oldest level (Ajuereado Complex) and, to a lesser extent, the one which follows (El Riego Complex) reveal a subsistence dependent to a great extent on hunting, and in an epoch which (in view of the C14 date for the Coxcatlan Complex) must be early post-glacial for the El Riego Complex and perhaps very late Pleistocene for the Ajuereado Complex. At this writing C14 dates for these two levels have not as yet been released.

These important excavations present unsuspected problems for Middle American Paleo-Indian archaeology. For example: (1) the association of Lerma points with Midland points (these last considered as an unfluted variety but with a typological-faunistical-geological context very similar to the Folsom points of the Great Plains) in the Ajuereado Complex of Coxcatlan cave (I have seen the supposed Midland point from Coxcatlan cave and feel that this identification must be reconsidered, an opinion shared by A. D. Krieger); (2) the association, in the El Riego level, of Plainview and Agate Basin points (until now, found *generally* in bison hunters' sites) with later points (Kent, Gary, and others), the cultural affiliations of which are with the so-called "Archaic" period of the southern United States; (3) the finding of this heterogeneous association (Plainview–Agate Basin–Kent–Gary–Abasolo) in a cultural level such as the El Riego materials reveal, that is, a phase of proto-agricultural gatherers, with squash cultivation, in which hunting had already passed to a secondary place among subsistence activities.

In concluding this section we should mention the discovery of an obsidian projectile point bearing a certain similarity to the Meserve or Dalton type (fig. 4,*f*), found in the archaeological zone of Huapalcalco, Hidalgo, Mexico (Müller, 1961), a site in which architectural structures of the Teotihuacan culture have been excavated. The identification of this point as a true Meserve is doubtful, since the convergence of its sides toward the distal end is at an angle very different from typical examples (E. M. Davis, 1953, fig. 133,*g,h*; Suhm, Krieger, and

Jelks, 1954, p. 450; Bell, 1958, p. 52). Meserve points have appeared in association with fossil bison in Nebraska, and on some occasions have been interpreted as reworked Plainview specimens. They seem to cover a very wide chronological margin (around 7000 to 2000 years B.C.), for they have been found in Archaic sites of North America. The Huapalcalco point is a puzzling discovery; it was found in a charred post-mold, sealed under ten archaeological floors, and in apparent association with a crude percussion-flaked obsidian pebble and a bison atlas vertebra (Müller, 1961). Later we shall discuss other data which suggest the presence of Early Man in Huapalcalco.

Further Evidences in the North of Mexico

Along ancient beach levels in the desiccated basin of Pleistocene Lake Chapala, in northern Lower California, Massey (1947) found worked flakes, projectile points, plano-convex scrapers, and other materials which demonstrate close typological relationships with early hunting complexes of the southern California desert, especially with the cultures of Lake Mohave, San Dieguito Playa, Gypsum Cave and Pinto Basin. Geological studies which correlate these materials with the fluctuations of the ancient lake appear to confirm their Pleistocene age (Arnold, 1957, pp. 249–80).

In Chorreras Arroyo, Tamaulipas, MacNeish discovered fossil mammoth bones associated with the remains of an ancient hearth containing abundant carbon fragments, burned bones, and other vestiges of human activity (MacNeish, n.d.*a*). Other mammoth bones associated with a crude nucleiform flint implement have been reported in Salinillas Arroyo, in the area now flooded by the Falcon dam, northern Tamaulipas (Aveleyra, 1951, pp. 42–44).

A fossil human skull was found in 1937 on the banks of Chinobampo Arroyo, 25 km. southwest of Novajoa, Sonora. It lay *in situ* in a hardened deposit, a limey clay accumulation known locally as "tierra blanca" or "caliche." In the immediate vicinity and at the same geological level were remains of a large camel (Camelops?), a complete horse skull, and the partial skeleton of a fossil wolflike carnivore. The human skull was 56 cm. below the upper limit of the Pleistocene formation, and careful excavation did not disclose evidence of intrusion or secondary deposition into the fossiliferous strata. The skull was found complete, although totally deformed by the pressure of the sediments in which it lay, and filled with hardened lime. This important discovery, which merits an exhaustive investigation of the area, was made by paleontologists and geologists of the Frick Laboratory of New York, during the course of a scientific expedition in southern Sonora. The skull is now in the American Museum of Natural History, New York; the exploration data, not yet edited, are reproduced here through the courtesy of Gordon F. Ekholm (Ekholm to Aveleyra, July 28, 1961; Blick, 1937).

PRIMITIVE HUNTERS IN THE VALLEY OF MEXICO

After the discoveries of the 19th century, reviewed in the first part of this article, the investigations concerning the geological antiquity of man in the central valley of Mexico came to a standstill which lasted for several decades. The studies of Arellano and Bryan on the stratigraphy of the sedimentary deposits which fill the basin (Arellano, 1946a; Bryan, 1946, 1948; De Terra, 1946) revived interest in this field and established a regional geological sequence, formed by a series of superimposed fossil soils. This geological column revealed, on the basis of paleo-climatological inferences, a regular alternation of humid and dry cycles represented respectively by *pedalfer* deposits and by soils of the *pedocal* category, the former composed of volcanic tuffs and alluvio-lacustrine beds of diverse types, and the latter by caliche crusts with a high content of calcium carbonates. The generalized stratigraphy, reconstructed as a result of these initial studies, can be described as follows, in order from least to greatest antiquity:

1. Noche Buena Formation, a recent humitic floor, containing the remains of archaeological cultures with pottery and agriculture, from the most ancient Preclassic (or Formative) to Aztec and later times.
2. Totolzingo Formation (pedalfer), probably of Early and Middle Recent age.
3. Barrilaco Caliche (pedocal), marking a severe dry period probably responsible for the extinction (or migration) of the Pleistocene fauna.
4. Upper Becerra Formation (pedalfer), with abundant fossils of extinct fauna of species typical of Upper and terminal Pleistocene.
5. Interformational Caliche (pedocal), absent in many localities, where it is generally replaced by an unconformity in the stratigraphy, revealing an erosive cycle of certain intensity and duration.
6. Lower Becerra Formation (pedalfer).
7. Morales Caliche (pedocal).
8. At the base, the Tacubaya Formation, almost devoid of fossils and of uncertain age.

This stratigraphic sequence was later correlated with the important lacustrine history of the region and with the series of glacial advances and retreats registered in the icecaps which permanently cover the high volcanic peaks marking the eastern limits of the basin (De Terra, 1947, 1949). All this evidence was, in its turn, correlated within the ampler and already established framework of the continental Pleistocene.

The Becerra Formation and the Barrilaco Caliche represent the periods of greatest interest for the study of the early hunting cultures in the Valley of Mexico. Both formations have been the object of special studies (Arellano, 1951a, 1953a). The first is of Upper Pleistocene age, probably contemporary in its later part with the Mankato-Valders phases of the Wisconsin glaci-

ation. The Barrilaco Caliche, on the other hand, could easily be a reflection of the climatic conditions prevailing during the Altithermal phase, defined in the Arid Southwest of the United States.

The Bryan–Arellano–De Terra interpretation of the basin's geology continues up to now to be valid in general terms, as a basic working hypothesis to which all recent discoveries have been subjected. Nevertheless, it is necessary to realize that these studies are still in their infancy in Mexico, and that later investigations will doubtless uncover new data which will modify the current ideas, perhaps radically. Palynological studies, of which there are already important contributions (Sears et al., 1955; Bopp, 1961), will play a prominent part in the re-evaluation of the evidence. Geological interpretations will have to depend increasingly on pedology, or the study of the genesis and profiles of soils, if we wish to obtain a greater knowledge of the paleoclimates and their important cultural implications. In this line of work, the contributions of Sokoloff and Lorenzo (1953), Arellano (1953a), Mooser, White and Lorenzo (1956), Lorenzo (1958a,b), González Rul and Mooser (1961), and Cornwall (1962) have paved the way for future researches.

The work of Bryan, Arellano, and De Terra culminated in the discovery of the celebrated Fossil Man of Tepexpan, embedded in the lacustrine facies of the Upper Becerra Formation (De Terra, 1949). The investigations leading to the discovery, as well as the actual discovery itself, need not be repeated here. It suffices to mention that the justly adverse criticisms of the method of excavation and recording (Black, 1949; Krieger, 1950) stimulated later studies which contributed new arguments in favor of the Pleistocene antiquity of the human remains (Arellano, 1951b).

Two other recent finds of human skeletal material have been postulated to be of preceramic antiquity in the Valley of Mexico.

In 1953, in soils removed by modern excavations at the edge of a spring near Santa Maria Astahuacan, D. F., George O'Neill discovered human bones of three strongly mineralized individuals (O'Neill, 1954). The remains were in a very confusing stratigraphical position, associated with pottery and some crude basalt artifacts. Morphologically, "primitive characteristics" have been noted in these skulls (Romano, 1955), a criterion which, needless to say, has no chronological significance when considered by itself. Romano qualifies the Astahuacan remains as "sub-fossils" (*ibid.*, p. 65) in spite of the fact that later, in the same article, he writes that the most important feature of the discovery was the advanced mineralization of the bones. Besides, on comparing the Astahuacan skulls with that of the fossil man of Tepexpan, Romano asserted (*ibid.*, pp. 67–68) that they were alike in color and in degree of "petrification" (*sic*), but that the weight of any of the Astahuacan skulls surpasses that of the Tepexpan. Therefore, it is evident that the term "sub-fossil," in this case, was not used to describe the *physical state* of the bones at the time of their discovery, but rather to give an unjustified chronological implication.

Fluorine tests on these remains revealed a minimum proportion of nitrogen (0.08) in contrast to a high content of fluorine (1.988). This would indicate for Astahuacan an even greater antiquity than that of Tepexpan Man, whose remains gave a result of 0.06 (nitrogen) and 1.540 (fluorine) (Heizer and Cook, 1959, p. 39). Such a situation is highly abnormal and tends to reveal the serious limitations which this method of dating still imposes. In conclusion, I believe that the uncertain stratigraphical situation of the Astahuacan remains and their association with ceramic fragments invalidate, unfortunately, any other consideration which tends to grant them preceramic antiquity. A similar opinion is shared by Lorenzo (1958a, pp. 67–68), who participated in the exploration and observed the remains before removal.

The second recent find of human bones, supposedly preceramic, was made early in 1955 by farmers digging a well near the village of San Vicente Chicoloapan, at Kilometer 29 on the highway between Mexico City and Texcoco. The bones were completely exhumed by the workers, who reburied them in the local graveyard with the exception of the skull, which was sent to the Museo Nacional de Antropología, where it remained unnoticed for some time among the collections of the Osteological Laboratory. Since 1954, Chicoloapan had been a locality well known for its sand pits bearing abundant remains of Pleistocene mammals. For this reason, when, in the company of the physical anthropologist Arturo Romano, I "discovered" the skull in the osteological collections of the museum, it was immediately resolved to locate the precise point of its discovery and undertake pertinent studies. The skull shows more pronounced "primitive characteristics" than the specimens from Tepexpan and Astahuacan. It lacks the basal and facial portions and is notable for its strong mineralization; it is dolichocephalic, with an index of 72.68, and has a cranial vault of medium height.

The exact location of the discovery proved to be in a water well, dug in lacustrine deposits, approximately 1.5 km. from the fossiliferous sand pits. In 1958 excavations were made by the Instituto Nacional de Antropología with the hope of obtaining some stratigraphic clue toward determining the original position of the human bones, extracted by the farmers nearly three years before. The stratigraphy revealed, in the upper levels, an alternation of sterile layers with strata yielding ceramic material of the latest archaeological horizons of the Valley of Mexico. At a depth between 2.25 and 3.76 m. was a fossil soil, devoid of pottery, and interpreted as the local equivalent of the Totolzingo Formation, of post-glacial age, possibly corresponding to the Medithermal. Toward the bottom of this deposit appeared clear vestiges of human occupation, such as hearths, calcinated stones, atypical and extraordinarily primitive utilized flakes, a distal fragment of a projectile point, and an obsidian blade with retouched edges. There were, in addition, large flat stones which could have been used as rudimentary metates, stone balls possibly used as manos or pestles, and many other materials which, since they were totally foreign to those of the ancient lacustrine bottom, must have been carried there by human agency. Below 3.76 m. appeared lacustrine silts of the Becerra Formation of Upper Pleistocene age.

The human skeleton was found, according to the farmers who uncovered it, at the base of the "Totolzingo" and with one of the large flat stones over the skull, a situation which suggests a ritual interment. It is regrettable that no opportunity presented itself for any investigator to observe the bones *in situ* before their removal by the workmen, but in spite of this it is quite probable that they were originally deposited in the preceramic level. In the first place, a fragment of human rib, which *probably* belonged to the same skeleton, was found still *in situ* at this level. In addition, the following combined secondary evidence, of varying significance, suggests post-Pleistocene, but preceramic, antiquity for Chicoloapan Man and his work: (1) the strong mineralization and primitive morphology of the skull; (2) the fluorine tests, indicative of considerable geological antiquity (Heizer and Cook, 1959, p. 39); (3) the tests by hydration of obsidian, on material recovered at the Totolzingo level of occupation, which gave dates of 5600 and 7000 years ago for two samples (Friedman and Smith, 1960, p. 513); (4) the complete absence of pottery and the primitive typology and technology revealed by the cultural remains found in this level.

The cultural stage which must be as-

396

signed to this discovery is uncertain, although it is quite possible that we have an occupation by a preceramic people with an economy still based partly on hunting but predominantly on gathering, and perhaps even with some kind of incipient cultivation. The few artifacts recovered appear to indicate this, notwithstanding their marked primitiveness and highly generalized form. Because of the nature of this deposit, no evidence of seeds or any other food remains was recovered. The pollen profiles, however, reveal a clear tendency toward a gradual increase in cultivated grasses, so that "agriculture appears well established throughout the Chicoloapan profile" (Bopp, 1961). It is possible that Chicoloapan Man and associated materials represent the first sure evidence that we have in the Valley of Mexico for the cultural phase transitional from hunters of extinct Pleistocene fauna to the ancient peasant farming and pottery-making villages of the Early Formative. De Terra (1959), on the basis of geological observations, offered a similar interpretation of this discovery in a very short note which so far is the only general published information on the matter.

Other manifestations of the activity of ancient man in the central basin of Mexico can be classed into two principal groups: artifacts found isolated in alluvial deposits or under other conditions suggestive of geological antiquity, and skeletons of fossil proboscidians in association with vestiges of human origin.

Artifacts Attributed to Early Man in the Valley of Mexico

De Terra attributed considerable geological antiquity to three groups of artifacts which he called "industries," although they lacked a well-defined typological characterization within a known chronologic lapse.

The so-called "San Juan Industry" consists of only 10 artifacts found in deposits of the Upper Becerra Formation, of an

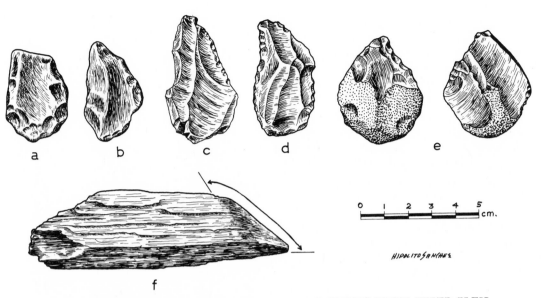

Fig. 5—ARTIFACTS OF DE TERRA'S "SAN JUAN INDUSTRY," FROM UPPER PLEIS-
TOCENE ALLUVIAL DEPOSITS
a,b,e, San Francisco Mazapa, Mexico. *c,* El Risco, Mexico. *d,f,* Tequixquiac, Mexico.

age considered similar, probably somewhat older, to that of Tepexpan Man. Six of these pieces were found in the San Francisco Mazapa area, adjacent to the archaeological site of Teotihuacan; one, in deposits of an ancient lacustrine beach at El Risco; and the remaining three in alluvial sediments in the rich fossiliferous Tequixquiac area (De Terra, 1946; 1949, pp. 65–70). Several of the 10 must be eliminated as true products of human workmanship, according to criteria already published (Aveleyra, 1950, p. 89 ff.). Others are doubtful, like the obsidian flake from El Risco (fig. 5,*c*), which is a product of simple percussion without any secondary retouching; and in the case of the "artifacts" of San Francisco Mazapa, they are so heavily waterworn that any traces of intentional flaking have been completely obliterated (fig. 5,*a,b,e*). The only two implements of undoubted human origin are both from Tequixquiac: a re-touched chalcedony flake (fig. 5,*d*) and a piece of fossil bone sharpened to a point by an intentional bevel, with obvious signs of polish and wear (fig. 5,*f*).

A second group of artifacts, called the "Tepexpan Industry" by De Terra, has even less evidence for its supposed antiquity. It consists of approximately 60 stone artifacts of all types and materials, all collected on the surface in the Tepexpan area (De Terra, 1949, pp. 70–72). This circumstance and their extremely mixed typology prohibit assigning to them either Pleistocene or even simply preceramic age (Aveleyra, 1950, pp. 94–95). Earlier in this article mention has been made of the artifact erroneously identified as a Folsom point and attributed to this "industry." Belonging to this same group is a fossil molar plate of a proboscidian, which De Terra (1949, p. 84) described as an artificial sculpture made in the form of a "human hand"; the reasons for considering this a very rash identification have been presented elsewhere (Aveleyra, 1950, pp. 92–94).

The extremely rich fossiliferous bone-beds of Upper Pleistocene age at Tequixquiac constitute one of the most promising sites for the study of Early Man in Mexico. The faunal remains comprise proboscidians, equines, bovines, camels, edentata, and felines; and there are certain indications that man was present there at an epoch which perhaps antedates the age assigned

397

to Tepexpan Man. It is very probable that through systematic excavation, Tequixquiac may very well produce the first real *industry* of the Mexican Pleistocene.

In addition to the carved sacrum mentioned earlier and the discoveries of De Terra, the Tequixquiac site has yielded other evidences of Paleo-Indian hunters. A hand-point of flint (fig. 6,*a*) was extracted from the fossiliferous gravels at the base of the Upper Becerra, which possibly substitutes, in this site, for the Interformational Caliche which marks the transition between the lower and upper levels of this Pleistocene formation (Maldonado-Koerdell and Aveleyra, 1949). The artifact has a close similarity to the one which Hamy reported in the last century, from "Quaternary alluvium" in Juchipila, Zacatecas (fig. 1,*c*), and also to one of the implements directly associated with the first mammoth of Santa Isabel Iztapan, in the Valley of Mexico (fig. 10,*f*).

Other interesting discoveries in Tequixquiac, made during numerous reconnaissances undertaken between 1951 and 1955 by the author and the field personnel of the Department of Prehistoric Research of the Instituto Nacional de Antropología, are described and illustrated for the first time in this article, in preliminary form. Only short and incidental mentions have been published previously (Aveleyra, 1954, pp. 44–45; Krieger, 1953, p. 239). These findings constitute nearly 20 implements of chipped stone and polished bone, undoubtedly manufactured by man and recovered *in situ*, in their entirety, at different points along the eroded gullies and small barrancas which cut through the Tequixquiac region. The precise stratigraphic situation of these artifacts has invariably been the bed of richly fossiliferous gravels and sands, which apparently form the base of the Upper Becerra here. The stone and bone artifacts were extracted directly from this conglomerate, in which they were imbedded and very solidly cemented. The associated fauna in-

398

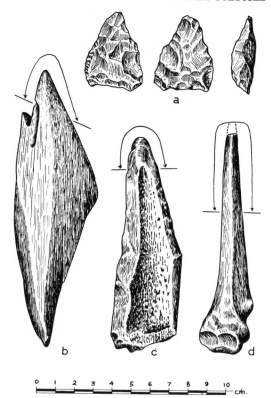

FIG. 6—UPPER PLEISTOCENE ARTIFACTS, TEQUIXQUIAC, MEXICO
Arrows indicate the extent of the worked and polished parts.

clude mammoth, mastodon, horse, bison, camel, various species of carnivores, glyptodon, ground sloth, and many other species. The richness and variety of the Tequixquiac fauna certainly do not reflect conditions proper to terminal Pleistocene times, when a dwindling fauna, on the verge of extinction, would be expected. This circumstance, together with certain stratigraphic considerations of a preliminary nature, lead me to believe that we may have in Tequixquiac one of the earliest and most important sites of the Paleo-Indian hunters in North America. Systematic archaeological excavations have not yet been attempted in this locality, although a few preliminary paleontological studies have been published (Hibbard, 1955; Maldonado-Koerdell, 1948).

The artifacts recovered at Tequixquiac,

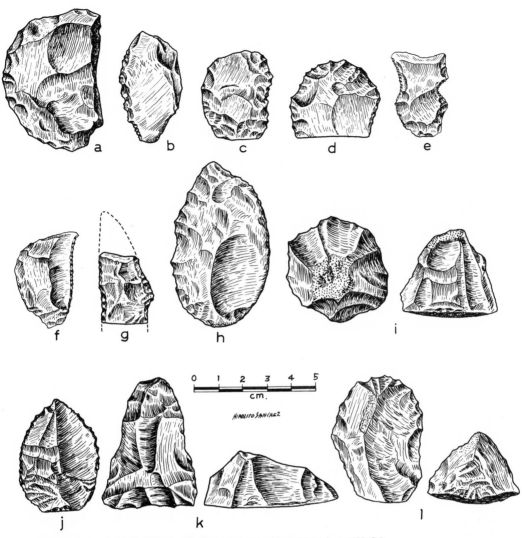

FIG. 7—UPPER PLEISTOCENE ARTIFACTS, TEQUIXQUIAC, MEXICO

as a whole, are relatively primitive and lack definite specialization or other diagnostic features which might define an industry typical of the area. The bone artifacts are principally awls, made on splinters, their tips carefully worked to a point with a circular section (fig. 6,b), or with the tip highly polished by use, in contrast to the sharp unworn edges of the rest of the piece (fig. 6,c). Another type of awl has been worked from a long mammalian bone; it is perfectly circular in section and sharp at the tip (fig. 6,d).

The stone tools include a variety of scrapers: side scrapers (fig. 7,a-c); end scrapers on thick blades (fig. 7,d,l); nucleiform scrapers (fig. 7,i) and keeled types (fig. 7,k). There are also unifacial blades with lanceolate contours, retouched by fine pressure on the edges (fig. 7,h,j) and two excellent small pieces with extremely fine marginal retouching so as to produce lateral notches and cutting edges, ending in a beaked point at the tip of the artifact (fig. 7,e,f). There is also a fragment of an asymmetrical bifacial knife (fig. 7,g) with a general shape which, curiously enough, is reminiscent of that of the well-known "Cody knives." These artifacts, together with Scottsbluff and Eden points, and as-

399

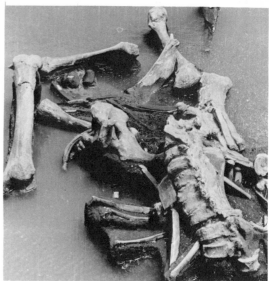

Fig. 8—MAMMOTH NO. 1 OF SANTA ISABEL IZTAPAN, MEXICO

sociated with fossil bison of the Great Plains, constitute the Cody Complex, proposed by Wormington (1957, pp. 127–37). One of the typical localities of this complex is the Horner site, near Cody, Wyoming, with a C14 date of 6920 ± 500 B.C. (Libby, 1955, p. 125).

The lithic assemblage from Tequixquiac is still far too scarce to be defined as an industry. Despite the absence of projectile points, the predominance of implements with a cutting or scraping function indicates subsistence activities derived from hunting. The presence of bone artifacts (and even bone carvings, such as the worked sacrum discovered in the last century) is important, and supports Krieger's theories about a possible primitive osseous industry accompanying the earliest lithic complexes in North America (Krieger, 1951, p. 78; 1953, p. 242). Bone artifacts identical with those of Tequixquiac have been discovered in several sites of North America, in conditions suggestive of great antiquity. For example, at the lower levels of Sandia cave (Hibben, 1941, p. 26), the Blackwater 1 site near Clovis (Sel-

lards, 1952, figs. 13, 14), and Tule Springs, Nevada (Wormington, 1957, pp. 197–98; Harrington and Simpson, 1961). Some other crude bone implements of considerable antiquity were reported in the Potter Creek Cave, California (Sinclair, 1904, fig. 7). In Friesenhahn Cave, Texas, crude flint artifacts were associated with a tubular bone implement and a rich fauna including more than 30 species, an Upper Pleistocene cultural-faunal complex possibly similar to that of Tequixquiac (Krieger to Martínez del Río, August 23, 1951; Sellards, 1952, fig. 43 and p. 94). In the Valley of Mexico other primitive bone tools have been found in fossiliferous sands in Totolzingo (De Terra, 1949, p. 86).

The primitive character of the stone and bone artifacts from Tequixquiac, their geological position at the base of the Upper Becerra, the fact that they show no signs of wear or abrasion in spite of their discovery *in situ* in alluvial gravels, and, finally, their association with a faunal complex which for its richness and variety of species is far from indicating paleo-ecological conditions favorable to approaching extinction,

400

are arguments which allow a considerable antiquity for these discoveries, prior to Tepexpan Man and the mammoth hunters of Iztapan, well within the Pleistocene and probably of a date beyond 12,000–15,000 years.

Articulated Mammoth Remains Associated with Artifacts

Almost all these discoveries have been made in the northeastern part of the basin, where particularly abundant fossil mammoth remains lay *in situ*, almost in perfect anatomical relation, in undisturbed sediments of the lacustrine bottom. The Tepexpan region has been known especially for its paleontological richness in fossil proboscidians (Reyes, 1923, 1927; Díaz Lozano, 1927).

A small obsidian flake, possibly used although without definite signs of human workmanship (fig. 12,*a*), was found by Arellano in 1945 in association with a mammoth skeleton excavated near Tepexpan (Arellano, 1946b). This was the first sure indication of the presence of ancient man in the region and, to some measure, one of the circumstances which stimulated the investigations resulting in the discovery of Tepexpan Man.

In March 1952 and in July 1954, two discoveries of mammoth bones associated with stone artifacts, in Santa Isabel Iztapan, hardly 2 km. from the site of Tepexpan Man, were minutely excavated and furnished definitive proof of the former existence of Paleo-Indian hunters in the area, besides valuable data about their subsistence, hunting methods, and butchering techniques (figs. 8, 9). The bones of both mammoths and the associated implements lay in the lacustrine facies of the Upper Becerra, in a geological position analogous to the remains of the human fossil. Both finds are too well known to repeat here the details (Aveleyra and Maldonado-Koerdell, 1952, 1953; Aveleyra, 1955, 1956, 1959; Martínez del Río, 1952a; Sellards, 1952, pp.

FIG. 9—MAMMOTH NO. 2 OF SANTA ISABEL IZTAPAN, MEXICO

42–46; Wormington, 1957, pp. 91–98). The associated artifacts reveal marked typological heterogeneity and are of diverse materials. There are obsidian side scrapers (fig. 10,*b*), one of them with lateral notches which could have served to smoothen and straighten dart foreshafts (fig. 10,*a*). Surprising is the presence of prismatic knives, identical to those which characterize the latest archaeological horizons of central Mexico (fig. 10,*c,d*), showing that this technique of stonework persisted unchanged for several millennia. There is also a flint blade with fine marginal retouching (fig. 10,*e*), a bifacial knife fragment (fig. 10,*g*), and a hand-point (fig. 10,*f*) similar to those found in Pleistocene deposits of Tequixquiac (fig. 6,*a*) and of Juchipila, Zacatecas (fig. 1,*c*). There are three distinctly different projectile points, their characteristics vaguely recalling types common among the Paleo-Indian hunters of North America. The first is a generalized point, perhaps typologically ancestral to the Scottsbluff variety of the Great Plains (fig. 10,*h*). The second, with lanceolate outline, fine marginal retouching, and an almost straight base (fig. 10,*i*) may

401

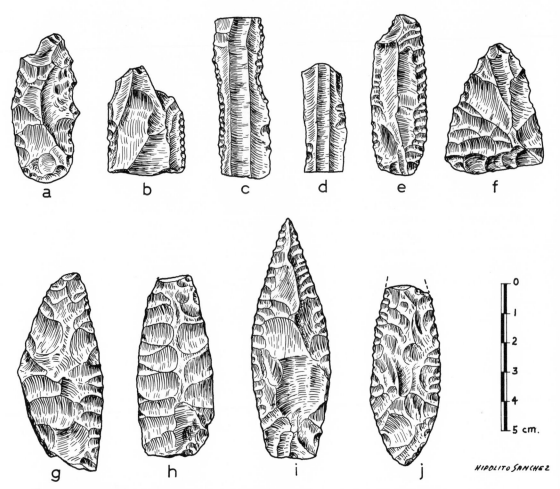

Fig. 10—ARTIFACTS ASSOCIATED WITH THE TWO MAMMOTHS OF SANTA ISABEL
IZTAPAN, MEXICO
a-f,h, Locality 1. g,i,j, Locality 2.

also be ancestral to the Angostura–Agate Basin margin of variability of these types, although it should be said that Wormington (1957, p. 95) does not consider this so. The third point is shaped like a bipointed laurel leaf, and closely resembles the Lerma points, described by MacNeish in the very lowest levels of his sequence in the Sierra de Tamaulipas and, very recently, by the same author, in the most ancient hunter's complex of Coxcatlan cave, Puebla (fig. 10,j).

Related to the dating of the Iztapan mammoths, and by extension the Tepexpan Man, are two C14 dates from wood (more than 16,000 years ago) and peat (11,003 ±

500) of the Armenta horizon of the Becerra Formation, a level which contains fossil remains characteristic of this Upper Pleistocene phase of the Valley of Mexico (Libby, 1955, p. 129). These dates, however, correspond to a locality in Ciudad de los Deportes, at the extreme southwest of the valley and at a stratigraphical level which may very well not correspond exactly to the lacustrine facies of the Becerra in which the Iztapan and Tepexpan remains were embedded. A sample taken from the sediment in which mammoth No. 1 lay, contained organic material which yielded a date of around 7000 B.C. (De Terra, 1957, p. 169). J. Laurence Kulp (personal com-

402

Fig. 11—MAMMOTHS IN MEXICO
a (*above*), Los Reyes Acozac, Mexico. b (*below*), San Bartolo Atepehuacan, D. F.

munication), who processed this sample in Lamont Laboratory of Columbia University, does not put too much reliance on it except that it probably represents a *reliable minimum age* (Kulp to Aveleyra, October 18, 1961).

Later discoveries of this type, in the Valley of Mexico, unfortunately remain for the most part unpublished by the parties who had charge of those excavations. Early in 1956 a perfectly controlled exploration by cartesian coordinates in an area of 144 sq. m. near the village of Los Reyes Acozac, disclosed remains of three mammoths and a few bones of other species (fig. 11,*a*). The marked scattering of the bones in sediments of a quiet and undisturbed deposition at a lake bottom suggests human intervention in the death and dismembering of these animals, a conjecture possibly confirmed by the discovery of two crude small flakes, one of basalt and the other obsidian, associated with these remains (fig. 12,*c,d*).

Another elephant excavated from Bercerra deposits in the suburb of San Bartolo Atepehuacan, in the northernmost part of Mexico City, in September 1957, is of major interest. The skull and the anterior part of the skeleton were unfortunately destroyed by public works before the controlled exploration (fig. 11,*b*). *In situ* with the rest of these bones was a utilized obsidian flake (fig. 12,*e*) and no less than 59 small chips of basalt and obsidian (fig. 12,*f-n*) which could not have had any practical function and which must be interpreted as waste products of stone flaking. This puzzling association with articulated remains and in deposits not removed by alluvial agencies seems to be unique, so far, in North America. The only explanation that occurs is that the mammoth hunters of Atepehuacan, after killing the animal, were busy resharpening the cutting edges of their blades and other butchering tools at the very spot of the kill. Along with the bones appeared three or four potsherds, surely intrusive from upper strata, and numerous carbon fragments of

probably human origin. These fragments yielded a C14 date of 7711 ± 400 years B.C. (sample no. M-776, University of Michigan Phoenix Memorial Project, H. R. Crane; J. B. Griffin to Martínez del Río, June 4, 1959). By the hydration of obsidian method, the chips associated with the Atepehuacan mammoth were dated at 7440 B.C. (Friedman and Smith, 1960, p. 513). Both dates seem to agree very well with the age assigned to the Santa Isabel Iztapan mammoths on the basis of geological observations and radiocarbon tests.

Through another discovery of mammoth remains between the villages of Tepexpan and Totolzingo, in March and April of 1958, the presence of man has been inferred from the fact that the dispersion of the skeleton was quite unnatural, and from certain cuts and incisions, of possible human origin, present in some bones.

ADDITIONAL DISCOVERIES IN OTHER REGIONS OF MESOAMERICA

Outside the Valley of Mexico certain evidence suggests the presence of primitive hunters in other regions of Middle America. Precise chronological-cultural characterization of these finds is difficult, owing to our limited knowledge of the geology and paleontology here. It is quite probable, nevertheless, that some of these finds may be closely related, culturally, with some in the Valley of Mexico, especially those in the central valleys (Puebla, Morelos, etc.) where, in Upper Pleistocene times, geological and ecological conditions practically identical to those of the central basin of Mexico must have prevailed.

The lake deposits of the state of Jalisco, western Mexico, have geological characteristics similar to those of the Valley of Mexico. The abundance of Upper Pleistocene mammalian fossils in the region of lakes Chapala, Zacoalco, and Sayula, and the possible presence of prehistoric beaches marking ancient levels of these lakes, make the zone of considerable potential impor-

404

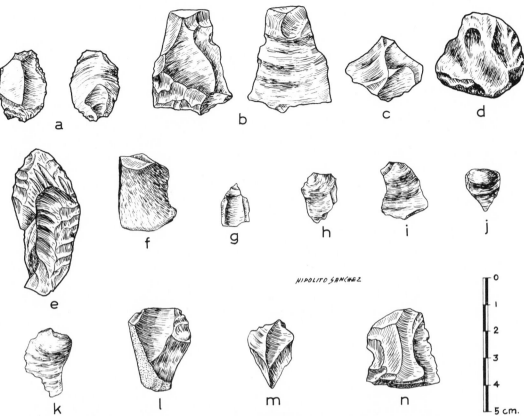

FIG. 12—CHIPPED STONE OF HUMAN WORKMANSHIP, FOUND IN ASSOCIATION
WITH FOSSIL MAMMOTH IN VARIOUS LOCALITIES IN MEXICO
a, Tepexpan, Mexico. *b*, Zacoalco, Jalisco. *c,d*, Los Reyes Acozac, Mexico. *e-n*, San Bartolo
Atepehuacan, D. F.

tance for the study of Early Man. In January 1957 a primary flake of obsidian, possibly an artifact, was found with the remains of an elephant in the vicinity of Lake Zacoalco. The find was made by Prof. Federico Solórzano Barreto and has been confirmed by the geologist Alberto R. V. Arellano, by whose courtesy the information and a drawing of the associated flake are recorded here (fig. 12,*b*).

In April 1954, in the state of Hidalgo, a short distance north of the archaeological zone of Huapalcalco, in the valley of Tulancingo, excavations in Chivo cave revealed a ceramic sequence between stucco floors. Resting on the rock floor of the cave in the deepest level, totally lacking pottery, was a large flint chopper (Müller, 1961). Additional discoveries in this site, of preceramic age, have recently been made by Cynthia Irwin. Precise information about these excavations is lacking at the time of this writing, but it seems that these ancient levels of Huapalcalco belong not to the phase of hunters of extinct fauna, but to the later and very important level of gatherers and preceramic incipient agriculturists, about whom little is yet known in Mesoamerica.

In the stratified cave of Chimalacatlan in the southern part of the state of Morelos, vague indications of human occupation have been reported at a supposedly preceramic level. The site has yielded remains of extinct fauna. The published information, however, is fragmentary and raises serious confusions and doubts on account of its deficiency (Arellano and Müller, 1948).

405

The area of the Valsequillo reservoir, south of the city of Puebla, has been known since the early part of the century as an important paleontological locality rich in Pleistocene mammals. The geological sequence in this region is more complete than in the Valley of Mexico since it includes deposits which possibly extend from Upper Pliocene to terminal Pleistocene and recent soils.

For several years, the amateur archaeologist, Juan Armenta Camacho, has scouted the Valsequillo area in search of evidences of ancient man. The results of this patient work have been the amassing of an extraordinarily rich paleontological collection, as well as certain associated materials which Armenta has tried to interpret as undoubtedly man-made.

At Cerro del Fortin, near the city of Puebla, and along the Alseseca river valley, were collected 10 "artifacts" said to be contemporaneous with extinct fauna (Armenta, 1957). The majority, however, are primary flakes and flint fragments with very doubtful intentional work, lying in alluvial deposits which contain, along with other transported material, scattered remains of Pleistocene fauna. A few of these artifacts are indeed the products of human workmanship, but their antiquity is uncertain because its original deposition in those levels is questionable.

In the same publication is described a fossil human statuette, carved in xylolite, found in an abandoned pit full of modern debris, "opened 40 years ago for mixing lime and sand for construction purposes." A Pleistocene age was proposed on the belief that the figure was first carved in natural wood, later petrified (Armenta, 1957, p. 11). However, this is a figurine of obvious Teotihuacan style, and was doubtless carved in a piece of already silicified wood, as is the case in numerous carvings belonging to different Mesoamerican cultures. Even projectile points have been found chipped in xylolite.

A more convincing discovery, in the same region, was made in 1958, in the San Pedro Zacachimalpa gorge, near the Valsequillo dam. This was a thick flint flake, almost circular in outline, with sharp edges apparently with secondary retouching along a small sector. It lay a few centimeters from an elephant tusk, in fluvial deposits (Armenta, 1959). This discovery has been the object of critical comments and observations, which serve to clarify typologic and stratigraphic ideas expressed in the original publication (Lorenzo, 1960).

In recent years Armenta has continued his investigations in the Valsequillo region, reporting new finds which remain still unpublished in scientific literature at present. Some of these discoveries have been prematurely divulged in more or less popular newspapers, magazines, and other publications, which have unfortunately stressed undue sensationalism.

The finds consist of abundant stone and bone objects, interpreted as artifacts, strongly cemented in a richly fossiliferous lime breccia which has been given the name of "Valsequillo gravels." The supposed cultural materials have been collected in four principal localities: Alseseca, Arenillas, Atepitzingo (near the village of Totimehuacan), and Tetela station, all of them in the area of the Valsequillo reservoir.

The fauna of this deposit is extraordinarily rich and varied; remains of about 30 different mammalian species, all heavily fossilized, have been recognized. The character of this faunal complex is very similar, in my opinion, to that of the Tequixquiac site in the Valley of Mexico. Not only are the same species found at both localities, but also the frequency with which one particular species appears, in relation to the others, is quite alike in both places. This consideration, together with other preliminary observations about the stratigraphy of both localities, leads me to believe that the so-called Valsequillo gravels, in which the pretended stone and bone artifacts have been recovered, must be of a very similar age of deposition, if not identical, to the one assigned to basal gravels underlying the Upper Becerra Formation at Tequixquiac and yielding, as we have seen, undoubted vestiges of human occupation.

The most diverse views have been expressed about the probable age of these Valsequillo deposits. In the early part of the century, H. F. Osborn (1905, p. 932) considered the faunal complex of Valsequillo to be Lower Pleistocene, or even Upper Pliocene. This attribution is surely much too early, and we know now that it was made in a period when little was known about the continental relations, precise stratigraphy, and even taxonomy of the mammalian faunas of North America. Paleontologist Manuel Maldonado-Koerdell, who has had an active part in the Valsequillo explorations, in collaboration with Armenta, is tentatively inclined (personal communication) to grant this fauna a pre-Wisconsin antiquity, within the Sangamon Interglacial.

A strictly preliminary geological report by Ian W. Cornwall and Federico Mooser, also unpublished, attributes the fossiliferous breccia to an age before the formation of the Clarion volcanic fracture, which gave origin to such volcanoes as the Popocatepetl, Malinche of Tlaxcala, and the Orizaba peak, among others. The Clarion fracture is supposed to have occurred toward the end of Pliocene times or during the initial Pleistocene, as least 600,000 years ago. This attribution is based on negative evidence, arguing that the Valsequillo gravels do not contain any of the typical mineralogical constituents emitted during the volcano-building period resulting from the Clarion fracture (Cornwall, 1962).

Undoubtedly a great deal of systematic research is badly needed in order to clear up these extremely opposed views. I reiterate, however, my early belief that the Valsequillo fossiliferous deposits must be of an age very close to that of the artifact-bearing gravels of Tequixquiac, within the Upper Pleistocene and not necessarily pre-Wisconsin, most probably corresponding to one of the major interstadials within Wisconsin times.

Most of the supposed stone "tools" recovered by Armenta in the Valsequillo gravels are amorphous pebbles or flakes, faceted irregularly by natural agents, such as alluvial transport. It is impossible to see, in any of these objects, the intelligent application of some kind of flint-work intended to produce a really effective working edge, useful for any particular function. On the other hand, the bone materials, interpreted as "awls," "knives," "cutting tools," "projectile points," and even "amulets" or "ornaments," are so doubtful that one must deny them, as a whole, any prehistoric significance.

A discovery from the same Valsequillo gravels, which merits separate consideration, is a fragment of fossil bone with incisions and scratches which Armenta believes depict various animals, including proboscidians and other extinct forms. The incisions were undoubtedly made by human hand, and that would suffice to prove the coexistence of man with the fossil fauna of this deposit. However, it should be said that the proposed interpretation of those designs, as figures of diverse animals, is extremely imaginative and scientifically unsupportable. Nevertheless, the fact remains that the incisions are of human origin. Other fossil bone splinters, later discovered in undoubted original position in the gravels, show additional cuts and incisions which just can not be explained away as caused by natural agencies. The association of man with Upper Pleistocene fauna at Zacachimalpa and Valsequillo seems, in this way, to be satisfactorily proved; important scientific results derived from any future research in the area must give full credit to the enthusiasm and persistence of Armenta, who, by provoking discussion and contro-

407

versy, has awakened interest in this zone.

Among other debatable discoveries are a charred mylodon bone, from the Acultzingo gorge, Veracruz (Müllerried, 1947a, p. 64), and a human skeleton which lay in apparent association with elephant bones in a clayish deposit of lacustrine origin, near the village of Tamazulapan, Oaxaca (Aveleyra, 1948).

In Central America finds have been scarce in spite of the great prehistoric potentialities of the isthmus, which must have been a necessary migration route for hunters of ancient fauna. Mention has already been made of the fluted points from Guatemala and Costa Rica; in addition, a few other discoveries, of an uncertain cultural affiliation, can be mentioned: In the valley of the Rio de la Pasion, Guatemala, was found a fossil mylodon bone, with three cuts or incisions made apparently by human hand (Shook, 1951, p. 93). At Copan, Honduras, Longyear (1948) excavated a sub-pottery deposit with charred bones, primary flakes and other remains separated by sterile levels from upper strata containing Maya ceramics of the Preclassic and Early Classic periods. El Cauce and other localities on the shores of Lake Managua, Nicaragua, have yielded traces of human footprints, impressed in hardened volcanic mud, together with tracks of several animals, among them two bison, underlying Preclassic pottery of the region (Williams, 1952b).

FINAL COMMENTS

Present information on the cultures of the Middle American Paleo-Indian is still scarce and scattered. Some provisional speculations can nevertheless be advanced.

The latest discoveries suggest the infiltration, in northern Mexico and Mesoamerica, of the two Paleo-Indian traditions recognized by Wormington (1957, p. 21) in the central and southern part of North America: the Paleo-eastern tradition of hunters of extinct fauna, and the Paleo-

western tradition, in some cases of similar age but defined principally by gathering subsistence. It is quite probable that both traditions may be partly fused in Mexico, a situation which could perhaps explain the typological heterogeneity observed in some of the sites of primitive man there.

A. D. Krieger, after reading this section, has remarked that it is highly inconvenient to discuss the Mexican sites in these terms, and to attempt to assign them to any of the early traditions proposed by Wormington. He states that even in the United States it is impossible in practice to work with that idea as a basis for a general classification of early cultures in North America. The Paleo-eastern tradition, for example, is supposed to be found in sites as far west as the Great Basin and Southwest; the Paleo-western, on the other hand, extends as far east as the Ohio valley. Also, Krieger says, the time factors appear to be all mixed up, partly due to the attempts to classify each site as "eastern" or "western" on the basis of economic life. Krieger further believes that, with a good number of sites, we are just not in position to say what the economy really was, because we seldom have camp or living sites, but only a few artifacts and fossil bones. Finally, he points out that it would be misleading to say that both traditions, Paleo-eastern and Paleo-western, appear to have partly fused in Mexico, because these traditions are "partly fused" all over the United States, too (Krieger to Aveleyra, October 8, 1961).

I acknowledge the fundamental truth behind Krieger's observations and recognize that, especially in Mexico, it is perhaps premature to make generalizations of this kind. However, I am of the opinion that until a better general scheme for the classification of the Paleo-Indian cultures of North America is advanced, Wormington's views represent a valuable attempt toward a global approach which might help to understand many obscure situations posed by current research. The need for a broad outlook of

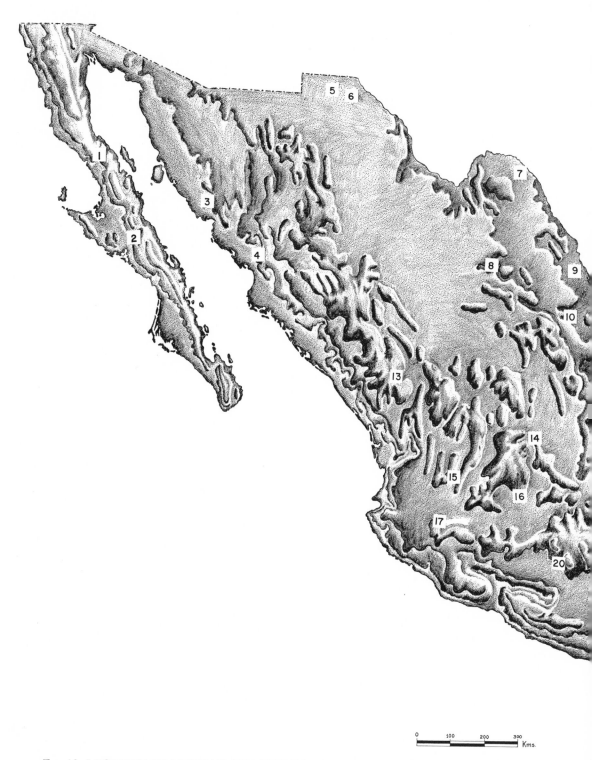

FIG. 13—LOCATION OF MEXICAN AND CENTRAL AMERICAN PREHISTORIC SITES DESCRIBED IN TEXT

1, Lago Chapala, Baja California. 2, San Joaquin, Baja California. 3, Cerro Guamas, Guaymas, Sonora. 4, Arroyo Chinobampo, Navojoa, Sonora. 5, Cuenca Tildio, Chihuahua. 6, La Mota, Samalayuca, Chihuahua. 7, La Chuparrosa, Villa Acuña, Coahuila. 8, Cueva Espantosa, Coahuila. 9, Presa Falcon, Tamaulipas. 10, San Isidro and Puntita Negra, Nuevo Leon. 11, Arroyo Chorreras, Tamaulipas. 12, Sierra de Tamaulipas. 13, Sitio Weicker, Durango. 14, Cueva San Pedro, San Luis Potosi. 15, Rio Juchipila, Zacatecas. 16, Cañada de Marfil, Guana 17, Lago de Zacoalco, Jalisco. 18, Huapalcalco, Hi 19, Chignahuapan, Puebla. 20, Amanalco de Be Mexico. 21, Valsequillo, Puebla. 22, Cueva de Ch catlan, Morelos. 23, Barranca de Acultzingo, Ver 24, Cueva de Coxcatlan, Puebla. 25, Rio de la I Guatemala. 26, San Rafael, Guatemala. 27, Copan, duras.

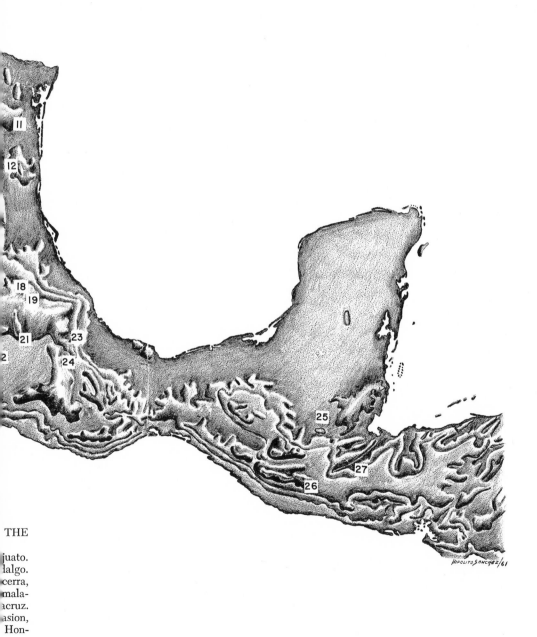

11

12

18

19

21 23

2 24

25

27

26

HIPOLITO SANCHEZ/61

THE

juato.
lalgo.
cerra,
mala-
acruz.
asion,
Hon-

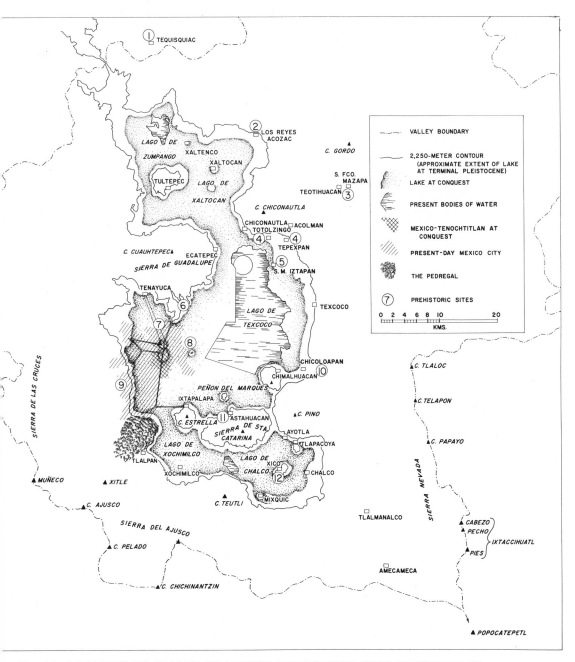

FIG. 14—LOCATION OF VALLEY OF MEXICO PREHISTORIC SITES DESCRIBED IN THE TEXT

1, Tequixquiac. 2, Los Reyes Acozac. 3, San Francisco Mazapa. 4, Tepexpan-Totolzingo. 5, Santa Isabel Iztapan. 6, El Risco. 7, San Bartolo Atepehuacan. 8, El Peñon de los Baños. 9, Cerro de las Palmas, Tacubaya. 10, San Vicente Chicoloapan. 11, Santa Maria Astahuacan. 12, Xico.

the many problems involved in the study of Early Man in the Americas has been acutely felt for some time by all students in this field, and Wormington's classification might very well be the starting point for this welcome change of attitude.

In Mexico and Central America, sites corresponding to what Wormington would call Paleo-eastern tradition are represented by a series of isolated finds, yielding fluted Clovis and Folsom projectile points and other varieties generally associated with extinct fauna, such as Angostura, Scottsbluff, Plainview, and possibly others. Aside from these artifacts, almost entirely recovered at the surface, the mammoths associated with evidences of human activity in Iztapan, Los Reyes Acozac, Atepehuacan, Zacoalco, and Zacachimalpa, and several other discoveries, like Tepexpan and Tequixquiac, are good examples of the presence of early hunting cultures in Middle America. The Tequixquiac and Valsequillo finds are of special importance; systematic excavations are badly needed at both sites, but at present it is perhaps permissible to infer that these localities could easily represent the earliest sites of ancient man so far recorded south of the Rio Grande, with a crude lithic and bone industry, possibly lacking projectile points, and, in short, with a cultural-faunal context similar to that of very early sites such as Tule Springs, Nevada.

The fluted points recovered so far in Mexico and Central America lie within the typological range of the Clovis family, with the unique exception of the Folsom point of Samalayuca, Chihuahua. In spite of the scarcity of these finds, it could perhaps be inferred that the mammoth hunters of the Llano Complex, invariably associated with Clovis points, had a wider distribution in these latitudes than the Folsom bison hunters. In North America the Folsom culture seems to have had circumscribed development, geographically, in the region of the Great Plains.

M. D. Coe (1960a) has indicated that the three fluted points found so far in the southernmost latitudes of Middle America (at Rancho Weicker, Durango; San Rafael, Guatemala; and in Costa Rica) are related to the Clovis varieties of eastern North America known as Cumberland points. This would indicate that part of the primitive Paleo-Indian population of Mesoamerica came from eastern United States, crossing the Rio Grande into the territory which today is Tamaulipas, Nuevo Leon, and Coahuila. However, A. D. Krieger (personal communication) does not think that those three points should be classified as Cumberlands, because of a number of valid typological reasons. Besides, short, thick, and slightly "fishtailed" Clovis fluted points, like the specimens from Durango, Guatemala, and Costa Rica, are frequent not only in eastern North America but also in the western part of the continent.

Bipointed leaf-shaped projectile points, known as Lerma by some authors, appear to have played an important role among the Paleo-Indian hunters of Middle America. They have been found under conditions indicating Pleistocene antiquity at three localities: the most ancient levels of the caves of the Sierra de Tamaulipas and Coxcatlan cave, southern Puebla, and directly associated with mammoth in Santa Isabel Iztapan, in the Valley of Mexico. The antiquity of the bipointed laureliform Lerma points in Mesoamerica may very well be even greater than in the periphery of this great cultural area. It is possible that these points may constitute an original development from the Paleo-Indian hunters of central Mexico, from where influences could have been sent to the north (Tamaulipas and southern Texas), and to the south (El Jobo, Venezuela). The results of the C14 tests on materials of the Lerma level of the Coxcatlan caves, as yet unavailable, could lend some support to this hypothesis. Nevertheless, it should be noted that the deposits in which the Santa Isabel Iztapan mammoths lay—one of them in clear association with a Lerma point—have given a C14 date of 9000 years ago. A good confirmation of the age of the mammoth hunters in the Valley of Mexico, has been provided by the San Bartolo Atepehuacan find, yielding a C14 date of 9670 ± 400 years ago. These dates seem to indicate that the extinction of the mammalian Pleistocene fauna in central Mexico was not as late as some authors have believed, and that it very well could have occurred contemporaneously with the disappearance of the great mammals from the North American Great Plains.

On the other hand, the possibility must be considered that the bipointed leaf-shaped points, associated with mammoth in central Mexico, may represent not precisely an original development there, but a cultural trait which persisted with great tenacity, derived from some cultures of the Siberian Upper Paleolithic in which these forms appear to have played an important role. Wormington, especially, has called attention to these east Asiatic developments, and has even suggested the possibility that the bipointed, leaf-shaped, bifacially flaked points may constitute the typological basis of an evolutionary sequence which would be followed by Sandia points, fluted Sandias, Clovis points, and Folsom points, in the order given (Wormington, 1962). In relation to this it should be remembered that, during the last years, Lerma-like points have won general acceptance as probable components of a widespread lithic complex of considerable geological antiquity, which apparently covers the whole continent, from the Pacific Northwest (Butler's "Old Cordilleran Culture"), through the southern Texas and Tamaulipas finds, Iztapan, Coxcatlan, El Jobo, and all the way down to Argentina (Rex González's Ayampitin Complex). I reiterate, however, that all these speculations must be taken with the greatest caution, because of reasons already pointed out in this article: Lerma-like points represent such a generalized, elementary, and scarcely diagnostic form that they are to be expected to be present in many different lithic assemblages and in almost any chronological situation.

The mammoths of the Valley of Mexico were also associated with points whose form seems to indicate a generalized prototype typologically ancestral to the Scottsbluff and Angostura varieties of the Great Plains, where they appear associated almost always with fossil bison, and at a later date about 5000 B.C. In consequence, the surprising possibility presents itself that these points could have had an original diffusion from a much more southerly latitude than it has been formerly believed.

Sites which could be identified with Wormington's Paleo-western tradition, represented in the United States by several localities of considerable antiquity (for example, Fort Rock Cave, Danger Cave, Pinto Basin, Bat Cave, Ventana Cave, and Cochise), have also been found in northern Mexico, as indicated by the discoveries of the Tildio Basin, Chihuahua, and of the Peralta Complex, Sonora (Fay, 1959), both related with the Cochise culture, in addition to the materials described by Massey and Arnold in Lower California.

Other discoveries attesting the southern extension of the primitive gatherers of this tradition, are from the Cueva Espantosa, Coahuila (W. W. Taylor, 1956); the majority of the ancient preceramic levels established by MacNeish in Tamaulipas; the Cueva del Chivo in Huapalcalco, Hidalgo; the sites of Chicoloapan and possibly El Peñon III, in the Valley of Mexico; the Coxcatlan Complex in southern Puebla; the Yuzanu site in Yanhuitlan, Oaxaca (Lorenzo, 1958c); and the Santa Marta rock shelter, near Ocozocuautla, Chiapas (MacNeish, 1961, p. 6).

To these groups of the Paleo-western

411

tradition must be attributed the creation and definitive implantation of the sedentary-agricultural-ceramic pattern, immediate source of the high civilizations of Middle America.

REFERENCES

Arellano, 1946a, 1946b, 1951a, 1951b, 1953a
—— and Müller, 1948
Arguedas and Aveleyra, 1953
Armenta, 1957, 1959
Arnold, 1957
Aschmann, 1952
Aveleyra, 1948, 1950, 1951, 1954, 1955, 1956, 1959, 1961, 1962, 1964
—— and Maldonado-Koerdell, 1952, 1953
Bárcena, 1882, 1887
—— and del Castillo, 1887
Bell, 1958
Black, 1949
Blick, 1937
Bopp, 1961
Brand, 1943
Bryan, 1946, 1948
Coè, M. D., 1960a
Cornwall, 1962
Cruxent and Rouse, 1956
Cuevas, 1940
Davis, E. M., 1953
De Terra, 1946, 1947, 1949, 1957, 1959
Díaz Lozano, 1927
Di Peso, 1955
Epstein, 1961
Fay, 1959
Field, 1948
Friedman and Smith, 1960
González Rul, 1959
—— and Mooser, 1961
Guillemin-Tarayre, 1867
Hamy, 1878, 1884
Harrington and Simpson, 1961
Heizer and Cook, 1959

Herrera, 1893
Hibbard, 1955
Hibben, 1941
Hrdlička, 1907
Krieger, 1950, 1951, 1953
León, 1921
Libby, 1955
Longyear, 1948
Lorenzo, 1953, 1958a, 1958b, 1958c, 1960
MacNeish, n.d. a, 1956, 1958, 1961
Maldonado-Koerdell, 1947, 1948
—— and Aveleyra, 1949
Martínez del Río, 1952a, 1952b
Massey, 1947
Mooser, White, and Lorenzo, 1956
Müller, 1961
Müllerried, 1947a
Newberry, 1887
O'Neill, 1954
Ordóñez, 1945
Osborn, 1905
Plancarte y Navarrete, 1923
Reyes, 1923, 1927
Romano, 1955
Sánchez, J., 1897
Sears et al., 1955
Sellards, 1941, 1952
Shook, 1951
Sinclair, 1904
Sokoloff and Lorenzo, 1953
Suhm, Krieger, and Jelks, 1954
Swauger and Mayer-Oakes, 1952
Taylor, W. W., 1956
Williams, 1952b
Wormington, 1957, 1962

12. The Food-gathering and Incipient Agriculture Stage of Prehistoric Middle America

RICHARD S. MAC NEISH

Our present knowledge of the food-gathering and incipient agriculture stage of prehistoric Middle America is based on only scant artifacts and bones and vegetal material from a few small excavations or tests, and on little more from the surface of sites that might possibly belong to this horizon. This evidence appears unconnected with the even sparser material from the so-called "Hunting or Paleo-Indian stage" (see Aveleyra, Article 11), except in the Tehuacan valley of Puebla (MacNeish, 1961). There the earliest Ajuereado phase, which is the largest well-excavated assemblage of "early man" artifacts in Mesoamerica, gradually developed into the El Riego phase, an excellent example of the "Incipient Agriculture Stage." Good links between the latter stage and the stage having early villages with full-time agriculture and pottery have been found so far only in the Tehuacan region (MacNeish, 1961; Willey, 1960a, pp. 6–10). The late ceramic and early ceramic phases of Tehuacan, with their abundant artifact remains, had not been thoroughly studied at the time of writing.

What little we have from most of central Mesoamerica and from the great bulk of unstudied material recently unearthed in southern Puebla, however, seems to be related to that from southern Tamaulipas, which has been thoroughly analyzed (MacNeish, 1958). Thus, for the present, one is forced to gauge the possible situation in the more nuclear southern regions by that from the northeastern peripheries.

In terms of absolute dates for this food-gathering and incipient agriculture stage, analysis of carbon-14 from stratified sites in southwestern Tamaulipas has yielded a long sequence (agreeing in main with the stratigraphy). These dates are: 6590 B.C. ± 450 (M500), 6250 B.C. ± 450 (M498), 3700 B.C. ± 350 (M497), 3280 B.C. ± 350 (M502), 2780 B.C. ± 300 (M504), 2630 B.C. ± 350 (M503), 1997 B.C. ± 334 (Kaplan and MacNeish, 1960, Table 1). There

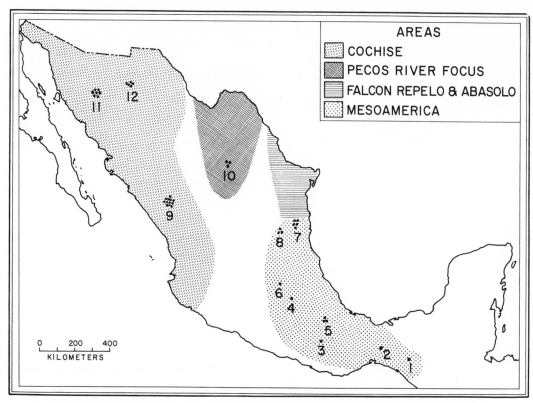

Fig. 1—SITES AND TENTATIVE CULTURE AREAS OF THE FOOD-GATHERING AND
INCIPIENT AGRICULTURE STAGE IN MEXICO
1, Comitan Cave (after J. L. Lorenzo). 2, Santa Marta Cave (after MacNeish and Petersen).
3, Yuzanu site (after Lorenzo). 4, Chicoloapan (after DeTerra). 5, Southern Puebla Caves
(after MacNeish). 6, Hidalgo Cave (after Irwin). 7, Sierra de Tamaulipas Caves (after Mac-
Neish). 8, Southwest Tamaulipas Caves (after MacNeish). 9, Central Durango sites (after
Kelley). 10, Coahuila Caves (after Taylor). 11, Peralta sites (after Fay). 12, Chihuahua Caves
(after Lister).

is also a date of 1700 B.C. ± 250 (M505a)
(*ibid.*) on a mixed sample from the latest
preceramic and earliest ceramic remains,
which may be considered an end date for
this horizon. In southern Tamaulipas wood
from the La Perra horizon has been dated
as 2495 B.C. ± 280 (C687) (Libby, 1952).
From southern Puebla charcoal associated
with a series of superimposed floors in a
number of caves has yielded a series of
dates which range from about 6700 to
about 2300 B.C. These floors contain artifacts of the El Riego, Coxcatlan, and Abejas
phases as well as evidence of the beginnings of corn domestication. In northern Oa-

xaca near Yanhuitlan two samples of charcoal from Yuzanu yielded dates of 2094 B.C.
± 200 (W497) and 1984 B.C. ± 200
(W480) (Lorenzo, 1958c). From near Ocozocautla, Chiapas, charcoal from cave floors
2 and 3 date the Santa Marta complex at
6780 B.C. ± 400 (M980) and 5360 B.C. ±
300 (M979) (MacNeish and Peterson,
1962). In the Valley of Mexico charcoal
from Tlatilco which was reputedly associated with the so-called "Chalco culture" gave
a date of 4439 B.C. ± 300 (C198) (Libby,
1952).

Slightly less absolute are the dates obtained from measuring the thickness of

obsidian rind. At Chicoloapan in the Valley of Mexico and at Coxcatlan Cave in southern Puebla pieces of obsidian associated with preceramic remains were evidently chipped during the fourth millennium B.C.

Floral, faunal, and petrological evidence shows the Nogales, La Perra (MacNeish, 1958, pp. 193–99), and Ocampo (MacNeish, n.d.*b*) cultures of southern Tamaulipas to have existed during a long dry period. Soil and fauna analysis of lower preceramic remains at Santa Marta, Chiapas, also indicate occupation during a dry warm climate (MacNeish and Peterson, 1962). Soil and pollen data from Chicoloapan (De Terra, 1959, p. 563), supposedly associated with the so-called Chalco complex (De Terra, 1949, pp. 51–53) of the Valley of Mexico, place it in a dry warm period. A number of specialists (MacNeish, 1958, pp. 193–99) have suggested the dry period of these cultures as being the Postglacial Optimum from 4500 to 7500 years ago (Clisby and Sears, 1955).

The absolute and relative dates indicate that cultures of this stage existed roughly from 7000 to 1500 B.C. Allowing for the appearance of villages earlier in some areas than in others and the existence in certain regions of fauna and flora that may have caused the shifts from hunting to food gathering to take place earlier or later, we find that a more realistic period for the food-gathering and incipient agriculture stage of Middle America would be from 6000 B.C. ± 1000 years to 1500 B.C. ± 500 years.

Sites belonging to this stage and period occur in Chiapas near Ocozocautla and Comitan. The former, called the Santa Marta rock shelter, was tested by an L-shaped trench 8 by 8 m. long, 3–5 m. wide, and 1–3 m. deep, which uncovered 107 preceramic artifacts in the lower five zones under early Formative and Classic strata. A year after this was undertaken by the New World Archaeological Foundation in 1959 (MacNeish and Peterson, 1962), José

Luís Lorenzo of the Instituto Nacional de Antropología e Historia tested a promising rock shelter near Comitan, where, although few preceramic artifacts occurred *in situ*, his surface collection indicates that the site has great potential and may contain a different assemblage than Santa Marta (Lorenzo, personal communication). In 1955 the same archaeologist dug the Yuzanu open site near Yanhuitlan, Oaxaca, where he carefully unearthed seven or eight artifacts and 58 flint chips from a well-defined deeply buried stratum that has become exposed in the bank of an arroyo (Lorenzo, 1958). Slightly farther north in southernmost Puebla the Tehuacan Archaeological-Botanical Project of the Robert S. Peabody Foundation for Archaeology has thoroughly excavated seven rock shelters (MacNeish, 1961), tested 12 more, and discovered 393 sites. Preliminary analysis of about 10,000 artifacts recovered early in the first season has revealed an unbroken sequence of culture from the "Paleo-Indian stage" to the Spanish conquest. Three cultural phases— El Riego, Coxcatlan, and Abejas—are germane to the "Incipient Agriculture stage."

In the Valley of Mexico, Helmut de Terra, in cooperation with the Instituto Nacional de Antropología e Historia, in 1957 excavated hearths and burials at Chicoloapan (De Terra, 1959), where he found about a dozen artifacts as well as skeletal material. He had earlier made surface collections from a number of sites in the Valley of Mexico which he classified as belonging to the Chalco and Tepexpan industries (De Terra, 1949). At the time this article was written, C. Irwin, a student at Harvard University, was surveying open sites, rock shelters, and caves from the Valley of Mexico, through the states of Hidalgo and Queretaro to San Luis Potosi. Her findings indicate that she had uncovered tools which seem to be of this stage.

Besides these investigations within Mesoamerica proper are those in the peripheral region of southeastern Tamaulipas (Mac-

Neish, 1958), where two archaeological zones have received preliminary study: one near the Canyon Infiernillo north of Ocampo in the Sierra Madre, the other in the Sierra de Tamaulipas. Our best information comes from three stratified caves in the Sierra Madre, where the earliest remains belong to the Infiernillo phase (5000–7000 B.C.), represented by two pure components (with abundant vegetal material and some artifacts), two probable components, and a possible component. These are overlaid by six components of the Ocampo phase (4000–3200 B.C.), three of which have many artifacts and foodstuffs. There are also surface collections from three possible components of the Ocampo phase. The Flacco phase (2200–1800 B.C.) is represented by two pure components and a number of possible ones; the Guerra phase (1800–1400 B.C.) is represented by two abundantly documented components and three probable or possible ones. In the Sierra de Tamaulipas we have three phases: Nogales (5000–3000 B.C.), La Perra (3000–2000 B.C.), and Almagre (2200–1800 B.C.). Only two components of La Perra had preserved vegetal remains and artifacts, though six other possible components occurred. Nogales had one well-represented component, though 17 others may belong to the phase; Almagre had two pure components and nine probable or possible ones.

Farther north in Mexico, and seemingly more distantly related, are a series of other sites, components, or phases that seem to be of the same period. In northern Tamaulipas and southern Texas are the poorly defined Repelo, Abasolo (MacNeish, 1958), and Falcon complexes (Suhm, Krieger, and Jelks, 1954, pp. 136–43). In Coahuila, Taylor has mentioned two complexes, Cienegas and Coahuila, as being of this period, but they have not been defined in publications. Adjacent to these materials, and possibly connected, are those of Pecos River focus

of the Big Bend region in Mexico and Texas (Kelley, Campbell, and Lehmer, 1940, pp. 22–27). In southern Durango are about "a dozen small camp sites with a Desert Culture–Archaic assemblage of traits" (Kelley to MacNeish, Apr. 24, 1959), one of the better-represented sites being Los Caracoles. J. C. Kelley, who has collected from the Laguna Medina site in the same area, made similar finds in rock shelters in the great barrancas cutting the Sierra Madre Occidental leading to the Sinaloa coast. In Sonora, G. E. Fay unearthed Cochise-like remains at seven sites which he calls the Peralta culture (Fay, 1955); Lister's excavation of caves in Chihuahua produced vegetal remains (including corn) with preceramic artifacts (Mangelsdorf and Lister, 1956, pp. 151–77). Archaeological surveys near the Mexico–New Mexico or Arizona border have revealed further Cochise-like materials. Finally, Massey has uncovered materials of this period in Lower California.

Although no thorough analysis has been made of this combined scant material, which is representative of the incipient agriculture stage of Middle America, the examples given in the previous paragraphs do share a number of Desert Culture-like traits: mullers and milling stones, choppers, large scrapers or scraping planes, Gary or Almagre points, and evidence of small temporary or seasonal camps of incipient agriculturists and/or food gatherers. Because of limited data it is difficult to subdivide Mesoamerica into archaeological zones but there are hints that some traits are confined to certain geographical or ecological zones.

From southern Tamaulipas to Chiapas there is one region characterized by triangular gouges, blades struck from polyhedral cores, Abasolo and/or Nogales and/or Tortugas points, Almagre points, disc scrapers, crude scraper planes, large mortars, bell-shaped pestles, mullers and pebble manos, gourd, pepper, corn and/or bean and/or

416

pumpkin and/or squash. All sites point to the existence of small bands of incipient agriculturists and food gatherers who dwelt in temporary or seasonal settlements.

In northwest Mexico (and perhaps lower California Cochise-like assemblages occur that have: Almagre and Langtry stemmed points, large and small side- and corner-notched Cochise points, choppers and scraping planes made from cobbles, relatively specialized mullers and milling stones, a similar settlement pattern, with incipient agriculture of sunflower, corn, pumpkin and, perhaps in the later stages, squash, bean, and gourd. The Big Bend–Coahuila area represents still another zone characterized by Shumla, Langtry and Almagre points, fewer choppers and scraping planes, milling stones and mullers, a similar settlement pattern but mainly a subsistence

TABLE 1—COMPLEXES OR PHASES OF THE INCIPIENT AGRICULTURE AND FOOD-GATHERING STAGE AND THEIR RELATIONS IN TIME AND SPACE

Dates	Northwest Chiapas: Santa Marta Excavations	Northern Oaxaca Sequence	Southern Puebla: Ajuereado Sequence	Valley of Mexico Sequence	Southwest Tamaulipas: 3 Infiernillo Excavations	Southeast Tamaulipas: 5 C. Diablo Excavations	
		Monte Alban I				Laguna	
1000 B.C.	Chiapa de Corzo I			El Arbolillo	Mesa de Guaje		← First Pottery
First Pottery →					Guerra		↑
2000 B.C.			Purron		Flacco	Almagre	
		Yuzanu				La Perra	
3000 B.C.			Abejas		Ocampo		
4000 B.C.							Incipient Agriculture and Food-gathering Stage
		Mitla Surface	Coxcatlan			Nogales	
5000 B.C.	↑				?		
				Chalco or Chicoloapan or			
6000 B.C.	Santa Marta		Abejas	Tepexpan	Infiernillo	?	
7000 B.C.	↓						↓ ← Paleo-Indian
	?	?	Ajuereado	Iztapan	?	Lerma Diablo	

+ signifies carbon-14 dates; italics indicate stratigraphy.
Incipient Agriculture and Food-gathering Stage

TABLE 2—COMPARISONS OF PRECERAMIC PHASES IN COMPONENTS IN MEXICO

Artifacts	Ajuereado	Santa Marta	Flacco	Almagre	Chicoloapan	Chalco	La Perra	Ocampo	Nogales	Infiernillo	Tepexpan	Yanhuitlan
Flake end scraper	X											
Pointed end scraper	X											
Flake biface		2										
Sinew stone	X	1										
Nutstone		1										
Needle		1	1									
Crude blade	X	22	1	7								
Conical polyhedral core	X	4	?	3								
Matamoras point	X	1	1 (?)	4								
End of blade scraper	X	3		8	X	X	1					
Spokeshave	X	3		1	X		1					
Battered nodule	X	1	2	3		X	14		1			
Boulder metates	X	3	2	10	X	X	9	5	2			
Ovoid biface	X	1	1	30	X	X	9		26			
Large plano-convex end scraper	X	5	11	30	X	X	6	7	2			
Flat scraping plane	X	9	16	1	?	X		8		7		
Split bone awl	X	1	2	1		X	2	1		3		
Gouge	X	1	1	8		X	5	3	7	3		
Domed scraping plane	X	3	2	22	X	X	10	8	5	15		
Pebble hammer	X	2	1	4	X	X	11	1	10	1		
Almagre stemmed point	X	3	1	8	X	X	3			4		
Slab chopper	X	5	124	2		X	1	26	1	47	X	
Abasolo point	X	1	9	35		X	23	17	64	3	X	
Nogales point	X	2	3	12		X	12	2	21		X	
Pebble mano	X	9	3	8	X	X	7	2	6			1
Nodule chopper or core	X	5	1	5	X	X	1	5	2	13	X	3
Thin flake side scraper	X	10	11	76	X	X	28	15	14	3	X	2
Thick flake side scraper	X	8	1	37	X	X	13	9	14	3	X	2
Shell beads			3	1			3	2	66	2		
Disc scraper	X	14		28		X	8	13	6	4		
Disc chopper	X	2		26		X	18	1	17	2		
Scraper-graver			1			X	2	2		3		
Mortars	X	1		4		X	3	1	5			
Tortugas point	X	8		25		X	32	8	10			
Antler flaker			2				1	2	1			
Catan point	X		1	2			1		1			
Pebble smoother	X			2			5		1	1		
Square-based biface	X			11		X	3		2			
Keeled scraper	?			21		X				1		
Gary stemmed point	X		6	25								
Flacco point	X		3	1								
Palmillas point				5								
Kent Point	X			11								
Ensor point	X			3								
Morhiss point				1								
Stone canine-like pendant				2								
Serrated scraper					X							
Ovoid biface graver									4			
Semilunar knife									1			
Infiernillo point										4		

418

based on food gathering with little or no incipient agriculture (pumpkin and gourd being possible exceptions). At present, these areas must be defined mainly on the basis of nonperishable materials whereas it may well be that perishable remains are better diagnostics. The first of these possible culture "areas" is perhaps the most representative of Middle America, that is, the area from southern Tamaulipas to Chiapas.

Despite our limited data, it is possible partially to reconstruct the way of life at this stage. Many of the tools and bones uncovered are related to subsistence directly or indirectly; many caves in Tamaulipas and the excavations in the Tehuacan valley, Puebla, produced vegetal foodstuffs and feces.

Only from southwest Tamaulipas has there been enough study to allow one to discern the changes within the subsistence pattern during the period from 7000 to 1500 B.C. (Whitaker, Cutler, and MacNeish, 1957), but the equally abundant unstudied foodstuffs from Tehuacan hint that this pattern will prove to be similar for some if not all the regions farther south.

In the Infiernillo phase about 50 per cent of foodstuff came from animals (hunting and trapping), 49 per cent from plants (food collecting), and only about 1 per cent from incipient agriculture. During the Ocampo phase hunting decreased, plant collecting greatly increased, and incipient agriculture grew slightly. During Flacco and Guerra incipient agriculture increased at the expense of both the other modes of food gathering. It seems that the shift from food gathering to food producing was not accomplished by any sudden realization of the potential of an agricultural economy, but was more likely to have been a slow steady accumulation (usually by slow diffusion) of more and more domesticated plants that gradually replaced the wild vegetal foodstuffs. Thus time and energy

for hunting and plant collecting become unconsciously usurped by agricultural activities such as clearing, planting, weeding, gardening, picking, harvesting, and food preparation. This meant that less energy was required to obtain more food, people were tied to their lands, and some of the time previously needed to gather food was freed for other pursuits.

Bones from many sites of this stage reveal that hunting and/or trapping had decreased in importance. In our stratified deposits in Tamaulipas the proportion of bone decreases as the number and bulk of vegetal foods increase from bottom to top (MacNeish, 1958, pp. 139–52). This also appears to be the case for the earlier phases in the Tehuacan valley (MacNeish, 1961). In the Santa Marta Cave the number of bones per cubic foot of refuse from Levels 10 to 5 also decreased (MacNeish and Peterson, 1962).

A large proportion of the mammal bones are split; some are scraped in the interior, indicating that marrow had been extracted and eaten. Some of the choppers may have served to break up the bones, for very few seemed to have been sawed or snapped in two. The occasional fragment of mammal bones in feces may indicate that bones were gnawed, or possibly crushed for soup or stew (personal communication from E. Callen, MacDonald College, Ste. Anne de Bellevue, Quebec). There are relatively few head bones, pelvic sections, or vertebrae but many ribs and limb fragments—an indication of the butchering techniques. Perhaps side scrapers and bifacial blades (knives) were the tools of the trade.

Some bones are burned, and a few feces from Tamaulipas contain burned meat (though almost all feces have charcoal fragments), tending to show the use of cooked meat. The numerous hearths with fire-cracked rock (often with burned bone) as well as the fire-cracked rock in the general refuse illustrate that some meat was roasted on the heated rocks. Perhaps the wooden fire-tongs from Infiernillo were used for turning meat over and/or plucking it from the hearths.

In Santa Marta, Tehuacan valley, and southwest Tamaulipas rock shelters the bones of small mammals, birds, and reptiles far outnumber those of larger ones such as white-tailed deer, tapir, jaguar, and buffalo, suggesting that people of this stage, in contrast to the earlier "big game" hunters, obtained much of their meat from trapping and snaring small animals. For some unknown reason fragments of spring traps appear in Flacco and Guerra but not in earlier horizons. Perhaps our sample of wooden tools is inadequate; perhaps the snares or traps were of the kind that could or would not be taken into caves; perhaps the fragments of string with slipknots, the nets, and the small notched and cut twigs were parts of traps. In Tehuacan, however, snare fragments and slip loops that may have been parts of snares do occur in some abundance in the Coxcatlan phase. Rabbit sticks occurring in the Guerra horizon could have been used to kill some of the small animals, as might also caches of nicely rounded pebbles found in Santa Marta.

The presence of larger mammal bones suggests that a few animals may have been killed by projectile points. The points that fitted into U-shaped notches at the end of pointed or rounded atlatl mainshafts were common in southwest Tamaulipas caves. The points were held in the notches by gum, by string wrapped around the stem, or, less commonly, by string tied around the foreshaft just below the notch and at the base of the point, thereby clamping the sides of the notch against the surface of the point. In Mexico these foreshafts fitted into hollow cane mainshafts, reinforced by string, to form darts, which probably were propelled by atlatls.

Darts seem to have been the most common weapon, but one point in a lance shaft occurred in Ocampo deposits. The suggestion that lances characterize the early hunters and atlatl darts the food gatherers lacks evidence in "early hunter" remains.

The fact that wild plants are the principal foods in refuse and feces in the Tamaulipas and Puebla caves points to plant collecting as the main subsistence activity. The wide variety of plants were probably gathered in the numerous nets, bags, baskets, and carrying loops of this stage and brought into caves or camps. Seeds and nuts were ground in boulder mullers by pebble manos or milling stones, crushed in nutstones, or roasted and possibly plucked from the embers by wooden fire-tongs. Perhaps some of the seeds were separated from the husk by shaking them in the open sifter-like baskets. Plants with stiff or fibrous leaves or stalks may have been cut by flake or side scrapers, or crushed or pounded by choppers or scraping planes. Certain plants were chewed, sucked, or masticated and the remaining quid spat out; many seeds, nuts, soft leaves, and flowers must have been eaten without previous preparation. Charred plant remains appeared in almost all feces from Tamaulipas, a sign that plants were commonly roasted. Feces also contained insects such as worms, grubs, and grasshoppers, that appear to have been eaten raw, besides snail shells (usually burned). Both burned and unburned shells are very common in sites of this period.

Throughout this stage of Middle American cultural development, incipient agriculture became increasingly important, apparently not as the result of domestication of more plants in a given area but rather from domestication of different plants in various areas and their diffusion to other regions. For example, pumpkins (pepo) seem to have been domesticated in or near Tamaulipas, beans south of it but north of Tehuacan; corn, squash, and avocados were probably domesticated near or south of Tehuacan. With time, hybridization and

420

selection enlarged the size of these plants and the amounts used. Feces give evidence that food habits based on domesticated plants underwent radical change. Pumpkins and squashes were at one time gathered for their seeds (often roasted), later for their flesh (often crushed). Beans in early times were eaten green (in or out of their pods), later eaten mature (after being soaked). Corncobs (perhaps green) were once masticated whole and then expectorated after the juice was sucked out; later, kernels were eaten off the cob, ground to flour, or made into leached dough. Much of the early corn was pod-pop but we have little evidence that it was popped. No artifacts seem to have been exclusively and specifically associated with agriculture; all those used for plant collecting could have served.

Besides the subsistence tools, people of this stage manufactured a whole series of other artifacts that may be considered industrial. One of the most important industries was flint knapping. Cylinders made from antler may have served as chipping hammers; antler tines with scarred tips, as pressure flakers. Most choppers were made by striking both faces on pebbles or slabs of flint. Scraping planes and disc scrapers were produced from split pebbles or nodules of flint shaped by a few blows on one face. A few flakes originally removed by percussion have been retouched on one surface to make side and end scrapers as well as gravers. The majority of tools, however, have been first roughed out by flaking and then retouched to form gouges, bifacial knife blades, and projectile points. A few points have been thinned by the removal of flakes from their bases; others are beveled at the tip by pressure flaking. Blades were struck from conical polyhedral cores or pressure flaked into drills and end scrapers; many show flaking scars that probably are the result of use.

Mullers, manos, sinew stones, and nut-stones were produced by grinding, more by use, I believe, than by conscious effort to shape them. Some of the stone beads were ground into shape and drilled with chipped stone bits. The bell-shaped pestles, mortars, stone ollas, and bowls from Tehuacan area show considerable skill and effort in making ground stone objects.

Woodworking was a major activity. It required gouges, spoke shaves, flake knives, or side scrapers. Caves contain few sticks over 2 inches in diameter. Small sticks could be got from trees by being merely broken off, being whittled in one direction around the branch of a small tree to weaken it and then snapped off, or (particularly those of cane) being encircled by a sawing motion and broken. A number of wooden tools have been whittled to their desired shape. Most have had their bark peeled off; some have been further smoothed by sandstone abraders or spokeshaves. A few ends of sticks have been pounded. The occurrence, in Flacco times, of flat sticks with ground shallow conical holes indicates the use of wooden fire-drills, but drilling of wood does not seem to have been one of their general woodworking techniques.

The method for making atlatl foreshafts is unique. A stick twice the desired length of the foreshaft was cut and shaved, then sawed a third of the way through first on one side and then on the opposite. A sharp pointed object was next pinned into the stick about an inch below the cut, just above the uncut third of the stick. Then, the two portions above and below the cut were bent back and forth in the direction of the edges of the two parallel cuts on the opposite sides, eventually causing two splits in the stick from the edges of the cuts to the indented portion. Further rocking caused the stick to break into two parts, one with a central tongue-like portion and the other with a corresponding central slot. The former was then used as a foreshaft. The hollow cane, roughly the same diameter as the foreshaft, was sawed into lengths and the portion near the ends reinforced by string wrappings. This became a mainshaft. Atlatls were gouged out of relatively flat or split sticks.

Barbed atlatl foreshafts, atlatl bunts, conical wedges, beveled sticks, fire-tongs, some knife handles, fire-drills, etc., were all whittled out of wood, their surfaces scraped and polished. Scraper handles, knife handles, lance shafts, flutes, and knives were of sawed or cut cane. Tools like spring traps, rabbit sticks, triggers for traps, rods for baskets, and other cut sticks were simply whittled without further work. Gourds were cut to make dishes and pierced to make handle holds.

Many tools usually associated with skin-working and scraping occurred in deposits of this horizon. Small snub-nose end scrapers and end-of-blade scrapers (inserted in handles) could have been used for fleshing; scraping planes, disc scrapers, or large plano-convex scrapers, for both fleshing and scraping. Although these tools were numerous, very few pieces of worked skin were found in the abundant perishable remains in southern Tamaulipas or Tehuacan. On these few only the flesh had been removed; the outer hair was untouched. Charcoal particles revealed in microscopic examination of the skin indicate that the pieces were probably cured by smoking. Skin-working does not seem to have been an important industry, however; probably the many so-called "skin scrapers" were not used for skin- or leatherworking. Perhaps wood-scraping or pulping of vegetal remains was their primary function. Likewise, the bone awls were apparently used not for leather-piercing but perhaps for weaving or for piercing gourds and the like.

Since woven items seem to have substituted for leather, basic tools must have been flint-flakes or side scrapers for cutting fibers and splitting leaves, pulpers or scrapers for softening fibers, pointed sticks and bone awls or punches and needles, and con-

ical wooden pegs or wedges for tying down looms.

The most common weaving materials of these incipient agriculturists were yucca, agave, or similarly leafed plants cut into strands. Next favored was yarn twisted from crushed, softened, or masticated leaf or root fibers. Hard fibers were twisted either clockwise S (slightly more common in later horizons) or counterclockwise Z, whereas softened (bast) fibers were predominantly S twist. A great deal of it had been S-twisted into two-yarn string, some into string of three, four, and six yarns. A very few lengths were braided. Yarn, cord, or string was often tied with overhand knots, square knots, lark's-head knots, slipknots, and granny knots. In the latest horizons of this period are a few hand-twisted fibers of what might be cotton. No string seems to have been made by use of a spindle whorl, and I would guess that most strings were made from fibers rolled against the thigh by the palm of the hand.

Some string has been woven into bags, nets, and kilts. Bags are mainly of the simple coil kind but Fuegian types occur, as well as knotless or laced, full-turned coiled, simple loop and twist, and knotted. In the later part of the horizon we find twined woven robes, warp-face plain-woven tumplines, and blankets. The last were probably woven on a simple belt loom.

More numerous and distinctive are mats, woven from strips of palm, agave, yucca, or similar leaves. At all times twilled rectangular mats were fairly common. In the early part of this stage a checker weave is quite frequent, later on a three-over-three-weave, and borders on squares marked off by a change in the number of strands passed over or under. These mats served as sleeping pads, as seats, and, when folded and sewn, as bags. So common are these mats that these people have been dubbed the Mat-Makers, in contrast to the Basket-Makers of the Southwest and the Blanket-Makers of Peru. Another contrast with the

Southwest lies in the apparent lack of sandals in our Mexican caves, although this may be due to our poor sample from southern Mesoamerica and a large sample from sandal-less Tamaulipas.

The basketry that does occur contrasts with the Southwest both in the types themselves and in the wider variety that our few specimens represent. Loop-twine and Fuegian-sifter baskets occur in early periods in Tamaulipas; these are joined by twilled baskets; and finally one-rod multiple stick and wrap-coiled baskets, interlocking-loop with or without twist-coiled baskets, and split-stitch baskets with rod or bundle foundation predominate. Recent excavations in southern Puebla have revealed an interesting evolution of coiled basketry with bundle foundation. There, coiled baskets with noninterlocking stitch appear in early El Riego, whereas in late El Riego and early Coxcatlan the stitch is interlocking. In late Coxcatlan one basket has both split stitch as well as interlocking stitch, and finally there is only split stitching. Only during the latest period do woven decorations appear on the baskets. The bone awls and pointed sticks may have been used in stitching the baskets.

The fragments of mats, baskets, and nets that have been put together with twisted yarn thread were probably sewn by bone or wooden needles.

Antler and bone tools are relatively rare in these horizons. Many of them—split bone, ulna and bird leg-bone awls, punches, needles, and antler cylinders—were ground to the desired form on sandstone abraders. The needles and some awls would have been pierced by drilling. Disc beads, tube beads, the geometric woven designs, and are a few examples. Other engraved wood leg-bones to their desired length.

A few objects, mainly ornamental, have been made from shell. Snail shells have been pierced for stringing as beads. Conch columella has been ground into cylinders, cut into lengths, and drilled. In La Perra a conch-shell fragment had been ground into a spoon or shallow dish.

Peoples of this stage reveal little interest in ornamental objects. The shell and bone beads, the geometric woven designs, and engraved wood are a few examples. Other attempts may be pictographs (if they prove to be connected with cultures of this horizon), which are mostly painted hands, stick figures, and tally-marks in black or red. A stained red dish from southwest Tamaulipas had been used to grind and mix paints, probably applied by strips of yucca or by fingers.

Evidence of trade or commerce is relatively scarce. Shells are sometimes found relatively distant from their points of origin. Obsidian and flint that are not common in the area of some sites appear to have been brought in by trade. In addition, it seems that domesticated plants slowly diffused over much of Middle America.

The evidence pertaining to industry shows that there were no full-time specialists at this period, little division of labor (other than possibly by sex and age), and few if any craftsmen.

Reconstruction of the industrial and subsistence activities of peoples of this stage is based on relatively firm, though scant data. The settlement pattern information is even less well known, but we can enlarge the picture by inferences drawn from the size and location of the sites, the thickness of deposits, and the seasonality of the plants used.

Sites or their components of this period occur often in caves or rock shelters, or in the open, along water courses (recent or extinct) flanking hills or canyons. In contrast to those of the Desert cultures, very few sites lay on the beaches of extinct lakes. Few were near the summits of high hills or mountains. Rarely did they lie in flat land away from water.

Except for a few pieces of wattle and daub from one Almagre site in the Sierra de Tamaulipas and from one mixed site containing Guerra remains in the Sierra Madre of Tamaulipas and a pit house in Tehuacan, no remains of permanent structures at any site of this period have so far been found.

Deposits of components are uniformly thin (never over 1 foot), from which we can conclude that the occupations were not lengthy and probably not permanent, nor were the people sedentary. Recent analysis of plant materials from 14 floors of this period from the Romero and Valenzuela Caves in the Sierra Madre of Tamaulipas gives more exact estimates of these short durations. This analysis was based on the assumption that remains of flowers and certain leaves, seeds, and tassels meant that the caves were occupied from February through May; that mature squash seeds, beans, corncobs, green nuts, and berries meant a summer or rainy season occupation, June through September; and that mature nuts and certain mature seeds or pods meant a fall occupation, October through January, the dry season. Of the 14 levels, 11 have plants representing only one season, indicating occupations of less than four months. In three of these thick refuse points to use during the whole season. Two levels have plants of two seasons, one level shows signs of three seasons. The latter occupations are considered semisedentary or seasonal. A slightly higher proportion of the occupation levels from the Tehuacan area and one of the two at La Perra also seem to have lasted for two seasons, possibly more. Thus we see occupations varying from temporary to semisedentary or seasonal.

Estimating the size of the groups is more difficult. Refuse in open sites ranges from 10 to over 200 m. in diameter; in caves, from the whole interior to only small portions. At the Sierra de Tamaulipas, it is often impossible to tell multiple small group (microband) occupation in adjacent areas in successive years, from a single occupation by a larger group (macroband)

over the whole area at one time. Be that as it may, no occupation of this period is large and it seems improbable that any group numbered over 100. Again our most reliable data come from Infiernillo Cave floors where no single floor seems to have been made by intermittent occupations. From the fact that nine of these floors cover less than 100 square feet, with two or less hearths associated, I believe that the occupation was by not more than three families, a microband. Five occupations, however, cover larger areas and have more than three hearths, refuse pits, and grass- or mat-lined sleeping areas. These floors I believe were laid down by groups of from three to eight families, macrobands. Lorenzo (1958) gives a similar picture at the Yanhuitlan open site, where he uncovered a very thin zone of refuse that most likely was deposited by a single occupation. The one definite firepit with four superimposed lenses of ash further shows continuous occupation over some time, perhaps several seasons. His maps plot artifacts and human remains over an area roughly 5 by 10 m., and there is the possibility that before erosion of one part of the site the zone of refuse was bigger. Within this area he illustrates at least five concentrations of burned and fire-cracked rocks (hearths) and three of these had concentrations of artifacts, deposited by possibly five or more family groups. It is more than likely that Yanhuitlan represents a seasonal camp occupied by a macroband.

Our limited data on settlement patterns seem to show that occupations were temporary or seasonal (never permanent) by microbands or macrobands. One might guess that during the dry season, when food was scarce, peoples of this stage broke up into nomadic microbands. At other times of year when the food supply was better, they could be sedentary, at least for a season or two. Also, during this period, wherever certain localities were favorable

424

concentrations of wild foodstuffs or to small agricultural plantings, these microbands coalesced to form macrobands. The very planting of a garden necessitated return to it for harvesting, implying that the yearly circle of wandering was confined to some vaguely defined territory.

In the light of our survey data from Tamaulipas as well as the new information from Puebla, one is tempted to speculate about how the above-described settlement pattern led to the establishment of villages. Is it not possible as the number of new agricultural plants utilized increased that the length of time that the microbands stayed in a single planting area also increased? In time could not perhaps one or more microbands have been able to stay at such a spot the year around? Then with further agricultural production is it not possible that the total macroband became sedentary? Such would, of course, be a village.

If our reconstruction of subsistence, settlement, and cultural ecology is correct and if Steward's generalization (1936) about patrilineal bands is also correct, we may be able to say something about the possible social organization. Steward has indicated that certain social features may be correlated and are functionally interrelated to factors of low population density (bands of less than 100 people due to food scarcity), seasonal nomadism (due to seasonal growth of food), hunting and gathering economy (confining the group to a particular environment), and transportation by human carrier. All these factors appear to be common to this cultural stage and to be accompanied by, and functionally interrelated with, such phenomena as patrilineal descent, patrilocal residence, band exogamy, band ownership of territories of food resources, weak and temporary leadership during group endeavors, and shamanism. Thus it is very possible that incipient agriculturists of 3000–9000 years ago had these social characteristics.

Although we have some knowledge of man's adaptation to his environment and some hypotheses about his social organization, we have practically no data about his relation with the supernatural. A few flexed burials in pits with a few grave goods indicate a belief in an afterlife. Perhaps the pictographs have magical significance and perhaps the red painted hands are connected with some sort of puberty rites. A small bag with herbs, an awl, some flint knives, string, and polished pebbles from Romero's Cave may be a medicine man's kit; perhaps shamanism existed. A male, a female, and a child in a richly furnished burial pit in a Guerra level in Romero's Cave, and the two adults and two children in a pit covered by rocks and grinding stones in Santa Marta, hint of burial ceremonies and perhaps human sacrifices. In the Tehuacan region four burials from the El Riego phase, ca. 6000 B.C., not only have abundant burial goods but suggest elaborate burial rites. All are secondary burials; two contain charred human bones (seemingly cannibalism, not cremation), and in two the heads had been severed and placed in baskets. One of these heads shows that the flesh had been scraped from it, the occiput broken, and the remainder roasted (perhaps to cook the brains). Further, in both this horizon and the Coxcatlan phase burned human bones occur in the refuse. For the most part our glimpse of the religious beliefs of this stage is vague and unsatisfactory, yet what little we have shows a complexity that is amazing for peoples of this subsistence level. One can but wonder if the rich ceremonialism of later Mesoamerican culture is only the culmination of a long tradition.

In conclusion I suggest that Lorenzo's preliminary testing and surface collections in Chiapas indicate possible important remains there. Miss C. Irwin has found a rock shelter in northwestern Hidalgo that should yield stratified components of this period. Work in northwest Mexico by Kelley and others should help to define the relationship between Cochise and related Mexican cultural phases. Rock shelters with preserved remains may also be found in western Oaxaca, northern Puebla, and Guerrero along the Rio Balsas.

The part of this stage of development that is particularly important for understanding the beginnings of civilization is the transitional period from preceramic to ceramic or from band to village life. So far, the only examples of the shift occur in southwest Tamaulipas and southern Puebla. The Tamaulipas example is poorly documented and obviously a peripheral situation where the preceramic Guerra descendants adopted ceramics from the Huasteca. The southern Puebla situation appears to be neither peripheral nor with insufficient materials. Unfortunately, most of these materials have not been analyzed nor have the relevant excavations been terminated.

The problem of the original domestication and spread of agriculture in the New World is now well on the way to being solved. The long period of incipient agriculture, the idea of multiple origins of many domesticated plants, and the very slow cultural changes that incipient agriculture wrought, have amazed many students of New World culture. It may very well happen that when we have comparable knowledge from similar stages in the Old World, many of our present reconstructions of this stage and the early aspects of the rise of civilization (neolithic revolution) will have to be radically revised.

REFERENCES

Armenta, 1959
Clisby and Sears, 1955
De Terra, 1949, 1959
Fay, 1955
Kaplan and MacNeish, 1960
Kelley, Campbell, and Lehmer, 1940
Libby, 1952
Lorenzo, 1958c

MacNeish, n.d. b, 1958, 1961
—— and Peterson, 1962
Mangelsdorf, MacNeish, and Galinat, 1956
—— and Lister, 1956
Steward, 1936
Suhm, Krieger, and Jelks, 1954
Whitaker, Cutler, and MacNeish, 1957
Willey, 1960a

13. Origins of Agriculture in Middle America

PAUL C. MANGELSDORF
RICHARD S. MAC NEISH
GORDON R. WILLEY

THE STORY of agriculture in Middle America begins with an era of "incipient cultivation." By this term it is meant that domesticated food plants played only a minor role in the subsistence of societies dependent for the most part on the collecting of wild plants and the hunting of small game. Gradually, the cultivated plants assumed greater economic importance. More plants were brought under domestication, and others were improved over the centuries by selection. Eventually, with agriculture becoming the primary and established subsistence mode, the era of incipient cultivation came to an end. We present here a summary of this early history of plant cultivation in Middle America. We will consider, in order, native wild plants of the area, circumstances favorable for their cultivation, a review of the archaeological evidence for plant domestication, plant genetics, plant distributions, and the place of Mesoamerican cultivation in the larger setting of the New World.

Let us first note, briefly, the position and context of the "era of incipient cultivation" which is to be our main concern (Willey, 1960a,b). The fully agricultural basis of life for pre-Columbian Mesoamerica is known from 16th-century records and from ethnographic observations of modern times. For the centuries immediately preceding the Spanish conquest, agriculture is known or inferred from a variety of archaeological evidences. Going back somewhat further in time, to the Preclassic period of the first and second millennia B.C., it is generally assumed that the earliest cultures of this period were supported by the cultivation of food crops (Willey, Ekholm, and Millon, Article 14). The "era of incipient cultivation" precedes the Preclassic period. Actually it is an era or period of food collecting together with "incipient cultivation." The societies of that time were small bands, living under seminomadic conditions and gaining a livelihood by collecting wild plants, killing and snaring small game, and, to a minor extent, planting and reaping. The span of time involved for such an era is estimated, on the basis of radiocarbon dates, to have been about 6000 B.C. ± 1000 years to 1500 B.C. ± 500 years (MacNeish, Article 12). It is believed that prior to 7,000 B.C. man's food quest in ancient Middle America was oriented more toward the pursuit and killing of large animals, under Pleistocene environmental conditions (Aveleyra, Article 11), than toward plants and small game. With the onset of a warmer, drier climate, following the Pleistocene, the small game-hunting and plant-collecting subsistence came into being; and, at least in certain Mesoamerican regions, plant domestication developed in this context.

PLANT CULTIVATION IN MIDDLE AMERICA

Circumstances Favorable for Development of Agriculture

There can be little doubt that the agriculture of the New World is an indigenous development. The Asiatic peoples who crossed Bering Strait on the wide land bridge, which almost certainly existed at a time when the sea level was 150–180 feet lower than at present (Hopkins, 1959), were undoubtedly strangers to the art of cultivation. Agriculture had not yet been invented in the Old World and, if it had, it would not have been extensively practiced in northeastern Asia, where these migrants to the New World originated, or successfully carried across the barren tundras of the strait into a not much more favorable area of what is now Alaska. Even after these peoples reached the region now the United States and southern Canada, which has subsequently proved to be well suited to agricultural enterprises, there were few plants which could have been successfully domesticated. Only one cultivated plant of any importance, the annual sunflower, has originated in the region now the United States; its domestication may have come relatively late (Heiser, 1955) and may have been inspired by the experience of successful domestication farther south.

Not until these nomadic hunting and food-gathering peoples reached the region now Mexico and northern Central America

did they encounter a combination of conditions which were conducive to the development of plant domestication and the practice of agriculture.

One of the factors involved in creating centers of domestication, according to Vavilov (1951), is a great diversity in the natural vegetation. As an example he cites the two small republics of Central America, Costa Rica and Salvador, which have areas about one hundredth that of the United States but which possess a number of species as great as is found in all of North America including the United States, Canada, and Alaska. Although taxonomists may question this particular statement, it is undoubtedly true that the floras of the countries of Middle America are rich and exhibit a great diversity of species and varieties. This diversity in vegetation is the product, in substantial part, of a corresponding diversity in habitats, which is provided by a wide range in altitude, temperature, and rainfall, and which promotes geographic differentiation in the genera and species inhabiting the area.

In addition to a rich flora, which is more likely to include plants amenable to domestication than a sparse one, there must be other factors and conditions which contribute to the invention and development of agriculture. On this point there is a variety of opinions.

Payne (1892) has suggested that agriculture probably originates first with root-crop culture, since the disturbance of the soil in the search for roots has in itself the character of tillage. Also the act of planting a root scarcely differs from that of digging one up; the implement used being the same for both, a simple fire-hardened stake, the universal implement of primitive agriculture. To Payne's arguments it should be added that no complex processing operations are required in preparing the majority of roots for consumption. Many can be eaten raw or cooked by simple means: roasted over hot coals or steamed in shallow pits over heated stones. No implements or utensils are needed for threshing, milling, or baking. The growing and processing of roots is undoubtedly more simple than comparable operations involving the cereals.

Sauer (1959), like Payne, has New World agriculture originating with root culture but for somewhat different reasons. He postulates that hunting and fishing people living a comfortable life began to cultivate the native, vegetatively propagated root crops not from necessity but because with leisure on their hands they had time to take steps to improve their lot by providing themselves with, among other things, a source of carbohydrates to supplement an otherwise highly proteinaceous diet. Sauer suggests that New World agriculture began in northern South America, perhaps in Colombia, with manioc, the native yam, arracacha, *Xanthosoma* (the American counterpart of the Old World taro), and other root crops. As this type of agriculture spread into the Andes other root or tuberous crops especially adapted to high altitudes, including oca, ulluco, año, and the potato, were added to the complex. The peanut was domesticated because a plant which buries its fruit resembles, superficially at least, the root crops which store their food reserves underground. This root-crop type of agriculture was also extended northward to its limits but was not adopted in Mexico in early times because no suitable root crops were available. Instead the requirements for a balanced diet were met by domesticating plants reproduced by seed, especially maize, beans, and squashes.

Sauer's hypothesis, though in many respects plausible, has little evidence to support it. True, there is some indication from the finding of griddles, presumably used in the preparation of manioc bread, that the cultivation of this plant began at a relatively early date, perhaps as early as 1000 B.C. (Cruxent and Rouse, 1958), but it is doubtful that it preceded the cultivation of maize, beans, and squashes in Mexico.

Recent archaeological evidence tends to support not Sauer but Spinden who (1917) expressed the opinion that agriculture would be more likely to originate under conditions that were hard rather than under those which were easy. An environment producing a healthy but hungry population, particularly a semiarid environment, would offer special inducements to the first agriculturists. Here they would encounter no heavy work in preparing the soil, and irrigation would make them the masters of nature.

Even before irrigation had been invented, however, there would have been obvious advantages in a semiarid climate where weeds, insect pests, and fungus diseases are less of a problem than in tropical lowlands and where living conditions in general are more healthful. Also the plants on which the earliest agriculture of Mexico was based —primitive maize, beans, and squashes— are plants better adapted to intermediate and fairly high altitudes, to a *clima medio*, than to the tropical lowlands. The beginnings of agriculture should be sought, we think, at intermediate altitudes in tropical regions which have distinct rainy and dry seasons and natural vegetations of great diversity. These conditions are met especially well in parts of Middle America and it is here where the earliest archaeological remains of several important American cultivated plants are found.

Review of the Archaeological Evidence for Early Plant Cultivation

The earliest occurrences of cultivated plants in Middle America and the most complete record of their development through time come from archaeological sites in the Mexican states of Tamaulipas and Puebla. The former region lies at the northeastern margin of Middle America; the latter is near the geographical center of the area. There are also evidences of early, probably cultivated, maize in pollen taken from soil borings made in the Valley of Mexico, and from cave deposits in Chiapas in southern Mexico.

The archaeological sites in Tamaulipas are dry caves in which the plants themselves, and plant particles in human feces, are found in deeply stratified layers of dusty refuse. The cultural contexts of these plant finds are described elsewhere (MacNeish, Article 12). In discussing the plants it will be necessary to refer to phase names, and dates, of two archaeological sequences, one for the Sierra de Tamaulipas and the other for the Sierra Madre Oriental of the southwestern part of the State of Tamaulipas. These sequences are closely related, and they are cross-referenced and dated in Table 1.

The earliest of the Tamaulipas culture phases with plant remains is the Infiernillo. It is dated at 7000–5000 B.C., and a number of plants are attributed to it. Some of these are definitely wild, such as the agave, the opuntia, and the runner bean (*Phaseolus coccineus*) (Kaplan and MacNeish, 1960; MacNeish, 1959). Possibly wild or possibly domesticates are the gourd (*Lagenaria*) and the chili pepper (*Capsicum annuum* or *C. frutescens*) (Whitaker, Cutler, and MacNeish, 1957; Callen and MacNeish, n.d.). The best case for a cultivated plant at this early time is the summer squash or pumpkin (*Cucurbita Pepo*). The plant, apparently, was first utilized for its seeds. Several of these seeds have been found in an Infiernillo deposit, and some authorities believe domesticates to be represented among them (Whitaker, Cutler, and MacNeish, 1957; MacNeish, 1959).[1]

Indisputable domesticates, yellow and red large beans (*Phaseolus vulgaris*), come into the Tamaulipas sequence in the phase succeeding the Infiernillo, the Ocampo, dated at 5000–3000 B.C. (MacNeish, 1958,

---

[1] Of the six pumpkin seeds (*Cucurbita Pepo*) in Infiernillo refuse, three are quite small and probably wild; but in the opinion of Whitaker and Cutler the other three seeds, all larger, appear to be domesticates.

430

TABLE 1.—CORRELATION OF TWO REGIONAL SEQUENCES OF TAMAULIPAS, WITH PHASE DATINGS BASED LARGELY UPON RADIOCARBON READINGS
(For more detailed presentation, discussion, and radiocarbon dates see MacNeish, 1958, Table 30 and pp. 193–99.)

	Sierra Madre	Sierra de Tamaulipas
A.D. 1750		
	San Antonio	
1300		Los Angeles
	San Lorenzo	? (hiatus)
900		
	? (hiatus)	
	(Late)	
		La Salta
500	Palmillas	
	(Early)	Eslabones
0	? (hiatus)	
	La Florida	Laguna
500		
	Mesa de Guaje	
		? (hiatus)
1400		
	Guerra	
1800		
		Almagre
	Flacco	
2200		
		La Perra
	(Late)	
3000	Ocampo	
4000	(Early)	Nogales
5000	? (hiatus)	
		? (hiatus following Paleo-Indian Phases)
B.C. 7000	Infiernillo	

pp. 167–68; 1959; Kaplan and MacNeish, 1960). Also, Ocampo pumpkins are a larger seeded variety than those of the preceding Infiernillo, and there is now no doubt that they are cultivated (Whitaker, Cutler, and MacNeish, 1957). A new wild plant, eaten

in Ocampo times, is *Panicum sonorum*, a type of millet (Callen and MacNeish, n.d.).

The great American Indian domesticated plant, maize (*Zea mays*), dates first from La Perra times, somewhere between 3000 and 2200 B.C. in the Tamaulipas sequence (MacNeish, 1958, p. 155).[2] It is a primitive corn, represented by two varieties (A and B) of the early *Nal-Tel* race (Mangelsdorf, MacNeish, and Galinat, 1956; Callen and MacNeish, n.d.).

After 2200 B.C. the Tamaulipas cave sequences show a rapid build-up of cultigens. The Bat Cave, or *Chapalote*, race of maize appears in the Flacco phase (2200–1800 B.C.), and in the Mesa de Guaje phase (1400–500 B.C.) both Bat Cave and new hybridized varieties of corn are present along with the maize-tripsacum cross, teosinte. In the Laguna phase (500 B.C.–0) there are three new important races of hybridized corn, *Breve de Padilla*, *Dzit-Bacal*, and *Nal-Tel* (Mangelsdorf and Reeves, 1959a,b; Mangelsdorf, MacNeish, and Galinat, 1956). Shortly after this, in early Palmillas phase times (0–A.D. 500), black beans, small red beans and the lima bean (*Phaseolus lunatus*) come into the sequence (Kaplan and MacNeish, 1960) and a great increase in the varieties of pumpkins (*Cucurbita Pepo*) occurs (Whitaker, Cutler, and MacNeish, 1957). In addition, the cushaw squash (*Cucurbita moschata*) is known from the Guerra phase (1800–1400 B.C.) and the Walnut squash (*Cucurbita mixta*) from the Palmillas (A.D. 300–800) (*ibid.*). *Amaranthus*, a well-known Mexican food plant, is as old as 2200 B.C., although its status as a wild or a cultivated one is uncertain (Callen and MacNeish, n.d.). Cotton (*Gossypium*) is first noted in the cave debris in the Guerra phase (1800–1400 B.C.), and the first tobacco (*Nicotiana rustica*) is placed in Palmillas (A.D. 300–800) (MacNeish, 1959). *Manihot*

dulcis, or sweet manioc, a possible domesticated food plant, is known from the Laguna phase (500 B.C.–0). This Tamaulipas manioc, although closely related to the *Manihot esculenta* of the South American lowlands, had a separate and local history of cultivation.

To sum up the Tamaulipas cave sequences and to relate the development of plant domestication in these sequences to other aspects of culture and society, we note the following trends. During the Infiernillo, Ocampo, and La Perra phases, or from about 7000 to 2200 B.C., domesticated food plants make up no more than 10 to 15 per cent of the total diet. The pumpkin and the bean were the earliest domesticates; maize, of a primitive sort, was added later. Communities were small and life probably seminomadic with only seasonal return to the cave sites. From 2200 to 500 B.C., in the Flacco, Almagre, Guerra, and Mesa de Guaje phases, cultigens increase to as much as 40 per cent of total diet by the terminal date. Sites are larger and some of them might be described as the village locations of semisedentary populations. New races of maize appear and are hybridized. Still later (500 B.C.–A.D. 500), more food plants are added to the complex, diet becomes essentially agricultural, and stable villages and towns appear (MacNeish, 1958, pp. 199–203; 1959).

It will be noted that this transition from early incipient to full village agriculture in Tamaulipas is chronologically somewhat behind the dating estimates given in the introduction to this article. By 1500 B.C., or even 1000 B.C., the cave dwellers and semisedentary villagers of the Tamaulipas mountains had not achieved a fully established agricultural economy. In fact, this does not seem to have been attained here until sometime between 500 B.C. and A.D. 500, well into Preclassic or even Classic times if measured against developments farther south in Middle America. The implications of this are that plant cultivation,

2 The evidence for maize in La Perra is from corncobs.

431

in both its incipient and fully established stages, are probably earlier near the "heart" of the Mesoamerican area than they are on the Tamaulipas peripheries. What archaeological plant evidence is there to support this hypothesis?

To date, the most significant discoveries pertaining to this problem have come from a dry cave at Aeyerado, near Coxcatlan, in southern Puebla. Although only test excavations have been carried out so far, six maize cobs were recovered from deep refuse levels. Three of these cobs are probably domesticates; but the other three from the very deepest levels are quite primitive in appearance and it is possible that these latter three represent the wild ancestor of cultivated maize. In the upper preceramic levels of Aeyerado Cave, maize cobs are definitely domesticates, and some show teosinte introgression. The Aeyerado sequence terminates with the appearance of Preclassic and Classic pottery and well-developed maize.[3] Although only a preliminary examination of the earliest Aeyerado artifacts has been made, the chipped stone tool types appear to correlate most closely with those of the upper preceramic levels (5000–3500 B.C.) of the Santa Marta Cave in Chiapas as well as with the Ocampo phase of the Tamaulipas sequence. If this correlation is supported by an early radiocarbon date for the lower Aeyerado levels, it would strongly suggest an early Mesoamerican hearth of maize domestication well to the south of Tamaulipas.[4]

The Puebla maize discoveries have some corroboration in studies of fossil pollen made in the Valley of Mexico, a short distance to the north but still well south of Tamaulipas. Here, pollen of what is probably domesticated maize has an early post-

Pleistocene geological estimated date (ca. 5000 B.C.). In this connection, it is interesting to note that there is still older maize pollen, presumably wild, from the Valley of Mexico (Barghoorn, Wolfe, and Clisby, 1954).[5]

The most significant generalization which emerges from all of the archaeological facts on plant cultivation in Middle America is that there were regional specializations at a very early time. In Tamaulipas, squash and then common beans were cultivated long before maize; in Puebla, maize has the earlier history.[†] By about 2000 B.C., however, there had been sufficient diffusion of cultivated plants within the Middle American area to produce a complex of agricultural foods—essentially maize, beans, squashes, and chili peppers—that revolutionized the whole nature of plant growing from a level of incipient cultivation to one of village agriculture. By the time of the advent of the Spanish the Middle American agricultural complex—augmented by new cultigens developed locally and imported from other American areas—was the richest assemblage of food plants in the western hemisphere.

Cultivated Plants of Middle America

The most intensive studies which have been made of the cultivated plants of the world are those of the Russian botanist, Vavilov, and his collaborators. These have involved numerous expeditions on a worldwide scale conducted between the two world wars and the most extensive collections of cultivated plants ever assembled. As a result Vavilov (1951) recognized eight world centers of origin of cultivated plants, one of which includes southern Mexico, Central America, and the Antilles and is

[3] Excavation of the Aeyerado Cave was carried out by MacNeish in early 1960. Mangelsdorf examined the maize cobs from Aeyerado in March of the same year. Aeyerado Cave was later called Coxcatlan Cave. See also Addendum.
[4] Samples have been sent to the University of Michigan Laboratory for radiocarbon analysis.

[5] See also Deevey (1944) for a record of maize pollen in soil borings, taken from vicinity of Lake Patzcuaro, Michoacan. Maize pollen in this sequence cannot be dated definitely although there is the reasonable likelihood that it may be as ancient as the early post-Pleistocene.
[†] See Addendum.

considered to be the center of origin of more than 50 cultivated species.

Vavilov's list is not complete, however, and is undoubtedly in error in assigning the origin of the sweet potato to this center and in omitting one of the most widely grown squashes, *Cucurbita Pepo*. More recently Dressler (1953) made an exhaustive study of the literature, including early historical sources as well as Vavilov's and other Russian works, which are concerned with the cultivated plants of Mexico. Dressler lists 88 different species, of which 71 are regarded as being of Mexican–Central American origin and 17 were introduced from elsewhere or are of uncertain origin. Although Dressler's work is concerned principally with Mexico, most of the species which he lists are grown also in Central America.

In Table 2 we have combined the data of these two authors, following the procedure of Vavilov in listing the plants in categories, based upon their use, but employing somewhat different categories, and following Dressler with respect to the Latin names, since he has made a special effort to determine for each species the correct Latin name which meets the requirements of the rules of botanical nomenclature. To make the table as complete as possible we have added the names of the families to which the species belong and we have indicated with asterisks those species which we consider not to be indigenous to Mesoamerica but to have been introduced from elsewhere. A few species are included in more than one category.

The list of plants set forth in Table 2 is impressive, not only in the large number of species which it includes but also, in calling attention to the fact that a number of genera, notably, *Phaseolus, Cucurbita, Annona, Opuntia, Theobroma, Agave,* and *Dahlia,* are each represented by several species. This provides tangible evidence of the fact, mentioned earlier, that the Mesoamerican floras, because of their richness and diversity, undoubtedly contained many species amenable to domestication and it suggests that the Mesoamerican people, once they had learned the art of domestication practiced it whenever they encountered such species. The list of cultivated plants also shows that the domestication of plants in Mesoamerica reached an advanced, indeed in some respects a highly sophisticated, state—a number of species being cultivated as ornamentals and several as host plants for "domestic" insects. However, the majority of the species listed in Table 2 are of minor agricultural importance and of limited usefulness in tracing the beginnings of agriculture in Mesoamerica. Consequently we shall confine further discussion to those species which are of major importance agriculturally and which may be critical in tracing the beginnings of agriculture and its subsequent spread to other parts of the hemisphere. These include maize, beans, squashes, the bottle gourd, cotton, and tobacco.[6]

SQUASHES. Both wild and cultivated squashes are represented in the vegetal remains of the Ocampo caves. Rinds and shells of the wild species, *Cucurbita foetidissima,* were found at all levels in the caves (Whitaker, Cutler, and MacNeish, 1957, p. 356). Since the flesh of the fruits of this species is quite unpalatable, as its Latin name may suggest, it is probable that this squash was used for its seeds which are nutritious. Carter (1945, p. 30) has suggested that the cucurbits in general first attracted attention for their seeds which are easily gathered, are palatable, and have a high oil content.

Three cultivated species of squashes—*C. Pepo, C. moschata,* and *C. mixta*—were identified among the archaeological remains of the caves. A fourth species, *C. maxima,* cultivated in Peru, has never been found

[6] For detailed information on other cultivated species not treated further here, the reader is referred to Dressler's paper and to its extensive bibliography of 220 titles.

TABLE 2—THE CULTIVATED PLANTS OF MIDDLE AMERICA
(After Vavilov, 1951, and Dressler, 1953)

COMMON NAME	LATIN NAME	PLANT FAMILY
	CULTIVATED FOR THEIR EDIBLE SEEDS	
Amaranth	*Amaranthus cruentus* L.	Amaranthaceae
Amaranth	*Amaranthus leucocarpus* S. Wats.	Amaranthaceae
Apazote	*Chenopodium Nuttalliae* Safford	Chenopodiaceae
Bean, common	*Phaseolus vulgaris* L.	Leguminosae
Bean, lima	*Phaseolus lunatus* L.	Leguminosae
Bean, runner	*Phaseolus coccineus* L.	Leguminosae
Bean, tepary	*Phaseolus acutifolius* A. Gray	Leguminosae
Bean, jack	*Canavalia ensiformis* (L.) DC.	Leguminosae
Chia	*Salvia hispanica* L.	Labiatae
Chia grande	*Hyptis suaveolens* Poit.	Labiatae
Maize	*Zea Mays* L.	Gramineae
Panic grass	*Panicum sonorum* Beal	Gramineae
Peanut*	*Arachis hypogaea* L.	Leguminosae
Sunflower*	*Helianthus annuus* L.	Compositae
	CULTIVATED FOR THEIR EDIBLE ROOTS OR TUBERS	
Coyolxóchitl	*Bomarea edulis* (Tuss.) Herb.	Amaryllidaceae
Manioc	*Manihot dulcis* (J. F. Gmel.) Pax	Euphorbiaceae
Manioc*	*Manihot esculenta* Crantz	Euphorbiaceae
Potato*	*Solanum tuberosum* L.	Solanaceae
Sweet potato*	*Ipomoea Batatas* (L.) Poir.	Convolvulaceae
Yam bean	*Pachyrrhizus erosus* (L.) Urban	Leguminosae
	CULTIVATED FOR THEIR EDIBLE GOURDLIKE FRUITS	
Chayote	*Sechium edule* Sw.	Cucurbitaceae
Squash, cushaw	*Cucurbita moschata* Duch.	Cucurbitaceae
Squash, summer	*Cucurbita Pepo* L.	Cucurbitaceae
Squash, walnut	*Cucurbita mixta* Pang.	Cucurbitaceae
Squash	*Cucurbita ficifolia* Bouché	Cucurbitaceae
	OTHER EDIBLE FRUITS	
Anona	*Annona purpurea* Moc. & Sessé	Annonaceae
Anona	*Annona glabra* L.	Annonaceae
Bullock's-heart	*Annona reticulata* L.	Annonaceae
Cherimoya*	*Annona Cherimolia* Mill.	Annonaceae
Ilama	*Annona diversifolia* Safford	Annonaceae
Soursop	*Annona muricata* L.	Annonaceae
Sweetsop	*Annona squamosa* L.	Annonaceae
Avocado	*Persea americana* Mill.	Lauraceae
Avocado	*Persea Schiedeana* Nees	Lauraceae
Caujilote	*Parmentiera edulis* DC.	Bignoniaceae
Capulin cherry	*Prunus serotina* Ehrh.	Rosaceae
Tejocote	*Crataegus pubescens* (HBK.) Steud.	Rosaceae
Cashew*	*Anacardium occidentale* L.	Anacardiaceae
Hog plum	*Spondias Mombin* L.	Anacardiaceae
Jocote	*Spondias purpurea* L.	Anacardiaceae
Coconut*	*Cocos nucifera* L.	Palmaceae
Elderberry	*Sambucus mexicana* Presl.	Caprifoliaceae
Guava	*Psidium Guajava* L.	Myrtaceae
Guayabilla	*Psidium Sartorianum* (Berg.) Niedenzu	Myrtaceae
Mamey colorado	*Calocarpum mammosum* (L.) Pierre	Sapotaceae
Sapote, green	*Calocarpum viride* Pitt.	Sapotaceae
Sapote, yellow	*Pouteria campechiana* (HBK.) Baehni	Sapotaceae
Sapodilla	*Manilkara Zapotilla* (Jacq.) Gilly	Sapotaceae
Matasano	*Casimiroa Sapota* Oerst.	Rutaceae
Sapote, white	*Casimiroa edulis* La Llave & Lex.	Rutaceae
Nance	*Byrsonima crassifolia* (L.) DC.	Malpighiaceae
Papaya	*Carica Papaya* L.	Caricaceae
Pineapple*	*Ananas comosus* (L.) Merrill	Bromeliaceae
Pitahaya	*Hylocereus undatus* (Haw.) Brit. & Rose	Cactaceae
Prickly pear	*Opuntia streptacantha* Lemaire	Cactaceae
Prickly pear	*Opuntia megacantha* Salm-Dyck	Cactaceae
Prickly pear	*Opuntia ficus-indica* (L.) Miller	Cactaceae

COMMON NAME	LATIN NAME	PLANT FAMILY
Ramón	*Brosimum Alicastrum* Swartz	Moraceae
Sapote, black	*Diospyros Ebenaster* Retz.	Ebenaceae

POTS HERBS AND OTHER VEGETABLES

Chaya	*Cnidosculus Chayamansa* McVaugh	Euphorbiaceae
Chipilín	*Crotalaria Longirostrata* Hook. & Arn.	Leguminosae
Pacaya	*Chamaedorea Wendlandiana* Hemsl.	Palmaceae
Tepejilote	*Chamaedorea Tepejilote* Liebm.	Palmaceae
Tomato	*Lycopersicon esculentum* Mill.	Solanaceae
Tomato, husk	*Physalis ixocarpa* Brot.	Solanaceae
Yucca	*Yucca elephantipes* Regel	Liliaceae

CONDIMENTS AND OTHER FLAVORING

Chili pepper	*Capsicum annuum* L.	Solanaceae
Chili pepper	*Capsicum frutescens* L.	Solanaceae
Vanilla	*Vanilla planifolia* Andr.	Orchidaceae

STIMULANTS AND NARCOTICS

Cacao	*Theobroma Cacao* L.	Sterculiaceae
Cacao	*Theobroma angustifolium* DC.	Sterculiaceae
Cacao	*Theobroma bicolor* Humb. & Bonpl.	Sterculiaceae
Maguey	*Agave atrovirens* Karw.	Amaryllidaceae
Maguey	*Agave latissima* Jacobi	Amaryllidaceae
Maguey	*Agave mapisaga* Trel.	Amaryllidaceae
Tobacco	*Nicotiana rustica* L.	Solanaceae
Tobacco*	*Nicotiana Tabacum* L.	Solanaceae

FIBER PLANTS

Cotton	*Gossypium hirsutum* L.	Malvaceae
Henequen	*Agave fourcroydes* Lem.	Amaryllidaceae
Maguey	*Agave atrovirens* Karw.	Amaryllidaceae
Maguey	*Agave tequilana* Weber	Amaryllidaceae
Sisal	*Agave sisalana* Perrine	Amaryllidaceae

DYE PLANTS

*Achiote**	*Bixa Orellana* L.	Bixaceae
Indigo	*Indigofera suffruticosa* Mill.	Leguminosae

CULTIVATED FOR ITS RESIN, USED AS INCENSE

Copal	*Protium Copal* (Schlecht. & Cham.)	Burseraceae

CULTIVATED AS HOSTS FOR WAX AND COCHINEAL INSECTS

Piñoncillo	*Jatropha Curcas* L.	Euphorbiaceae
Cochineal cactus	*Nopalea cochenillifera* (L.) Salm-Dyck	Cactaceae

FRUITS USED AS UTENSILS

Bottle gourd	*Lagenaria siceraria* (Mol.) Standl.	Cucurbitaceae
Calabash	*Crescentia Cujete* L.	Bignoniaceae

PLANTS USED FOR LIVING FENCES

Dahlia	*Dahlia Lehmannii* Hieron	Compositae
Pitayo	*Pachycereus emarginatus* (DC.) Brit & Rose	Cactaceae
Yucca	*Yucca elephantipes* Regel	Liliaceae
Piñoncillo	*Jatropha Curcas* L.	Euphorbiaceae

ORNAMENTAL PLANTS

Cypress	*Taxodium mucronatum* Ten.	Pinaceae
Dahlia	*Dahlia coccinea* Cav.	Compositae
Dahlia	*Dahlia excelsa* Benth.	Compositae
Dahlia	*Dahlia Lehmannii* Hieron.	Compositae
Dahlia	*Dahlia pinnata* Cav.	Compositae
Marigold	*Tagetes erecta* L.	Compositae
Marigold	*Tagetes patula* L.	Compositae
Tiger flower	*Tigridia pavonia* (L.f.) Kerr.	Liliaceae
Tuberose	*Polianthes tuberosa* L.	Amaryllidaceae

*Probably not native to Mesoamerica.

archaeologically in Mesoamerica, a fact which furnishes one of a number of examples of independent domestication in the two regions.

1. Pumpkin and Summer Squash, *Cucurbita Pepo* L. This species in modern horticulture includes many varieties: the golden fall pumpkin; a diversity of summer squashes including yellow crookneck squashes, acorn squashes, scallop or pattypans, zucchinis, vegetable marrows; and the small inedible gourds grown for ornamental purposes. This species makes its first appearance in Mexico in the Infiernillo phase, 7000–5000 B.C. However, of these earliest seeds, those illustrated by Whitaker *et al.* (1957) in their figure 4, are very small and may well represent wild squashes. Somewhat larger seeds which may be those of cultivated squashes were also found at this level (see note 1), as well as in the Mesa de Guaje culture dated at 1400–500 B.C. The absence of *C. Pepo* in Peru, like the absence of *C. maxima* in Middle America, is evidence that the domestication of the squashes was, to some extent at least, independent in the two regions.

2. Cushaw Squash, *Cucurbita moschata* Duchesne. This squash, represented in contemporary horticulture in the United States by the cushaw of the southern states and butternut squash of the northern states, definitely makes its appearance in the Ocampo Caves at 1400–500 B.C., and there is one peduncle, probably of this species, dated at 1800–1400 B.C. (Whitaker *et al.*, 1957, p. 357). It is impossible to determine from these early specimens—all peduncles —whether they are wild or cultivated. This species is also represented in the early levels of Huaca Prieta site in Peru dated at about 2000 B.C. (Whitaker and Bird, 1949). The fact that *C. moschata* has its center of diversity in Central America and northern South America indicates that this may be the primary center of domestication. The criterion of diversity, however, is far from infallible and can result in serious errors

436

such as that which Vavilov (1951) made when he placed the origin of *C. Pepo* in the Near East because the greatest diversity of its varieties occurs in Asia Minor. Centers of diversity may be centers of convergence as well as centers of origin.

Although *C. moschata* occurs in both Middle America and Peru and although it makes its first appearance in the two regions at about the same date,† it is represented by distinct types, a brown-seeded one in South America and a white-seeded one in Mexico. These are sufficiently different to be regarded by some authorities as distinct subspecies (Bukasov, 1930).

It cannot be said, at least with any degree of confidence, that *C. moschata* was first domesticated in Peru and later introduced into Mexico or vice versa. If any conclusion is to be drawn at this point it would be that domestication of *C. moschata* probably occurred independently in the two regions from somewhat different wild geographic races or subspecies.

3. Walnut Squash, *C. mixta* Pang. This species, coming quite late† (A.D. 150–850) in the cultural sequence and never reaching South America, has little bearing either on the beginnings of agriculture or on its subsequent spread.

BEANS. Four species of beans—the tepary bean, the runner bean, the lima bean, and the common bean—are known today in Middle America and with the exception of the first† all have now been found archaeologically, as noted above, in this region. The relatively early dates at which they occurred suggest that they may be native to the region and there is support for this supposition in the occurrence of wild forms of several of these species.

1. Tepary Bean, *Phaseolus acutifolius* A. Gray. Wild forms of the tepary bean occur in northern Mexico and in the southern part of the southwestern United States (Carter, 1945) and since this species is unknown in South America either archaeologically or as commonly grown cultigen in modern

times, there can be little doubt that it originated either in Mesoamerica or near its northern periphery. It has not yet been found archaeologically in early Mexican sites and may represent a comparatively recent addition to the Middle American agricultural complex.†

2. Runner Bean, *Phaseolus coccineus* L. This bean, like the tepary, is clearly not of South American origin since it is unknown there archaeologically and is little used in contemporary agriculture. Wild plants of this species have been collected in Guatemala and in the states of Puebla, Zacatecas, Coahuila, Mexico, Jalisco, and Chiapas in Mexico (Kaplan and MacNeish, 1960). These authors also conclude that the runner beans found archaeologically in the Infiernillo phase of Romero's Cave, dated at 7000–5000 B.C., may have been those of wild plants although this species is not known in the wild in Tamaulipas today. They suggest that a second thermal period may have been the cause of the extinction of *P. coccineus* from this part of its native range.

3. Lima Bean, *Phaseolus lunatus* L. Since the lima bean does not occur archaeologically in Middle America until A.D. 0–500 and has been identified from preceramic levels dated at 2000 B.C. in the Huaca Prieta site in Peru (Towle),[7] it might be supposed that this species represents an introduction into Middle America from South America. However, the lima beans in the two areas are quite different, the Peruvian form being a large-seeded type and the Mexican a small-seeded type known to horticulturists as the "sieva" lima. Mackie (1943) has placed the origin of the lima bean in the Guatemala-Chiapas area, where wild forms of a small-seeded type have been collected. Recently a lima bean has been collected in Peru growing on the terraces of Ollantaitambo in the Urabamba Valley by Ing. Alexander Grobman of the National School of Agriculture. Because of its hard, thick-

ened shell, which differs from that of any cultivated lima, this bean has been identified as a wild form by Dr. R. W. Allard, University of California. The same form is reported by Ing. Alfonso Cerrate to be common in the Department of Ancash in Peru.[8] This wild lima has seeds much larger than those of the wild lima of Guatemala. It seems probable, therefore, that the lima beans of Mesoamerica and of South America represent separate domestications of two distinct wild races or subspecies.

4. Common Bean, *Phaseolus vulgaris* L. The situation with respect to the common or kidney bean is in some respects a counterpart of that involving the lima bean. Wild beans of this species, or one closely related to it, have been found in both Middle America and South America (Kaplan and MacNeish, 1960, p. 53), which suggests at once the possibility of an independent domestication of beans in the two regions. Furthermore the modern bean varieties of Mexico and South America, although regarded as belonging to the same species, are quite different in many of their horticultural characteristics, including various physiological responses to environmental conditions, disease resistance, and productivity. Nevertheless, the fact that this species appears quite early in Mexico, 5000–3000 B.C., and relatively late, 400 B.C., in South America is consistent with the hypothesis of a Middle American origin and a later spread to South America. More data on the genetic and cytological relationships of the cultivated varieties to the various wild forms are needed before final conclusions on this problem can be reached.

MAIZE. Of all the cultivated plants of Middle America, maize was by all odds the most important. There was no well-developed, prehistoric agriculture in any part of this region in which maize was not the principal crop. Even today there are millions of "indígenas" in Guatemala and Mexi-

---

[7] Personal communication, M. A. Towle, 1960.

[8] Personal communication, A. Grobman, 1960.

co to whom maize is quite literally the staff of life and whose agriculture is based upon the growing of this plant.

Whether maize originated in this region, and only here, are questions to which complete answers have not yet been found. The evidence is conflicting and authorities do not agree. Earlier students of maize were virtually unanimous in postulating a South American origin: St. Hilaire assigning it to Paraguay, DeCandolle to New Granada, and Darwin to Peru (cf. Mangelsdorf and Reeves, 1939). Later when the close relationship of maize and teosinte was discovered the scene shifted from South America to Mexico. Except for Sturtevant, who still held to a South American origin, opinions were almost unanimous that maize had its beginnings in Mexico and argument was confined, as Collins once stated, "to the rival claims of particular Mexican localities." Harshberger, Collins, Kempton, Kempton and Popenoe, Vavilov, Kuleshov, Weatherwax, and later Randolph, all postulated a Mexican or Central American–Mexican origin primarily because teosinte, the closest relative of maize, is confined to this general region and is unknown in South America except where it is rarely cultivated (Mangelsdorf and Reeves, 1939).

Mangelsdorf and Reeves (1939), on the basis of their cytogenetic studies of maize and its relatives, concluded that teosinte is a hybrid of maize and Tripsacum rather than the progenitor of maize, and postulated that maize as a wild plant originated in the lowlands of South America and that the Andean region became the primary center of diversification. Later, however, when fossil maize pollen was discovered in the Valley of Mexico (Barghoorn et al., 1954), Mangelsdorf (1954) concluded that "maize undoubtedly had at least one center of origin in Middle America."

In spite of conflicts of opinion certain facts are reasonably clear. There is little doubt that maize is an American plant. There have been periodic attempts to place

its origin in Asia but there is no tangible evidence of any kind—archaeological, ethnographic, linguistic, ideographic, pictorial, or historical—of the existence of maize in Asia before 1492 (Mangelsdorf and Oliver, 1951). On the other hand, there is overwhelming evidence of its American origin, among the most convincing of which is the recent discovery of fossil maize pollen, mentioned above, in the Valley of Mexico. This fossil pollen not only proves that there was once a wild maize native to this hemisphere but also suggests strongly that cultivated maize may have had one center of origin in Mexico.

There is archaeological evidence to support this suggestion. As noted, the most primitive prehistoric maize so far found in Mesoamerica are the tiny cobs from Aeyerado Cave which may be wild maize.† This maize has definite affinities with a cultivated race, *Chapalote*, still found in Mexico. Archaeological specimens of this same race have been found in the lowest levels of Swallow Cave in Chihuahua (Mangelsdorf and Lister, 1956) and it is possible that the earliest corn of Bat Cave is also of this race (cf. Mangelsdorf and Lister, 1956).

The earliest maize of La Perra Cave in Tamaulipas, dated at 4450 years, is related to another living Mexican race, *Nal-Tel* (Mangelsdorf, MacNeish, and Galinat, 1956) and shows that even at this early date there were already distinct races of maize in Mexico. This indicates either that domestication had already proceeded to the point of producing considerable diversification in cultivated maize or that distinct geographical races of wild maize occurred in various parts of Mexico and were domesticated wherever they were found.

It is now possible to identify with respect to race these archaeological specimens of maize in Mexico because of the comprehensive studies of living maize of Mexico made by Wellhausen et al. (1952). These authors recognized in Mexico four primitive races: *Palomero Toluqueño, Arrocillo Amarillo,*

438

Chapalote, and *Nal-Tel,* which they designated as "Ancient Indigenous" because there is no evidence of their having been introduced from elsewhere. Four additional races, *Cacahuacintle, Harinoso de Ocho, Olotón,* and *Maíz Dulce,* were designated as "Pre-Columbian Exotic Races" because they clearly have affinities with the maize of South America and because several of them became the parents of hybrid races which are known, from replicas on funerary urns, impressions in lava, and actual prehistoric specimens (including those of *Breve de Padilla* and *Dzit-Bacal* mentioned earlier), to have originated in pre-Columbian times. The South American affinities of these exotic races are well established by the subsequent studies of Roberts *et al.* (1957) on the races of maize of Colombia and of Wellhausen *et al.* (1957) on Guatemalan maize. The latter shows that several other races in addition to the four Mexican races mentioned above were introduced into Middle America from South America. It may be worth noting in passing that all these introductions of South American maize occurred in western parts of Guatemala. This is also true of three of the Mexican exotic races.

These introduced races from South America were more productive than the indigenous races. Why, if maize originated in Middle America, it should have evolved more rapidly in South America than in its native region, is a question not yet completely answered, although there is evidence that there has been hybridization in South America, not only between distinct races, but also with corn's hardy wild relative *Tripsacum* (Mangelsdorf and Reeves, 1959a, pp. 400–04; 1959b, pp. 421–22). The important fact for the present discussion is that the introduction of these productive South American races and their subsequent hybridization with indigenous races and with teosinte to produce still better races, the "Prehistoric Mestizos" of Wellhausen *et al.,* undoubtedly had a revolutionary

effect on the agriculture of Mesoamerica. Indeed it is quite possible that the flowering of civilization in Mesoamerica is related to the arrival in that region of the agriculturally superior South American races.

The old idea, that agriculture in this hemisphere came into full development when maize was domesticated, is no longer tenable. The wild maize with which domestication began was certainly not a particularly promising food plant—both beans and squashes were probably more productive in the early stages of agriculture. That maize eventually became the basic food plant of the pre-Columbian cultures and civilizations of the New World is due to its remarkable ability to evolve rapidly in a man-made environment.

COTTON. The New World cultivated cotton, *Gossypium hirsutum* L. of Mexico and *G. barbadense* L. of Peru are 26-chromosome allopolyploid hybrids between two 13-chromosome cottons, one of which must have resembled the wild cotton, *G. Raimondii* of Peru, and the other, one of the Old World cottons, *G. arboreum* or *G. herbaceum.* There is general agreement among students of cotton on this basic fact. Opinions differ, however, on the question of when this hybridization occurred. Hutchinson, Silow, and Stephens (1947) postulated that the hybridization took place in relatively recent times after man, crossing the Pacific by raft or canoe, introduced the Old World cultivated cotton, *G. arboreum,* into Peru where it came within the range of the native wild cotton, *G. Raimondii,* with which it hybridized. The cultivated Peruvian species, *G. barbadense,* and the Mexican species, *G. hirsutum,* as well as the wild 26-chromosome Hawaiian species, *G. tomentosum,* are assumed to have evolved from this original hybrid.

There are numerous objections to this theory, one of the most formidable being that it does not allow time enough for the differentiation of the New World 26-chromosome cotton into three distinct species

439

and a number of well-differentiated varieties, *punctatum* and *marie-galante* of *G. hirsutum* and *brasiliense* of *G. barbadense*. Especially difficult to reconcile with the theory is the wild *G. tomentosum*, a typical Hawaiian endemic, a lintless cotton far removed in many of its characteristics from its mainland relatives. Other students of cotton, although recognizing the hybrid nature of the 26-chromosome species, have assumed that this hybridization occurred before the New World and Old World species had become completely separated in their ranges at a time in the remote geological past when the floras of parts of America and parts of the Old World, South America and Africa, for example, were more or less continuous. This assumption has received support from recent cytological studies which indicate that *G. barbadense*, the cultivated cotton of Peru, is probably more closely related to *G. herbaceum*, the cultivated cotton of Africa, the Near East, and India, than it is to *G. arboreum*, the cultivated cotton of western India, China, and other parts of Asia.

Whatever their origin, the two American cultivated cottons are quite distinct and probably represent separate domestications. *G. hirsutum* appears to have its center of diversity in southern Mexico and Guatemala with one of its two varieties, *punctatum*, extending into the Greater Antilles and the other, *marie-galante*, into the Antilles and northern South America. *G. barbadense* is the cotton of Peru and western South America with one of its varieties, *brasiliense*, spreading into northeastern South America and through the Antilles. Hutchinson *et al.* assumed that this spread from the original centers is recent but we are convinced that it is ancient, much, if not most, of it having occurred before man arrived on the scene.

The earliest archaeological remains of *G. hirsutum* in Mexico and of *G. barbadense* in Peru occur at about the same time, 1700

years B.C. for the former† and 2000 years B.C. for the latter. The similarity in dates is probably a coincidence. Both remains probably represent wild cotton and the domestication of the two species was probably quite independent.

TOBACCO. Tobacco, like cotton, is represented by two cultivated species, *Nicotiana Tabacum* L. and *Nicotiana rustica* L. The former is South American in origin but it is possible that its use spread to parts of Central America and southern Mexico in pre-Columbian times. In most of Mexico, however, as well as throughout the southwestern and eastern United States and eastern Canada the cultivated tobacco was *N. rustica*, which has a nicotine content three to four times as high as that of *N. Tabacum*, a fact which may account for the circumstance that many tribes used the toxic weed only ceremonially and not for pleasure.

The tobaccos, like the cottons, are allopolyploid hybrids. *N. Tabacum* has never been found in the wild but its putative parents, *N. sylvestris* and a species of the section *Tomentosae*, *N. otophera*, are in contact today in northwestern Argentina and adjacent Bolivia which suggests that this may be the original area of its natural distribution (Goodspeed, 1954, p. 373).

The other cultivated species, *N. rustica*, apparently has for its progenitors *N. paniculata*, which has a range comprising nearly the entire length of western Peru, and *N. undulata*, which ranges from northern Peru to northwestern Argentina. The hybrid species, *N. rustica*, is highly polymorphic with a long history as a cultigen. It is unknown in the wild with the exception of the variety, *pavoni*, which ranges from southwestern Ecuadorian inter-Andine highlands through the western flanks of the Andes of southern Peru and adjacent northern Bolivia (Goodspeed, 1954, p. 355). This wild variety is quite different from the cultivated forms which probably had their origins in Mesoamerica.

440

It is probable that the domestication of *N. rustica* in Middle America was independent of that of *N. Tabacum* in South America.

BOTTLE GOURD. Belonging to the same family as the edible squashes is the inedible bottle gourd, *Lagenaria siceraria* (Mol.) Standl. Remains of this gourd represented by fragments of rinds were found in all levels of the Ocampo Caves beginning at 7000–5000 B.C.; however, seeds, which furnish a more positive identification, did not appear until the Mesa de Guaje phase at 1400–500 B.C.

If we accept the identification of the early specimens based on rinds alone, we are presented with a puzzling problem. *Lagenaria* has never been found in the wild in America and it is known to be an Old World cultigen probably of considerable antiquity. How did it reach Tamaulipas in Mexico at so early a date? Towle (1952, p. 182) has suggested that the fruits of this species may have been carried to America from Africa by ocean currents and the experiments of Whitaker and Carter (1954) on floating fruits in sea water have shown this to be a possibility. It might be supposed, however, that such ocean currents would have introduced the plant into the eastern part of South America, and it may be as Sauer (1950, p. 506) has stated that, "The theory of its accidental dissemination involves, in addition to the undamaged transit of an ocean, a waiting agriculturalist who carried it in from the sea shore to a suitable spot of cultivation."

If this assumption has validity, then agriculture in America must have had its beginnings not in Mexico or Peru but in eastern South America, not with a native seed plant but with a root-culture tradition, probably based on manioc, serving as the ready recipient for the ocean-borne *Lagenaria*, an exotic species whose fruits were useful primarily as utensils. The culture of *Lagenaria*, minus the manioc, must then have spread at very early dates to both Mexico and Peru. Such an hypothesis demands an improbable number of fortuitous circumstances.

Perhaps the time has come to take a broad new look at the genus *Lagenaria*. Perhaps it, like the genus *Gossypium* and many other genera both living and fossil, was common to both America and Africa and its great diversity, even in the earliest times, is the product, not of centuries of domestication but of millions of years of evolution in nature. The bottle gourd, perhaps more than any other species involved in tracing the origins of American agriculture, needs the attention of taxonomists, geneticists, and cytologists.

MIDDLE AMERICAN PLANT CULTIVATION IN THE NEW WORLD SETTING

In pre-Columbian times Mesoamerica enjoyed a cultural dominance on the New World scene. Along with Peru it was one of the geographic centers from which the influences of civilization radiated outwards to areas of lesser cultural intensity. To what extent was this role of dominance a function of priority in the development of agriculture? Although centers of cultural elaboration are not necessarily centers of origin as well, archaeological evidence strongly suggests that Middle America was an important primary hearth, as well as a zone of climax, for plant cultivation. It is highly likely that maize, beans, and squashes—those three staples of native American diet—were all first cultivated within or very near to Mesoamerica.

The earliest archaeological occurrence of domesticated squash or pumpkin (*Cucurbita Pepo*) comes from northern Middle America in Tamaulipas. These Infiernillo and Ocampo appearances of pumpkin seeds antedate the New Mexican Bat Cave findings of pumpkin by more than a thousand years (C. E. Smith, 1950) and the Adena pumpkin remains of the Ohio Valley by several thousand years (Goslin in Webb and Baby, 1957). South of Tamaulipas, in Mesoamerica, the pumpkin is not abundantly documented from archaeological levels.[9] Still farther south, in Peru, this pumpkin does not occur. These data, few though they are, virtually establish a point of domestication in or near Middle America. Another squash, the *C. moschata,* is placed at about 2000 B.C. in both Tamaulipas and in distant Peru (Whitaker and Bird, 1949). These findings, together with the discovery of *moschata* in preceramic Aeyerado Cave in Puebla as well as the greatest modern diversity for *moschata* being established in southern Middle America, hint at a southern Middle American primary domestication well before 2000 B.C. with a subsequent spread northward and southward at least to northwestern South America. *C. mixta,* the walnut squash, seems to be the latest of the three as a domesticate. It has been found in both Tamaulipas and in Ventana Cave, Arizona, at about A.D. 300 (Whitaker, Cutler, and MacNeish, 1957). Almost certainly, it is a north Mexican or Mesoamerican domesticate.

The cultivated common bean, *Phaseolus vulgaris,* is known first from the Ocampo phase in Tamaulipas, at 5000–3000 B.C. In the Southwestern United States *P. vulgaris* is found in Bat Cave at about 1000 B.C. (C. E. Smith, 1950), and in the eastern United States it is no earlier than the Hopewellian horizon of the time of Christ or later (Wedel, 1943, p. 26). In Peru, *P. vulgaris* does not appear until approximately 400 B.C. (Bennett and Bird, 1949, p. 142). These dates and distributions favor Middle America as the first seat of domestication of *P. vulgaris,* although it should be remembered that the Peruvian form of this bean may have had a separate and independent domestication. Within Middle America it is not likely that Tamaulipas was the original

[9] MacNeish (Article 12) refers to a *Cucurbita Pepo* seed in late preceramic levels of Aeyerado Cave, southern Puebla.

442

point of cultivation. The presence, today, of a wild variety of bean in southern Mexico and Guatemala argues for a southern Mesoamerican homeland (Dressler, 1953). The lima bean, *P. lunatus,* is no earlier than the early Palmillas phase (A.D. 0–500) in the Tamaulipas sequence, but in Peru it is one of the oldest domesticates, dating back to 2000 B.C. Again, as mentioned earlier, this does not signify a south-to-north diffusion, as the Middle American and Peruvian varieties of *P. lunatus* are clearly different and it is likely that they represent separate and independent domestications of wild beans (see note 7).

For *Zea mays* or American Indian corn the archaeological evidence is predominantly on the side of a Middle American primary domestication. Most likely, this was a southern Mexican domestication beginning as early as 2000 B.C. or before.[†] It would appear that the earliest diffusions of this primitive but cultivated maize were northward from this center, to Tamaulipas, Sonora (Mangelsdorf and Lister, 1956), and the southwestern United States (Mangelsdorf and Smith, 1949; Irwin and Irwin, 1959). Even at this very early date (ca. 3000–2000 B.C.) there were two races of *Z. mays.* The Sonoran, Southwestern Tamaulipas, and Bat Cave New Mexican specimens belong to a pod-pop type which has affinities with the modern race, *Chapalote,* while that from the Sierra de Tamaulipas caves is an early *Nal-Tel* type (*ibid.;* Mangelsdorf, MacNeish, and Galinat, 1956). Apparently, the spread of primitive Middle American maize to Andean South America was somewhat later than this. On the north Peruvian coast it is dated between 1400 and 1200 B.C. (D. Collier, 1959). Whether or not maize had also been domesticated independently in Peru before this, is an interesting question. If, as Mangelsdorf and Reeves (1959b, p. 422) have suggested, the great diversification of maize in Peru is the result of hybridization between the early and primitive Mesoamerican popcorn with the

Peruvian popcorn, *Confite Morocho*, then it might be argued that *Confite Morocho* resulted from a separate Peruvian domestication of local wild maize. As yet, however, this problem is not resolved.

Several other important plants have an early history in Middle America although they did not necessarily originate there, nor is it certain they are all early domesticates. The chili pepper (*Capsicum annuum* and *C. frutescens*), the ubiquitous Middle American condiment, is one of these. It occurs in Tamaulipas in the Infiernillo phase (7000–5000 B.C.), and in Peru it is known from the earliest Huaca Prieta levels (ca. 2000 B.C.) (Bird, 1948). As wild chili ranges, intermittently, over an area from the southwestern United States to Brazil, it is possible that domestication took place, independently, in several localities (Dressler, 1953). Although it is difficult to tell wild from cultivated varieties, the absence or scarcity of the wild species of *Capsicum* in highland Tamaulipas today suggests that the archaeological specimens of the plant found in that region are domesticates (MacNeish, 1959).

New World cotton occurs as two species. *Gossypium hirsutum* is as early as 1700 B.C. in Tamaulipas† and a closely related variety is in the southwestern United States by the first millennium B.C. (Martin *et al.*, 1952). The other species, *G. barbadense*, is found in Peruvian preceramic contexts at 2000 B.C. (Bennett and Bird, 1949). Apparently these were separate and independent domestications. The story of tobacco is probably similar. *Nicotiana Tabacum* seems to have been first cultivated in the South American tropical lowlands, spreading from there to the West Indies and possibly to Central America and Southern Mexico. *N. rustica*, the species known earliest from Middle America and eastern North America, probably originated as a domesticate in Middle America and gradually spread northward from there to the southwestern and eastern United States and eastern Can-

ada. This was the tobacco known in the Mississippi Valley as early as the first millennium B.C. (Webb and Baby, 1957). *Lagenaria*, the bottle gourd, which dates from the Infiernillo phase in Tamaulipas, is also early in Peru (Bennett and Bird, 1949; Towle, 1952), in Bat Cave, New Mexico (C. E. Smith, 1950), and in the eastern United States (Funkhouser and Webb, 1929). The ambiguities and problems surrounding the history of this particular plant have been discussed in detail above. In any case this plant is not the most critical for the rise of Mesoamerican agriculture as are some others.

A number of "root crops," belonging to a South American tropical lowland tradition of "vegetative planting," were introduced into Middle America as domesticates in relatively late prehistoric times (Sauer, 1959). Among these the peanut (*Arachis hypogaea*), the sweet potato (*Ipomoea Batatas*), and manioc (*Manihot esculenta*) were the most important. Manioc occurs at Huaca Prieta in Peru on a time level of 750–400 B.C. (D. Collier, 1959); in Tamaulipas it is first found at 500 B.C.–0 when it probably was not a domesticate but the wild Mexican *M. dulcis* (MacNeish, 1959). It is almost certain that it was cultivated in northeastern South America much earlier than any of these dates (Willey, 1960a).

To conclude, within the larger New World setting Middle America was a primary center for plant domestication. Native agriculture developed slowly here at first over a span of several millennia which we have designated as an "era of incipient cultivation." Then, as plants were improved through cultivation and selection they were also interchanged throughout the area so that by the beginning of the first millennium B.C., if not considerably before, Middle America became essentially dependent on an agricultural way of life. From the very earliest beginnings of incipient cultivation there appears to have been diffusion of plants and ideas concerned with their

443

domestication out of the Middle American area. Then, with the establishment of full village agricultural subsistence, Middle America became even more of a heartland for the propagation of agriculture to lands beyond its borders. Conversely, it also assimilated cultivated plants originating in other areas; and it was the recipient of new improved secondary types of old Middle American cultigens which elsewhere had hybridized with other races and wild relatives, and thus had evolved more rapidly than the primary types in their original center. Such, very briefly, is the history behind the amazing agricultural richness and diversity of Middle America which Cortés viewed in the early 16th century.

ADDENDUM

Since this article was written in the early summer of 1960, there have been a number of significant developments related to the origins of agriculture in Middle America. Especially important are the results that have come from the excavations conducted by MacNeish and his associates in a number of once-inhabited caves in the Valley of Tehuacan, Mexico (MacNeish, 1964; Mangelsdorf, MacNeish, and Galinat, 1964; C. E. Smith and MacNeish, 1964). These show a transition, over a period from 7200 B.C. to A.D. 1540, from a hunting and food-gathering subsistence to a full-fledged agriculture which included many species of plants and employed a well-developed system of irrigation.

The earliest remains of plants occurred in the El Riego phase, 7200–5200 B.C., and included a number of species later domesticated: a species of squash, C. mixta, chili peppers, avocados, and cotton. In the Cox-

catlan phase, 5200–3400 B.C., gourds, amaranths, tepary beans, yellow and white sapotes, another squash, C. moschata, and, most important of all, maize had been added to the list. Some of these plants may have been cultivated; the maize was almost certainly wild and is the first prehistoric wild maize to be uncovered (Mangelsdorf, MacNeish, and Galinat, 1964).

The Abejas phase, 3400–2300 B.C., shows definite evidence of agriculture and the addition to the food plants of common beans, P. vulgaris, another squash, C. Pepo, and cultivated maize.

The Purron phase, 2300–1500 B.C., is poor in plant remains, but in the succeeding phase, Ajalpan, 1500–900 B.C., the people were full-fledged agriculturalists, growing a hybridized corn, three species of squashes, beans, chili peppers, amaranths, and cotton.

Irrigation may have had its beginnings in the Santa Maria phase, 900–200 B.C. It was certainly employed systematically by full-time agriculturalists in the Palo Blanco phase, from 200 B.C. to A.D. 700.

The final phase, Venta Salada, A.D. 700–1540, was characterized by a highly developed and productive agriculture with irrigation capable of supporting a large population living in secular cities or towns —a population perhaps 5000 times as large as the original number of inhabitants of the valley, which is estimated to have consisted of not more than three microbands of four to eight people each.

Although providing earlier dates than were previously available for several of the plants discussed above, the new evidence tends, to a rather remarkable degree, to support the principal conclusions set forth in the earlier part of this article.

REFERENCES

Barghoorn, Wolfe, and Clisby, 1954
Bennett and Bird, 1949
Bird, 1948
Bukasov, 1930
Callen and MacNeish, n.d.
Carter, 1945
Collier, D., 1959
Cruxent, 1958
Deevey, 1944
Dressler, 1953
Funkhouser and Webb, 1929
Goodspeed, 1954
Heiser, 1955
Hopkins, 1959
Hutchinson, Silow, and Stephens, 1947
Irwin and Irwin, 1959
Kaplan and MacNeish, 1960
Mackie, 1943
MacNeish, 1958, 1959, 1964
Mangelsdorf, 1954
—— and Lister, 1956

——, MacNeish, and Galinat, 1956, 1964
—— and Oliver, 1951
—— and Reeves, 1939, 1959a, 1959b
—— and Smith, 1949
Martin, 1952
Payne, 1892
Roberts et al., 1957
Sauer, 1950, 1959
Smith, C. E., 1950
—— and MacNeish, 1964
Spinden, 1917
Towle, 1952
Vavilov, 1951
Webb and Baby, 1957
Wedel, 1943
Wellhausen et al., 1952, 1957
Whitaker and Bird, 1949
—— and Carter, 1954
——, Cutler, and MacNeish, 1957
Willey, 1960a, 1960b

445

14. The Patterns of Farming Life and Civilization

GORDON R. WILLEY
GORDON F. EKHOLM
RENÉ F. MILLON

THE DISTINCTIVE CULTURES and civilizations of Mesoamerica[1] emerged with or shortly after the establishment of agriculture and sedentary communities. This new way of life, as opposed to incipient cultivation and less sedentary existence, seems to have been well established a millennium or even a millennium-and-a-half before the beginning of the Christian Era.[2] At about the same time appeared the art of pottery making, which, because it provides an archaeological record, serves to document this early Mesoamerican stage. Sedentary life may be still older than pottery, but from at least this point forward we know that channels were open for the evolvement of a new way of life for the peoples of the area, and within a few centuries these channels were so deepened that they influenced the direction of native cultural development down to the present day.

We shall here briefly describe the form and qualities of pre-Columbian Mesoamerican society and culture as a whole and its regional variations. After passing on to relative and absolute chronology, we finally consider some of the major social and cultural trends from the beginnings of village farming to the rise of cities and empires. This summary, as does all our knowledge of Mesoamerica, derives from four principal sources: (1) archaeological data including sites, monuments, artifacts, and hieroglyphics; (2) native writings and semilegendary histories of the Spanish conquest period bearing on the past; (3) early descriptions and histories written by Europeans who were eyewitnesses to events of the 16th century or who drew upon firsthand accounts; and (4) inferences from modern ethnology and linguistics which throw light on conditions in earlier times.

FORM AND QUALITIES OF MESOAMERICAN SOCIETY AND CULTURE

Basic Technologies

Plant cultivation became the primary subsistence activity in pre-Columbian Middle America by 1000 B.C., if not before (see

[1] See Kirchhoff (1943), Kidder, Jennings, and Shook (1946), Kroeber (1948), for definitions of Mesoamerica as a culture area.
[2] See Article 12 by MacNeish and Article 13 by Mangelsdorf, MacNeish, and Willey.

446

Fig. 1—PYRAMID OF THE MOON, TEOTIHUACAN, MEXICO

MacNeish, Article 12, and Mangelsdorf, MacNeish, and Willey, Article 13). Maize, planted in *milpas*, was the principal staple, together with red and black beans, lima beans, pumpkins, squash, and chili peppers; these were supplemented by sweet manioc, agave, sweet potatoes, sunflower seeds, amaranth, chenopodium, cacao, aguacates, tomatoes, and other fruits and vegetables.[3] The lands for these crops were cleared with stone tools, the fallen trees burned, and the seeds or cuttings planted with the aid of a fire-hardened digging stick.[4] This system of clearing and planting was, and is, widespread in Mesoamerica, with adaptations

to the particular environment. In some regions the soil is sufficiently fertile to allow for annual rotation and fallowing, alternating between two fields or plots (*barbecho* or fallowing system); in others, usually in lowland tropical forests, a field may be planted for one or two years and left to return to bush for perhaps five (*roza* or slash-and-burn system) (Palerm, 1955). More intensive cultivation was possible in humid

[3] See Mangelsdorf, MacNeish, and Willey, Article 13.

[4] A modification of this was the copper-shod or pointed digging stick used in western Mexico (Armillas, 1951, p. 29).

447

FIG. 2—TEMPLE II, TIKAL, GUATEMALA
(ARTIST'S RECONSTRUCTION)
Maya Classic terraced pyramid and surmounting temple. The temple is adorned with an ornately sculp-
tured roof comb. (After Proskouriakoff, 1946.)

in granaries or in subterranean pits. The
corn was prepared by boiling it in lime
water and then grinding it while wet on a
stone *metate* with a handstone or *mano*. In
some parts of Mesoamerica the resulting
paste, *masa*, was made into thin cakes, or
tortillas, by being roasted on a flat pottery
griddle or *comal*, and eaten with beans and
chili. The masa was prepared in a number
of other ways, but the most common in the
lowland regions was the mixing of it with
water to make thin gruel, *pozole*. A drink
of low alcoholic content was *pulque*, made
from the sap of the maguey plant, a variety
of agave. The cacao bean was the source
of a chocolate drink; honey, from beekeep-
ing, was a sweetener; and salt was derived
from deposits around inland lake beds or
from near the sea. The dog, sometimes
raised as a source of food, and the turkey
were the only animal domesticates (see
Wolf, 1959, pp. 63–66 for a summary of
foods and food preparation). The degree of
dependence on hunting, fishing, and wild
foods must have varied considerably. It is
probable that a small but significant addition to the primarily vegetarian diet was
supplied by deer, peccaries, iguanas, fish,
insects, and birds of many kinds (see Roys,
1943, as an example; also Deevey, 1957).

At the time of the Spanish conquest
Mesoamerican civilization was essentially
on a stone-age level of technology. Metals
were known but employed mainly for ornaments; copper tools, in use in parts of western Mexico and, to a lesser extent, in Oaxaca and central Mexico in late pre-Columbian times, were the exception. Most of the
area depended on tools or weapons of
chipped or ground stone. Celts or axes of
chipped chert or of ground stone were used
in land clearing and in agriculture, and it is
possible that these same implements served
the stone mason in the trimming of limestone or tuff. Knives, daggers, projectile
points, scrapers, and drills were made of
chert and obsidian. Among the most com-

valley bottoms with rich soils, or was made
possible by agricultural terracing, canal irrigation, and construction of *chinampas* or
"floating gardens." Generally, intensive cultivation techniques were followed in upland
regions tending to semiaridity. The construction of chinampas—small artificial islands of mud and reeds in shallow lakes—
was widespread in the Valley of Mexico in
Aztec times and may well represent an
ancient tradition in the Valley. (For cultivation practices see Armillas, 1949; West and
Armillas, 1950; Palerm, 1955; Wolf and
Palerm, 1955; Millon, 1959; Wolf, 1959, pp.
48–68.)

Corn and other seed foods were stored

FIG. 3—MAYA ARCHITECTURE IN THE NORTHERN LOWLANDS (ARTIST'S RECON-
STRUCTION)
The Monjas or Nunnery quadrangle, Uxmal, Yucatan, Mexico. Temple of the Dwarf, or Magi-
cian, stands at the right. Pure Florescent. (After Proskouriakoff, 1946.)

FIG. 4—NUNNERY ANNEX AND IGLESIA, CHICHEN ITZA, YUCATAN
Pure Florescent. (Photo by Otto Done.)

er flat, rectangular, and made to be hafted, or clublike and unhafted, both bear characteristic grooved surfaces.

Mesoamerican architecture—as exemplified by palaces, pyramids, and temples—is one of the outstanding accomplishments of pre-Columbian America (see Marquina, 1951). As early as the first millennium B.C. temple and palace platform mounds of imposing size were built of earth, rock, rubble, and adobe; and by the beginning of the Christian Era pyramidal platforms and their surmounting buildings were faced with cut stone masonry set in lime mortar. Roofs of the buildings were spanned by either wooden or stone beams laid flat across upright supports, or, in some Mesoamerican regions, a corbeled-arch principle was employed in the construction of a stone vault. Among the major architectural features were stairways, both raised and inset, balustrades, terraces, plinths and moldings, columns, and superstructural additions to temples and palaces such as flying façades and roof combs. True

FIG. 5—NEPHRITE CELT, COSTA RICA
(Photo by Middle American Research Institute, Tulane University.)

mon household artifacts of the past, as well as today, are the stone metates and manos for corn grinding. Metates are either trough-shaped and fitted with a short, rectangular mano or they are flat from side to side and used with a long mano that extends out over the sides. Sometimes the metates are legged. Bark beaters, for pounding bark into cloth or paper, are another ground-stone artifact frequently found in domestic refuse. Wheth-

FIG. 6—ONYX MASK, MEXICO
Alexander Kirk Collection. (Photo by Middle American Research Institute, Tulane University.)

450

storied buildings are rare although this effect was sometimes achieved by placing one series of rooms above another with the upper rooms set back and resting on solid construction. Domestic houses were usually small, one- or two-room affairs with pole, wattle-and-daub, adobe, or stone walls. These were roofed with wood and grass or palm thatch. In some places ordinary dwellings were constructed as agglutinated clusters of buildings or rooms, apartment-house fashion; in others the individual houses were isolated.

The sculptor's art was especially well developed in native Mesoamerica. It is expressed both in small objects of stone (figs. 5, 6), and in monumental sculpture, for which the area is famous. The latter includes freestanding statues and stelae (fig. 7) carved in both high and low relief as

FIG. 8—STUCCO BAS-RELIEF, WALL OF TOMB, COMALCALCO, MEXICO (RESTORED)
(Photo by Middle American Research Institute, Tulane University.)

FIG. 7—STELA B, COPAN, HONDURAS
A beautiful example of Late Classic Maya ornate sculpture. (Courtesy, Gordon R. Willey.)

well as bas-relief and stucco-relief wall decoration (fig. 8). Such monuments are associated with major sites and ceremonial precincts, either individually or as architectural adornment. Mural painting (figs. 9, 10) was another important element of ceremonial architecture in certain regions (Ruppert, Thompson, and Proskouriakoff, 1955).

Native Mesoamericans everywhere were adept ceramists (figs. 11–14). Pottery was constructed by hand modeling, by annular additions (coils, rings, etc.), or by the use of molds. The wheel was not used to "throw" pottery, although it is probable that vessels were sometimes rotated on unpivoted turntables during their manufac-

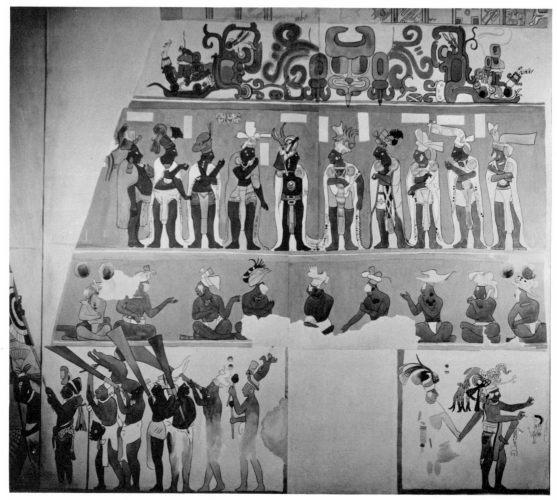

FIG. 9—MURAL, BONAMPAK, CHIAPAS, MEXICO
Late Classic. (Photo by Otto Done.)

ture.[5] The basic pottery shapes are bowls, plates, jars, and bottles occurring in a great variety of forms. Annular and ring bases, handles, lids, stirrup-spouts and straight spouts were all known as were a variety of human and animal effigy forms. A widespread item is the incense burner or *incen-*

sario, often ornately modeled. Ceramic decorative techniques include modeling and other plastic treatments, incising, carving, and painting. Single or multicolored wares were usually painted before firing, but there are varieties of postfired painting in which brilliant colored paints were combined with a thin stucco-layer coating. Rarer but quite widespread in central and western Mexico is the decorative technique known as *paint cloisonné.* Resist or negative painting is an unusual process of decorating pottery that

[5] See Foster, 1955, 1959a, and R. H. Thompson, 1958, for native Mesoamerican pottery-making methods still used in modern times. For the relationship between such methods and the use of the potter's wheel, see Foster, 1959a and 1959b.

452

FIG. 10—MURAL, TEMPLE OF THE WARRIORS, CHICHEN ITZA, YUCATAN
Modified Florescent. (Photo by Otto Done.)

FIG. 11—THIN ORANGE HUMAN-EFFIGY JAR
FROM KAMINALJUYU, GUATEMALA
Early Classic. (Courtesy, J. Haveman.)

FIG. 12—POLYCHROME VASE, CHAMA, GUA-
TEMALA
Late Classic. (After M. Louise Baker.)

FIG. 13—POLYCHROME VASE, RATINLIXAL,
ALTA VERAPAZ, GUATEMALA
Late Classic. (After M. Louise Baker.)

FIG. 14—POTTERY VESSEL, HUASTECA RE-
GION, MEXICO
(Photo by Middle American Research Institute,
Tulane University.)

FIG. 15—POTTERY FIGURINE, XUPA, CHIA-
PAS, MEXICO
Jaina style, Late Classic (Photo by Middle Amer-
ican Research Institute, Tulane University.)

FIG. 16—JAINA-STYLE FIGURINE, PROBABLY FROM CAMPECHE, MEXICO
(Courtesy, Peabody Museum, Harvard University.)

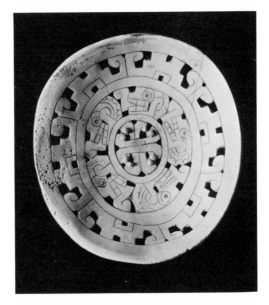

FIG. 17—SHELL ORNAMENT, HUASTECA REGION, MEXICO
(Photo by Middle American Research Institute, Tulane University.)

appears early in Mesoamerica. In addition to vessels, figurines, both handmade and moldmade and in human and animal forms, are abundant products of Mesoamerican ceramic manufacture (figs. 15, 16). Other items are whistles and rattles, earplugs, roller and flat stamps or seals, smoking pipes, and spindle whorls.

The work of the Mesoamerican sculptor was not confined to ceramics and stone. Bone and shell ornaments (fig. 17) and occasionally preserved wooden objects reveal delicate skills. Rare finds from the muck and water of the Cenote of Sacrifice of Mayan

Chichen Itza include wooden knife handles and other objects handsomely and intricately carved, as well as items of bone and gourd. Wooden drums and atlatls, of which a number of Aztec and Mixtec examples still exist, are superbly carved, and it is known that wood was widely used for decorative house fittings and furniture.

Mosaic work in stone or shell on bases of wood or stone was another highly developed Mesoamerican craft, as was the use of colored feathers for the adornment of shields, for insignia and headdresses, and for cloaks. The weaving of textiles was apparently universal, but the nature of the productions in this craft can only be inferred from the garments represented in sculptures and paintings, from those described at the time of the conquest, and the occasional shreds of cloth turned up in archaeological contexts. Cotton and agave were the principal fibers woven; the dyes were various. Paper in the form of bark

455

cloth was manufactured for clothing and for books.

Metallurgy was a Mesoamerican craft with a relatively brief tradition in the area, probably not appearing before A.D. 800. At the time of the Spanish conquest, goldsmiths were highly respected artisans; gold was cast by the "lost-wax" or "wax-model" method to make exquisite jewelry (fig. 18). Copper was used both for ornaments and utensils.[6]

Land transportation in native Mesoamerica was confined to foot travel and to litters borne by humans (fig. 13); there were no draft animals. That the principle of the wheel was known is indicated by the presence of wheeled toys of clay, but there is no archaeological evidence that it was ever put to practical use (Ekholm, 1946a). The traveler was aided by well-known and marked trails and roads throughout all of the area. These were the routes taken by Cortés and other conquerors in the 16th century. In Yucatan prepared roadways were constructed aboriginally between some of the major ceremonial centers. One of these roads or causeways is as much as 100 km. long (J. E. S. Thompson, 1954, p. 66). For the most part such carefully prepared roads were not common in Mesoamerica. Canoe travel was important in many places. The Spanish conquistadores refer to the numerous canoes and boats on Lake Texcoco; produce was carried to the Aztec capital of Tenochtitlan from surrounding communities by this means. Canoes also must have served for river transportation; aboriginal paintings at Chichen Itza, in Yucatan, apparently show coastwise use of canoes (fig. 10). Other evidence indicates that coastal canoe traffic was relatively extensive in Yucatan and surrounding regions when the Spanish arrived (Columbus, 1867, p. 292; Oviedo, 1851–55, 1: 235; Torquemada, 1723, 1: 335).

[6] Vaillant (1941, pp. 139–68) gives a good summary account of craftsmanship in Aztec times.

FIG. 18—GOLD MASK OF THE GOD XIPE, FROM MONTE ALBAN, OAXACA
Late Postclassic, probably Mixtec in origin. (Courtesy, René F. Millon.)

Organization of Society

The organization of ancient Mesoamerican society is reflected, to some extent, in settlement patterns which can be studied archaeologically. The term *settlement pattern* refers to the size and grouping of dwellings, the relationship of these to public or ceremonial buildings, and the relation of all these to natural environment, thus affording inferences as to the economic, social, political, and religious aspects of ancient Mesoamerican societies. Ethnohistoric documents and modern ethnological studies supplement the settlement data in significant ways.

The basic settlement in Mesoamerica was the agricultural village. From historic and modern ethnological sources we may infer that the households of a village were the residences of nuclear or extended families and that kinship was structured in either bilateral or patrilineal terms. There were

Fig. 19—THE ACROPOLIS, COPAN, HONDURAS (ARTIST'S RECONSTRUCTION),
SHOWING PYRAMIDS SURMOUNTED BY TEMPLES, PALACES ON PLATFORMS, AND
OTHER BUILDINGS OF THE CEREMONIAL CENTER
Late Classic. (After Proskouriakoff, 1946.)

two types of village settlement: concentrated and dispersed. In the former, dwellings were placed close together to compose a visible, compact community; in the latter, households were scattered, occurring individually or in small hamlet clusters, with farming lands interspersed between them. Both these types persist throughout the prehistory of agricultural Mesoamerica, the normal pattern being the long persistence of one type or the other in a given region or subarea.

We have little reliable information on how the social order was structured in pre-Columbian times. In general, it would appear that leadership, both religious and secular, was inherited, and that succession,

if not determined strictly by a descent principle, tended to be restricted to families or to small aristocratic groups. It seems certain that social classes were a feature of ancient Mesoamerica, at least in its Classic and Postclassic periods. The basic stratum was the peasantry;[7] at the top was an aristocracy of civic, religious, and military leaders; occupying an intermediate position, at least in

[7] We are using this term in the sense attributed to it by Redfield (1956). The rise of temple centers and cities in Mesoamerica undoubtedly basically altered the way of life of the ordinary farmer. The transformation was almost certainly more profound in some regions than others, but just as clearly does not seem to have been dependent on the formation of urban centers. See below, p. 489.

457

Fig. 20—THE ACROPOLIS, PIEDRAS NEGRAS, GUATEMALA (ARTIST'S RECON-
STRUCTION)
A Maya Late Classic architectural complex of platforms, pyramids, courtyards, palaces, temples,
and stairways. (After Proskouriakoff, 1946.)

some instances, were artisans, traders, the lower echelons of the priesthood, and minor officials.

The temple or ceremonial center (figs. 19–21) appears early in the Mesoamerican agricultural era. These centers are marked by platform mounds and other monuments which clearly differentiate them in function from ordinary dwelling units. Sometimes they are associated with concentrations of dwellings; in other instances they occur as more or less isolated entities surrounded by dispersed villages. In the later pre-Columbian periods urban communities or cities grew up around some of these centers. At the same time, in other parts of Mesoamerica, great ceremonial centers of obvious importance developed without accompanying urban types of settlements. Both the true city and the nonurban ceremonial center seem to have served as political, religious, and perhaps trading "capitals" for geographic zones which embraced villages and other lesser settlement units.[8]

[8] A *community* settlement pattern refers to the community unit alone, the village, town, etc.; a *zonal* settlement pattern describes the integration of villages and centers making up the interdependent system of economic, social and political life of a region. See W. T. Sanders, 1956; Mayer-Oakes, 1959, pp. 368–70.

Fig. 21—AERIAL VIEW OF CHICHEN ITZA, YUCATAN, MEXICO, WITH TEMPLE OF THE WARRIORS AND COLONNADE IN FOREGROUND, MAIN PYRAMID, OR CASTILLO IN CENTER, AND THE CARACOL, NUNNERY, AND OTHER BUILDINGS IN BACKGROUND
The buildings in background pertain to the earlier, or Pure Florescent, Mayan occupation of the site; the Temple of the Warriors and the Castillo belong to the Toltec, or Toltec-related, Modified Florescent occupation. (Courtesy, Compañía Mexicana Aerofoto.)

In late pre-Columbian times, at least, and possibly earlier, political aggregates of substantial territorial size were a part of the Mesoamerican scene. The Aztec "empire" is the best known of these. It extended from the capital of Tenochtitlan, in the Valley of Mexico, to both sea coasts. A great many lesser regional or city "states" were under its suzerainty. This "empire" was held together by military force and, to some extent, by trade. It had not developed the kind of bureaucratic control and stability that seems to have characterized the Inca empire of Peru; for its numerous vassal lords were in somewhat tenuous subjection or allegiance to the Aztecs so that successive conquests, revolts, and reconquests marked its history.[9]

Dominant Themes

Mesoamerican culture can be characterized by certain dominant themes. They are not all, except in their stylistic peculiarities, unique to Mesoamerica. Most of them might be considered intensified and elaborated expressions of more widely held New World patterns. It is in their intensification and elaboration, however, that they have become distinctively Mesoamerican (Kirchhoff, 1943).

One predominant theme is a distinctive fatalistic cosmology, manifested in elaborate religious systems, with powerful, often capricious gods before whom man is in-

[9] For a description of Aztec political organization see Katz, 1956, 1958; Caso, 1954; Wolf, 1959, pp. 132–51; Prescott, 1843; Vaillant, 1941.

Fig. 22—BALL COURT, COPAN, HONDURAS (RESTORED)
Note markers in central playing alley and at top of playing benches. Buildings surmounted the
side platforms. Maya· Late Classic. (After Longyear, 1952.)

significant and impotent. All the testimony of archaeology attests to the strength of such complex religious beliefs extending deep into the past. Architecture is largely devoted to religion, and the major arts are rich in religious iconography of this sort. In spite of many regional and local variations of expression, certain Mesoamerican religious concepts and symbols had an area-wide, or nearly area-wide, distribution. The water god Tlaloc, the jaguar, the serpent, and the feathered-serpent motifs are examples.

Bound up with the beliefs and rituals of this distinctive religious orientation were hieroglyphic writing, mathematics, astronomy, and a complex calendrical system. These were most highly developed among the ancient Maya of the lowlands, but they

occur in similar but less elaborate forms in most regions of Mesoamerica. For example, an annual calendar of 18 months of 20 days each, plus five additional days, was widely employed. This was combined with an even more widespread 260-day ritual calendar formed by the permutation of 20 day signs and 13 numbers, to form a 52-year cycle. The counting and periodization of time, and the endowing of time with religious and ritual meaning, is a characteristic feature of pre-Columbian Mesoamerica.

Human sacrifice is another religious element that can be considered a theme in Mesoamerican culture. It, too, was a part of religious belief. Apparently of some antiquity, it was intensified in the last centuries before the Spanish conquest when the Aztecs were offering thousands of annual

460

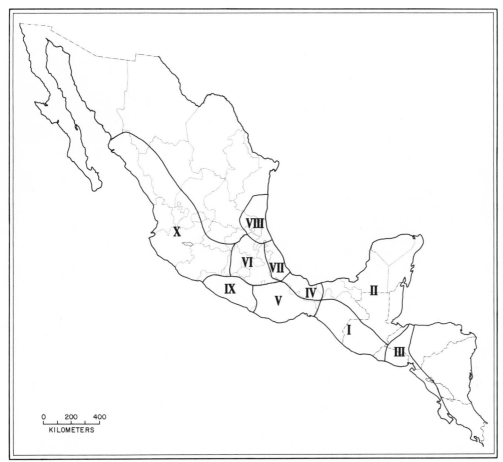

Fig. 23—MAP OF THE MESOAMERICAN CULTURE AREA WITH REGIONAL DIVI-
SIONS
I, Maya Highlands. II, Maya Lowlands. III, Southern Periphery. IV, Southern Veracruz-Tabas-
co. V, Oaxaca. VI, Central Mexico. VII, Central Veracruz. VIII, The Huasteca. IX, Guerrero.
X, Western Mexico and the Northern Frontier.

sacrificial victims to their gods. Although
not carried to such extremes elsewhere, it
was practiced widely. For example, in Yucatan "backsliding" from Christianity to old
pagan beliefs and rituals was sometimes
accompanied by human sacrifice (J. E. S.
Thompson, 1954, pp. 243–45).

Two ritual games qualify as distinctly
Mesoamerican. One of these was the famous sacred ball game, played with a rubber ball between two teams on a specially
constructed playing field or ball court.
These courts have been identified archaeologically as has some of the paraphernalia
associated with the game (Blom, 1932b;
Ekholm, 1946b; Stern, 1948). Courts are

known for the Classic (fig. 22) and Postclassic periods, and figurines representing
ball players are evidence of an even greater antiquity of the complex. Ball games
similar to that of Mesoamerica are found
elsewhere in the New World, and this is a
clear case of specialized elaboration of a
more widely shared pattern. The other
ritualized "game" is the *volador* ceremony
in which four men dressed as gods or birds
descend through the air at the ends of ropes
that unwind over a revolving platform at
the top of a tall pole. It is still performed
by Indians in several parts of Mesoamerica.

Markets were emphasized in native Mesoamerica as they are today. From Preclassic

461

Fig. 24—ZACULEU, GUATEMALAN HIGHLANDS
Postclassic period. (Courtesy, A. Ledyard Smith.)

period times we have archaeological evidences of interregional trade, and from the ethnohistoric picture of 16th-century Tenochtitlan, Tlatelolco, and other cities we can infer that the institution of the market and its location in plazas around which temples are grouped has considerable antiquity in Mesoamerica. The high development of the market as an institution and the rise of specialized merchants is distinctively Mesoamerican as compared with the other great area of native American civilization, Peru. There interregional and much of the intraregional distribution of goods, raw materials, and produce was controlled by the Inca state.[10]

Finally, subtle emphases are shared by the great art styles of Mesoamerica. These are thematic, emphatic, and repetitive qualities which imply some basic common heritage of ways of perceiving the world. Maya, Teotihuacan, Totonac, Zapotec, Olmec, Toltec, Mixtec, and Aztec styles are all geographically and chronologically distinct. Yet

they are linked by such practices as the use of rhythmic curves to delineate forms, the adaptation of grotesques or combined natural-grotesque forms as ornaments, and the great emphasis on the scroll element and the "stepped fret" as design elements (Proskouriakoff, 1958).

REGIONAL DIVERSITY

Along with this over-all unity of Mesoamerican agrarian society and culture, we find, on another level of viewing, considerable diversity. This is expressed spatially and is undoubtedly due in large part to the extraordinary topographic and climatic diversity within the Mesoamerican area. The salient social and cultural differences that exist are to be seen in the separate, although interrelated, histories of the several regions (see map, fig. 23).

Maya Highlands

The region of the Maya highlands is the upland country of Guatemala and Chiapas and its bordering Pacific slopes and coasts. Our best information on the archaeology of the region comes from the highland basin of Guatemala City and the Kaminaljuyu site zone. Village and town concentrations

[10] For contrast see the account of the Aztec market in Tlatelolco in Vaillant, 1941, pp. 234–36, and statements about Inca trade in Rowe, 1946, pp. 270–71; S. F. Moore, 1958, pp. 86–89.

and ceremonial platform mounds of earth and adobe appear early here, dating back to the Early Preclassic phase of Arevalo (Shook, 1951). Ceramics and handmade figurines were abundant and well developed. By Middle Preclassic times Kaminaljuyu was a large ceremonial and residential center (Shook and Kidder, 1952). There is an early sophistication to highland Preclassic culture expressed in fine jade carving, richly furnished burials, a monumental stone carving style, and hieroglyphics.[11] Curiously, the early start in monumental stone carving and hieroglyphics of the Preclassic is not followed up. The Guatemalan highland Classic phases lack distinctive local stylistic flavor; architecture (fig. 24) is strongly influenced by the Teotihuacan civilization of central Mexico; and ceramic arts are either Teotihuacan-inspired or in Maya lowland traditions (Kidder, Jennings, and Shook, 1946). In the Late Classic period Mexican influence is seen in the Cotzumalhuapa sculptural style and glyphic material of the Guatemalan Pacific slopes.[12] The influence is neither that of Teotihuacan nor of Tula although it is possible that it is a reflection of early Toltec expansion. Early Postclassic was the horizon of the diffusion of plumbate wares which appear to have radiated from southern Guatemala and Salvador in Early Postclassic times (A. O. Shepard, 1948). During the late Postclassic period the Maya highlands underwent a "time of troubles." Settlements for the period are mostly hilltop fortified locations (A. L. Smith, 1955; Shook and Proskouriakoff, 1956).

Maya Lowlands

The lowlands of the Peten in Guatemala and the adjacent tropical forests of Chiapas, Tabasco, the Yucatan Peninsula, British Honduras, and western Honduras constituted the seat of classic Maya civilization *par excellence*. The civilization is characterized by the greatest architectural elaboration in Mesoamerica, by a major art style, and by outstanding developments in writing, astronomy, and calendrics (J. E. S. Thompson, 1954). The earlier Preclassic beginnings of this civilization appear rather unimpressive although there is some evidence for mound and ceremonial center building (Brainerd, 1954, pp. 12–20, and see Andrews, vol. 2, Article 12).[12a] Vaulted buildings, calendrics, hieroglyphics, characteristic Maya art, and polychrome pottery have their beginnings in the Late Preclassic and Early Classic periods and brilliantly and rapidly effloresce. To what extent this efflorescence was locally generated or influenced from other regions such as the Maya highlands or Southern Veracruz-Tabasco is not yet clear. For example, monumental sculpture, hieroglyphics, and a system of numeral notation are found in these other regions earlier than in the Maya lowlands, or so it appears.[13] Despite this, the societies of the Maya lowlands had outstripped all other Mesoamerican societies in these activities by the end of the southern Early Classic and the northern Early period. In the Late Classic of the south (figs. 19, 20) and the Florescent of northern Yucatan (fig. 3) there was a proliferation of ceremonial centers. These appear to have been politico-religious and perhaps economic capitals for dispersed farming populations living in hamlet-type communities (W. R. Bullard, 1960). In the southern part of the Maya lowlands the Classic period closes with either the abandonment or a

[11] See Miles, volume 2, Article 10.
[12] J. E. S. Thompson, 1948. The Cotzumalhuapa style may have been the work of the Pipil. Recent excavations in Pacific Guatemala by the Milwaukee Public Museum have led some archaeologists to believe that the Cotzumalhuapa style may date to the Early rather than to the Late Classic period (Lee A. Parsons, personal communication, 1963).
[12a] Recent excavations by University of Pennsylvania archaeologists at Tikal, northeastern Dept. of Peten, have revealed considerable architectural, aesthetic, and intellectual elaboration in the Late Preclassic period.
[13] See this article, pp. 462, 465, and Drucker, Heizer, and Squier, 1959, pp. 248–71.

FIG. 25—TEMPLE OF THE INSCRIPTIONS, A LATE CLASSIC BUILDING AT THE
MAYA SITE OF PALENQUE, CHIAPAS, MEXICO
(Courtesy, Robert F. Heizer.)

marked cessation of constructional activity in its great centers. The causes of this collapse of Maya lowland civilization in the south have been much debated, and there is no agreement on the subject among scholars (J. E. S. Thompson, 1954, pp. 91–130; Morley, 1946, pp. 67–72). Failure of water supply, soil exhaustion, prolonged drought, overpopulation, internal revolt, and pressures of warlike central Mexican nations have all been suggested. In the north there was no such decline, and a further renaissance occurred of the Modified Florescent of Yucatan, at first under Toltec guidance. There is reason to believe that Toltecs, or Toltec-related peoples, overran Chichen Itza at the beginning of Modified Florescent times (fig. 21, Tozzer, 1957). A fusion of Mexican and Mayan architectural styles resulted. In the latter part of the Postclassic "Decadent" period Maya and Mexican cultural elements were blended although the conquerors seem to have been absorbed, for when the Spanish entered Yucatan, Maya speech was universal.

Southern Periphery

Salvador, the Ulua Valley–Lake Yohoa country of Honduras, and the Pacific coast of Nicaragua and northern Costa Rica compose a southern peripheral region where Mesoamerican culture merges with that of Central America. Similarities in ceramics indicate a close link with Mesoamerica in the Preclassic (Strong, 1948). Later, in the Classic period, strong influences from Maya civilization are apparent in both pottery and architecture (Strong, 1948; Longyear, 1944). In the 16th century Salvador and western Honduras were occupied by the Nahua-speaking Pipil and the linguistically independent Lenca and Jicaque, but evidences of a former Maya occupation are indicated by Maya linguistic enclaves as well as by the archaeology (Lothrop, 1939). Postclassic Mesoamerican influences are found not only in Honduras and Salvador

but as far south as Pacific Nicaragua and the Nicoya Peninsula of Costa Rica.[14]

Southern Veracruz–Tabasco

This region of the lowlands of the Gulf of Mexico coast is defined by the distribution of sites of the "Olmec" or La Venta style and culture.[15] The eastern boundary is the Laguna de Carmen, just short of the Maya site of Comalcalco; the western and northern boundary is set in the vicinity of Cerro de las Mesas (Drucker, 1943a). Ancient "Olmec" culture apparently had its beginnings in the Early or Middle Preclassic period. By 800–400 b.c. the site of La Venta (figs. 26, 27) was an important ceremonial center with large artificial platform and burial mounds, carved stone altars, stelae, and huge human heads (fig. 28). The sculptural style of La Venta features humans with "baby-faces," round or pear-shaped heads, heavy, drooping mouths, swollen oblique eyes, and, sometimes, a fusion of jaguar elements with the human. The style is expressed in both monumental

[14] The Naco site in western Honduras is representative of Late Postclassic influences and migrations (Strong, Kidder, and Paul, 1938, pp. 27–34). The Nicarao of Pacific Nicaragua were Nahua in speech, and the Nicoya Polychrome pottery style (Lothrop, 1926, pp. 390–410) is linked to Mesoamerican Postclassic ceramics. The southern boundary of the Mesoamerican area at the time of the Spanish conquest may be drawn to include Pacific Nicaragua and the Nicoya Peninsula (see Kirchhoff, 1943).

[15] The term "Olmec" (Spanish: cultura olmeca) has come to refer to a civilization and art style which appears to have reached its zenith in Preclassic times. It is in many respects an unfortunate term, because the Olmecas (Spanish: los olmecas) were a people who played a prominent role in Postclassic times in Central Mexico, in particular at Cholula (Jiménez-Moreno, 1959, pp. 1022, 1075 ff.). While people identified as Olmeca seem also to have occupied the southern Veracruz-Tabasco region in the 16th century, there is no reason to assume that the "Olmec" of the Preclassic were their ancestors. In an effort to avoid this confusion, Jiménez-Moreno (1959, p. 1022) has recently proposed that the term "Tenocelome" ("people of the jaguar mouth") be applied to the Preclassic civilization and art style now called "Olmec."

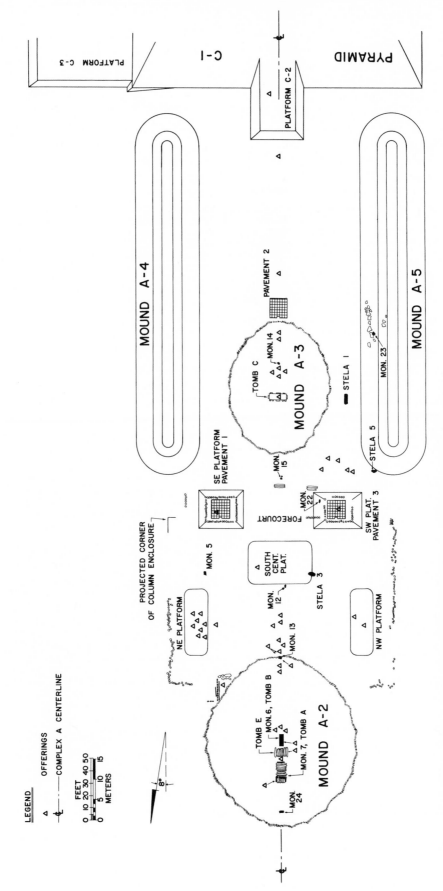

Fig. 26—GROUND PLAN OF LA VENTA CEREMONIAL CENTER, TABASCO, MEXICO
Preclassic. (After Drucker, Heizer, and Squier, 1959.)

FIG. 27—COLUMNAR BASALT TOMB CONSTRUCTION, LA VENTA, TABASCO, MEXICO. Preclassic. (Courtesy, Gordon R. Willey.)

FIG. 28—GREAT STONE HEAD IN OLMEC STYLE, LA VENTA, TABASCO, MEXICO Preclassic. (Courtesy, Philip Drucker.)

FIG. 29—"DANZANTE" FIGURE, MONTE ALBAN I PHASE, OAXACA Preclassic. (Courtesy, René F. Millon.)

467

Fɪɢ. 30—MONTE ALBAN, OAXACA, MEXICO.
"Danzante" figures on stelae in foreground. (Photo by Otto Done.)

Fɪɢ. 31—AIR VIEW OF THE CIUDADELA, PRESUMABLY A CEREMONIAL ENCLO-
SURE, WITH THE TEMPLE OF QUETZALCOATL AS THE PRINCIPAL BUILDING,
TEOTIHUACAN, VALLEY OF MEXICO
Classic. (Courtesy, Compañía Mexicana Aerofoto.)

work and small figurine carvings of jade. In
scope, including both realism and conven-
tionalizations, in beauty and power, in general feeling, and in execution it is one of the
great Mesoamerican styles.[16] Bar-and-dot
numerals are also known from these early
"Olmec" sites (Stirling, 1940; M. D. Coe,
1957a). La Venta was apparently abandoned by Late Preclassic times and the
"Olmec" style had declined by the beginning of the Classic period. Tres Zapotes
continued to be a center of importance and
Cerro de las Mesas developed into a great
center, but both came under strong influence from the Teotihuacan civilization of
central Mexico.

Oaxaca

The mountainous Oaxaca region was occupied by the Zapotecs and Mixtecs in the
16th century and had long been the homeland of at least the former. Monte Alban,

[16] Drucker, 1952; see also Covarrubias, 1957,
who gives an artist's as well as an archaeologist's
appraisal of Olmec art.

the site of ancient Zapotec civilization, has
a history going back to Middle Preclassic
times. Monte Alban I style stone carvings,
the peculiar "danzante" human figures (figs.
29, 30), and numbers and hieroglyphs are
probably contemporaneous with the florescence of the "Olmec" style and at least distantly related to it. Monte Alban may, or
may not, have been occupied by Zapotecan-
speakers at this time, but by Classic times it
almost certainly was. The main part of the
ceremonial center, situated on a hillspur
overlooking the Valley of Oaxaca, dates
from the Classic (Caso, 1938). Construction is monumental, of earth and rubble fill
and well-fitted stone masonry facings (fig.
30), but there is little architectural ornament. Chamber tombs, built in many of
the mounds, contained magnificent funerary urns modeled to represent grotesque
humans and gods. In the Early Classic II–
IIIA and IIIA phases there are a number
of relationships and cross-ties with Teotihuacan (Caso, 1938; Bernal, 1949). Monte
Alban continued to be occupied in Post-

Fig. 32—MURAL, TEMPLE OF AGRICULTURE, TEOTIHUACAN, MEXICO
Classic. (Photo by Otto Done.)

classic times, probably by Zapotecs and then by invading Mixtecs. The latter, perhaps best known archaeologically at Coixtlahuaca in the northwest, were the local makers of the famed Cholula-Mixtec polychrome pottery, a ware found in Monte Alban V graves and elsewhere in central Oaxaca (Caso, 1941, pp. 56–60; Bernal, 1950, p. 47; Bernal, 1948–49).

Central Mexico

The region of central Mexico consists of the Valley or Basin of Mexico, eastern portions of the State of Mexico, southern Hidalgo, Tlaxcala, Puebla, and Morelos. This region has been the center of cultural, social, political, and economic power in colonial and modern Mexico; and in pre-Co-

lumbian Mexico its populations played central roles as well. From this region stemmed the four great waves of artistic, social, and cultural influence in Classic and Postclassic times in Mesoamerica—Teotihuacan, Toltec, Aztec, and in part that of Mixteca-Puebla. It is the most densely populated region in Mexico today, as it was in pre-Columbian times.

Village farmers who lived along the shores of Lake Texcoco in the Valley of Mexico are among the best known of the Early Preclassic inhabitants of central Mexico (Piña Chan, 1955; Vaillant, 1930, 1935). They were versatile potters and figurine-makers, rivaling their Preclassic contemporaries of highland Guatemala in skill. In the Late Preclassic period or earlier

Fɪɢ. 33—A RECONSTRUCTED RESIDENTIAL (?) COURTYARD AND BUILDINGS, ATETELCO SECTION, TEOTIHUACAN, MEXICO
Classic. (Courtesy, René F. Millon.)

they built big ceremonial mounds; and, during the Middle and Late Preclassic the Valley of Mexico became a sort of crossroads and melting pot of new strains of stylistic influence and, perhaps, peoples. The "Olmec" style, seen in the figurines of the Tlatilco phase, is one such strain (Porter, 1953; Piña Chan, 1958). It seems likely that Teotihuacan in the Valley of Mexico, the seat of the civilization and art style of that name, was a big town or city even in the Late Preclassic (Millon, 1957b, 1960b). Its Classic period dimensions are immense. The combined ceremonial, palace, and residential sections cover 5 or more square miles.[17] Architecture is severely plain but often of enormous bulk, the famed Pyramid of the Sun being one of the largest structures of native America (fig. 40). Palace

and residential units are of a distinctive and characteristic plan, and were frequently decorated with elaborate mural paintings (fig. 32). Rooms are arranged around rectangular courtyards, and sometimes a small platform or altar has been placed in the center of the household court or plaza figs. 33, 34). Interestingly, this residential unit pattern, which is also found at Tula (Marquina, 1951, p. 94; Charnay, 1880, pp. 520–27, 1888, pp. 104–10), spread northwestward in Mexico and is found at such sites as distant from the Valley of Mexico as La Quemada.

It is probable that the Valley of Mexico was economically and politically united under the leadership of Teotihuacan. Azcapotzalco and Portesuelo, two of the large contemporary sites, may have been residential and trading centers, allied to Teotihuacan but lacking its ceremonial and

[17] Millon, unpublished 1959 field data.

471

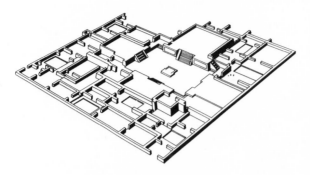

FIG. 34—GROUND PLAN OF XOLALPAN SECTION
OF TEOTIHUACAN (IN PERSPECTIVE)
Classic. (After Linné, 1934.)

and moldmade figurines, radiated out of the
Valley of Mexico during the Early Classic
period, and it is, indeed, possible that Teotihuacan was the center of an empire which
reached beyond the valley. The truly urban
conditions of Teotihuacan and its satellites
raise the question of how such large concentrations of population were fed, and it
has been suggested that intensive irrigation
was practiced at Teotihuacan although this
has not been demonstrated archaeologically
(Armillas, 1951, p. 24; Palerm, 1955, p. 35;
Millon, 1957a). It is certain, however, that
canal irrigation was extensive in the Valley
of Mexico in later Postclassic times (Palerm,
1954, 1955; Wolf and Palerm, 1955). After
the fall and destruction of Teotihuacan it
may be that leadership in the Valley of
Mexico passed to Azcapotzalco, but by the
beginning of the Postclassic period, Tula

political functions. Numerous villages dotted over the valley must have served as
homes for supporting farming populations
(Mayer-Oakes, 1959; Tolstoy, 1958; Millon,
1957b). Trade and influence, reflected in
Thin Orange ware, slab-footed tripod jars

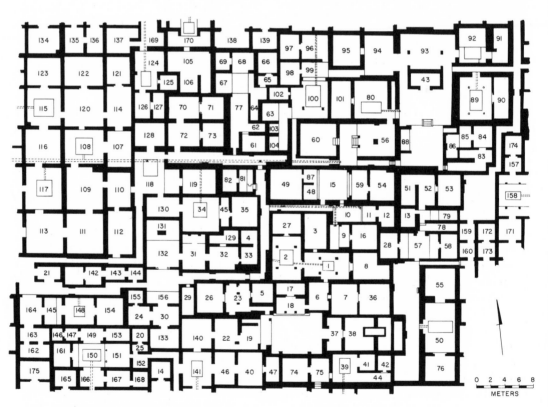

FIG. 35—GROUND PLAN OF CONJOINED ROOMS, COMPLEXES AND ALLEYS, TLAM-
IMILOLPA SECTION OF TEOTIHUACAN
Classic. Broken lines: drains. (After Linné, 1942.)

472

FIG. 36—TEMPLE B COMPLEX, TULA, HIDALGO, MEXICO
Postclassic. (Courtesy, René F. Millon.)

(fig. 36) in southern Hidalgo, and the great center of Cholula in western Puebla, were the power centers of the Central Mexican region (Acosta, 1940, 1944, 1945; Noguera, 1954; Jiménez Moreno, 1959). The fall of Tula and the restriction of the influence of Cholula were succeeded by the rise of various city states in the Valley of Mexico and neighboring areas that were eventually amalgamated in large part into the empire of the Aztecs of Tenochtitlan (Jiménez Moreno, 1954–55; Krickeberg, 1956).

Central Veracruz

The Central Veracruz region consists of the coastal lowlands and interior of that state from the vicinity of Cerro de las Mesas north to Tuxpan. The largest and most important Preclassic site in this region is Remojadas, in the southern part of the region. This was also an important center during the Classic period, and through most of its history it evidences close ceramic and artistic relationships with Teotihuacan, relationships that are as yet poorly understood. The famous smiling or laughing heads as well as complete figures are found at Remojadas in Classic association but seem to have been more common at several sites just to the south of Remojadas (Medellín Zenil, 1953, 1955a; García Payón, 1953; Covarrubias, 1957, pp. 192–95; Spratling, 1960; Medellín Zenil and Peterson, 1954).

In the northern part of the Central Veracruz region the Tajin or Classic Veracruz art style is the dominant feature of the Classic period (Proskouriakoff, 1954). This style is characterized by linked or interlaced ribbon-scrolls which embellish serpent, jaguar, frog, and human motifs. It is best seen in architectural reliefs at El Tajin and on carved stone "yokes," mirrorbacks, and thin stone heads (Covarrubias, 1957, pp. 171–95). El Tajin is a compact cluster of stone-faced pyramids (fig. 37), platforms, plazas, and ball courts. Although the latter may have been constructed relatively late in the history of Tajin, the antiquity of the "yokes," believed to have been paraphernalia associated with the game, goes back to the Middle Preclassic period (Ekholm, 1946b, 1949; García Payón, 1954). It is possible that the rubber-ball game originated in these Veracruz lowlands

473

FIG. 37—THE PYRAMID OF THE NICHES, TAJIN, VERACRUZ
Classic. (Courtesy, René F. Millon.)

where rubber was grown. The first and second ceramic phases at Tajin date to the Late Preclassic and Classic periods, the latter cross-tying with the expansion of Teotihuacan styles. The site seems to have continued in use into Postclassic time as indicated by ceramics, but there was little building activity after the close of the Classic (García Payón, 1943, 1949a, 1954; Du Solier, 1945). After the abandonment of Tajin, Cempoala became the leading center. This was the capital of the Totonac nation which Bernal Díaz describes as an urban establishment of 30,000 people. Its ruins cover an area of 2 square miles (García Payón, 1949b; Krickeberg, 1918–22, 1925; Covarrubias, 1957, p. 197). Like Remojadas and the other sites where the smiling heads occur, it is located in a semiarid zone of tropical Veracruz.

474

The Huasteca

The lowland coast from Tuxpan north to Soto la Marina and the country lying to the interior in southern Tamaulipas, San Luis Potosi, and Hidalgo constitute the region known as the Huasteca. In the interior zones a long incipient agricultural sequence terminates in sedentary agricultural village cultures of the Early or Middle Preclassic period. The latter were influenced in their ceramic and other practices by the coastal peoples of the Panuco area, and this same dependence on the coast continued into Classic times. In turn, the cultures of the Panuco area had a generally peripheral relationship to those of Central Veracruz and Central Mexico.[18] The cultural climax of

[18] See MacNeish, 1954, 1958, for a discussion of relationships between interior Tamaulipas and

the Panuco area as indicated by mound construction and monumental sculpture was in the Postclassic period, the Las Flores and Panuco phases (Ekholm, 1944, pp. 373–91). The ties to Toltec sculptural art and the Quetzalcoatl cult are obvious. The Las Flores phase, and probably the earlier phases of the Panuco region, can be attributed to the Huastec-speaking peoples. Very late Huastec pottery is in a distinctive black-on-white style (Staub, 1920). The Postclassic cultural florescence of the coastal Huastecs is not matched in the interior. There the late pre-Columbian phases undergo a decline, perhaps as a result of the progressive desiccation of the semiarid inland environment (MacNeish, 1958).

Guerrero

The present state of Guerrero is little known archaeologically, and an assessment of the region must depend on scattered reports and numerous "collectors' items" in the form of small stone sculptures that have been found. Preclassic and Classic ceramics occur in sequence at Acapulco on the Costa Grande (Ekholm, 1948), and the finding of many Olmec-style stone figurines and "Teotihuacan" masks—in greater abundance than could be accounted for by trade—indicates the presence of fairly complex cultures. A notable local style of stone carving, known as the Mescala style, centers in the upper Balsas drainage of central Guerrero and merges with both Olmec and Teotihuacan influences in various ways (Covarrubias, 1957, pp. 104–13). Later influences from the Mixteca-Puebla complex and the Aztec occupation of some portions of the region are also apparent. In far western Guerrero, relationships with the cultures of Michoacan appear to be dominant. Thus, while the cultures of Guerrero are at present identified in large part by

the apparent influences from other regions, the ability of the local populations to absorb these elements and the occurrence of some fairly large ceremonial sites attest to the region's having been of considerable importance in Mesoamerican history.

Western Mexico and the Northern Frontier

This large region includes all of the semi-arid and mountainous country to the west and northwest of Central Mexico extending to the Pacific coast and the northern limits of Mesoamerica (Lister, 1955).[19] It is a region containing a number of distinctive cultural expressions, all somewhat less highly developed and seemingly peripheral to the major centers of civilization in regions farther to the east.

Some ceramics and figurines of the region resemble those of the Preclassic peoples of Central Mexico (Porter, 1956), but there are as yet no indications of Middle or Late Preclassic ceremonial developments such as the temple mounds found elsewhere in Mesoamerica at this time level, except, perhaps, for the El Opeño tombs of Michoacan (Noguera, 1942). Nor is there a Classic florescence in the region with monumental architecture, sculpture, hieroglyphics, or calendrics. The Classic phases show, however, some contacts with the east and south. In Michoacan, for example, the "pre-Taras-can" phase (Rubín de la Borbolla, 1948) and the Delicias and Apatzingan phases (Kelly, 1947) are local developments that apparently cross-date with Classic Teotihuacan. It is not clear if ceremonial mound building—such as the "yacatas" of Michoacan—is this early or if it is confined to the Postclassic.[20] In the Jalisco-Colima area the

coastal Tamaulipas sequences and for wider geographical sequence comparisons. See also Ekholm, 1944, p. 503.

[19] The region of Western Mexico is variously defined. It usually does not include the frontier area of Zacatecas and Durango and often includes Guerrero. Greater standardization of areal divisions will be possible only when more is known of the archaeology of the entire region.

[20] Isabel Kelly (1947) is of the opinion that some of the yacatas may be this early; Rubín de la Borbolla (1948) feels they are later in the vicinity of Tzintzuntzan.

FIG. 38—COLONNADE AT LA QUEMADA, ZACATECAS, MEXICO
Postclassic. (Courtesy, Gordon R. Willey.)

Ortices phase deep-shaft tombs appear to belong to the Classic period, a phase noted for its amazing pottery of modeled life forms—dogs, men, women, warriors, and plants. This tradition, with local variations in style, extends northward into Nayarit (Kelly, 1947, pp. 194–95; Arte Precolombino del Occidente de Mexico, 1946; Gifford, 1950; Covarrubias, 1957, pp. 87–94). Late Classic phases have also been identified in the northern Nayarit-Sinaloa subregion (Kelly, 1938) and in the sequence known for Zacatecas and Durango in the highlands (Kelley, 1957).

It seems to have been only in Postclassic times that this region reached its full development in terms of larger populations and ceremonial centers equivalent to those of other Mesoamerican regions. In the Postclassic the Tarascans were the great nation of the west with their capital of Tzintzuntzan. Large platform structures and stone sculpture of a distinctive style, but including the chac-mool form common to Tula and Chichen Itza, appear, as well as many

476

objects of metal. The presence here of an advanced metallurgical tradition as well as stirrup-spouted vessels has suggested connections with Ecuador and Peru—by a coastal route or by sea—on a late time level.

The coastal area of northern Nayarit and Sinaloa forms a distinctive subregion with the sites of Chametla, Culiacan, and Guasave, revealing a sequence from Late Classic to apparently conquest times (Ekholm, 1942, p. 123; Kelley, 1957). The Rio Fuerte in northern Sinaloa is the approximate boundary beyond which the patterns of Mesoamerica dissolve into a region of relatively simple cultures and then into those of the Southwestern United States. In the highlands east of the Sierra Madre in Zacatecas and Durango a series of larger ceremonial sites such as La Quemada (fig. 38), Alta Vista de Chalchihuites, and Schroeder mark the approximate frontier of Mesoamerica (Lister and Howard, 1955; Kelley, 1956, 1957; Kelley and Winters, 1958). Apparently of both Classic and Postclassic date these ceremonial centers were the work of populations undergoing acculturation to the ways of civilization or of peoples emigrating from regions to the south and east. The sequence of phases in the Chalchihuites area can be cross-dated by trade items with the sequence of Nayarit and Sinaloa, with the most intensive contacts occurring in late prehistoric times. In both areas strong Mixteca-Puebla influences, composing a major element in the later Postclassic remains in Central Mexico and elsewhere, were an important factor.

CHRONOLOGY

Terminology

Three major chronological horizons are generally recognized within the agricultural era of pre-Columbian Mesoamerica. The earliest is the horizon of settled village farming, in effect, an American "neolithic" threshold; the next in time is the horizon of the florescence of civilization as reflected in monumental architecture and art; and the third horizon encompasses the more recent civilizations which followed the seeming break-up of the former and which existed when the Spanish arrived in the 16th century. This tripartite chronological division was first established for the Valley of Mexico early in the 20th century, with the local cultural terms of "Archaic," "Toltec," and "Aztec" (Boas, 1911–12; Gamio, 1921; Tozzer, 1921).[21] Over the years other culture sequences or chronologies were developed for other regions and subareas of Mesoamerica (R. E. Smith, 1940; Hay and others, 1940; J. E. S. Thompson, 1943, 1945; Spinden, 1917; Vaillant, 1938).

These first Mesoamerican sequential classifications were essentially chronological in their treatment of the data; but it is frequently difficult to adhere to a purely chronological classification when the synchronization of many local and regional sequences is dependent on stylistic and element comparisons rather than absolute dates. Partly as a result of this, descriptive generalizations in terms of "culture types" have become incorporated in many Mesoamerican chronological classifications (J. E. S. Thompson, 1943, 1945, 1954; Covarrubias, 1957; Ekholm, 1958). The major periods or horizons of the area have come to be designated by such terms as "Classic," which have configurational and developmental implications, or by names such as "Mexican Absorption," which carry processual connotations. Some sequential classifications have been consciously directed toward developmental or historical-developmental interpretation (Armillas, 1957; Caso, 1953b; Willey and Phillips, 1958; Wauchope, 1950; Brainerd, 1954, 1958; Morley, 1956; M. D. Coe, 1957b; Lathrap, 1957; Holden, 1957; Levine, 1958). Others are less so. This ambiguity between strict chronology, on the one hand, and the characterization of social and cultural con-

figurations and similarities through time, on the other, has given rise to confusion and misunderstanding. Should Phase A be assigned to the Preclassic period because relative and absolute dating techniques indicate such a chronological placement for it? Or should it be assigned to the "Classic" because it exemplifies certain qualities of esthetic excellence in architecture and art? Obviously we are dealing with two kinds of classification here. Classification may be made on the basis of either set of criteria, but the criteria used must be made explicit, and should be designed to order only one set of phenomena at a time.

In dealing with Mesoamerican chronology and periods we are concerned, first, with the criteria of relative and absolute time and their application to the various prehistoric remains of the area. Problems of process—social and cultural evolution or development—are of great interest in Mesoamerican archaeology. But such problems can be approached more effectively when the data of spatial-temporal placement have been assembled. We shall review such matters farther along; here our immediate interest is in the establishment and application of a terminology that is as strictly chronological as it is possible to make it.

The sequential classificatory system for Mesoamerica most generally accepted now is the threefold one of the *Preclassic, Classic* and *Postclassic* periods.[22] We shall adhere to this terminology, because it has been used in most of the existing literature and will be followed by most of the authors writing for the present Handbook. It is true, of course, that it carries the disadvantage of configurational and developmental connotations. The terms suggested as possible substitutes (Millon, 1960a)—*pre-Initial Series, Initial Series,* and *post-Initial*

[21] The term "Toltec" was then applied to the Teotihuacan culture, not to Tula as it is at present.

[22] Synonyms for Preclassic in Mesoamerican archaeology include Archaic, Formative, and Developmental; for Classic, Regional, Florescent, and Theocratic; for Postclassic, Historic, Mexican, and Militaristic.

NATURAL ENVIRONMENT AND EARLY CULTURES

Series respectively—refer to the Maya calendar, whose dates form the basis for much of our chronological structure; but unfortunately, these alternatives are almost without precedent in the archaeological literature, and we feel it would be inadvisable to introduce it here. In northern Yucatan, however, Andrews has shown that the period corresponding chronologically most closely with the Early Classic of the south is by no means the "classic" expression of culture there, the true cultural flowering of Yucatan coming in a subsequent period that he calls "Florescent."

Period Definition

Our most objective chronological baselines for the establishment of periods are the dates for the beginning of the Classic, for the close of that period, and for the Spanish entry into Mesoamerica. The last is A.D. 1520; the other two dates are less certain. The beginning of the Classic period is set at the Maya calendar katun ending of 8.12.0.0.0.[23] The Christian calendrical equivalent of this in the Goodman-Martínez-Thompson correlation of the Maya and Christian calendars[24] is A.D. 278 which may be modified to the round figure of A.D. 300. The termination of the Early Classic corresponds to the Maya calendric katun ending of 9.8.0.0.0, read as A.D. 593 or, in round numbers, A.D. 600 (G-M-T correlation). The Late Classic ends at either 10.3.0.0.0 or 10.4.0.0.0 in the Maya calendar, rendered as A.D. 889 and 909, respectively, or, in approximate figures, A.D. 900 (G-M-T correlation). These dates are subject to a downward revision of 256 years by application of the Spinden correlation, so that the Early Classic begins and ends at A.D. 50 and 350, respectively, and the Late Classic closes at A.D. 650.[25] The chronological Chart 1 follows the Goodman-Martínez-Thompson correlation, that of Chart 2 follows the Spinden.

Prior to the Classic period, estimated dates for the Preclassic are based largely on radiocarbon tests. The Preclassic is believed to have begun sometime between 1500 and 1000 B.C., depending on which particular radiocarbon dates are accepted as most reliable. Figure 2 combines the Goodman-Martínez-Thompson correlation with the earlier Preclassic radiocarbon dates; figure 3 combines the Spinden correlation with the later Preclassic radiocarbon dates. The Preclassic period has three subdivisions. In Chart 1 the Early Preclassic extends from 1500 to 1000 B.C., the Middle Preclassic from 1000 to 300 B.C., and the Late Preclassic from 300 B.C. to A.D. 300. In Chart 2 the Early Preclassic runs from 1000 to 500 B.C., the Middle Preclassic from 500 to 300 B.C., and the Late Preclassic from 300 B.C. to A.D. 50.

The final pre-Columbian epoch, the Postclassic period, extends from A.D. 900 to 1520, with the Goodman-Martínez-Thompson correlation; and it is divided into Early and Late divisions at A.D. 1200 (Chart 1). In the Spinden correlation the Postclassic period extends from A.D. 650 to 1520 with an Early and Late dividing point also at A.D. 1200 (Chart 2).

Relative and Absolute Dating

Before we consider this Mesoamerican chronology, some comments are in order on the validity of the various types and combinations of relative and absolute dating that

[23] The earliest known stela date from the Maya lowlands is an 8 baktun 12 katun inscription from Tikal (W. R. Coe, 1959a), which is dated as A.D. 292 in the Goodman-Martínez-Thompson correlation, a few years later than 8.12.0.0.0.
[24] The Goodman-Martínez-Thompson correlation of Maya and Gregorian Christian calendars is based upon the correspondence of the year 1539 with the 11 baktun 16 katun ending of the projected Maya Initial Series or Long Count system of dating (see J. E. S. Thompson, 1935; Satterthwaite, vol. 2, Article 24).
[25] The Spinden correlation is based upon the correspondence of the year 1536 with the 12 baktun 9 katun ending of the projected Long Count. In this correlation the katun ending 8.12.0.0.0 is A.D. 21, 9.8.0.0.0 is A.D. 333, and 10.3.0.0.0 is A.D. 629.

are available. Our chronology for all Meso-america is dependent in very large degree on the sequence in the Maya lowlands and the absolute dating of the Classic portion of this one regional sequence by calendrical correlations. This extension of a chronology from a single region to the entire area is fraught with difficulties and limitations. Extension is based on cross-finds demonstrating cultural influences and trade between the Maya lowlands and other regions; but unfortunately, the Maya were relatively isolated, and direct ties are often lacking. Much depends, therefore, on the correlation of the Classic period of the Maya lowlands with Teotihuacan, for there are many evidences of relationships between that site and other regions of Mesoamerica. Even these basic correlations, however, are of a kind that allow only a very loose network of cross-dating. There are many weak spots and missing pieces in the total fabric that must be filled in by future research.

Closely interlocked with this extension of the Maya sequence and chronology to other regions of Mesoamerica by cross-dating is the evidence provided by radiocarbon dates. These are available from a good many Mesoamerican archaeological sites and most of the regions; but they are still too few and relatively unreliable to resolve the most pressing chronological problems. For example, although radiocarbon dates have seriously shaken the Goodman-Martínez-Thompson correlation of the Maya-Christian calendars, they have still provided no final answer to this problem.[26]

[26] In this connection see Broecker, Olson, and Bird, 1959. However, as this manuscript was being completed, Linton Satterthwaite Jr. presented information on a number of radiocarbon runs from wooden beams of Temple IV of the Classic period site of Tikal, all of which indicate a Late Classic dating of ca. A.D. 750 for the temple and support thereby the Goodman-Martínez-Thompson or 11.16.0.0.0 correlation (paper presented by Satterthwaite at New Haven meeting of the Society for American Archaeology, May 1960). The tests in question were made by the University of Penn-

Pages 480–481
CHART 1—CHRONOLOGY CHART FOR
MESOAMERICAN REGIONS
This arrangement follows the Goodman-Martínez-Thompson correlation of Maya and Christian calendars and relies on an "early" group of radiocarbon dates for the Preclassic period.

For *Southern Periphery* see Longyear, 1944; Strong, 1948; Canby, 1951; Willey, 1958.

For *Maya Highlands* see Shook, 1951; Shook and Kidder, 1952; M. D. Coe, 1959; Thompson, 1948; Dixon, 1959. It should be noted that the reversal of the positions of the Las Charcas and Arevalo phases in the Kaminaljuyu sequence, making Arevalo the older, follows an opinion of E. M. Shook (September 1959). The Chiapas sequence follows the conclusions of the Chiapas conference of September 1959.

The *Maya Lowlands* column relates to R. E. Smith, 1955, Brainerd, 1958, and Andrews, 1960.

Southern Veracruz–Tabasco is based principally on findings of Drucker, Heizer, and Squier, 1959.

Oaxaca follows the interpretations of Caso, 1938, and Bernal, 1949.

Central Veracruz is based on Bernal and Davalos, 1953, particularly the chronological charts in the end of the volume.

The *Huasteca* follows the work of Ekholm, 1944, and MacNeish, 1954, 1958.

The *Central Mexico* column utilizes Vaillant, 1941; Piña Chan, 1955, 1958; Armillas, 1950; Linné, 1956; Acosta, 1945; Dutton, 1955; Noguera, 1954; Tolstoy, 1958; Franco, 1949; Bernal, 1948–49.

Western Mexico is put together with the aid of Lister, 1955; Rubín de la Borbolla, 1948; Porter, 1956; Kelly, 1947; Covarrubias, 1957; and Gifford, 1950.

The *Northern Frontier* column relies on Lister and Howard, 1955; Lister, 1955; J. C. Kelley, 1956, 1957; and J. C. Kelley and Winters, 1958.

In addition, we have consulted the general Mesoamerican chronological charts of Hay and others, 1940; Bernal and Dávalos, 1953; Ekholm, 1958; Jiménez Moreno, 1959; Millon, 1960a.

For pertinent radiocarbon dates see appendix.

Pages 482–483
CHART 2—CHRONOLOGY CHART FOR
MESOAMERICAN REGIONS
This arrangement follows the Spinden correlation of Maya and Christian calendars and relies on a "late" group of radiocarbon dates for the Preclassic period. See caption to Chart 1 for further comment and bibliographic references.

sylvania laboratory, the most exhaustive examination of radiocarbon dating and the Maya calendrical correlation question to be reported to date.

CHART IA—CHRONOLOGICAL CHART

PERIODS	DATES G-M-T	SOUTHERN PERIPHERY Honduras	SOUTHERN PERIPHERY Salvador	MAYA HIGHLANDS Guatemala Highlands	MAYA HIGHLANDS Guatemala Coast	MAYA HIGHLANDS Chiapas	MAYA LOWLANDS Peten	MAYA LOWLANDS Yucatan	SOUTHERN VERACRUZ—TABASCO	OAXACA
Postclassic Late	1520 / 1200	Naco		Chinautla		Chiapa XII		Decadent Transition	Soncautla	Monte Alban V
Early	900		Plumbate	Tohil		Chiapa XI		(Modified) Florescent (Pure)	Upper Cerro Las Mesas	Monte Alban IV
Classic Late	600	Ulua Mayoid	Copador	Pamplona Amatle	Cotzumalhuapa	Chiapa X	Tepeu	Transition Early (2nd phase)		Monte Alban III B / Monte Alban III A-B
Early	300		Esperanza	Esperanza Aurora		Chiapa IX / Chiapa VIII	Tzakol	Early (1st phase)	Lower Cerro Las Mesas II / Upper Tres Zapotes	Monte Alban III A / Monte Alban II-III A
Preclassic Late	A.D. / B.C. / 300	Ulua Bichrome	Cerro Zapote	Santa Clara / Arenal	Izapa	Chiapa VII / Chiapa VI / Chiapa V	Matzanel ←	Transition / Dzibilchaltun Formative III	Lower Cerro Las Mesas I / Middle Tres Zapotes ?	Monte Alban II
Middle	1000	Playa los Muertos		Miraflores Providencia Majadas / Las Charcas Conchas		Chiapa IV / Chiapa III / Chiapa II	Chicanel / Mamom	Transition Dzibilchaltun Formative IIb / Dzibilchaltun Formative IIa / Dzibilchaltun Formative I	? ? / Lower Tres Zapotes / ←La Venta→ ?	Monte Alban I
Early	1500	Yarumela I		Arevalo	Ocos	Chiapa I				

Chart 1B—CHRONOLOGICAL CHART

PERIODS	DATES G-M-T	CENTRAL VERACRUZ Dry Zone	CENTRAL VERACRUZ Tajin	THE HUASTECA Panuco	THE HUASTECA Interior	CENTRAL MEXICO Valley of Mexico		CENTRAL MEXICO Cholula	WEST MEXICO and NORTHERN FRONTIER Michoacan	Colima	Sinaloa	Durango-Zacatecas
Postclassic Late	1520 1200	Cempoala IV Cempoala III	Castillo	Panuco	San Antonio- Los Angeles	Aztec IV Aztec III Aztec II		Cholulteca III	Tzintzuntzan	Periquillo	Culiacan	
Early	900	Cempoala II Cempoala I	de Teayo Tajin III	Las Flores	San Lorenzo	Aztec I	Tula- Mazapan	Cholulteca II Cholulteca I	Tarascan	Colima		Calera Rio Tunal
Classic Late	600	Upper		Zaquil	La Salta	Coyotlatelco Ahuitzotla-Amantla (Fall of Teotihuacan)		C h o l			Aztatlan	Las Joyas Ayala
Early	300	Remojadas II	Tajin II	Pithaya	Palmillas Eslabones	Xolalpan Tlamimilolpa	?	u l a	Apatzingan- Delicias	Ortices	Chametla ?	Alta Vista ?
Preclassic Late	A.D. B.C. 300	Upper Remojadas I	Tajin I	El Prisco		Miccaotli Tzacualli		P r e c l a	Chupicuaro			
Middle	1000	Lower Remojadas Trapiche		Chila Aguilar	Laguna Mesa de Guaje	Cuicuilco-Ticoman Tlatilco		s s i c ? Middle Zacatenco	? El Opeño			
Early	1500			Ponce Pavon ?				Early Zacatenco El Arbolillo I				

CHART 2A—CHRONOLOGICAL CHART

PERIODS	DATES Spinden	SOUTHERN PERIPHERY Honduras	Salvador	MAYA HIGHLANDS Guatemala Highlands	Guatemala Coast	Chiapas	MAYA LOWLANDS Peten	Yucatan	SOUTHERN VERACRUZ—TABASCO	OAXACA
Postclassic Late	1520 1200	Naco		Chinautla		Chiapa XII		Decadent Transition	Soncautla	Monte Alban V
Early	650		Plumbate	Tohil		Chiapa XI		(Modified) Florescent (Pure)	Upper Cerro Las Mesas	Monte Alban IV
Classic Late	350	Ulua Mayoid	Copador	Pamplona Amatle	Cotzumalhuapa	Chiapa X	Tepeu	Transition Early (2nd phase)		Monte Alban III B
Early	A.D. 50		Esperanza	Esperanza Aurora	Izapa	Chiapa IX Chiapa VIII	Tzakol	Early (1st phase) Transition	Lower Cerro Las Mesas II / Upper Tres Zapotes	Monte Alban III A
Preclassic Late	300 B.C.	Ulua Bichrome	Cerro Zapote	Santa Clara Arenal Miraflores Providencia	Izapa	Chiapa VII Chiapa V Chiapa IV	Matzanel Chicanel	Dzibilchaltun Formative III	Lower Cerro Las Mesas I / ? Middle Tres Zapotes ? / ? ← La Venta → ?	Monte Alban II
Middle	500	Playa los Muertos		Majadas Las Charcas Conchas	Ocos	Chiapa III Chiapa II	Mamom	Dzibilchaltun Formative IIb	Lower Tres Zapotes / La Venta	Monte Alban I
Early	1000	Yarumela I		Arevalo	Ocos	Chiapa I		Dzibilchaltun Formative I, IIa	?	

CHART 2B—CHRONOLOGICAL CHART

PERIODS	DATES (Spinden)	CENTRAL VERACRUZ — Dry Zone	CENTRAL VERACRUZ — Tajin	THE HUASTECA — Panuco	THE HUASTECA — Interior	CENTRAL MEXICO — Valley of Mexico	CENTRAL MEXICO — Cholula	WEST MEXICO and NORTHERN FRONTIER — Michoacan	Colima	Sinaloa	Durango-Zacatecas
Postclassic Late	1520	Cempoala IV	Castillo ←	Panuco	San Antonio-Los Angeles	Aztec IV / Aztec III / Aztec II	Cholula III	Tzintzuntzan	Periquillo	Culiacan	Calera / Rio Tumal / Las Joyas
	1200	Cempoala III									
Early	650	Cempoala II / Cempoala I	de Teayo / Tajin III	Las Flores	San Lorenzo	Aztec I	Cholula II / Cholula I	Tarascan	Colima	Aztatlan	Ayala ←
Classic Late	350	Upper	Tajin II ←	Zaquil	La Salta / Palmillas	Coyotlatelco / Ahuitzotla-Amantla (Fall of Teotihuacan) →	Cholula				
Early	A.D. 50	Remojadas II		Pithaya	Eslabones	Xolalpan / Tlamimilolpa →		Apatzingan-Delicias	Ortices	Chametla → ?	Alta Vista → ?
Preclassic Late	300 B.C.	Upper Remojadas I / Lower Remojadas	Tajin I	El Prisco	Laguna ←	Miccaotli / Tzacualli	Preclassic	Chupicuaro → ?			
Middle	500	Trapiche		Chila / Aguilar	Mesa de Guaje	Cuicuilco-Ticoman ←	Middle Zaca-tenco	El Opeño			
Early	1000			Pavon	?	Tlatilco	Early Zacatenco / El Arbillo				

Radiocarbon dates published to the present time and bearing on Mesoamerican chronologies are listed in the appendix. It is too soon to offer conclusive appraisals of these dates or to make final acceptances or eliminations. There are numerous contradictions both between radiocarbon dates and between dates and stratigraphic evidence. It is impossible to arrange a detailed archaeological chronology of Mesoamerica which is consistent in all of its radiocarbon, Maya calendric, and archaeologic interpretations. Neither of our two charts (Charts 1 and 2) has such consistency although we have tried to approach it. Rather than discuss, in detail, the possible applications of all Mesoamerican radiocarbon dates to archaeological chronologies, we refer the reader to our appendix, where the dates are arranged by region and archaeological phase.

Relative dating on the Preclassic level has been effected with certain styles and markers, mostly pottery and figurines, which have partial but not complete Mesoamerican-wide distributions (Willey and Phillips, 1958, pp. 29–34; L. A. Parsons, 1957). The "Olmec" style is one of these. Baby-face and jaguar-human-face figurines of pottery and jadeite link such phases as La Venta in southern Veracruz–Tabasco, Tlatilco in the Central Mexico region, Trapiche in Central Veracruz, and Aguilar in the Huasteca. According to one chronology, this partial horizon style diffused at about 1000–800 B.C. (Chart 1); following another the date was nearer 500 B.C. (Chart 2). In neither chronology can these "Olmec"-style occurrences be pinned down to a relatively brief span of time although more finely drawn stylistic studies at La Venta and elsewhere may make this possible eventually. For example, there is reason to suspect that the "Olmec" style persisted for several centuries at La Venta; but, as yet, no specific phase in the La Venta sequence has been matched with Olmec-style occurrences in other regions or subareas.

484

Apparently related to "Olmec" stylistic diffusions are features which in themselves do not comprise a style but may serve as markers for cross-dating. Rocker-stamped pottery decoration is one of these. It is widespread in Mesoamerica, occurring in the Preclassic in Honduras, in the Ocos phase of Pacific Guatemala, and in the aforementioned La Venta, Tlatilco, and Trapiche contexts. The exact chronological value of rocker-stamping is still uncertain although it appears to have its most important vogue in the Early to Middle Preclassic. Usulutan ware is a ceramic marker for the Middle and Late Preclassic periods. This is a kind of resist or negative-painted pottery which seems to have had its origins in highland or Pacific Guatemala and to have spread from there over much of southern Mesoamerica. In Guatemala it has an Early Preclassic inception, but elsewhere it is confined largely to the Late Preclassic. Another horizon marker is the Late Preclassic mammiform tetrapodal pottery support, found in southern Mesoamerica.[27] There are also sequence synchronizations of more limited geographic scope than the foregoing. An example would be the linking of the Mamom phase of the Maya lowlands with the Las Charcas of the Maya highlands.

Absolute dates for the Preclassic period fall into two groups of radiocarbon results sharply at variance with each other. Five dates from Kaminaljuyu in the Guatemalan highlands represent the "early" group. They are associated with phases from Las Charcas through Miraflores and range from 1500 to 500 B.C.[28] Fourteen other Kaminaljuyu

[27] L. A. Parsons (1957) summarizes Preclassic horizon markers. Other analyses of Preclassic relative and absolute dating are Wauchope, 1950, 1954; MacNeish, 1954; Sorenson, 1955; M. D. Coe, 1957b; Piña Chan, 1958. The reader is also referred to citations in the captions to Charts 1 and 2.

[28] See dates C-885,-886,-879,-884,-887 in appendix. A 240-year Suess-effect correction may be made, making these readings that much earlier. All dates in this group come from the Chicago laboratory.

dates belong to a "late" group. These come from phases from Arevalo through Aurora, and the span is from about 400 B.C. to 400 A.D.[29] In the Valley of Mexico there is a similar discrepancy with a set of "early" dates running from 1400 to 400 B.C.[30] while a set of "late" dates, paralleling the same sequence of phases, goes from 500 B.C. to A.D. 500.[31] Preclassic dates from the Huasteca region[32] and from Chiapa de Corzo[33] coincide, more or less, with the "early" group whereas some from the Conchas phase of the Guatemalan Pacific coast and from southern Veracruz–Tabasco could be interpreted as favoring either the "early" or "late" group.[34]

The Teotihuacan civilization of the Central Mexico region exerted the most profound influences on other parts of Mesoamerica during the Classic period, and, as noted, these influences are the prime means of cross-dating for the period. These irradiations from Teotihuacan were the result of trade, of the spread or influence of a religion or a cult, or, perhaps, of actual migrations or conquests. They are a feature of the Early rather than the Late Classic period and pertain largely to the Xolalpan and Tlamimilolpa phases at Teotihuacan. Although it was once thought that Xolalpan was the earlier of these two, recent findings make this less certain; and it has been argued that Tlamimilolpa has priority (Armillas, 1950; Linné, 1956). It is also pos-

sible that the two are contemporaneous and represent social rather than chronological differences in the great urban site which are reflected in somewhat different ceramic styles (Millon, 1960b). In the lowland Maya Tzakol phase ceramic features that reflect Teotihuacan include Thin Orange ware, cylindrical tripod vessels with slab feet, knobbed lids for many of these vessels, and the postfired application of polychrome stucco decoration to vessel surfaces (R. E. Smith, 1955, 1: 34, 152, 23, 81–83, 137, 153; J. E. S. Thompson, 1939, pp. 91–94; Longyear, 1952, pp. 57–58). Although it cannot be demonstrated that any of these ceramic practices originated at Teotihuacan, it is virtually certain that they spread over much of Mesoamerica from this center. During the Esperanza phase, along with architectural elements, they reached Kaminaljuyu in the Guatemalan highlands where their presence has been interpreted as the result of invasion and conquest on the part of people from central Mexico (Kidder, Jennings, and Shook, 1946, pp. 254–56; Lathrap, 1957). Some of them appear in Monte Alban II-111A and IIIA (Lathrap, 1957; Caso, 1938; Bernal, 1949, 1958), in Upper Remojadas II (Medellín Zenil, 1953, 1955a,b), in Lower Cerro de las Mesas II (Drucker, 1943a; Lathrap, 1957) and Upper Tres Zapotes (Drucker, 1943b, pp. 16, 120–22), phases of Veracruz, in the Zaquil phase of the Panuco region (Ekholm, 1944, p. 419), and in Guerrero (Ekholm, 1948; Covarrubias, 1957, pp. 110–13) and in Ortices phase tombs in Colima (Kelly, 1949, pp. 194–95). It is not certain at just what point in time these Teotihuacan irradiations ceased although this undoubtedly differed in different regions. Perhaps the abandonment of the city after its presumed destruction corresponds to its cessation as a center of widespread influences. On the other hand, it may be that the power of Teotihuacan as an expansive social and cultural force was lessened well in advance of the actual fall of the city (Millon, 1960a).

[29] See Yale laboratory dates for the Kaminaljuyu site, Guatemala highlands, in appendix. Shook now feels that the Arevalo phase precedes the Las Charcas, and we have placed it so on Charts 2 and 3; but it will be noted that these Yale dates indicate Las Charcas to be slightly older.
[30] See dates C-196,-199,-202,-200,-203 in appendix.
[31] See dates M-662,-660; Y-437,-644; M-612,-611,-664,-663 in appendix.
[32] A date from Mesa de Guaje phase in interior Tamaulipas, see M-505 in appendix.
[33] See Groningen dates in appendix. All these dates are susceptible to Suess-effect correction of 240 years (backward in time).
[34] See dates M-535,-529,-534,-532,-531,-530,-528,-536,-533; W-836,-837 in appendix.

For the Late Classic period there are no Mesoamerican stylistic or element spreads comparable in scope to those of Teotihuacan in the Early Classic. A few phenomena of more limited geographic range serve for cross-dating between some regions; Maya Late Classic polychrome pottery influence in Honduras and Salvador, resulting in the Ulua Mayoid and Copador phases, is an example (Strong, 1948; Longyear, 1944). Architectural similarities between the Maya lowlands and Tajin (E. S. Spinden, 1933; García Payón, 1943, 1949a, 1954) and Xochicalco (Escalona Ramos, 1953) are others. In Western Mexico and the Northern Frontier the red-on-buff wares have some kind of relationship to Teotihuacan and post-Teotihuacan styles of the Valley of Mexico, but these have not been sharply defined (Kelley and Winters, 1958). In general, although the Late Classic may have been the beginning of troubled times in Mesoamerica—marked by the first large population disruptions and migrations— this does not seem to be reflected in horizon phenomena in the archaeological record.

Absolute dating on the Classic level has been discussed with reference to the Maya calendar and Long Count dates, expressed according to the two principal correlations of the Maya and Christian calendars in Charts 1 and 2. As already noted, radiocarbon readings are inconclusive in supporting either correlation consistently or in providing a firm basis for refined chronological assignments for the Classic period. In the Valley of Mexico terminal Preclassic radiocarbon dates range from about 500 B.C. to A.D. 500[35] and those from Teotihuacan also show a wide spread. A Classic Teotihuacan date of 235 ± 65 A.D. (Linné, 1956) has, perhaps, the most reliable association of any Teotihuacan date and is identified as Tlamimilolpa phase. Our chart placements of Xolalpan-Tlamimilolpa are in accord with

this date and with the cross-dating by pottery of Xolalpan-Tlamimilolpa and Maya lowland Tzakol. The Tzakol phase has a radiocarbon date of 170 ± 60 A.D.[36] which favors the Spinden correlation placement in Chart 2A although two other presumably Early Classic dates are at about 500 A.D., which may be interpreted as lending support to the Goodman-Martínez-Thompson correlation in Chart 1A.[37] In the Guatemalan highlands there are no Esperanza dates from Kaminaljuyu, but the immediately preceding Aurora phase has four dates between about A.D. 100 and 400 which support either chart.[38] A Monte Alban IIIA date of 298 ±185 A.D.[39] also supports either chart, as does a Palmillas phase date from the Huasteca region of 230 ± 150 A.D.[40] In general, radiocarbon dates for the Early Classic period for Mesoamerica indicate a time range from about A.D. 100 to 500. Finer shading is impossible at the present time, but the earlier of the two calendrical correlations seems favored.

Late Classic radiocarbon dates include one from the Guatemalan highlands of 780 ± 60 A.D., which supports the Goodman-Martínez-Thompson correlation of Chart 1A.[41] This is more than counterbalanced by three readings from Tikal, in the Maya lowlands, which check with the Spinden correlation of Chart 2A.[42] Another Tikal radiocarbon date for the Tepeu phase is much later.[43] There is also a Tepeu date from Uaxactun which is 630 ± 70 A.D. and which could be interpreted in the direction of

---

[35] See Cuicuilco-Ticoman, Tzacualli (Teotihuacan I), and Teotihuacan Classic dates in appendix.

[36] Y-367.

[37] Rands and Rands (1960) present two dates from the Humble Oil Company laboratories (charcoal specimens 396 and 397) which may be interpreted in this way. On the other hand, two other dates from these laboratories (specimens 639 and 641), from the Palenque site and from levels presumably later than those of the above-mentioned specimens, fall at 384 and 409 A.D. (± 105), respectively. These dates, if from Late Classic refuse, are in line with the Spinden correlation.

[38] Y-396,-378,-405,-629.

[39] C-426.   [40] M-506.   [41] Y-383.

[42] C-949,-948; L-113.   [43] Y-392.

[44] Y-368.   [45] M-857, Y-627, W-707.

either correlation.[44] Three dates from Yucatecan Late Classic contexts are early and in line with the Spinden correlation,[45] whereas another from Yucatan and two from British Honduras favor Goodman-Martínez-Thompson.[46] To sum up, the Late Classic dates from Maya country are divided between a dating which precedes and one which follows A.D. 600 although the earlier or Spinden dating holds a definite edge.

The rise of Tula as a center of power is an event of the Early Postclassic period which is reflected archaeologically in the spread of Tula art styles and architectural forms (Acosta, 1945; Dutton, 1955). The outstanding example is the founding of the Tula-related portion of the Chichen Itza site in Yucatan either by invading Toltecs or by peoples under strong Tula-Toltec influence (Tozzer, 1957). More widespread than Tula art, and more useful as horizon markers, are the two Early Postclassic trade wares, Tohil Plumbate (fig. 39), and X Fine Orange (A. O. Shepard, 1948; Wauchope, 1948, pp. 143–45; Brainerd, 1958, pp. 56–59, 78–79, 94–95, 276–82, 372; R. E. Smith, 1955, 1: 28–30). Plumbate is an unique ware with a glazelike surface of exceptional hardness and beauty. Vessels were frequently modeled in effigy forms and were evidently highly prized, being widely traded and imitated. Tohil Plumbate is most abundant in Chiapas, southern Guatemala, and El Salvador; but it links chronologically such widely separated centers as Tula, Isla de Sacrificios, a Postclassic occupation of the Teotihuacan zone, Cerro de las Mesas Upper I, Monte Alban IV, Uxmal, Chichen Itza, and the Tohil phases (Ayampuc level) in the Guatemalan highlands. X Fine Orange is a pottery of great excellence made with a fine dense paste. It is some-

FIG. 39—PLUMBATE EFFIGY JAR
Early Postclassic. Copan, Honduras. (After Longyear, 1952.)

times painted, sometimes incised, and sometimes carved after firing. It, too, provides linkages over much of Mesoamerica in Early Postclassic times. The place of origin of X Fine Orange is unknown but is thought to be on the Tabasco or Veracruz coast. Another Postclassic horizon marker, contemporaneous with Plumbate and X Fine Orange but lasting longer, is the colorful polychrome pottery of Cholula and the Mixteca. Cholula was probably its major center of dissemination and perhaps also the locus of its initial florescence (Noguera, 1954; L. A. Parsons, 1957; Jiménez Moreno, 1959, p. 1075). In the Early Postclassic the style spread over large parts of Mesoamerica and later became part of the Aztec ceramic tradition.

The Late Postclassic period is less well knit with archaeological horizon markers although the extension of the Aztec Empire into Guerrero, Oaxaca, and coastal Veracruz is marked by the occurrence of Aztec pottery and sculptural styles. Other than this, relative dating on this time level is effected

[46] GRO-613. A correction of 240 years should be made on GRO-613 which would bring it back to A.D. 650. The British Honduras dates are BM-37 and -67.

487

by more limited comparisons between adjoining regions and by linkages seen in historical accounts of the time of the Spanish conquest.

The dates of the Postclassic depend, of course, on the calendrical correlation question (see Charts 1 and 2). Radiocarbon datings have been of little value so far, although again they tend to favor the Spinden correlation. There is a Tohil phase (Early Postclassic) Guatemalan highland date of 1190 ± 60 A.D. which would coincide with the end of the Plumbate horizon in the Goodman-Martínez-Thompson correlation.[47] Opposed to this are dates of 800 ± 70 A.D. and 820 ± 100 A.D.[48] for Toltec Chichen Itza, which are more in line with Spinden's correlation as is a Tulum date (presumably Late Postclassic) of 1080 ± 60 A.D.[49] Of three presumably Late Postclassic dates from the site of Mayapan in Yucatan, one can be interpreted as favoring the Spinden correlation; the other two may be interpreted either way.[50] On the northern frontier two Postclassic dates from the Huasteca region are late, but the contexts in which they are found are too remote from the Maya scene to help much in the correlation question.[51] Northwest Mexican dates could be taken as favoring either Goodman-Martínez-Thompson or Spinden, depending on the dates cited or the cross-dating of the phases involved.[52]

Major Trends

An idealized sequence of social and cultural development for the agricultural era of pre-Columbian Mesoamerica might be constructed as follows: first, the appearance of sedentary farming villages; second, the rise of small temple or ceremonial centers; third, the development of civilization with populations clustering around temple centers in true urban zones or living in temple-center-with-outlying-hamlet arrangements; and fourth, the formation of expansionistic civilizations dominating large territorial states and empires. To what extent does this sequence square with the facts of Mesoamerican prehistory as we now know them?

Before turning to a review of the evidence for such major trends in Mesoamerican prehistory, let us make clear that the data of archaeology are not only very incomplete but notoriously intractable to interpretation in terms of living situations and institutions. Mesoamerican archaeologists and anthropologists are a long way from understanding just how and why certain social and cultural changes came about in the past. They are still largely concerned with the outward forms of these changes.

The concept of the sedentary agricultural village is linked to "established cultivation." The latter means that a stable community is supported primarily by the growing of food plants. This condition is conceived of as the threshold of agricultural Mesoamerica. Such a community is sedentary in that its inhabitants exploit a restricted geographic zone of farming land. The village may be a concentration of dwellings which remain in one place over a considerable period of time, or it may be a scattering of hamlets or households whose locations are shifted about over a radius of a few miles. In either case the village as a social entity remains centered in one place, and this centering is obviously of great importance in all spheres of life—social, economic, political and religious.

According to our hypothetical sequence of development, such a stage of simple sedentary farming villages would have existed more or less uniformly over significantly large portions of Middle America prior to the appearance of more complex forms of settlement;[53] but the evidence for

[47] Y-369. [48] Y-626 and Y-626 bis. [49] Y-393.
[50] GRO-452,-1166,-450 should all be made 240 years earlier. GRO-452 favors the Spinden correlation.
[51] M-501, C-207. [52] M-592,-432,-431,-430.

[53] See Wauchope, 1950; M. D. Coe, 1957b, for a discussion of "Village Formative."

this is inconclusive. The best examples of Early Preclassic remains which appear to represent the archaeological vestiges of simple farming villages are those of the Chiapa I phase in Chiapas (MacNeish, personal communication, 1959; Lowe, 1959), the Early Zacatenco and El Arbolillo I phase in central Mexico (Vaillant, 1941), Pavon on the Huasteca coast (MacNeish, 1954), Mani in Yucatan (Brainerd, 1958), Yarumela I in Honduras (Canby, 1951), and, probably, the Mesa de Guaje phase in interior Tamaulipas (MacNeish, 1958). These are represented by remains which lack associated temple centers or ceremonial architecture. On the other hand, the Arevalo and Ocos phases of highland and Pacific Guatemala—which may be as early as those listed above—may have special temple-mound components (Shook, 1951; M. D. Coe, personal communication, 1959); the same is probably true for the earliest phases at La Venta, Tabasco (Drucker, Heizer, and Squier, 1959). In brief, the dawn of settled village farming in Mesoamerica seems to involve some societies which appear to be more complexly organized than is consistent with the concept of "simple village farming." It is possible, of course, that the seeming absence of ceremonial structures in the first-mentioned group of sites is due only to our knowing the earliest cultures represented from the bottoms of stratigraphic pits, or by otherwise incomplete finds, and that the societies may have been more advanced in this direction than we now realize. In this event the theoretical stage of simple village farm- . ing may have been associated only with preceramic or as yet undiscovered early ceramic horizons.

We place great stress upon the "temple center" or "ceremonial center" in this discussion of major trends in the growth and changes of ancient Mesoamerican society. It is from such centers that we draw most of our inferences of past social, political, and religious organization. Our starting point is the 16th century, when we know that pyramid mounds and artificial platforms were the locations of the temples, palaces, and other public buildings in native communities which were used by priests, rulers, and other dignitaries. We also know that plazas in these temple centers served as marketplaces. Undoubtedly, the organization of pre-Columbian societies varied greatly at different times and places, but the appearance of plazas, temples, and other public buildings in any local or regional Mesoamerican sequence is the most reasonable point at which to postulate the beginnings of changes leading from relatively undifferentiated to relatively highly differentiated societies.

We have noted that temple mounds were features of some of the Early Preclassic phases in Mesoamerica and infer from this that such societies were already at that time relatively highly differentiated, at least in the religious sphere; but it is in the Middle and Late Preclassic period that the temple center rises to notable importance over much of Mesoamerica. Almost certainly this event was accompanied by a general population increase. Temple-center formation may have involved a process whereby daughter villages hived off from parent villages without breaking kinship and other social, political, and religious bonds. Certain villages, perhaps the older ones, may have been revered as the homes of leaders and the hearths of tribal tradition. These might have become the seats of political and religious authority to which pilgrimages were made and where the notable dead were buried. Perhaps many or most of them also served as marketplaces, although the antiquity of this important temple-center function remains to be determined. The development of various arts and crafts and of formal learning was presumably fostered by the resident leadership as its members rose to positions of greater status and prestige. This was, perhaps, primarily due to the increasing proliferation of the needs of the

489

Fig. 40—PYRAMID OF THE SUN, TEOTIHUACAN, MEXICO
Late Preclassic to Classic. (Photo by Otto Done.)

temple-center cult as interpreted by its earthly representatives.

Whether the process was shaped in this or other ways, it is clear that the outcome in many regions of Mesoamerica was the development of civilized societies. How do we define civilization? V. Gordon Childe has attempted to tie the rise of civilization to the development of cities. He has further suggested certain criteria, presumably deducible from archaeological data, which may be taken to define the emergence of an urban society and civilization (Childe, 1950, 1952). However, the correlation of civilization and city is only partial in Mesoamerica. For this reason we have chosen to define civilization in Mesoamerica somewhat differently. Our criteria are modified paraphrases of some of Childe's and are as follows: (1) monumental public architecture, (2) great art styles involving artistic representations in many media, (3) development of practical sciences and means of recording (astronomy, calendars, numeral notation systems, accounting systems, and, often but

not always, writing), (4) populations of relatively great size and density, often but not always including large densely populated settlements, (5) differentiation of the population into a number of more or less distinguishable social classes, ordered in hierarchical fashion with differential access to privilege and probably with differential access to knowledge or the acquiring of skills in both the practical and ideological spheres (priests, secular officials, artists, craftsmen, peasants, and sometimes merchants), (6) concentration of natural and human resources for public enterprises, and (7) extensive foreign trade.

We further infer, although this is not directly deducible from archaeological data, that in Mesoamerica the integration of a civilized society was effected at least in part through the medium of a formalized political system which was closely related to an elaborated, hierarchically administered religious system. The most dramatic manifestation of this is the great pyramid-temple. On the basis of comparative cross-cultural evidence we may assume that the duties required of the individual by the social order were performed because people were internally motivated to meet their obligations. They had been socialized on the household and wider levels to believe that the demands made upon them were moral and just. Those occupying subordinate positions in the hierarchy must have accepted the inevitable inequities of a markedly stratified society and would not have seriously questioned either the justice of their obligations or the right of their superiors to exact these obligations. The fact that pyramids, temples, and other public buildings were built at all is a sufficient indication of concensus, since coercion alone could not account for their existence.

Although it might be difficult to demonstrate that all of the above criteria are inferrable from our present knowledge of any single archaeological site, it is clear that most of them can be so inferred at many sites over wide areas of Mesoamerica.

When does civilization as so defined first appear on the Mesoamerican scene? In some parts of Mesoamerica it appears in the Middle Preclassic period (La Venta, Monte Alban, Kaminaljuyu). And certainly by the opening of the Classic period civilized societies were well established in a number of regions. Centers of civilization in Mesoamerica may be divided into two types. One was truly urban in the sense of extensive and densely settled, internally differentiated populations living around great temples in compact aggregations of dwellings, building complexes, streets and alleys. The other type lacked these formal properties of urbanism; rather, it was a greatly magnified temple center, with a relatively small resident population, the remainder of the population living in dispersed villages and hamlets. Both types seem to have their origins in the smaller temple centers of the Preclassic period.

The Mesoamerican city had its origin in the upland valley basins of central Mexico,

Oaxaca, and Guatemala. In the Valley of Mexico, at Teotihuacan, the Late Preclassic Tzacualli phase is represented by a broad zone of architectural and other remains more than a kilometer in length (Millon, 1957b); it seems probable that the great Pyramid of the Sun (which contains 30,-000,000 cubic feet of earth and stone) (fig. 40)[53a] was built towards the end of this phase. In the Classic period, as noted above, the Teotihuacan urban zone covered at least 5 square miles. There can be little doubt that Teotihuacan was a highly differentiated, stratified society in which priests fulfilled important political as well as religious functions and that craft specialization and social classes were concomitants of the city's grandeur. Long-distance trade radiated from this capital, and a good case can be made for an extensive conquest state centered at Teotihuacan. However, so far lacking at Teotihuacan are clear evidences of the use of writing, of a developed system of numeral notation, and of allied advances.[54]

In highland Guatemala Kaminaljuyu was densely populated in Middle Preclassic times; and the ceremonial mounds, richly furnished tombs, sculptures, and hieroglyphics of its Miraflores phase attest to the attainment of civilization well before the Classic period (Shook and Kidder, 1952). Similarly, the early developments of civilization in Oaxaca, in the Monte Alban I phase, antedate the Classic period (Caso, 1938).

The other type of civilization center in Mesoamerica, the magnified temple center,

---

[53a] Recent ceramic analyses carried on by R. E. Smith indicate the construction of this great pyramid to have been an event of the Early Classic period (R. E. Smith, personal communication, 1963).

[54] Some evidence of writing, numeral notation and the use of the 260-day ritual calendar exists at Teotihuacan in the form of bar-and-dot numerals combined with what appear to be hieroglyphs. Other isolated elements may also be glyphs. So far the evidence is fragmentary, however. See Caso, 1937; Franco, 1959, p. 378.

is essentially a lowland, tropical forest development. It has been argued, and probably correctly, that it is a correlate of slash-and-burn farming, with the necessity for constantly shifting cultivation fields. In such lowland tropical regions, land must be allowed to return to bush for long periods after it is cultivated. This situation encourages relatively dispersed settlement, even though population density per square mile may be relatively high (Cowgill, 1959). Thus, although the temple center was an important focus of social, political, religious and, perhaps, economic life, it did not become a densely settled urban zone. In spite of this, such centers were manifestly the seats of great civilizations. The famed lowland Maya sites of the Classic period are the ideal examples of the magnified temple center, among the greatest being Tikal, Copan, and Palenque. It is possible that Tikal, the greatest of all, was a true urban center. Although Maya society of the Classic period probably was tightly integrated, it is doubtful if most individual lowland Maya societies were more than relatively localized temple-center–hamlet networks. In the Maya lowlands the great temple centers probably were in formation in the late Preclassic although they are best known from the Classic period. However, in the adjacent Tabasco lowlands, in tropical forest terrain similar to that of the Maya country, the La Venta ceremonial center presents most of the aspects of civilization by the opening of the Middle Preclassic period if not before. There is no evidence for densely settled populations at La Venta, but there can be no doubt that the site had extraordinary prestige in its region and time. Located on a small island within a swamp, La Venta is marked by a number of earthen platforms, the largest of which measures 420 by 240 feet at its base and is 103 feet high (Drucker, Heizer, and Squier, 1959, p. 11). Other features of the site include stelae and altars executed in a commanding art style, mosaic pave-

ments laid out in mask designs, and enclosures of huge basalt columns (figs. 26, 27). The labor involved in the construction of such a site is astounding when we realize that the nearest natural supply of stone is 60 miles distant.

One of the primary problems posed by these early Mesoamerican civilizations is how they were internally integrated. What were the political, social, religious, and economic ties that bound these societies together? Obviously, the manpower resources of these societies could be and were mobilized for great collective enterprises; yet how this was accomplished remains obscure. Important in this regard is the problem of how economically self-sufficient the peasant populations of these societies were. To what extent were external and internal trade and/or the requirements of irrigation and other forms of intensive agriculture significant integrative factors? Were prehistoric temple centers and cities also formal market centers? If so, at what point in time did the temple-center–market come into being? Similarly, to what extent was endemic warfare an integrative factor favoring the internal development of centralized authority to meet external threats? So far only partial and fragmentary answers to these questions are possible. However, we can infer from the archaeological evidence that religion played an important integrative role, both in the concentrated urban and in the dispersed temple-center societies. It is also evident that the problem of integration was quite different in dispersed tropical lowland societies from what it was in highland regions and we may expect that the means employed for effecting integration differed significantly from region to region.

Certain aspects of the integrative problem are, perhaps, better understood for the final pre-Columbian era, the Postclassic period. A number of expansionistic states or empires passed across the scene at this time, of which that of the Aztecs is best known. Military force and tribute exactions were among the integrative means employed. We also have archaeological evidence of war, strife, and mass migrations throughout much of Mesoamerica beginning with the Early Postclassic period. This, for instance, is the period to which most Mesoamerican forts and fortified sites are dated (Armillas, 1948, 1951; Palerm, 1956). Also, semilegendary histories from central Mexico and the Guatemalan highlands attest to this "time of troubles." In sum, the Postclassic was a period of war and empire building; the question for the archaeologist to settle is the extent to which similar conditions prevailed earlier. Classic Teotihuacan may have been an expansionistic state, like those of later times, but we cannot yet be certain of this.

In reviewing these main trends of Mesoamerican social and cultural development we see the village farming community as the *sine qua non* of the Early Preclassic period. In some regions, particularly the southern part of Mesoamerica, temple centers appear to be contemporaneous with the very earliest stable agricultural communities; but farther north the oldest villages do not have temple or ceremonial constructions in association. The Middle and Late Preclassic periods are a time of population increase and of the rise of ceremonial centers. Such centers are found in nearly all parts of the area, the West Mexican and northern frontier region being a possible exception. In the highland valleys of Mexico and Guatemala temple centers were the foci around which urban populations clustered into cities; in the lowland forest country of Guatemala, Yucatan, and Veracruz-Tabasco the temple centers grew in size and importance as the politico-religious (and economic?) nuclei of scattered village and hamlet dwellers. The Mesoamerican city thus had relatively ancient origins although it is best known from the time of the Classic period. During this emergence of the temple center and the city in the central and

southern portions of Mesoamerica the trends in the north and west probably were neither fully parallel nor synchronous. Ceremonial center construction seems to have lagged in this region, and it is unlikely that cities or temple centers made their appearance here until well after their inception in the Valley of Mexico and elsewhere. In the Postclassic period there are definite evidences of political expansionism, through both military might and trade. The limitations of archaeological evidence make it difficult or impossible to be certain if such conditions of expansionism and state building had earlier roots in the area. In any event, the rise of empire in pre-Columbian Mesoamerica is inextricably linked with the phenomenon of the city.

To return to the idealized sequence of Mesoamerican social and cultural development outlined at the beginning of this discussion of trends, we see that our first level, that of sedentary village farming society, cannot be defined as fully distinct from, and antecedent to, a second level of village plus temple center. Whether this is because a tradition of ceremonial-center construction antedates village agriculture, is exactly coexistent with it in parts of Mesoamerica, or because the archaeological record is still too incomplete, we do not know. The possibility also exists that migrations or influences from other advanced centers—in Asia—may have played some role in sparking the growth of Mesoamerican civilization, even though at the present state of archaeological research this cannot be demonstrated satisfactorily. The second level, that of the small temple center, grades into the third, that of cities and great temple centers. With this third level the city appears to come into being in the upland valleys of regions such as the Valley of Mexico or the Guatemalan highlands whereas greatly enlarged temple centers are found in the lowlands. It is clear that such achievements of civilization as elaborations in art, architecture, writing, and calendrics are

493

not necessarily associated with the city and arose without it. In fact, many of the earliest appearances of monumental sculptural art, writing, and calendrics in Mesoamerica are correlated with the lowland and upland temple centers. On the other hand, there is some reason to suspect that it was only the concentrated urbanism of the uplands that provided the base from which the third level passed to the fourth or in which these true cities became the capitals of empires.

APPENDIX

LIST OF PERTINENT MESOAMERICAN RADIOCARBON DATES BY REGION, PERIOD, AND ARCHAEOLOGICAL PHASE*

MAYA HIGHLANDS REGION
Preclassic period (all Kaminaljuyu zone except Y-374)
Arevalo phase
Y-402 . . . 110 B.C. ± 50 (Deevey, Gralenski, and Hoffren, 1959).
Y-401 . . . 280 B.C. ± 60 (*ibid.*).
Las Charcas phase
C-885 . . . 1546 B.C. ± 800 (Libby, 1955).
Y-384 . . . 380 B.C. ± 50 (Deevey, Gralenski, and Hoffren, 1959).
Majadas phase
C-886 . . . 1020 B.C. ± 200 (Libby, 1955).
Y-390 . . . 375 B.C. ± 50 (Deevey, Gralenski, and Hoffren, 1959).
Providencia phase
C-879 . . . 1196 B.C. ± 300 (Libby, 1955).
Y-370 . . . 110 A.D. ± 60 (Deevey, Gralenski, and Hoffren, 1959).
Sacatepequez phase (not in Kaminaljuyu zone but believed contemporaneous with Providencia phase)
Y-374 . . . 160 B.C. ± 60 (Deevey, Gralenski, and Hoffren, 1959).
Miraflores phase
C-884 . . . 1192 B.C. ± 240 (Libby, 1955).
C-887 . . . 540 B.C. ± 300 (*ibid.*).
Y-391 . . . 65 B.C. ± 60 (Deevey, Gralenski, and Hoffren, 1959).
Y-382 . . . 40 A.D. ± 60 (*ibid.*).
Y-377 . . . 20 A.D. ± 60 (*ibid.*).
Santa Clara phase
Y-406 . . . 160 A.D. ± 60 (Deevey, Gralenski, and Hoffren, 1959).
Aurora phase (may also be considered as Classic period)
Y-396 . . . 100 A.D. ± 60 (Deevey, Gralenski, and Hoffren, 1959).
Y-378 . . . 175 A.D. ± 60 (*ibid.*).
Y-405 . . . 299 A.D. ± 60 (*ibid.*).
Y-629 . . . 400 A.D. ± 70 (*ibid.*).
Classic period
Late Pokom phase (Zacualpa zone; probably very Late Classic)
Y-383 . . . 780 A.D. ± 60 (Deevey, Gralenski, and Hoffren, 1959).
Postclassic period
Tohil phase (at Nebaj site; probably Early Postclassic)
Y-369 . . . 1190 A.D. ± 60 (Deevey, Gralenski, and Hoffren, 1959).

* Laboratories are: Y—Yale University; C—Chicago University; GRO—Rijks University, Groningen; L—Lamont Laboratory, Columbia University; Humble Oil—Humble Oil Co. of Texas; BM—British Museum; S—Stockholm; W—U.S. Geological Survey. Recent statements by physicists in charge of the Groningen and other radiocarbon laboratories indicate that all the Groningen and Chicago dates on these lists should be revised backward by 240 years to allow for the Suess-effect correction (Munnich, Ostlund, De Vries, and Barker, 1958).

PACIFIC COAST OF GUATEMALA (may be considered part of Maya highlands region)
   Preclassic period
      Conchas phase (Ocos, Guatemala)
         W-836   . . . 190 B.C. ± 240 (Rubin and Alexander, 1960).
         W-837   . . . 120 B.C. ± 240 (*ibid.*).

CHIAPAS (may be considered part of either highlands or lowlands region; all dates from Chiapas de Corzo zone)
   Preclassic period†
      Chiapa I phase
         GRO-774 . . . 1050 B.C. ± 150 (Dixon, 1959, p. 41).
      Chiapa II phase
         GRO-1172 . . . 928 B.C. ± 60 (Dixon, 1959, p. 41).
         GRO-1512 . . . 813 B.C. ± 50 (*ibid.*).
         L-427   . . . 770 B.C. ± 150 (Olson and Broecker, 1959).
      Chiapa III–V phase
         GRO-1056 . . . 172 B.C. ± 60 (Dixon, 1959, p. 41).
         GRO-1524 . . . 312 B.C. ± 45 (*ibid.*).
      Chiapa VI phase
         GRO-1525 . . .   27 A.D. ± 50 (Dixon, 1959, p. 41).
      Chiapa VII phase
         GRO-1589 . . . 278 A.D. ± 45 (Dixon, 1959, p. 41).

MAYA LOWLANDS REGION
   Preclassic period
      Dzibilchaltun site (Formative III-IV Transition)
         LJ-279 . . . 240 B.C. ± 90 (Andrews, 1962, p. 33). La Jolla Lab.
         C-425 . . . 310 B.C. ± 80 (*ibid.*). Isotopes, Inc.
   Classic period
      Tzakol phase (Uaxactun site)
         Y-367   . . . 170 A.D. ± 60 (Deevey, Gralenski, and Hoffren, 1959).
      Palenque site (Classic phases)
         Humble Oil, Spec. 396 . . . 558 A.D. ± 100 (Rands and Rands, 1960).
         Humble Oil, Spec. 397 . . . 508 A.D. ± 100 (Rands and Rands, 1960).
         Humble Oil, Spec. 639 . . . 384 A.D. ± 105 (Rands and Rands, 1960).
         Humble Oil, Spec. 641 . . . 409 A.D. ± 105 (Rands and Rands, 1960).
      Tepeu phase (Tikal site)
         C-949   . . . 434 A.D. ± 170 (Libby, 1955).
         C-948   . . . 470 A.D. ± 120 (*ibid.*).
         L-113   . . . 481 A.D. ± 120 (Kulp, Feely, and Tryon, 1951).
         Y-392   . . . 1159 A.D. ± 50 (Deevey, Gralenski, and Hoffren, 1959).
      Tepeu phase (Uaxactun site)
         Y-368   . . . 630 A.D. ± 70 (Deevey, Gralenski, and Hoffren, 1959).
      Dzibilchaltun site (probably Tepeu 1 equivalent)
         M-857   . . . 460 A.D. ± 200 (Crane and Griffin, 1959).
         W-707   . . . 510 A.D. ± 200 (Rubin and Alexander, 1960).
      Uxmal site (probably Late Classic)
         GRO-613 . . . 893 A.D. ± 100 (De Vries and Waterbolk, 1958).
         Y-627   . . . 570 A.D. ± 50 (Deevey, Gralenski, and Hoffren, 1959).
      British Honduras (Late Classic or Early Postclassic)
         BM-37   . . . 1040 A.D. ± 150 (Las Cuevas) (Barker and Mackey, 1959).
         BM-67   . . . 840 A.D. ± 50 (Rio Frio) (Barker and Mackey, 1960).
   Postclassic period
      Balankanche cave (Modified Florescent)
         LJ-272 . . . 870 A.D. ± 90 (Andrews, 1962, p. 33). La Jolla Lab.
         LJ-273 . . . 870 A.D. ± 100 (*ibid.*). La Jolla Lab.

† It should be noted that here, as on the chronology charts, the Chiapa de Corzo sequence follows the new enumeration used at the Chiapas conference of September 1959.

Chichen Itza–Toltec phase (Modified Florescent)
  Y-626 . . . 800 A.D. ± 70 (Deevey, Gralenski, and Hoffren, 1959).
  Y-626 bis . . . 820 A.D. ± 100 (Stuiver, Deevey, and Gralenski, 1960).
Tulum site (Late Postclassic?)
  Y-393 . . . 1080 A.D. ± 60 (Deevey, Gralenski, and Hoffren, 1959).
Mayapan site (Late Postclassic)
  GRO- 452 . . . 1250 A.D. ± 95 (De Vries and Waterbolk, 1958).
  GRO-1166 . . . 1550 A.D. ± 55 (De Vries and Waterbolk, 1958).
  GRO- 450 . . . 1615 A.D. ± 90 (De Vries and Waterbolk, 1958).

SOUTHERN PERIPHERY REGION
  Preclassic period (probably Late Preclassic)
  Cerro Zapote site (below volcanic deposits)
    C-891 . . . 1039 B.C. ± 360 (Libby, 1955).

SOUTHERN VERACRUZ–TABASCO REGION
  Preclassic period
  La Venta I phase
    M-535 . . . 1160 B.C. ± 300 (Drucker, Heizer, and Squier, 1957).
    M-529 . . . 910 B.C. ± 300 (*ibid.*).
    M-534 . . . 720 B.C. ± 300 (*ibid.*).
    M-532 . . . 700 B.C. ± 300 (*ibid.*).
    M-531 . . . 610 B.C. ± 300 (*ibid.*).
  La Venta II phase
    M-530 . . . 810 B.C. ± 300 (*ibid.*).
  La Venta Post–IV phase
    M-528 . . . 450 B.C. ± 250 (*ibid.*).
    M-533 . . . 280 B.C. ± 300 (*ibid.*).
    M-536 . . . 580 B.C. ± 300 (*ibid.*).

OAXACA REGION
  Preclassic period
  Monte Alban I phase (Tilantongo site)
    C-424 . . . 650 B.C. ± 170 (Libby, 1955).
  Monte Alban II phase (Monte Alban site)
    C-425 . . . 273 B.C. ± 145 (Libby, 1955).
  Classic Period
  Monte Alban IIIA phase (Chachoapan)
    C-426 . . . 298 A.D. ± 185 (Libby, 1955).

CENTRAL MEXICO REGION
  Preclassic period
  Early Zacatenco phase (Early Preclassic)
    C-196 . . . 1360 B.C. ± 250 (Libby, 1955).
    M-662 . . . 500 B.C. ± 250 (Crane and Griffin, 1958b).
  Tlatilco phase (Early-to-Middle Preclassic)
    C-199 . . . 1457 B.C. ± 250 (Libby, 1955).
    M-660 . . . 575 B.C. ± 250 (Crane and Griffin, 1958b).
  Loma del Tepalcate phase (Late Preclassic)
    C-202 . . . 615 B.C. ± 200 (Libby, 1955).
  Cuicuilco-Ticoman phases (Late Preclassic)
    C-200 . . . 472 B.C. ± 250 (Libby, 1955).
    M-664 . . . 520 A.D. ± 20 (Crane and Griffin, 1958b).
    M-663 . . . 90 A.D. ± 200 (*ibid.*).
    Y-437 . . . 34 A.D. ± 60 (*ibid.*).
    M-612 . . . 9 A.D. ± 200 (Crane and Griffin, 1959).
    M-611 . . . 309 A.D. ± 200 (*ibid.*).
  Tzacualli or Teotihuacan I phase
    C-203 . . . 484 B.C. ± 500 and
              431 A.D. ± 200 (Libby, 1955).
    Y-644 . . . 30 A.D. ± 80 (Stuiver, Deevey, and Gralenski, 1960).

Classic period
Teotihuacan II-III (Miccaotli and Tlamimilolpa-Xolalpan) phases
    C-422   . . . 294 B.C. ± 180 (Libby, 1955).
    C-423   . . . 1474 B.C. ± 230 (ibid.).
    S-162   . . . 235 A.D. ± 65 (Tlamimilolpa) (Linné, 1956).

HUASTECA REGION
Preclassic period
Mesa de Guaje phase (probably Early Preclassic)
    M-505   . . . 1700 B.C. ± 250 and
                     1490 B.C. ± 250 (Crane and Griffin, 1958a).
Classic period
Palmillas phase
    M-568   . . . 230 A.D. ± 150 (Crane and Griffin, 1958a).
Postclassic period
San Lorenzo phase
    M-501   . . . 1430 A.D. ± 200 (Crane and Griffin, 1958a).
Los Angeles phase
    C-207   . . . 1299 A.D. ± 150 (Libby, 1955).

NORTHERN FRONTIER REGION
Classic period
Ayala phase
    M-592   . . . 810 A.D. ± 200 (Crane and Griffin, 1959).
La Quemada site (phase uncertain; possibly Postclassic)
    M-432   . . . 740 A.D. ± 200 (Crane and Griffin, 1958a).
    M-431   . . . 1170 A.D. ± 200 (ibid.).
    M-430   . . . 1060 A.D. ± 200 (ibid.).
Pre–Las Joyas (phase uncertain)
    M-613   . . . 408 A.D. ± 250 (Crane and Griffin, 1958b).

REFERENCES

Acosta, 1940, 1944, 1945
Armillas, 1948, 1949, 1950, 1951, 1957
Arte Precolumbino, 1946
Barker and Mackey, 1959, 1960
Bernal, 1948–49, 1949, 1950, 1958
—— and Dávalos Hurtado, 1953
Blom, 1932b
Boas, 1911–12
Brainerd, 1954, 1958
Broecker, Olson, and Bird, 1959
Bullard, W. R., 1960
Canby, 1951
Caso, 1937, 1938, 1941, 1953b, 1954
Charnay, 1880, 1888
Childe, 1950, 1952
Coe, M. D., 1957a, 1957b, 1959
Coe, W. R., 1959a
Columbus, 1867
Covarrubias, 1957
Cowgill, 1959
Crane and Griffin, 1958a, 1958b, 1959
Deevey, 1957
——, Gralenski, and Hoffren, 1959
DeVries and Waterbolk, 1958
Dixon, 1959

Drucker, 1943a, 1943b, 1952
——, Heizer, and Squier, 1957, 1959
Du Solier, 1945
Dutton, 1955
Ekholm, 1944, 1946a, 1946b, 1948, 1949, 1958
Escalona Ramos, 1953
Foster, 1955, 1959a, 1959b
Franco, 1949, 1959
Gamio, 1921
García Payón, 1943, 1949a, 1949b, 1953, 1954
Gifford, 1950
Hay et al., 1940
Holden, 1957
Jiménez Moreno, 1954–55, 1959
Katz, 1956, 1958
Kelley, 1956, 1957
——, Campbell, and Lehmer, 1940
—— and Winters, 1958
Kelly, 1938, 1945–49, 1947
Kidder, Jennings, and Shook, 1946
Kirchhoff, 1943
Krickeberg, 1918–22, 1956
Kulp, Feely, and Tryon, 1951
Lathrap, 1957
Levine, 1958

Libby, 1955
Linné, 1934, 1942, 1956
Lister, 1955
—— and Howard, 1955
Longyear, 1944, 1952
Lothrop, 1926, 1939
Lowe, 1959
MacNeish, 1954, 1958
Marquina, 1951
Mayer-Oakes, 1959
Medellín Zenil, 1953, 1955a, 1955b
—— and Peterson, 1954
Millon, 1957a, 1957b, 1959, 1960a, 1960b
Moore, S. F., 1958
Morley, 1946, 1956
Morris, Charlot, and Morris, 1931
Münnich, Ostlund, De Vries, and Barker, 1958
Noguera, 1942, 1954
Olson and Broecker, 1959
Oviedo y Valdes, 1851–55
Palerm, 1954, 1955, 1956
Parsons, L. A., 1957
Piña Chan, 1955, 1958
Porter, 1953, 1956
Proskouriakoff, 1946, 1954, 1958
Rands and Rands, 1960
Redfield, 1956
Roys, 1943
Rowe, 1946
Rubin and Alexander, 1960
Rubín de la Borbolla, 1948

Ruppert, Thompson, and Proskouriakoff, 1955
Sanders, W. T., 1956
Shepard, A. O., 1948
Shook, 1951
—— and Kidder, 1952
—— and Proskouriakoff, 1956
Smith, A. L., 1955
Smith, R. E., 1940, 1955
Sorenson, 1955
Spinden, E. S., 1933
Spinden, H. J., 1917
Spratling, 1960
Staub, 1920
Stern, 1948
Stirling, 1940
Strong, 1948
——, Kidder, and Paul, 1938
Stuiver, Deevey, and Gralenski, 1960
Thompson, J. E. S., 1935, 1939, 1943, 1945, 1948, 1954
Thompson, R. H., 1958
Tolstoy, 1958
Torquemada, 1723
Tozzer, 1921, 1957
Vaillant, 1930, 1935, 1938, 1941
Wauchope, 1948, 1950
West and Armillas, 1950
Willey, 1958
—— and Phillips, 1958
Wolf, 1959
—— and Palerm, 1955

REFERENCES AND INDEX

REFERENCES

ACOSTA, J. R.
1940 Exploraciones en Tula, Hidalgo, 1940. *Rev. Mex. Estud. Antropol.*, 4: 172–94.
1944 La tercera temporada en exploraciones arqueológicas en Tula, Hidalgo, 1942. *Rev. Mex. Estud. Antropol.*, vol. 6, no. 3.
1945 La cuarta y quinta temporada de excavaciones en Tula, Hidalgo. *Rev. Mex. Estud. Antropol.*, 7: 23–64.

AGUILAR Y SANTILLÁN, R.
1908 Bibliografía geológica y minera de la República Mexicana, completada hasta el año de 1904. *Bol. Inst. Geol. de Mex.*, no. 17.
1918 Bibliografía geológica y minera de la República Mexicana, 1905–1918.
1930 Bibliografía geológica y minera de la República Mexicana, correspondiente a los años de 1919 a 1930.

AGUILERA, J. G.
1907 Les volcans du Mexique dans leur relations avec le rélief et la tectonique du pays. *10th Int. Cong. Geol., Compte Rendu*, 2: 1155–68.

—— AND E. ORDÓÑEZ
1895 Excursión científica al Popocatépetl.

AGUILERA HERRERA, N.
1955 Los suelos tropicales de Mexico. Inst. Mex. Recursos Naturales Renovables, mesas redondas sobre problemas del trópico mexicano, pp. 3–24.
1959 Suelos. *In* Beltrán, 1959, pp. 177–212.

AHLMANN, H. W.
1953 Glacier variations and climatic fluctuations. *Amer. Geog. Soc., Bowman Memorial Lectures*, 3d ser.

ALBRITTON, C. C.
1958 Quaternary stratigraphy of the Guadiana Valley, Durango, Mexico. *Bull. Geol. Soc. Amer.*, 69: 1197–1216.

ALCALÁ, M.
1906 Sondeos en las lagunas o ciénegas de Almoloya y Lerma. *Bol. Soc. Geol. Mex.*, 2: 15–34.

ALLEN, P. H.
1956 The rain forests of Golfo Dulce. Univ. Florida.

ALLEN, W. E.
1939 Surface distribution of marine plankton diatoms in the Panama region in 1933. *Bull. Scripps Inst. Oceanogr., Univ. Calif., Tech. Ser.*, 4: 181–95.

ANONYMOUS
1957 Data report: surface water temperatures at shore stations, United States west coast and Baja California, 1955. SIO Reference 57-28, 5 July 1957. (Baja California data taken under direction of Carl L. Hubbs, pp. 50–56.)

ARELLANO, A. R. V.
1946a Datos geológicos sobre la antigüedad del hombre en la cuenca de Mexico. *Mem. 2d Cong. Mex. Cienc. Sociales*, 5: 213–19.
1946b El elefante fósil de Tepexpan y el hombre primitivo. *Rev. Mex. Estud. Antropol.*, 8: 89–94.
1951a The Becerra formation (latest Pleistocene) of central Mexico. *18th Int. Cong. Geol.*, pt. 11 (Proc. sec. K: Correlation of Continental Vertebrate-bearing Rocks), pp. 55–62. London.
1951b Some new aspects of the Tepexpan Man case. *Bull. Texas Archaeol. and Paleontol. Soc.*, 22: 217–24.
1953a Barrilaco Pedocal, a stratigraphic marker ca. 5,000 B.C. and its climatic significance. *19th Int. Cong. Geol., Compte Rendu*, sec. 7 (Déserts actuels et anciens, fascicule 7), pp. 53–76. Algier.
1953b Estratigrafía de la cuenca de Mexico. *Mem. Cong. Cien. de Mex.*, 3: 172–85.

—— AND F. MÜLLER
1948 La cueva encantada de Chimalacatlan, Morelos. *Bol. Soc. Mex. Geog. y Estad.*, 66: 483–91.

ARGUEDAS R. DE LA BORBOLLA, S., AND L. AVELEYRA ARROYO DE ANDA
1953 A Plainview point from northern Tamaulipas. *Amer. Antiquity*, 18: 392–93.

ARMENTA, J.
1957 Hallazgos prehistóricos en el valle de

Puebla. *Centro de Estud. Hist. de Puebla*, no. 2.

1959 Hallazgo de un artefacto asociado con mamut, en el valle de Puebla. *Inst. Nac. Antropol. e Hist.*, Pub. 7. Mexico.

ARMILLAS, P.
1948 Fortalezas mexicanas. *Cuad. Amer.*, 41: 143–63.

1949 Notas sobre sistemas de cultivo en Mesoamerica. *An. Inst. Nac. Antropol. e Hist.*, 3: 85–113.

1950 Teotihuacan, Tula, y los Toltecas. Las culturas post-arcaicas y pre-Aztecas del centro de Mexico. Excavaciones y estudios 1922–50. *Runa*, 3: 37–70. Buenos Aires.

1951 Tecnología, formaciones socio-económicas y religión en Mesoamerica. *In* Tax, 1951, pp. 19–30.

1957 Programa de historia de la America indígena. Pt. 1: America precolombina. *Pan Amer. Union, Social Sci. Monogr.*, no. 2. (Also published in English, 1958.)

ARNOLD, B. A.
1957 Late Pleistocene and Recent changes in land forms, climate, and archaeology in central Baja California. *Univ. Calif. Pub. Geog.*, 10: 201–318.

ARTE PRECOLOMBINO DEL OCCIDENTE DE MEXICO
1946 Secretaría de Educación Pública. Mexico.

ASCHMANN, H.
1952 A fluted point from Baja California. *Amer. Antiquity*, 17: 262.

1959 The central desert of Baja California: demography and ecology. *Ibero-Amer.*, no. 42.

1960 The subsistence problem in Mesoamerican history. *Pan Amer. Union, Social Sci. Monogr.*, 10: 1–11.

ATWOOD, W. W.
1933 Home of the ancient Maya civilization in Central America. *Proc. 5th Pac. Sci. Cong.*, 2: 1379–89. Toronto.

AUBERT DE LA RÜE, E.
1958 L'homme et les volcans. Paris.

AVELEYRA ARROYO DE ANDA, L.
1948 El hombre de Tamazulapan. *Mem. Acad. Mex. de Hist.*, 7: 3-15.

1950 Prehistoria de Mexico. Ediciones mexicanas., S.A.

1951 Reconocimiento arqueológico en la zona de la Presa Internacional Falcón, Tamaulipas y Texas. *Rev. Mex. Estud. Antropol.*, 12: 31–59.

1954 Productos geológicos del valle de Mexico: marco cultural. *Rev. Mex. Estud. Antropol.*, 14: 41-52.

1955 El segundo mamut fósil de Santa Isabel Iztapan, Mexico, y artefactos asociados. *Inst. Nac. Antropol. e Hist.*, Pub. 1.

1956 The second mammoth and associated artifacts at Santa Isabel Iztapan, Mexico. *Amer. Antiquity*, 22: 12–28.

1959 Los cazadores del mamut, primeros habitantes de Mexico. *In* Esplendor del Mexico Antiguo, pp. 53–72. Centro Invest. Antropol. de Mex.

1961 El primer hallazgo Folsom en territorio mexicano y su relación con el complejo de puntas acanaladas en Norteamerica. *In* Homenaje a Pablo Martínez del Río, pp. 31–48.

1962 Antigüedad del hombre en Mexico y Centroamerica: catálogo razonado de localidades y bibliografía selecta (1867–1961). *Cuad. Inst. Hist., Ser. Antropol.*, no. 14.

1964 El sacro de Tequixquiac. *Cuad. Mus. Nac. Antropol.*, no. 2.

—— AND M. MALDONADO-KOERDELL
1952 Asociación de artefactos con mamut en el Pleistoceno Superior de la cuenca de Mexico. *Rev. Mex. Estud. Antropol.*, 13: 3–29.

1953 Association of artifacts with mammoth in the valley of Mexico. *Amer. Antiquity*, 18: 332–40.

BAKER, C. L.
1930 Natural regions of Mexico. *Pan-Amer. Geol.*, 53: 311–12.

BAKER, P. T., et al.
1962 Ecology and anthropology: a symposium. *Amer. Anthropol.*, 64: 15–59.

BAKER, R. H.
1963 The geographical distribution of terrestrial mammals in Middle America. *Amer. Midland Nat.*, 70: 208–49.

—— AND J. K. GREER
1962 The mammals of the Mexican state of Durango. *Pub. Mus., Michigan State Univ. Biol. Ser.*, 25: 25–154.

BANCROFT, H. H.
1876 The native races of the Pacific states of North America. Vol. 5. New York.

1886 The works of Hubert Howe Bancroft.

502

Vol. 5: The native races, primitive history. San Francisco.

BÁRCENA, M.
1882 Descripción de un hueso labrado, de llama fósil, encontrado en los terrenos posterciarios de Tequixquiac. *An. Mus. Nac. Mex.*, ep. 1, 2: 439–44.
1887 Contestación a las observaciones de la carta anterior. *La Naturaleza*, 1st ser., 7: 286–88.
—— AND A. DEL CASTILLO
1887 Noticia acerca del hallazgo de restos humanos prehistóricos en el valle de Mexico. *La Naturaleza*, 1st ser., 7: 257–64.

BARGHOORN, E. S., M. K. WOLFE, AND K. H. CLISBY
1954 Fossil maize from the valley of Mexico. *Bot. Mus. Leafl., Harvard Univ.*, 16: 229–40.

BARKER, H., AND C. J. MACKEY
1959 British Museum natural radiocarbon measurements I. *Amer. Jour. Sci., Radiocarbon Suppl.*, 1: 81–86.
1960 British Museum natural radiocarbon measurements II. *Amer. Jour. Sci., Radiocarbon Suppl.*, 2: 26–30.

BARTLETT, H. H.
1935 A method of procedure for field work in tropical American phytogeography based upon a botanical reconnaissance in parts of British Honduras and the Peten forest of Guatemala. *Carnegie Inst. Wash.*, Pub. 461, pp. 1–25.

BEAL, C. N.
1948 Reconnaissance of the geology and oil possibilities of Baja California. *Geol. Soc. Amer.*, Mem. 31.

BEARD, J. S.
1944 Climax vegetation in tropical America. *Ecology*, 25: 125–58.
1955 The classification of tropical American vegetation types. *Ecology*, 36: 89–100.

BELL, R. E.
1958 Guide to the identification of certain American Indian projectile points. *Oklahoma Anthropol. Soc.*, Special Bull. 1.

BELTRÁN, E., ed.
1959 Los recursos naturales del sureste y su aprovachamiento. Pt. 2; Estudios particulares, vol. 2. Inst. Mex. Recursos Naturales Renovables.

BENASSINI, A., AND A. GARCÍA QUINTERO
1955–57 Recursos hidráulicos de la República Mexicana. *Ingeniería Hidráulica en Mexico*, vols. 9–11. Mexico.

BENNETT, E. B.
1963 An oceanographic atlas of the eastern tropical Pacific based on data from "Eastropic" Expedition, Oct.–Dec. 1955. *Bull. Inter-Amer. Tropical Tuna Comm.*, 8: 31–196.
—— AND M. B. SCHAEFER
1960 Studies of physical, chemical, and biological oceanography in the vicinity of the Revilla Gigedo Islands during the "Island Current Survey" of 1957. *Bull. Inter-Amer. Tropical Tuna Comm.*, 4: 217–317.

BENNETT, H. H.
1925 The soils of Central America and northern South America. Rep. 5th Ann. Meeting, *Amer. Soil Survey Assoc.*, Bull. 6, vol. 1.
1926 Agriculture in Central America. *Ann. Assoc. Amer. Geog.*, 16: 63–84.
1929 Soil reconnaissance of the Panama Canal Zone and contiguous territory. U.S. Dept. Agriculture. Tech. Bull. 94.
1945 Soil conservation in Latin America. *In* Verdoorn, 1945, 165–69.

BENNETT, W. C., AND J. B. BIRD
1949 Andean culture history. *Amer. Mus. Nat. Hist., Handbook Ser.*, no. 15.
—— AND R. M. ZINGG
1935 The Tarahumara, an Indian tribe of northern Mexico. Univ. Chicago Press.

BERNAL, I.
1948-49 Exploraciones en Coixtlahuaca, Oaxaca. *Rev. Mex. Estud. Antropol.*, 10: 5–76.
1949 La cerámica de Monte Alban IIIA. Tésis para doctorado en letras, Univ. Nac. Autónoma de Mex.
1950 Compendio de arte mesoamericano. *Encic. Mex. Arte*, no 7.
1958 Monte Alban and the Zapotecs. *Bol. Estud. Oaxaqueños*, no. 1 Mexico City College.
—— AND E. DÁVALOS HURTADO
1953 Huastecos, Totonacos y sus vecinos. *Rev. Mex. Estud. Antropol.*, vol. 13, nos. 2 and 3.

BEYER, H.
1933 Shell ornament sets from the Huasteca, Mexico. *Tulane Univ., Middle Amer. Research Inst.*, Pub. 5, pp. 153–215.

BIRD, J. B.
1948 Preceramic cultures in Chicama and Viru. *In* W. C. Bennett, Reappraisal of Peruvian archaeology. *Soc. Amer. Archaeol.*, Mem. 4.

BLACK, G. A.
1949 Tepexpan Man, a critique of method. *Amer. Antiquity*, 14: 344–46.

BLACKBURN, M.
1962 An oceanographic study of the Gulf of Tehuantepec. *U.S. Fish and Wildlife Service, Spec. Sci. Rept.—*Fisheries, no. 404.

1963 Distribution and abundance of tuna related to wind and ocean conditions in the Gulf of Tehuantepec, Mexico. *FAO Fisheries Rept. No. 6*, 3: 1557–82.

AND ASSOCIATES
1962 Tuna oceanography in the eastern tropical Pacific. *U.S. Fish and Wildlife Service, Spec. Sci. Rept.—*Fisheries, no. 400.

BLÁSQUEZ LÓPEZ, L.
1943 La edad glacial en Mexico. *Bol. Soc. Mex. Geog. y Estad.*, 58: 263–305.

1956 Bosquejo fisiográfico y vulcanológico del occidente de Mexico. *In* Volcanismo terciario y reciente del eje volcánico de Mexico. Excursión A-15, pp. 9–17. *20th Cong. Geol. Int.* Mexico.

BLICK, J. C.
1937 Chinobampo skull. MS, Frick Laboratory, New York.

BLOM, F.
1932a Commerce, trade, and monetary units of the Maya. *Tulane Univ., Middle Amer. Research Inst.*, Pub. 4, no. 14.

1932b The Maya ball-game *pok-ta-pok*. *Tulane Univ., Middle Amer. Research Inst.*, Pub. 4, no. 13.

BOAS, F.
1911–12 Album de colecciones arqueológicas. *Pub. Escuela Int. Arqueol. y Etnol. Amer.* Mexico.

BOEKELMAN, H. J.
1935a Ethno- and archeo-conchological notes on four Middle American shells. *Maya Research*, 2: 255–77.
1935b Shell beads in the Caracol, Chichen Itza. *Maya Research*, 2: 401–04.

BOGERT, C. M., AND J. A. OLIVER
1945 A preliminary analysis of the herpetofauna of Sonora. *Bull. Amer. Mus. Nat. Hist.*, 83: 301–425.

BOLTON, H. E.
1916 Spanish exploration of the Southwest, 1542–1706. New York.
1927 Fray Juan Crespi: missionary explorer on the Pacific coast, 1769–1774. Univ. California Press.

BONET, F.
1953 Datos sobre las cavernas y otros fenómenos erosivos de las calizas de la Sierra de El Abra. *Mem. Cong. Cien. Mex.*, 3: 238–66.

BOPP, M.
1961 El análisis de polen, con referencia especial a dos perfiles polínicos de la cuenca de Mexico. *In* Homenaje a Pablo Martínez del Río, pp. 49–56.

BORAH, W.
1951 New Spain's century of depression. *Ibero-Amer.*, no. 35.
1954 Early colonial trade and navigatior between Mexico and Peru. *Ibero Amer.*, no. 38.

BOTERO ARANGO, G.
1942 Contribución al conocimiento de la petrografía del batolito antioqueño. *Minería*, 20: 9318–30.

BRAINERD, G. W.
1954 The Maya civilization. Southwest Mus. Los Angeles.
1958 The archaeological ceramics of Yucatan. *Anthropol. Records*, no. 19. Univ. California Press.

BRAMBILA, M.
1942 Mapa de suelos de Mexico. Sec. Agricultura y Fomento, Com. Nac. Irrigación. (Rev. eds. 1946, 1957.)

BRAND, D. D.
1943 A note on the preceramic man in northern Mexico. *In* El Norte de Mexico y el Sur de Estados Unidos, p. 164. Tercera reunión de mesa redonda sobre problemas antropológicos de Mexico y Centro America. Mexico.
1957 Coastal study of southwest Mexico. 2 vols. Dept. of Geog. Univ. Texas.

BRANDHORST, W.
1958 Thermocline topography, zooplankton standing crop, and mechanisms for fertilization in the eastern tropical Pacific. *Jour. Conseil. Int. Expl. Mer*, 24: 16–31.

BRETZ, J. H.
1955 Cavern-making in a part of the Mexican plateau. *Jour. Geol.*, 63: 364–75.

BRIGGS, J. C.
1951 A review of the clingfishes (Gobieso-

cidae) of the eastern Pacific with descriptions of new species. *Proc. Calif. Zool. Club,* 1: 57–108.

1955 A monograph of the clingfishes (order Xenopterygii). *Stanford Ichth. Bull.,* 6: 1–224.

BRITISH HONDURAS LAND USE SURVEY TEAM
1959 Land in British Honduras. *Colonial Research Pub. 24.* London.

BRODKORB, P.
1943 Birds from the gulf lowlands of southern Mexico. *Univ. Mich., Mus. Zool.,* Misc. Pub. 55.

BROECKER, W. S., E. A. OLSON, AND J. B. BIRD
1959 Radiocarbon measurements on samples of known age. *Nature,* 183: 1582–84.

BROOKS, C. E. P.
1925 The distribution of thunderstorms over the earth. *Geophys. Mem.,* no. 24. British Meteorological Office. London.

BRYAN, K.
1946 Comentario e intento de correlación con la cronología glacial. *Mem. 2d Cong. Mex. Cien. Sociales,* 5: 220–25.

1948 Los suelos complejos y fósiles de la altiplanicie de Mexico, en relación a los cambios climáticos. *Bol. Soc. Geol. Mex.,* 13: 1–20.

BUDOWSKI, G.
1956 Tropical savannas, a sequence of forest felling and repeated burnings. *Turrialba,* 6: 23–33. Inst. Interamer. Cien. Agrícolas. Turrialba, Costa Rica.

1959a Algunas relaciones entre la presente vegetación y antiguas actividades del hombre en el trópico americano. *Actas 33d Int. Cong. Amer.,* 1: 257–63.

1959b The ecological status of fire in tropical American lowlands. *Actas 33d Int. Cong. Amer.,* 1: 264–78.

BUKASOV, S. M.
1930 The cultivated plants of Mexico, Guatemala, and Colombia. *Bull. Appl. Bot. Gen. and Plant Breeding,* Suppl. 47. (English summary, pp. 470–553.)

BULLARD, F. M.
1956 Volcanic activity in Costa Rica and Nicaragua in 1954. *Trans. Amer. Geophys. Union,* 37: 75–82.

1957 Active volcanoes of Central America. *20th Int. Cong. Geol.,* sec. 1: Vulcanología del Cenozoico, 2: 351–71.

BULLARD, W. R., JR.
1960 The Maya settlement pattern in northeastern Peten, Guatemala. *Amer. Antiquity,* 25: 355–72.

BURKART, J.
1836 Aufenthalt und Reisen in Mexiko in den Jahren 1825 bis 1824. Stuttgart.

BURT, W. H.
1938 Faunal relationships and geographic distribution of mammals in Sonora, Mexico. *Univ. Mich., Mus. Zool.,* Misc. Pub. 39.

CAIN, S. A., AND G. M. DE OLIVEIRA CASTRO
1959 Manual of vegetation analysis. New York.

CALLEN, E., AND R. S. MACNEISH
n.d. Prehistoric Tamaulipas food remains as determined by a study of fecal remains. MS.

CALVERT, P. P.
1908 The composition and ecological relations of the odonate fauna of Mexico and Central America. *Proc. Acad. Nat. Sci. Philadelphia,* pp. 460–91.

CANBY, J. S.
1951 Possible chronological implications of the long ceramic sequence recovered at Yarumela, Spanish Honduras. *In* Tax, 1951, pp. 79–85.

CÁRDENAS, H.
1955 Informe agroeconómico de Jamiltepec, Oax. *Inst. Nac. Indigenista,* Ser. Mimeo., no. 8. Mexico.

CARDOS DE M., A.
1959 El comercio de los Mayas antiguos. *Acta Anthropol.,* ep. 2, vol. 2, no. 1. Mexico.

CARPENTER, R. H.
1954 Geology and ore deposits of the Rosario mining district and the San Juancito mountains, Honduras, Central America. *Bull. Geol. Soc. Amer.,* 65: 23–38.

CARR, A. F.
1949 La Montaña Llorana. *Sci. Monthly,* 68: 225–35.

1950 Outline for a classification of animal habitats in Honduras. *Bull. Amer. Mus. Nat. Hist.,* 94: 563–94.

1952 Handbook of turtles: the turtles of the United States, Canada, and Baja California. Ithaca, N.Y.

—— AND L. GIOVANNOLI
1957 The ecology and migrations of sea turtles: two results of field work in

Costa Rica. *Amer. Mus. Novitates,* no. 1835.

CARREÑO, A. DE LA O.
1951 Las provincias geohidrológicas de México. *Inst. Geol., Univ. Nac. Autónoma de Mex.,* Bol. 56.

CARRIKER, M. A., JR.
1910 An annotated list of the birds of Costa Rica including Cocos Island. *Ann. Carnegie Mus.,* 6: 314–915.

CARTER, G. F.
1945 Plant geography and culture history in the American southwest. *Viking Fund Pub. Anthropol.,* no. 5.
1957 Culture trails in the Pacific. *Johns Hopkins Mag.,* February.

CASARES, D.
1905 A notice of Yucatan with some remarks on its water supply. *Amer. Antiquarian Soc. Papers,* n.s., 17: 207–30.

CASO, A.
1937 ¿Tenían los Teotihuacanos conocimiento del Tonalpohualli? *El Mex. Antiguo,* 4: 131–43.
1938 Exploraciones en Oaxaca, quinta y sexta temporadas, 1936–37. *Inst. Panamer. Geog. e Hist.,* Pub. 34.
1941 Culturas Mixtecas y Zapotecas. *Bib. del Maestro, El Nacional.* Mexico.
1953a El Pueblo del Sol. Mexico.
1953b New World culture history: Middle America. *In* Kroeber, Anthropology today, pp. 226–37.
1954 Instituciones indígenas precortesianas. *In* Caso, Métodos y resultados de la política indigenista en Mexico. *Mem. Inst. Nac. Indigenista,* vol. 6.

CASTETTER, E. F., AND W. H. BELL
1951 Yuman Indian agriculture. Univ. New Mexico Press.

CHAPEL, L. T.
1927 Winds and storms on the Isthmus of Panama. *Monthly Weather Rev.,* 55: 519–30.

CHAPMAN, A.
1957 Port of trade enclaves in Aztec and Maya civilizations. *In* Polanyi, 1957, pp. 114–53.
1960 Los Nicarao y los Chorotega según las fuentes históricas. Univ. Costa Rica.

CHAPMAN, F. M.
1917 The distribution of bird-life in Colombia. *Bull. Amer. Mus. Nat. Hist.,* no. 36.
1926 The distribution of bird-life in Ecua-

dor. *Bull. Amer. Mus. Nat. Hist.,* no. 55.

CHARNAY, D.
1880 The ruins of Central America. Pt. 4. *North Amer. Rev.,* 131: 519–27.
1888 The ancient cities of the New World. New York.

CHEVALIER, F.
1952 La formation des grands domaines au Mexique. *Travaux et Mémoires de l'Institut d'Ethnologie, Univ. Paris,* vol. 56. Paris.

CHILDE, V. G.
1950 The urban revolution. *Town Planning Rev.,* 21: 3–17. Univ. Liverpool.
1952 The birth of civilization. *Past and Present,* no. 2, pp. 1–10. London.

CLAYTON, H. H.
1927 World weather records. Washington.
1944 World weather records, 1921–1930. Washington.
—— AND F. L. CLAYTON
1947 World weather records, 1931–1940. Washington.

CLISBY, K. H., AND P. B. SEARS
1955 Palynology in southern North America. Pt. 3: Microfossil profiles under Mexico City correlated with sedimentary profiles. *Bull. Geol. Soc. Amer.,* vol. 66.

COE, M. D.
1957a Cycle 7 monuments in Middle America: a reconsideration. *Amer. Anthropol.,* 59: 597–611.
1957b Pre-classic culture in Mesoamerica: a comparative survey. *Kroeber Anthropol. Soc. Papers,* no. 17, pp. 7–37. Univ. California.
1959 Una investigación arqueológica en la costa del Pacífico de Guatemala. *IDAEH,* 11: 5-11. Guatemala.
1960a A fluted point from highland Guatemala. *Amer. Antiquity,* 25: 412–13.
1960b Archaeological linkages with North and South America at La Victoria, Guatemala. *Amer. Anthropol.,* 62: 363–93.

COE, W. R.
1959a Tikal, 1959. *Expedition, Bull. Univ. Pennsylvania Mus.,* 1: 7–11.
1959b Piedras Negras archaeology: artifacts, caches, and burials. *Mus. Monogr., Univ. Pennsylvania.*

COLE, L. J.
1910 The caverns and people of northern

Yucatan. *Bull. Amer. Geog. Soc.*, 42: 321–36.

COLEMAN, S. N.

1946 Volcanoes, new and old. New York.

COLLIER, A.

1958 Gulf of Mexico physical and chemical data from *Alaska* cruises. U.S. Dept. Interior, *Fish and Wildlife Service*, Special Sci. Rept.: Fisheries, no. 249.

—— AND J. W. HEDGPETH

1950 An introduction to the hydrography of tidal waters of Texas. *Inst. Marine Sci.*, 1: 123–94.

COLLIER, D.

1959 Agriculture and civilization on the coast of Peru. MS presented at annual meeting, Amer. Anthropol. Assoc.

COLUMBUS, F.

1867 Vita di Cristoforo Colombo, descritta da Ferdinando, e tradotta da Alfonso Ulloa. London.

GONGRESO GEOLÓGICO INTERNACIONAL

1956 Carta geológica de la República Mexicana.

CONNELL, C. H., AND J. B. CROSS

1950 Mass mortality of fish associated with the protozoan *Gonyaulax* in the Gulf of Mexico. *Science*, 112 (2909): 359–63.

CONSERVATION FOUNDATION

1954 Soil erosion survey of Latin America. In collaboration with Food and Agriculture Organization of the United Nations. Reprinted from *Jour. Soil and Water Conservation*, vol. 9, July, Sept., Nov.

CONTRERAS, D., AND H. CEREZO

1958 Geografía de Guatemala. Guatemala.

COOK, O. F.

1909 Vegetation affected by agriculture in Central America. U.S. Dept. Agriculture, *Bur. Plant Industry*, Bull. 145.

1921 Milpa agriculture, a primitive tropical system. *Smithsonian Inst.*, ann. rept. 1919, pp. 307–26.

COOK, S. F.

1946 The incidence and significance of disease among the Aztecs and related tribes. *Hisp. Amer. Hist. Rev.*, 36: 320–25.

1949a The historical demography and ecology of the Teotlalpan. *Ibero-Amer.*, no. 33.

1949b Soil erosion and population in central Mexico. *Ibero-Amer.*, no. 34.

1958 Santa Maria Ixcatlan: habitat, population, subsistence. *Ibero-Amer.*, no. 41.

—— AND L. B. SIMPSON

1948 The population of central Mexico in the sixteenth century. *Ibero-Amer.*, no. 31.

COOKE, C. W.

1931 Why the Mayan cities in the Peten district were abandoned. *Jour. Wash. Acad. Sci.*, 21: 283–87.

CORNWALL, I. W.

1962 Volcanoes, lakes, soils, and early man in and near the Mexico basin. *Man*, 86: 55–58.

COVARRUBIAS, M.

1957 Indian art of Mexico and Central America. New York

COWGILL, U. M.

1959 Agriculture and population density in the southern Maya lowlands. MS presented at annual meeting, Amer. Anthropol. Assoc.

CRANE, H. R., AND J. B. GRIFFIN

1958a University of Michigan radiocarbon dates II. *Science*, 127 (3306): 1098–1105.

1958b University of Michigan radiocarbon dates III. *Science*, 128: 1117–23.

1959 University of Michigan radiocarbon dates IV. *Amer. Jour. Sci., Radiocarbon Suppl.*, 1: 173–98.

CROMWELL, T.

1958 Thermocline topography, horizontal currents and "ridging" in the eastern tropical Pacific. *Bull. Inter-Amer. Tropical Tuna Comm.*, 3: 133–64.

—— AND E. B. BENNETT

1959 Surface drift charts for the eastern tropical Pacific Ocean. *Bull. Inter-Amer. Tropical Tuna Comm.*, 3: 215–37.

CRUXENT, J. M., AND I. ROUSE

1956 A lithic industry of Paleo-Indian type in Venezuela. *Amer. Antiquity*, 22: 172–79.

1958 An archaeological chronology of Venezuela. *Pan Amer. Union, Social Sci. Monogr.*, no. 6, pp. 263–65.

CUEVAS, M.

1940 Historia de la nación mexicana. Mexico.

DANSEREAU, P.

1951 Description and recording of vegetation upon a structural basis. *Ecology*, 32: 172–229.

507

DARLINGTON, P. J., JR.
1957 Zoogeography: the geographical distribution of animals. New York.
DAUBENMIRE, R. F.
1938 Merriam's life zones of North America. *Quar. Rev. Biol.*, 13: 327–32.
DAVIS, A. P.
1900 Hydrography of Nicaragua. *U.S. Geol. Survey*, 20th ann. rept., pt. 4, pp. 563–637.
DAVIS, C. C.
1948 *Gymnodinium breve* sp. nov., a cause of discolored water and animal mortality in the Gulf of Mexico. *Bot. Gaz.*, 109: 358–60.
DAVIS, E. M.
1953 Recent data from two Paleo-Indian sites on Medicine Creek, Nebraska. *Amer. Antiquity*, 18: 380–86.
DAWSON, E. Y.
1944 Some ethnobotanical notes on the Seri Indians. *Desert Plant Life*, 16: 132–38.
1945 Marine algae associated with upwelling along the northwestern coast of Baja California, Mexico. *Bull. Southern Calif. Acad. Sci.*, 44: 57–71.
1951 A further study of upwelling and associated vegetation along Pacific Baja California, Mexico. *Jour. Marine Research*, 10: 39–58.
1952 Circulation within Bahia Viscaino, and its effects on marine vegetation. *Amer. Jour. Botany*, 39: 425–32.
1960 The biogeography of California and adjacent seas. Pt. 2: A review of the ecology, distribution, and affinities of the benthic flora. *Syst. Zool.*, 9: 93–100.
DE BUEN, F.
1943 Los lagos michoacanos I: El lago de Zirahuen. *Rev. Soc. Mex. Hist. Natural*, 4: 211–32.
1944 Los lagos michoacanos II: Patzcuaro. *Rev. Soc. Mex. Hist. Natural*, 5: 99–125.
1945 Resultados de una campaña limnológica en Chapala y observaciones sobre otras aguas exploradas. *Rev. Soc. Mex. Hist. Natural*, 6: 129–44.
DE CSERNA, Z.
1956 Tectónica de la Sierra Madre Oriental de Mexico, entre Torreon y Monterrey. Mexico.
1958 Notes on the tectonics of southern Mexico. *In* Habitat of Oil (Amer. Assoc. Petroleum Geol.).

DEEVEY, E. S.
1943 Intento para datar las culturas medias del valle de Mexico mediante análisis de polen. *Ciencia*, 4: 97–105.
1944 Pollen analysis and Mexican archaeology: an attempt to apply the method. *Amer. Antiquity*, 10: 135–49.
1955 Limnological studies in Guatemala and El Salvador. *Internationale Vereinigung für theoretische und angewandte Limnologie*, Verhandlungen, 12: 278–83.
1957 Limnologic studies in Middle America with a chapter on Aztec limnology. *Trans. Connecticut Acad. Arts and Sci.*, 39: 213–28.
———, L. J. GRALENSKI, AND V. HOFFREN
1959 Yale natural radiocarbon measurements IV. *Amer. Jour. Sci., Radiocarbon Suppl.*, 1: 144–72.
DEGER, E. C.
1932a Las cenizas y arenas volcánicas de Guatemala y El Salvador en relación con su rol en la formación del suelo agrícola. Guatemala.
1932b Zur kenntnis der mittelamerikanischen Aschen. *Chemie der Erde*, 11: 249–55.
1939 Album petrográfico de la America Central. I: La zona de Amatitlan. Guatemala.
1942 Diferenciaciones magmáticas en la edificación de la Cordillera Andina de Centro-America. *Proc. 8th Amer. Sci. Cong.*, 4: 459–60.
DENEVAN, W. M.
1958 The upland pine forests of Nicaragua. M.A. thesis, Univ. California.
1961 The upland pine forests of Nicaragua: a study in cultural plant geography. *Univ. Calif. Pub. Geog.*, 12: 251–320.
DE TERRA, H.
1946 New evidence for the antiquity of early man in Mexico. *Rev. Mex. Estud. Antropol.*, 8: 69–88.
1947 Teoría de una cronología geológica para el valle de Mexico. *Rev. Mex. Estud. Antropol.*, 9: 11–26.
1949 Early man in Mexico. *In* Tepexpan man, pp. 13–86. *Viking Fund Pub. Anthropol.*, no. 11.
1950 Los cambios climatológicos y la conservación del suelo en Mexico. *Turrialba*, 1: 28–31.
1957 Man and mammoth in Mexico. London.
1959 A successor of Tepexpan man in the

valley of Mexico. *Science,* 129 (3348): 563–64.

——, J. ROMERO, AND T. D. STEWART, eds.
1949 Tepexpan man. *Viking Fund Pub. Anthropol.,* no. 11.

DEVRIES, H., AND H. T. WATERBOLK
1958 Groningen radiocarbon dates II. *Science,* 127 (3290).

DÍAZ-LOZANO, E.
1917 Diatomeas fósiles mexicanas. *An. Inst. Geol. de Mex.,* 1 (1): 1–27.
1920 Depósitos diatomíferos en el valle de Toxi, Ixtlahuaca, Mexico. *An. Inst. Geol. de Mex.,* 1 (9): 1–19.
1927 Los restos fósiles de elephas encontrados en terrenos de la hacienda de Tepexpan, Mexico. *An. Inst. Geol. de Mex.,* 2 (6–10): 201–202.

DICCIONARIO DE MOTUL
1929 Maya-Español. Juan Martínez Hernández, ed. Merida.

DICE, L. R.
1943 The biotic provinces of North America. Univ. Michigan Press.
1952 Natural communities. Univ. Michigan Press.

DICKEY, D. R., AND A. J. VAN ROSSEM
1938 The birds of El Salvador. *Field Mus. Nat. Hist., Zool. Ser.,* no. 23.

DI PESO, C. C.
1955 Two Cerro Guamas Clovis fluted points from Sonora, Mexico. *Kiva,* 21: 13–15.

DIRECCIÓN GENERAL DE IRRIGACIÓN
1954–55 Estadística hidrológica. Servicio de Hidrometría Nacional. Tegucigalpa, Honduras.

DIXON, K. A.
1959 Ceramics from two pre-classic periods at Chiapa de Corzo, southern Mexico. *New World Archaeol. Found.,* Pub. 4, Paper 5.

DOLLFUS, A., AND E. DE MONTSERRAT
1868 Voyage géologique dans les républiques de Guatemala et de Salvador. Paris.

DONDOLI, C.
1940a Rocas de Costa Rica, determinación y estudio petrográfico (cuarzo-diorita andesino). *Centro Nac. Agronómico,* pp. 73–78. San Jose, Costa Rica.
1940b Rocas de Costa Rica, determinación y estudio petrográfico (andesita labradorítica). *Bol. Técnico Dept. Nac. de Agricultura,* no. 32. San Jose, Costa Rica.
1943a La región de El General, condiciones geológicas y geoagronómicas de la zona. *Bol. Técnico Dept. Nac. de Agricultura,* no. 44. San Jose, Costa Rica.
1943b Relación entre el terreno y la roca. *Bol. Técnico Dept. Nac. de Agricultura,* nos. 45, 46. San Jose, Costa Rica.

DOZIER, C. L.
1958 Indigenous tropical agriculture in Central America. *Nat. Acad. Sci., Nat. Research Council,* Pub. 594.

DRESSLER, R. L.
1953 The pre-Columbian cultivated plants of Mexico. *Bot. Mus. Leafl. Harvard Univ.,* 16: 115–72.

DRUCKER, P.
1943a Ceramic stratigraphy at Cerro de las Mesas, Veracruz, Mexico. *Smithsonian Inst., Bur. Amer. Ethnol.,* Bull. 141.
1943b Ceramic sequences at Tres Zapotes, Ceracruz, Mexico. *Smithsonian Inst., Bur. Amer. Ethnol.,* Bull. 140.
1952 La Venta, Tabasco: a study of Olmec ceramics and art. *Smithsonian Inst., Bur. Amer. Ethnol.,* Bull. 153.

——, R. F. HEIZER, AND R. J. SQUIER
1957 Radiocarbon dates from La Venta, Tabasco. *Science,* 126: 72–73.
1959 Excavations at La Venta, Tabasco, 1955. *Smithsonian Inst., Bur. Amer. Ethnol.,* Bull. 170.

DRUMMOND, K. H., AND G. B. AUSTIN
1958 Some aspects of the physical oceanography of the Gulf of Mexico. *In* A. Collier, 1958.

DUELLMAN, W. E.
1960 A distributional study of the amphibians of the Isthmus of Tehuantepec, Mexico. *Univ. Kansas Pub., Mus. Nat. Hist.,* 13: 19–72.

DUNN, E. R.
1931 The herpetological fauna of the Americas. *Copeia,* 3: 106–19.
1940 Some aspects of herpetology in lower Central America. *Trans. New York Acad. Sci.,* 2: 156–58.

DURHAM, J. W., AND E. C. ALLISON
1960 The biogeography of Baja California and adjacent seas. Pt. 1: The geologic history of Baja California and its marine faunas. *Syst. Zool.,* 9: 47–91.

DU SOLIER, W.
1945 La cerámica arqueológica de El Tajin. *An. Mus. Nac. Arqueol., Hist. y Etnog.,* ep. 5, vol. 3.

509

DUTTON, B. P.
1955 Tula of the Toltecs. *El Palacio, 62:* 195–251.

EARDLEY, A. J.
1951 Structural geology of North America. New York.
1954 Tectonic relations of North and South America. *Bull. Amer. Assoc. Petroleum Geol.,* 38: 707–73.

EDWARDS, C.
1954 Geographical reconnaissance in the Yucatan Peninsula. Rept. field work carried out under ONR Contract 222(11) NR 388 067. Univ. Calif., Dept. Geog.
1957 Quintana Roo: Mexico's empty quarter. *Ibid.*

EDWARDS, J. D.
1956 Estudio sobre algunos de los conglomerados rojos del Terciario Inferior del centro de Mexico. *20th Cong. Geol. Int.*

EGLER, F. E.
1942 Vegetation as an object of study. *Philosophy of Sci.,* 9: 245–60.

EISENMANN, E.
1955 The species of Middle American birds. *Trans. Linn. Soc. New York,* vol. 7.

EKHOLM, G. F.
1942 Excavations at Guasave, Sinaloa, Mexico. *Anthropol. Papers Amer. Mus. Nat. Hist.,* vol. 38, pt. 2.
1944 Excavations at Tampico and Panuco in the Huasteca, Mexico. *Amer. Mus. Nat. Hist., Anthropol. Papers,* vol. 38, pt. 5.
1946a Wheeled toys in Mexico. *Amer. Antiquity,* 11: 222–27.
1946b The probable use of Mexican stone yokes. *Amer. Anthropol.,* 48: 593–606.
1948 Ceramic stratigraphy at Acapulco, Guerrero. *In* El Occidente de Mexico, pp. 95–104. Soc. Mex. Anthropol.
1949 Palmate stones and thin stone heads: suggestions on their possible use. *Amer. Antiquity,* 15: 1–9.
1958 Regional sequences in Mesoamerica and their relationships. *In* Willey, Vogt, and Palerm, Middle American anthropology, pp. 15–24. *Pan Amer. Union, Social Sci. Monogr.,* no. 5.

EKMAN, V. W.
1905 On the influence of the earth's rotation on ocean currents. *Ark. Mat.,*

Astr. och Fysik, K. Svenska Vetenskapsakad., 2 (11): 1–52.

EMERY, K. O.
1960 The sea off southern California: a modern habitat of petroleum. New York and London.

EPSTEIN, J. F.
1961 The San Isidro and Puntita Negra sites: evidence of early man horizons in Nuevo Leon, Mexico. *In* Homenaje a Pablo Martínez del Río, pp. 71–74.

ERBEN, K. G.
1957a Paleogeographic reconstructions for the Lower and Middle Jurassic and for the Callovian of Mexico. *20th Cong. Geol. Int.,* sec. 2, El Mesozoico del hemisferio occidental y sus correlaciones mundiales, pp. 35–41.
1957b New biostratigraphic correlations in the Jurassic of eastern and south-central Mexico. *Ibid.,* pp. 43–52.

ESCALONA RAMOS, A.
1953 Xochicalco en la cronología de America Media. *In* Huastecos, Totonacos y sus vecinos, pp. 351–70.

FARRINGTON, O. C.
1897 Observations on Popocatepetl and Ixtaccihuatl, with a review of the geographic and geologic features of the mountains. *Field Columbian Mus., Biol. Ser.,* 1: 66–120.

FAY, G. E.
1955 Pre-pottery lithic complex from Sonora, Mexico. *Science,* 121 (3152): 777–78.
1959 Peralta complex, a Sonoran variant of the Cochise culture: new data, 1958. *El Palacio,* 66: 21–24.

FELIX, J., AND H. LENK
1892 Über die tecktonischen Verhältnisse der Republik Mexiko. *Zeit. der Deutschen Geol. Gesellschaft,* 44: 303–23.

FENNEMAN, N. M.
1928 Physiographic divisions of the United States. *Ann. Assoc. Amer. Geog.,* 18: 261–353.

FIELD, H.
1948 Early man in Mexico. *Man,* 48 (14–24): 17–19. London.

FIGUEROA A., J.
1960 Mexican national report on seismology. 12th General Assembly of the I.U.G.G., Helsinki, Finland. Inst. de Geofísica, U.N.A.M., Mexico (mimeographed).

510

FLEMING, R. H.
1935 Oceanographic studies in the Central American Pacific. Doctoral dissertation, Univ. Calif.
1938 Tides and tidal currents in the Gulf of Panama. *Jour. Marine Research,* 1: 193–206.
1941 A contribution to the oceanography of the Central American region. *Proc. 6th Pacific Sci. Cong.,* 3: 167–75.

FORDE, C. D.
1934 Habitat, economy and society: a geographical introduction to ethnology. London.

FOSHAG, W. F.
1955a Jadeite from Manzanal, Guatemala. *Amer. Antiquity,* 21: 81–83.
1955b Chalchihuitl, a study in jade. *Amer. Mineral.,* 40: 1062–70.
—— AND J. GONZALES REYNA
1956 Birth and development of Paricutin volcano, Mexico. *U.S. Geol. Survey,* Bull. 965-D.

FOSTER, G. M.
1955 Contemporary pottery techniques in southern and central Mexico. *Tulane Univ., Middle Amer. Research Inst.,* Pub. 22, pp. 1–48.
1959a The Coyotepec *molde* and some associated problems of the potter's wheel. *SW. Jour. Anthropol.,* 15: 54–63.
1959b The potter's wheel: an analysis of idea and artifact in invention. *SW. Jour. Anthropol.,* 15: 99–119.

FRANCO, J. L.
1949 Algunos problemas relativos a la cerámica azteca. *El Mex. Antiguo,* 7: 162–208.
1959 La escritura y los códices. *In* Esplendor del Mexico Antiguo, 1: 361–78. Centro Invest. Antropol. de Mex.

FRIEDLAENDER, I.
1930 Über die mexikanischen Vulkane Pico de Orizaba, Cerro de Tequila, und Colima. *Zeit. für Vulkanologie,* 13: 154–64.
—— AND R. A. SONDER
1923 Über das Vulkangebiet von San Martin Tuxtla in Mexiko. *Zeit. für Vulkanologie,* 7: 162–87.

FRIEDMAN, I., AND R. L. SMITH
1960 A new dating method using obsidian. Pt. 1: The development of the method. *Amer. Antiquity,* 25: 476–522.

FRIES, C.
1960 Geología del estado de Morelos y partes adyacentes de Mexico y Guerrero, región central meridional de Mexico. *Inst. Geol., Univ. Nac. Autónoma de Mex.,* Bol. 60.

FUGLISTER, F. C.
1947 Average monthly sea surface temperatures of the western North Atlantic. *Papers Physical Oceanogr. and Meteorol.,* 10: 3–25.

FUNKHOUSER, W. D., AND W. S. WEBB
1929 The so-called "ash caves" in Lee County, Kentucky. *Univ. Dept. Anthropol. and Archaeol.,* vol. 1, no. 2.

GADOW, H.
1930 Jorullo: the history of the volcano Jorullo and the reclamation of the devastated district by animals and plants. Cambridge.

GALTSOFF, P., ed.
1954 Gulf of Mexico: its origin, waters, and marine life. U.S. Dept. Interior, *Fish and Wildlife Service,* Fishery Bull., vol. 55.

GAMIO, M.
1921 Album de colecciones arqueológicas, texto. Escuela Int. Arqueol. y Etnol. Amer.

GARBELL, M. A.
1947 Tropical and equatorial meteorology. New York and Chicago.

GARCÍA PAYÓN, J.
1943 Interpretación cultural de la zona arqueológica de El Tajin. Univ. Nac. Autónoma de Mex.
1949a Arqueología del Tajin. Univ. Nac. Autónoma de Mex.
1949b Zempoala. Compendio de su estudio arqueológico. *Uni-Ver,* vol. 1, no. 8. Univ. Veracruzana.
1953 ¿Qué es lo Totonaco? *In* Huastecos, Totonacos y sus vecinos, pp. 379–87.
1954 El Tajin: descripción y comentarios. *Uni-Ver,* 4: 18–43.

GARFÍAS, V. R., AND T. C. CHAPÍN
1949 Geología de Mexico. Mexico.

GARTH, J. S.
1960 The biogeography of Baja California and adjacent seas. Pt. 2: Distribution and affinities of the brachyuran Crustacea. *Syst. Zool.,* 9: 105–23.

GERHARD, P.
1964 Emperor's dye of the Mixtecs. *Natural Hist.,* 73: 26–31.

GERSTENHAUER, A.
1960 Der tropische Kegelkarst in Tabasco

(Mexico). *Zeit für Geomorphologie, Suppl.*, 2: 22–48.

GERTH, T. H.
1955   Der geologische Bau der Südamerikanische Kordillere. Berlin.

GIERLOFF-EMDEN, H. G.
1959   Die Küste von El Salvador. Eine morphologische-ozeanographische Monographie. *Acta Humboldtiana, Series Geog. et Ethnog.*, no. 2. Wiesbaden.

GIFFORD, E. W.
1950   Surface archaeology of Ixtlan del Rio, Nayarit. *Univ. Calif. Pub. Amer. Archaeol. and Ethnol.*, vol. 43, no. 2.

GILMORE, R. M.
1950   Fauna and ethnozoology of South America. *In* Handbook of South American Indians, 6: 345–463. *Smithsonian Inst., Bur. Amer. Ethnol.*, Bull. 143.
1957   Whales aground in Cortes' sea. *Pacific Discovery*, 10: 22–27.
1959   On the mass strandings of sperm whales. *Pacific Naturalist*, 1: 9–16.

GINSBURG, I.
1930   Commercial snappers (*Lutianidae*) of Gulf of Mexico. *U.S. Bur. Fisheries*, Bull. 46, pp. 265–76.

GODSKE, C. L, T. BERGERON, J. BJERKNES, AND R. C. BUNDGAARD
1957   Dynamic meteorology and weather forecasting. Amer. Meteorol. Soc. and Carnegie Inst. Wash.

GOLDMAN, E. A.
1920   Mammals of Panama. *Smithsonian Inst., Misc. Coll.*, vol. 69, no. 5.
1951   Biological investigations in Mexico. *Smithsonian Inst., Misc. Coll.*, vol. 115.
—— AND R. T. MOORE
1946   The biotic provinces of Mexico. *Jour. Mammology*, 26: 347–60.

GONZÁLEZ RUL, F.
1959   Una punta acanalada del rancho La Chuparrosa. *Inst. Nac. Antropol. e Hist.*, Pub. 8.
—— AND F. MOOSER
1961   Erupciones volcánicas y el hombre primitivo en la cuenca de Mexico. *In* Homenaje a Pablo Martínez del Río, pp. 137–41.

GOODSPEED, T. H.
1954   The genus *Nicotiana*. Chronica Botanica.

GRISCOM, L.
1926   Nicaragua. *In* Shelford, 1926, pp. 604–07.
1932   The distribution of bird-life in Guatemala. *Bull. Amer. Mus. Nat. Hist.*, no. 44.
1934   The ornithology of Guerrero, Mexico. *Bull. Mus. Comp. Zool., Harvard Univ.*, 75: 365–422.
1935   The ornithology of the Republic of Panama. *Bull. Mus. Comp. Zool., Harvard Univ.*, 78: 260–382.
1940   Origin and relationships of the faunal areas of Central America. *Proc. 8th Amer. Sci. Cong.*, 3: 425–30.
1950   Distribution and origin of the birds of Mexico. *Bull. Mus. Comp. Zool., Harvard Univ.*, 103: 341–82.

GROVES, G. W., AND J. L. REID, JR.
1958   Estudios oceanográficos sobre las aguas de Baja California. Mem. Primer Cong. de Hist. Regional. Dir. General de Acción Cívica y Cultural, Gobierno del Estado de Baja California, Mexicali, pp. 81–121.

GUILLEMIN-TARAYRE, E.
1867   Rapport sur l'exploration minéralogique des régions Mexicaines. *Archives Com. Sci. du Mexique*, 3: 173–470. Paris.

GUNTER, G.
1941   Relative numbers of shallow water fishes of the northern Gulf of Mexico, with some records of rare fishes from the Texas coast. *Amer. Midl. Nat.*, vol. 26, no. 1.

GUZMAN, E. J., AND Z. DE CSERNA
1960   Outline of the tectonic history of Mexico. MS.

HADEN-GUEST, S., J. K. WRIGHT, AND E. M. TECLAF, eds.
1956   A world geography of forest resources. New York.

HALL, E. R., AND K. R. KELSON
1959   The mammals of North America. 2 vols. New York.

HAMMOND, E. H.
1954   A geomorphic study of the cape region of Baja California. *Univ. Calif. Pub. Geog.*, 10: 45–112.

HAMY, E. T.
1878   L'ancienneté de l'homme au Mexique. *La Nature*, revue des sciences et de leurs applications aux arts et a l'industrie, no. 251, pp. 262–64. Paris.
1884   Anthropologie du Mexique. Recherches zoologiques pour servir a

l'histoire de la faune de l'Amérique Centrale et du Mexique. Paris.

HANSON, H. C.
1958 Principles concerned in the formation and classification of communities. *Botanical Rev.*, 24: 65–125.

HARDY, A.
1960 Was man more aquatic in the past? *New Scientist*, 7: 642–45.

HARRINGTON, M. R., AND R. D. SIMPSON
1961 Tule Springs, Nevada, with other evidences of Pleistocene man in North America. *Southwest Mus. Papers*, no. 18.

HARSHBERGER, J. W.
1911 Phytogeographic survey of North America. A consideration of the phytogeography of the North American continent, including Mexico, Central America and the West Indies, together with the evolution of North American plant distribution. Leipzig.

HATT, R. T.
1953 Faunal and archeological researches in Yucatan caves. *Cranbrook Inst. Sci.*, Bull. 33.

HAY, C. L., et al.
1940 The Maya and their neighbors. New York.

HEACOCK, J. G., AND J. L. WORZEL
1955 Submarine topography west of Mexico and Central America. *Bull. Geol. Soc. Amer.*, 66: 773–76.

HEILPRIN, A.
1891 Geological researches in Yucatan. *Proc. Philadelphia Acad. Natural Sci.*, pp. 136–58.

HEIM, A.
1934 El Bernal de Horcasitas, a volcanic plug in the Tampico plain. *Zeit. für Vulkanologie*, 15: 254–60.
1940 The front ranges of Sierra Madre Oriental, from C. Victoria to Tamazunchale. *Ecologae Geol. Helvetiae*, 33: 313–62. Basel.

HEISER, C. B., JR.
1955 The origin and development of the cultivated sunflower. *Amer. Biol. Teacher*, 17: 161–67.

HEIZER, R. F.
1943 Aboriginal use of bitumen by the California Indians. *Calif. Div. Mines*, 118: 73–75.

—— AND S. F. COOK
1959 New evidence of antiquity of Tepexpan man and other human remains from the valley of Mexico. *SW. Jour. Anthropol.*, 15: 36–42.

—— AND W. C. MASSEY
1953 Aboriginal navigation off the coasts of Upper and Baja California. *Bur. Amer. Ethnol., Anthropol. Papers*, no. 39, Bull. 151, pp. 285–311.

HELBIG, K. M.
1959 Die Landschaft von Nordost-Honduras. *Petermanns Mitt.*, Ergänzungsheft 286. Gotha.

HERBERTSON, A. J.
1905 The major natural regions of the world. *Geog. Jour.*, 25: 300–10. London.

HERNÁNDEZ, J.
1923 The temperature of Mexico. *Monthly Weather Rev.*, Suppl. 23.

HERRERA, A. L.
1893 El hombre prehistórico de Mexico. *Mem. Soc. Cien. Antonio Alzate*, 7: 17–56.

HERSHKOVITZ, P.
1958 A geographical classification of Neotropical mammals. *Fieldiana* (Zoology), 36: 581–620.

HESS, H. H.
1938 Gravity anomalies and island arc structure with particular reference to the West Indies. *Proc. Amer. Phil. Soc.*, 79: 71–96.

HESTER, J. A., JR.
1954 Natural and cultural bases of ancient Maya subsistence economy. Doctoral dissertation, Univ. Calif.

HEYERDAHL, T., AND A. SKJÖLSVOLD
1956 Archeological evidence of pre-Spanish visits to the Galapagos Islands. *Soc. Amer. Archaeol.*, Mem. 12.

HIBBARD, C. W.
1955 Pleistocene vertebrates from the Upper Becerra (Becerra Superior) formation, valley of Tequixquiac, Mexico, with notes on other Pleistocene forms. *Univ. Michigan, Contrib. Mus. Paleontol.*, 12 (5): 47–96.

HIBBEN, F. C.
1941 Evidences of early occupation of Sandia Cave, New Mexico, and other sites in the Sandia-Manzano region. *Smithsonian Inst., Misc. Coll.*, vol. 99, no. 23.

HILDEBRAND, S. F.
1925 Fishes of the Republic of El Salvador. *U. S. Bur. Fisheries*, Bull. 41, pp. 237–87.
1938 A new catalogue of the fresh-water

fishes of Panama. *Field Mus. Nat. Hist., Zool. Ser.,* 22: 219–359.

HILL, R. T.
1898 The geological history of the Isthmus of Panama and portions of Costa Rica. *Bull. Mus. Comp. Zool., Harvard Univ.,* 28: 151–285.

HOFFSTETTER, R., et al.
1960 Lexique stratigraphique international. Vol. 5: Amérique Latine. Paris.

HOLDEN, J.
1957 The postclassic in Mesoamerica. *Kroeber Anthropol. Soc. Papers,* no. 17.

HOLDRIDGE, L. R.
1947 Determination of world formations from simple climatic data. *Science,* 105 (2727): 367–68.

1956 Middle America. *In* Haden-Guest et al., 1956, pp. 183–200.

HOLMES, R. W., AND M. BLACKBURN
1960 Physical, chemical, and biological observations in the eastern tropical Pacific Ocean Scot Expedition, April–June 1958. *U.S. Fish and Wildlife Service, Spec. Sci. Rept.—Fisheries,* no. 345.

HOOPER, E. T.
1952 A systematic review of the harvest mice (genus *Reithrodontomys*) of Latin America. *Univ. Michigan, Mus. Zool.,* Misc. Pub. 77.

HOPKINS, D. M.
1959 Cenozoic history of the Bering land bridge. *Science,* 129: 1519–28.

HOSTOS, A. DE
1948 The ethnography of Puerto Rico. *In* Handbook of South American Indians, 4: 540–42. *Smithsonian Inst., Bur. Amer. Ethnol.,* Bull. 143.

HOVANITZ, W.
1958 Distribution of butterflies in the New World. *Zoogeography, Amer. Assoc. Advancement Sci.,* Pub. 51, pp. 321–68.

HOVEY, E. O.
1905 The western Sierra Madre of the state of Chihuahua. *Bull. Amer. Geog. Soc.,* 37: 531.

1907 A geological reconnaissance in the western Sierra Madre of the state of Chihuahua. *Amer. Mus. Nat. Hist.,* Bull. 23, pp. 401–42.

HRDLICKA, A.
1907 Skeletal remains suggesting or attributed to early man in North America. *Smithsonian Inst., Bur. Amer. Ethnol.,* Bull. 33.

HUASTECOS, TOTONACOS Y SUS VECINOS
1953 Huastecos, Totonacos y sus vecinos. Ed. by Bernal and Davalos Hurtado. *Rev. Mex. Estud. Antropol.,* vol. 13, nos. 2 and 3.

HUBBS, CARL L.
1948 Changes in the fish fauna of western North America correlated with changes in ocean temperatures. *Jour. Marine Research,* 7: 459–82.

1952 Antitropical distribution of fishes and other organisms. *In* Symposium on problems of bipolarity and of pan-temperate faunas. *Proc. 7th Pacific Sci. Cong.,* 3: 324–29.

1958 Recent climatic history in California and adjacent areas. Proc. Conference on Recent Research in Climatology, Scripps Inst. Oceanogr. Comm. on Research in Water Resources, Univ. Calif., pp. 10–22.

1960a Quaternary paleoclimatology of the Pacific coast of North America. *Repts. Calif. Coop. Oceanic Fish. Invest.,* 7: 105–12.

1960b The biogeography of Baja California and adjacent seas. Pt. 2: The marine vertebrates of the outer coast. *Syst. Zool.,* 9: 134–47.

——, G. S. BIEN, AND H. E. SUESS
1960 La Jolla natural radiocarbon measurements I. *Amer. Jour. Sci., Radiocarbon Suppl.,* 2: 197–223.

1962 La Jolla natural radiocarbon measurements II. *Radiocarbon,* 4: 204–38.

—— AND L. C. HUBBS
1960 Shoreline surface-temperature data between La Jolla, California, and Punta Baja, Baja California. *In* Surface water temperatures at shore stations. U.S. west coast and Baja California, 1956–59. SIO Reference 60–27, 15 Sept. 1960, pp. 78–95.

1961 *Idem,* 1960. SIO Reference 61–14, 28 Apr. 1961, pp. 38–43.

1962 *Idem,* 1961. SIO Reference 62–11, 2 Apr. 1962, pp. 36–41.

1963 *Idem,* 1962. SIO Reference 63–17, 17 June 1963, pp. 34–39.

HUBBS, CLARK
1952 A contribution to the classification of the blennioid fishes of the family Clinidae, with a partial revision of the eastern Pacific forms. *Stanford Ichth. Bull.,* 4: 41–165.

514

1953 Revision of the eastern Pacific fishes of the clinid genus *Labrisomus*. *Zoologica*, 38: 113–36.

HUMBOLDT, A.
1811 Essai politique sur le royaume de la Nouvelle-Espagne. 5 vols. Paris.

HUMPHREY, W. E.
1956 Tectonic framework of northeast Mexico. *Trans. Gulf Coast Assoc. Geol. Soc.*, 6: 26–35.

HUMPHREYS, E. W.
1916 *Sphenozamites rogersianus* Fontaine, an addition to the Rhaetic flora of San Juancito, Honduras. *Jour. New York Bot. Garden*, 17: 52–58.

HURD, W. E.
1929a Tropical cyclones in the eastern north Pacific. *Monthly Weather Rev.*, 57: 43–49.
1929b Northers in the Gulf of Tehuantepec. *Monthly Weather Rev.*, 57: 192–94.

HUTCHINS, L. W.
1947 The bases for temperature zonation in geographical distribution. *Ecol. Monogr.*, 17: 325–35.

HUTCHINSON, J. B., R. A. SILOW, AND S. G. STEPHENS
1947 The evolution of Gossypium. Oxford Univ. Press.

HYMAN, L. H., ed.
1960 Symposium: the biogeography of Baja California and adjacent areas. Pt. 3: Terrestrial and fresh-water biotas. *Syst. Zool.*, 9: 47–232.

IMLAY, R. W.
1939 Possible interoceanic connection across Mexico during the Jurassic and Cretaceous periods. *Proc. 6th Pacific Sci. Cong., Geophys. and Geol.*, pp. 423–27.
1943 Jurassic formations of the gulf region. *Bull. Amer. Assoc. Petroleum Geol.*, 27: 1407–1533.
1944a Correlation of Cretaceous formations of the Greater Antilles, Central America and Mexico. *Bull. Geol. Soc. Amer.*, 55: 1005–45.
1944b Cretaceous formations of Central America and Mexico. *Bull. Amer. Assoc. Petroleum Geol.*, 28: 1077–98.
1952 Correlation of the Jurassic formations of North America, exclusive of Canada. *Bull. Geol. Soc. Amer.*, 63: 953–62.

IRWIN, H. J., AND C. C. IRWIN
1959 Excavations at the Lodaiska site in the Denver, Colorado, area. *Proc. Denver Mus. Nat. Hist.*, no. 8.

IVES, R. L.
1935 Recent volcanism in northwestern Mexico. *Pan-Amer. Geol.*, 63: 335–38.

JACKS, G. V.
1954 Multilingual vocabulary of soil science. Food and Agriculture Organization of the United Nations.

JAEGER, E. C.
1957 The North American deserts. Stanford.

JAEGER, F.
1926 Forschungen über das Diluviale Klima in Mexico. *Petermanns Mitt.*, Ergänzungsheft 190. Gotha.

JAMES, P. E., AND C. F. JONES, eds.
1954 American geography: inventory and prospect. Syracuse Univ. Press.

JAUREGUI, S.
1948 Estudio del izote (*Yucca elephantipes*) como planta auxiliar. *Café de El Salvador* (April), pp. 277–91.

JIMÉNEZ MORENO, W.
1954-55 Síntesis de la historia precolonial del valle de Mexico. *Rev. Mex. Estud. Antropol.*, 14: 219–36.
1959 Síntesis de la historia pretolteca de Mesoamerica. *In* Esplendor del Mexico Antiguo, 2: 1019–1108. Centro Invest. Antropol. de Mex.

JOHANNESSEN, C. L.
1957 Man's role in the distribution of the corozo palm (*Orbignya* spp.). *Yearbook Assoc. Pacific Coast Geog.*, 19: 29–33.
1959 The geography of the savannas of interior Honduras. Univ. Calif., Dept. Geog.
1963 Savannas of interior Honduras. *Ibero-Amer.*, no. 46.

JORDAN, D. S., AND B. W. EVERMANN
1896–1900 The fishes of North and Middle America. *Smithsonian Inst., U.S. Nat. Mus.*, Bull. 47, 4 vols.

KAPLAN, L., AND R. S. MACNEISH
1960 Prehistoric bean remains from caves in the Ocampo region of Tamaulipas, Mexico. *Bot. Mus. Leafl., Harvard Univ.*, 19: 33–56.

KATZ, F.
1956 Die Sozialekonomischen Verhältnisse bei den Azteken im 15 und 16 Jahrhundert. *Ethnographisch-Archeologisch Forschungen*, vol. 3, pt. 2. Berlin.
1958 The evolution of Aztec society.

515

Past and Present, no. 13, pp. 14–25. London.

KELLEY, J. C.
1956 Settlement patterns in north-central Mexico. *In* Willey, 1956, pp. 128–39.
1957 North Mexico and the correlation of Mesoamerican and southwestern cultural sequences. MS.

——, T. N. CAMPBELL, AND D. J. LEHMER
1940 The association of archaeological materials with geological deposits in the Big Bend region of Texas. *West Texas Hist. and Sci. Soc.,* no. 10.

—— AND H. D. WINTERS
1958 Graphic survey of work at the Schroeder site (LCAJI-I), Durango, Mexico. MS.

KELLOGG, C. E.
1949a The soils that support us. New York.
1949b Special issue of *Soil Science* (vol. 67, no. 2) devoted to soil classification.

KELLY, I. T.
1938 Excavations at Chametla, Sinaloa. *Ibero-Amer.,* no. 14.
1945–49 The archaeology of the Autlan-Tuxcacuesco area of Jalisco. *Ibero-Amer.,* nos. 26, 27.
1947 Excavations at Apatzingan, Michoacan. *Viking Fund Pub. Anthropol.,* no. 7.

KIDDER, A. V.
1947 Artifacts of Uaxactun. *Carnegie Inst. Wash.,* Pub. 576.

——, J. D. JENNINGS, AND E. M. SHOOK
1946 Excavations at Kaminaljuyu, Guatemala. *Carnegie Inst. Wash.,* Pub. 561.

KIRCHHOFF, P.
1943 Mesoamerica, sus límites geográficos, composición étnica y carácteres culturales. *Acta Amer.,* 1: 92–107.
1946a Cronología de la historia precolombia de Mexico. *In* Vivó, 1946, pp. 99–108.
1946b El papel de Mexico en la America precolombia. *In* Vivó, 1946, pp. 82–90.

KOEPPEN, W.
1900 Versuch einer Klassifikation der Klimat, vorzugsweise nach ihren Beziehungen zur Pflanzenwelt. *Geog. Zeit.,* 6: 593–611, 657–79. Leipzig.
1948 Climatología. Mexico.

—— AND R. GEIGER, eds.
1930-39 Handbuch der Klimatologie. 4 vols. Berlin.

KOHL, J. G.
1863 Aelteste Gesichte der Entdeckung und Erforschung des Golf von Mexiko und der ihn umgebenden Küsten durch die Spanier von 1492 bis 1543. *Zeit. für Allegemeine Erdkunde,* 15: 1–40, 169–94. Berlin.

KOVAR, P. A.
1945 Idea general de la vegetación de El Salvador. *In* Verdoorn, 1945, pp. 56–57.

KRAMER, F. L.
1957 The pepper tree, *Schinus molle. Economic Botany,* 11: 322–26.

KRICKEBERG, W.
1918-25 Die Totonaken: ein Beitrag zur historischen Ethnographie Mittelamerikas. *Baesseler Archiv,* 7: 1–55; 9: 1–75.
1956 Altmexikanische Kulturen. Safari-Verlag. Berlin.

KRIEGER, A. D.
1950 *Review of* De Terra, Romero, and Stewart, Tepexpan Man. *Amer. Antiquity,* 15: 343–49.
1951 Notes and news: early man. *Amer. Antiquity,* 17: 77-78.
1953 New World culture history: Anglo-America. *In* Kroeber, Anthropology today, pp. 238–64.

KROEBER, A. L.
1948 Anthropology. Rev. ed. New York.

KRYNINE, P. D.
1935 Arkose deposits in the humid tropics: a study of sedimentation in southern Mexico. *Amer. Jour. Sci.,* 229: 353–63.

KULP, J. L., H. W. FEELY, AND L. E. TRYON
1951 Lamont natural radiocarbon measurements I. *Science,* 114: 565–68.

LANDA, DIEGO DE
1864 Relación de las cosas de Yucatan.
1938 *Ibid.,* 7th ed.
1941 *See* Tozzer, 1941.

LATHRAP, D. W.
1957 The classic stage in Mesoamerica. *Kroeber Anthropol. Soc. Papers.,* no. 17, pp. 38–74.

LAUER, W.
1956 Vegetation, Landnutzung und Agrarpotential in El Salvador (Zentralamerika). *Schriften Geog. Inst. Univ. Kiel,* no. 16.
1959 Klimatische und pflanzengeograph-

516

ische Grundzüge Zentralamerikas. *Erdkunde*, 13: 344–54.

LEÓN, N.
1921 Huellas humanas impresas sobre roca en el territorio mexicano. *El Mex. Antiguo*, 1: 204–10.

LEOPOLD, A. S.
1950 Vegetation zones of Mexico. *Ecology*, 31: 507–18.
1959 Wildlife of Mexico: the game birds and mammals. Univ. Calif. Press.

LEVINE, M. H.
1958 An area co-tradition for Mesoamerica. *Kroeber Anthropol. Soc. Papers*, no. 18.

LIBBY, W. F.
1952 Chicago radiocarbon dates III. *Science*, 116 (3023).
1955 Radiocarbon dating. 2d ed. Univ. Chicago Press.

LINDIG, W.
1959 Die Seri: ein Hoka-wildbeuterstamm in Sonora, Mexiko. Leiden.

LINNÉ, S.
1934 Archaeological researches at Teotihuacan, Mexico. *Ethnog. Mus.*, Pub. 1. Stockholm.
1942 Mexican highland cultures: archaeological researches at Teotihuacan, Calpulalpan, and Chalchicomula in 1934–35. *Ethnog. Mus.*, Pub. 7. Stockholm.
1956 Radiocarbon dates in Teotihuacan. *Ethnos*, 21: 180–93.

LISTER, R. H.
1955 The present status of the archaeology of western Mexico: a distributional study. *Univ. Colorado Studies, Anthropol. Ser.*, no. 5.
—— AND A. M. HOWARD
1955 The Chalchihuites culture of northwestern Mexico. *Amer. Antiquity*, 21: 122–29.

LONGYEAR, J. M., III
1944 Archaeological investigations in El Salvador. *Mem. Peabody Mus., Harvard Univ.*, vol. 9, no. 2.
1948 A sub-pottery deposit at Copan, Honduras. *Amer. Antiquity*, 13: 248–49.
1952 Copan ceramics: a study of southeastern Maya pottery. *Carnegie Inst. Wash.*, Pub. 597.

LÓPEZ DE LLERGO, R.
1953 Las provincias fisiográficas de la República Mexicana. *Mem. Cong. Cien. Mex.*, 4: 274–77.

LÓPEZ RAMOS, E.
1956 Visita a las localidades tipo de las formaciones del Eoceno, Oligoceno y Mioceno de la cuenca sedimentaria de Tampico-Misantla, en la llanura costera del Golfo de Mexico, entre Poza Rica, Ver. – Tampico, Tamps. y Ciudad Valles, San Luis Potosi. *20th Cong. Geol. Int.*, Field Guide, no. 1.

LORENZO, J. L.
1953 A fluted point from Durango, Mexico. *Amer. Antiquity*, 18: 394–95.
1958a Préhistoire et Quaternaire récent au Mexique: etat actuel des connaissances. *L'Anthropologie*, 62: 62–83. Paris.
1958b Una hipótesis paleoclimática para la cuenca de Mexico. *Misc. Paul Rivet Octogenario Dicata*, 1: 579–84. Univ. Nac. Autónoma de Mex.
1958c Un sitio precerámico en Yanhuitlan, Oaxaca. *Inst. Nac. Antropol. e Hist.*, Pub. 6.
1959a Glaciología mexicana. *Bol. Bibl. Geofísica y Oceanogr. Amer.*, 1: 131–36.
1959b Los glaciares de Mexico. *Monogr. Inst. Geofísica*, no. 1. Univ. Nac. Autónoma de Mex.
1960 Sobre un hallazgo de carácter prehistórico en el estado de Puebla. *Tlatoani*, ep. 2, no. 13, pp. 37–40.

LOTHROP, S. K.
1926 Pottery of Costa Rica and Nicaragua. *Contrib. Mus. Amer. Indian, Heye Found.*, no. 8. 2 vols.
1939 The southeastern frontier of the Maya. *Amer. Anthropol.*, 41: 42–54.

LOWE, G. W.
1959 The long sequence of preclassic architectural development at Chiapa de Corzo, Chiapas. 24th ann. meeting, Soc. Amer. Archaeol., abstracts of papers, p. 38.

LOZANO GARCÍA, R.
1945 El gas natural y la turba en la cuenca de Mexico. *Inst. Geol., Univ. Nac. Autónoma de Mex., Estud. Geol.-Econ.*, no. 1.

LUMHOLTZ, C.
1902 Unknown Mexico. 2 vols. New York.

LUNDELL, C. L.
1934 Preliminary sketch of the phytogeography of the Yucatan peninsula.

Carnegie Inst. Wash., Pub. 436, Contrib. 12.

1937 The vegetation of the Peten. *Carnegie Inst. Wash.,* Pub. 478.

1945 The vegetation and natural resources of British Honduras. *In* Verdoorn, 1945, pp. 270–73.

McBirney, A. R.

1958 Active volcanoes of Nicaragua and Costa Rica. Catalogue of Active Volcanoes of the World, pt. 4, pp. 107–46. Naples.

McBryde, F. W.

1947 Cultural and historical geography of southwest Guatemala. *Smithsonian Inst., Inst. Social Anthropol.,* Pub. 4.

McEwen, G. F.

1916 Summary and interpretation of the hydrographic observations made by the Scripps Institution for Biological Research of the University of California, 1908 to 1915. *Univ. Calif. Pub. Zool.,* 15: 255–356.

McGee, W J

1901 The Seri Indians. *Smithsonian Inst., Bur. Amer. Ethnol.,* ann. rept., 17 (1895–96): 1–344.

MacGillavry, H. J.

1934 Some rudistids from the Alta Verapaz. *Proc. Koninklijke Nederlandsche Akad. van Wetenschappen Amsterdam,* 37: 232–38.

1937 Geology of the province of Camaguey, Cuba, with revisional studies in rudistid paleontology. Dissertation, Univ. Utrecht.

Macías Villada, M.

1954 Estudio agrológico de gran visión de la península de Yucatan. Sec. Rec. Hidráulicos.

1960 Suelos de la República Mexicana. *Ingeniería Hidráulica en México,* 14: (2) 51–71; (3) 63–73.

Mackie, W. W.

1943 Origin, dispersal and variability of the lima bean, *Phaseolus lunatus. Hilgardia,* 15: 1–29.

McKusick, M. B.

1960 Aboriginal canoes in the West Indies. *Yale Univ. Pub. Anthropol.,* no. 63.

MacNeish, R. S.

n.d.,*a* Midseason report of the second Tamaulipas archaeological expedition. MS, File 565, Technical Archives, Inst. Nac. Antropol.

n.d.,*b* Culture and agriculture in prehistoric southwest Tamaulipas, Mexico. MS.

1954 An early archaeological site near Panuco, Veracruz. *Trans. Amer. Phil. Soc.,* n.s., vol. 44, pt. 5.

1956 Prehistoric settlement patterns on the northeastern periphery of Mesoamerica. *In* Willey, 1956, pp. 140–47.

1958 Preliminary archaeological investigations in the Sierra de Tamaulipas, Mexico. *Trans. Amer. Phil. Soc.,* n.s., vol. 48, pt. 6.

1959 Origin and spread of some domesticated plants as seen from Tamaulipas, Mexico. MS presented to annual meeting, Amer. Anthropol. Assoc.

1960 Restos pre-cerámicos de cueva Aeyerado en el sur de Puebla. Dir. Prehistoria.

1961 Restos precerámicos de la cueva de Coxcatlan en el sur de Puebla. *Inst. Nac. Anthropol. e Hist.,* Pub. 10.

1964 Ancient Mesoamerican civilization. *Science,* 143: 531–37.

—— and F. Peterson

1962 Santa Marta rock-shelter, Ocozocoautla, Chiapas. *New World Archaeol. Found.*

Maldonado-Koerdell, M.

1947 Antecedentes del descubrimiento del hombre de Tepexpan. *Anthropos,* 1: 33–36.

1948 Los vertebrados fósiles del Cuaternario en Mexico. *Rev. Soc. Mex. Hist. Natural,* 9: 1–35.

1952 Formaciones con fusulínidos del Permo-Carbonífero Superior de Mexico. *Ciencia,* 12: 235–47.

1953a Plantas del rético-liásico y otros fósiles Triásicos de Honduras (Centroamerica). *Ciencia,* 12: 294–96.

1953b Mamíferos recientes y fósiles de Mexico. *Ciencia,* 13: 79–84.

1954a La formación y carácteres del pedregal de San Angel. *Tlatoani,* nos. 8, 9, pp. 2–6.

1954b Nomenclatura, bibliografía y correlación de las formaciones arqueozoicas y paleozoicas de Mexico. *Bol. Asoc. Mex. Geol. Petroleros,* 6: 113–38.

1954-55 La historia geohidrológica de la cuenca de Mexico. *Rev. Mex. Estud. Antropol.,* 14: 15–21.

1958a Recientes adelantos en geofísica y geología submarinas en las areas del océano Pacífico próximas a Mexico. *Ciencia*, 18: 105–13.

1958b Nomenclatura, bibliografía y correlación de las formaciones continentales (y algunas marinas) del Mesozoico de Mexico. *Bol. Asoc. Mex. Geol. Petroleros*, 10: 287–308.

1958c Bibliografía geológica y paleontológica de America Central. *Inst. Panamer. Geog. e Hist.*, Pub. 204.

—— AND L. AVELEYRA ARROYO DE ANDA
1949 Nota preliminar sobre dos artefactos del Pleistoceno Superior hallados en la región de Tequixquiac, Mexico. *El Mex. Antiguo*, 7: 154–61.

MANGELSDORF, P. C.
1954 New evidence on the origin and ancestry of maize. *Amer. Antiquity*, 19: 409–10.

—— AND R. H. LISTER
1956 Archaeological evidence on the evolution of maize in northwestern Mexico. *Bot. Mus. Leafl., Harvard Univ.*, 17: 151–78.

——, R. S. MacNEISH, AND W. C. GALINAT
1956 Archaeological evidence on the diffusion and evolution of maize in northeastern Mexico. *Bot. Mus. Leafl., Harvard Univ.*, 17: 125–50.

1964 Domestication of corn. *Science*, 143: 538–45.

—— AND D. L. OLIVER
1951 Whence came maize to Asia? *Bot. Mus. Leafl., Harvard Univ.*, 14: 263–91.

—— AND R. G. REEVES
1939 The origin of Indian corn and its relatives. *Texas Agric. Expt. Sta.*, Bull. 574.

1959a The origin of corn. III: Modern races, the product of teosinte introgression. *Bot. Mus. Leafl., Harvard Univ.*, 18: 389–411.

1959b The origin of corn. IV: Place and time of origin. *Bot. Mus. Leafl., Harvard Univ.*, 18: 413–27.

—— AND C. E. SMITH
1949 New archaeological evidence on evolution in maize. *Bot. Mus. Leafl., Harvard Univ.*, 13: 213–47.

MANÓ, J. C.
1883a Primer informe presentado a la secretaría de fomento, por . . . comisionado por el supremo gobierno para estudiar la República de Guatemala bajo el punto de vista mineralógico. *An. Soc. Geog. e Hist. de Guatemala*, 16: 304–07 (1939–40).

1883b Segundo informe. . . . *Ibid.*, 16: 384–400 (1939–40).

MARMER, H. A.
1926 The tide. New York and London.

MARQUINA, I.
1951 Arquitectura prehispánica. *Inst. Nac. Antropol. e Hist.*, Mem. 1.

MARTIN, PAUL SIDNEY
1952 Mogollon cultural continuity and change. *Fieldiana* (Anthropology), vol. 40.

MARTIN, PAUL SCHULTZ
1958 A biogeography of reptiles and amphibians in the Gomez Farias region, Tamaulipas, Mexico. *Univ. Michigan, Mus. Zool.*, Misc. Pub. 101.

MARTÍNEZ DEL RIO, P.
1952a El mamut de Santa Isabel Iztapan. *Cuad. Amer.*, año 11, no. 4, pp. 149–70.

1952b Los orígenes americanos. 3d ed. Mexico.

MASSEY, W. C.
1947 Brief report on archaeological investigations in Baja California. *SW. Jour. Anthropol.*, 3: 344–59.

MAYER-OAKES, W. J.
1959 A stratigraphic excavation at El Risco, Mexico. *Proc. Amer. Phil. Soc.*, vol. 103, no. 3.

MAYR, E.
1946 History of the North American bird fauna. *Wilson Bull.*, 58: 1–41.

MEDELLÍN ZENIL, A.
1953 Secuencia cronológico-cultural en el centro de Veracruz. *In* Huastecos, Totonacos y sus vecinos, pp. 371–78.

1955a Desarrollo de la cultura prehispánica central veracruzana. *An. Inst. Nac. Antropol. e Hist.*, 7: 101–110.

1955b Exploraciones en la Isla de Sacrificios. Gobierno del Estado de Veracruz, Dept. Antropol.

—— AND F. A. PETERSON
1954 A smiling head complex from central Veracruz, Mexico. *Amer. Antiquity*, 20: 163–69.

MEEK, S. E.
1904 The freshwater fishes of Mexico north of the Isthmus of Tehauntepec. *Field Columbia Mus., Zool. Ser.*, Pub. 93, vol. 5.

1907 Synopsis of the fishes of the Great Lakes of Nicaragua. *Field Columbia Mus., Zool. Ser.*, Pub. 121, 7: 97–157.

1908 Zoology of lakes Amatitlan and Atitlan, Guatemala, with special reference to ichthyology. *Field Columbia Mus., Zool. Ser.,* Pub. 127, 7: 159–206.

MEJÍA, J. V.
1927 Geografía de la República de Guatemala. 2d ed. Guatemala.

MENARD, H. W.
1955 Deformation of the northeastern Pacific basin and the west coast of North America. *Bull. Geol. Soc. Amer.,* 66: 1149–98.
1959 Geology of the Pacific sea floor. *Experientia,* 15: 205, 244.
1960 The east Pacific rise. *Science,* 132: 1737–46.

MENDIZABAL, M. O. DE
1946 Influencia de la sal en la distribución geográfica de los grupos indígenas de Mexico. *In* his Obras completas, 2: 181–340.

MERCADO SÁNCHEZ, P.
1959 Breve reseña sobre las principales artes de pesca usadas en Mexico. Sec. Industria y Comercio, Dir. General de Pesca e Industrias Conexas, pp. 1–79.
1961 Corrección y modernización del sistema de captura del camarón en aguas interiores del noroeste de Mexico. *Acta Zool. Mex.,* 4: 1–11.

MERRIAM, C. H.
1891 The geographic distribution of life in North America. *Smithsonian Inst.,* ann. rept., pp. 365–415.
1898 Life zones and crop zones of the United States. U.S. Dept. Agriculture. *Biol. Survey,* Bull. 10.

MERZ, A.
1906 Beiträge zur Klimatologie und Hydrographie Mittelamerikas. *Mitt. des Vereins für Erdkunde zu Leipzig,* 1906: 1–96.

METEOROLOGICAL OFFICE
1956 Monthly meteorological charts of the eastern Pacific Ocean. *British Meteorological Office,* 518: 1–122. London.

MEYER-ABICH, H.
1952 Das Erdbeben von Jucuapa en El Salvador vom 6 und 7 Mai 1951. *Neues Jahrbuch für Mineralogie und Geologie,* Abhandlungen, 95: 311–36.
1952–53 Consideraciones generales acerca de la planta eléctrica proyectada en el lugar "Chorrera del Guayabo" en el Rio Lempa. *Comunicaciones Inst. Tropical Invest. Cien. Univ. El Salvador,* 1: 1–6.
1953 Los ausoles de El Salvador, con un sumario geológico-tectónico de la zona volcánica occidental. *Ibid.,* 2: 55–94.
1956 Los volcanes activos de Guatemala y El Salvador. *An. Servicio Geol., El Salvador,* Bol. 3.
1958 Active volcanoes of Guatemala and El Salvador. Catalogue of the Active Volcanoes of the World, pt. 4, pp. 37–105. Naples.

MEZA CALIX, U.
1916 Geografía de Honduras. Tegucigalpa.

MILLER, G. S., AND R. KELLOGG
1955 List of North American recent mammals. *Smithsonian Inst., U.S. Nat. Mus.,* Bull. 205.

MILLER, R. R.
1958 Origin and affinities of the freshwater fish fauna of western North America. *In* Zoogeography, Amer. Assoc. Advancement Sci., Pub. 51, pp. 187–222.

MILLON, R. F.
1957a Irrigation systems in the valley of Teotihuacan. *Amer. Antiquity,* 23: 160–66.
1957b New data on Teotihuacan I in Teotihuacan. *Bol. Centro Invest. Antropol. de Mex.,* no. 4, pp. 12–18.
1959 La agricultura como inicio de la civilización. *In* Esplendor del Mexico Antiguo, 2: 997–1018. Centro Invest. Antropol. de Mex.
1960a Chronological and developmental classifications in Mesoamerican prehistory. MS presented to annual meeting (1959), Amer. Anthropol. Assoc.
1960b The beginnings of Teotihuacan. *Amer. Antiquity,* 26: 1–10.

MIRANDA, F.
1947 Rasgos de la vegetación de la cuenca del Rio de las Balsas. *Rev. Soc. Mex. Hist. Natural,* 8: 95–114.
1948 Datos sobre la vegetación en la cuenca alta del Papaloapan. *An. Inst. Biol. Univ. Nac. Autónoma de Mex.,* 19: 333–64.
1952–53 La vegetación de Chiapas. 2 vols. Tuxtla Gutierrez, Dept. Prensa y Turismo.
1959 Estudios acera de la vegetación. *In* Beltrán, 1959, pp. 215–71.

—— AND A. J. SHARP
1950 Characteristics of vegetation in certain temperate regions of eastern Mexico. *Ecology*, 31: 313–33.

MONGES CALDERA, J.
1960 Trabajos gravimétricos en las Americas. *Bol. Biblio. Geofísica y Oceanogr. Amer.*, 2: 341–51.

MOORE, R. T.
1945 The transverse volcanic biotic province of central Mexico and its relationship to adjacent provinces. *Trans. San Diego Soc. Nat. Hist.*, 10: 217–36.

MOORE, S. F.
1958 Power and property in Inca Peru. New York.

MOOSER, F.
1957 Los ciclos de vulcanismo que formaron la cuenca de Mexico. *20th Cong. Geol. Int.*, pp. 337–48.
1958 Active volcanoes of Mexico. Catalogue of the Active Volcanoes of the World, pt. 4, pp. 1–36. Naples.

—— AND M. MALDONADO-KOERDELL
1961 Tectónica penecontemporanea a lo largo de la costa mexicana del Oceano Pacifico. *Geofísica Int.*, 1: 3–20.

——, H. MEYER-ABICH, AND A. R. McBIRNEY
1958 Catalogue of the active volcanoes of the world. Pt. 4. Int. Volcanological Assoc. Naples.

——, S. E. WHITE, AND J. L. LORENZO
1956 La cuenca de Mexico: consideraciones geológicas y arqueológicas. *Inst. Nac. Antropol. e Hist.*, Pub. 2.

MORLEY, S. G.
1938 Inscriptions of Peten. 5 vols. *Carnegie Inst. Wash.*, Pub. 437.
1946 The ancient Maya. Stanford Univ. Press.
1956 The ancient Maya. 3d ed., rev. by G. M. Brainerd. Stanford Univ. Press.

MORRIS, E. H., J. CHARLOT, AND A. A. MORRIS
1931 The Temple of the Warriors at Chichen Itza, Yucatan. *Carnegie Inst. Wash.*, Pub. 406.

MÜLLER, F.
1961 Tres objetos de piedra de Huapalcalco, estado de Hidalgo. *In* Homenaje a Pablo Martínez del Río, pp. 319–22.

MÜLLERRIED, F. K. G.
1942a The Mesozoic of Mexico and northwestern Central America. *Proc. 8th Amer. Sci. Cong.*, 4: 124–47.

1942b Contribution to the geology of northwestern Central America. *Proc. 8th Amer. Sci. Cong.*, 4: 469–82.
1942c Valle de Tixtla, cuenca de desagüe subterráneo temporal en el estado de Guerrero. *Rev. Geog.*, 2: 17–48.
1944 El mapa geológico de la America Central. *Rev. Geog. Inst. Panamer. Geog. e Hist.*, 4: 35–64.
1945 Contribución a la geología de Mexico y noroeste de America Central. Mexico.
1947a Acerca del descubrimiento del hombre de Tepexpan (valle de Mexico). *Bol. Biblio. Antropol. Amer.*, 9: 60–64.
1947b El mapa geológico de Centro-America. *An. Soc. Geog. e Hist. de Guatemala*, 22: 143–65.
1948 Las facies de fauna y flora del Mesozoico en el noroeste de la America Central (del Istmo de Tehauntepec a Nicaragua). *18th Int. Geol. Cong.*, Volume of Titles and Abstracts, sec. J, Faunal and Floral Correlations, p. 71.
1949a Rectificación de la estratigrafía del Mesozoico en el noroeste de America Central (del Istmo de Tehauntepec a Nicaragua). *Ciencia*, 9: 219–23.
1949b La orogénesis del sur y del sureste de Mexico. *Bol. Soc. Geol. Mex.*, 14: 73–101.

MÜNNICH, K. O., H. G. OSTLUND, H. DE VRIES, AND H. BARKER
1958 Carbon 14 activity during the past 5000 years. *Nature*, 182: 1432–33.

MULLER, C. H.
1939 Relations of the vegetation and climatic types in Nuevo Leon, Mexico. *Amer. Midl. Naturalist*, 21: 687–729.
1947 Vegetation and climate of Coahuila. *Madroño*, 9: 33–57.

MURRAY, G. E.
1961 Atlantic and gulf coast geology of North America. New York.

NELSON, E. W.
1921 Lower California and its natural resources. *Mem. Nat. Acad. Sci.*, vol. 16, no. 1.

NEWBERRY, J. S.
1887 Discusiones acerca del hombre del Peñón. *La Naturaleza*, 1st ser., 7: 284–85.
1888a Rhaetic plants from Honduras. *Amer. Jour. Sci. and Arts*, 3d ser., 36: 342–51.

1888b Triassic plants from Honduras. *Trans. New York Acad. Sci.*, 7: 113–15.

NEWELL, N. D.
1959a Corals. Pt. 1: Questions of the coral reefs. *Natural Hist.*, 68: 118–31.
1959b The coral reefs. Pt. 2: Biology of the corals. *Natural Hist.*, 68: 226–35.

NOGUERA, E.
1942 Exploraciones en "El Opeño," Michoacan. *27th Int. Cong. Amer.*, 1: 574–86.
1948 Estado actual de los conocimientos acerca de la arqueología del noroeste de Michoacan. *In* El Occidente de Mexico, pp. 38–39.
1954 La cerámica arqueológica de Cholula. Mexico.

NYGREN, W. E.
1950 Bolivar geosyncline of northwestern South America. *Bull. Amer. Assoc. Petroleum Geol.*, 34: 1998–2006.

OAKES, H., AND J. THORP
1950 Dark-clay soils of warm regions variously called Rendzina, black cotton soils, regur, and tirs. *Proc. Soils Sci. Soc. Amer.*, 15: 347–54.

OLSON, E. A., AND W. S. BROECKER
1959 Lamont natural radiocarbon measurements V. *Amer. Jour. Sci., Radiocarbon Suppl.*, 1: 1–28.

OLSON, E. C., AND P. O. McGREW
1941 Mammalian fauna from the Pliocene to Honduras. *Bull. Geol. Soc. Amer.*, 52: 1219–44.

OLSSON, A. A.
1932 Contributions to the Tertiary paleontology of northern Peru. Pt. 5: The Peruvian Miocene. *Bull. Amer. Paleontol.*, 19: 1–272.

O'NEILL, G.
1954 Notes and news: early man. *Amer. Antiquity*, 19: 304.

ORDÓÑEZ, E.
1903–06 Los xalapazcos del estado de Puebla. *Inst. Geol. de Mex., Parergones*, 1: 295–393.
1906 Guide géologique au Mexique. Pt. 8: De Mexico á Patzcuaro et Uruapan. *10th Cong. Geol. Int.* Mexico.
1936 Principal physiographic provinces of Mexico. *Bull. Amer. Assoc. Petroleum Geol.*, 20: 1277–1307.
1941 Las provincias fisiográficas de Mexico. *Rev. Geog.*, 1: 133–81.
1945 Las huellas de pisadas humanas en Rincon de Guadalupe, Amanalco de Becerra, estado de Mexico. MS, Inst. Geol. library. Mexico.

OROZCO Y BERRA, M.
1864 Memoria para la carta hidrográfica del valle de Mexico. Mexico.

ORTIZ, F.
1947 El huracán. Mexico.

ORTIZ MONASTERIO, R.
1950 Reconocimiento agrológico regional del estado de Yucatan. *Bol. Soc. Mex. Geog. y Estad.*, 69: 245–324.
1955–57 Los recursos agrológicos de la República Mexicana. *Ingeniería Hidráulica en Mexico*, vols. 9–11. Sec. Recursos Hidráulicos.

OSBORN, H. F.
1905 Recent vertebrate paleontology: fossil mammals of Mexico. *Science*, 21 (546): 931–32.

OSORIO-TAFALL, B. F.
1943 El Mar de Cortes y la productividad fitoplanctónica de sus aguas. *An. Escuela Nac. Cien. Biol.*, 3: 73–118.
1946 Algunos problemas de la hidrología mexicana. *In* Tamayo, 1946, pp. 385–417.

OVIEDO Y VALDÉS, G. F. DE
1851–55 Historia general y natural de las Indias, islas y tierra firme del mar océano. 4 vols. Madrid.

OWER, L. H.
1928 Geology of British Honduras. *Jour. Geol.*, 36: 494–509.

PAGE, J. L.
1930 Climate of Mexico. *Monthly Weather Rev.*, Suppl. 33.

PALERM, A.
1954 La distribución del regadío en el área central de Mesoamerica. *Cien. Sociales*, 5 (25–26): 2–15, 64–74.
1955 The agricultural basis of urban civilization in Mesoamerica. *In* Steward et al., Irrigation Civilizations: a comparative study. *Pan Amer. Union, Soc. Sci. Monogr.*, no. 1.
1956 Notas sobre las construcciones militares y la guerra en Mesoamerica. *Cien. Sociales*, 7 (39): 189–202.

PALMER, R. H.
1926 Tectonic setting of Lago de Chapala. *Pan-Amer. Geol.*, 45: 125–234.

PAN AMERICAN INST. GEOGRAPHY AND HISTORY
1953–54 Los estudios sobre los recursos naturales en las Americas. 9 vols. Mexico.

PANAMA
1958 Carta hidrológica. Inst. Fomento Económico.

PARR, A. E.
1935 Report on hydrographic observations in the Gulf of Mexico and the adjacent straits made during the Yale oceanographic expedition on the *Mabel Taylor* in 1932. *Bull. Bingham Oceanogr. Coll., Peabody Mus. Natural Hist., Yale Univ.*, vol. 5, art. 1.
1937 A contribution to the hydrography of the Caribbean and Cayman seas. *Ibid.*, vol. 5, art. 4.
1938 Further observations on the hydrography of the eastern Caribbean and adjacent Atlantic waters. *Ibid.*, vol. 6, art. 4.

PARSONS, J. J.
1955 The Miskito pine savanna of Nicaragua and Honduras. *Ann. Assoc. Amer. Geog.* 45: 36–63.

PARSONS, L. A.
1957 The nature of horizon markers in Middle American archaeology. *Anthropol. Tomorrow*, 5: 98–121. Anthropol. Club, Univ. Chicago.

PASSARGE, S.
1919 Grundlagen der Landschaftskunde. 2 vols. Hamburg.

PATIÑO, L. R.
1955 Posibilidades agrícolas y de colonización de la zona costanera de Oaxaca entre los ríos Salado y Mixtepec. Informes agroeconómicos de la Mixteca de la Costa. *Inst. Nac. Indigenista*, Ser. Mimeo., no. 8.

PATTULLO, J., W. H. MUNK, R. REVELLE, AND E. STRONG
1955 The seasonal oscillation in sea level. *Jour. Marine Research*, 14: 88–155.

PAYNE, E. J.
1892 History of the new world called America. New York.

PAYNTER, R. A., JR.
1955 The ornithogeography of the Yucatan peninsula. *Peabody Mus. Natural Hist., Yale Univ.*, Bull. 9.

PEARSE, A. S., et al.
1936 The cenotes of Yucatan. *Carnegie Inst. Wash.*, Pub. 457.

PEÑAFIEL, A.
1884 Memoria sobre las aguas potables de la capital de Mexico. Sec. Fomento. Mexico.

PENDLETON, R. L.
1943 General soil conditions in Central America. *Proc. Soil Sci. Soc. Amer.*, 8: 403–07.
1945 Some important soils of Central America. *In* Verdoorn, 1945, pp. 163–65.

PETERS, J. A.
1955 Use and misuse of the biotic province concept. *Amer. Naturalist*, 89: 21–28.

PETERSON, C. L.
1960 The physical oceanography of the Gulf of Nicoya, Costa Rica, a tropical estuary. *Bull. Inter-Amer. Tropical Tuna Comm.*, 4: 137–216.

PETTERSSEN, S.
1941 Introduction to meteorology. New York and London.

PILSBRY, H. A.
1926 The land mollusks of the Republic of Panama and the Canal Zone. *Proc. Acad. Nat. Sci. Philadelphia*, pp. 57–133.
1930 Results of the Pinchot South Seas expedition. Pt. 2: Land mollusks of the Canal Zone, the Republic of Panama, and the Cayman Islands. *Proc. Acad. Nat. Sci. Philadelphia*, pp. 339–65.

PIÑA CHAN, R.
1955 Las culturas preclásicas de la cuenca de Mexico, Mexico. Fondo de Cultura Económica. Mexico.
1958 Tlatilco. *Investigaciones*, nos. 1 and 2. Inst. Nac. Antropol. e Hist.

PITTIER, H. F.
1912 Kostarika. Beiträge zur Orographie und Hydrographie. *Petermanns Mitt.*, Ergänzungsheft 175. Gotha.

PLANCARTE Y NAVARRETE, F.
1923 Prehistoria de Mexico. Tlalpan, D.F.

POCOCK, R. I.
1902 Arachnida, scorpiones, pedipalpi, and solifugae. *In* Biologia Centrali-Americana, Zoology, vol. 12.

POLANYI, K., et al.
1957 Trade and market in the early empires. Glencoe, Ill.

POPENOE, H.
1960 Effects of shifting cultivation on natural soil constituents in Central America. Doctoral dissertation, Univ. Florida.

POPENOE, W.
1926 Guatemala. *In* Shelford, 1926, pp. 596–601.

PORTER, M. N.
1953 Tlatilco and the pre-classic cultures

of the New World. *Viking Fund Pub. Anthropol.*, no. 19.

1956 Excavations at Chupicuaro, Guanajuato, Mexico. *Trans. Amer. Phil. Soc.*, vol. 46, pt. 5.

POWERS, S.
1918 Notes on the geology of eastern Guatemala and northwestern Spanish Honduras. *Jour. Geol.*, 26: 507–23.

PRESCOTT, W. H.
1843 History of the conquest of Mexico. 2 vols. New York.
1930 Climate of Mexico. *Monthly Weather Rev.*, Suppl. 33.

PALERM, A.
1927 Notas preliminares sobre vestigios glaciales en el estado de Hidalgo y en el valle de Mexico. *Mem. y Rev. Soc. Cien. Antonio Alzate*, 48: 1–13.

PROSKOURIAKOFF, T.
1946 An album of Maya architecture. *Carnegie Inst. Wash.*, Pub. 558.
1954 Varieties of classic central Veracruz sculpture. *Carnegie Inst. Wash.*, Pub. 606, Contrib. 58.
1958 Studies on Middle American art. *In* Willey, Vogt, and Palerm, Middle American Anthropology, pp. 29–35. *Pan Amer. Union, Social Sci. Monogr.*, no. 5.

RADCLIFFE, L.
1922 Fisheries and market for fishery products in Mexico, Central America, South America, West Indies, and Bermudas. Rept. U.S. Comm. Fisheries, App. 8.

RADLEY, J.
1960 The physical geography of the east coast of Nicaragua. Rept. field work carried out under ONR Contract 222(11) NR 388 067. Univ. Calif., Dept. Geog.

RAISZ, E.
1959 Landforms of Mexico. [Map with text.] Cambridge, Mass.

RANDS, R. L., AND B. C. RANDS
1960 Ceramic investigations at Palenque. *Bol. Biblio. Antropol. Amer.*, vol. 21–22.

RAY, S. M., AND W. B. WILSON
1956 The occurrence of *Gymnodinium breve* in the western Gulf of Mexico. *Ecology*, 2: 388.

RECINOS, A., ed.
1947 Popol Vuh. Las antiguas historias del Quiche. Mexico.

RECORD, S. J., AND R. W. HESS
1943 Timbers of the New World. New Haven.

REDFIELD, R.
1956 Peasant society and culture: an anthropological approach to civilization. Univ. Chicago Press.

REED, W. W.
1923 Climatological data for Central America. *Monthly Weather Rev.*, 51: 133–41.
1926 Climatological data for the West Indian islands. *Monthly Weather Rev.*, 54: 133–60.

REESIDE, J. B., JR., et al.
1957 Correlation of the Triassic formations of North America, exclusive of Canada. *Bull. Geol. Soc. Amer.*, 68: 1151–1614.

REGAN, C. T.
1906–08 Pisces. *In* Biologia Centrali-Americana, Zoology, vol. 8.

REID, J. L., JR., ed.
1960 The NORPAC atlas. Oceanic observations of the Pacific, 1955. Univ. California Press and Univ. Tokyo Press.

——, G. I. RODEN, AND J. G. WYLLIE
1958 Studies of the California Current system. *Calif. Coop. Fisheries Invest.*, Progress Rept., 1956–58, pp. 27–57.

REVELLE, R.
1950 1940 *E. W. Scripps* cruise to the Gulf of California. Pt. 5: Sedimentation and oceanography: summary of field observations. *Geol. Soc. Amer. Mem.*, 43: 1–6.

REYES, A. E.
1923 Los elefantes de la cuenca de Mexico. *Rev. Mex. Biol.*, 3: 227–44.
1927 Ejemplar no. 213 del Museo Paleontológico del Instituto Geológico de Mexico. *An. Inst. Geol. de Mex.*, 2: 203–04.

RICHARDS, P. W.
1957 The tropical rain forest: an ecological study. Cambridge Univ. Press.

ROBERTS, L. M., U. J. GRANT, R. RAMIREZ E., W. H. HATHEWAY, AND D. L. SMITH in collaboration with P. C. MANGELSDORF
1957 Races of maize in Colombia. *Nat. Acad. Sci., Nat. Research Council*, Pub. 510.

ROBERTS, R. J., AND E. M. IRVING
1957 Mineral deposits of Central America. *U. S. Geol. Survey*, Bull. 1034.

REFERENCES

ROBLES RAMOS, R.
1942 Orogénisis de la República Mexicana en relación a su relieve actual. *Irrigación en Mex.*, 23: 6–61.
1944 Algunas ideas sobre la glaciología y morfología del Iztaccihuatl. *Rev. Geog. Inst. Panamer. Geog. e Hist.*, 4: 65–98.
1950 Apuntes sobre la morfología de Yucatan. *Bol. Soc. Mex. Geog. y Estad.*, 69: 27–106.
1959 Geología y geohidrología. *In* Beltrán, 1959, pp. 55–92.

RODEN, G. I.
1958 Oceanographic and meteorological aspects of the Gulf of California. *Pacific Sci.*, 12: 21–45.
1959 On the heat and salt balance of the California Current region. *Jour. Marine Research*, 18: 36–61.
1960 On the nonseasonal variations in sea level along the west coast of North America. *Jour. Geophys. Research*, 65: 2809–26.
1961a On seasonal temperature and salinity variations along the west coast of the United States and Canada. *Calif. Coop. Oceanic Fisheries Invest.*, Rept. 8, pp. 95–119.
1961b On the wind driven circulation in the Gulf of Tehuantepec and its effect upon surface temperatures. *Geofis. Internac. Mex.*, 1: 55–76.
1962 Oceanographic aspects of the eastern equatorial Pacific. *Geofis. Internac. Mex.*, 2: 77–92.
1963 Sea level variations at Panama. *Jour. Geophys. Research*, 68: 5701–10.
1964 Oceanographic aspects of the Gulf of California. *In* Marine Geology of the Gulf of California, *Bull. Amer. Assoc. Petroleum Geol.* (in press).

—— AND G. W. GROVES
1959 Recent oceanographic investigations in the Gulf of California. *Jour. Marine Research*, 18: 10–35.

ROMANO, A.
1955 Nota preliminar sobre los restos humanos sub-fósiles de Santa Maria Astahuacan, D. F. *An. Inst. Nac. Antropol. e Hist.*, 7: 65–74.

ROSEN, D. E., AND R. M. BAILEY
1963 The poeciliid fishes (Cyprinodontiformes), their structure, zoogeography, and systematics. *Bull. Amer. Mus. Nat. Hist.*, 126: 1–176.

ROSENBLATT, R. H.
1959 A revisionary study of the blennioid fish family Tripterygiidae. Doctoral dissertation, Univ. California.

ROSSBY, C. G.
1954 Las bases científicas de la moderna meteorología. *Bol. Soc. Mex. Geog. y Estad.*, 78: 103–87.

ROUSE, I.
1948 The West Indies. *In* Handbook of South American Indians, 4: 495–565. *Smithsonian Inst., Bur. Amer. Ethnol.*, Bull. 143.

ROWE, J. H.
1946 Inca culture at the time of the Spanish conquest. *In* Handbook of South American Indians, 2: 183–330. *Smithsonian Inst., Bur. Amer. Ethnol.*, Bull. 143.

ROY, S. K.
1957 The present status of the volcanoes of Central America. *Fieldiana* (Geology), 10: 335–39.

ROYS, R. L.
1939 The titles of Ebtun. *Carnegie Inst. Wash.*, Pub. 505.
1943 The Indian background of colonial Yucatan. *Carnegie Inst. Wash.*, Pub. 548.

RUBIN, M., AND C. ALEXANDER
1960 United States Geological Survey radiocarbon dates V. *Amer. Jour. Sci., Radiocarbon Suppl.*, 2: 129–85.

RUBÍN DE LA BORBOLLA, D. F.
1948 Arqueología tarasca. *In* El Occidente de Mexico, pp. 29–33.

RUPPERT, K., J. E. S. THOMPSON, AND T. PROSKOURIAKOFF
1955 Bonampak, Chiapas, Mexico. *Carnegie Inst. Wash.*, Pub. 602.

RYAN, R. M.
1963 The biotic provinces of Central America as indicated by mammalian distribution. *Acta Zool. Mex.*, 6: 1–55.

SÁENZ, M. A.
1940 Bosquejo geo-edafalógico de Costa Rica y el Instituto Interamericano de Ciencias Agrícolas. *Inst. Defensa del Café de Costa Rica*, 17: 141–48.

SÁNCHEZ, J.
1897 Importancia de la historia natural en el estudio de la historia antigua y la arqueología americanas. *Actas 11th Cong. Int. Amer.*, pp. 386–96.

SÁNCHEZ, P. C.
1935 Importancia geográfica del "Eje volcánico," cordillera que atraviesa la República Mexicana. *Panamer. Inst. Geog. e Hist.*, Pub. 11.

1937 Centro America, dónde principia, dónde termina. Regiones geológicas, unidades geográficas. Su vida y desarrollo, según las enseñanzas de la geografía moderna. Sus volcanes y sismos en relación con las anomalías de la gravedad. *Inst. Panamer. Geog. e Hist.*, Pub. 25.

SANDERS, E. M.
1921 The natural regions of Mexico. *Geog. Rev.*, 11: 212–26.

SANDERS, W. T.
1956 The central Mexican symbiotic region: a study in prehistoric settlement patterns. *In* Willey, 1956, pp. 115–27.

SAPPER, K.
1894 Grundzüge der physikalischen Geographie von Guatemala. *Petermanns Mitt.*, Ergänzungsheft 113.

1896 Sobre la geografía física y la geología de la península de Yucatan. *Inst. Geol. de Mex.*, Bol. 3.

1899 Über Gebirgsbau und Boden des nördlichen Mittelamerika. *Petermanns Mitt.*, Ergänzungsheft 127.

1901 Die Alta Verapaz (Guatemala), eine landeskundliche Skizze mit 5 Karten. *Mitt. der Geographischen Gesellschaft in Hamburg*, 17: 78–224.

1902a Beiträge zur physichen Geographie von Honduras. *Zeit. der Gesellschaft für Erdkunde zu Berlin*, 1902: 33–56, 143–64, 231–41.

1902b Die geographische Bedeutung der mittelamerikanischen Vulkane. *Zeit. der Gesellschaft für Erdkunde zu Berlin*, 1902: 512–36.

1903 Der Ausbruch des Vulkans Santa Maria in Guatemala (Oktober, 1902). *Centralblatt für Mineralogie, Geol. und Palaeontol.*, 1903: 33–44, 65–70.

1905 Über Gebirgsbau und Boden des südlichen Mittelamerika. *Petermanns Mitt.*, Ergänzungsheft 151.

1913 Die Mittelamerikanische Vulkane. *Petermanns Mitt.*, Ergänzungsheft 178.

1926 Die vulkanische Tätigkeit in Mittelamerika im 20 Jahrhundert. *Zeit. für Vulkanologie*, 9: 156–203, 231–70.

1932 Klimakunde von Mittelamerika. *In* Koeppen and Geiger, 1932, vol. 2, pt. 2.

—— AND W. STAUB
1937 Handbuch der regionalen Geologie. *Mittelamerika*, vol. 8, no. 29.

SARKISYAN, A. S.
1960 On the determination of the steady wind currents in a baroclinic layer. *In* A collection of articles on dynamic meteorology. *Soviet research in geophysics in English translation*, 1: 58–72. Tr. from Sbornik statei po dinamicheskoi meteorologii, Trudy Geophys. Inst., Akad, Nauk, USSR, no. 37 (164), published in 1956.

SAUER, C. O.
1925 The morphology of landscape. *Univ. Calif. Pub. Geog.*, 2: 19–24.

1934 The distribution of aboriginal tribes and languages in northwestern Mexico. *Ibero-Amer.*, no. 5.

1941 The personality of Mexico. *Geog. Rev.*, 31: 353–64.

1950 Cultivated plants of South and Central America. *In* Handbook of South American Indians, 6: 487–543. *Smithsonian Inst., Bur. Amer. Ethnol.*, Bull. 143.

1952 Agricultural origins and dispersals. New York.

1959 Age and area of American cultivated plants. *Actas 33d Int. Cong. Amer.*, 1: 215–29.

SAYRE, A. N., AND G. C. TAYLOR, JR.
1951 Ground-water resources of the Republic of El Salvador, Central America. *U.S. Geol. Survey, Water-Supply Paper 1079-D.*

SCHAEFER, M. B., Y. M. BISHOP, AND G. V. HOWARD
1958 Some aspects of upwelling in the Gulf of Panama. *Bull. Inter-Amer. Tropical Tuna Comm.*, 3: 77–132.

SCHMIDT, K. P.
1943 Corollary and commentary for "Climate and Evolution." *Amer. Midl. Naturalist*, 30: 241–53.

1954 Faunal realms, regions and provinces. *Quar. Rev. Biol.*, 29: 322–31.

SCHMITHÜSEN, J.
1959 Allgemeine Vegetationsgeographie. Berlin.

SCHOLES, F. V., AND R. L. ROYS
1948 The Maya Chontal Indians of Acalan-Tixchel. *Carnegie Inst. Wash.*, Pub. 560.

SCHOTT, A.
1866 Die Küstenbildung des nördlichen

Yukatan. *Petermanns Mitt.*, 12: 127–30.

SCHOTT, G.
1935 Geographie des Indischen und Stillen Ozeans. Hamburg.

SCHUCHERT, C.
1929 The geological history of the Antillean region. *Bull. Geol. Soc. Amer.*, 40: 337–60.
1935 Historical geology of the Antillean-Caribbean region. New York.

SCLATER, P. L.
1858 On the general geographical distribution of the members of the class Aves. *Jour. Proc. Linn. Soc.* (Zoology), 2: 130–45.

SCRIPPS INST. OCEANOGRAPHY
1957 Oceanic observations of the Pacific, 1949. Univ. California Press.
1960a *Idem*, 1950.
1960b *Idem*, 1955.
1963a *Idem*, 1951.
1963b *Idem*, 1956.
n.d. *Idem*, 1952–54, 1957–59. MS.

SEARS, P. B.
1952 Palynology in southern North America. Pt. 1: Archaeological horizons in the basin of Mexico. *Bull. Geol. Soc. Amer.*, 63: 241–54.
1955 [with others] Palynology in southern North America. *Bull. Geol. Soc. Amer.*, 66: 471–530.

—— AND K. H. CLISBY
1955 Palynology in southern North America. Pt. 4: Pleistocene climate in Mexico. *Bull. Geol. Soc. Amer.*, 66: 521–30.

SELLARDS, E. H.
1941 Stone images from Henderson County, Texas. *Amer. Antiquity*, 7: 29–38.
1952 Early man in America: a study in prehistory. Univ. Texas Press.

SERVICIO METEOROLÓGICO MEXICANO
1945 Atlas climatológico de Mexico. Mexico.

SHARP, A. J.
1946 Informe preliminar sobre algunos estudios fitogeográficos efectuados en Mexico y Guatemala. *Rev. Soc. Mex. Hist. Nat.*, 7: 35–40.

SHELFORD, V. E., ed.
1926 Naturalist's guide to the Americas. Baltimore.

SHEPARD, A. O.
1948 Plumbate, a Mesoamerican trade ware. *Carnegie Inst. Wash.*, Pub. 573.

SHEPARD, F. P.
1950 1940 *E. W. Scripps* cruise to the Gulf of California. Pt. 3: Submarine topography of the Gulf of California. *Mem. Geol. Soc. Amer.*, 43: 1–32.

SHOOK, E. M.
1951 The present status of research on the pre-classic horizons in Guatemala. *In* Tax, 1951, pp. 93–100.

—— AND A. V. KIDDER
1952 Mound E-III-3, Kaminaljuyu, Guatemala. *Carnegie Inst. Wash.*, Pub. 596, Contrib. 53.

—— AND T. PROSKOURIAKOFF
1956 Settlement patterns in Mesoamerica and the sequence in the Guatemalan highlands. *In* Willey, 1956, pp. 93–100.

SHREVE, F.
1934 Vegetation of the northwestern coast of Mexico. *Bull. Torrey Bot. Club*, 61: 373–80.
1939–40 Observations on the vegetation of Chihuahua. *Madroño*, 5: 1–13.
1951 Vegetation of the Sonoran desert. *Carnegie Inst. Wash.*, Pub. 591.

SHUMWAY, G., C. L. HUBBS, AND J. R. MORIARTY
1961 Scripps Estates site, San Diego, Calif.: a La Jolla site dated 5460–7370 years before the present. *Ann. New York Acad. Sci.*, 93: 37–131.

SIMMONS, C. S., J. M. TÁRANO, AND J. H. PINTO
1959 Clasificación de reconocimiento de los suelos de la República de Guatemala. Inst. Agropecuario Nac., Servicio Coop. Inter-Amer. de. Agricultura, Ministerio de Agricultura.

SIMPSON, G. G.
1943 Turtles and the origin of the fauna of Latin America. *Amer. Jour. Sci.*, 241: 413–29.

SIMPSON, L. B.
1952 Exploitation of land in central Mexico in the sixteenth century. *Ibero-Amer.*, no. 36.

SINCLAIR, W. J.
1904 The exploration of the Potter Creek cave. *Univ. Calif. Pub. Amer. Archaeol. and Ethnol.*, vol. 2, no. 1.

SKUTCH, A. F.
1950 Problems in milpa agriculture. *Turrialba*, 1: 4–6.

SMITH, A. L.
1955 Archaeological reconnaissance in cen-

527

tral Guatemala. *Carnegie Inst. Wash.*, Pub. 608.

—— AND A. V. KIDDER
1951 Excavations at Nebaj, Guatemala. *Carnegie Inst. Wash.*, Pub. 594.

SMITH, C. E.
1950 Prehistoric plant remains from Bat Cave. *Bot. Mus. Leafl., Harvard Univ.*, 14: 157–80.

—— AND R. S. MacNEISH
1964 Antiquity of American polyploid cotton. *Science,* 143: 675–76.

SMITH, H. M.
1939 The Mexican and Central American lizards of the genus *Sceloporus. Field Mus. Nat. Hist., Zool. Ser.*, no. 26.
1949 Herpetogeny in Mexico and Guatemala. *Ann. Assoc. Amer. Geog.*, 39: 219–38.

—— AND E. H. TAYLOR
1945 An annotated checklist and key to the snakes of Mexico. *Smithsonian Inst., U.S. Nat. Mus.*, Bull. 187.
1948 An annotated checklist and key to the amphibia of Mexico. *Smithsonian Inst., U.S. Nat. Mus.*, Bull. 194.
1950 An annotated checklist and key to the reptiles of Mexico exclusive of the snakes. *Smithsonian Inst., U.S. Nat. Mus.,* Bull. 199.

SMITH, R. E.
1940 Ceramics of the Peten. *In* Hay et al., 1940, pp. 242–49.
1955 Ceramic sequence at Uaxactun, Guatemala. 2 vols. *Tulane Univ., Middle Amer. Research Inst.*, Pub. 20.

SOIL SURVEY STAFF
1960 Soil classification: a comprehensive system (prepared by) soil survey staff. 7th approximation. U.S. Soil Conservation Service.

SOKOLOFF, V. P., AND J. L. LORENZO
1953 Modern and ancient soils at some archaeological sites in the valley of Mexico. *Amer. Antiquity,* 19: 50–55.

SORENSON, J. L.
1955 A chronological ordering of the Mesoamerican pre-classic. *Tulane Univ., Middle Amer. Research Rec.*, vol. 2, no. 3.

SPINDEN, E. S.
1933 The place of Tajin in Totonac archaeology. *Amer. Anthropol.*, 35: 271–87.

SPINDEN, H. J.
1917 The origin and distribution of agri-

culture in America. *Proc. 19th Int. Cong. Amer.*, pp. 269–76.

SPRATLING, W.
1960 More human than divine. Univ. Nac. Autónoma de Mex.

SPRINGER, V. G.
1958 Systematics and zoogeography of the clinid fishes of the subtribe Labrisomini Hubbs. *Pub. Inst. Marine Sci.*, 5: 417–92.

STANDLEY, P. C.
1920–26 Trees and shrubs of Mexico. *Contrib. U.S. Nat. Herbarium*, vol. 23.
1926 The Republic of El Salvador. *In* Shelford, 1926, pp. 602–04.
1928 Flora of the Panama Canal Zone. *Contrib. U.S. Nat. Herbarium*, vol. 27.
1936 The forests and flora of British Honduras. *Field Mus. Nat. Hist., Bot. Ser.*, vol. 12.
1937 Flora of Costa Rica. *Field Mus. Nat. Hist., Bot. Ser.*, vol. 18.

—— AND J. A. STEYERMARK
1945 The vegetation of Guatemala, a brief review. *In* Verdoorn, 1945, pp. 275–78.
1946–62 Flora of Guatemala. *Chicago Natural Hist. Mus., Fieldiana: Botany*, vol. 24, pts. 1–7.

STARR, F.
1900 Notes upon the ethnography of southern Mexico. *Proc. Davenport Acad. Sci.*, 8: 1–98.

STAUB, W.
1920 Neue Funde und Ausgrabungen in der Huaxteca (Ost-Mexiko). Beiträge zum Jahresbericht über die Ethnographische Sammlung. Bern.

—— AND C. LAGER
1922 Über eine erloschene Vulkanische Tätigkeit in der Golfregion des Nordöstlichen Mexiko. *Zeit. für Vulkanologie,* 5: 103–13.

STEGGERDA, M.
1941 Maya Indians of Yucatan. *Carnegie Inst. Wash.*, Pub. 531.

STEINBECK, J., AND E. F. RICKETTS
1941 The sea of Cortez: a leisurely journal of travel and research. New York.

STERN, T.
1948 The rubber-ball game of the Americas. *Amer. Ethnol. Soc.*, Monogr. 17.

STEWARD, J. H.
1936 The economic and social basis of

primitive bands. *In* Essays in Anthropology, pp. 331–50. Presented to A. L. Kroeber. Univ. California Press.

STEYERMARK, J. A.
1950 Flora of Guatemala. *Ecology*, 31: 368–72.

STILLE, H.
1955 Recent deformation of the earth's crust in the light of those of earlier epochs. *In* Crust of the Earth, pp. 171–92. *Geol. Soc. Amer.*, Special Paper 62.

STIRLING, M. W.
1940 An initial series from Tres Zapotes, Vera Cruz, Mexico. *Nat. Geo. Soc., Contrib. Tech. Papers, Mex. Archaeol. Ser.*, vol. 1, no. 1.

STRONG, W. D.
1948 The archaeology of Honduras. *In* Handbook of South American Indians, 4: 71–120. *Smithsonian Inst., Bur. Amer. Ethnol.*, Bull. 143.

——, A. KIDDER II, AND A. J. D. PAUL, JR.
1938 Preliminary report on the Smithsonian Institution Harvard University archaeological expedition to northwestern Honduras. *Smithsonian Inst., Misc. Coll.*, vol. 97, no. 1.

STUART, L. C.
1943 Taxonomic and geographic comments on Guatemalan salamanders of the genus *Oedipus*. *Univ. Mich., Mus. Zool.*, Misc. Pub. 56.
1954a A description of a subhumid corridor across northern Central America, with comments on its herpetofaunal indicators. *Contrib. Lab. Vertebrate Biol., Univ. Michigan*, no. 65.
1954b Herpetofauna of the southeastern highlands of Guatemala. *Contrib. Lab. Vertebrate Biol., Univ. Michigan*, no. 68.
1956 El ambiente del hombre en Guatemala. *Seminario Integración Social en Guatemala*, Pub. 3, pp. 17–30.
1958 A study of the herpetofauna of the Uaxactun-Tikal area of northern El Peten, Guatemala. *Contrib. Lab. Vertebrate Biol., Univ. Michigan*, no. 75.
1963 A checklist of the herpetofauna of Guatemala. *Misc. Pub.* Mus. Zool., Univ. Michigan, 122.

STUDHALTER, R. A.
1936 *In* Studies of the Yaqui Indians of Sonora, Mexico. *Texas Tech. College Bull.*, vol. 12, no. 1.

STUIVER, M., E. S. DEEVEY, AND L. J. GRALENSKI
1960 Yale natural radiocarbon measurements V. *Amer. Jour. Sci., Radiocarbon Suppl.*, 2: 49–61.

SUHM, D. A., A. D. KRIEGER, AND E. B. JELKS
1954 An introductory handbook of Texas archaeology. *Bull. Texas Archaeol. Soc.*, vol. 25.

SVERDRUP, H. U.
1941 The Gulf of California: preliminary discussion of the cruise of the *E. W. Scripps* in February and March, 1939. *Proc. 6th Pacific Sci. Cong.*, 3: 161–66.
1943 Oceanography for meteorologists. New York.

——, M. W. JOHNSON, AND R. H. FLEMING
1942 The oceans: their physics, chemistry, and general biology. New York.

SWAUGER, J. L., AND W. J. MAYER-OAKES
1952 A fluted point from Costa Rica. *Amer. Antiquity*, 17: 264–65.

SYKES, G. G.
1937 The Colorado delta. *Carnegie Inst. Wash.*, Pub. 460.

TAMAYO, J. L.
1941 Morfología de la República Mexicana y división regional de la misma. *Rev. Geog.*, 1: 221–35.
1946 Datos para la hidrología de la República Mexicana. Mexico.
1949 Geografía general de Mexico. 2 vols. and atlas. Mexico.
1958 El aprovechamiento del agua y del suelo. Mexico.
1959a Geografía de America. 2d ed. Mexico.
1959b Mexico y Centro America. *Geog. Universal*, vol. 18. Barcelona.

TAX, S., ed.
1951 The civilizations of ancient America. Selected papers of the 29th Int. Cong. Amer.

TAYLOR, E. H.
1951 A brief review of the snakes of Costa Rica. *Univ. Kansas Sci. Bull.*, 34: 3–188.
1952a The salamanders and caecilians of Costa Rica. *Univ. Kansas Sci. Bull.*, 34: 695–791.
1952b The frogs and toads of Costa Rica. *Univ. Kansas Sci. Bull.*, 35: 577–942.
1956 A review of the lizards of Costa Rica. *Univ. Kansas Sci. Bull.*, 38: 3–322.

TAYLOR, W. W.
1956 Some implications of the carbon 14

dates from a cave in Coahuila, Mexico. *Bull. Texas Archaeol. Soc.*, 27: 215–34.

TERMER, F.

1927 Observaciones geográficas en los Altos Cuchumatanes. *An. Soc. Geog. e Hist. de Guatemala*, 4: 7–13.

1932 Geologie von Nordwest-Guatemala. *Zeit. Gesellschaft für Erdkunde zu Berlin*, pp. 241–48.

1933 Paisajes geográficos del norte de America Central. *Bol. Soc. Geog. Nac.*, 60: 19–34, 92–103.

1936 Zur Geographie der Republik Süd-Guatemala. *Mitt. Geog. Gesellschaft in Hamburg*, 44: 89–275.

1950 La densidad de población en los imperios Mayas como problema arqueológico y geográfico. *Bol. Soc. Mex. Geog. y Estad.*, 70: 211–39.

1954 Die Halbinsel Yucatan. *Petermanns Mitt.*, Ergänzungsheft 253.

TERMIER, H., AND G. TERMIER

1958 The geological drama. New York.

1960 Atlas de paléogéographie. Paris.

TERRY, R. A.

1956 A geological reconnaissance of Panama. *Calif. Acad. Sci., Occasional Papers*, no. 23.

THAYER, W. H.

1916 The physiography of Mexico. *Jour. Geol.*, 24: 61–94.

THOMPSON, J. E. S.

1929 Comunicaciones y comercio de los antiguos Mayas. *An. Soc. Geog. e Hist. de Guatemala*, 6: 40–44.

1935 Maya chronology: the correlation question. *Carnegie Inst. Wash.*, Pub. 456, Contrib. 14.

1939 Excavations at San Jose, British Honduras. *Carnegie Inst. Wash.*, Pub. 506.

1943 A trial survey of the southern Maya area. *Amer. Antiquity*, 9: 106–34.

1945 A survey of the northern Maya area. *Amer. Antiquity*, 11:2–24.

1948 An archaeological reconnaissance in the Cotzumalhuapa region, Escuintla, Guatemala. *Carnegie Inst. Wash.*, Pub. 574, Contrib. 44.

1949 Canoes and navigation of the Maya and their neighbors. *Jour. Royal Anthropol. Inst.*, 79: 69–78.

1954 The rise and fall of Maya civilization. Univ. Oklahoma Press.

1959 La civilización Maya. Mexico.

THOMPSON, M. L., AND A. K. MILLER

1944 The Permian of southernmost Mexico and its fusulinid fauna. *Jour. Paleontol.*, 18: 481–504.

THOMPSON, R. H.

1958 Modern Yucatecan Maya pottery making. *Soc. Amer. Archaeol.*, Memoir 15.

THORADE, H.

1909 Über die Kalifornische Meeresstromung. Oberflächentemperaturen und Strömungen an der Westküste Nordamerikas. *Ann. Hydrog. und Mar. Meteorol.*, 37: 17–34, 63–76.

THORPE, J. AND G. D. SMITH

1949 Higher categories of soil classification: order, suborder, and great soil groups. *Soil Sci.*, 67: 117–26.

THOULET, M. J.

1898 Oceanography. *Smithsonian Inst.*, ann. rept., pp. 407–25.

TOLSTOY, P.

1958 Surface survey of the northern valley of Mexico: the classic and post-classic periods. *Trans. Amer. Phil. Soc.*, n.s. vol. 48, pt. 5.

TORQUEMADA, J. DE

1723 Los veinte i un libros rituales i monarchia Indiana. 3 vols. Madrid.

TOWLE, M. A.

1952 The pre-Columbian occurrence of Lagenaria seeds in coastal Peru. *Bot. Mus. Leafl., Harvard Univ.*, 15: 171–84.

TOWNSEND, C. H.

1901 Dredging and other records of the U.S. Fish Commission steamer *Albatross. Rept. U.S. Comm. Fish and Fisheries* (1900), pp. 387–562.

TOZZER, A. M.

1921 Excavation of a site at Santiago Ahuitzotla, D.F., Mexico. *Smithsonian Inst., Bur. Amer. Ethnol.*, Bull. 74.

1941 Landa's Relación de las Cosas de Yucatan. A translation. *Papers Peabody Mus., Harvard Univ.*, vol. 18.

1957 Chichen Itza and its cenote of sacrifice: a comparative study of contemporaneous Maya and Toltec. *Mem. Peabody Mus., Harvard Univ.*, vols. 11 and 12.

TROLL, C.

1952 Das Pflanzenkleid der Tropen in seiner Abhängigkeit von Klima, Boden und Mensch. *Deutscher Geog. Frankfurt, 1951*, Tagungsber. und wiss. Abh., Remagen, pp. 35–56.

530

TUAN, YI-FU
1960   Coastal land forms of central Pan-
          ama. Rept. field work carried out
          under ONR Contract 222(11) NR
          388 067. Univ. Calif., Dept. Geog.
UNITED STATES BUREAU OF COMMERCIAL FISH-
ERIES, SAN DIEGO LABORATORY
1960   [Monthly] Sea-surface temperature
          charts, eastern Pacific Ocean. (Con-
          tinued in Calif. Fishery Market News
          Monthly Summary, pt. 2, Fishing In-
          formation.)
UNITED STATES COAST AND GEODETIC SURVEY
1915   Pacific coast tide tables for western
          North America, eastern Asia, and
          many island groups for the year
          1916. General Tide Tables.
1956   Surface water temperatures at tide
          stations: Pacific coast of North and
          South America and Pacific Ocean
          islands. Special Pub. 280. 5th ed.
1957   Density of sea water at tide stations:
          Pacific coast of North and South
          America and Pacific Ocean islands.
          Pub. 31–4. 5th ed.
UNITED STATES DEPARTMENT OF AGRICULTURE
1938   Soils and men. Yearbook.
UNITED STATES GEOLOGICAL SURVEY
1954   Compilation of records of surface
          waters of the United States through
          September 1950. *Water-Supply Pa-
          per 1313.*
1958   Surface water supply of the United
          States, 1956. *Water-Supply Paper
          1434, 1441, 1442.*
UNITED STATES HYDROGRAPHIC OFFICE
1947   Atlas of surface currents: northeast-
          ern Pacific Ocean. Pub. 570.
1951   Sailing directions: west coast of
          Mexico and Central America. Pub.
          84. 9th ed.
UNITED STATES WEATHER BUREAU
1930–52 Climatological data, West Indies
          and Caribbean service.
1947   Weather summary, West Indies.
          Hydrographic Office, Pub. 530.
1948   Weather summary, Central America.
          Hydrographic Office, Pub. 531.
1949   Weather summary, Mexico. *Hydro-
          graphic Office*, Pub. 532.
1955–60 Climatological data. National
          Summary, vols. 6–11.
1959   World weather records, 1941–50.
VAILLANT, G. C.
1930   Excavations at Zacatenco. *Amer.
          Mus. Nat. Hist., Anthropol. Papers,*
          vol. 32, pt. 1.
1935   Early cultures of the valley of Mex-

ico: results of the stratigraphical
project of the American Museum of
Natural History in the valley of Mexico, 1928–1933. *Amer. Mus. Nat.
Hist., Anthropol. Papers,* vol. 35, pt.
3.
1938   A correlation of archaeological and
          historical sequences in the valley of
          Mexico. *Amer. Anthropol.,* 40: 535–
          73.
1941   Aztecs of Mexico. New York.
VAN MARTENS, E.
1890–1901 Terrestrial and fluviates Mol-
          lusca. *In* Biologia Centrali-Ameri-
          cana, Zoology, vol. 9.
VAN ROSSEM, A. J.
1945   A distributional survey of the birds
          of Sonora, Mexico. *Louisiana State
          Univ., Mus. Zool., Occasional Papers,*
          no. 21.
VAVILOV, N. I.
1951   Phytogeographic basis of plant
          breeding. *Chronica Botanica,* 13:
          14–54.
VERDOORN, F., ed.
1945   Plants and plant sciences in Latin
          America. Chronica Botanica.
VERMEER, D. E.
1959   The cays of British Honduras. Rept.
          field work carried out under ONR
          Contract 222(11) NR 388 067.
          Univ. Calif., Dept. Geog.
VIVÓ, J. A.
1943   Los limites biogeográficos en Ameri-
          ca y la zona cultural mesoamérica.
          Rev. Geog., 3: 109–31.
1946   Mexico prehispánico: culturas, dei-
          dades, monumentos. Mexico.
1958a La conquista de nuestro suelo. Mex-
          ico.
1958b Geografía de Mexico. Mexico.
1959   Geografía humana de Mexico. Es-
          tudio de la integración territorial y
          nacional de Mexico. Mexico.
——— AND J. C. GÓMEZ
1946   Climatología de Mexico. Mexico.
WADELL, H. A.
1938   Physical-geological features of Peten,
          Guatemala. *In* Morley, 1938, 4:
          331–48.
WAGNER, H. R.
1930   Pearl fishing enterprises in the Gulf
          of California. *Hisp. Amer. Hist.
          Rev.,* 10: 188–203.
WAGNER, P. L.
1955   Parras: a case history in the deple-
          tion of natural resources. *Land-
          scape,* 5: 19–28.

531

1958   Nicoya: a cultural geography. *Univ. Calif. Pub. Geog.*, 12: 195–250.

WAIBEL, L.

1933   Die Sierra Madre de Chiapas. *Mitt. Geog. Gesellschaft in Hamburg*, 43: 12–162.

1946   La Sierra Madre de Chiapas. *Soc. Mex. Geog. y Estad.* Ser. Geogr., no. 2.

WAITZ, P.

1906   Les geysers d'Ixtlan. *10th Cong. Geol. Int.* Guide Géologique du Mexique, pt. 12. Mexico.

1910a   Excursión al Nevado de Toluca. *Bol. Soc. Geol. Mex.*, 6: 113–17.

1910b   El Nevado de Toluca, uno de los dos grandes volcanes de Mexico a que ascendió Humboldt. *Memoria de Humboldt*, pp. 59–62.

1914–15 Der gegenwärtige Stand der mexikanischen Vulkane und die letzte Eruption des Vulkans von Colima. *Zeit. für Vulkanologie*, 1: 247–74.

1943   Reseña geológica de la cuenca de Lerma. *Bol. Soc. Mex. Geog. y Estad.*, 58: 123–38.

WALFORD, L. A.

1958   Living resources of the sea. New York.

WALKER, B. W.

1960   The biogeography of Baja California and adjacent seas. Pt. 2: The distribution and affinities of the marine fish fauna of the Gulf of California. *Syst. Zool.*, 9: 123–33.

WALLACE, A. R.

1876   The geographical distribution of animals. 2 vols. New York.

WALLÉN, C. C.

1955   Some characteristics of precipitation in Mexico. *Geog. Annaler*, 37: 51–85.

1956   Fluctuations and variability in Mexican rainfall. *Amer. Assoc. Advanc. Sci.*, Pub. 43, pp. 141–55.

WAUCHOPE, R.

1948   Excavations at Zacualpa, Guatemala. *Tulane Univ., Middle Amer. Research Inst.*, Pub. 14.

1950   A tentative sequence of pre-classic ceramics in Middle America. *Tulane Univ., Middle Amer. Research Rec.*, vol. 1, no. 14.

1954   Implications of radiocarbon dates from Middle and South America. *Tulane Univ., Middle Amer. Research Rec.*, 2: 19–39.

WEBB, W. S., AND R. S. BABY

1957   The Adena people, no. 2. Ohio State Univ. Press.

WEBBER, B. N., AND J. OJEDA R.

1957   Investigaciones sobre lateritas fósiles en las regiones sureste de Oaxaca y sur de Chiapas. *Inst. Nac. Invest. Recursos Minerales de Mex.*, Bol. 37.

WEBER, H.

1959   Los páramos de Costa Rica y su concatenación fitogeográfica con los Andes suramericanos. *Inst. Geog. Nac.*, San Jose, Costa Rica.

WEDEL, W. R.

1943   Archaeological investigations in Platte and Clay counties, Missouri. *Smithsonian Inst., U.S. Nat. Mus.*, Bull. 183.

WEED, W. H.

1902   Notes on a section across the Sierra Madre Occidental of Chihuahua and Sinaloa, Mexico. *Trans. Amer. Inst. Min. Eng.*, 32: 444–58.

WEEKS, L. G.

1956   Paleogeografía de America del Sur. Lima.

WELLHAUSEN, E. J., L. M. ROBERTS, AND E. HERNANDEZ X. in collaboration with P. C. MANGELSDORF

1952   Races of maize in Mexico. Bussey Inst., Harvard Univ.

——, A. FUENTES O., AND E. HERNANDEZ X. in collaboration with P. C. MANGELSDORF

1957   Races of maize in Central America. *Nat. Acad. Sci., Nat. Research Council*, Pub. 511.

WERCKLÉ, C.

1909   La subregión fitogeográfica costarricense. San Jose, Costa Rica.

WEST, R. C.

1948   Cultural geography of the modern Tarascan area. *Smithsonian Inst., Inst. Social Anthropol.*, Pub. 7.

1961   Aboriginal sea navigation between Middle and South America. *Amer. Anthropol.*, 63: 133–35.

—— AND P. ARMILLAS

1950   Las chinampas de Mexico. *Cuad. Amer.*, 2: 165–82.

WEYL, R.

1955a   Geologischen Studien in der Cordillera de Talamanca von Costa Rica. *Neues Jahrbuch für Geol. und Palaeontol.*, Monatsheft, 6: 262–69.

1955b   Vestigios de una glaciación del Pleistoceno en la cordillera de Talamanca, Costa Rica, A. C. *Informe Trimes-*

tral (Julio a Setiembre) del Inst. Geog. de Costa Rica, pp. 9–32.

1955c Beiträge zur Geologie El Salvadors, VI–Die Laven der jungen Vulkane. *Neues Jahrbuch für Geol. und Palaeontol.*, Abh. 101: 12–38.

1956a Geologische Wanderungen durch Costa Rica. *Natur und Volk*, 86: 13–24, 93–102, 211–19, 380–90, 410–21.

1956b Eiszeitliche Gletscherspuren in Costa Rica (Mittelamerika). *Zeit. für Gletscherkunde und Glazialgeologie*, 3: 317–25.

1956c Costa Rica, die Schweiz Mittelamerikas. *Zeit. für Schulgeographie*, 8: 470–74.

1961 Die Geologie Mittelamerikas. Berlin.

WHITAKER, T. W., AND J. B. BIRD
1949 Identification and significance of the cucurbit materials from Huaca Prieta, Peru. *Amer. Mus. Novitates*, no. 1426.

—— AND G. F. CARTER
1954 Oceanic drift of gourds—experimental observations. *Amer. Jour. Botany*, 41: 697–700.

——, H. C. CUTLER, AND R. S. MACNEISH
1957 Cucurbit materials from three caves near Ocampo, Tamaulipas. *Amer. Antiquity*, vol. 22, no. 4.

WHITE, S. E.
1951 Geologic investigations of the late Pleistocene history of the volcano Popocatepetl, Mexico. Doctoral dissertation, Syracuse Univ.

1956 Probable substages of glaciation on Iztaccihuatl, Mexico. *Jour. Geol.*, 64: 289–95.

1960 Late Pleistocene glacial sequence for west side of Iztaccihuatl, Mexico. Abstract. *Bull. Geol. Soc. Amer.*, 71: 2001.

WIELAND, G.
1913 The Liassic flora of the Mixteca Alta: its composition, age and source. *Amer. Jour. Sci. and Arts*, 4th ser., 36: 251–81.

1914 La flora Liásica de la Mixteca Alta. *Inst. Geol. de Mex.*, Bol. 31.

WILLEY, G. R.
1956 [ed.] Prehistoric settlement patterns in the New World. *Viking Fund Pub. Anthropol.*, no. 23.

1958 Estimated correlations and dating of south-central American culture sequences. *Amer. Antiquity*, 23: 353–78.

1960a New World prehistory. *Science*, 131 (3393): 73–86.

1960b Historical patterns and evolution in native New World cultures. *In* Tax, Evolution after Darwin, 2: 111–41. Univ. Chicago Press.

1962 The early great styles and the rise of the pre-Columbian civilizations. *Amer. Anthropol.*, 64: 1–14.

—— AND P. PHILLIPS
1958 Method and theory in American archaeology. Univ. Chicago Press.

WILLIAMS, H.
1950 Volcanoes of the Paricutin region, Mexico. *U.S. Geol. Survey*, Bull. 965-B.

1952a Volcanic history of the Meseta Central, Costa Rica. *Univ. Calif. Pub. Geol. Sci.*, 29: 145–80.

1952b Geologic observations on the ancient human footprints near Managua, Nicaragua. *Carnegie Inst. Wash.*, Pub. 596, Contrib. 52.

1952c The great eruption of Cosigüina, Nicaragua, in 1835, with notes on the Nicaraguan volcanic chain. *Univ. Calif. Pub. Geol. Sci.*, 29: 21–46.

1960 Volcanic history of the Guatemalan highlands. *Univ. Calif. Pub. Geol. Sci.*, 38: 1–86.

—— AND H. MEYER-ABICH
1955 Volcanism in the southern part of El Salvador, with particular reference to the collapse basins of lakes Coatepeque and Ilopango. *Univ. Calif. Pub. Geol. Sci.*, 32: 1–64.

WILSON, W. B., AND A. COLLIER
1955 Preliminary notes on the culturing of *Gymnodinium breve* Davis. *Science*, 121 (3142): 394–95.

WITTICH, E. L. M. E.
1935 Bergfenster und Naturbrücken in Mexiko. *Mitt. über Höhlen u. Karstforschung*, 1935: 1–9.

1935–38 Höhlen und Karsterscheinung in Mexiko. *Mitt. über Höhlen u. Karstforschung*, 1935, 3: 81–87; 1936, 1: 1–16; 1937, 1: 16–30; 2–3: 74–82; 1938, 1–2: 42–44.

WOLF, E. R.
1959 Sons of the shaking earth. Univ. Chicago Press.

—— AND A. PALERM
1955 Investigation in the old Acolhua do-

main, Mexico. *SW. Jour. Anthropol.*, 11: 265–81.

WOODRING, W. P., AND T. F. THOMPSON
1949   Tertiary formations of Panama Canal Zone and adjoining parts of Panama. *Bull. Amer. Assoc. Petroleum Geol.*, 33: 223–47.

WOODSON, R. E., R. W. SCHERY, et al.
1943–62   Flora of Panama. *Ann. Missouri Bot. Garden*, vols. 30–33, 35–37, 45–49.

WOOLLARD, G. P., AND J. MONGES CALDERA
1956   Gravedad, geología regional y estructura cortical en Mexico. *An. Inst. Geofis.*, 2: 60–112.

WOOSTER, W. S.
1959   Oceanographic observations in the Panama Bight: *Askoy* Expedition, 1944. *Bull. Amer. Mus. Nat. Hist.*, 118: 113–52

—— AND T. CROMWELL
1958   An oceanographic description of the eastern tropical Pacific. *Bull. Scripps Inst. Oceanogr.*, 7: 169–282.

—— AND F. JENNINGS
1955   Exploratory oceanographic observations in the eastern tropical Pacific, January to March, 1953. *Calif. Fish and Game*, 41: 79–90.

WORMINGTON, H. M.
1957   Ancient man in North America. 4th ed., rev. *Denver Mus. Nat. Hist., Popular Ser.*, no. 4.
1962   A survey of early American prehistory. *Amer. Scientist*, 50: 230–42.

YOSHIDA, K., AND H. L. MAO
1957   A theory of upwelling of large horizontal extent. *Jour. Marine Research*, 16: 40–54.

YUNCKER, T. G.
1945   The vegetation of Honduras, a brief review. *In* Verdoorn, 1945, pp. 55–56.

ZOPPIS DE SENA, R.
1957   El volcán Masaya de Nicaragua. *Bol. Servicio Geol. Nac. de Nicaragua*, 1: 45–64.

INDEX

A. and M. College of Texas: research in Gulf of Mexico by, 126
abalone: 150–151, 168
Abasolo complex: of northern Tamaulipas, 416
Abasolo points: 392, 416
Abeillia: 343
Abejas phase: plants of, 444
Abelardo Rodríguez Luján dam: on Sonora River, 103
Abies, distribution of: *A. guatemalensis*, 239, 374; *A. religiosa*, 241, 242, 372
Acacia: distribution of, 228, 242, 246–250 *passim*, 254, 255, 257, 367–370 *passim*, 372–374 *passim*, 377, 378, 381; *A. farnesiana*, 252; *A. cymbispena* and *A. unijuga*, 253; *A. macracantha*, 253, 254; *A. vernicosa*, 256
Acaena: 235, 236
acahual: 231
Acanthaceae: distribution of, 227, 229, 235. SEE ALSO *Bravaisia, Thunbergia*
Acanthothamnus: 253
Acaponeta River: drainage of, 103
Accipitridae: 322
Achillea: 240
Achras: distribution of, 226, 228, 247
Achras sapodilla: 247
Achras sapota: as source of chicle, 226, 231; distribution of, 226, 231, 376
Acmaea: of Baja California Pacific coast, 168; in Baja California shell middens, 178
Acnistus: 234
Acrocomia: 247, 248
Acrostichum: 262
Actinocheita: 252
Actopan River: drainage of, 92
Acuitze Catapeme: as possible rain god of Tarascans, 205
Acultzingo: human skeleton with mammoth at, 408
Adelphicos: 343
Aechmea: 229
Aeyerado Cave: maize at, 432, 438
Agate Basin points: association of, with Plainview and Archaic types, 392; in Mexico, 392, 401–402
Agave: distribution of, 241, 253, 254, 255, 367, 381; *A. lechuguilla*, 256, 257, 367; in Infiernillo phase, 430
Ageratum: 247
Agkistrodon: 330
Agonandra: 253
agoutis: distribution of, 319, 382
agriculture: of Cahita, 103, 209, 369; *chinampa* system of, 111, 267, 276, 296, 448; northward diffusion of, in Mexico, 114, 209–210; modern, in Comarca Lagunera, 115; milpa, in Meso-

america, 231, 244, 245, 374, 447; theories concerning origin of, 428–429; terracing in, 448; canal irrigation in, 448, 472; fallowing system in, 447; tools for, 447
Agriocharis ocellata: 322, 343
aguacate. SEE *Persea*
aguadas: in Yucatan, 99–100, 377
Aguan River: drainage of, 88, 96
Aguilar: Olmec art style at, 484
Ahuautlea mexicana: as Aztec food, 111
air masses: over eastern Pacific, Gulf of Mexico, and Caribbean, 189, 193
air movements: over Middle America, complexity of, 197–198
Ajuereado complex: age and artifacts of, 392
Ajuereado phase: early hunting culture of, 413
akalché: in Peten and Yucatan Peninsula, 101
Alaminos, Anton de: Caribbean currents known by, 126
Alamo River: waterflow of, 89
Alash Higuito River: drainage of, 96
Alaudidae: 325
albatrosses: 321
Albizzia: distribution of, 246, 247, 248, 377, 381
Alcedinidae: 323
Alchemilla: distribution of, 235, 236, 240
Alchornea: 227
alder. SEE *Alnus*
Alfaroa: 234
algal scum: as Aztec food, 111
alluvial fan formation: in Mexican Pliocene, 19
Alluvial soils: distribution of, 279 (fig. 2), 284 (fig. 6), 289–292, 294, 296, 298, 300, 305, 306, 307, definition of, 288, 289; Indian use of, 289
alluvial terraces: in Mexican Quaternary, 28
Almagre phase: components of, 416; time span of, 416; wattle and daub in, 423–424
Almagre points: in Mexico, 392, 416, 417
Alnus: *A. acuminata*, 235; distribution of, 236, 241, 256; pollen of, at El Peñon de los Baños, 386–387
Alouatta: 317
Alpine Meadow soils: origin of, 287; use of, by Indians, 287; distribution of, 291–292, 294, 296
Alseseca: Valsequillo gravels at, 406
altars: in Mesoamerica, 465, 492
Alta Vista de Chalchihuites: Mesoamerican frontier site of, 476. SEE ALSO Chalchihuites culture
Altiplanicie Meridional: definition of, 102, 104
Altiplanicie Septentrional: arid basins in, 110, 114
Alvaradoa: 249
Alvaro Obregón dam: on Yaqui River, 104
Amacuzac River: drainage of, 106
Amanalco de Becerra: human footprints in rock at, 387

Atlantic-Pacific connection: across Isthmus of Te-
huantepec, 15; across Panama and Colombia, 18
Atlapates: 325
atlatls: in Mesoamerica, 322, 455
atmospheric pressure: seasonal distribution of, in
Mexico and Central America, 199–200
Atoyac River: drainage of, 64 (fig. 15), 107
Atoyac Poblano River: drainage of, 106
Atriplex: 254
Attalea: 247
Aurora phase: radiocarbon dates for, 485, 486, 494
Austral Zone: 350, 352
Austrocentral Province: 351
Austro-occidental Province: 351
Avenidas de Pechuca River: drainage of, 91
Avicennia: 262
avocado: in El Riego phase, 444. SEE ALSO *Persea*
axes, stone: uses of, in Mesoamerica, 448
axolotl: 331
Ayala phase: radiocarbon date for, 497
Azcapotzalco: as residential and trading center,
471; political position of, 472
azonal soils: types and distribution of, 288
Aztec-Maya trade route: across Yucatan Peninsula,
95
Aztecs: trade of, 95, 97, 376; gold tribute received
by, 106; capital city of, 111; foods of, 111;
chinampas of, 448; empire of, 459, 475, 487;
human sacrifice by, 460–461; art style of, 462;
artifacts of, value for cross-dating, 470, 487–488;
political position of, 473

Baccharis: 239, 253
badger: 319
bagres: 334
Baja California: geohistory of, 9, 13, 16, 56; shoreline features of, 56; deserts of, 56; batholith in,
56; Indians of, 56, 143, 177, 180, 182, 416;
springs and water resources of, 102, 369; radiocarbon dates from shell middens of, 144 (fig. 1),
145; Punta Minitas site in, 144 (fig. 1), 145;
shell middens of, 144 (fig. 1), 145, 150–151,
171–173, 177–178, 180, 369; plankton blooms
along coast of, 150; marine fishes of, 150, 180;
shellfish of, 150–151, 168, 172, 178; salinity
variation along coast of, 151; heat balance
studies along coast of, 151, 153; crustaceans of,
168, 180; flora of, 169, 177, 221, 369, 381;
climate of, 171–173, 189, 203, 208, 381; biotic
changes in, 172; Laguna Seca Chapala site,
173, 393; fishing methods in, 180; sea mammals
of, 182; use of beach cobbles and asphaltum in,
182; land mammals of, 369; characteristics of,
as a natural region, 369–370; Clovis point in,
388, 389 (fig. 3)
Balaenoptera physalus: 182
Balaenopteridae: 320
Balankanche Cave: radiocarbon dates for, 495
Balboneura: 337
ball game: in Mesoamerica, 460 (fig. 22), 461,
473–474
balsa: 232. SEE ALSO *Ochroma*
Balsas Basin: view of, 61 (fig. 13); archaeological

sites in, 381; fauna of, 381; human interference
in vegetation of, 381
Balsas Province: 360
Balsas River: drainage of, and seasonal waterflow
regime of, 61 (fig. 13), 106
Baluarte River: drainage of, 103
balustrades: in Mesoamerican architecture, 450
bamboo: 232, 234, 236. SEE ALSO *Chusquea*
banana: 247
barbecho. SEE fallowing
barberry. SEE *Berberis*
barbets: 324
bari. SEE *Calophyllum*
bark beaters: in Mesoamerica, 450
barrancas. SEE canyons
barrier beaches: of Pacific coastal lowlands, 380
barrier reef: on Yucatan coast, 73
Barrilaco Caliche: stratigraphic position of, 394
Bartlett Trough. SEE Cayman Trench
Basiliscus: 328, 343
basilisk: 328
basins: in Mexico and Central America, 44, 48,
50, 63, 77, 79, 92, 110, 114
basketry, coiled: in Coxcotlan and El Riego phases,
423
Bassaricyon: 319
Bassariscus: 319
basses, black: 334
basswood: 373
basureros: 329
Bat Cave: *Chapalote* maize in, 438
Bat Cave maize. SEE *Chapalote* maize
batholiths: in Colombia, 7, 9; in Baja California,
56; in Southern Mexican Highlands, 63; in
Highlands of Chiapas, 67; in Volcanic Bridge
of Costa Rica and Panama, 79; in Costa Rica,
374
Bathysiredon: 331, 339
bats: distribution of, 317; vampire, as carriers of
rabies, 317
Bauhinia: 249, 253
beach cobbles: use of, in Baja California, 182
beach ridges: of Pacific coastal lowlands, 380
beans, domestication of, 429; in Ocampo phase,
430, 442; in Palmillas phase, 431; in Coxcatlan
and Purron phases, 444
beans, lima: wild and domesticated forms of, 437
bears: 319
Beaucarnea pliabilis: 250
beaver: 318
Becerra Formation: age of, 30, 394. SEE ALSO
Upper Becerra Formation, Lower Becerra
Formation
bee: wild forms of, 337; domestication of, in
Mesoamerica, 448
beech: 373
Befaria: 238
begonia: 235, 246
Belize River: drainage and seasonal regime of, 95
Belonesox: 343
Benassini, A. and García Quintero, A.: on hydrologic resources of Mexico, 85

Cecropia: genera of, 228, 230, 246, 247, 248; *C. obtusifolia,* 231

cedar: distribution of, 235, 247, 376, 378. SEE ALSO *Cedrela*

cedar waxwing: 325

Cedrela: genera of, 229, 233, 238, 246, 248, 376, 378; *C. mexicana,* 231

Ceiba: genera of, 229, 242, 248, 249, 252, 253; *C. pentandra,* 227, 376, 378

Celtis: genera of, 226, 228, 252, 254, 255; *C. monoica,* 237

celts, stone: in Mesoamerica, 448; in Costa Rica, 450 (fig. 5)

Cempoala: Totonac capital at, 474

Cenote of Sacrifice: Chichen Itza, objects retrieved from, 455

cenotes: origin of, 99; fauna of, 99; mentioned, 72, 377

Cenozoic: of Mexico, 3–4, 9, 14, 15, 18, 19, 22, 23, 28–30 *passim,* 42, 174, 410, 415; of Central America, 3–4, 9, 14, 16, 17, 23, 24, 29, 70, 74–76, 79, 174. SEE ALSO Tertiary, Quaternary, Paleocene, Eocene, Oligocene, Miocene, Pliocene, Pleistocene, Recent

Central America: Cenozoic in, 3–4, 9, 17, 74–76, 174; seismic activity in, 3–4; volcanic activity in, 3, 9, 17, 22, 23, 74–76, 113, 373; geological studies in, 5, 23, 33–34; Paleozoic in, 7–10; tectonic activity in, 7–8; Archeozoic in, 7, 9; Mesozoic in, 10–13 *passim,* 79; Tertiary in, 14 (fig. 7), 16 (fig. 8), 17, 70, 74, 76, 79; Quaternary in, 23, 24, 29, 74–76; evidence of man under volcanic deposits of, 76; limnological studies in, 85; hydrologic studies in, 85; wind regimes of, 160, 163, 165; Pacific coastal waters of, 163–167; climate of, 160, 163, 165, 173, 187–189, 193, 195–201, 202 (figs. 7–12), 203, 210–213, 373–374; isthmian development in, 174; rain gods and rain cults of, 203–205; soils and soil studies in, 265–266, 301 (fig. 7), 305, 308 (fig. 8); South American cultures in, 366; aboriginal population density in, 373; Clovis point in, 388, 389 (fig. 3); Mixteca-Puebla cultures in, 470

Central American Trench: relationship of, to San Andreas fault, 22

Central Mexico: as a cultural area, 469 (fig. 31), 470–474, 484, 485, 490 (fig. 40)

Central Veracruz: as a cultural area, 473; culture periods of, 473–474; Olmec style in, 474, 484; Huasteca influenced by, 474

Centrarchidae: distribution of, 334, 339, 359

Centrolenellidae: 332

Centropogon: 238, 240

Centropomidae: 335

Centruroides suffusus: 337

Cephaelis: 229, 238

Cephalocereus: genera of, 252, 253; *C. mezcalensis,* 252

ceramics: in Mesoamerica, 451–452, 455, 463, 484. SEE ALSO pottery wares

Cerastium: 242

Cerathyla: 332

Cercidium: distribution of, 252, 253, 254, 257, 369

Cercocarpus: 242

ceremonial centers: in Mesoamerica, 371, 457 (fig. 19), 458, 463, 465, 467 (fig. 26), 469, 471, 472–474, 476, 489–492, 493

Cereus: 246

Cerro de las Mesas: Teotihuacan influence at, 469, 485; Tohil Plumbate at, 487

Cerro de las Palmas: artifact in Pleistocene deposit at, 385

Cerro del Fortin: evaluation of artifacts found at, 406

Cerro Guamas: Clovis point at, 389 (fig. 3)

Cerro Zapote: radiocarbon date for, 496

Certhiidae: 324–325, 342

Cervidae: 320, 341

Cespedesia macrophylla: 235

Cestrum: 234

Cetacea: 320

Cetopidae: 345

Chac: association of, with Itzamna, 204; as Maya rain god, 204–205

chachalacas: distribution of, 320, 322, 343, 382

chac-mool: in Tarascan area, 476

Chaetoptelea: genera of, 226, 228, 234, 237; *C. mexicana,* 238

Chagas' disease. SEE tripanosomiasis

Chalchihuites culture: distribution of, 48; environmental basis of, 367; trade contacts of, 476; Mixteca-Puebla influences on, 476

Chalchiuhtlicue: association of, with Tlaloc, 204

Chalco culture: radiocarbon date for, 414; climate during period of, 415

Chama: polychrome pottery from, 453 (fig. 12)

Chamaedorea: distribution of, 226, 229, 234, 374

Chamaeidae: 324, 339

Chamelecon River: structural depression drained by, 88

Chametla: sequence at, 476

Changuinola River: delta of, 82

Chapalote maize: in Flacco and Mesa de Guaje phases, 431; in Bat and Swallow caves, 438

Chapultepec: springs of, 111

Characidae: distribution of, 333, 339, 341, 343, 345, 359, 360

Charadriidae: 322

Chejel River: drainage of, 93. SEE ALSO Rio Grande de Chiapas

Chelonia mydas: distribution of, 140, 181, 327

Cheloniidae: 327

Chelydridae: 326

Chenopodium: 247

Chepo River: drainage of, 109

Chernozem soils: distribution of, 281, 282, 291, 293, 295, 296, 297, 306, 309

cherry, wild. SEE *Prunus*

chert: uses of, in Mesoamerica, 448

Chestnut soils: distribution of, 277 (fig. 1), 281, 282, 291, 292, 293, 294, 296, 297, 306, 309

Chiapa de Corzo: radiocarbon dates from, 485, 495

Chiapa I phase: as example of Preclassic agricultural village, 489

Chiapas: Archeozoic in, 7; Paleozoic in, 9, 67;

Mesozoic in, 13, 67; Tertiary in, 67; springs in, 93; Tohil Plumbate in, 487

Chiapas-Guatemalan Highland Province: 357, 358

Chiapas-Guatemalan Los Altos Province: 358 n. 20

Chiapas, Valley of: vegetation in, 381

Chichen Itza: agricultural experiment at, 304; architecture at, 449 (fig. 4), 459 (fig. 21); murals at, 453 (fig. 10); objects from Cenote of Sacrifice at, 455; boats in murals at, 456; Toltecs at, 465, 487; Tohil Plumbate at, 487; radiocarbon dates from, 488, 496

Chichimecs: salt trade of, 50; in Rio Grande drainage, 89; linguistic affiliation of, 209; natural environment of, 294; post-Conquest history of, 294; at El Gran Tunal, 367

chicle: source of, 226, 231

Chicoalapan: obsidian dating at, 396, 415; hearths and burials at, 415

Chicoloapan Man: fluorine test of, 387, 396; evaluation of, 395, 396

chicosapote: 376

Chihuahua: volcanic activity in, 16; Casas Grandes culture of, 48; springs in, 115; Folsom point in, 388, 389 (fig. 3); Cochise artifacts in, 388; caves of, 416

Chihuahua culture: settlement pattern of, 292

Chihuahuan Province: 351, 354, 355

Chihuahua-Zacatecas Province: 351

Chilean-Peruvian Geosyncline: relationship of, to Cordilleran Geosyncline, 13

chili pepper: 430, 443. SEE ALSO *Capsicum*

Chilopsis: 255

Chimalacatlan Cave: evidence of early human occupation in, 405

Chimarrhis: 229

chinaberry. SEE *Cedrela, Guarea*

chinampas: in Mesoamerican agriculture, 111, 267, 276, 296, 448

Chinandegan Province: 357 n. 19

Chinantec: location of, 92

Chinobampo Arroyo: human skull and fossil animals in, 393

Chionactis: 339

Chione: 178

chipmunks: 318

Chiranthodendron pentadactylon: 238

Chironectes: 317

Chiroptera: 317

Chirostoma: 109, 335, 360

Chirripo River: drainage of, 98

Chivo Cave: large chopper from, 405

Chixoy River: drainage of, 93. SEE ALSO Usumacinta River

Chlorofora: distribution of, 229, 246, 253

Choco: location of, 109

Cholula: political position of, 473; polychrome pottery of, 487

Cholula-Mixtec polychrome pottery: at Coixtlahuaca and Monte Alban, 470

Chomelia: 246, 247

Chorotegan culture: distribution of, 77, 79, 80; as southern Mesoamerican extension, 380

Chorreras Arroyo: man and mammoth in association at, 393

chronological classifications: in Mesoamerica, 476–478, 480–483

Chrysemys: 326

Chrysophyllum: distribution of, 228, 229, 237, 246, 250

chuckwallas: 328

Chucunaque River: drainage of, 109

Chusquea: distribution of, 236, 237, 375

Ciboney Indians: boats used by, 128

Cichlasoma: distribution of, 97, 113, 114, 335; *C. managuense,* 97

Cichlidae: distribution of, 333, 335, 339, 341, 342, 359, 360

Ciconiidae: 321

Cienegas complex: of Coahuila, 416

Cinclidae: 324–325, 342

cinder cones: distribution of, 43 (fig. 6), 44, 77, 371, 373

cirio: 369

Cirsium: 240, 242

Cissampelos: 233

Citellus: 318, 339

Citharexylum: 233

cities. SEE urban communities

clams: in Baja California, 150–151, 172; Seri use of, 179

Claravis: 323

Clarion Fracture Zone: relationship of, to Neovolcanic Axis of Mexico, 20–21, 23, 34, 42; relationship of, to Middle American Trench, 25; possible connection of, with Cayman Trench, 38; age of, 407

classes, social: in Mesoamerica, 457

Classic period: in Maya area, 448 (fig. 2), 451 (fig. 7), 452 (fig. 9), 453 (figs. 11, 12), 454 (figs. 13, 15), 457 (fig. 19), 458 (fig. 20), 460 (fig. 22), 463, 464; in Southern Periphery, 465; in Oaxaca, 469; in Central Mexico, 469 (fig. 31), 470–472, 485, 490 (fig. 40); in Central Veracruz, 473–474; in the Huasteca, 474; in Western Mexico and Guerrero, 475; in Jalisco-Colima area, 475–476; in Zacatecas, Nayarit-Sinaloa area, and Durango, 476; synonyms for, 477 n. 22; subdivisions of, 478, 480–483; duration of, 478, 480–483; cross-dating in, 485–486; radiocarbon dates for, 486–487, 494–497

classifications: chronological, in Mesoamerica, 476–478

Claudius: 326, 343

Clematis: 233

Clemmys: 326

Clethra: distribution of, 236, 237, 238, 241

Cleyera: 238, 241

Clidemia: 233

climate: of Mexico, 31, 171, 187–189, 193–203 *passim,* 206, 208–213 *passim,* 270, 381, 415; of Central America, 173, 187–189, 193, 195–201, 202 (figs. 7–12), 203, 210–213, 373–374; controls of, 188–189; Koeppen classification of, 205–206; distribution of types of, 207 (fig. 14); during La Perra, Nogales, and Ocampo phases,

541

415; during Santa Marta Cave occupation and at time of Chalco culture, 415
Clipperton Fracture Zone: intersection of, with Middle American Trench, 25, 26, 38
Clipperton Island: origin of, 175
cloth: Maya trade in, 129
Clovis points: in Mexico and Central America, 388, 389 (fig. 3)
Clusia: 224, 237
Cnemidophorus: 329
Coahuila: *bolsóns* of, 49 (fig. 9); Clovis point from Amistad reservoir of, 388, 389 (fig. 3)
Coahuila complex: 416
Coahuiltec: culture and language of, 212
coati: 319, 382
Coatzacoalcos River: volume of, 87; navigability of, 88; drainage of, 92
Cobaea: 238
Coban Formation: 13
cobbles (beach): use of, in Baja California, 182
cochineal insect: 337
Coccoloba: distribution of, 226, 227, 237, 246, 247, 248; *C. roseiflora,* 235
Cochimi: language spoken by, 209
Cochise culture: evidence of, in northwestern Mexico, 388, 416, 417, 426
Cochlospermum: distribution of, 246, 248, 249, 252
Cocijo: as Zapotec rain god, 205
Coclé culture: of Panama, 379–380
coconut: 247
Coco River: drainage of, 88, 97
Cody knives: in Mexico, 399–400
Coe, M. D. and Krieger, A. D.: on Cumberland points in Middle America, 388, 410
Coerebidae: 325
Cointzio dam: on Rio Grande de Morelio, 111
Coixtlahuaca: Mixtec culture at, 470
Coldenia: 255
cold fronts, effects of, 193
Coleonyx: 327
Colinus: 322
colluvium: definition of, 289
Colombia: Ordovician in, 7, 9; batholith in, 7, 9; Tertiary Atlantic-Pacific connection across, 18
Colombia Basin: description of, 123
Colon-Darien Province: 356 n. 18
Colonia Formation: 13
colonnades: in Mesoamerica, 450, 459 (fig. 21)
Colorado River: drainage of, in Mexico, 102; effect of, on salinities of Golfo de California, 157–158; tidal bore in, 165
Colubridae: 329–330, 341
Colubrina: 249, 257
Columbigallina: 323
Columbus: as first oceanographer of the Caribbean, 126
columns: in Mesoamerican architecture, 450, 459 (fig. 21)
comal: use of, in Mesoamerican cooking, 448
Comalcalco: Maya site of, 94–95; stucco bas-relief at, 451 (fig. 8)
Comarca Lacustre. SEE Peten lake region

Comarca Lagunera: irrigation agriculture in, 115
Comecrudos: linguistic affiliation of, 370
Comisión Nacional de Irrigación: soil mapping in Mexico by, 266
Comitan rock shelter: investigations at, 415
Commission Scientifique du Mexique: 19th-century investigations of, 384–386
community settlement pattern: definition of, 458 n. 8
Comocladia: 249, 252
Compositae: distribution of, 227, 233, 235
Compsoneura: 229
conch shell: use of, in La Perra phase, 423
Conchas phase: radiocarbon dates for, 485, 495
Conchos: agriculture of, 89, 210
Conchos River (of Coahuila): as major tributary of Rio Grande, 89; settlement pattern along, 292
Conchos River (of Nuevo Leon-Tamaulipas): waterflow of, 90
Condalia: 254, 255
Conepatus: 319
Conestegia: 233, 238
Confite Morocho maize: possible separate domestication of, 442–443
congrejo: 337
Conocarpus: 262
Conophis: 343
Conopophagidae: 345
Conopsis: 339
Conservation Foundation: soil erosion survey by, 267
continental shelf: in Caribbean and Gulf of Mexico, 123 (fig. 1), 124, 137 (fig. 9)
Conzattia: 252
Cook, S. F.: on soil erosion in relation to population density, 267
cooking: methods of, in Mesoamerica, 448
coots: 322, 372
Copador phase: Maya polychrome influence in, 486
copal: 377, 378
Copan: preceramic culture at, 408; stela at, 451 (fig. 7); Acropolis at, 457 (fig. 19); ball court at, 460 (fig. 22); plumbate effigy jar from, 487 (fig. 39)
copper, in Mesoamerica: 448, 456
Coraciiformes: 323
coral reefs: elevation of, in Costa Rica and Nicaragua, 22; on eastern coasts of Costa Rica and Panama, 82; on Pacific coast, 175; comparisons of, 185
coral tree. SEE *Erythrina*
corbinas: in Baja California middens, 180
Cordia: distribution of, 228, 246, 248, 249, 254, 257, 370, 378
Cordilleran Geosyncline: relationships of, 9, 13; location of, 9, 10; disappearance of, 11, 16
Coriaria: 239
cormorants: 321
Cornus: 238, 241
Corozo oleifera: 262
corozo palm: 379
Corythophanes: 328

Jumanos: salt sources of, 114
Juncus: 236
Juniperus: genera of, 240, 256, 372; *J. Standleyii,* 240; *J. flaccida,* 241
Jurassic: geosynclines of, 11; in Guatemala, Honduras, Mexico, and Nicaragua, 12
Justicea: 228
jute: 337

Kaminaljuyu: strategic location of, 77; Thin Orange ware at, 453 (fig. 11); Preclassic period at, 463; radiocarbon dates for, 484–485; 494; Teotihuacan traits at, 485; urbanism at, 491
karst topography: 53, 55, 67–68 and 68 (fig. 17), 70, 72, 99, 116, 373
Karwinskia: distribution of, 248, 254, 257
Kekchi: agriculture of, 306
kelp: on Pacific coast of Baja California, 150, 168
Kent points: in El Riego Complex, 392
killifishes: distribution of, 101, 109, 113, 334, 359
kingfishers: 323
kinkajou: distribution of, 319, 339, 382
Kinney points: in El Riego Complex, 392
Kinosternidae: 326, 343
Kinosternon: 326, 327
Klinge, H.: soil surveys in El Salvador by, 266
Koeppen system of climate classification: 205–206
Krieger, A. D., and M. D. Coe: on Cumberland points in Middle America, 388, 410

La Angostura Reservoir: on Rio Bavispe, 103
La Antigua River: drainage of, 92
Lacanji River: drainage of, 93
Lacantun River: drainage of, 93
Lacertilia: 327
Lachesis: 330, 342
La Chuparrosa: fluted point at, 389 (fig. 3)
Ladenbergia: genus of, 234; *L. Brenesii,* 235
Laemanctus: 343
Laetia: 226, 228
Lafoensia: 248
Lagenaria: in Infiernillo and Mesa de Guaje phases, 430, 441, 443; transmission of, to New World, 441
Lagomorpha: 318
Laguna de Guzman: description of, 114
Laguna de las Palomas: salt deposits of, 115
Laguna del Carmen: salt formation in, 286
Laguna de los Patos: desiccation of, 114
Laguna de Mayran: decline of, 115–116
Laguna de Santa Maria: desiccation of, 114
Laguna de Tlahualilo: location of, 115
Laguna de Viesca: desiccation of, 115
Laguna Medina: site of, 416
Laguna phase: time span of, 431; maize in, 431, 439; manioc in, 441, 443
Laguna Seca Chapala: site of, 173, 393
Laguncularia: 262, 379
lahars: in Mesa Central, 45
Lake Amatitlan: archaeological sites near and fishes in, 113
Lake Apam: location of, 113

Lake Apoyo: *Cichlasoma* in, 114
Lake Arenal: as source of Rio Arenal, 98
Lake Asososco: *Cichlasoma* in, 114
Lake Atescatempa: location of, 113
Lake Atitlan: fauna of, 113
Lake Atocha: location of, 113
Lake Ayarza: location of, 113
Lake Azufrado: location of, 113
Lake Bacalar: origin of saline waters of, 100
Lake Catemaco: drainage from, 92
Lake Chalco: *chinampa* agriculture of, 111; drainage of, 286–287
Lake Chapala: geographic position of, 104; fish resources and geologic history of, 105
Lake Chichancanab: origin of, 100
Lake Coatepeque: description of, 113
Lake Cuitzeo: reduction in size of, 111; salt formation in, 286
Lake Cuscachapa: description of, 113–114
Lake Güija: location of, 113
Lake Huehuechoca: location of, 113
Lake Ilopango: description of, 114
Lake Ixpaco: 113. SEE ALSO Lake Azufrado
Lake Izabal: drainage of, 95
Lake Macanche: origin of, 100
Lake Magdalena: 109, 111
Lake Managua: outlet change of, 97; human and animal footprints in volcanic mud near, 408
Lake Masaya: *Cichlasoma* in, 114
Lake Nicaragua: history, drainage, and fishes of, 97
Lake Patzcuaro: as center of Tarascan culture, 111; use of atlatl on, 322 n. 2
Lake Peten Itza: fluctuating level of, 101
Lake Puerco: location of, 113
Lake Sayula: reduction in size of, 111
Lake Tecocomulco: location of, 113
Lake Tepancuapan: as example of karst lake, 101
Lake Texcoco: drainage of, 109; Aztec capital on, 111; salt formation in, 111, 286; use of boats on, 456
Lake Totolcingo: disappearance of, 113
Lake Xaltocan: saline waters of, 111
Lake Xochimilco: *chinampa* agriculture of, 111
Lake Xolotlan. SEE Lake Managua
Lake Yaxha: origin of, 100; fluctuating level of, 101
Lake Yojoa: drainage of, 96
Lake Yuriria: 16th-century artificial reservoir of, 105
Lake Zacapu: disappearance of, 111
Lake Zapotitan: disappearance of, 114
Lake Zirahuen: description of, 111; view of, 112 (fig. 6)
Lake Zocoalco: mammoth and artifact associated near, 405
Lake Zumpango: saline waters of, 111
La Laguna District. SEE Comarca Lagunera
lakes: Quaternary sequence of, in Valley of Mexico, 30–31, 371–372; basins of, in Mesa Central, 47; recent drainage of, in Mesa Central, 47; fault-depression origin of, in Yucatan, 100; decline and disappearance of, in Mexico, 107, 109,

Mauria: 234, 235

Maya: salt production and salt trade of, 73, 129, 132; effect of subsurface drainage on agriculture of, 85, 304; ceremonial centers of, 93–94, 100; sites of, on natural levees, 95; trading centers of, 96; cacao trade of, 96, 376; settlement patterns of, 99, 302, 305; water sources of, 99–101; environment of, 101, 213, 298; occupation of Flores Island by, 101; foods of, 101, 138–139, 141; improbability of voyages to Cuba by, 127–128; boats used by, 128–129; maritime trade of, 128–129; cloth trade of, 129; fishing and fishes used by, 129, 138–139; use of shells for lime by, 180; hurricane deification by, 195–196; rain god of, 204–205; plants associated with archaeological sites of, 228, 231, 247; soils and soil knowledge of, 267, 287, 298, 301 (fig. 7), 303–304; population estimates of, 299, 304; decline of, soil depletion hypthesis for, 302; sacred tree of, 376; Classic period of, 448–464 *passim;* architecture of, 449; human sacrifice by, 461; influence of, on other cultures, 486. SEE ALSO Mesoamerica

Maya-Aztec trade: route used in, 95; in gold, 97

Maya-Christian calendar correlation: by Goodman-Martinez-Thompson, 478, 479, 480–481; by Spinden, 478, 482–483

Maya Highlands: definition of, 462; cultural characteristics and periods of, 463

Maya Lowlands: definition and periods of, 463; theories concerning abandonment of, 464–465

Mayapan: radiocarbon dates at, 488, 496

Mayo: agriculture of, 103, 209, 369; linguistic affiliation of, 209

Mayo River: Mocuzari dam on, 104; Indians along flood plain of, 369

Maytenus: 249, 253

Mazahua: natural environment and post-conquest history of, 294, 295

Mazama: 320, 382

Mazatec: location of, 92

meadow-beauty: 235. SEE ALSO *Blakea, Topobea*

Meadow soils. SEE Humic Glei soils

measles: effect of, on native populations, 199

medicine: flowers of *Cymbopetalum penduliflorum* used for, 226

Megaptera novaeangliae: on Pacific coast, 182

Mejocote River: drainage of, 96

Melaniris sardina: in Lake Nicaragua, 97

Melastomaceae: 226, 233, 263. SEE ALSO *Clidemia, Conostegia, Miconia*

Meleagrididae: 322, 342

Meleagris gallopavo: 322

Meliosoma: 241

Melocactus: 250

Mendocino Fracture Zone: location of, 25

Mephitis: 319, 342

Mesa Central: volcanic features of, 44–45, 47–48, 371; landscape of, 46 (fig. 8); prehistoric settlements on lakes of, 47; Pleistocene lakes of, 110, 371–372; ceremonial and urban centers of, 371; flora of, 371–372

Mesa de Guaje phase: maize in, 431; time span of,

431; squash in, 436; as an agricultural village, 489; radiocarbon dates for, 497

Mesa del Norte: cultures in, 48; volcanic features of, 48; basins and *bolsones* in, 48, 50; pediments in, 50; salt deposits of, 50–51; flora of, 367

Mescala style: in Guerrero, 475

mesereum. SEE *Daphnopsis*

Meserve point: at Huapalcalco, 391 (fig. 4), 392-393

Mesoamerica: concept of, 3, 4 (fig. 1), 293 n. 15, 366 (fig. 2), 380; trade in, 70, 73, 95, 96, 97, 129, 132, 178–179, 320, 326 n. 5, 376, 461–462, 471, 472, 476, 485, 487, 491; agriculture of, 111, 267, 276, 296, 448, 472; weapons of, 322, 455; use of feathers in, 326 n. 5, 455; southern limits of, 366, 371, 380, 465; northern limits of, 366 (fig. 2), 371, 381, 476; ceremonial centers in, 371, 457 (fig. 19), 458, 463, 465, 469, 471, 473–474, 476, 489–492, 493; cultivated plants of, 443, 447; salt, beverages, and domesticated animals of, 448; food preparation and storage in, 448, 450; stone tools of, 448, 450; metals in, 448, 456; architecture in, 449, 450–451; 458 (fig. 20), 459 (fig. 21), 460, 469, 471 (fig. 33), 493; platform mounds in, 450, 457 (fig. 19), 458, 465, 473, 476, 489, 492; ceramics in, 451–452, 455, 463, 484; sculpture in, 451, 463, 465, 467 (fig. 28), 469, 476; murals in, 451, 452 (fig. 9), 453 (fig. 10), 470 (fig. 32), 471; paint cloisonné in, 452; mosaics in, 455; musical instruments in, 455; wood-working in, 455; use of gourds in, 455; textiles in, 455; shell and bone ornaments in, 455; use of paper in, 455–456; transportation and use of wheel in, 456; settlements in, 456–457, 488–489, 493; social organization in, 457, 492–493; urbanism in, 458, 472, 489–494; religion in, 459–461, 465, 492–493; cultural themes of, 459–462; empires of, 459, 472–473, 487, 492–493; art in, 460, 462, 463, 465; ball games in, 460 (fig. 22), 461, 473–474; astronomy, mathematics, and calendrical systems of, 460, 463, 469; writing in, 460, 463, 469; regional subdivisions of, 461 (fig. 23); markets in, 461, 462, 489; altars and burial mounds in, 465; chronological classifications of, 476–478; dating problems in, 478–479, 484–488; list of radiocarbon dates for, 494–497

Mesozoic: formation of Mexican Geosyncline in, 6, 11; in Mexico, 7–13 *passim,* 38, 67; southward extension of Marathon-Ouachita axis in, 10; in Central America, 10–13 *passim,* 79. SEE ALSO Triassic, Jurassic, Cretaceous

Mesquital River: non-tropical fish in, 103; drainage and canyon of, 103, 115

mesquite: distribution of, 254, 255, 256, 257, 367, 370, 381. SEE ALSO *Prosopis*

Metachirus: 317

metals: use of, in Mesoamerica, 448

metallurgy: first appearance of, in Mesoamerica, 456; in Tarascan area, 476

metate: use of, in Mesoamerica, 448, 450

Metapan Formation: 13

Mexican Geosyncline: location of, 6; formation of, 6, 11; disappearance of, 15

Mexican Plateau: emergence of, 17; appearance of volcanoes in, 42

Mexico: seismic activity in, 3–4; Cenozoic in, 3–4, 9, 14, 15, 18, 19, 22, 23, 28–30 *passim*, 42, 174, 410, 415; volcanic activity in, 3, 9, 15, 18–19, 22, 23, 42; Archeozoic in, 7; Paleozoic in, 7–10; tectonic activity in, 7–8; Precambrian in, 7, 9; Mesozoic in, 7, 9, 10, 11, 12, 13; marine transgressions in, 11; plateau formation and land subsidence in, 14; Tertiary in, 14, 15, 18, 19, 42; alluvial fan formation in, 19; Tarango Formation in, 19, 30; San Andreas fault in, 21, 22; Quaternary in, 22, 23, 28, 29–30, 42, 410, 415; intrusive bodies in, 24; alluvial terraces in, 28; soil formation in, 29–30; glaciation in, 29, 42; Becerra and Totolzingo formations in, 30; geological investigations in, 33–34; Clarion Fracture Zone in, 38; limnological and hydrologic studies in, 85; springs and subterranean streams in, 90, 91; karst topography in, 116; climate of, 187–189, 193–203 *passim*, 206, 208–213 *passim*, 270, 415; rain gods and cults in, 203–205; jaguar cult in, 204; Athabascan languages in, 209; aboriginal agriculture in, 209–210, 432, 448; soils of, 266, 269, 274, 298, 305, 370, 373; caliche in, 269, 298, 394, 395; leaching in, 305; flora of, 370, 373; initiation of prehistoric studies in, 384; human footprints in volcanic rock in, 387; projectile point types in, 389, 392, 401–402, 410, 416, 417; food-gathering and incipient agriculture zone of, 416–417, 419; pictographs in, 423; maize in, 438–439; culture periods of, 475, 476

Mexico, Valley of: Quaternary lake sequence in, 30–31; 393–395; Quaternary biotic changes in, 31; early hydrologic studies in, 85; as source of Panuco River, 91; artificial drainage changes in, 91; aqueduct construction by Nahua of, 111; springs and lakes of, 111; surface water resources of, 117–121; mammoth and man associated in, 401–402, 404; *chinampas* of, 276, 296, 448; saline lakes in, 286; effects of altitude on agriculture in, 296; stratigraphic studies in, 384, 393; Pleistocene man at Cerro de las Palmas in, 385; human skeletons at El Peñón de los Baños in, 386–387; human mandible and fossil horse in, 387; carved sacrum of fossil camelid at Tequixquiac in, 387; Clovis points in, 388, 389 (fig. 3); fluted point at Tepexpan in, 388; caliche in, 394–395; San Juan Industry in, 396–397; bone tools at Totolzingo in, 400; locations of prehistoric sites in, 409; Chalco culture of, 415; Irwin's site survey of, 415; Tepexpan culture in, 415; fossil maize pollen in, 432, 438; radiocarbon dates from, 485, 495

Mescala River: drainage of, 106

Mezcala River: drainage of, 106
jalva River

mice: distribution of, 318, 319, 339, 340, 343, 345, 382

Michoacán: Brand's coastal study in, 4–5; Tertiary

in, 15, 43; prehistoric occupation of, 104; gold and springs in, 106; salt lakes in, 286; Apatzingan and Delicias phases of, 475; El Opeño tombs of, 475; Postclassic period in, 475; "pre-Tarascan" phase of, 475; Teotihuacan influences in, 475; yacatas in, 475

Miconia: distribution of, 227, 228, 233, 235, 238

Microchera: 343

Microhylidae: 332

Microtus: 319, 342

Micruridae: 330

Middle America: geological concept of, 3, 4 (fig. 1); geological provinces of, 5–7; cultivated plants of, 434–435

Middle American Continent: location of, 6

Middle American Trench: location of, 7; effect of, on coastal geomorphology, 23; description of, 25; association of, with Clarion Fracture Zone, 25; association of, with Clipperton Fracture Zone, 25, 26, 38; relationships of, to San Andreas fault, 25, 36; studies of, 26; as epicenter of earthquakes, 77

Midland points: in Mexico, 392

Miguel Hidalgo dam: on Rio Fuerte, 104

Mije: location of, 92

millet: in Ocampo phase, 431

milpa agriculture: 231, 244, 245, 374, 447, 457

Mimidae: 325

Mimosa: genera of, 233, 242, 254, 256, 374, 381; *M. pudica*, 247

minnows: distribution of, 333, 334, 359, 360

Minquartia: 229

Miocene: origin of San Andreas fault in, 16; appearance of Peninsula of Lower California in, 16; peninsula formation in Costa Rica and Panama during, 16; of Mexico, 16, 17, 20; in Central America, 16–18, 20; emergence of Mexican Plateau and Sierra Madre Occidental in, 17; volcanic activity in Central America during, 17–18; animal migrations of, 20 (fig. 10)

Miraflores phase: radiocarbon dates for, 484, 494

Misanteca: 228

Miskito: location of, 81, 97; culture of, 97, 214

Misquito. SEE Miskito

Mississippi Delta: encroachment of, on continental shelf, 124

Mississippian-Pennsylvanian: in Mexico, 8

mistletoe. SEE *Dendrophthora, Gaiadendron*

Mitla: site of, 63, 373

Mixtec culture: area of, 63; sites of, 373; art style of, 462; at Coixtlahuaca, 470; in Oaxaca, 469–470

Mixteca-Puebla culture: in Central Mexico, 470; influence of, in Guerrero, 475; influence of, on Chalchihuites culture and on Nayarit-Sinaloa area, 476

Mixtecs: Tzahui as rain god of, 205

moccasin, water: 330

mockingbirds: 325

Moctezuma River (of eastern Mexico): as boundary of Mesoamerican culture, 371

Moctezuma River (of Sonora): drainage of, 103

Neovolcanic Range: agriculture and karst topography in, 55
newts: 331
Nexapa River: drainage of, 106
Nezahualcoyotl, dike of: in Valley of Mexico, 111
Nicaragua: Precambrian in, 7; Paleozoic in, 7, 8–9; Mesozoic in, 12, 13, 17 (fig. 9), 20 (fig. 10); subsidence in, 14; Tertiary in, 14, 17, 21, 22, 70, 74, 76; volcanic activity in, 17, 23; coral reef elevation in, 22; Quaternary in, 23, 76; gold in, 76; hydrologic studies in, 85; Indians of, 97–98; crater lakes in, 114; shell tools in, 180; soil studies in, 265; human footprints in volcanic mud in, 408
Nicaraguan depression: canal through, 98
Nicaraguan Montane Province: 358 n. 20
Nicarao: sea travel by, 184; linguistic affiliation of, 465 n. 14
Nicotiana: origin and distribution of, 443
Nicotiana otophera: as possible parent of *N. Tabacum,* 440
Nicotiana paniculata: as possible parent of *N. hirsutum,* 440; distribution of, 440
Nicotiana rustica: in Palmillas phase, 431; origin and distribution of, 440, 441
Nicotiana sylvestris: as possible parent of *N. Tabacum,* 440
Nicotiana Tabacum: origin and distribution of, 440, 441
Nicotiana undulata: as possible parent of *N. hirsutum,* 440
Nicoya polychrome style: linkage of, with Mesoamerican ceramics, 465 n. 14
nightshade: 235. SEE ALSO *Solanum*
niño dormido: 331
Nito: as Maya trading center, 96
Noche Buena Formation: cultures associated with, 394
Nogales Cave: Plainview point in, 390
Nogales phase: culture represented by, 390; Plainview point in, 390; climate during, 415; components and time span of, 416
Nogales points: in Mexico, 416
nomads: effect of, on agricultural peoples of northern Mexico, 210
Non-Calcic Brown soils: distribution of, 285, 291, 306
North Coastal Zone: 356
Northeast Trade Winds: relationship of, to Pacific currents, 145–146; effect of, on rainfall in Middle America, 192
North Equatorial Current: description of, 145–146; local temperature effects of, 151
Northern Highlands of Central America: sources of jadeite in, 67; karst topography of, 67–68; Maya cacao derived from, 70; gold in, 70
northers (*nortes*). SEE cold fronts
Nothocercus bonapartei: 321
Notropis: 359
Nuclear America: Spinden's hypothesis of, 183
nuclear Central America: 357
Nuevo Leon: Clovis point in, 388; Plainview points in, 389, 391 (fig. 4)

nuthatches: 324
nutmeg: 235
Nyctibiidae: 323
Nyctomys: 319, 333, 339, 343
Nymphalidae: 336
Nyssa: 238

oaks: distribution of, 228, 233, 235, 236, 240–245 *passim,* 248, 251, 254, 256, 257, 259, 350, 353, 357, 370–375 *passim.* SEE ALSO *Quercus*
Oaxaca: Archeozoic in, 7; Paleozoic in, 8; Triassic in, 10; Mesozoic in, 13; Tertiary in, 15; gold in, 106; culture periods of, 469–470; Mixtec and Zapotec cultures in, 469–470; expansion of Aztec empire into, 487
obsidian and other volcanic rocks: uses of, 47–48, 448
obsidian dating: at Chicoloapan, 396, 415; at San Bartolo Atepehuacan, 404; at Coxcatlan Cave, 415
oca: domestication of, 429
Ocampo phase: climate during, 415; components of, 416; time span of, 416, 430; foods of, 419; plants of, 430, 431, 433, 442
ocelot: distribution of, 320, 375, 382
ochna: 235. SEE ALSO *Cespedesia*
Ochroma: 246, 247
Ocos phase: rocker-stamped pottery in, 484; cultural status of, 489
Ocotea: distribution of, 228, 229, 233, 246
ocotilla: 254, 256. SEE ALSO *Fouquieria*
Odocoileus: 320
Odonata: 336
Odontophorus: 322
Oecopetalum: 238
Ogcodeia: 229
"Old Antillia": location of, 38. SEE ALSO Caribbean Land
Oligocene: plateau formation during, 14; in Mexico and Central America, 14; marine transgressions in, 15
olingo: 319
Oliva shell: ornaments of, 140
Olmec culture: area of, 59, 95, 377, 465; climatic association of, 213; influence of, on other cultures, 213, 469, 471, 473, 475; association of, with lateritic soils, 282; art style of, 462, 465, 467 (fig. 28), 469, 471, 473, 475, 484; beginning date for, 465; confusing terminology for, 465 n. 15; bar-and-dot numerals in, 469; date for diffusion of, 484
Olmedia: 229
Olmediella: 238
Olneya: 254
Olotón maize: in Mexico, 439
onchoceriasis: 337
Opata: agriculture of, 209, 371
Ophidia: 329–330
Opizia: 253
opossums: distribution of, 317, 382
Opsiandra: 228
Opuntia: distribution of, 254, 255, 258, 367, 370; in Infiernillo phase, 430

556

visions of, 478, 480–483; rise of Tula in, 487; radiocarbon dates for, 488, 494–497
Postglacial Optimum: in Mexico, 415
potato, Irish: domestication of, 429
potato, sweet: introduction of, into Middle America, 443
Potentilla: 240
potoos: 323
Potos: 319, 339
Potosi River: waterflow of, 90
pottery wares: Thin Orange, 453 (fig. 11), 485; polychrome, 453 (fig. 12), 454 (fig. 13), 470, 486, 487; black-on-white, 475; rocker-stamped, 484; Usulutan, 484; red-on-buff, 486; Tohil Plumbate, 487; X Fine Orange, 487. SEE ALSO ceramics
Poulsenia: 229
Pourouma: 229, 235
Pouteria: 229
pozas. SEE springs
pozole: preparation of, in Mesoamerica, 448
prairie dogs: 318
Prairie soils: distribution of, 279 (fig. 2), 281 (fig. 4), 282, 291, 295, 297, 306
Precambrian: in Central America, 7, 9; in Mexico, 9. SEE ALSO Archeozoic
precipitation and vegetation: 202 (figs. 10, 11), 220–221
precipitation gradient: in Middle America, 221
Preclassic period: association of, with Totolzingo Formation, 30; in Maya area, 463; in Southern Periphery, 465; in Southern Veracruz-Tabasco, 467 (figs. 26–28); in Oaxaca, 467 (fig. 29), 469; in Central Mexico, 470–476, 490 (fig. 40); in Central Veracruz, 473–474; in the Huasteca, 474; in Western Mexico and Guerrero, 475; synonyms for, 477 n. 22; subdivisions of, 478, 480–483; time span of, 478, 480–483; association of rocker-stamped pottery with, 484; relative dating of, 484; radiocarbon dates for, 484–485, 486, 494–497; agricultural villages of, 489, 493
Pre-Las Joyas: radiocarbon date for, 497
Pre-Paleozoic arc: location of, 9
Presidio River: drainage of, 103
Priapella: 334, 343
prickly pear: 367, 370. SEE ALSO *Opuntia*
priests: as first weather forecasters, 205
Primates: 317–318
Prinzapolca River: drainage of, 97
Prioria: 229, 246
Pristis: 335
Procellariidae: 321
Procinura: 339
Procyon: 319
Profundulus: 334, 360, 361
pronghorn: 320
Prosopis: genera of, 254, 255, 381; *P. juliflora,* 252, 253, 367
Protium: genera of, 228, 229; *P. copal,* 231
Providencia phase: radiocarbon dates for, 494
Prunus: genera of, 228, 236, 238, 239, 241, 244; *P. Salasii,* 237

Pseudemys: 327
Pseudochama: of Baja California Pacific coast, 168; in Baja California shell middens, 178
Pseudoeurycea: 331, 342
Pseudolmedia: genera of, 226, 228; *P. oxyphyllaria,* 226; *P. spuria,* 231
Pseudomodingium: 242, 252
Pseudo-phoenix sargentiana: 250
Pseudotsuga: genus of, 256; *P. mucronata,* 372
Psidium: distribution of, 237, 244, 246, 247, 248
Psilorhinus: 343
Psophiidae: 345
Psychotria: distribution of, 228, 229, 237, 249
Pternohyla: 332
Pterocarpus: genera of, 229, 262; *P. officinalis,* 261
Ptilogonatidae: 325, 342
Ptychohyla: 332, 343
Puebla: caves of Coxcatlan and El Riego in, 391–392; Valsequillo gravels in, 406; artifacts with extinct fauna in, 406; Armenta's investigations in, 406–408
Pueblo Indians: flood irrigation by, 89
puffbirds: 324
pulque: preparation of, in Mesoamerica, 448
puma: 382
pumpkin: in Ocampo phase, 430; in Palmillas phase, 431. SEE ALSO squash
Punta Arenas-Chiriqui Province: 357 n. 19
Punta Gorda River: drainage of, 97
Punta Minitas: site of, 144 (fig. 1), 145
Puntita Negra: Clovis point at, 388
Pure Florescent period: Maya architecture during, 459 (fig. 21)
Purpura patula pansa: as source of purple dye, 180
Purron phase: cultivated plants of, 444; time span of, 444
Puuc area: as Mayan center, 72
Puya: 236
Pyramid of the Moon: view of, 447 (fig. 1)
Pyramid of the Sun: size of, 471, 491; view of, 490 (fig. 40); construction period of, 491
pyramids: examples of, 447 (fig. 1), 448 (fig. 2), 458 (fig. 20), 459 (fig. 21), 471, 474 (fig. 37), 490 (fig. 40)
pyrophytes: examples of, 379, 381
python: 329

quail-doves: 323
quails: distribution of, 322, 339, 369
Quararibea funebris: 226
Quassia: 229, 246
Quaternary: in Central America, 23, 24, 29, 74–76; volcanic activity during, 23, 44, 74–76; in Mexico, 24, 28, 29, 30–31, 44, 56; soil formation during, 28; alluvial terraces of, 28; glaciation during, 29; caliche formation during, 30; lake sequence of, 30–31; climatic sequence of, 31; biotic changes during, 31
Quercus: genera of, 228, 256, 370; pollen of, at El Peñon de los Baños, 386–387; species of, *Q. Skinnerii,* 226, 238, 239; *Q. costaricensis,* 234, 237; *Q. irazuensis,* 237; *Q. acatenangensis,* 238, 239; *Q. brachystachys, candicans, corrugata,*

oocarpa, peduncularis, polymorpha, and *sebifera,*
239; *Q. conspersa,* 239, 242; *Q. affinis, lanigera,
laurina, magnoliaefolia, reticulata,* and *urbanii,*
241; *Q. glaucoides, glaucophylla, Liebmanii,*
and *obscura,* 242; *Q. chihuahuensis,* 255
Queretaro: Irwin's site survey in, 415
quetzal: use of, for headdresses, 223, 326 n. 5;
distribution of, 323, 375
Quetzalcoatl: association of, with Tlaloc, 204;
Temple of, at Teotihuacan, 469 (fig. 31)
Quetzalcoatl cult: in Panuco area, 475
Quiché: hurricane deification by, 195–196

rabbits: distribution of, 318, 339, 369, 372, 375,
382
rabbit sticks: in Guerra phase, 420
rabies: vampire bats, as carriers of, 317
raccoons: 319
racers: 329–330
radiocarbon dates: from Baja California shell
middens, 144 (fig. 1), 145; from Santa Isabel
Iztapan, 402, 403, 410; San Bartolo Atepehuacan, 404, 410; for Tamaulipas culture sequence,
413–414, 497; for Chalco culture, Santa Marta
complex, Valley of Tehuacan, La Perra phase,
and Yuzannu, 414; for Kaminaljuyu, 484–485,
494; for Preclassic period, 484–485, 486, 494–
497; for Las Charcas and Miraflores phases,
484, 494; for Aurora phase, 485–486, 494;
for the Huasteca, 485, 488, 497; for Arevalo
phase, 485, 494; for Valley of Mexico, Conchas
phase, and Chiapa phases, 485, 495; for Veracruz-Tabasco region, 485, 496; for Classic
period, 486–487, 494–497; for Palenque, Tikal,
Uaxactun, Tepeu and Tzakol phases, 486, 495;
from Monte Alban, 486, 496; for Teotihuacan,
486, 496–497; for Palmillas and Tlamimilolpa
phases, 486, 497; for Tohil phase, 488, 494;
for Postclassic period, 488, 494–497; for Chichen Itza, Mayapan, and Tulum, 488, 496; for
Nebaj and Santa Clara, Pokom, Majadas,
Providencia, and Sacatepequez phases, 494; list
of, for Mesoamerica, 494–497; for Balankanche
Cave, Dzibilchaltun, British Honduras, and
Modified Florescent, 495; for La Venta, Cerro
Zapote, Tlatilco, and Tzacualli, Cuicuilco-
Ticoman, Loma del Tepalcate, and Early
Zacatenco phases, 496; for La Quemada, Pre-
Las Joyas, Mesa de Guaje, San Lorenzo, Los
Angeles, and Ayala phases, 497
radiocarbon dating: Suess-effect correction in,
484 n. 28, 485 n. 33
rafts: use of, by Seri, 183
rails: 322
rainfall: effect of Northeast Trade Winds and subtropical calms on, 192; distribution of, 200–201,
203, 270; seasonal, 201, 203; year-to-year variability of, 204 (fig. 13); effect of, on soils, 270
rain gods and cults: of Mexico and Central America, 203–205
Rallidae: 322
Rama: location and economy of, 97
ramón tree. SEE *Brosimum*

Ramos River: drainage of, 115
Rana: 332
Randia: 234, 242
Ranidae: 332
Ranunculus: 242
Rapanea: 238, 241
Raphia: genus of, 262; *R. taedigera,* 262
Rathbunia: 254
Ratinlixal: polychrome pottery from, 454 (fig. 13)
rats, varieties of: true, 318–319; spiny and rice,
319; vesper, 319, 339, 343; wood, 319, 340, 342;
opossum, 345; kangaroo, 318, 339; cotton, 319;
climbing, 319, 343; in tropical lowlands, 382
rattlesnakes: distribution of, 330; in Mesoamerican
art and rain cults, 330 n. 6
Rattus: 318–319
Rauwolfia: 247
Ravenia: 229
Recent: origin of Totolzingo Formation during,
30; Baja California climatic changes during,
171–173
Red Desert soils: definition of, 280, 291, 293;
distribution of, 277 (fig. 1), 280, 281, 282, 309
Reddish Brown soils: distribution of, 277 (fig. 1),
281, 285, 293, 299, 309
Reddish-Brown Lateritic soils: distribution of, 306,
307, 310
Reddish Chestnut soils: distribution of, 277 (fig.
1), 281, 282, 291, 293, 298
Reddish Prairie soils: distribution of, 279 (fig. 2),
282, 297, 298, 309
red-on-buff wares: possible Teotihuacan connections of, 486
Reduviidae: 337
Red-Yellow Podzolic soils: distribution of, 307
Red-Yellow Podzolic-Lateritic soils: distribution
of, 285, 305
Regosols: definition of, 288, 289; distribution of,
288–294, 297, 307
Reinhardtia: 229
Reithrdontomys: distribution of, 319, 344 (fig. 3)
relative humidity: gradients, seasonal contrasts,
and human comfort effects of, 200, 202
religion: in Mesoamerica, 459–461, 492–493; re-
lationship of, to art and architecture, 460
Remojadas: periods represented at, 473; Olmec art
style at, 473; Teotihuacan traits at, 473, 485
remora: use of, by Arawak, 139–140
Rendzina soils: distribution of, 284 (fig. 6), 287,
290, 293, 298, 300, 303, 370, 376; origin of,
287; use of, by Maya, 287, 298, 301 (fig. 7)
Renealmia: 229
Repelo complex: of northern Tamaulipas, 416
Reventazon River, drainage of, 98
Rhamdia: distribution of, 99, 113, 334
Rhamnus: 238, 256
Rheedia: 228
Rheomys: 319, 343
Rhinocheilus: 339
Rhinocryptidae: 324, 342
Rhinophrynidae: 331, 343
Rhizophora: 261, 262
Rhus: distribution of, 239, 255, 256